Twentieth-Century Culture

Twentieth-Century Culture,
Modernism to Deconstruction

Norman F. Cantor

PETER LANG

New York · Berne · Frankfurt am Main · Paris

Library of Congress Cataloging-in-Publication Data

Cantor, Norman F.
    Twentieth-century culture.

    Bibliography: p.
    1. Civilization, Modern—20th century.   2. Modernism
(Art)   3. Modernism (Literature)   I. Cantor, Mindy.
II. Title.   III. Title: 20th century culture.
CB425.C28   1987   909.82   87-17024
ISBN 0-8204-0358-X

Printed by Lang-Druck AG, Berne, Switzerland

Preface

I hope that scholars, critics, and college teachers will find this book useful and illuminating because of its synthetic quality, its bringing together of information from a wide variety of disciplines and because of its effort to depict the development of culture and thought in the twentieth century in broad and comprehensive categories. Whatever the controversial quality of such interdisciplinary interpretation, it can be valuable to see conventionally known facts in a somewhat different and original perspective.

This book is not, however, only expository. It does have a specific thesis relating to the nature of Modernism and its destiny. I am aware that this thesis is controversial and that it will be challenged by some. I hope that out of the ensuing debate, greater attention to and clarification of the issues raised in this book will arise. We now know enough about the details of twentieth–century cultural and intellectual history to begin to find a pattern of development that will in turn give a context to the meaning of current cultural trends. If this book contributes to that end, it will have served scholars, critics, and college teachers.

Aside from views on the nature and destiny of Modernism, the other idea in this book that might be construed as controversial is that I have tried to take rightist political culture seriously as well as leftist doctrine. Granted that what the right has accomplished intellectually still falls short of the elaboration of Marxist theory, I believe that a rightist position also merits intellectual consideration. I hope that by trying to delineate the history of rightist doctrine, I will make a contribution to novel speculation from that end of the political spectrum. Although I am not a supporter of Marxism, I have tried to present an informed overview of Marxist theory, some of which represents an important contribution to the culture of this century.

This book is written in such a way as to make it readily accessible to the educated layman, the college student, and the beginning graduate student in the humanities and social sciences. My hope is that the layman will find this discussion useful and stimulating, and that the student will see that it was critically necessary to have this background.

During three decades of teaching undergraduate and graduate students in medieval and English legal history, I have had frequent occasion to refer to some basic doctrine or leading thinker of the twentieth century and to get an uncomfortable or even bewildered response that reveals at best a vague name recognition but no real comprehension. It seemed to me it would be valuable to put into the hands of laymen and students a relatively concise account that provides a map of the intellectual and cultural history of the twentieth century. No such comprehensive book existing, I began in 1981 to read widely and, after trial runs in a course called "The Usable Past," in the spring semesters of 1985 and 1986, to sharpen my ideas and clarify the exposition by teaching a course at N.Y.U. entitled "From Modernism to Structuralism." With the positive response from students in this course—most of them first year students in a liberal education program for mature adults—I have been able to develop this book which could be entitled "Everything you always wanted to know about T.S. Eliot, Durkheim, Freud, Jung, Wittgenstein, Heidegger, Adorno, Habermas, Lévi-Strauss, Derrida, etc., but were afraid to ask."

The purpose of this book is therefore liberal education, to compensate for the lamentable failure of our colleges to teach comprehensive and systematic overviews of twentieth-century thought and culture. The educated layman and college student is often better informed on an overview of classical and Renaissance thought than of the culture and doctrines of his own century. This book will remedy that deficiency to a significant degree.

I am favorably impressed by the interdisciplinary thrust of the academic subset called literary theory which in the past decade has been by far the most vigorous and creative branch of the humanities. Yet I have good reason to believe that because of the many disciplines that literary theory draws upon, the best journals in the field frequently publish articles that are not fully comprehensible even to relatively advanced humanities students. One of the special purposes of this book is to facilitate the reading of learned articles and books in literary theory. Another special purpose is to contribute to the revival of cultural and intellectual history. I have made contributions to this historical subdiscipline in regard to medieval and English history. It seemed to me crucial that the history of modern times also be explored from this point of view in a synthetic way.

I have tried in this book to keep technical terms to a minimum and to write in plain English as much as possible. Where I have had to use jargon, I have tried to explain such terms in a manner that the lay reader will readily comprehend, and not always in the way the thinker himself or herself would have explained the term. I hope that this pedagogical device will not be regarded as vulgar or otherwise vulnerable. Sitting in learned conferences or participating in seminars, I have often felt that many people present, even Ph.D's and published scholars, really do not know precisely what is being said and that a few words of explanation and definitions would clarify the proceedings in a major way. That is what I have tried to do here. Even Wittgenstein and Heidegger are not particle physics or molecular biology. I believe their main ideas can be expounded and comprehended without much strain. And as a matter of fact even the main theories of modern physics or biology can be succinctly stated. That of course does not mean that I pretend to have mastered these fields, immeasurably far from it. But I believe that it is time we created a universe of discourse on twentieth-century as well as sixteenth- or eighteenth-century ideas. This is what the program of humanism is all about.

The Bibliography is not intended to be comprehensive. It is suggestive only.

It lists books, mostly of recent vintage, that I found particularly illuminating or insightful in some way, and I expect the reader will too. I have not listed books in foreign languages. There are enough good books written in English or translated into English to go around.

I wish as far as possible to acknowledge the assistance I have received in preparation of this book:

To Mindy Cantor for sharing with me her deep knowledge of the visual arts of this century, providing many additional comments of critical value, and particularly for preparing the accompanying picture essays that constitute independently an overview of twentieth–century art.

To Judy and Howard Cantor for advice on recent and current cultural trends.

To New York University for providing special secretarial, copying, research, and travel assistance.

To Samuel Lipman and Hilton Kramer of the *New Criterion* for advice and encouragement.

To the John M. Olin Foundation for continuing support of my work.

To Dean Michael Miller and Dean Arthur Williamson for allowing me to teach courses that enabled me to explore many of the ideas in this book.

To my friends and colleagues William Nelson, Robert Hanning, and Perry Meisel for reading large sections of the manuscript in draft form and providing both trenchant criticism and inspiring encouragement; their advice has been immeasurably valuable.

To Steve Brams who gave me learned and perceptive criticism and much encouragement.

To David Berry and the faculty of Essex County Community College, Newark, New Jersey, for whom I conducted a faculty seminar in 85–86 on the major ideas incorporated in this book. I benefited from their comments and suggestions. The faculty seminar was sponsored by the N.J. State Education Department.

To Barbara Kern for encouragement and advice during the years I worked on this book.

To the following current or former students who helped me appreciably by technical assistance and/or useful comments: Charles Dellheim, Nathalia King, James Cohen, and Michela Mago.

To Marc Aronson who read the manuscript with an eye to fact-checking and saved me from several errors.

To Sanford Greenberg who generously allowed the use of material in his possession.

To James Banko and Deniz Sengel who over a period of many months helped in preparation of the manuscript through successive drafts; their commitment to this book was exceptional.

To my editor Jay Wilson of Peter Lang Publishing for his criticism and encouragement and to Mr. Peter Lang himself for being the kind of idealistic publisher devoted to learning and thought that is extremely rare nowadays.

And to the many students who made comments on my lectures and saved me from error or forced me to clarify my interpretations or got me thinking in new directions.

One of my former students, Frank Stella, generously gave me color transparencies of two of his own paintings in his private collection. They are both used in this book, one on the jacket.

None of these acknowledgements should be construed to mean agreement with anything I have said. I alone am responsible for any errors of fact or judgment in this book. In specific instances, I know that some of the colleagues, friends, and students mentioned above have strongly dissented from what I say. I have taken their comments into account as much as I could, but ultimately I had to go my own way.

Washington Mews
Greenwich Village, N.Y.C.
September 15, 1986

TO MY STUDENTS THROUGH THE PAST
THREE DECADES OF LEARNING AND TEACHING

The sense of justice and injustice is not derived from nature, but arises artificially, though necessarily, from education and human invention.

David Hume

Contents

Chapter Four. Marxism and the Left

Chapter Five. Traditions on the Right

Chapter Six. Structuralism, Deconstruction, and Post-Modernism

List of Illustrations

Pablo Picasso, *Les Demoiselles d'Avignon*, 1907
Oil on canvas, 8′ × 7′ 8″
Collection, The Museum of Modern Art, New York.
Acquired through the Lillie P. Bliss Bequest.

Marcel Duchamp, *Nude Descending a Staircase, no. 2*, 1912
Oil on canvas, 58″ × 35″
Philadelphia Museum of Art.
Louise and Walter Arensberg Collection.

Robert Delaunay, *Simultaneous Contrasts: Sun and Moon*, 1913
Oil on canvas, 53″ diameter
Collection, The Museum of Modern Art, New York.
Mrs. Simon Guggenheim Fund.

Umberto Boccioni, *The City Rises*, 1910
Oil on canvas, 6′ 6½″ × 9′ 10½″
Collection, The Museum of Modern Art, New York.
Mrs. Simon Guggenheim Fund.

Wassily Kandinsky, *Black Lines*, December 1913
Oil on canvas, 51″ × 51 5/8″
The Solomon R. Guggenheim Museum, New York.
Photo: David Heald

Franz Marc, *Stables*, 1913–14
Oil on canvas, 29 1/8″ × 62¼″
The Solomon R. Guggenheim Museum, New York.
Photo: Robert E. Mates

Paul Klee, *Lost in Thought—Self-Portrait—Portrait of an Expressionist*, 1919
Watercolor lithograph
Kunstmuseum Bern.
© Copyright ARS, NY/SPADEM 1987

Egon Schiele, *Self-Portrait Masturbating*, 1911
Pencil, watercolor, and gouache on paper, 18½″ × 12¼″
Graphische Sammlung Albertina, Vienna.
Photo courtesy Galerie St. Etienne, New York

Paula Modersohn-Becker, *Self-Portrait with Lemon*, 1906
Oil on canvas
Private collection
Photo: Courtesy Galerie St. Etienne, New York

Amedeo Modigliani, *Head*, 1911–13
Limestone, 25″ high
The Solomon R. Guggenheim Museum, New York.
Photo: Robert E. Mates

Wilhelm Lehmbruck, *Standing Youth*, 1913
Cast Stone, 7' 8" high, at base 36" × 26 3/4"
Collection, The Museum of Modern Art, New York.
Gift of Abby Aldrich Rockefeller.

Alexander Archipenko, *Médrano II*, 1915
Painted tin, wood, glass, and painted oilcloth, 49 7/8" × 20¼" × 12½"
The Solomon R. Guggenheim Museum, New York.
Photo: Robert E. Mates

Piet Mondrian, *Composition*, 1922
Oil on canvas, 15" × 13 3/4"
Collection Judith Rothschild, New York.
Photo: UHT

Ben Nicholson, *White Relief*, 1935
40" × 65½"
The Tate Gallery, London.

Fernand Léger, *The City*, 1919
Oil on canvas, 90 3/4" × 117¼"
Philadelphia Museum of Art.
A. E. Gallatin Collection.

Kasimir Malevich, *Suprematist Composition, Black Trapezium and Red Square*, 1915
Oil on canvas, 101.5 cm × 62 cm
Stedelijk Museum, Amsterdam.

Salvador Dali, *The Persistence of Memory*, 1931
Oil on canvas, 9½" × 13"
Collection, The Museum of Modern Art, New York.
Given anonymously.

Jean Arp, *Objects Arranged According to the Law of Chance* or *Navels*, 1930
Varnished wood relief, 10 3/8" × 11 1/8"
Collection, The Museum of Modern Art, New York.
Purchase.

Max Ernst, *Celebes*, 1921
Oil on canvas, 49.37" × 42½"
The Tate Gallery, London.

Paul Delvaux, *Phases of the Moon*, 1939
Oil on canvas, 55" × 63"
Collection, The Museum of Modern Art, New York.
Purchase.

Francis Bacon, *Painting*, 1946
Oil and tempera on canvas, 6' 5 7/8" × 52"
Collection, The Museum of Modern Art, New York.
Purchase.

Jean Dubuffet, *Jules Supervielle, Grand Portrait Bannière*, 1945
Oil on canvas, 51½" × 38½"
Gift of Mr. and Mrs. Maurice E. Culberg
The Art Institute of Chicago.
Photo: Courtesy of The Art Institute of Chicago.

Henry Moore, *Reclining Figure*, 1939
Carved elm, 37" × 6' 7" × 30"
Copyright 1987 The Detroit Institute of Arts,
Gift of the Dexter M. Ferry, Jr. Trustee Corporation

Alexander Calder, *Black Widow*, 1959
Painted sheet steel, 7' 8" × 14' 3" × 7' 5"
Collection, The Museum of Modern Art, New York.
Mrs. Simon Guggenheim Fund.

Matta (Sebastian Antonio Matta Echaurren), *Le Vertige d'Eros*, 1944
Oil on canvas, 6' 5" × 8' 3"
Collection, The Museum of Modern Art, New York.
Given anonymously.

Arshile Gorky, *Agony*, 1947
Oil on canvas, 40" × 50½"
Collection, The Museum of Modern Art, New York.
A. Conger Goodyear Fund.

Willem de Kooning, *Woman, I*, 1950–52
Oil on canvas, 6' 3 7/8" × 58"
Collection, The Museum of Modern Art, New York.
Purchase.

Hans Hofmann, *Spring*, 1944–45
Oil on wood panel, 11 ¼" × 14 1/8"
Collection, The Museum of Modern Art, New York.
Mrs. Simon Guggenheim Fund.

Jackson Pollock, *Convergence*, 1952
Oil on canvas, 93½" × 155"
Albright-Knox Art Gallery, Buffalo, New York.
New York. Gift of Seymour H. Knox, 1956.

Barnett Newman, *Vir Heroicus Sublimis*, 1950–51
Oil on canvas, 7' 11 3/8" × 17' 9¼"
Collection, The Museum of Modern Art, New York.
Gift of Mr. and Mrs. Ben Heller.

Robert Motherwell, *Elegy to the Spanish Republic, 54*, 1957–61
Oil on canvas, 70" × 7' 6¼"
Collection, The Museum of Modern Art, New York.
Given anonymously.

Ad Reinhardt, *Number 87*, 1957
Oil on canvas, 9' × 40"
Collection, The Museum of Modern Art, New York.
Purchase.
Photo: Eric Pollitzer

Frank Stella, *Valpariso Flesh and Green*, 1963
Metallic paint on canvas, 78" × 135¼"
Collection: Frank Stella
Photo: Steven Sloman

Andy Warhol, *100 Cans*, 1962
Oil on canvas, 72" × 52"
Albright-Knox Art Gallery, Buffalo, New York.
Gift of Seymour H. Knox, 1963.

Roy Lichtenstein, *WHAAM!*, 1963
Acrylic on canvas, 1727 mm × 4064 mm
The Tate Gallery, London.

Robert Rauschenberg, *Bed*, 1955
Combine Painting, 75¼" × 31½ × 6½"
Photo: Courtesy of Leo Castelli Gallery, New York.
Photo: Rudolph Burckhardt

Jasper Johns, *Target with Four Faces*, 1955
Encaustic on newspaper over canvas 26" × 26" surmounted by four tinted
   plaster faces in wood box with hinged front.
Box, closed, 3 3/4" × 26" × 3½". Overall dimensions with box open, 33 5/8"
   × 26" × 3".
Collection, The Museum of Modern Art, New York.
Gift of Mr. and Mrs. Robert C. Scull.

Claes Oldenburg, *Soft Toilet*, 1966
Vinyl filled with kapok, wood, liquitex, chromed metal rack, 50½" ×
    32 5/8" × 30 7/8"
Courtesy of Leo Castelli Gallery, New York.
Collection of Mr. and Mrs. Victor Ganz
Photo: Geoffrey Clements

David Smith, *Cubi XIX*, third view, 1964
Stainless steel, Height 112"
The Tate Gallery, London.

Sol Lewitt, *Untitled Cube (6)*, 1968
Painted steel, 15¼" × 15¼" × 15¼"
Collection of the Whitney Museum of American Art, New York.
Gift of the Howard and Jean Lipman Foundation, Inc.
Photo: Geoffrey Clements

George Segal, *Walk, Don't Walk*, 1976
Plaster, cement, metal, painted wood and lights, 104" × 72" × 72"
Collection of the Whitney Museum of American Art, New York.
Purchase, with funds from the Louis and Bessie Adler Foundation, Inc.,
    Seymour M. Klein, President; the Gilman Foundation, Inc.; the Howard
    and Jean Lipman Foundation, Inc.; and the National Endowment for the
    Arts.
Photo: Jerry L. Thompson

Christo, *Surrounded Islands, Project for Biscayne Bay, Greater Miami, Florida*,
    1983
Collage in two parts: 11" × 28" and 22" × 28"
Fabric, pastel, charcoal, pencil, crayon, enamel paint and photographic
    map
Copyright Christo
Photo: Wolfgang Volz

Joseph Beuys, *Aus Berlin: Neues Vom Kojoten*, 1979
(Photo shows installation in Ronald Feldman Fine Arts, Inc., New York,
    1986)
Plaster, wood lathing and other rubble, newspapers, felt hat, toenails, hair,
    felt, musical triangle, gloves, flashlight, wood cane, acetylene lanterns,
    arc lamp, wood sticks, fire extinguishers, hay, and sulphur.
Collection of the Dia Art Foundation, New York.
Courtesy Ronald Feldman Fine Arts Inc., New York.
Photo: D. James Dee

Richard Serra, *Vertical Parallelogram*, 1983
Sandblasted corten steel (five plates), 41 3/4" × 24" × 24"
Photo: Courtesy of Leo Castelli Gallery, New York

Susan Rothenberg, *For the Light*, 1978–79
Acrylic on canvas, 105″ × 87″
Collection of the Whitney Museum of American Art, New York.
Purchase with funds from Peggy and Richard Danziger.
Photo: Geoffrey Clements

Marcus Lupertz, *Bewohner: Mittag (Das Collier des Siegers)*, 1983
Oil/linen, 65″ × 52½″
Mary Boone Gallery, New York.
Photo: Zindman/Fremont.

Francesco Clemente, *Two Painters*, 1980
Gouache on nine sheets of handmade paper with cloth backing, 94 1/8″ × 68″
Courtesy of Sperone Westwater Fischer, New York.

Sandro Chia, *Poetic Declaration*, 1983
Oil on canvas, 96″ × 96″
The Soloman R. Guggenheim Museum, New York.
Courtesy Sperone Westwater, New York.

Roger Brown, *The Modern Story of Life: A Civics Diatribe*, 1983
Oil on canvas, 72¼″ × 96″
The Metropolitan Museum of Art, George A. Hearn Fund, 1983.
Photo: William H. Bengtson, Courtesy Roger Brown and the Phyllis Kind Gallery, Chicago/New York.

Mies van der Rohe, The Seagram Building, New York, 1958
Photo: Ezra Stoller
Courtesy of Joseph E. Seagram & Sons, Inc.

Robert Venturi, Vanna Venturi House, Chestnut Hill, Pennsylvania, 1962
Photo: Rollin La France

Richard Meier & Partners Architects, Museum für Kunsthandwerk [Decorative Arts], Frankfurt, 1979–84
Photo: Copyright Ezra Stoller/ESTO

John Burgee Architects with Philip Johnson, AT&T Corporate Headquarters, New York, 1978
Photo: Copyright Richard Payne, A.I.A. 1985

Jacket: Frank Stella, #2 Diavolozoppo, 1984
Oil, Urethane Enamel, Florescent Alkyd, Acrylic and Printing Ink on Canvas, Etched Magnesium, Aluminum and Fiberglass.
139⅛ × 169¾ × 16⅛″
Collection Frank Stella
Photo: Steve Sloman

1

The Nineteenth-Century Foundations of Twentieth-Century Culture

The Four Cultural Revolutions

The foundations of twentieth-century culture consist of formulations in the late nineteenth century—what was happening in Europe around 1900 that produced the cultural revolution called Modernism, the critical development in twentieth-century culture.

Twentieth-century cultural history has a unifying theme, that of Modernism: The emergence of Modernism, its impact in multiple areas as diverse as painting, philosophy, and anthropology, and how it evolved. We are now living in a period that is called the age of Postmodernism because we are not quite certain what it is. What we do know is that it follows upon the Modernist era whose high-point was from about 1900 to 1940, and that we are the legatees of the Modernist heritage.

The exhibition in New York in 1986 of the work of Mies van der Rohe, the prominent Modernist architect, is an example of our persistent concern with Modernism. Hardly a month goes by without a showing in New York of some form of Modernist art. Much of our time and attention within both university humanities departments and cultural weeklies and quarterlies is devoted to Modernist literature and its influence. Modernism in fact remains dominant in the publishing world, among leading purveyors of poetry and fiction, more than it probably does in culture as a whole. It continues to have a major and not always fortunate influence on what is published in poetry and fiction. The physics and microbiology that is central to natural scientists is rooted in the Modernist view of the world, and is inconceivable without it. Psychoanalysis, sociological research and anthropological theory as taught in our universities are alike products of Modernism.

Modernism is one of the four great cultural revolutions in Western civilization since 1500. By cultural revolution is meant a great upheaval in consciousness, perception, value systems and ideology which has affected the way we think of ourselves and our world, and which has had a seminal impact in literature, philosophy, religion, political theory and the visual and performing arts.

The first of these cultural revolutions was the Reformation of the sixteenth century, which not only generated Protestantism but involved the reshaping of the Catholic Church as well. It produced the Calvinist ethos and the great manifestations of baroque art and music.

The Protestant reformers taught that all is dung and dross in comparison with Christ. Each individual is driven back upon one fundamental fact of human existence, his relationship to God. The "works," or institutions, of the Church pale into insignificance when confronted with this existential fact. The only redemptive force in human life was ultimately God's love of man, His creature. And the only liberty or righteousness of which men are capable flowed from faith in God. This was Martin Luther's "Liberty of a Christian Man": "No external thing, by whatever name it may be called can in any way conduce to Christian righteousness or liberty." Thus the Protestant Reformation, at the same time as it declared the awesome majesty and omnipotence of God, taught the incomparable dignity and privilege of the individual human conscience. No other civilization has so privileged individual liberty and conscience. And this message has not vanished entirely in the twentieth century, even in the most adverse environments, in the Gulag or Auschwitz.

The second legacy of the Reformation was John Calvin's doctrine, deriving from Jewish, early Christian and medieval eschatological traditions, of the holy community. State and society should be controlled by the godly, by those who have demonstrated their reception of God's grace. Nineteenth-century liberalism, which drew heavily upon Calvinist tradition, softened this doctrine into the belief that if good and idealistic men could only take over the reins of government, the problems of industrial society would be resolved. This assumption endures in the program of the Democratic Party and the pages of *The New York Times* and *The Washington Post*.

The third legacy of the cultural revolution of the Reformation was the distinctive attitude and style of life that is called the Puritan ethos or the Protestant work ethic: piety, frugality, long and intensive labor, postponed gratification, simplicity in dress and diet, a repressive sexual code, preservation of the nuclear family, and service to the local community. This ethos was particularly pronounced among English and American Calvinists, and its influence on the development of Britain and the United States before 1900 was profound.

Although the Reformation received its initial dynamic impetus from the Protestant churches, the impact of this cultural revolution was sufficient also to reshape the Catholic Church and affect the way of life of millions of people in Catholic countries. There was a Catholic as well as Protestant Reformation. In several ways, Catholic Ireland, locked in a time warp, is the country in the Western world that is today still vestigially closest to the pristine attitudes and behavior patterns generated by the sixteenth-century Reformation.

The second cultural revolution was the eighteenth-century Enlightenment, the liberal rationalism that eventually produced the American and French revolutions and modern political liberalism, and that helped make the Constitution with which we are still trying to live, and sometimes trying to ignore.

The *philosophes* of the Enlightenment regarded John Locke's thesis that human understanding is the product of experience—the result of the impress of the environment on the mind—as a liberating doctrine. Men and women were not limited by a cast of mind or set of ideas they were born with, as claimed by Plato and Descartes. Men could know anything and be conditioned in any direction by the circumstances of environment, education, and experience. Man's future was unlimited—a comforting doctrine for the tidewater planters who faced the uncoiled expanse of the American continent and the uncertain prospects of a new republic. The *philosophes* argued that Newton's discovery of the laws of the physical world had demonstrated the infinite capacity of the human mind, given mankind the key to the mastery of nature, and opened the possibility of solving social problems and creating a much better world for men and women to live in.

From these assumptions Jean Jacques Rousseau extrapolated the principle that prevailing political institutions were merely artificial constructs that retained neither the sanctions of nature nor of ethics. They can and should be overturned: "It is plainly contrary to the laws of nature, however defined, that children should command old men, fools wise men, and the privileged few should gorge themselves with the superfluities while the starving multitude are in want of the bare necessities of life." Here is the voice and temperament of revolution, drawing hazardous sustenance from moral indignation.

Enlightenment intellectuals like Thomas Jefferson taught that life is an end in itself and that all the resources of society and mind should be committed to the pursuit of human happiness. This doctrine has inspired modern liberal and radical political movements and the effort to apply science to technology in order to improve the circumstances of everyday life. Although the *philosophes* lived in a preindustrial, preponderantly aristocratic and landed society, their faith has deeply affected the modern industrial and democratic world.

The third cultural revolution was Romanticism which prevailed between 1790 and 1850. Romanticism produced an immense change in human consciousness and feeling and had a vast effect in philosophy and the arts. Indeed, it generated whole new art forms or transformed existing ones, such as lyric poetry and the opera. It made historical writing central rather than peripheral in literature.

The main idea of Romanticism was transcendentalism; the enhancement of individual grandeur by uniting the individual with an irresistible force outside himself, such as art, history, the nation or the beloved. The shrinking of the individual and the dimunition of his freedom threatened by the coming of industrial economy and the bureaucratic state were resisted by Romanticism's compensatory vision of the individual's symbiosis with some "Mighty Being" which was, in William Wordsworth's articulation "awake/and doth with eternal motion make/a sound like thunder everlastingly." Thus Romanticism sought to preserve the freedom and dignity of the individual that the two previous cultural revolutions, the Reformation and the Enlightenment, had posited, the former on religious and the latter on scientific grounds.

To affirm this continuing freedom, Romanticism enunciated the philosophy of act. Ideals must be strenuously lived from day to day and freedom and redemption lie in the experience of the struggle itself. So we have Goethe's Faustian hero: "He only earns his freedom and his life/Who takes them everyday by storm." And the Byronic hero: "To rise/I knew not whither."

From the Faustian/Byronic ideal of life as act comes a long tradition that embraces "The Man on Horseback." The Romantic novelist Stendhal said he respected a single man, Napoleon. This same tradition glorifies the uncompromising revolutionary storming of the barricades; the bohemian artist; the perpetually adolescent lover. These are types that permanently entered into Western culture.

Finally, there is Modernism, the twentieth-century cultural revolution. If one looks at conventional histories of the twentieth century, one will usually find a few pages about Modernism tucked here and there, in the shape of brief comments about Picasso and Proust. One does not see Modernism treated as a crucial cultural dynamic, comparable to the Reformation, the Enlightenment, or Romanticism in terms of its vast impact.

Why has Modernism not been seen as a seminal transformation in human values? First we are still trying to live with and come to terms with Modernism. We are still living at its edges or perhaps we are culturally within its extension. We have not determined whether the Postmodernist era is a revived or altered Modernism, or whether it is a late stage of Modernism, a rebellion against it or something quite different from it. Whatever the response, Modernism remains something very close to us, something in which we are still engaged. Gaining a historical perspective on Modernism, therefore, is a complex undertaking.

The second reason why Modernism has not been perceived in its full dimensions as a cultural revolution is that twentieth-century history has been largely written in political and economic terms rather than as cultural explication. There is no accessible general work on the cultural history of the twentieth century.

The groundwork has indeed been laid to write the cultural history of the twentieth century. There has been in recent years a vast outpouring of books on various aspects of the arts, literature, philosophy and science in this century and some of these are enduringly valuable. The biographies of leading intellectual and artistic figures since 1900 have been particularly detailed and illuminating. Drawing on these works, we may try to understand the full range of cultural history since 1900 and the relationship within a social context among the arts, humanities, and social and physical sciences. Until these dimensions are explained the significance of Modernism cannot be perceived.

Modernism's failure to develop a distinctive political ideology constitutes the third reason why Modernism has not been fully and appropriately understood. The other cultural revolutions such as the Reformation and the Enlightenment eventually turned into political revolutions. In the case of the Reformation, modern statism, the centralized bureaucratic state, was rapidly entrenched. The Enlightenment fostered political liberalism. Romanticism's political outcome, on the other hand, was polarized. It produced a leftist ideology, Marxism, as well as a rightist one, a highly conscious and determined conservative nationalism. Romanticism thus generated coherent political and social theories to such an extent that we are still trying to extricate ourselves from them. We are still living through the consequences of the political and ideological outcomes of Romanticism. Today, most of the world is governed through either varieties of Marxism or a kind of pervasive nationalism, both of which are residual political legacies of Romanticism.

Modernism never generated a clear political consequence. Strenuous efforts, which will be discussed in a later chapter, were made, particularly in the United States in the 1930's, to relate Modernism to the left. Although the attempt to conjoin Marxism and Modernism has produced no obvious results, the issue still receives attention—in the pages, for instance, of the *Partisan Review*, *New York Review of Books* and *The Village Voice*. In the Germany and Italy of the 1930's, there were also efforts to join Modernism with the right; and to some extent, Fascism was a consequence of joining right-wing traditions with Modernism.

But the elucidation of Modernism's political formation has never been actualized. Modernism had its recognized impress in all other areas of human culture, in the visual and performing arts, literature, philosophy, and the natural and social sciences, but its political outcomes remained confused. Owing to the tendency among historians to make the political sphere their focal point, Modernism has not been given its central place in twentieth-century history, for it never developed a clear political outcome. If the only way to write history is in political terms, then Modernism becomes peripheral rather than a central focus.

It is perhaps the case in Western Civilization that with each subsequent cultural revolution the West undergoes, the cultural revolution's political effect becomes less lucid. The Reformation's politics revealed its direction quickly. Almost from the very beginning it was clear that the Reformation was going to end medieval pluralism and establish state absolutism and centralization. It took perhaps about fifty years for the political consequence of the Enlightenment to become fully visible. The Enlightenment began in the areas of science, literature and religion, and only slowly did it turn into an extremely powerful political movement. Romanticism ultimately produced strong bipolar political outcomes. Rather than a unified political consequence, it generated as strong a leftist stance as a rightist one.

Modernism never produced a clear political consequence. Interrupted by other concurrent upheavals in the socio-economic and political spheres such as the two World Wars and the Great Depression, it produced a host of ambiguities and ambivalences. These had—as we shall see later—on the whole a negative effect on the articulation of Modernism. Although there was some impetus to Modernism from World War I, the war also produced negative consequences for the movement's development. The Great Depression and World War II further generated Neo-Victorian tendencies and revivals of nineteenth-century attitudes, and thereby impaired the road Western society had taken with Modernism. That is why even though we continue to extrapolate implications from Modernism, we can nevertheless claim that as a coherent cultural movement Modernism ended around 1940.

Still, despite the fact that Modernism did not acquire a distinct political stance, it was nevertheless a cultural revolution. It represents a transformation as profound as the Reformation, the Enlightenment, and Romanticism, albeit more elusive and harder for us to encapsulate. It is easier to describe

Modernism's attributes than it is to define and establish its sociological model or cultural typology.

At this point we may use as a working definition of Modernism that it was a cultural movement flourishing in the first four decades of this century and that it emphasized ahistorical, non-narrative or "synchronic" ways of thinking; the microcosmic, small-scale dimension; self-referentiality; and moral relativism. Above all, Modernism was a revolt against Victorianism. We shall explain these and other aspects of Modernism in the next chapter. For the moment, this definition will be useful as we explore the nineteenth-century background to Modernism.

*   *   *

Foreshadowings of Modernism

Modernism emerged around 1900 as a coherent movement. However, certain manifestations appear already in the last two decades of the nineteenth century, signaling its emergence. In the 1940's, a husband-wife sociological team at Columbia, Helen and Robert Lynd, in a pioneering study identified the 1880's as the major historical turning point in the modern world. To an extent this is true. In the 1880's, there was a shift in consciousness and attitudes, particularly reflected in a new appreciation of sexuality and an involvement with new social concerns, which indicates that the pattern of nineteenth-century, "Victorian" thought was in the course of erosion.

Modernism does not distinctly begin until about 1900, but the first signs of the change in values and attitudes become discernible in the 1880's. In the year 1884, George Bernard Shaw, then an obscure Irish drama critic living in London, wrote that there were two things in the world that he hated: "My duty and my mother."—this, even though (or perhaps because) his mother supported him until he was about forty years old. Shaw's comments herald the beginning of a shift whose emergence Shaw was one of the first to perceive. Though some of his critical writings were shallow and naive, and though he did not fully understand what was happening, between 1895 and 1910 Shaw wrote some of the earliest essays that identified a cultural change of great importance.

If we go back to the 1880's, we can see certain writers who are moving in a new direction that heralds the Modernist movement. They are not themselves what we might call Modernist writers. Still embedded in Victorian preconceptions, they display differences from Victorians proper. In Émile Zola's novel *Germinal*, dealing with miners in France, for example, we see an appreciation of the sensibility and circumstances of ordinary people that conflicts with the normal tendency of Victorian thought, that is, with the inclination to concentrate on the politically dominant and wealthy strata of society. Zola not only understands and appreciates the workings of life among the miserable, but also shows himself capable of genuine sensitivity toward working-class experiences.

The presence of a new consciousness is even stronger in the novels of Thomas Hardy, particularly in his most revolutionary and controversial novel

Tess of the D'Urbervilles. Thomas Hardy was outside the established English cultural world. Trained as an architect's apprentice, he lacked a university education. He lived in Dorset in the southwestern part of England and came from a lower middle class and peasant background. Although he usually kept his opinions private and gave vent to them only in his novels, he was extremely hostile toward the comfortable world of the upper middle class. *Tess of the D'Urbervilles* is an assault on the fundamental assumptions of the Victorian world. Particularly Hardy's treatment of the theme of underprivileged women makes *Tess of the D'Urbervilles* a devastating account of the exploitation, misery and abuse experienced by women who came from outside and below the middle class.

Another outsider writing in the late nineteenth century was "Joseph Conrad", the English pseudonym of a novelist who came from a noble Polish family. Conrad left Poland upon being charged with subversive activities against the Russian state, and became a merchant captain. He began to write novels about coastal society in Africa and the Orient, concentrating mainly on life within the British Empire. *Heart of Darkness* is one of his most famous and successful novels, as well as his shortest. (It is the novel on which the film *Apocalypse Now* is confusedly based.) *Heart of Darkness* has a dual message. One is that imperialism could not succeed because it tried to contend with cultures that were too vital, too old, too powerful and too mysterious for the West. Hence the West will not be able to maintain its foothold in Africa and Asia for long. Conrad envisioned this around 1890. He has been proved a visionary. Africa is a great Other which cannot be understood by the Western mind.

The second emphasis in Conrad's novel exposes the terrible loneliness that we all experience when we try to establish a life based upon wealth and power. In so doing we are engaged in a slow process of self-destruction. The pursuit of wealth and power constitutes a process of dehumanization. The two ideas are presented in the novel as congenial: Imperialism is a massive dehumanization and desensitization of the West which will slowly erode Western morality. To some extent that has also been proved true.

Another writer who worked in the 1880's was Henrik Ibsen, regarded by many as the founder of modern drama, whatever that elusive term may mean. Ibsen came from a lower middle-class family in Norway. He failed miserably as the director of a theater in Norway; in fact, he failed twice. For seventeen years, from various places in Germany and Italy, particularly in Munich and Rome, he tried to turn himself into a successful dramatist before returning to Norway to spend the closing years of his life.

Ibsen did triumph. To the new literary generation of the eighties and nineties, he was an intellectual and artistic liberator. Around 1900, George Bernard Shaw published a book called *The Quintessence of Ibsenism*. For Shaw, Ibsen became the prophet of the Modernist revolt against Victorian culture. Even though Ibsen wrote about thirty plays, most of which are in prose and some early ones in verse, his best known work today is *A Doll's House*. Ibsen intended *A Doll's House* to be not only a narrative of female liberation, which is the way it is interpreted today. It is a play that deconstructs the

Victorian family, that questions values which it finds to be against the needs, humanity and desire for self-realization of a middle-class woman. But Ibsen understood this drama to portray the needs of everybody's humanity, male or female, and to show the antagonism to the individual from the demands of social institutions.

There is a Neo-Romantic strain in Ibsen and hence we are not altogether comfortable with him today. He is not a Modernist, but a pre-Modernist, or, actually, a late Romantic. He is a kind of Kierkegaardian and Nietzschean who pits a strong individual against society. But he heralds a shift in ideology and values that was fundamental and timely.

At the same time in the 1880's, it was recognized in vanguard scientific and literary circles that human sexuality is a complicated thing that can affect people's behavior in a variety of ways, including some that are not obvious and anticipated, and that sado-masochistic feelings are, if not normal, at least very common. This new understanding of sexuality and its place in human life was a significant departure from dominant Victorian opinions. We must understand that Freud drew upon this new perception of sexuality. He extended it greatly, but he did not invent it. If this conception had not been gaining credence since the 1880's, Freud probably could not have produced his work. Early in his career, in 1885, Freud conducted postdoctoral work in Paris with the psychologist Jean Martin Charcot, a pioneer in the use of hypnosis as a means to understand and probe the unconscious. From the work of Charcot as well as from that of several other psychiatrists in Paris and Vienna, Freud began to build his own conception of the structure and method of psychoanalysis.

Another important departure from Victorianism occurred in England in the 1880's with the development of a new conception of history. As we shall shortly discuss, Victorianism depended deeply on historicism. If all phenomena (even natural ones) are seen in continuous temporal terms and if in order to understand something, a full account of its nature is given and this history is seen as evolutionary, with each step in the process building on the preceding, the point of view is teleological, deterministic, and essentially Victorian. In the 1880's a professor of law at Cambridge University, Frederick William Maitland, began to take a very different approach to the understanding of history.

Maitland offered a new perspective for comprehending the history of English law which avoided historical continuity and rejected long-term teleological determinism. Maitland concentrated on the analysis of short-term phenomena. He looked at the intervention of will, and found that at a certain point in time the will of some people or group or even of an individual can change everything in ways which cannot be anticipated. What happens in history is unanticipated, according to Maitland. It is fortuitous, chancy, and not determined over a long term. It is accidental and immediate. There are breaks and discontinuities in history, rather than a seamless, inevitable flow.

To take an example from the twentieth century: One should not determine why Hitler arose in Germany in terms of events that occurred three hundred years before in German history, or even by incidents of fifty years before, but in terms of occurrences that perhaps took place three months or three days before Hitler came to power. Hitler's rise, therefore, was not predetermined by long-term circumstances, but by very immediate, discontinuous, accidental, even absurd happenings. That is the new approach Maitland adopted in his history of English law, which constituted a radical departure from Victorian thought. The importance of Maitland's work was not begun to be appreciated until about the time of his death in 1906 and this appreciation occurred mainly in the United States. But even though his writings were not fully understood for a long time (until the 1950's), they exemplify an intellectual change which emerged in the 1880's.

There are a number of other figures in the late nineteenth century who are more familiar to us today. There is Friedrich Nietzsche, for example, who is nowadays often regarded as the prophet of the twentieth century. This is a controversial opinion. In some ways Nietzsche was the last of the great Romantics rather than the first of the Modernists. He was a German professor of philosophy who went mad at the age of forty-five, probably from syphilis, and although he did not die until 1900, he had written all he was going to by 1880. It took a while for his work to begin to be read and appreciated. His impact was not felt until the 1890's.

Nietzsche says some original things—although often in a confused and inconsistent manner—which, if taken seriously, represent a new direction in thought. First, he expressed a strongly relativistic view of ethics. He regarded the prevailing system of Christian morality to be determined by the interests of certain groups and individuals and believed that, as such, this system bore no intrinsic legitimacy. He wanted new systems of ethics to emerge. He proclaimed the death of God, that is, the ending of the dominance of Christian values, and searched for a new system of values in a changed world. This inclination towards ethical relativism is a theme that runs through twentieth-century thought. It had profound effects in the first twenty years of the twentieth century, and has undergone a great revival since about 1965.

Nietzsche's ethics had a supporting—although not causal—influence on Modernism and in turn contributed to Postmodernism, or what is termed the deconstructionist cultural movement of the 1970's. Particularly in France Nietzsche has become very popular again.

Nietzsche also proposed the view of the "undiscovered country" far beyond contemporary Western Civilization. Western Civilization, having exhausted itself, had to be transcended. Nietzsche proclaimed a going beyond everything that was imaginable in the nineteenth century, a penetration into undiscovered areas of the mind, a supersession and replacement of Victorian culture. His vision of the undiscovered country, of transcendence, and of a cultural revolution of momentous and unimaginable consequences, is perhaps his greatest contribution to laying the background for Modernism. Yet Nietzsche was not a Modernist. He believed Richard Wagner's operas, the essence of Victorianism, to be the ultimate in art. His attitude to women is extremely patronizing and sadistically cruel.

There are other familiar late nineteenth–century phenomena which indicate the germination of cultural upheaval. One of these was the movement in

French painting in the 1870's and 80's called Impressionism. Impressionism generated a new interest in color and its use, and by concentrating on the materials of painting as well as what is represented, it pointed the way toward the non-representational art of the early twentieth century. Impressionism tried to improve representation by the careful use of color and of the materials of painting. When the representation of objects ceased to be a concern, and painting concentrated on its materials and their possible applications to the canvas, we can speak of Modernist, nonrepresentational, abstract painting. Impressionism was therefore a transitional stage between Victorian painting which focused on subject matter and Modernist painting which emphasized the materials themselves.

We can also regard the late nineteenth-century artistic (and poetic) movement of Symbolism as a further herald of cultural transformation. Nineteenth-century art is full of symbolism, but its symbolism is largely drawn from classical mythology, Christianity or from very familiar, traditional literary motifs. The symbolism of the 1880's and 90's on the other hand, creates new symbols that are divorced from traditional classical and Christian motifs. Thereby symbolism too is an artistic movement that is transitional between Victorianism and the new art of the twentieth century. It separates itself from Christian and classical symbolism in order to create new symbols, often the product of psychology or psychoneurosis, that show people in torture and torment. The feeling generated in the viewer by this contemporary, secular form of torment was more persuasive than the by now formalistic motifs of Christian hellfire. This is the beginning of something radically different in art.

Also in the 1880's, we find a new concern with the Orient and oriental culture. This is not the first time the West has felt such an interest. The Enlightenment, in the first half of the eighteenth century, had generated enthusiasm for oriental style and culture. The interest was above all in Chinese art and style (especially interior decoration), or in what the eighteenth century thought was Chinese art, in "chinoiserie," and to a lesser extent, in Indian art. Historians of the Enlightenment find this to be the beginning of a break away from European parochialism and the first time Europe begins to appreciate another culture. This Enlightenment interest in the Orient was revolutionary in its implications. The appreciation of different artistic styles led to thinking about other political systems and to the idea that, like culture, political systems too can be superseded. Once you have Chinese wallpaper, you may very well start thinking about the possibility of a different form of government.

In the 1880's and 90's, there was a novel interest in Japanese and Buddhist art and culture, and to some extent in the Indian and Middle Eastern visual traditions. How accurate and professional a knowledge the late nineteenth century actually had of these cultures is beside the point. We know that oriental studies were poorly developed in the West at the time. Hardly anybody knew the languages; translations were often inadequate. Nevertheless this new interest in Buddhism, and particularly in Japanese forms of Buddhism, emerged in the 1880's and became an important ingredient in Modernist culture in the first twenty-five or thirty years of the twentieth century. German Expressionism, which runs through the period from about 1910 to 1930, reveals a deep fascination with these oriental traditions which had already begun in the 1880's.

Finally, in the 1890's, we come upon the movement called art nouveau or "aestheticism" which is in a sense the first movement which we can properly call Modernist. Art nouveau was concerned with detail. It displayed an aesthetic appreciation not for the grand and the large, but for the small. How to make a dramatic window or a better door, and specifically a more attractive stairway were among its preoccupations. Just as the artists of the eighteenth century had spent a lot of time on doorways (Robert Adam), art nouveau occupied itself with the improvement of stairways (Victor Horta), wallpaper and chairs. Originally called "the aesthetic movement," art nouveau was an effort to bring beauty, sensibility and maximum utility to objects we experience most immediately at close range. A piece of household furniture, a decorative object, tableware, wallpaper, lithographs, were examined close up in detail, thereby articulating significant ingredients of Modernism, Art nouveau (called *Jugendstil* in Germany) was an important transition from the beginnings of cultural upheaval in the 1880's, to the actual focusing of a movement which around 1900 became Modernism.

Art nouveau, especially in England, can be viewed as an outgrowth of a desire to return to allegedly "pure," pre-industrial "folk" forms of art. This artistic puritanical populism was led in England by the utopian socialist William Morris and his disciples. In the United States a similar movement produced the "natural" breakfast food (Kellogg's Corn Flakes), anticipating the health food craze of our recent decades. It also encouraged a revival of furniture styles (Shaker, Pennsylvania Dutch) that were simpler and lighter than the heavy, fussy and ornate objects Victorians had come to prefer. A related development in Germany was a novel organization of youth groups for camping and mountain-climbing, in turn inspiring the Anglo-American Boy Scout movement after 1900.

From William Morris and the folk art movement, the 1890's derived a marginal but significant aesthetic focus on the small beauties of everyday life. This was a departure from traditional Victorian attitudes but it was still characterized by the integration of aesthetics with ethics that was a fixation of the Victorian mind. Morris turned this obsession in a somewhat novel direction. He and his disciples on both sides of the Atlantic sought to recover a more spontaneous, pre-industrial communal life whose art, it was believed, represented an authentic manifestation of a free human spirit. Perhaps this was not much more than an updated version of early 19th century transcendentalism, of Blake, Emerson, and Thoreau. The Morris dancers were late Walden.

At the same time, there emerged a self-conscious aestheticism that separated beauty from ethics and made total concentration on art a positive life-style. In England this attitude was associated principally with Walter Pater and Oscar Wilde and in Western Europe generally it was regarded as an expression of a fin-de-siècle decadence far removed on the cultural spectrum from Morris' folk art, fresh air movement. There was a lot of posturing involved in this art for art sake movement in the 90's and in reading Pater's fruity essays on the

Renaissance, we are still separated substantially from the Modernist temperament. Reading Pater on Renaissance art conjures up Edwardian drawing rooms with brocade wallpaper, port and cigars in an Oxford common room, and sodomy.

But there was something here that contributed to Modernism, if only to give confidence to the new generation that emerged after 1900 by allowing them to feel that their rebellion against Victorian ethical triumphalism was not unprecedented. Wilde's aphorism that life imitates art more than art imitates life forecasts a principal theme in the Modernist challenge to Victorian culture.

*   *   *

Characteristics of Victorian Culture

Modernism was a revolt against Victorian culture. Therefore, in order to understand Modernism, we first have to comprehend the dimensions, the characteristic attitudes and the fundamental assumptions of the nineteenth century. As has already been pointed out, the first fundamental characteristic of Victorian culture was historicism, that is, the notion that the explanation of the nature of things is gained from the description of their histories. The nineteenth century applied this idea to everything from an individual to an entire society as well as to scientific phenomena. In each case, whether national constitutions or biological species, history would provide the explanation of the nature of the thing through its longitudinal evolution. What is x? Tell me its story so I can know it. That is the Victorian way of thinking.

This attitude advantageously produced an unprecedented interest in biography. The biographies the nineteenth century produced were unprecedented for their voluminous detail and they are still valuable even if they are rather tiresome for us to read. They are usually blind to psychological factors.

The interest in biography was accompanied by concentration on national history. For the purpose of understanding current politics, it was deemed necessary to investigate political life in the middle ages or even of earlier periods. Nineteenth-century Germany, the world of Bismarck, for example, could be understood by tracing the nation's teleological development from its existence in the forests under the barbarian chieftains. In order to understand English politics in 1870, one began one's study by describing politics in 1270. This seems a trifle absurd and futile to us since with respect to the study of history we have gone in a direction quite different from the Victorians. Between 1967 and 1982, the percentage of graduating BA's majoring in history in the United States declined from 5.7% to 1.8%. We have not only gone beyond the Victorians in downgrading the value of historical explanation; we have gone twice beyond them, once in the early twentieth century, and again in the 1960's and 70's.

It is difficult for us to comprehend the Victorian addiction to history. After the Bible the most popular book in Victorian England was Thomas Macaulay's *History of England* in which the author—a liberal politician and retired Indian civil servant—gave lengthy descriptions of obscure political machinations by seventeenth–century aristocrats. He never got past 1695, but Victorian readers still thought the book was very relevant to contemporary events. When the French historian Jules Michelet lectured in the University of Paris in the 1830's, no theater could be found large enough for his audience. He was the rock star of his day. Hundreds of people lined up to hear Michelet talk about Joan of Arc, expecting that this account would somehow clarify events in modern France.

In light of the popularity of history, it is not surprising that Victorian art and literature exhibited a strong historicist tendency. Even when paintings and sculptures, novels and poems were not treating subjects evoking the distant or recent past—and that occurred frequently—there was a dominant trend towards the depiction of a narrative. In Victorian literature and art, the conscious concern is with telling a story. Narrative is paramount over other considerations. The Victorian belief that truth and reality is found in temporal projections was what the audience wanted all writers and artists to address: Which narrative does the poem, novel, painting, or sculpture illustrate? What is the story? Victorian art was shaped by these questions.

This historicist mentality has made Victorian painting and sculpture of small interest to us today, despite recent valiant attempts by art historians to find qualities in them beyond the narrative line. Nineteenth–century poetry, between the exhaustion of Romanticism in the 1830's and the symbolist anticipation of Modernist poetry in the eighties and nineties, likewise has little appeal to us. Victorian poetry has a strong proclivity to historicism and dramatic narrative and is furthermore suffused with moral preaching. In spite of the academic effort in recent years to rehabilitate Tennyson, the cultural barrier between his poetry and our attitudes and taste is too great. "To strive, to seek, to find and not to yield." Even as history, this lacks conviction; Tennyson's Ulysses is a Protestant missionary. "Grow old along with me/The best is yet to be." Browning's Rabbi Ben Ezra is a tedious schoolmaster at prize day.

Historicism does, however, perpetuate a function for Victorian novels—not normally to read them (because of their inordinate length and bewildering array of characters) but to adapt their story lines for transference to musical comedy, film, and especially TV series. Since the latter media are fixated primarily on narrative presentations, the Victorian novel maintains a half-life in that form, more readily than the Modernist novel that succeeded it.

The counterpart of historicism in the sciences was organicism. The examination of long-term biological developments was the purpose of Darwin's *The Origin of Species*. Darwin explains biology through organic evolution of biological species. He placed species in a sequential order and tried to account in terms of time for existing biological features and for the capacity of certain species to survive. It turned out that chance and environmental adaption ("natural selection") played the decisive roles. Darwin's is a biology very different from the vanguard biology of today.

Contrary to common belief, Darwinian biology did not shatter the Victorian frame of mind. On the contrary, Darwinist biology was expressed in the conventional historicist framework of Victorian thought. While the factor of chance rather than divine creation upset some people then and now, chance could be explained away as God's instrumental mechanism. With regard to the general theory he propounded, Darwin was not devastating Victorian thought. On the contrary, he was carrying out a value salvage operation, protecting historicism from the impact of scientific data.

Darwin, a reclusive gentleman autodidact, had two historical theories to account for the evolution of all animate species over time. The first was the theory of common descent of all species from one source. It was this theory that aroused noisy controversy when he published it in 1859 because it deprivileged humanity, by placing humans, like apes and monkeys, in the general pattern of common descent of all species from some pristine animate matter. This was held by conservative people for a while (and in some instances still today) to be blasphemous and to deny the Biblical view of man's creation in God's image.

The second theory that Darwin propounded is more interesting to us nowadays because of its decisive role in biological science: the theory of natural selection. In the evolution of species, including the human one, there is an infinite supply of genetic variation, the product of chance mutation. But which of these individual genetic variations become a species mutation depends on their suitability for adaption to environmental conditions. That one giraffe has a longer neck than others is a chance variation. But in so far as the idiosyncratic longer-necked giraffes are better suited to feed on trees and thereby survive, they participate in a process of natural selection and evolving modification of the species. By this theory Darwin's macro-historical vision accounts for life forms.

Today, biology does not give priority to speculating on what occurred in nature causing certain animals to disappear, or to wondering about the fate of the extinct organisms which now exist only as fossils on South American islands. These kinds of historical speculation are now a marginal concern of biological science. In the nineteenth century they were considered to be central. The fate of dinosaurs may still engage the attention of the popular press but the big grants from foundations and contracts from corporations go to the molecular biologists, not the emulators of Darwin. The leaders of biological science, the Nobel laureates, are today in the lab, scrutinizing the screens on their electron microscopes, not in the boondocks collecting flora and fauna.

Nineteenth-century linguistics was historical philology. It posited that there had been an original "Indo-European" language that existed millenia ago somewhere between Turkey and Calcutta, and it was preoccupied with discovering how European languages evolved out of this allegedly pristine Indo-European language. Remote even from the linguistics that is studied in elementary school today, it has nothing whatsoever to do with current transformational grammar. There is in fact hardly anyone left today in the United States who knows about historical philology, except perhaps a few aged scholars. It has completely disappeared from the university curriculum.

Historicism, then, was the first characteristic of Victorianism. The second was the tendency to macrocosm, for the big picture, for large-scale views. The Victorians thought that big is better. They believed not only in national history, but in world history. When Hegel produced a philosophy of history in which he presented a pattern of world history in 400 pages, people took him seriously. One could make such claims in the nineteenth century; one could attempt to devise comprehensive systems.

Hegel tells us that "the history of the World has been a rational process." What distinguishes this process is the activity of "a World-Spirit . . . which unfolds this its one nature in the phenomena of the World's existence." What does this mean? It means that the triumph of reason and World-Spirit is represented by Protestant Christianity and the Prussian State. We may find this outcome anti-climactic, even a bit absurd, but there is no doubt that Hegel had a perception of the big historical picture.

In the sciences the macro level was likewise stressed by the Victorians. Science aimed at general biology, general physics, a general theory of chemistry. The purpose of physics was to propound universal laws. The purpose of chemistry was to discover all possible elements and map them on a "periodic" table, showing their relationships to one another. On the walls of some high school chemistry labs one can still see the faded periodic table which was put together in 1890 by a Russian chemist. This tabulation of chemical elements has little to do with chemistry today. Most chemists today would not even know the periodic table, nor would they have a use for it.

The proclivity of nineteenth-century science to grand macrocosmic schemes of evolution in contrast to twentieth-century science's emphasis on the microcosmic level, or the smallest discernible unit, is demonstrated by the strange scientific career of Gregor Mendel. An Austrian monk teaching physics and other natural sciences in a provincial Catholic school after studying at the University of Vienna, Mendel did massive statistical studies of the growth and breeding of peas, and in 1866 published a revolutionary paper that established the basis of modern genetics. He was able to show the mathematical ratio (3–1) between dominant and recessive genes in each generation. This was a conceptual and methodological breakthrough of the greatest importance.

Only seven years after Darwin's *Origin of Species*, Mendel anticipated not only twentieth-century genetics, but the essential microcosmic spirit of post-Victorian science: "The distinguishing characteristics of two plants can, after all, be caused only by differences in the composition and grouping of the elements existing in dynamic interaction in their primordial cells." The enunciation of scientific reality as lying in dynamic interaction in primordial cells was a trumpet call for modern science. Yet Mendel's work was entirely ignored until 1900 when geneticists thinking along similar lines rediscovered his paper and realized that Mendel had largely anticipated their work several decades earlier.

The failure of Mendel to gain any recognition in his day, even though more than 100 scientific libraries in Western Europe received published copies of his 1866 paper, reveals the dominance of macro-historicism in Victorian science which blinded scientists to a novel way of thinking—micro and statistical— that would have taken them well beyond Darwin into the revolutions of twentieth-century science. Mendel's story is paradigmatic of the way in which the dominant mind-set conditions the course of scientific as well as other forms of theory.

The purpose of Victorian social science was the development of a universal theory of social evolution. The most prominent names under this heading were the Americans Lewis Morgan and William Graham Sumner and the prolific Englishman Herbert Spencer. Spencer tried to provide a general theory of sociology which could be applied to all peoples. At the one end of the scientific spectrum was presumed to be the periodic table of chemical elements; at the other, the hierarchy of societies from the primitive to the advanced, from the simple to the most complex.

It is not difficult to imagine who occupied the lower end and who the higher. The social theory according to which American Indians and the people of Africa constituted the simple peoples and occupied the lower end of the hierarchical ladder became known as social Darwinism. Europeans were the more complicated peoples, it was held, and in course of the universal process called "the struggle for existence" had built the more advanced societies. Obviously this Victorian effort to see the large sociological picture by positing a hierarchy of peoples was propaganda for imperialism. But Victorians believed it was social science.

When it came to social science, Victorian semiotics and iconology were not very subtle. Everyone knew what the "survival of the fittest" in the evolutionary struggle for existence signified. It meant lithe, handsome, blond Englishmen playing cricket on the lawn of the Calcutta or Mombassa country club while quiescent natives in starched uniforms served gin and tonics to the chaste bosomy wives and daughters of the master race. In the social macrocosm everyone had his or her designated place. The function of a general theory of society was to assure this disciplinary situation.

Nineteenth-century painting also aimed at telling a story which would make the beholder macrocosmically recollect as many things as possible. Victorians painted huge, cluttered canvasses in the 1850's and 60's. The pictures presented Biblical stories or episodes from Virgil and Homer. The purpose behind this was ultimately to stimulate in the viewer recollections of a cultural universe. Through viewing a detailed and dramatic scene from the Bible or classical mythology, the Victorian was supposed immediately to be reminded of the elaborate, tightly integrated cultural system he had imbibed from school and church. The function of art was principally to reinforce values and ideas. While an occasional critic like John Ruskin would struggle against this view that art was better the more it provided pedagogical and mnemonic services to the general ideas embedded in a cultural macrocosm, it remained a fixation of the Victorian mind and became a prime target of Modernism.

 In addition to historicism and macrocosm, the third Victorian characteristic was a rigid system of normative ethics. Nineteenth-century people could conceive of the good and of the bad, of the way to behave and not to behave, and they believed in the righteous imposition of their code through institutional power. There was authority in the world, represented usually by the father, the adult male, and the state, to enforce the system of ethics whose code derived from the Bible, from the Old and the New Testament, from the churches as well as from the behavioral pattern of a hierarchical family structure. The code, in other words, was set down by authority. What served the interests of pastors, fathers, lawyers, generals, and businessmen was given absolute moral sanction. In the twentieth century, we see very little advantage in this inflexible system of ethics. Our century has spent much time undermining it.

By the 1970's, there was a tremendous erosion of this Victorian moral code, preceded by the first enervating wave in the first three decades of the twentieth century. Currently, however, there are some people who look back at Victorian ethics with nostalgia. They find that, despite the fact that it may have done some harm, nevertheless it inculcated a powerful work ethic, unequivocally condemned street crime, alcoholism and narcotic addiction, and allegedly did not require (or more accurately allow) as many abortions as we have today.

Above all, Victorian morality fostered the nuclear family. During the first four or five decades of the nineteenth century, Victorian society witnessed an alarming level of urban crime, alcoholism, and family dislocation, particularly among the industrial working-class. All the moral resources of Western society transmitted by church, state, school, and the popular press were recruited to combat these indices of social pathology. The conventional family unit with two parents, children in residence through adolescence, and with dominance allocated to the father, was deemed the institutional realization of moral doctrine. Ethics meant family, with the middle class model imposed on the working class as a norm that would make the latter respectable, secure, and prosperous.

This ethical legitimization of the nuclear family model was successful: there was a strong trend towards the stable family unit in the late nineteenth century. We, who have experienced a severe trend towards family disintegration and who might look with some envy on the Victorian situation, have to remember that the triumph of the Victorian family was not only the product of impersonal social and material forces. It was essentially made possible by strenuous moral teaching, which the Modernist movement began to unravel after 1900. Today, there is widespread concern about the decline of family stability and the increasing prominence of the one parent family. Disagreement arises about the utility of restoring Victorian ethics as the means to rebuilding family structure.

The fourth characteristic of Victorian thought was Western chauvinism or the justification of imperialism. The West was perceived as an advanced society while the people of Africa, for example, were regarded as primitives. The nineteenth century did not find much wrong in this respect with Chinese and Indian societies, for these were old cultures, but they were, in turn, regarded as effete and decadent. The West was the ideal social model whereas other societies were either decadent or primitive. The West, neither hot nor cold, was just right, as in the story of Goldilocks. In the words of Rudyard Kipling's poem, written in honor of Teddy Roosevelt (who remarked to a friend that Kipling's encomium was bad poetry but good theory), it was not only the West's privilege but its moral duty to "take up the White Man's burden" and help the less fortunate colored races of mankind.

This patronizing imperialist doctrine gained overwhelming credence, especially in the second half of the nineteenth century. If pervasive faith in this doctrine had not existed, there would not have been a Western imperialism. At most, there would have been a few commercial stations here and there, to pursue business interests, but certainly no British domination of India, nor American rule over "the little brown brothers" in the Philippines, nor the European carving up of Africa.

Around 1850, the West still controlled little of Africa. But by 1900 its rule over the continent was complete. Only the concept of chauvinistic Western superiority justified this dominion, making it appear valuable and necessary. The majority of these newly acquired European colonies in Africa were fiscally burdensome to the imperial power. Without an imperialistic and racist mentality, European involvement in Africa would have been marginal.

Imperialism was profitable to only a handful of people, to army officers, a few businessmen and administrators, and occasionally to missionaries. By and large, the balance sheet of imperialism was negative. Even though the Indian people were taxed to defray expenditure for government and defence, it cost the British more to rule India than they ever gained from it, with the result that, impoverished by World War II, they had to leave precipitously in 1947.

Over two long centuries of the British Raj, there were only two tangible as distinct from psychic advantages that the British people gained from the Jewel in the Crown. India provided a large reservoir of military manpower, useful in the First World War and critically necessary in the Second. Furthermore the Indian civil service, law courts, and army provided a steady pool of creative and challenging jobs. In the words of an early nineteenth-century anti-imperialist, the Empire and especially the Raj was "the great system of outdoor relief for the British upper classes." After 1947 such people had to become advertising executives, Oxbridge dons, BBC producers, or migrate to America to become Jaguar salesmen, newspaper editors or Ivy League professors. Such is the menial denouement of the pith helmet brigade.

Indo-China (Vietnam) was a fiscal sinkhole for the liberal French Third Republic; only for generals and Catholic missionaries was there an immediate advantage to be gained from the French Vietnamese involvement. It had to be justified on grounds of disseminating French "civilization" among less fortunate people.

The notion that the West had a destiny and an obligation, and that it was at the right point of development between primitivism and decadence to shoulder the white man's burden, was believed in by educated people as well as the masses stirred up by the popular press. This attitude is difficult for us to conceive today; there is very little of it left. Only the Afrikaners in South Africa, with nothing to lose, would today dare assert publicly the white man's superiority. But in the late nineteenth-century, Western triumphalism was powerfully present, a fact to which much Victorian literature bears witness. Even generous liberals like Tom Macaulay believed that it would be many decades, perhaps centuries, before the people of India would be ready to govern themselves. Self-government for Africans was not even a subject for speculation.

Rudyard Kipling, the poet laureate of the white man's burden, inserted a paradoxical note of pessimism into the imperialist doctrine. The non-Europeans he cautioned, "half savage and half child" couldn't appreciate the fine things the English, Americans, and other colonial powers were doing in their empires: imperialism would recede in coming decades. He was right.

The fifth characteristic of Victorian thought was philosophical idealism. The more abstract, general, and theoretical thought became, the more it could propound universal theorems, the closer it was to the truth. Truth did not reside in the particular, but in universal propositions. This was, in a way, the philosophical aspect of historicism and the macrocosm, but it can also be regarded as a distinct category. Professional philosophy in the nineteenth century, that is, what was taught by professors in the universities, was overwhelmingly idealist until about 1900.

The most influential philosopher of the nineteenth century was the German Hegel, who believed in a kind of developmental Platonism. As we have seen, truth, according to Hegel, lay in general ideas which moved through time and history, evolving toward a grand finale (currently the Prussian state, he claimed). The purpose of thinking was to refine all away all empirical data and attain pure abstraction, the most universal propositions ("the Absolute").

It may be hard for us to know what to make of such views, but they spelled truth itself for the nineteenth century. There were three reasons for the dominance of philosphical idealism in nineteenth-century thought. First, it drew upon strong currents in the three previous cultural revolutions—the Reformation, the Enlightenment, and Romanticism. Idealism was a reformulation of the most continuous philosophical movement in Western Civilization, namely Platonism, and cheap and relatively accurate new translations into all the main European languages had recently made the Greek philosopher accessible to the Victorian educated public.

Secondly, philosophic idealism was in the Victorian mind a secularized substitute for Christianity. Idealism became a half-way house for middle class intellectuals who had lost their faith in Christian revelation ("the long-withdrawing roar" of the mid-century, in Matthew Arnold's words) but who wanted to preserve a certain way of looking at the world and human behavior compatible with the churches' teaching in many areas. Thirdly, idealism was a philosophy for the sexually repressed. If Victorians in most (but not all) instances resisted coming to terms with sexual drives, idealism buttressed this severe repression, since truth lay only in general propositions (secularized Christian ethics) but not in empirical data (e.g. dreams and neurotic behavior patterns).

Even in 1900, German universities were respectful of Hegelianism. Hegel preserved his importance in British universities too for a long time. The philosophy department of Princeton University remained entirely Hegelian at the turn of the century. Still Hegelian in 1900 was a prominent professor of philosophy at Harvard. Hegelianism collapsed quite suddenly. Ten years later, at least outside Germany, it had almost disappeared. Overnight, as it were, Hegelian idealism had gone up in smoke. But at the end of the nineteenth century it was still dominant.

In the 1890's a radically modified, non-Hegelian form of philosophical idealism began to gain visibility in the heartland of idealism, the philosophy faculties of the German universities. Going back beyond Hegel to Immanuel Kant, neo-Kantian philosophy sustained the authenticity of intuitive general propositions about ethics and religion but also allowed the power of the human mind to derive empirically based models or types from the study of particular phenomena. Here was a half-way house between idealism and empiricism: the recognition of general propositions that were rationally created by human consciousness out of data. Using these neo-Kantian assumptions, Wilhelm Dilthey developed a cultural history that provided a high degree of patterning without the rigid, arbitrary, and unverifiable abstractions favored by Hegel and his disciples. Dilthey's colleague Max Weber also in the 1890's set about fashioning his sociology of ideal-types (based on accumulation and generalization from empirical data) such as the charismatic leader and bureaucratic government.

Nevertheless, while neo-Kantianism differed from Hegelianism, it remained a form of idealist philosophy: it found reality in the general forms that consciousness creates.

The sixth quality of Victorian thought was the concept of order, which was always regarded as preferable to disorder. The Enlightenment had a strong proclivity to system-building; the Romantic movement somewhat diminished the centrality of order. The mid-Victorians brought back systemic order to the foreground of cultural and social value. Coherence, organization, hierarchy, systematization constituted the desiderata. In line with this penchant, one dealt with a problem by dividing it into the upper and the lower, the left and the right, thereby devising a system of order. The marginal, the disorderly, the particular, the uncontrolled, and the unpredictable were relegated to the realm of the negative. The determined and the predictable could be placed in sets of early and late, upper and lower, and were therefore good.

Some commentators see this penchant for order as a reaction to the Industrial Revolution. The Industrial Revolution created upheaval and chaos, and such social and environmental change that in response to it, there was a desperate attempt to create order, an attempt which began with the family. From there, one hierarchically proceeded to build other invincible organizations and institutions.

The Victorians in their pursuit of order created the police force. There was very little in the way of a police organization anywhere in the West before the nineteenth century. The Victorian age established penitentiaries and the penal system. In some ways, this was a reflection of all aspects of Victorian thought, that is, of a macrocosmic, idealist, historicist, and normative way of thinking, but it was also a reflection of fear of the disorder generated by the upheaval of the Industrial Revolution.

Thomas Mann's first novel *Buddenbrooks* is concerned primarily with this fascination with order and its debilitating consequences in individual lives of his North German family. Writing in 1901 Mann claimed that middle-class families payed a harsh psychological price for the constant stress upon social order. What would he say after studying the activities of crack pushers, valley girls, and porno video shops?

Finally, the seventh feature of Victorianism was simplification and popularization. The nineteenth century believed that thought should not be esoteric, that it should not be the exclusive domain of professionals and scholars, just as it believed that poetry was not only for poets, nor paintings for artists. Ideas should be communicated and made accessible to society as a whole, or at least to the educated middle class, which, due to the role of secondary education, either free or inexpensive, was very much on the increase in the second half of the nineteenth century.

To take complicated ideas and make them available to educated people, which in practice meant anyone with high school education, was central to the Victorian cultural program. There was a tremendous urge to what the French call "high vulgarization," or to what we might call simplification and popularization. Whether novelists or philosophers, scientists or theologians, nineteenth century intellectuals tried to address a broad, educated public and to express their ideas in ordinary, non-technical language. Artists and poets used themes easily recognizable by the public. Culturally, the Victorians tended towards democracy and away from elitism.

The very small proportion of Victorian men—and virtually no women— who attended university before the 1880's was a factor that contributed to this cultural populism. Even among intellectuals and professional people, only a minority were college graduates. To gain an audience, Victorian thinkers and writers had to use the language and conceptual level concomitant with secondary education (equivalent to the sophomore level in an American college today).

But there was more to the Victorian zeal for simplication and popularization than this social factor. They had a missionary calling to spread higher culture as far as possible in the middle class and among the more reliable and sober working class.

Victorians believed passionately in cultural accessibility. As a result, whether it was poetry, fiction, literary criticism, or even scientific theory, anyone with a high school education could gain immediate access to the major works, for which there was consequently a substantial market. Victorian booksellers, like our own, sold a lot of trash, but they also sold major works of both fiction and non-fiction. The leading edge of serious current literature that in New York City today is sold in only a half-dozen esoteric bookstores in the whole metropolitan area, Victorians could purchase at a kiosk in a railway station. Consequently there exists the paradoxical situation that Heine, Stendhal, Arnold, Mill, and Darwin are much easier even for us to read than comparable classics of Modernism and Postmodernism. That is why in secondary school curricula, perhaps even in college curricula, there is today a disproportionate favoring of Victorian as against Modernist and Postmodernist writings: the Victorians are much easier to read.

This phenomenon, of intellectual accessibility in the nineteenth century, is admirable. It is, in fact, currently admired: the effort that is now being made to establish core curricula in American colleges is, in a way, a neo-Victorian statement. The effort at re-establishing a simplified base of knowledge available to everybody is certainly not something the Modernist movement would have advocated. Modernism tended in an entirely different direction.

*   *   *

Causes of the Modernist Cultural Revolution

Before establishing a model of Modernism in the next chapter, it is necessary to discuss why the large-scale transformation occurred around 1900, what factors precipitated it, and why the Modernist revolution came about specifically at the turn of the century. Why cultural revolutions occur, why there has been a Reformation, an Enlightenment or Romanticism, is something that historical science has not been able to explain persuasively. In the past four decades the fashion in academic historiography has been almost exclusive attention to durable structures and avoidance of even considering the causes of change. A few suggestions, however, may be offered explaining why Modernism came about when and where it did.

First, there is the factor of entropy, or exhaustion. It is a fact of history that after a period, a cultural movement or a world view exhausts itself. It maintains its central position for a period of time. It is taught, believed in, but then, at a certain point, it seems to have solved its problems and said everything it could within the framework of its cardinal principles. No artist can achieve further visibility, no poet can attain a remarkable breakthrough, no philosopher can envision something new following the old assumptions. The assumptions lose their plasticity, and the cultural movement exhausts itself.

This is an old story. In 1600 Western Europeans had an insatiable taste for hearing about Christian doctrine. By 1680, however, people in Europe were no longer much interested in the dispute between Protestant and Catholic theology. By 1740 Voltaire could get a big laugh by simply listing the main themes of Reformation theology. Similarly, at a certain point (1790) the Enlightenment appeared tiresome, even shallow, and by the middle of the nineteenth century Romanticism found itself exhausted. Already in the second decade of the century Byron wrote: "So we'll go no more aroaming/So late into the night,/Though the heart be still as loving/ and the moon be still as bright," expressing his weariness with Romanticism.

Victorianism was such a rich culture, affirming its characteristics in such powerful ways, that by 1900, at least for artists and intellectuals, it had become tiresome and ineffectual. There seemed to be nothing more to be obtained from it. Victorian culture lost its resiliency and its main assumptions appeared trivial and redundant. Intellectuals entered the way of rebellion, searched for new ways to express themselves, and developed points of view that ran counter to Victorian premises.

Therefore, the first cause of the emergence of Modernism was the over-success of Victorianism and the corresponding entropy of Victorian culture. In the 1890's Victorian culture was broad and elaborate but it was thin—it increasingly lacked conviction, inspiration, vitality. It appeared to the emerging generation of 1900 to be unimaginative and banal and indeed it was. It may be conceded that this explanation sounds like a tautology: Victorianism ended because it ended. But there is no better explanation for major cultural changes than the entropic model.

Thomas Kuhn's celebrated explanation of the cause of scientific revolutions—the old paradigm can no longer absorb and reconcile new data—is essentially the same as the entropic explanation for cultural revolutions, and equally tautological.

The second explanation for the emergence of Modernism was the demoralization that began to occur in the Victorian world for social reasons. Victorians became conscious of the fact that they were having difficulties solving what they called the "social problem," a problem which still remains largely unsolved. Victorians faced the problems of the poor and homeless and, although there was much less in the late nineteenth century than what we have today, of crime. They felt pressed to resolve the prevalence of poverty and social pathology.

These concerns were exacerbated by the great depression the entire Western world underwent between 1873 and 1895. There was bankruptcy, unemployment, credit shortage, in short, every characteristic of a depression, duly accompanied by confusion as to how to resolve these difficulties. It took twenty years to get out of them. Historians are pretty sure as to the causes of the depression. For one thing, we know that nineteenth-century banking and credit institutions were deficient. But historians are uncertain as to how the Western world emerged from the depression. We can conjecture that with the discovery of gold mines in South Africa, the infusion into the Western world of gold advantageously increased the money supply.

At any rate, the Victorians faced debilitating and apparently insoluble social problems and then a great depression which further undermined confidence in their doctrines. With so much concentrated social misery and poverty in the 1880's and early 1890's, belief in historicism, macrocosm, and traditional Christian ethics began to evaporate.

The third cause for the rise of Modernism was that imperialism began to turn sour. The strangest facet of European imperialism is that it began its collapse at the moment it reached its zenith. Although it took until the 1920's for this fact to become fully manifest and to emerge in actual political movements for colonial liberation, we have seen that Rudyard Kipling was already in 1897 predicting the downfall of the white man's empire. The decline of imperialism was accompanied by the proliferation of ideologically anti-imperial sentiment in Europe and the increasing feeling that imperialism was a hoax set up by soldiers and a few capitalists, particularly those engaged in mineral extraction like the "randlords" in South Africa, who were its only visible beneficiaries.

Two events of the 1880's demoralized many reflective people and inevitably raised questions about imperialism and Western chauvinism. One was the massacre of Zulus in South Africa by the British army at the behest of white settlers who wanted the natives' land. Magnificent Zulu warriors were mercilessly mowed down by modern British machine guns. The other incident was the suppression of the French-Indian métis, or the "halfbreeds" as the English called them, and the Indians in Saskatchewan, Canada. The French-

Indians tried to establish an independent democratic republic in Saskatchewan; they too were crushed by a British army. The métis leader was tried and hanged for treason, becoming a perpetual martyr for French-speaking Canada.

These ugly events prompted rethinking about the purpose and utility of imperialism and signaled the diminution of imperialist enthusiasm. The Boer War that began in South Africa in 1898 inflicted on imperialism a mortal blow. Strange as it may seem now, rebellious Afrikaner (Boer, Dutch) settlers trying (in the end, unsuccessfully) to throw off British rule were seen as heroes by the European left. It was not noted that one reason they wanted independence was to be able to treat the black population more severely.

The guns were barely stilled in South Africa when the myth of the natural superiority of the white man and effete quality of the Asian peoples was devastated by the Russo-Japanese War of 1904–5. After the Japanese had taken Russia's far eastern fortress of Port Arthur, the Russian Baltic Fleet, allegedly one of the more powerful in the world, sailed proudly more than half-way around the globe to confront the Japanese navy. The Russian fleet was sent to the bottom by the Japanese in an hour, anticipating the events of December 7, 1941. An obscure British-educated Indian lawyer Mohandas K. Gandhi soon emerged as the leading opponent of the Raj. Gandhi drew from the Russian naval catastrophe the lesson that the European empires in Asia were paper tigers, and he began his four decades of persistent campaigning for Indian freedom.

With the decline of imperialism, the general unraveling of Victorian thought also accelerated. Since Victorianism and imperialism were entwined, when imperialism began to collapse, it brought down with it other aspects of the surrounding culture.

This is essentially the theme of E. M. Forster's novel about imperialism, *A Passage to India*. Although published in 1924, it was written several years earlier, and describes the Indian Raj of 1914. It is not only that imperialism, in Forster's view, is base, that it is terribly demoralizing and raises very grave questions about Western ethics. More fundamentally, Forster believes that Indian civilization and the Indian middle class constitute a great Other which even generous-minded Englishmen cannot comprehend. India is an endless dark cave that disorients and bewilders Westerners; they had best pack up and go home. This message is similar to that propounded by Conrad three decades earlier, but significantly it was now set forth in an acerbic manner, with very little sympathy for the imperial master class. They appear in Forster's novel not as tragic but as diminished, foolish, petty.

In Forster's view, imperialism is tattered and chintzy. Far from being grand, it is beginning to look sordid and soiled around the edges, even in its physical aspects. Although Forster's Indian novel was not written in Modernist style, he himself was a close associate of Modernist writers and artists, and in his mind was the idea that the decline of imperialism was related to the emergence of the new culture.

A third factor that helped generate the cultural revolution of Modernism was the proliferation, to which we have already referred, of a large, educated middle class. Beginning in the 1870's throughout the Western world, first in

Germany, then in France and the United States, and finally, rather late in 1904, in England, virtually free secondary education became available, although of course it remained highly selective. From 1870 to 1900, the high school population rose from 2% to 10% of the male 13–17 age group and in response to a voracious demand for office workers, women increasingly gained access to secondary education. (The Underwood typewriter did more for the liberation of women than all the feminist theory propounded before 1900). Although university populations remained small, compared to previous generations there was also a major expansion in higher education.

The educated middle class registered a quantum leap in one generation, which certainly led to concurrent changes in the arts, literature and intellectual pursuits. The conservative academies that had set the style and motifs for the visual arts in particular, and to some extent for the performing arts, could no longer exert the same control. The educated became so numerous, as did people with aesthetic taste and cultivation who could make discretionary expenditures on the arts and books, that a vanguard could emerge by 1900 eluding the authority of conservative institutions. That is, once a relatively large educated middle class came into being, it became impossible to control the socialization, education and intellectual propensity of an entire rising generation or to sustain the hold of traditional cultural values.

There would henceforth be those at the social margin who would join the avant-garde. The Victorians believed very much in education, and made enormous strides in it. But they undermined their own system by producing a surplus of cultivated people, many more than their traditional intellectual and artistic institutions could control or absorb.

A host of additional social and material factors should also be mentioned that interactively played special roles in forging the new consciousness.

One of these was the end of the great depression in 1895. Between 1895 and 1906, the West witnessed great prosperity. The employment rate was high, inflation was low, and it was relatively cheap to live. Such periods of high employment and low inflation are infrequent in history, and they produce momentous cultural developments. A similar phenomenon recurred for a few years in the 1920's and in the 1960's. When a rising generation of educated people does not have to worry about securing its livelihood, about choice of profession, when it does not feel obliged to become accountants or lawyers, and can risk becoming artists or philosophers, or founding new theaters, or writing poetry, because it knows that it can always find a means for making a living, that period witnesses a cultural explosion. Such was the case between 1895 and 1906.

After 1906, the rapid rise of inflation was followed by the high unemployment that began three or four years before the first World War. Labor problems, strikes, lay-offs, and cut-backs were features of the period leading up to World War I, which contrasted sharply with the fondly remembered gay 90's. The epithet "gay 90's" is based on the social fact that young people could easily find jobs as well as pursue the arts in the decade after 1895.

The second material factor that contributed to the Modernist cultural revolution was inexpensive housing. Analogous to the principle of material determinism in history, one can cite a relationship between affordable living quarters in a period and cultural history. Extrapolating from this principle, we can easily claim that New York is now doomed as a cultural center. The future cultural vanguard of the United States will be located in places like Minneapolis; Burlington, Vermont; Tulsa, Oklahoma; Louisville, or Seattle.

The period of our concern was a time of unprecedented, phenomenally cheap housing in great metropolitan centers throughout the world. Reading the biography of Picasso, one finds out that around 1912, Picasso in Paris decided that he needed a new and larger studio which he rented within a few hours for a trifling sum. Picasso was at the time still a relatively unknown artist. Nowadays a young artist could never afford a large studio in Montmartre, a very attractive part of Paris. This is the period that saw the emergence of New York's Greenwich Village as an artists' colony, of Bloomsbury in London's West End as the habitat of intellectuals, writers and philosophers. Virginia Woolf and her sister Vanessa Bell leased Bloomsbury houses which are today affordable only by stockbrokers or advertising executives, not by aspiring novelists and painters.

The availability of good housing around 1900 for artists, intellectuals, and academics was due to changes in metropolitan transportation. In the 1880's and 90's the tram or trolley car systems were developed, electric railroads were introduced, and most important of all, the first subways were built. The early subways were so salubrious and safe that riding them was deemed a privilege rather than a burden. Entrance kiosks on the Vienna and Paris subways are still treasured as wonderful examples of art nouveau; ladies and gentlemen entered the New York IRT in evening dress to travel to the opera; London subways had special smoking cars. An enormous urban expansion inevitably followed the building of the new metropolitan transport lines around 1900. What enabled, for example, Columbia University to move from Manhattan's center to Morningside Heights in 1903 was the opening of the IRT subway line. When Columbia moved to its present location, the area was vacant land. In fact, someone suggested to Nicholas Murray Butler, then president of Columbia, that he buy the large meadow called Harlem that lay below Morningside Heights. He rejected it on grounds that no one would ever move and live up there "in the country."

In 1880 ninety per cent of New York's population lived below Central Park, about seventy per cent lived below Forty-Second Street. In the 1890's, the population density in Manhattan's Lower East Side was 500,000 people per square mile—what it is in Hong Kong today. This situation changed very rapidly in the later years of the nineteenth and early twentieth century. The working class moved to Brownsville, Brooklyn, Queens and the Bronx. There was nothing in the Bronx until the early years of the twentieth century except farmland. Queens too was largely unsettled. Similar transformations occurred in all the large cities of the Western world. Entire new areas emerged for the working class on the periphery of cities which, as a result, expanded rapidly, vastly extending their territorial borders.

At the same time many in the middle class moved to the suburbs. This is the period of the musical comedy song "Forty-Five Minutes to Broadway." It was

Yonkers, the residential area for businessmen and the first bedroom community, that was forty-five minutes to Broadway, or more precisely, to Grand Central or Penn Station. These departures—by the working class to the peripherey and the affluent class to the suburbs—left vacant and underutilized housing in the heart of the metropolitan areas, such as the West End of London, New York City below 14th street, the area around the university in Munich, parts of Berlin, the Left Bank and Montmartre in Paris, central Vienna—all of which provided superb opportunities for artists and intellectuals. They took over the housing abandoned by the working class, or, in some cases, by the middle class.

The new apartment blocks for the working class on the edge of old Vienna eased pressure on the housing stock in the central city, allowing young Dr. Freud and other impecunious intellectuals to rent comfortable homes or flats. Paradoxically, some of the new working class housing was so attractive that in the twenties it was much sought after by artists and writers. The Chelsea section of London experienced a similar history.

Not until decades later, after the Second World War, did these housing opportunities finally disappear. In the 1920's they were still there. An erosion of real estate opportunities for the avant-garde threatened in the thirties but the depression dammed this trend. It was not until the 1950's that housing facilities for artists and intellectuals began their absolute decline. Since in the sixties and seventies in Paris and to a lesser extent elsewhere there was again some working class move to peripheral developments, the avant-garde real estate situation in Europe is not quite as bad as in New York, where it has become catastrophic.

Another factor in the emergence of Modernism was the rise of fringe countries and provincial cities. The great centers of Modernism were Berlin, London, Paris, Vienna and New York, but there were other participating places: Dublin, the locale of the Irish Renaissance, was the city of Joyce and Yeats; Chicago and Glasgow were two of the important centers for Modernist architecture; Oslo bred two great dramatists of the early twentieth century. Chicago was an important center in social science; Cambridge, Mass., in philosophy and psychology.

Some scientists of the Modernist era came from very distant places. Ernest Rutherford, who along with Einstein is one of the two most important physicists of the early twentieth century, came from New Zealand—and Einstein did his early, seminal work in Zurich, the home of Jung, and final refuge of Joyce. Rutherford did most of his early research at McGill University in Montreal, which in the early years of the century was a lively place intellectually. Another important physicist, Niels Bohr, worked in Copenhagen. Marie Curie was a Pole who immigrated to Paris.

There was, in short, a major expansion in intellectual activity which drew on the Western population in a comprehensive way. Places which had once constituted the provinces became secondary metropolitan centers of Western culture. Newly founded or greatly expanded universities outside the old metropolitan centers—Johns Hopkins, Chicago, Manchester, Göttingen, Strasbourg—moved rapidly to the forefront of learning and research.

In the twenty years before World War I, Russia's contribution to Western culture, especially in music, attained not only an unprecedented level but a peak that it has never regained under Communist rule. The cultural connection between St. Petersburg and Paris in the early Modernist years was a close and productive one. Emigrés from the Tsarist Empire dominated French ballet and were prominent in painting both in Paris and Berlin.

New media played a role in shaping the context of Modernism. The revolution in the printing trades evolved into the late nineteenth-century appearance of the paperback book which meant fast and low-cost printing. People could now buy a softcover novel or a work in philosophy at the railway station kiosk before boarding their train. This novelty of the 1890's was made possible by new high speed printing and cheap paper. With the technological revolution in the printing trades—the greatest since Gutenberg—hand-presses became obsolete and were, in turn, bought by intellectuals who used the old, abandoned hand-presses to turn out small magazines and vanguard books.

One of the great Modernist scenes in the early 1920's is Virginia Woolf standing in the basement of her Bloomsbury house over an obsolete hand-press which she and Leonard Woolf had bought for a few pounds, setting type for the first edition of T.S. Eliot's *The Waste Land*. She and her husband founded their own press, called The Hogarth, which is still in business although they do not use hand-presses any more. They were the first to publish Eliot's poem.

They were by no means the only writers and intellectuals to undertake such activity. The Modernist era in literature was made possible by "little magazines" and small publishing houses. Joyce's *Ulysses* was originally published by an American bookstore proprietor in Paris and the first edition of Proust's *Swann's Way* by a fledgling publishing house after being rejected by more prominent Parisian editors. Some of the most celebrated names among New York publishers became prominent and eventually affluent in the twenties and thirties as patrons of Modernist fiction. Little magazines with paid circulation of less than a thousand each transformed literary and art criticism, and public taste.

Another novelty in the printing trade was color lithography, which became a major medium in modern art around 1900 and for a while was almost synonymous, along with stairways, with *art nouveau*. Some of the first manifestations of Expressionist art appear in color lithographs that were produced around this time. Two of the pioneers of Modernism, Edvard Munch, in his first important work, and Gustav Klimt, in some of his early production, utilized this medium before they concentrated on painting. Some of Paul Klee's early work was done in lithographs. This new medium played an important part in the formation of Modernist art. Now one could actually hold an original work of art, bought for little money, in one's hands, and not just a reproduction.

The role of photography in the emergence of Modernism is not a simple story. First, photography was one of the ways in which secular symbolism expressed itself. Many of the early photographers of the 1880's and 90's were artists. They looked upon photography not so much as a way of depicting the real world, but as a method for representing a symbolic dimension. Photography was in its early decades the new medium for the creation and communication of original artistic forms and ideas. It was to take its place alongside paint and canvas, stone and metal, as an art form. This expectation has never entirely disappeared, and in recent years it has again become prominent.

Photography's second role in the making of Modernist culture lay in precisely the opposite direction from this symbolic art photography. The effectiveness of the camera in reproducing images of the real or natural world made it seem superfluous for painting to pursue this task, as it had done through much of the nineteenth century as well as earlier. In 1914 art critc Clive Bell remarked: "Who doubts that one of those Daily Mirror photographers ... can tell us far more about 'London by day' than any royal academician?" The painter or sculptor was no longer called upon to illustrate scenes from life or the human face and body as they appeared to the eye: photographs could do that well enough, and as the mobility of the camera improved and the chemistry of celluloid film became more sophisticated, it could do it better and far more cheaply and rapidly than the artist.

At the turn of the century, in London's Chelsea, Paris' Left Bank, or New York's Greenwich Village, the artist—unless he or she was a commercial illustator—felt increasingly impelled to make a mark by depicting a non-realistic world, the world seen by the inner imaginative but not physical eye; finally, a non-representational, abstract world. It is too simple to say that the Kodak camera made Picasso and Kandinsky inevitable, but there is a core of truth in this statement.

Finally photography and—although in 1900 it was still cumbersome and expensive—especially color photography revolutionized art education. In 1870 only the wealthy, or the beneficiaries of affluent patronage, could gain the rudiments of education in the visual arts because only they could afford to travel to galleries and museums. In 1900 people of modest means could, however, get some sense of what great painting and sculpure looked like by studying photographs. The new women's colleges that were founded at this time were the first institutions to realize clearly the educational possibilities that art photography represented and established basic courses in art history and criticism. Talented people in the provinces could now glimpse what was occurring in the metropolitan centers of avant-garde art and gain inspiration for joining the aesthetic vanguard.

Furthermore, they did not have to stay in the provinces. They could get on a train and for a reasonably priced ticket be on the Left Bank, in London's Bloomsbury, or in Greenwich Village in a matter of hours. Modernism emerged in that strange and ephemeral technological moment, the railroad era, which for practical purposes endured only from 1880 to 1955. It took until 1880 for the national railway networks to be built and after 1955 the airplane for long journeys and automobile and bus service for shorter trips made the utility of the railroad marginal or even negligible.

Economic historians tell us that the railroad was never a technological necessity in Western Europe and the United States. If the magnificent canal system built in the eighteenth and early nineteenth centuries had been maintained and expanded, it could have distributed goods and people just as well (although not to precisely the same locations as the railroads) and could have done so more cheaply and with less ravaging of the countryside.

Railroads were built as speculative capitalist ventures or to suit the vanity of heads of government, or facilitate the mobility of armies. From the beginning these fiscally leveraged, ruinously expensive enterprises made very little money as transportation systems: they survived out of land and mineral concessions or direct government subsidies. In some ways, railroads were extravagant Potemkin villages, like the bloated, unnecessary European empires that flourished at precisely the same time.

But the railways were built and they made a difference. They brought to all areas outside metropolitan centers the possibility of rapid communication with these centers, and greatly expanded the market for information, educational materials, popular literature and journalism. For centuries there had been one capital in each country in Europe as a whole, a small handful of central cities, while the majority of the population lived like medieval peasants, in darkness and ignorance, outside the circle of communication and learning. Provincial cities were dull, stifling, and vulgar enclaves.

The railways changed all that very rapidly in the last two decades of the nineteenth century. Through the information and communication network established by the railways, there was an overwhelming proliferation of ideas, knowledge, the performing arts, and popular culture just as there came about a rapid transition of people. Steamships greatly reduced the time and discomfort of trans-Atlantic travel and modified American intellectual isolation. In the new railroad and steamship era, Americans travelled to Europe in significant numbers to obtain M.D. and Ph.D. degrees.

Ordinary people, ordinary in terms of their means, could now move unprecedented distances. They could transport themselves to the metropolitan center in search of education and an artistic life. They could move rapidly and often across continents in large numbers. One of the reasons one should read Richard Ellmann's splendid biography of James Joyce is that Joyce's life demonstrates the impact of the railroad on Modernism. He moved extensively over Europe—Ireland, England, Italy, France and Switzerland, living in different cities, never hesitating to pack up and move on when it suited him, devastating as the moves were to his wife and children. It had become feasible even to try a city like Trieste. Living in Trieste in 1870 would have been completely alienating and stupifying. In 1910 Joyce did not feel cut off from the cultural and information network. He did some of his best writing in Trieste and supported himself by working in the tourist trade, teaching English in a Berlitz school.

If an intellectual in the railroad era came from an affluent family, he could become a continental cosmopolite, moving easily from place to place in search of gurus and inspiration. Thus from 1906 to 1912 the young Viennese engineer and philosophy student, Ludwig Wittgenstein, moved back and forth between Berlin and Cambridge seeking guidance and testing his ideas. His face to face encounter with Bertrand Russell at Cambridge changed philosophy permanently.

The transportation network created by railways moved not only immigrants and workers, but also artists and intellectuals, and thereby made its own significant contribution to Modernism. The speed and ease with which literary and artistic products could now be sent through the mails also helped to foster Modernism as a trans-European and trans-Atlantic phenomenon. The climactic moment in the early biography of Modernist novelists and poets was the anxious dispatch of a manuscript through the railroad-carried mails to friend, patron, or publisher and the expectation of prompt reply.

In the years after 1900 the railroad and steamship era made the literary and artistic expatriate a central figure in the Modernist movement. Kandinsky and Klee, a Russian and Swiss respectively, headed the Berlin expressionist movement in painting. Two Americans—Ezra Pound and T.S. Eliot—were the leaders of literary modernism in Britain. In Paris in the twenties, three American women, Gertrude Stein, Sylvia Beach, and Peggy Guggenheim played important fostering roles in literature and the arts. The Irishman Joyce, the Italian Modigliani, and American Hemingway (fresh from working on a Toronto newspaper) and the Canadian Morley Callaghan as well as the East European Jews Chagall and Soutine were prominent in the vibrant life of the Left Bank and Montmartre. Modernism was built on cheap metropolitan housing and steam transportation.

Railroads and railroad terminals by their nature gave psychological reinforcement to would-be expatriates or provincials heading for the cultural metropolis. In European and U.S. cities railroad depots were located in the city centers and had been built in the nineteenth century in the style of Greek temples or the baths of Caracalla or Gothic cathedrals. Entering a terminal to make the traumatic move to the bohemian sections of the metropolis, the undiscovered artist or writer from St. Louis, Toulouse, Wiesbaden, or Birmingham was making a public declaration of his (or her) new artistic commitment in an awesome structure. He could not but feel that he had undertaken a sacred journey. Compare this with a similar artistic person heading for the metropolis by air in the 1960's: he or she would take a scruffy bus to a desolate airport terminal at the edge of the city. Embarking by air was, and is, a furtive, plebian, almost guilty act.

Taking a train to and from the likes of old Pennsylvania Station or Euston Station or the Gare du Nord was on the contrary a celebratory, public, ego-boosting act. Thomas Wolfe's 1930's novel, *Look Homeward, Angel*, a best-seller in its day but almost entirely forgotten now, evokes very well the epiphany of artists' and writers' journeys in the railroad/Modernist era. So do the novels of an equally forgotten Canadian novelist of the 1920's, Frederick Philip Grove.

Around 1900 the introduction of the automobile appeared to be bringing to a climax what electric light and steam transportation had started—the most profound changes in the circumstances of human life, especially in ever-expanding urban areas, that had occurred since neolithic times. Shortly educated people were aware that in universities the most important discoveries about the laws of the physical world were being made since the age of Newton. This technological and scientific transformation contributed towards the reconstruction of art, literature, philosophy, and social theory so as to question received values and modes of expression.

A changed environment encouraged a cultural revolution that would provide a system of sensibility, reason, and learning for the new century. Perhaps even more radically, the culture of Modernism eroded the restraining hold of traditional values and world-views and allowed the new technology and science to shape social life in relatively emancipated fashion.

Yet just as each of the previous three cultural revolutions was related to the other, Modernism was faced with choosing to break with attributes of the previous cultural movements or to reaffirm their focal message. The Reformation posited freedom and dignity of individual conscience on theological grounds. The Enlightenment secularized this message, proclaiming the freedom and power of the rational mind shaped by a salubrious environment. Romanticism tried to protect this humanist tradition against materialism and power by transcendentalist projection.

Modernism addressed the question: did modern society, technology, and learning demand a rupture with the humanist tradition, or a further reconstitution of this now venerable idea of freedom and dignity in the light of new experience and circumstances of living? This was the most difficult issue that Modernism faced. It explored this issue intensively but never clearly resolved it. We have not definitively resolved it after passage of so many decades and such dramatic events.

Modernism never had full opportunity to address this problem. By the 1930's and 40's resurgent neo-Victorianism in the forms of Marxism and Fascism plus additional cultural trends during and after World War II, forestalled a definitive Modernist response to the humanist traditions derived from previous cultural revolutions. The decline of the metropolis as a middle class habitat after 1945 also undermined the modernist capacity to face critical questions.

Whether the generation of the early twenty-first century will benefit or suffer from the interruption of Modernist speculation on individuality and freedom is a moot issue, suitable now only for the ever-expanding literature of science fiction.

*   *   *

The Victorian Achievement

Cultural revolutions happen and we ought to try to understand why and how in the specific instances, in this case the emergence of Modernism. But we would be falling into the Victorian mode of historicism were we to celebrate the change as an unmitigated triumph and denigrate consistently what went before.

We are in some respects so distanced from the Victorian ambience that we are awed and mystified by aspects of their cultural system. We cannot refrain from a patronizing and contemptuous attitude to some dimensions of nineteenth-century culture. But it is necessary to stress the Victorian accomplishment within this cultural context.

The nineteenth century was the century of the Long Peace. There were no major wars in Europe between the Battle of Waterloo in 1815 and August 1914. The Crimean War in the 1850's was a squalid and miserable affair but it did not last long and involved small armies. The Franco-Prussian War of 1870 was over in a few months and involved one major battle. The only terrible conflict of the nineteenth century, in many ways a foreshadowing of the first and second World Wars, was the American Civil War, an ideological conflict fought with remorseless savagery as a war of attrition. The nineteenth century knew no holocausts within Europe (the imperial scene was a different story but not for long without censure). Again apart from the American Civil War, civilian populations were treated with restraint and generosity.

Aside from spanning a century of peace, Victorian culture presided over the greatest technological and economic upheaval since the Neolithic era—the Industrial Revolution—with, after much initial confusion and misery (inspiring Marx and Engels), a high degree of rationality and humanity. There was during the nineteenth century an enormous growth in the size of the middle class, and a vast improvement in the welfare of the working class. The increase in the level of education and literacy was unprecedented.

The Victorian era also was a time of increased political democracy and recognition of civil liberties—of course not consistently in each country—but on the whole there was political and legal progress almost everywhere. In 1900 the British (in both the United Kingdom and in their dominions overseas), the French, Germans, Scandinavians and Italians enjoyed a very high degree of freedom both intellectual and political. Even the evil empire of the nineteenth century, Tsarist Russia, looks relatively benign compared to what occurred in the same country in the 1930's. To compare the Berlin or Munich of 1900 with the same city four decades later is to move from an extremely beneficent and cultivated environment to the abyss of tyranny and barbarism.

One of the great questions in human history is why did Western society as it broke away from the confinements and superseded the limitations of Victorian culture at the same time enter an age of iron and terror? How are these phenomena related?

In the late 1920's the Viennese novelist Robert Musil perceived the disturbing ambiguity of the Modernist cultural upheaval. He wrote in *The Man Without Qualities* of a Europe rising in 1900 ambivalently and explosively to rebel against tradition.

This was an era in which both "the Superman was adored and the Subman was adored . . . one had faith and was skeptical, one was naturalistic and precious, robust and morbid." It was a time when "one dreamed . . . of vast horizons . . . the uprisings of slaves of toil, men and women in the primeval Garden and the destruction of society." No one evoked more dramatically the intellectual crisis at the beginning of the new century.

By 1938 Musil, one of the leading Modernist writers, was fleeing with his Jewish wife from Vienna to Switzerland as the Nazis took over the old imperial city.

2

Modernism

A Model of Modernism

In 1918, the British writer Lytton Strachey published *Eminent Victorians*, a biographical account of four prominent figures of Victorian England. Strachey came from a prominent literary and political family and was a close friend of Virginia Woolf, her sister the artist Vanessa Bell, as well as of other members of the Bloomsbury group. Educator Thomas Arnold, health care administrator Florence Nightingale, military hero General Chinese Gordon, and Cardinal Manning, head of the Roman Catholic Church in England during its great expansion in the late nineteenth century, were the personages portrayed in *Eminent Victorians*.

The book, which became an immediate bestseller, was a humorous and savage prostration of these Victorian icons. Thomas Arnold appears a snob and a bigot. Florence Nightingale is a busybody and a petty tyrant, General Gordon, a racist and grotesque incompetent, and Cardinal Manning, a vulgarian hypocrite. With the possible exception of General Gordon, who seems to have been a psychopath by all accounts, most biographers today would question Strachey's characterizations. *Eminent Victorians* was enormously popular, despite its questionable validity, and represented the reflexive anti-Victorianism which constituted a primary ingredient of Modernism.

Rebellion against the Victorian world, hostility or contempt or at least a profound lack of sympathy for it, remained a hallmark throughout the Modernist movement during the first half of the twentieth century. Just as we have posited, in our culture, that everything the American establishment did in the 1960's with respect to the Vietnam War was wrong, just as it once sufficed to mention names like Lyndon Johnson, McGeorge Bundy or Richard Nixon to elicit visceral negative reactions, justified or unjustified, so by the second decade of the twentieth century, one only had to name prominent Victorians much admired in their own day, in order to get a similar unfavorable response.

In addition to this reflexive anti-Victorianism that continued throughout the heyday of Modernism and well into the 1950's, specific ideas and attitudes characteristic of Modernism manifested themselves in fields ranging from literature and art to science and philosophy. By identifying these fundamentals, the Modernist mentality can be reconstructed.

First of all, Modernism was anti-historicist. It did not believe that truth lay in telling an evolutionary story. Modernism cared little for history; it was in fact hostile to it. Truth-finding became analytical, rather than historical. As

T.S. Eliot, a prime theoretician of Modernism, wrote in 1923, the "narrative method" had been replaced by the "mythic method." The historical approach, in Eliot's view, was superseded by the very different program of concentrating on direct, inner, symbolic meaning, that was both completely external to history and irrelevant to considerations of temporality.

Again in the early 1930's, T.S. Eliot wrote that "All time is unredeemable/ What might have been and what has been point toward the same end,/Which is always the present." Reality is an ahistorical, unredeemable present. This negation of temporality was precisely opposed to the Victorian proclivity to place everything in sequential time.

Another way of stating this concept would be to say that Modernist anti-historicism concentrated upon immediate understanding, direct analysis, or upon what is later termed "close reading," the intensive examination of the object removed from historical sequence. It will become apparent that this attitude had revolutionary consequences in many fields, but particularly in fiction, literary criticism, painting and the social sciences. The anti-historicism or the analytical, mythic method made a strong comeback in the 1970's, which removes us twice from nineteenth-century historicism: first through the Modernist rebellion, and again through the upheaval witnessed in the last ten years, which is sometimes referred to as the structuralist movement, or variously as deconstruction or Postmodernism. Using the terminology of this later structuralism, Modernism stressed the synchronic rather than the diachronic plane.

The second intellectual characteristic of Modernism was its departure from the macrocosmic, universalist tendencies of nineteenth-century thought, and instead placed its focus on the microcosmic dimension. As has been already pointed out, the nineteenth century believed in the superior value of the big picture. Modernist thought adhered to the notion that the small was more and beautiful. The physics of the time, for example, has been called "particle physics," for it emphasized the sub-atomic particle, making it the prime subject of interest and research. Focus on a minute particle— of human experience or art as well as nature—conditioned all of Modernist culture.

Throughout Modernist culture it was held that the smallest segment would reveal an entire world when subjected to microcosmic, microscopic analysis, that it was the most minute conceivable or comprehensible unit that would establish the connection with reality rather than the investigation on the generalized macrocosmic level. The latter could yield nothing but empty words.

The emphasis here is upon the precise and exact word, and on the concrete image, which are terms used by Modernists themselves, along with the "particle" of science, the "data" of social science, and the "microcosmic world" of the arts. This total shift in the level addressed by the mind—from the big to the small, from the general to the particular—made much of nineteenth-century thought, its philosophy, science, and social science, not only wrong, but totally meaningless.

A third characteristic of Modernism was the preoccupation with what is called self-referentiality or textuality, meaning that anything that is examined constitutes a self-enclosed world. To understand it, you take it first of all, and often in the last analysis too, in terms of itself. The entity refers back to itself; it is self-referential. The text is simply what it is, and it is this self-enclosure of the text that should be studied. The painting does not represent something external to itself; the poem does not illustrate a story. Both exist in and for themselves, and are enclosed in and show a world that always refers back to itself. The text is finite rather than illustrative.

The American expatriate in Paris, Gertude Stein, saw with dramatic clarity in the early years of the century that self-referentiality was at the center of the whole Modernist movement. Words, she said, "were not imitations either of sounds or colors or emotions," as the Victorians believed. She intended to write "as if the fact of writing were continually becoming true and completing itself, not as if it were leading to something." Six decades later the Postmodernist critic Susan Sontag expressed the same idea about the essence of Modernism in somewhat more elaborate form: "The idea that depths are obfuscating, demagogic, that no human essence stirs at the bottom of things, and that freedom lies in staying on the surface, the large glass on which desire circulates—this is the central argument of the modern aesthetic position."

A fourth quality of Modernism was a penchant for the fragmented, the fractured, and the discordant. In opposition to the Victorians who showed a predilection for the finished and the harmonious, Modernism foregrounded the disharmonious and the unfinished, the splintered world, the piece that had broken off, the serendipitous, and pursued this preference to the point of making it an aesthetic principle.

The fifth feature of Modernist culture was lack of predetermined pattern. Modernism favored random access. In attempting to understand something, one cannot presuppose either a spatial or temporal succession that is predetermined. A sequence may be ultimately established, but this must be done empirically from within the object itself. Sequentiality cannot be imposed upon it externally, nor can it be anticipated. There may not be a sequence involved at all in the object of study, for one may very well be face to face with discontinuity. If there is in fact a continuity in the object, it is never one that can be presupposed in any predetermined program.

One of the weaknesses of Victorian thought certainly was this predisposition to continuity and to assuming prior knowledge of exact sequence. Among the problems this led to was to make much of Victorian social science hopeless or useless. Modernism began by questioning the assumption about continuity, whether it existed, and if it did, what its precise nature was.

Similarly, a sixth point in Modernism's departure from Victorian thought was its rejection of philosophical idealism, especially Hegelian theory. The favorite philosophy of the nineteenth century was one that removed the empirical in order to arrive at the most general proposition, and at the purist concept that could be imagined by consciousness, or at what Hegel called "the absolute." This notion disappeared rapidly after 1900. Philosophical idealism was faulted and abandoned on two accounts: it was insufficiently empirical, and impervious to concrete data; and it only dealt with the realm of the conscious and ignored the unconscious. Ignorant of the empirical and the unconscious, nineteenth-century philosophy was perceived to be empty, and therefore invalid.

The seventh intellectual quality of Modernism was functionalism. This term found particular application in the fields of architecture, where it is still in use (although not always in a laudatory way), and in sociology and anthropology. Once the object of analysis is understood as microcosmic, self-referential and exterior to predetermined spatial and temporal sequentiality, what remains to be studied is how the object functions in and for itself. It can be concluded that functionalism was a product of other main characteristics of Modernism. It can be viewed in another way, as expressing anti-historicism. External to history, the object exists in terms of its function.

Time and time again Modernism asks how a thing works, and further, how it works in and for itself. From this functionalist point of view modern experimental physics was born, as well as field research in the social and behavioral sciences.

An eighth characteristic of Modernism was its antipathy for, or rejection of, absolute polarities. Victorians assumed the polarity of male and female, of object and subject, the higher and lower, the early and late, mass and energy, time and space. They were certain that the world and human life operated in terms of absolute, separable polarities. Modernism questioned this notion by claiming that these polarities were integrated with one another, that they were interactive and not absolute. It viewed them as convenient ways of talking about phenomena, which, when observed closely, revealed themselves to be related to one another, or, in other words, to be functions of one another.

The weakening or even abandonment of absolute polarities was central to Modernism and had revolutionary consequences in many area of thought and behavior. The Victorians reflexively separated things; the Modernists felt compelled to integrate them. The interactive nature of apparent polarities and their possible symbiosis was a leading characteristic of both Modernist art and science.

The ninth aspect of Modernism, a particularly difficult and controversial one, was that in contrast to nineteenth-century culture which strongly tended to vulgarization and popularization, it was elitist. Nineteenth- century scholars and writers believed that social science, philosophy and, above all, literature and art could be expressed in a way that was readily accessible by at least anyone with high school education. Modernism, to the contrary, believed in complexity and difficulty. It addressed a narrow, highly selective, learned and professional audience. Its audience was the vanguard.

This is a feature that runs through Modernist culture in a fundamental way. From science to literature and art, Modernism was a culture of the elite. It required sophistication, learning, intense application. In any given area, Modernism was not accessible to the naive and unprepared person, to the common man. Whether in art, philosophy, or science, Modernist culture was only open to the specially prepared and specifically cultivated mind.

This particular quality of elitism presented important problems for Modernism and constituted one of its fundamental tensions for the many Modernists who also belonged to the political left. They naturally had difficulty reconciling their elitism with their political democracy. This issue still churns away in the leftist weeklies and quarterlies.

A tenth characteristic of Modernism was greater openness with regard to sexuality. There has been much research done recently about what the Victorians did in bed or around—or on—the kitchen table. Whether their practices differed greatly from our own we still do not know (the data is too anecdotal and fragmentary), but their way of talking about it was certainly different. Modernism produced a new frankness in the exchange about sexual relationships, and indeed had a tendency toward the scatalogical, to what the Victorians would have regarded as "vulgar" and "dirty talk." At first the Modernists were very self-conscious about this new sexual frankness. Virginia Woolf makes the use of the dread word "semen" at one of her early Bloomsbury parties an earth-shattering event. By the twenties, intellectuals talked about sex as familiarly as Victorians conversed about God. Of course, Freud and psychoanalysis made a major difference.

Modernism also was sympathetic toward feminism and homosexuality and expressed an interest in the androgynous and the bisexual, another manifestation of the Modernist tendency to break down polarities. Modernism was not committed to the separation of the male and the female on moral, biological, or psychological grounds as the Victorians had been.

An eleventh quality of Modernism was its attention to the outcomes of a technological culture. Modernism can be looked upon as an effort to address the cultural consequences of a new technological world and of a mass culture. The recognition that culture had changed as a result of the application of science to the needs of everyday life and particularly the revolution in transportation and communication systems, and the emergence of widespread, near universal literacy, marks Modernism. Dealing with the implications of such transformations is something we are still very much engaged in. How the artist and philosopher should respond to a situation in which mechanization takes command and a revolutionary scientific paradigm has been attained is a continuing Modernist concern.

On the one side Modernism was a product of the age of railroad and steamship and was fashioned by the rapid and easy means of transportation and commitment to the urban culture and the trans-Atlantic metropolitan centers. On the other side Modernism was concerned with preservation of rationality, art and learned intelligence in the age of mechanical reproduction and mass culture. The latter concern is reflected in the elitist quality of Modernism.

A twelfth characteristic of Modernism can be located in the area of ethics. Although not shared by all Modernists, there was a tendency in the movement towards moral relativism and departure from a normative code of ethics. It is conventional to say that Modernism represented a relativistic rebellion against the puritanical normative ethics of the nineteenth century.

The issue, however, might be stated somewhat differently. Nineteenth-century ethics focused on the nuclear family and its value to society. Its entire ethical system was designed to maintain the nuclear family as the social norm. Modernism weakened this Victorian conception. On the one hand it gave a new authenticity to individualism and to individual search for values, and on the other, it valorized a unit larger than the family, namely, culture as a whole. It sought for a moral theory and system that stemmed from the entire culture. While emphasizing the authenticity of individual ethics, it also stressed extended cultural solidarity.

Along with a deep but not universal tendency toward relativism, this perception undermined severely an ethic focused on the preservation of the family. The decline of the nuclear family began around 1900, owing to complex reasons, of which the emergence of Modernism was probably the most critical.

In the nineteenth century, in the context of urbanization and salaried employment ouside the home in an industrial economy, the family had become less of an economic agency, and more of an affective, reproductive, and educational unit. The Victorian increase of sentiment in family relationships combined with the family ideology to bring the nuclear family to its zenith. By attacking patriarchal authority and questioning sexual repression that the Victorian family fostered, as well as by stressing individualism and the demands of a cultural solidarity beyond the family, by a relativist frame of mind that eroded legitimacy that had conventionally come to adhere to the nuclear family, Modernism precipitated a social and ethical revolution which is still unwinding, for better or worse, in our own day.

A thirteenth characteristic of Modernism, which has had consequences for social policy as well as for aesthetics, was the conviction that humanity is in its most authentic, truly human condition, when it is involved with art, whether literary, visual, or performing in kind. In spite of monumental artistic achievements in the arts in the nineteenth century, the Victorians retained the Christian Augustinian conviction that humanity achieves its highest and purest nature in moral action. The Modernists replaced the superiority of the ethical dimension with the primacy of not only artistic creation but also common entitlement to participation in and consumption of art. This meant that the positive purpose of government and social institutions was not the fostering of a moral code but the provision of opportunities for realization of entitlement to art.

Finally, Modernism displayed a tendency towards cultural despair. Victorianism was by and large optimistic, or at least transcendental. It either believed that things were improving or, when this did not seem credible, it held that matters would improve eventually. Even Nietzsche, who found little to approve in his own times, felt certain about a stepped-up future betterment. Modernism, however, tends towards pessimism and despair. The world in Modernist imagery is often a bleak, devastated urban landscape. The world as a hospital, not a very hopeful one, where people are dying of terminal illness, or as a downscale tavern, or a brothel, or a cruel law court where there is no justice, are among its favorite social images and metaphors. Elias Canetti, the Viennese novelist and social philosopher, succinctly expressed Modernism's harshly realistic and sad view of human nature: "Human beings . . . accuse themselves by representing themselves as they are, and this is self-indictment, it does not come from someone else."

While Victorians were comforted by history, the Modernists pessimistically considered it a nightmare from which we are trying to awake, in James Joyce's phrase, and not successfully. "Force, hatred, history, all that," says Joyce's spokesman Leopold Bloom. "That's not life for men and women." Similarly, Marcel Proust advises us that the only paradise is the one we have lost.

It should be noted that this formulation of a model of Modernism as integral to the culture of the early decades of the century is controversial. Some historians and critics believe in some such model, some do not. The skeptics, speaking in 1986 through the Irish critic Denis Donoghue, claim that "a motive supposedly held in common" by the writers, artists, and composers of the period 1910–1925 "would have to be described in such general and abstract terms as to be virtually meaningless. We could designate it as modernism only if we were willing to ignore differences and to preserve at any cost a semblance of common purpose." This view we have shown to be mistaken, because a general model of Modernist culture embraces specific ideas, motifs, and attitudes. Donoghue's skeptical view of Modernism is itself inspired by a neo-Victorian mindset that by denying that the writers and artists of the first thirty years of the century belong to a cohesive cultural movement seeks to postulate an unbroken continuity with Victorianism and late Romanticism.

The fourteen characteristics of Modernism that we have specified achieve validity not only as a general model that provides a persuasive order to complex phenomena. It also is a heuristic device for exploring particular aspects of literature, the arts and sciences. It teaches us what to look for. At the same time, the discovery of Modernist qualities in many diverse areas of culture inductively and empirically leads us back to confirmation of the model.

Of course, Donoghue and his followers have the option not to think along general lines, not to seek cultural patterns and not to develop a historical model, but in a skeptical, nominalist way to list endless names of writers, artists, and composers without "a semblance of common purpose." This nominalist method precludes historical understanding and cultural analysis. The Donoghue approach prevents us from confronting the meaning of the complex intellectual, artistic, and scientific developments of the first four decades of the century, which are conditioned by a common mentality.

On the basis of the general model of Modernism, particular manifestations of it can be examined in a variety of areas, in order to see how these characteristics were expressed. Modernism affected nearly every area of culture, and for us today, it is memorialized most dramatically in the novel and poem, architecture, in painting, philosophy, physics and anthropology.

✳   ✳   ✳

The Novel, Poetry, and Criticism

There was a radical change in the novel around 1900 and in the following four decades in the entire Western world, including the United States. The novel became a prime vehicle of Modernist expression and the most readily accessible to educated people.

The Victorian novel, with its strong narrative and historicizing tendency, was for the most part popular literature. The Modernist novel distinguishes itself radically from the Victorian in this respect. The novel becomes the literary form the Modernist intellectual focuses on. It is the genre around which much literary criticism develops and which soon occupies a central place in the university curriculum. The Modernist novel is today still held up as the fictional ideal by critics and publishing houses.

The Modernist novel met with initial strong resistance, but recognition did come quickly. By the mid-twenties, it was widely appreciated that a new form of novel had emerged which presented a distinct departure from the Victorian, and that this vanguard form of literature was extremely important and valuable. For educated people of refined tastes, the novel was consistently one of the most accessible forms of Modernist culture.

Without doubt, the Anglo-American Henry James in the last decade of the nineteenth century was the forerunner of the Modernist novel. James readily recognized the writers after 1900 who were his disciples, particularly James Joyce and Marcel Proust, and understood the purpose and importance of their effort. Other prominent European novelists of the movement were Virginia Woolf and D.H. Lawrence in England; Franz Kafka in Prague, where there was found a large German-Jewish population from which he emerged, and Robert Musil, Elias Canetti, and Hermann Broch in Vienna—these were the writers from the Austro-Hungarian Empire.

Leading Modernist novelists in Germany were Heinrich Mann and his brother Thomas Mann, at least in the latter's middle period. Thomas Mann's first novel *Buddenbrooks* was Victorian in style and his later series on Joseph and his brothers is an early example of Postmodernist fabulism. But *Death in Venice* and to a certain extent *The Magic Mountain* are novels from Mann's intermediary stage which represent Modernist efforts. Thomas Mann was like Picasso in that he could adopt any style and work in it, and for a while he was a Modernist.

The leading American Modernist novelists were Ernest Hemingway and William Faulkner. Hemingway was the most visible of the post-World War I generation of American expatriates in Paris and his novels also reflect a self-conscious Midwestern muscularity. The technique of most of his fiction in centrally in the Modernist tradition. Two methods distinguish all of Hemingway's novels. The action is moved forward mostly by dialogue and the reader is not clearly informed about key events that occur earlier or off-stage. Faulkner, writing mostly in the 30's and 40's in Mississippi, consciously drew upon the local color of the Southern tradition. But he subtly altered it in the way Joyce exploited the British tradition of the provincial novel while pursuing intense examination of segments of universal experience.

The extremely talented F. Scott Fitzgerald could never quite decide where he stood between Victorian and Modernist traditions. Nevertheless, *The Great Gatsby* is frequently called a major Modernist novel. *The Day of the Locust*, by Nathaniel West, received little attention when it was published in 1939, but is now regarded as a quintessential Modernist work. Thomas Wolfe is now neglected but was celebrated as a Modernist exponent in the 30's.

Isak Dinesen, who has recently become a celebrity, can be cited as the Modernist fiction writer from Denmark. There are many others but these are the most prominent novelists of the movement.

Getting started was usually not easy for these novelists. Ellmann and other biographers describe the bizarre way in which Joyce had his first great Modernist novel *Ulysses* published, with customers of Sylvia Beach's Parisian bookstore assigned to make fair copy for the printers and editing Joyce's precious text in idiosyncratic and unauthorized ways, and French typesetters who knew no English. Proust was initially turned down by leading publishing houses in Paris and found acceptance only from a newly established vanguard publisher; the last third of *Remembrance of Things Past* was still in manuscript when he died. Similarly when Robert Musil died in 1940, only half of his *The Man Without Qualities* had been published. Some of Kafka's novels were published only posthumously. For many years in mid-career, D.H. Lawrence was an anathema to publishers, who would not read his manuscripts.

But by and large, these writers certainly received recognition by the late twenties. If they were not wealthy like Proust or did not have a secure executive job like Kafka or did not have an understanding spouse like Woolf, they found generous patrons, as did Joyce and Lawrence. Hemingway began as a journalist and this experience affected even his fiction. He provided terse bulletins from the front lines. Both Fitzgerald and Faulkner worked for a time as Hollywood film writers.

The fundamental characteristic of the Modernist novel, particularly when compared with the Victorian, was stated by Marcel Proust in 1918. He said that the purpose of the novel was the discovery of what he called "a different self." The aim is not to tell a story, expound a moral or even to describe a social situation, although he certainly did the latter. It is to achieve a breakthrough to a different self, through writing on the part of the author, and through reading on that of the reader. The self sought is different from the ordinary familial and social being known in everyday life.

The burden of the Modernist novel is existential discovery of a deeper, mythic, more human self. The exploration of a sensibility replaces the Victorian purpose of telling a story. The Modernist novel does contain a story which may be by turns elaborate and minimal, but it serves only as a vehicle for the exploration of sensibility on the part of the author, which helps the reader to discover himself. This feature still continues in what is known as "*The New Yorker* Short Story," which preserves the Modernist value placed upon the exploration of sensibility.

It is also characteristic of the Modernist novel that it supposes the possibility of a penetration or fragile transference from the conscious to the unconscious at any given time. A novel exists at the point of the meeting of the two, and is the exploration of their precarious interaction. The 1920's term "stream of consciousness" refers to this quality but not accurately.

The Modernist novel communicates not a programmed narrative but the confusion, hesitancies, and partial perception of fragmented individual experience. In the Modernist novel, we do not stand with the Victorian author on some distant Napoleonic height surveying the course of the action. We are close up, seeing and especially hearing—the action is often revealed through only partly coherent dialogue—what is happening from the limited point of view of one or two characters.

In the Modernist novel we are immersed in the surface of things. We only slowly or never get the big picture or readily comprehend the general pattern of events. Indeed the major dramatic happenings will often occur somewhere offstage and we will be given only the impact on a particular consciousness. The Victorian novel was the fiction of sense, the Modernist novel that of sensibility. If after reading five pages, we do not comprehend what is happening but we have a close perception of someone's consciousness, and/or glimpses into their unconscious, we are in a Modernist novel.

Because of this focus on the surface confusion of experienced happenings and this enclosure within consciousness and unconsciousness, the Modernist novel has deprivileged the author, who no longer stands outside the event as an imperial and omniscient manipulator of the action. The author is more a reporter than commander of events. Thereby the Modernist novel liberated to significant degree the reader from the author's authority and allowed the reader an autonomous condition, to shape the action and determine the meaning in his or her own mind.

George Eliot (Mary Ann Evans), the prominent Victorian novelist and Virginia Woolf were women of similar character—very learned, extremely opinionated, masterful. Each, invited to a dinner party, would completely dominate the conversation, crushing male egos with a resounding crash. Yet the effect on the reader experiencing Eliot's *Adam Bede* compared with Woolf's *To the Lighthouse* is quite different. Eliot controls her novel to such an extent that she becomes something of a bore; we wish she would get out of the way. *Adam Bede* may be a more interesting and complex person than Eliot allows; we wish she would moderate her incessant historicizing and moralizing and let the novel play. Woolf gets us much closer to her characters, gives them much more autonomy, allows us to internalize them to a degree separately from her. That Woolf herself was an insufferable snob does not prevent us from discoursing directly with her middle class characters.

The difference between the Victorian and Modernist novels comes down to this. In the Modernist novel we are seated in the third row of the theater, can hear and see everything, including the actors' perspiration, and we can make our own judgment as to what is going on. In the Victorian novel we are seated in the eighth row of the balcony in a cavernous theater and have to strain to see and hear what is occurring on stage. Furthermore, a companion in the next seat keeps whispering in our ear what he thinks is happening on stage and freely interprets the action for us.

The Modernist novel is a study in frustration and disappointment. It rarely presents an epiphany, but is an examination of the disappointments of modern life, of the difficulty of achieving ambitions, fulfilling love and even of communicating, which becomes a frequent theme. A cognate theme is the tremendous exertion it takes to overcome these limitations, engage in a simple act of love or any other form of communication, and terrible sense of loneliness, alienation, and defeat that often enervates the individual. If these impediments are overcome, it still leaves the individual exhausted, used up. If there is a moment of intense triumph, it is a very brief moment indeed.

All fiction occurs in someone's memory. What was distinctive in the Victorian novel was the wide screen of memory and the steady pace of events projected on it. The narrator was omniscient or at least sufficiently well informed to recall in reportorial detail a broad front of events. Unless the novel was placed in a distant past, the events most frequently occurred about twenty to thirty years ago and from this starting-point, clearly demarked, the narration moved steadily toward the present.

Memory in the Modernist novel is much more narrowly focused. The time events usually appear to have occurred recently, although related to an earlier trauma, and the sequential time sequence is normally interrupted and distorted. Some physical act or a surge from the unconscious to the conscious mind activates images about an intensely visualized experience or set of connected experiences. Modernist memory gains in density and high luminosity for what it abandons in comprehensiveness and sequentiality. The focus of the Modernist novel is on the memory of a compelling short-term experience (second, minute, day) and reflection on the implication of that experience.

Thus the mythic plane replaces the narrative projection. The Modernist novel supersedes the Victorian assumption of sequential time with a microcosmic particle of remembered feeling. Stop/Time substitutes for extended time. Memory summons up the Stop/Time moment that can consist of an image of sitting in a deck chair on a beach (Woolf), biting into a *madeleine* (Proust), lying naked on a bed (Joyce), standing dry-mouthed before a judicial hearing (Kafka), some gesture of sexual arousal, in a cabaret dressing room (H. Mann) or in the snow (Lawrence). Memory of taste and smell frequently accompanies the visual image. The coded image opens onto an infinite world of activated sensibility, concretely visualized happenings, and recurring symbols. The parallel with psychoanalysis is obvious.

These characteristics are present in all the cited novelists in one way or another, despite the fact that they differ from each other in some other respects. A common pattern of what they are trying to achieve through the novel form is discernible in their works.

By the late 1920's it became clear that there was a market for this kind of difficult and provocative literature, and the more established publishing houses began to show themselves receptive to it. With the development of professional literary criticism, and of college departments of English, the Modernist novel also received the kind of defined public support that was important for its further development and dissemination.

It is significant, however, that the great era of the Modernist novel was as brief as from about 1905 to 1930. The moment a certain degree of social triumph sets in, that is, when the established publishers welcome and support the genre, buying the publishing rights from the obscure vanguard houses or the literary executors, the size of the cadre of achieving Modernist novelists begins to decrease precipitously. By 1940 there were very few of the literary giants still at work.

The history of the Modernist novel resembles that of another artistic phenomenon that has crucially affected Western culture—the painting of the High Renaissance. It too was the work of barely more than one phenomenal generation. The greatest writers of the movement, who are also among the literary giants of all time, emerged in one generation, between 1905–1930, and were soon monumentalized. They were appreciated in an endless series of commentaries and explications which continues unabated. But the giants departed and were not replaced.

Modernism itself as a cultural movement was weakened in the 1930's, affected by the rise of Communism, Fascism, the Great Depression and various forms of Neo-Victorianism. One discerns a failure of nerve as it were, in Modernist culture, when it is faced with this revival of nineteenth-century modes of thinking, and the Modernist novel particularly does not remain outside the disintegration.

The pattern of development in Modernist poetry was similar to that of the novel. It forms a radical break from the nineteenth century, and presents a new poetic form. Modernist poetry too reached its peak around 1930, but it did not exhaust itself as rapidly as its novelistic counterpart, although it was certainly already over the zenith by 1940. The poets as well generated a canon, an authorized body of writing, which set the standard for subsequent twentieth-century poetry. After the Modernist poets, in order to receive recognition as poet, it was necessary to write within the conventions of their canon.

Just as the Modernist novel finds a forerunner in Henry James, Modernist poetry has precursors in the 1880's French poet Stephen Mallarmé and in the English poet Gerard Manley Hopkins of the 1890's. Mallarmé and Hopkins anticipate the poetry that will be written after 1900, whose most influential figures in the English-speaking world were the two Anglo-Americans, T.S. Eliot and Ezra Pound.

Tom Eliot came from a wealthy St. Louis family, studied at Harvard under the conservative classicist Irving Babbit, and received a Ph.D. in philosophy. He migrated to England, and married there a genteel but unfortunately psychotic English woman whom he eventually divorced and put in an insane asylum. A play, not very flattering to Eliot, has recently been written and produced about this marriage. Eliot became the dominant transatlantic poet of the inter-war years, not only through his poetic work, but also owing to his critical essays. Quite simply, it was Eliot who established, in essays as well as by his poetry, what poetry was henceforth supposed to be.

Eliot's colleague Ezra Pound was also an American. He too migrated, first to England, later to Italy where he became a strong supporter of Mussolini. Pound became legally a traitor during the Second World War, making broadcasts on behalf of Mussolini. After the war, just before he was about to be tried and condemned for treason, his friends found a prominent psychiatrist in Washington who certified him insane. Pound died in an asylum in Washington.

There is no doubt that Pound's reputation has steadily increased in recent decades and now that he is evaluated in terms of his actual work—*The Cantos*—he has begun to be regarded as Eliot's equal if not even as his superior. The more Eliot's biography is explored, and this is not a very easy task since his second wife has suppressed personal material and witheld it from the public, the more it becomes evident how much Eliot learned and benefited from Pound. Ezra Pound was the editor of Eliot's early and perhaps most famous poem *The Waste Land* (1922). The original work was considerably longer than the published version before Pound worked on it. Using Modernist principles, which were not yet fully clear in Eliot's mind, Pound reduced the poem by about one third and sharpened its effect.

A prominent Modernist poet of the German language was the Austrian Hugo von Hofmannsthal who was also the librettist for some of Richard Strauss' operas. Strauss' *The Woman Without Shadows* consists of a series of Modernist poems by Hofmannsthal. The German Rainer Maria Rilke also stands alongside Eliot and Pound as one of the most accomplished of twentieth-century Modernist poets. As with all Modernist poets, his work is very difficult to translate.

Like Eliot and Pound, Rilke was very much aware of the poetic revolution he was conducting. He had a broad view of the Modernist movement, and published pioneering criticism on Modernist art. For Rilke, the Modernist program was "to achieve the conviction and substantiality of things, a reality intensified and potentiated to the point of indestructibility by . . . experience of the object."

The Frenchman Paul Valéry also belongs in this group, as well as the Irishman William Butler Yeats, whose contemporary and posthumous reputation has been extremely controversial because of Yeats' neo-Victorian proclivity to historicism and moralizing.

Two Americans, Robert Frost and Wallace Stevens should be placed in the forefront of the Modernist trend in poetry. Frost was an extremely ambitious man who assiduously promoted himself as American visionary and poetic sage. His unpalatable personal qualities have retrospectively somewhat diminished his reputation as a poet, which deserves to be placed high.

Stevens' reputation has continued to grow. He now stands with Eliot, Pound and Rilke as the most eminent of modernist poets. Stevens was a modest man who made a living as an insurance executive in Hartford. He did not promote himself much and was not very well known until the 1950's and 1960's. Stevens' conception of poetry is the same as Proust's view of the Modernist novel. The self is bifurcated into the half that adheres to "common earth" and the half that reaches for "moonlit extensions" of reality. In the search for these moonlit extensions, Stevens believed, the poet attains a more creative and authentic identity.

In the opinion of many critics, the English poet W.H. Auden, who migrated to the United States in 1939, represents the late blossoming of Modernism. His one-time associate, Stephen Spender, who is still alive and much venerated as a living memorial to the great Modernists, already decidedly belongs in the epigone category.

One of the giants of Modernist poetry is today almost unknown outside of

Israel. This is Chaim Nachman Bialik, whose earlier work was written mostly in Yiddish and later poems mostly in Hebrew. Bialik's huge output contains neo-Romantic work in the vein of Pushkin and Tennyson. But there is also a corpus of Modernist poetry of the front rank, to which fragmentary English translations have not given access.

What exactly is this "Modernist poetry" on which English, French and German literature departments today concentrate so intensely and which to characterize in summary fashion is nothing less than presumptuous on the one hand, and necessary on the other? Modernist poetry is, first of all, not Victorian. It is not narrative and is usually very short. It is what is designated as lyric poetry. Even longer Modernist poems like Eliot's *The Waste Land* and *Four Quartets* are really cycles of short poems.

Modernist poetry propounds no moral, nor a popular message, and it is above all very difficult. An invariable quality of Modernist poetry is that rather than admitting of easy reading, it calls for scrupulous and intensive study. Victorian poetry on the other hand was meant to be declaimed and easily read. Modernist poetry is extremely dense, contrived, and intellectual. Modernist poetry takes immense pains to be precisely accurate in communicating ideas and sensibility. This accuracy often requires opaque language because the ideas and sensibility are complex.

Under Modernist aegis the term "poetics" came to mean the theory of poetry. In view of the intense intellectualism of Modernist poetry, this conjunction is appropriate.

Eliot never held an academic post, although he could have obtained one easily. He preferred to make his living first as a banker, and later as a publisher. But he did consent to giving public lectures at universities. Many of his lectures are devoted to defining what Modernist poetry is. The definition he gave in lectures delivered in England and the United States in 1931 is characteristically concise and persuasive: "To find the word and give it the utmost meaning in its place; to mean as many things as possible; to make it [the word or the poem] both exact and comprehensive, and really to *unite* the disparate and the remote." The latter part of the definition contains the description of the Modernist project in general, namely to unite the disparate and the remote. "To give them a fusion and a pattern with the word," that is to say, to bring together and contain them in the word—"surely this is the mastery at which the poet aims."

In other words, Modernist poetry is self-referential and textual. The poem is; it is a thing in and of itself, its meaning lies within it: it is not meant to illustrate, nor to refer to things, nor to propound a message or tell a story. It is a thick culture that stands by itself. The poem is something that is capable of absorbing, drawing into itself everything that it wants to express, and of containing it in concrete imagery.

Eliot as well as Valéry, Rilke and Stevens aimed at exactitude which, they believed, could be achieved by an extremely dense imagery which was at the same time concrete, and which would express deep feeling. Eliot hated Victorian poetry, and he even detested Milton, whom he denied the title of poet, on grounds that these writers were sloppy, imprecise, not concrete and accurate. The Victorian poet, so Eliot said, expresses whatever comes to his mind. His imagery falls apart under the slightest scrutiny precisely because it is not exact and comprehensive, containing, as it does, ideas merely thrown together. The Victorians—and Milton—failed to understand the principle of the "objective correlative," which is that sensibility must be fully and intrinsically communicated in the language of the poem, not just vaguely described or referred to. The poem does not declaim feeling, it is feeling.

Eliot's poet, pursuing the method of the objective correlative, is marked by his complete mastery of imagery and by the ability to achieve density. The poem is a thick presentation of sensibility. This conception still informs the perception of what twentieth-century poetry is and should be. The popular bardic quality that was prominant in Victorian poetry was completely abandoned in favor of a piercing intellectuality. Wallace Stevens saw contemporary culture as intrinsically unstable, "a postcard from the volcano," the new consuming the old. It is the function of poetry to embody this transition. In the hands of the Modernists, poetry became a particularly exalted and sophisticated form of cultural criticism.

The rise of Modernist novel and poetry was closely connected to the emergence of literary criticism. Every new form of literature needs a validating system that legitimizes and authenticates it, that establishes the criteria of judgment by which the literary work can be evaluated aesthetically. It needs a critical system, that is, which is active in authorizing publications, convincing universities and media that the fictive or poetic work carries the stamp of greatness, and in the awarding of prizes for literary achievement.

The nineteenth century had its own criteria which were often based on popularity which, in turn, found their ready measure in the number of copies a work sold. There were critical journals in the nineteenth century too, which praised or condemned literary works, as well as academies, often extremely conservative, which handed out prizes. Now these institutional authorities were superseded.

The rise of the Modernist novel and poetry was accompanied between 1910 and 1930 by the rise of literary criticism as we know it. This is a kind of literary criticism very different from the one that had existed in the nineteenth century, not only in attitude but in vocation too, as criticism became increasingly academic and technical.

It is rather difficult for us to imagine that there were no departments of English in 1900 except in a few American state universities and other vanguard institutions. Oxford and Cambridge did not have an English department at the turn of the century. The first important English departments began to take shape around 1910, and became really habilitated in the major universities in the early 1920's. English Departments rose contemporaneously with Modernist novel and poetry, and they reinforced each other. Modernist novel and poetry became the particular province or subject in whose interpretation English departments specialized. The genres, in brief, found their authentication in these institutions' work, and acquired a legitimacy which would otherwise have been difficult to obtain.

The English departments acclaimed Modernist novels and poems not only as real literature, but as literature of almost unprecedented quality as well. By 1930, unless one had read Joyce, Proust, Eliot and Rilke, one could not pretend to being an educated person or an intellectual—so said the academic literary critics.

Just as Henry James effected the transition to the modern novel, and Mallarmé and Hopkins to the corresponding poetry, so the Londoner Edmund Gosse was the first Modernist critic. Gosse occupies the transition point between the Victorian "man of letters" and the twentieth-century critic. The man of letters had been a person of reading and breeding who expounded his views on literature, within the limits of his contemporaries' taste, and did so in a rather loose and unrigorous way. He provided literary appreciation rather than criticism. Close reading and evaluation were not his domain. He wrote short pleasant essays which often had a strong historical flavor to them, to be published in magazines and journals. Gosse too began in this fashion, but became increasingly technical and analytical in his work, although he never fully achieved the thickness or rigor of Modernist criticism. Therefore, by the 1920's, he was regarded as out-of-date and old-fashioned. Nevertheless, for his day, in 1910, he was a seminal figure who was leaving behind the easy-going Victorian man of letters, and anticipating the close-reading, analytically-oriented modern critic.

Furthermore, Edmund Gosse was capable of appreciating the new trends. He was not in a position to grasp exactly what was going on, but he was generous in his evaluation of the new novels and poetry; and since he enjoyed tremendous prestige in his day, his judgment was influential and served as an early authentication of this literature.

Eliot himself is the first and most important of the Modernist critics. He gained enormous influence and prestige, through his academic lectures and the journal of criticism he founded, *The Criterion*, which became an extremely important one. In addition, Eliot was a force in the publishing world as a consultant to publishers and a partner in a leading house. What he determined to be publishable was published. He was a power-broker, one might say, of Modernist literature in the 1920's and 1930's.

After the First World War, Cambridge University decided to constitute a Faculty of English. A senior professor who already occupied a post at Cambridge, Hector Munro Chadwick, a remnant of nineteenth–century literary historians but a scholar with a strong inclination towards anthropology, and who was a pioneer in comparative literature, recruited the new faculty. Chadwick himself was a medievalist, but the people he invited to join the new English department of Cambridge were young critics interested in modern, and even contemporary, literature. Chadwick was a tough-minded person of great vision who could imagine new things and wider horizons.

He hired two remarkable people who arrived in Cambridge still wearing their immobilized-army uniforms. The two men who were going to have powerful influence on the discipline of English literature and literary criticism between the two wars and whose impact is still felt, were F.R. Leavis and I.A. Richards. They, along with T.S. Eliot, dominated literary criticism in the transatlantic world in the 1920's and 30's, and had much to do with the development of the new academic criticism which was hospitable to, and in many cases actively promoted, the new literature.

Frank Leavis, a complicated and still highly controversial figure, was actually part of a husband and wife team. His wife Queenie Leavis may have been the more brilliant of the two. Mrs. Leavis did not get much opportunity in her day. Contemporaneously with the German critic Walter Benjamin, she published the first studies of the impact of mass culture on literature. Yet Queenie Leavis was never offered an academic post at Cambridge except for an occasional invitation to teach an extension course. She did, however, play a major role in the development of the discipline. The couple edited a new journal entitled *Scrutiny*. Along with Eliot's *The Criterion*, *Scrutiny* was the most important and influential English language journal of literary criticism in the twenties and thirties in the United States as well as in England and its back issues have again been put in print and are still studied.

Almost single-handedly Leavis created the reputation of D.H. Lawrence. He decided that Lawrence was an important novelist who belonged to the great nativist tradition of English novelists of which Jane Austen, Dickens, George Eliot and, to a certain extent, Henry James, were exclusive members. This occurred at a time when Lawrence lived in extreme isolation, and faced great difficulties in publishing his novels, occupying, as it were, the margins of both material and professional existence. Lawrence then found a patron, the eccentric American Mabel Dodge, who took him and his German aristocratic wife to New Mexico where the writer died in 1930. Without Leavis, Lawrence would have never achieved in his own lifetime much public recognition beyond his very first novel, the autobiographical *Sons and Lovers*.

I.A. Richards, a remarkable man whose biography remains to be written, was certainly one of the cultural heroes of the Modernist world. Born in the 1880's, he lived close to a century, until 1979. He had three careers; the last, beginning in the late thirties was devoted to the Basic English movement, bringing English literacy to China and the Third World. In his first career Richards became a Cambridge critic and the founder of the Cambridge school which based itself on Eliot's poetic principles of density, concrete imagery, self-referentiality, and textuality. Richards brought the Eliot message into the university and became its spokesman. Then he moved to Harvard and revolutionized the Harvard English Department, which up to then had been largely historicist. He became the founder of that Modernist American movement in criticism which was called "New Criticism."

By no means did the Modernist or New Critics concentrate on or alter the understanding of only Modernist literature, although that was their first consideration. They showed how masterpieces of the past could greatly benefit from close reading, the fussy screen of historicizing having been put aside. The more difficult and learned an old masterpiece was, the more attractive the New Critics found it. Dante, Petrarch and Donne became popular texts among the New Critics. Old literature that was dense and learned particularly attracted New Critics.

The achievement of the Modernist critics is hard to demonstrate because they were so successful that their approach dominated the way literature was taught in all colleges in at least the English-speaking world. What literature teaching was like before New Criticism is hard to recall. In 1910 a literature professor lecturing on the medieval German epic the *Niebelungenlied* would begin by telling his audience how many manuscripts survived (34) and into what recensions they were divided; then he would tell the students about the earlier poems on which the author of the *Niebelungenlied* may have drawn; then he would recount the history of the period in which the poem was written. By this time the semester was almost over and all that was left was for the professor to utter a few vague bromides about the aesthetic quality of the poem.

The New Critic changed all that. He boyantly came into class the first day, insisted that the students have their copies of the text in front of them, and without dipping into the murky river of scholarship and history, he simply proceeded to read the poem word by word and to try to understand what the poet was saying and to ferret out the techniques the poet used. Or he analyzed the novel page by page, studying dense paragraphs scrupulously. Images and symbols were thoroughly scrutinized. Nor did the New Critic insist that everything in the novel or poem be articulated into common meaning. As self-referential literature, it was allowed to be, up to a point, opaque and mysterious.

The New Critic worked on the principle that literature had been created by a powerfully constructive mind and his or her job was to encounter that mind and reconstruct its conscious operation from the text of the poem or novel. Close reading and keen attention to the words and phrases of the work was what was needed, not the dumping of erudite libraries on the students' heads.

The New Critics carried out an educational as much as a critical revolution. At a time when college and university education was becoming more accessible, there was a pressing question concerning what the literature curriculum should concentrate on. What was to be the core of humanistic education? The New Critics said the literary work itself, and this approach fitted in neatly with the classroom situation. Very few colleges could in fact afford to stock their libraries with the background scholarship. But students could be told to go to the bookstore and buy a cheap edition of Eliot or a reasonably accurate translation of Dante. The New Critics, to the delight of parsimonious university presidents and the relief of boards of trustees, said that expensive libraries were not necessary and in fact got in the way. What was necessary was directly to encounter the writer's mind, to read closely, to pour over the self-referential text.

Furthermore, Leavis and Eliot held that an ultimate purpose of humanistic studies in the university was to inculcate a common culture that would conserve social solidarity. The best way to do that was by universal study of a core of prescribed texts. In this way, the delibitating consequences of mass culture could be countervailed.

So the New Criticism satisfied at the same time the demands of literary study, cheap universal education, and the conservative fostering of cultural community. This was an unbeatable combination and hence until the 1960's the heirs of Eliot, Leavis, and Richards overwhelmingly dominated English and other literature departments.

After 1940 as the Modernist movement ran down and neo-Victorian historicism made a partial comeback, the radical self-confidence of the New Critics was slowly drained and close reading and textuality was somewhat softened by a partial reassertion of an historicist and ideological attitude to literature and humanistic education. Yet close reading remains the nucleus of literary study, around which everything else has been built.

New Criticism was the dominant force in the English departments, literary criticism, journals and as time went on inevitably also in the publishing houses of the twenties and the thirties. New Criticism propagated Eliot's message. Its proponents scorned the old-fashioned historical approach which Leavis satirized as asking useless questions like "How many children had Lady Macbeth?", and turned to examining what the text itself contained. The New Critics could concentrate on two pages of Joyce, one of Proust, ten lines from Eliot, or on six from Rilke, and could study them for days, if not for weeks or for a life-time. By 1930 novels and poems were commonly studied in American as well as British colleges not for the story they told, the social ambiance they reflected or the traces of the author's biography they contained—for these, it was held, had nothing to do with criticism—but for the work in itself, submitting it to an intense close reading.

Nor did the legitimate line of Modernist critics run out. In the war years of the forties the work of Cyril Connolly was deemed so important in Britain that his critical journal, *Horizon*, was granted special paper allocations by the government. The great tradition of modernist critics was perpetuated after the War by V.S. Pritchett who at an advanced age still writes in British journals and in *The New Yorker*.

The role of literary criticism in the development of French Modernist literature was also dominant. In 1909 the critic and Modernist novelist André Gide founded the *Nouvelle Revue Française* which immediately acquired hegemonic influence in Parisian cultural circles. *NRF* also established a publishing house which acquired immense prestige; by 1914 to be published by the *NRF* publishing house and warmly praised in the pages of its journal was enough to make a literary career.

Ironically, Gide initially rejected *Swann's Way*, the first volume of Marcel Proust's incomparable Modernist series *Remembrance of Things Past*. Gide soon realized his potentially disastrous error, humbly begged Proust's pardon, and after painful negotiations obtained the publications rights to *Swann's Way* from the publishing house that had dared to undertake Proust's work—partly because the privately wealthy novelist had heavily subsidized his own novel.

The *NRF* continued to dominate French letters until the Second World War, during which its reputation became clouded because of its collaboration with the Nazi occupiers of Paris. The most prominent collaborationist editor committed suicide and the journal was suppressed at the time of the liberation in 1944. But under the appropriate title of *Modern Times*, the Modernist group of critics resumed their important, although no longer as dominant role in French literary life.

One of the key ways in which the Nazis harmed German literature was by taking over or suspending the Berlin journals and publishing houses dedicated to Modernism—either on racial or ideological grounds. The Modernist tradition in German literature never recovered from the rupture.

In the United States, New Criticism spread out in the late twenties from Harvard to Yale and eventually through the entire country. Kenyon College, a small college in Ohio, became a center of New Criticism, and published a very influential journal, *The Kenyon Review*, which is still in existence. New Criticism spread among Southern universities as well, and became particularly strong in The University of the South in Sewanee, Tennessee. It became associated with the renaissance of Southern culture.

For white educated people in the Southern United States in the 1930's, New Criticism came to represent an elitist, patrician culture, the intellectualized shield of revived Southern humanism. While this attitude had conservative and racist overtones, the Southern devotion to New Criticism and Modernist literature was not a regional reactionary fantasy. T.S. Eliot, Ezra Pound, and F.R. Leavis held similar views. The Southern commitment to New Criticism and Modernism is still strong in literature departments in that part of the country.

When states in the Southwest became temporarily flushed with oil wealth in the sixties and seventies, both public and private universities in that region set about building monuments to Modernist poets and novelists. Anyone today who wishes to do serious research on Joyce has to make his way to Tulsa, Oklahoma; the same holds for the manuscripts of D.H. Lawrence and many other writers at Austin, Texas. There is an authentic story about a poet of the Irish Renaissance who in his geriatric years sat down and copied out anew all his poems from published versions and sold these manuscripts to an eager Southwestern library.

The prominent American names of New Criticism were Cleanth Brooks, a professor at Yale who exerted immense influence in the 1930's, John Crowe Ransom, Allen Tate, and Robert Penn Warren who is known today more as a novelist and a poet than as a critic. In the late thirties, Brooks and Warren published a textbook entitled *Understanding Poetry* which was used for almost two generations in American colleges for the teaching of the methods and close reading procedures of New Criticism. One other well-known American name of this school is R.P. Blackmur who taught at Princeton in the 1940's and 50's. Blackmur, a severe alcoholic who never received a Bachelor's degree, is now considered one of the greatest American critics of the twentieth century.

The development of academic English, which had a very distinct perception of language, literature and education, helps explain the rise of Modernist novel and poetry. Certainly, without men like Richards and Leavis, and in the United States, without Brooks and Blackmur, the penetration of these two Modernist genres as canonic standards would have been much less prevalent.

*   *   *

Drama, Music, and Dance

Modernist drama, however, cannot claim similar success. Particularly before 1940, it has no record of achievement comparable to the novel and poetry. If we are to examine Modernist drama in strict accordance with Modernist theory, we would have to focus on the period after the second World War, and search for it in the works of Samuel Beckett, Harold Pinter, and more recently Sam Shepard and David Mamet. Nevertheless, there were some important efforts early in the century.

At the beginning of the century, theater was still the prime vehicle of popular entertainment—alongside drinking and prostitution. People attended the theater to have their prevailing assumptions about ethics and society reinforced in a diverting manner, not to be challenged and given new insights. They were easily shocked and a great uproar could ensue. Thus Ibsen's dramas had aroused plenty of furious controversy in the nineties. And works which we now see as only marginally Modernist, and more of historical than dramatic interest, were vehemently damned and also praised at their first performance.

This was the case with several new plays, products of the Irish Renaissance, put on at the avant-garde Abbey Theater in Dublin in the first decade of the century. This theater was founded and supported by a visionary wealthy woman of progressive attitudes, Lady Gregory. In 1907 Dublin was shaken and many professed themselves scandalized by John Millington Synge's *The Playboy of the Western World*, which was held to denigrate the noble Irish peasant and blaspheme the Church. Nowadays, there are more blasphemous and amoral things to be seen on any given evening on American TV. Synge's work now seems pretty tame stuff, but it was important in its day because it heralded a theater that would be critical rather than celebratory of contemporary values and institutions.

George Bernard Shaw wanted to become the great Modernist dramatist. Many thought at the time that he succeeded, and he himself claimed to have been a cultural revolutionary. His dramas were published with long prefaces in which he announced himself as the great Modernist dramatist. Increasingly, this appears not be the case. His dramas are infrequently produced today, and when they are, they are not very well received.

Shaw is a difficult transitional figure. His work is marked by historicism and is for the most part narrative. His plays are replete with a pastiche of trendy—but now sadly dated—ideas. He was still writing for a popular audience whose taste had been shaped by Victorian drama. Therefore he did not do what he probably could have done. The careful control and meticulously structured density which are the characteristics of Modernist literature, are absent in his work. Shaw is much too sloppy by Modernist standards: an occasional scene that is clearly in the Modernist mode can be followed in his plays by one that looks like the Edwardian follies. Shaw could not decide who he wanted in his audience.

Critics today think that the Swedish August Strindberg, who was writing in the first fifteen years of the twentieth century, stands out as the greatest of Modernist playwrights. Strindberg acquires this title particularly because of his very direct approach to questions of sexuality and his explorations of the unconscious. His work has been regarded as the staged version of Freudian theory, even though there is no direct evidence that Strindberg ever read Freud. There is evidence, however, that Freud read Strindberg. Strindberg's plays are so rarely produced, at least in the English speaking world, that it is hard to make a judgment on his work.

Bertolt Brecht is often regarded as a leading Modernist dramatist. Brecht's problem was that he was a German Marxist ideologue and Marxism is still a Victorian worldview that drew on Hegelian philosophy and historicism. These are features that do not mix well with Modernism. Brecht was aware of and sometimes tried to work around this problem. There are examples of his work which are clearly in the Modernist mode. Especially the opera *The Rise and Fall of the City of Mahagonny* on which he collaborated with the composer Kurt Weill and which was produced once in Germany, in 1930, before it was banned by the Nazis, can be cited in this context. This opera was finally produced by New York's Metropolitan Opera in 1979. The production followed Brecht's and Weill's conception closely: discordant, intense, pessimistic, violent, it was an marvelous example of German Expressionism in drama and opera.

Brecht and Weill had curious careers. Before *Mahagonny*, they had an immense success with the expressionist musical comedy *The Threepenny Opera*, which is still popular. When they were on the verge of a breakthrough in German Expressionist opera and drama, they were exiled. Brecht spent fifteen years in Hollywood where he wrote screenplays which nobody produced. But he always got paid for them. Upon encountering political difficulties in the McCarthy era, he went to East Germany where he became the director of the State Theater. Only a small number of these later plays which belong to the agit-prop genre, have been translated and produced outside of East Berlin. Putting aside the Modernist style he had been developing, Kurt Weill took up the American musical comedy. He wrote "September Song," which can still be heard on popular radio stations.

It is today widely recognized that the American Eugene O'Neill was one of the leading Modernist dramatists. This is more valid with reference to his later work. Particularly plays from the forties and early fifties such as *Long Day's Journey into Night* and *The Iceman Cometh*, through their intensity and pessimism, are works that partake of the Modernist sensibility. O'Neill was a poor craftsman; his major dramas are long, tedious, and awkwardly stitched together, but his reputation appears to be secure as a leading Modernist dramatist. There are some twenty or thirty minute segments of O'Neill's two major works that are hallmarks of Modernist drama. The problem is that the plays run for four hours, as verbose and gloomy as the Jansenist Irish-American culture in which they are set.

Confusion about reality is the theme of much of the work of Luigi Pirandello, an Italian dramatist whose plays were enthusiastically received in the 1920's. Pirandello's dramas were self-consciously experimental in format and his ideas in the vanguard of the time. Who is mad? Who is sane? Is not a private illogical universe a higher kind of rationality that offers escape and comfort from the ugly, corrupt world? These questions were provocative in the twenties, conventional nowadays. Pirandello's plays are rarely produced today. He is admired as a pioneer but his place in the dramatic canon is a small one.

It cannot thus be claimed with as great certainty as in the case of the novel and poetry, that drama in the first four decades of this century achieved a breakthrough that can be properly designated as Modernist. In a sense, drama was the first form of literature to signal a breakthrough to Modernism on a grand scale in the work of Henrik Ibsen in the 1880's and 90's. Ibsen anticipates many of Modernism's features. But aside from the work of Strindberg, and some of the work of Brecht and O'Neill, a comprehensive transformation of the genre did not occur. Because of the costs of production and the need to gain audiences, it was more difficult for dramatists than for novelists and poets to pursue the Modernist style.

There is no doubt that the supreme, quintessential Modernist dramatist is the Irishman Samuel Beckett, who built most of his career in Paris. He began writing in the 1930's, but did not achieve much visibility until the fifties. Beckett's plays are minimalist, dense, difficult, self-referential, discordant, and gloomy—all key qualities of Modernism. The work of the Englishman Harold Pinter in the fifties and early sixties also fully cultivates the Modernist style.

The record of what can be termed Modernist music is of ambivalent nature, for a conscious effort was made in Europe and the United States along severely Modernist lines, but with rather strange results. There is no doubt that there is a very strong and elaborate Modernist tradition of dissonant and atonal music which can be described as disharmonious, fractured, intense, concrete, and thick. The technical term for this kind of Modernist music is "serialism." The prominent composers of this music were Arnold Schoenberg, Paul Hindemith, Alban Berg, Anton Webern, and to some extent, the American Charles Ives. It is Alban Berg's opera *Lulu*, which also received only one staging before it was shut down by the Nazis, that, along with Brecht and Weill's opera, stands as the most remarkable achievement in dissonant Modernist music.

The tradition of Modernist serialist or atonal music has continued in the United States in the work of Roger Sessions, Milton Babbitt, and several other composers. The problem is that their work has not received much popular support even among educated audiences. It has been played infrequently and to limited audiences. The impact of atonal, discordant, disharmonious Modernist music has been meager, and despite the efforts of a substantial number of composers to parallel the achievement of Modernist novelists and poets, the mode continues to address itself to a narrow group of listeners. The educated public has not accepted this music in the way it has accepted Modernist literature. Modernist music has not been able to receive the authenticating, legitimizing attention that the novel and poetry have obtained. Serialism has remained marginal.

An indicative phenomenon occurred in New York City in the early seventies when the French vanguard composer and conductor Pierre Boulez, who was strongly committed to Modernism, miraculously became the conductor of the New York Philharmonic and tried to involve the orchestra in performances of Modernist music. The result was intense hostility: subscriptions were cancelled, attendence fell, the critics of the popular press were cold, to say the least, and the orchestra itself rebelled. Boulez had to give up his project and was forced to resign, although he was easily the most distinguished conductor of the Philharmonic since Bruno Walter in the early fifties. Now Boulez runs what might be called a museum of Modernist music in Paris. This strange interlude is symbolic of the problem of Modernist music.

There was programmatically no difference between the direction taken by the dissonant and atonalist composers and the Modernist poets of the first four decades of the twentieth century. Even the idea of what we now call electronic music—then it was produced by electro-mechanical means— that would free composers from the limitations of traditional instruments appeared very early in the Modernist era. The visionary Ferruccio Busoni, learning in 1907 that someone had invented a two hundred ton machine that allegedly could generate any kind of sound by electrical means, speculated, "In what direction does the next step lead? To abstract sound, to unhampered technique, to unlimited tonal material."

Busoni was clear-eyed about the Modernist program in music. Not only should electronic music be pursued but its general dissonance was to replace Victorian "thematic" composition. Dissonance represented "nature." What Busoni acheived as a composer rather than as a critic and theorist is not as self-evident. A recent British production of his opera *Dr. Faustus* has been hailed in some quarters as masterly and intensely personal.

There was nothing shallow or timid about the Modernist musical intention, and there was a lot of experimental effort. Then why did the Modernist poets become the canonical force in poetry while the serialists remained at the margin of the musical world? It was much easier for the poets to publish than for the Modernist composers to get their work performed frequently enough and by major orchestras so as to have a strong impact on public taste. By and large, the Modernist composers of thick, disharmonious, dense music failed to obtain an appropriate hearing—and still lack a forum.

Even more important, the Modernist poets gained the overwhelming support of the major literary critics both within and outside the academic world. Critical support for Modernist dissonant music was again decidedly marginal. It never extended to the popular press and even in the cultural journals atonal music received only a moderate endorsement. The new serialist music lacked the support of opinion makers of the quality of T.S. Eliot and Cleanth Brooks. This made a very substantial difference. But above all, even the more educated public found atonal music uninteresting and uninspiring. It appeared to be composed by intellectual formula and not created by musical feeling.

If atonal music had been performed enough, especially by prominent orchestras, it would perhaps have effected significant changes in taste. There are still prominent conductors like Sir George Solti who will very rarely perform anything later than Mahler, who was the last of the Victorian composers.

In spite of the intrinsic achievements of dissonant, atonal, and electronic music, a simple physical problem was and is an obstacle to its social acceptance. Difficult and thick as Joyce's novels or Pound's poetry are, the reader has the flexibility of pacing the required close reading over relatively short attention spans. Listening to serialist disharmony, particularly in a concert hall—and in the twenties, thirties, and forties it was principally in live performance—can be a test of endurance.

Aside from serialism, a shift from the elaborate symphonic form to short pieces designed to express intensely perceived themes—"tone poems"—marks Modernist music. This became the dominant trend among composers between 1920 and 1940. The famous examples are Igor Stravinsky's *Rite of Spring*, which was originally written for ballet, and the prolific work of Richard Strauss, including *Don Juan*. (One of Strauss' tone poems, *Thus Spake Zarathustra*, later became popular as the soundtrack for the film *2001*.)

Debussy, Ravel, Respighi, Sibelius, Prokofiev and Ralph Vaughan Williams followed the same method as these composers. Although they wrote an occasional formal symphony, they concentrated on the short piece designed to be the direct, concise expression of a particular theme. This kind of expressionist music was well-received. Its specimens were performed as soon as they were composed, became popular, and continue to enjoy a high degree of popularity.

There are close ties between this twenties' musical expressionism and the Hollywood soundtrack of the late thirties and forties. Composers, usually good ones although not the most illustrious, who worked for the film companies brought elements of the expressionist school into their commercial work. Some of the soundtracks of the Hollywood films from these two decades are of high quality musically.

A change, therefore, did occur in music, wherein strenuous efforts were made to parallel Modernist poetry and novels in atonal compositions. But whereas the efforts in serialist music did not receive much visibility and acceptance despite the considerable work that had been done both quantitatively and qualitatively, the expressionist short piece, the tone poem, that emerged alongside the atonal compositions, by and large replaced the symphony as the favorite genre, and gained a wide audience.

The pinnacle of what might be called modernist classical music was reached in the earlier work of Sergei Prokofiev in the 1920's and the work of Bela Bartok in the thirties and forties. This comes very close to an effective combination of two strands of modernist music—blending experimental disharmony with expressionism or the programmatic tone poem. Some critics see the same achievement in the work of Charles Ives, the American composer in the twenties (Ives, like the poet Wallace Stevens, was an insurance executive). Sergei Rachmaninov was a successful continuator of nineteenth century music, but Dmitri Shostakovich was certainly within the modernist tradition. Shostakovich, along with Prokofiev, was concerned with the integration of music with other art forms. Both composed extensively for film.

One of Shostakovich's later symphonies uses symbolist poetry as a text. Nevertheless, the commitment of Prokofiev and Shostokovich was restrained by the repressive Stalinist atmosphere in which they worked and the opposition of the Soviet authorities to modernist art forms.

Modernist music was also subject to an unfortunate historical circumstance in Germany. In 1930 and 1931, respectively, in Brecht and Weill's opera *The Rise and Fall of the City of Mahagonny* and in Alban Berg's *Lulu*, Modernist music may have reached its peak and found its most suitable form in the expressionist opera. But no sooner were these works performed than they were suppressed by the Nazis, and their authors driven into exile. Recent opera companies have shown small interest in these works. It is to the credit of The Metropolitan Opera that it has mounted productions, in some ways remarkable ones, of these works. But the original productions of these Modernist operas found no successors, not even in the work of Brecht, Weill and Berg themselves. These complicated works are difficult and expensive to stage. They require singers who are also unusually capable actors.

The above argument leads to the provocative view that the most successful forms of Modernist music were neither atonal serialist nor the expressionist tone-poem, although the latter became popular and is still frequently performed, but in fact two other forms the Modernist movement has occasioned: the baroque revival and American jazz. Both of these forms are self-referential, textual, pure forms of music. Their prominence in the Modernist era was not accidental.

The great baroque revival that began after the First World War was partly the result of a technical factor. From this time until the 1950's, the low-fidelity phonograph record made it much more possible than ever before to obtain a truer impression of baroque music than of subsequent modes such as the nineteenth-century symphony which required the high-fidelity stereo record of the 1960's in order to be heard with any degree of honesty. Baroque music was ideal for phonograph, and Scarlatti and Vivaldi, who had hardly been played in two centuries, became immensely important and remained so. In a way, we can think of Vivaldi as the most performed Modernist composer.

Simultaneously with this development, came the upsurge of jazz which achieved the unusual stature of being at once a popular art and one taken seriously by many intellectuals. The origins of jazz lie in African music that accompanied the Black slaves to the New World. Out of this background came blues, Black folk music recounting traumas in the lives of these repressed people after their legal emancipation during the Civil War. At the turn of the century, blues music was written down in musical notation. At the same time, popular ragtime provided another source for jazz, which emerged in New Orleans among extraordinarily talented Black musicians in the early years of the century.

Jazz migrated with Black people to Chicago and other northern cities in the first two decades of the century, and with the help of night club and tavern owners, often Italian or Jewish, began to find a white audience. Phonograph records were also important in winning a general audience for Black jazz. The first great jazz performer with a white following, Louis Armstrong, joined New

Orleans jazz with swing, the emerging trend in popular music, and arranged jazz to accompany ballroom dancing in the twenties, further increasing its audience.

Yet this vulgarization or democratization of jazz did not detract from its fundamental Modernist qualities, particularly in the work of the first great jazz composer Ferdinand Jelly Roll Morton, and first prominent white jazz musician Bix Beiderbecke. Jazz remained a highly self-referential, non-sequential, partly disharmonious, and above all intensely improvisatory and individualistic form of music. The driving beat of the best Black jazz gave it a personal impact that was lost in the atonal music of the Modernist era.

This self-referential, thickly textual kind of music experienced a further development in the 1940's and 1950's—bebop or progressive jazz, a more abstract variety with complicated harmonies that marks the work of Charlie Parker, Charles Mingus, and John Coltrane. This later jazz, composed and played by well-trained and extremely sophisticated musicians was the most original and creative product of the Modernist era in music. Jazz's capacity to develop ever more complex and unique variants distinguished its intrinsic status as a major art form.

What endures in the work of the most celebrated American composer of the thirties, George Gershwin, is his partly successful efforts to blend blues and jazz motifs with the mainstream forms of popular music. He received lavish praise for this syncretic form in his day. In retrospect, his efforts appear idiosyncratic, because jazz itself has become mainstream, central to indigenous American culture as much as Hemingway or Jackson Pollock.

Aaron Copland's musical efforts were similar to Gershwin's. He made use of blues, jazz, and folk songs, trying to express a native music. Copland is still alive and he has received more attention in recent years. His work of the 1940's has come to receive considerable appreciation.

In the early years of the twentieth century in Paris, Sergei Diaghilev's *Ballet Russe* made its appearance with its great performer and choreographer Nijinsky. The company met with a remarkable reception followed by equally profound impact. What the Diaghilev Ballet showed was that a ballet did not necessarily have to follow traditional forms, that it could adjust to more recent departures in music, and especially that demands could be put upon dancers to undertake body movements that did not exist in nineteenth-century ballet.

The Russian group in Paris also tried new work. In 1908 the Diaghilev company performed the *Polovetsian Dances*, which is a Romantic piece from the late nineteenth century. This sentimental composition by Aleksandr Borodin appealed to the Modernist temperament through its emphasis on folk music. Proust attended the premiere performance.

More radical in its Modernist style was the Diaghilev ballet's production of *The Afternoon of a Faun* in 1910. The ballet, with choreography by Nijinsky, featured Debussy's setting of a poem by Mallarmé. Nijinsky aimed to fulfill Mallarmé's vision that "the ballerina is not a girl dancing . . . She is not a girl but rather a metaphor. She does not dance but rather, writing with her body, she suggests things." Proust again attended *The Afternoon of a Faun* and noted that Nijinsky's choreography achieved a clarity that did not banish all mystery—a good description of Modernist performance art. "My own inclinations are 'primitive'," Nijinsky announced to a reporter's queries about his choreography. An extensive set of drawings and photographs of *The Afternoon* production has survived. They show an effort to create costumes that combine classical Greek style as seen on vases with a touch of the primitive. The dancers' poses are angular, intentionally abstracted.

Then, most important, in 1913 the Diaghilev group gave the first performance of *The Rite of Spring* whose music was written by Stravinsky, and choreography executed by Nijinsky. The costumes used in this first production of *The Rite of Spring* were those of Ukranian peasants—again the folk or William Morris motif—as can be ascertained from the photographs of the performance. Unfortunately we do not have a record of the choreography, but we do know that the production created an uproar, and was even found shocking. The angular body movements, probably seen as sexually suggestive, were certainly not customary. The music too was provocative, although not exactly disharmonious, since Walt Disney incorporated Stravinsky's tone poem into his ambitious feature-length cartoon *Fantasia* in 1940. Nevertheless, to the ear of 1913, Stravinsky's music sounded original and disturbing.

In the early years of the century, it was customary for audiences to show their disapproval or appreciation by applauding, hooting, howling, and for the popular press to give vent to its outrage or approval in undisguised terms. People looked upon the theater and the opera as places they went to to have their ideas confirmed. They attended performances for the reinforcement of their expectations, and they always knew what to expect. Nineteenth-century opera, for example, conformed to those expectations. There are only a few operas from that period—Verdi's *Don Carlo* and a couple of the *Ring* operas of Wagner—which have the capacity to tax their audience's minds.

Early in the twentieth century, therefore, when the major departures in the performing arts began to take place, audiences were far from being ready to understand the new conceptions of the purpose of performance. They did not understand that they were there to explore, along with the artists, what Proust termed "the different self," that they were attending the performance to undergo the shock of recognition that led to an altered or more refined sensibility and not in order to have reinforced and reconfirmed what they already believed. Seeing, therefore, a ballet so different from what they were accustomed to, caused nothing less than an outrage among these audiences.

Nevertheless, with the work of Nijinsky in particular, ballet did manage to turn in a new direction. The choreographer who succeded Nijinsky in opening up the ballet as a creative art form was George Balanchine. He was a Russian who worked in the 1930's first in Paris and then in New York, where in the late thirties he founded a major ballet company. He was fortunate enough to find a collaborator in Lincoln Kirstein, a patron of the arts who understood the new forms of ballet and who organized and managed the company for which Balanchine did the modernist choreography.

Finally, the "modern dance" movement of the twenties and the thirties was consciously committed to Modernism. The Americans Isadora Duncan, Ruth St. Denis and Martha Graham played leading roles in the modern dance movement, which has been perpetuated in our day by Merce Cunningham. Between 1920 and 1940, the manifestations of this movement seemed to be the quintessence of Modernism in dance, and they were certainly intended to be so. They were free-flowing in every respect, employed original sets and costumes, were set to expressionist music, intended to provoke, and had a strong sexual content.

The modern dance movement peaked in the thirties and forties. It has not been able to find again the social recognition it enjoyed then. Nor has it in recent decades been taken as seriously expressive of Modernism as the ballet. The ballet has continued to develop as a creative art form, and incorporating some of the ideas of Martha Graham into its own field, it has become a combination of the traditional ballet and modern dance forms.

The modern dance movement, as presented by Duncan and Graham, has not achieved the recognition that its admirers in the forties expected. Whereas in the late forties, in order to see Modernist dance, one still went to Jacob's Pillow in the Berkshires where Ruth St. Denis and Ted Shawn, the teachers of Martha Graham, were performing, today it is to Lincoln Center, with its presentations of vanguard ballet, that one goes to in order to see the highest achievement in Modernist dance. Nijinsky has triumphed over Isadora Duncan, a development not foreseen in the 1920's.

The Modern dance movement resembles Ravel's *Bolero* and other prominent tone poems of the twenties. Its contrived and determined effort at Modernism has not worn well. Just as the tone poem developed into the Hollywood music sound track, so did modern dance, beginning with Agnes De Mille's choreography for *Oklahoma!* in 1943, achieve popular adulation on the musical comedy stage. This represents a major social impact but Modernism was an elitist, vanguard movement and it was in the instance of modern dance as well as the tone poem fragmented by popularization.

*　　*　　*

The Visual Arts

While the record of Modernism in music and dance is somewhat difficult to assess and is controversial, its achievement in painting was seminal and overwhelming. The Modernist movement in painting created the most important and productive era in terms of the application of color to canvas since the early sixteenth century, since, that is, the era of the high Renaissance that produced da Vinci, Michelangelo, Raphael and El Greco. Since the Renaissance, there had not been as impressive a period of creation in the visual arts and such fundamental transformation as occurred in the first thirty years of the twentieth century. The Tate Gallery in London, several galleries in Paris, the Museum Ludwig in Cologne, and New York museums such as The Museum of Modern Art, the Whitney and the Guggenheim are monuments to that effect, as is too the current insatiable appetite of the art market for Modernist work.

First among the social and material factors that contributed to the formation of the Modernist era in painting, came the proliferation of photography, and specifically its success in giving a realistic, or allegedly realistic, view of the world. Painting was pressed to take a different approach. Once the Kodak camera made its appearance, it became necessary for artists to move towards more nonrepresentational portrayals because the camera coopted what had hitherto been the characteristic province of the painter, namely, to depict what the eye saw. Now the painter had to concentrate increasingly on what the inner eye saw.

Secondly, the cheapness of painting materials, due to advances in chemistry, was another contributing reason. The most successful industry in the late nineteenth century was chemistry, and one by-product of this achievement was the production of inexpensive paint and canvas, and hence their accessibility for artists of modest means. Painting was no longer the exclusive domain of the academician or of artists in the carriage trade. Almost anybody could seriously attempt the artist's career.

Thirdly, the opening of museums and art galleries to the public strongly affected Modernist painting. These were supported by the state or, more frequently, by private benefactors and collectors who initially gathered art works for their own interest (for example, the Frick Collection) and then willed them to the public. What this meant above all, and here we have to take into account the aiding factor of affordable railroad transportation, was that artists could simply go and see the important work that had been and was being done in their field. That is, they now had immediate access not only to the work of their contemporaries, but to the techniques developed by the old masters as well. The ways in which a painter handles the brush-work, how he solves the problems of perspective and color are questions to be answered only through the close study of actual paintings in a museum. These features cannot be observed in photographs. And only in the early years of this century did the works of previous as well as contemporary artists become accessible to the public.

The importance of the availability of cheap housing and food in metropolitan centers in the first forty years of the century has been already mentioned as a factor in the development of Modernist painting. This allowed persons to undertake the artist's hazardous career. The economic circumstances of the early decades of this century enabled a rather large group of artists to survive. There were hundreds of painters at work in Paris in the 1920's, many of whom never became well-known but could nevertheless continue to paint because of the low cost of living.

Another reason for the Modernist renaissance in painting was the development of an art market, owing firstly to the emergence of a large middle class whose taste was becoming increasingly more sympathetic to Modernist forms, and secondly to the rise of the art dealer in the later years of the nineteenth century. Initially, art dealers were interested only in the masters of the old school, mainly in the painters of the Renaissance. But increasingly, especially starting with the 1920's, they began to buy more recent work as well and became patrons to promising young artists. The Modernist movement in painting rose along with the art market and the proliferation of commercial galleries.

A further factor that was intellectual as well as social, was the increasing recognition that a technological civilization required a new kind of art. This view emerged particularly during and shortly after the First World War, and was referred to at times as constructivism, and at others as futurism or surrealism, all of which terms signified the recognition that the painter now had a new subject, that of the impact of technological civilization. He had to convey this awareness in ways different from those used by nineteenth-century artists which had been, it was believed, expressive of a pre-technological civilization.

Before all else, however, the great artistic movement occurred because of a phenomenal generation of artists especially in France and the German–speaking countries. We cannot very well work around the fact that a remarkable number of artistic people appeared at a particular time in history. Historians cannot adequately explain such generational phenomena. In the United States, as a matter of fact, the Modernist movement was stillborn in the 1920's and 30's. Not that there were not enough artists who knew what they wanted to achieve, but rather that they could not realize their intentions very well. The great Modernist movement in the United States—Abstract Expressionism—did not appear until the late forties and fifties, even though the ideas and the intention had been in existence long before then. But in Europe the Modernist breakthrough in painting came at the same time as in the novel and poetry—the first three decades of the century.

The principles of Modernist painting are today common knowledge and self-evident to educated people. First, it is not the depicted subject but the craftsmanship that is paramount, particularly the use of color and the application of paint to canvas. What becomes central is the activity of the painter. Regardless of whether he is painting a Duchess, a Parisian backstreet, a fruit bowl or six lines, the painter must foreground and concentrate on his technique and his use of color. This is the Modernist principle of textuality or self-referentiality.

Secondly, the artist is engaged in a symbolic representation of a world that borders consciousness and unconsciousness, oscillating between the two sides of the dividing line. Art is the product of the interaction of the conscious and unconscious domains. The realm of symbolism and fantasy is central to art. This too constitutes a fundamental Modernist principle.

Third comes the principle that non-representational or abstract art has a special claim to authenticity and aesthetic value. Despite the problems it met with in its beginnings, the recognition of nonrepresentational art, especially among younger intellectuals, as an important and authentic art form, came very rapidly. In Paris, London and Berlin, abstract art had gained wide recognition among young intellectuals even before the First World War. Nonrepresentational art is entirely mythic or symbolic and this is why it is pure art.

Finally, there was the tendency to exoticism. The appreciation of oriental motifs and ideas appeared early in Modernist art. In Modernism, a strong movement toward neo-primitivism was also discernible, at least in the shape of a recognition or even valorization of the primitive. Orientalism and primitivism are qualities that run through earlier Modernist art.

It is the opinion of art historians that the forerunner of Modernism in painting was Paul Cézanne working in the late 1880's. Just as Henry James was a forerunner of the Modernist novel, and Mallarmé and Gerard Manley Hopkins forecast Modernist poetry, Cézanne anticipated Modernist painting, not only with respect to his work, but also in terms of his statements on painting. Cézanne clearly articulated the Modernist principles. He claimed that a picture, first of all, "should represent nothing but color." Further, "art is a harmony parallel to nature," which is to say that art does not imitate nature. It generates its own world parallel to nature. Art is a harmony, not derivative of nature, but one that exists in and for itself. Cézanne had a clear and revolutionary program for the painter.

Cézanne's work was carried on at the turn of the century by Vincent van Gogh and Paul Gauguin. In December 1910, there occurred in London an exhibition of the work of the Post-Impressionist School, as Cézanne, van Gogh and Gauguin came to be called. It had been organized by the art critic Clive Bell, brother-in-law of Virginia Woolf and husband of Vanessa Bell. Although the exhibition caused quite a furor, it found immediate acceptance among the younger generation that had come to agree with Virginia Woolf that the world had changed fundamentally, that a new art and a new culture had come into being. Similarly in New York in 1913, the Armory show introduced Modernist painting to the general public. Marcel Duchamp's quasi-abstract "Nude Descending a Staircase" caused a media sensation.

Around this time, Henri Matisse had begun his work in Paris. Matisse, who lived until 1954, played the important role of bridging the generations between van Gogh and the rise of American Abstract Expressionism through his sixty-year career as painter. He began to paint as a near-contemporary of Van Gogh and died as a contemporary of Jackson Pollock and the New York school.

In the work of Gauguin, the efforts at orientalism and primitivism are clearly observable. Gauguin lived in Tahiti for several years in order to find what he called "the grandeur, the profundity and the mystery of Tahiti," that is, an abstract form for immediate truth, the mythic image of a primitive culture. At the same time in Paris, Henri Rousseau achieved a different kind of primitivism, one that found its source in the artist's own mind. Rousseau, a genuine, self-taught primitive artist explored the entirely private world of fantasy.

Van Gogh and Matisse were crucial for the early development of Modernist painting for the reason that they showed the subject matter of art to be inconsequential. Van Gogh painted human subjects such as Belgian workers, then flowers and fields seen from his window in the south of France. Matisse's favorite subjects were Parisian street scenes and coastal fishing villages. Both focused on the application of color to the painting surface, and the arbitrary, and wide, range of the subject matter helped place the subject in the background in favor of the technique and materials of painting. They took the stock subjects of Victorian art, such as flowers and street scenes, and transformed them by a radical technique which bespoke an altered sensibility.

At the same time, exploration of the unconscious, the world of dream and fantasy had become a prime motif. The three artists who took the lead in the artistic meditation on the borders of the conscious and the unconscious were the Norwegian Edvard Munch, the Austrian Gustav Klimt and the French expressionist Odilon Redon. The work of these artists deals with what Redon termed "the coming of the unconscious." Their interest is in the dream, the fantasy, and the primal scream. Their work informs the background of the Dadaism and Surrealism of the 1920's, as well as much of later science-fiction imagery. In fact, elements of the iconography of contemporary science-fiction film can be traced back directly to the paintings of Munch, Klimt and Redon. "Nothing is small nothing is great—", wrote Munch. "Inside us are worlds."

Around 1910, Georges Braque and Pablo Picasso began to experiment with abstract forms in Paris, producing, for the first time since Anglo-Irish art of the eighth century, wholly non-representational art. They were trying to get at what Picasso called "the abominable forms." This movement came to be called Cubism because of a tendency to focus on rectangular lines and is now viewed as the seminal development in early twentieth–century painting. Out of simple lines and what were considered ugly patterns, out of rectangles, circles, and discordant traces, they generated the self-referential world of the canvas— painterly, or pure painting.

After the First World War, Braque and Picasso were followed by a large group of painters who joined the abstract or non-representational movement, among whom the most outstanding perhaps were Piet Mondrian and Jóan Miró. As has been pointed out above, just as this movement began to erode in Paris in the thirties, it emerged forcefully around 1940 in the United States in the work of Jackson Pollock and Willem de Kooning. From the Left Bank cafés, abstract art moved to Greenwich Village studios and to the Cedar Tavern, an unpretentious bar on University Place that became the clubhouse of the Abstract Expressionists. Later in the 50's Pollock and de Kooning moved to East Hampton, L.I.—because it was then considered cheap!

The Modernist movement in sculpture was not as vast in productivity as in painting, primarily because of the great cost of working in sculpture. Whereas painterly materials were rather inexpensive in this period, materials for the latter, such as stone or metal, remained almost unaffordable. Sculpture is an art that entails difficult and slow work, and requires advance commissions. Picasso did some early work in sculpture and demonstrated his incredible talent in this medium as well. But he soon largely confined his work to canvas. Nevertheless, in the 1920's, in the work of Modigliani and Giacometti, the beginnings of sculptural abstract expressionism becomes discernible. Even more recognized was the work of Henry Moore starting with the 1930's. Moore, who was greatly influenced by Gauguin as well as by Picasso, combined abstract expressionism with the worship of the primitive. Moore is now regarded as the leading Modernist sculptor.

Again, around the same time, there was a very important movement in the Soviet Union, called Constructivism. This was a movement parallel and related to the Paris School. Painters like Marc Chagall and Chaim Soutine shuttled back and forth between Paris and Russia, participating in both movements. The most prominent names of the Constructivist movement were Naum Gabo, both a painter and a sculptor, and Kasimir Malevich the painter. Malevich's variety of Constructivism was also called Suprematism, after his statement that he aimed at "the supremacy of pure sensitivity in creative art." From the handful of Malevich's canvases that are available in the West, he appears to have anticipated the work of the American Abstract Expressionists like Pollock and de Kooning. He is possibly one of the leading painters of this century. However, in 1922, Modernism was declared to be a decadent bourgeois art by Lenin and Trotsky, and repressed by the Soviet government. In many cases, the painters were imprisoned or exiled, thus bringing the great Russian Constructivist movement to an end. Many of the Constructivist works that are held by Soviet museums have never been publicly exhibited.

A movement similar to Constructivism, called Futurism, can be seen in Italy during this period. Its leading exponent was Gino Severini. Both Constructivism and Futurism were dedicated not only to abstract art, but more specifically to abstract art that arose in response to contemporary events, technological culture, and to the First World War. The most effective artistic responses to the war came from these two movements.

Although the Futurist movement declined in the 1920's under Mussolini, Italian design—in furniture, clothes, and automobiles—was permanently influenced by it. The long-term success of Italian design from the 1920's to the present is the heritage of Futurism.

The influence of the Russian and Italian movements on the French Surrealism of the 1920's, which attempted to present a very provocative nonrepresentational art and visceral anarchism, was powerful enough to enable us to designate the latter movement as a continuation of the traditions of Constructivism and Futurism. The leading surrealist figure in the 1920's was André Breton, not much of an artist per se, but a theorist and spokesman of considerable import. Breton is a prototype of the artistic pundit that anticipates the counter-culture hero of the 1960's. He was certainly a very visible figure in his day.

Beginning around 1910 and continuing into the twenties, there was another great movement in painting—Expressionism—this time in Germany. The two figures that predominate in this movement, Wassily Kandinsky, who was originally a Russian, and Paul Klee, a Swiss-German, stand, in the opinion of most critics, as the greatest of Modernist painters along with Picasso and Braque. This German movement was originally known as the "Blue Rider" school, after a journal of art and social critique that its leaders published at this time. The German Expressionst movement was influenced in its early years by the French painter Robert Delauney, whose reputation is currently on the rise.

Kandinsky, Klee and some other members of the Blue Rider school joined the Bauhaus in the 1920's. The Bauhaus was an institute devoted to architecture, painting and design, aiming at a revolutionary new era in the visual arts in conformity with Modernist principles, new technology and, to some extent, with socialism. Kandinsky and Klee taught painting in the Bauhaus. With the rise of Hitler to power, the went into exile, along with other Bauhaus members and Brecht, Weill and Berg. Klee went to Switzerland, Kandinsky to Paris, where he died in 1944. Klee died in 1940 in Berne.

In his last years in Paris, Kandinsky had to struggle to find buyers and patrons. His paintings, along with those of Van Gogh and some early Picasso work, now command the highest prices of any Modernist artist. Kandinsky's influence on American Abstract Expressionism was more direct than any other European artist. Kandinsky humanized the abstract character of the Parisian school. His nonrepresentational paintings are more personal, emotional, and sometimes mystical and whimsical.

Klee was the theorist of the painterly Modernism of the 1920's. Picasso wrote very little, perhaps because he was too occupied producing painting upon painting. Klee, however—who sold few paintings in his lifetime— wrote extensively about Modernist art, and particularly about its abstract school. He maintained that his intention was to communicate "the primordeal realm of psychic improvisation," which was necessary, he claimed, to release abstract structures which "transcend all schematic intent and to achieve a new naturalism." The abstract structures rose above all language and achieved a natural realm of their own. Klee was also very much influenced by Chinese and Indian art and philosophy, and to a degree, by Middle Eastern art as well. He made a trip to Tunisia before the First World War, where he acquired a taste for Middle Eastern art forms. Klee's abstract art is highly symbolic, mythological, fantastic, and intensely personal.

By the 1920's, these artists, as well as many others less well-known, had attained the status of celebrities. Yet Modernist paintings which are sold today for between half a million to two million dollars, could still be bought in Paris in the late twenties for anywhere between two hundred and two thousand dollars. Painters made enough to live on, but substantial rewards were slow in coming. The situation was altered with the entry of the American buyers and art dealers into the market, the establishment of the Museum of Modern Art in 1937, and the compiling of the Whitney collection, all of which were factors that contributed to the rise in the prices of Modernist paintings. The sculptor Henry Moore, for example, had become wealthy by the late thirties. Indeed, by the 1940's, there was no metropolitan bank or corporate executive office that felt secure without a Henry Moore primordial figure reclining on its premises. Picasso by 1940 had become a mythic figure, like Einstein, and the embodiment in the popular imagination of what an artist should do and how he should live.

Obviously, this market phenomenon was not altogether glorious, but it is indicative of the way Modernist art achieved a central role in cultural life as well as popular support, and thereby changed people's aesthetic values. Today, what we wear, the colors we use, the furniture we sit on, the shape of our rooms, the imagery that appears nowadays in our stage-sets and in our films have all been shaped through and by Modernist painting. We see the world differently than did people before 1900. Not only are Modernist painters themselves venerated, but they have actually transformed the visible world.

The Modernist design style of the twenties and thirties, art deco, was a conscious and contrived reflection of Modernist painting and its motifs and assumptions. Whereas a leading theme in art nouveau in the early years of the century reflected the folk-art, fresh air movement of the 1890's, art deco sought for a mode of interior design that reflected the lines and bold patterns—Picasso's "abominable forms"—of the Parision school. Instead of art nouveau's natural-grained wood and woven carpets, art deco favored lacquered wood furniture, parquet floors, and especially the use of burnished metallic objects indicative of a high-tech culture. Or it devised a few deeply colored pieces of furniture against an all-white background. The great monument to art deco is the foyer of Radio City Music Hall in New York. The Scandinavian design of the fifties represented a peculiar effort to combine elements of both art nouveau (natural-grained wood) and art deco (white walls, metal and glass tables), a kind of all-star Modernist style.

Modernist art was helped by the emergence of critics and art historians. Just as Modernist poetry and novel achieved their penetration with the collaboration of critics and scholars, and just as serialist music, because it never quite achieved similar critical support, remained culturally marginal, so painting and sculpture benefited from the emergence of art criticism as a distinct intellectual force and profession. This emergence occurred principally in the twenties and thirties.

The first modern art critic and the prototype of the profession was Bernard Berenson, an immigrant Jew from the slums of Boston who won a scholarship to Harvard in the 1880's, and became a self-taught, self-advertised expert on the Italian Renaissance. He collaborated with a rather flamboyant and unscrupulous art dealer named Lord Duveen from the 1890's until the twenties, and between them they dominated the market for Renaissance paintings. Duveen found Renaissance works in the back alleys of Siena and Florence, Berenson conveniently authenticated his colleague's finds, and the paintings sky-rocketed in value. This showed what an art critic of competence, taste, learning, and a not-too-tender conscience could do. Although Berenson himself was never devoted to Modernist art, and confined himself to the Renaissance, he created the prototype of the art critic who, as we well know by now, can be a very powerful figure in the art market.

Berenson had a disciple, a precocious Englishman named Kenneth Clark who came from an extremely wealthy family. Clark studied with Berenson after leaving Oxford, and devoted himself, following his master, not only to the Renaissance, but also to Modernist art. At the age of thirty-one, Clark became the director of the Tate Gallery in London, and proceeded to validate and popularize Modernist art. In the early thirties, Clark purchased for the Tate Van Gogh, Gauguin, Cézanne and other Modernist painters in large blocks at unimaginably low prices. The exhibitions he devised greatly enhanced the reputation of these works.

Clark singlehandedly made a significant contribution to the inflation of the Modernist art market and fostered the legitimacy of the Parisian school in gentry eyes. This is the same Sir Kenneth Clark who used to tell us the story of civilization on Public Television in the 1970's. At one point in his dealings, Clark came upon a group of Matisse drawings for sale. Not having gallery funds to purchase them, he acquired them for a modest sum for his personal collection. These drawings alone by the 1960's made Sir Kenneth a multi-millionaire.

Two influential and perceptive art critics appeared in the United States in the 1930's: Clement Greenberg and Meyer Schapiro. Greenberg was a largely self-educated person who wrote for *The Partisan Review* and other intellectual quarterlies. Eventually, in the forties, he became an art critic for *New Yorker* magazine, and the primary spokesman for the American school of Modernist painting and Abstract Expressionism. Greenberg made Jackson Pollock the way F.R. Leavis made D.H. Lawrence. Greenberg's essays are still readable. He found an illuminating way of encapsulating the Modernist principle of self-referentiality. In Modernist culture a "discipline criticizes itself by its own methods."

Meyer Schapiro was a colorful figure and was still active in the 1980's. Again, mostly self-taught and with close personal ties to the New York painterly school, he did get a Ph.D. at Columbia and became a medieval art historian, since entry into the academic art world was not possible in the 1930's unless one taught medieval or Renaissance art, and he did some very fine work in that area. Schapiro gained a tenured professorship of art history at Columbia, where his lectures drew standing room only audiences. No one, in fact, has written more persuasively than Meyer Schapiro about Romanesque art, to which there is a proto-expressionist quality. But Schapiro's greatest interest was in Modernism, and his essays on the subject, which go back to the thirties, are still very readable. From the influential vantage of his Columbia professorship, Schapiro could foster a public critical acceptance for Modernism.

With the opening of the Museum of Modern Art, Modernism acquired in New York of the thirties an aura of elite orthodoxy. Only a quarter of century had transpired since the media had heaped contempt on Marcel Duchamp and the pioneering Armory Show. Even the *New York Times* eventually surrendered to the Modernist tide. *The Times* hired the astute and learned Harvard graduate, Hilton Kramer, a disciple of Greenberg and Schapiro in his commitment to Modernism, as its art critic because, so the editors told Kramer, the *Times* wanted to keep even with the aesthetic preferences of its readers.

That all three critics were Jewish was not accidental. New York Jewish intellectuals in the thirties and forties, having no investment in Gentile and genteel Victorian art, could enthusiastically embrace Modernist aesthetics for its intrinsic values of cultural liberation.

At the same time as the development of professional art criticism, the 1920's also saw the creation of another new field of scholarship, art history. This was largely a German creation—*Kunstgeschichte*—and owed some of its original conceptions to nineteenth-century philosophical idealism. But there was very much a Modernist slant to the emergence of the field. Art history as we know it, as distinct from nineteenth-century connoisseurship or art appreciation, was a method of close analysis, and it was founded by two German scholars, Abby Warburg and Erwin Panofsky.

Warburg came from the prominent German-Jewish banking family. He developed the method of art history which is called iconology or iconography, after the medieval word for "image." The purpose of the art historian, according to Warburg, is to carry out a close reading of a particular image as it appears in medieval manuscript illumination or in stained glass, say, in Chartres, as well as in all the other particular manifestations of the same icon. The art historian's task was to map out the entire field of the icon's meaning, use and influence, including the literary motifs that helped generate the pictorial image, and everything that was entailed in the craftsmanship. Every image was ultimately related to a literary text.

Until Warburg, the approach of the art historian had been devoid of a rigorous method. It had consisted mainly of learned but idiosyncratic connoisseurship—aesthetic appreciation of pretty pictures. Warburg displaced this with precepts for systematic and technical close reading very much like those generated by the New Critics for the study of literature and with special interest in iconological symbolism.

Warburg left Germany in 1928 upon the rise of the Nazis, went to London and reestablished his institute there. He persuaded an English textile family, the Courtaulds, to give him additional funds and created the Warburg-Courtauld Institute. The Institute now comprises the graduate department of art history of the University of London. Its thought-world remains remarkably rooted in the Berlin culture of the 1920's.

Erwin Panofsky was a student of Warburg's, and followed the same method of close reading or iconographic study. He came to the United States in the thirties where his first activity was to transform the Institute of Fine Arts of New York University into by far the most eminent school of art history in the United States. In the forties, he moved to the Institute for Advanced Study in Princeton where too he helped create a distinguished department of art history at Princeton University.

Although art historians were initially interested in medieval and Renaissance art, eventually in the forties and fifties, they came to incorporate the study of Modernist art into their canon. The art history departments in women's colleges like Bennington, Wellesley, Smith, Sarah Lawrence and Bryn Mawr, were the first to make art history a discipline to be taught even to undergraduates, to release it from being a specialization for graduate students and researchers, and to make it central to the humanistic education of post-adolescents. They were also the first to give priority to the study of Modernist art in their curricula. Bennington, which was founded in the late thirties, was a vehemently progressive college for affluent young women that placed its primary emphasis on the study of Modernist dance, poetry and art, and to some extent, still does. When in the 1950's Oxford University finally established a chair in art history, the first appointment to its chair—Edgar Wind—was a German émigré scholar of the Renaissance who had taught at Smith College for many years.

From these colleges, art history departments spread first through the Ivy League schools and then through the state universities, and decisively contributed to the creation of a public taste. They generated a much larger market, consisting of knowledgeable people with a practiced eye and a sense of the scope of art history. The growth of art history as an academic subject was linked as closely to the profusion of galleries, museums and the market for Modernist art, as the New Critics' activities were connected to the creation of a publishing market for Modernist poetry and novel in the twenties and thirties.

Modernist architecture was often designated, especially in its first generation, as the functionalist style, and in the 1940's and 50's, as the international style. It was born in four different cities at about the same time but independently of each other, in the early years of the century—in Barcelona, Glasgow, Chicago and Berlin.

The Barcelona architect was Antonio Gaudi, who was perhaps the most imaginative and creative art nouveau architect. He used flowing lines creating buildings that looked like settings for science fiction films. They had strong decorative elements, and a sense of fantasy. Gaudi, who died in 1926, was not really appreciated until the 1960's.

The Glasgow architect was Charles Rennie Mackintosh who had been locally trained, was, in fact, an autodidact, but who had traveled widely on the continent. He was a professor of architecture and design at the Glasgow School of Art. Macintosh designed only a few buildings, most of which were local houses and schools. He has a single monumental public building, the Glasgow School of Art, which was built between 1910 and 1912. This is the first functionalist or Modernist building in Britain, and it still is one of the most important and successful works of Modernist architecture in terms of both its interior and exterior design.

Macintosh was certainly very much a product of the Art Nouveau movement. He was influenced by William Morris and the folk-art ethos of the late nineteenth century. His aims were to reduce a building to its essentials, to communicate a populist feeling, to use pure materials such as local stone on the outside and almost entirely wood on the inside, and to create the building in which all elements were totally integrated. To this latter end, even the furniture and the entire decor of the building would be designed by the architect and his staff. The chief member of his staff was his wife who was a prominent designer—she made her living for forty years designing wallpaper.

Macintosh was an important, pioneering figure in the development of Modernist architecture. Unfortunately, he had difficulty getting commissions, and, whether out of disappointment or for another reason, he became a severe alcoholic, which eventually led to a breakdown. Although he did not die until the late 1930's, he produced very little work after the First World War.

The first great name, and certainly the most versatile one in the history of American architecture, was Louis Sullivan. One of Sullivan's important buildings in Chicago is the Auditorium. A great achievement of 1890's Victorian architecture, it is in the shape of a Roman basilica, emphasizing the horizontal, and holds three thousand people. The Auditorium was originally designed as an opera house, but is currently used—after complete restoration in the 1970's—as a concert hall. This marvelous work of architecture was also a pioneer in the use of electric illumination. The original electric bulbs were recreated at exorbitant cost as part of the restoration work.

In the early years of the century, Sullivan worked on his first Modernist building, the first architectural artifact approaching a skyscraper in appearance, although it was only twelve stories. A vertical-functional edifice of what later came to be called the international style, this is the Carson, Pirie, Scott Department Store on State Street in Chicago. Sullivan was aware of the new possibilities for building relatively tall buildings opened up by the emerging steel frame and the new pneumatic elevator which used compressed air. The Carson, Pirie, Scott building signaled the direction of twentieth-century architecture made possible by these technological advances.

Despite Sullivan's immense skill at decorating the facades of buildings, the relatively unadorned face of the Carson building also indicated a new trend. Nineteenth-century buildings were held up by their heavy stone walls which the architect then adorned—this was called the Beaux Arts style. Thick walls became unnecessary in the engineering revolution of the early twentieth century, and the facades of buildings lost their decorative character to the sparse functionalist style. The Carson building still has some marvellously delicate ironwork. Nevertheless, in comparison with the beaux arts style, it inaugurated the transition to Modernist minimalism.

Sullivan was fully conscious of what he was undertaking. Although they have not been published, his private papers have been exhibited, and reveal that Sullivan was very much influenced by Nietzsche. He certainly had a proto-Modernist, radical temperament. He was sensitive to the new ideas that were appearing in a variety of fields at the turn of the century. Although Sullivan had immense success with the Auditorium and other horizontally focused, heavily decorated buildings, he realized that it was both possible and necessary to create a new style. The Modernist style would have a relatively plain exterior and the building would simply demonstrate its function rather than memorialize some cultural heritage.

Sullivan's disciple was the Midwestern native, Frank Lloyd Wright, who received his education as an apprentice in Sullivan's firm, and became his partner for a while before starting his own firm. Wright is one of the leading Modernist architects even though he did not build skyscrapers and emphasize the vertical plane. He stressed the horizontal plane and to some extent, he was not entirely a functionalist. There is a highly decorative tone to Wright's work. In New York, there is only one building of his design, the Guggenheim Museum which was built in the early sixties and which reflects some of his main ideas: the emphasis is on integration and more on the horizontal than on the vertical; it stresses rounded rather than sharp corners.

But in order to understand Wright, one has to go to the Midwest where his early work, and particularly his first houses, can be seen. Wright's major involvement was in domestic architecture, perhaps out of necessity since he received very few public commissions. A flamboyant character and a utopian visionary, he had a rather stormy personal life. His first wife was killed under tragic circumstances, by an axe-murderer in Wisconsin, which became a media sensation and cast somehow a lurid light on him. In the 1920's Wright moved to Taos, New Mexico and created there a utopian art colony which is still in existence. His somewhat nonconformist life style may have discouraged patrons. Aside from the Guggenheim Museum, his major surviving public work in the United States consists of an office building for the Johnson Wax company in Wisconsin and a bank in a very small town in Minnesota.

Wright's most important and characteristic work, in domestic architecture, displays substantial Japanese influence. Wright loved the Orient, and designed a hotel in Tokyo which endured for three decades. Wright may also have been influenced by the Mayan architecture of Central America. His domestic buildings are dispersed from Pennsylvania through the Midwest.

Wright can be seen at his peak in the Johnson House in Racine, Wisconsin. It was built for the family that owned Johnson's Wax, but is now used as a conference center. It incorporates all the ideas that are now found in expensive modern domestic architecture. The style Wright developed in this construct later became known first as the California style, and then as the Long Island style. He also designed the interior of the Johnson House of which one innovative feature was the central fireplace and another was the blond furniture.

Many of Wright's ideas, such as the central fireplace, have been so frequently used, particularly during the suburban development in the forties and fifties, that they now appear a trifle redundant. Aside from the Johnson House, among Wright's other well-known domestic work is the Robie House, which is on the campus of what is now the University of Chicago. Built before the university occupied the area, it is now open to the public.

The most admired and imitated of Wright's many private houses is the Kaufmann House in Bear Run, Pennsylvania (1936–7). Here Wright's evocation of Mayan pyramidal temples and his efforts to integrate interior living space with outdoor terraces and a waterfall signals a neo-Romantic attitude that has been emphasized in the sixties and seventies in the works of Philip Johnson and John Burgee and the Postmodernist architects. Like that of all of the great artists, Wright's work transcended categories and embraced the whole architectural history of the century.

Wright's conception of architecture entails the idea of authenticity, and the notion that a house is a machine for living and that therefore it cannot be formidable and overpower its inhabitants; it is a humanistic machine. He stresses the use of local materials, the heavy use of wood, and the integration of the furniture with the design. The Art Nouveau influence on Wright, while not as pronounced as in the case of Mackintosh, was substantial, especially in his interior decoration and furniture.

It is, however, the German Bauhaus school that fully developed the Modernist architecture that swept Europe and particularly the United States after World War II. It created Park Avenue in New York as we know it, as well as Third Avenue. Perhaps because of the over-enthusiasm with which the Bauhaus style was received and applied, it produced a reaction, if not a rebellion, against itself, which was inaugurated by Philip Johnson in the late sixties and which still continues—although Frank Lloyd Wright's work can be seen as a Modernist alternative to the Bauhaus skyscraper style.

Walter Gropius, Ludwig Mies van der Rohe and Marcel Breuer were the three remarkable originators of functional Modernist skyscraper architecture.

Gropius was the leading architect of the Bauhaus and van der Rohe and Breuer were his disciples. After the Nazis came to power, Gropius bacame an architecture professor at Harvard. Mies van der Rohe and Breuer followed Gropius to the United States, where they had successful careers. In 1954 Mies van der Rohe built the Seagram building on Park Avenue, which served as the prototype of the International Style in New York City. Breuer designed the Whitney Museum. He probably would not have objected to the current project of adding onto the top and sides of the existing building.

Gropius was a visionary and a socialist. He believed in a new architecture for the new day and the new technology that would use concrete, steel, and glass and be simple and direct. He built several factories around Berlin, most of which did not survive the Second World War. There are only about three left. They are small structures that do not look particularly imposing, but they constituted a significant breakthrough. They are memorable for the unprecedented expansion of glass and use of glass bricks, a hallmark of art deco style, and a medium also favored by Frank Lloyd Wright. Gropius' factory buildings around 1910 unequivocally proclaim an architectural revolution.

According to Gropius, a building was simply what it was. A factory building was a factory building, not a Roman temple, and what you saw, therefore, too had to be precisely that: a factory building. The interior of the structure was to be predictable from the outside, and the building materials were to be cheap and accessible. Gropius' favorite project was working class housing. His more comprehensive vision was the new technological city with rapid transportation and great concrete blocks of working class housing. That such housing has become for us a symbol not of liberation but of misery demonstrates the downside of utopian expectations.

Mies van der Rohe, Gropius' prime disciple, aimed at elaborating on his teacher's project, and in 1921, he generated designs toward what he called the "city of the future." The design included vast circular towers forty to fifty stories high which would house the working class of the future, pull them out of the slums, and literally elevate them above the city. Mies van der Rohe's plans presupposed the new metropolitan rapid transit systems. Had he been forced to ride on the IRT of the 1980's, he might have had second thoughts about the city of the future.

Mies van der Rohe received his opportunities not in Germany but in Chicago, where he went in 1937, four years after the Nazi dissolution of the Bauhaus. In Chicago he became a professor at the Illinois Institute of Technology, and eventually an associate of the largest American architectural firm, Skidmore, Owings, & Merrill. On Lakeshore Drive in Chicago, one can see his series of four semi-circular constructs which were erected in the late fifties by the architect and his disciples, not, as it turned out, as working class housing, but as Chicago's most expensive apartment complex. Mies van der Rohe remained loyal to his architectural principles, adopting them, however, to a different social environment—upper middle class America.

Mies van der Rohe's simple skycraper effect, seen in the Seagram Building in New York, furnished the model for innumerable lesser buildings in the fifties and sixties. These buildings can be recognized by their emphasis on the steel

Vincent Van Gogh, *The Night Café*, 1888

Edvard Munch, *The Shriek*, 1896

Gustav Klimt, *Fulfillment I*, Stoclet Frieze, 1905

Paul Gauguin, *The Moon and the Earth*, 1893

Henri Rousseau, *The Dream*, 1910

Ernst Kirchner, *Girl with Japanese Umbrella*, 1909

Paul Cézanne, *Mont Sainte Victoire*, 1902-04

Henri Matisse, *The Moroccans*, 1916

Georges Braque, *The Portuguese*, 1911

Jean Metzinger, *Portrait of Albert Gleizes*, 1912

Pablo Picasso, *Les Demoiselles d'Avignon*, 1907

Marcel Duchamp,
Nude Descending a Staircase, no. 2, 1912

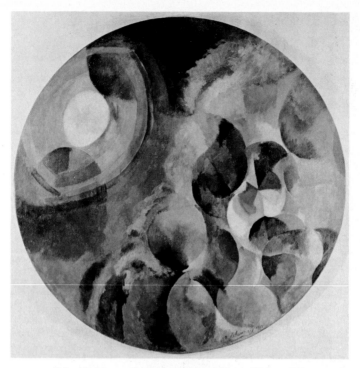

Robert Delaunay, *Simultaneous Contrasts: Sun and Moon*, 1913

Umberto Boccioni, *The City Rises*, 1910

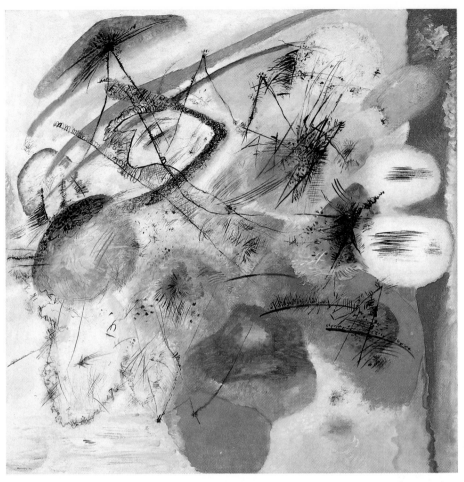

Wassily Kandinsky, *Black Lines*, December 1913

Franz Marc, *Stables*, 1913-14

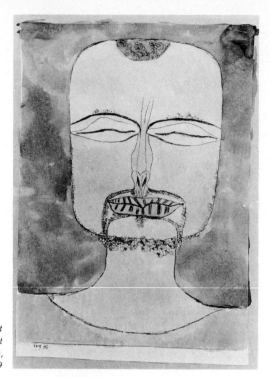

Paul Klee, *Lost in Thought*
Self-Portrait
Portrait of an Expressionist,
1919

Egon Schiele, *Self-Portrait Masturbating*, 1911

Paula Modersohn-Becker, *Self-Portrait with Lemon*, 1

Amedeo Modigliani, *Head*, 1911-13

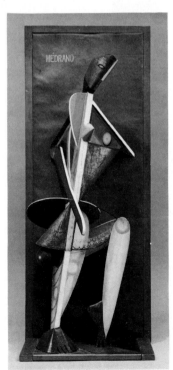

Alexander Archipenko, *Medrano II*, 1915

Wilhelm Lehmbruck, *Standing Youth*, 1913

Piet Mondrian, *Composition*, 1922

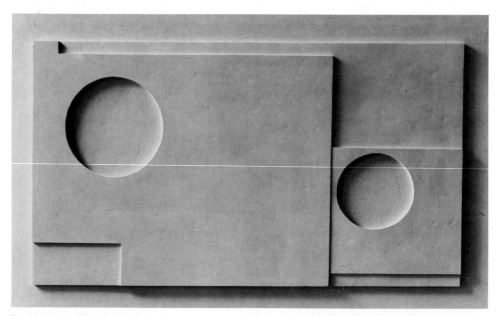

Ben Nicholson, *White Relief*, 1935

Fernand Léger, *The City*, 1919

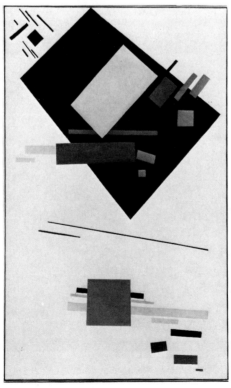

Kasimir Malevich, *Suprematist Composition,
Black Trapezium and Red Square*, 1915

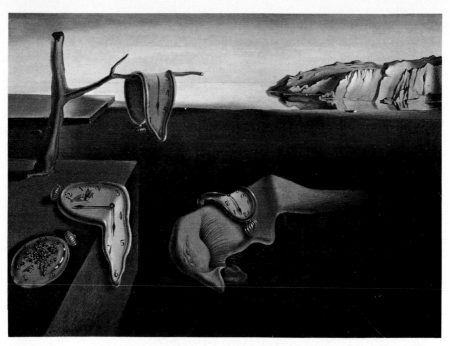

Salvador Dali, *The Persistence of Memory*, 1931

Jean Arp, *Objects Arranged According to the Law of Chance* or *Navels*, 1930

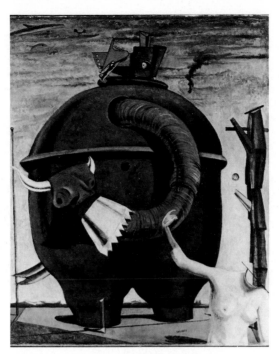

Max Ernst, *Celebes*, 1921

Paul Delvaux, *Phases of the Moon*, 1939

Clockwise From Left:
Constantin Brancusi, *Bird in Space*, 1928?
Alberto Giacometti, *Spoon Woman*, 1926
Hans Bellmer, *La Poupée*, 1937
Oskar Schlemmer, *Abstract Figure*, 1921

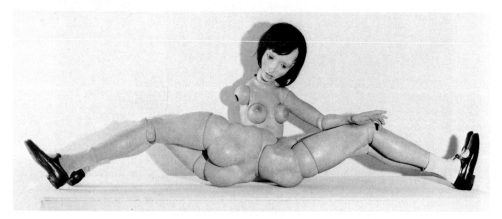

Hector Guimard, Paris Métro, 1900

Louis Sullivan, Carson Pirie Scott Department Store,
Chicago, 1899-1904

Victor Horta, Stairhall of Tassel House,
Brussels, 1892-93

Josef Hoffmann, Palais Stoclet,
Brussels, 1905-11

Erich Mendelsohn, Einstein Tower, Potsdam, 1921

Walter Gropius, *Bauhaus*, Dessau, 1925-26

Charles Rennie Mackintosh,
Glasgow School of Art,
Interior, Library Wing, 1897-1909

Le Corbusier, Villa Savoye, Poissy, 1928-29

Frank Lloyd Wright, Robie House, Chicago, 1909

frame, treating the brick, concrete and glass as mere curtains which take no share in holding up the building. This style also emphasizes the high-speed elevator. And since the use of air conditioning had become widespread in the fifties, these buildings easily accommodated air conditioning ducts. The old horizontal, heavy block buildings were difficult to air condition.

Gropius' and Mies van der Rohe's functional style envision buildings that can harbor elements of modern technology while not occupying much space. It was ideal for New York City and it was also used extensively—although not exclusively—in rebuilding devastated Western Europe after 1945. On the skyline of West German cities the Bauhaus spirit has come home. Even in Paris the beaux arts ambience has been infiltrated by the Bauhaus heritage.

The phenomenal popularity of the Bauhaus international style in the fifties and sixties was the consequence of its compatability with the technological capabilities and commercial interests of the period. The hundreds of corporate executives and commonplace architects who imitated the Seagram building were motivated by other than aesthetic concerns—but this too was part of the functionalist ethos.

Marcel Breuer's prime accomplishment in Germany was not in architecture, although he was a major architect, but in furniture design. He was the developer of the Breuer or Bauhaus chair, which can nowadays be purchased in every department store for $99. Using chrome or steel in its back and the seat made of cane, it was the functional chair, and has, in the meantime, become the universal chair whose imitations are used even in classrooms. Breuer became professor of architecture at Harvard, and supported by Harvard's prestige, he validated Modernist architecture in the United States. He tried, however, in his later work to moderate the technological severity of the Bauhaus style. The Whitney Musuem is Modernist architecture in its humanist form.

Another exponent of the effort to humanize Bauhaus functionalism was the work of the Swiss-French architect Le Corbusier. His imaginative use of geometric forms other than rectangles and his bold use of poured concrete gave a sparkling vitality to functionalist principles. Le Corbusier worked in Brazil in the late thirties, fomenting a renaissance in building and city planning that made the country a vanguard architectural center. The new interior capital of Brasilia was created in the fifties by Le Corbusier's disciples. His most famous work in the large scale urban mode was a provincial capital in Punjab, India, designed around a pool of water, and begun in 1951. His own masterpiece was the Church of Notre Dame du Haut in Ronchamp, France, completed in 1955, a decade before the end of his long life. This church combines stark but sloping and rounded concrete walls with a monumental flying concrete roof. The main structure closely resembles a nun's traditional headdress.

There is no doubt that in the Bauhaus, as there was in Sullivan and Mackintosh, there was a very strong ideological content. Bauhaus architects were idealistic and had social commitments. Yet the Bauhaus architects were commercially oriented, since it is not possible to work as an architect without such orientation. Frank Lloyd Wright, who subscribed least to commercial concerns, suffered for his nonconformist attitude. Regardless of how their achievement may be evaluated retroactively, the Modernist architects conceived of themselves as creating an architecture for a new society and from Berlin to London to New York and Chicago their style now dominates the metropolitan skyline. If the harshness and repetitiveness of the result makes some long for the good old days of the beaux arts style, the fault does not lie with Gropius and his colleagues: their urban vision was developed in the context of the earlier twentieth century, not its closing years. We have seen that Wright, Breuer, and Le Corbusier made strenuous efforts to avoid the redundancy and harshness of the international style.

Technically speaking, the development of film was largely the work of Americans and Frenchmen. Americans and the French developed film as a popular medium. Charlie Chaplin and Mack Sennett first attracted large audiences with one and two reeler slapstick comedies. Nowadays it is debatably held that Chaplin went much further, and drawing upon his roots in British musical hall performance, created in his Little Tramp a universal figure of sentimental pathos and indomitable courage who naively confronts the forces of power and technology. That Chaplin intended this to be the message of his feature length film *Modern Times* (1936) is evident and it can also be interpreted as the theme of *The Gold Rush* (1925).

Whatever Chaplin's place in the development of film, D.W. Griffith is now recognized as the first master of film for his extended narrations and the devising of many of the basic techniques of filmmaking. Griffith's *The Birth of a Nation* (1915) in its original form ran for more than three hours and signaled the emergence of a potential new art form. This lachrymose celebration of the Old South and the Ku Klux Klan, rife with anti-Black racism, reflected Griffith's southern background and his early experience in travelling theatrical companies devoted to popular melodrama. Griffith was a bizarre combination of vanguard technique and obsolete Victorian culture. Therefore he could not intellectually exploit, in spite of several later efforts, his pioneering mastery of technique. It was left to the German and Russian filmmakers to do so.

The expressionist art film was chiefly the achievement of Germans and Russians. It was the Germans in the 1920's who first tried to appropriate into film the techniques of expressionist painting as developed by Kandinsky, Klee and their disciples, as well as to adopt radical ideas from the Modernist novel.

The two films that mark the great achievement of German expressionist film are Fritz Lang's *M* (1931), which is about a child murderer and involves sado-masochist motifs, and Josef Von Sternberg's *Blue Angel* (1930) which is based on Heinrich Mann's powerful Modernist novel *Professor Unrat* and is about the savage humiliation and destruction of a repressed high school teacher (Emil Jannings) by a cruel cabaret girl (Marlene Dietrich). It is one of the great films of all time. A comparison of these films with the art of Klee and Kandinsky, and fantasists like Klimt and Munch immediately demonstrates the influence of Modernist painting on German expressionist film. The introduction of sound around 1930 provided further opportunity for deployment of intellectual themes in film.

The Russian achievement in film was entirely the work of one man, Sergei Eisenstein. A devoted Bolshevik, in the twenties Eisenstein concentrated mostly on the propaganda film, although traces of expressionist technique are already visible in the two remarkable films he produced in this period to commemorate the Revolution, *The Battleship Potemkin* (1925) and *Ten Days That Shook the World* (or *October*) (1928). The latter is a romanticized version of what really went on in the Winter Palace in 1917.

In the 1940's, Eisenstein became more independent and boldly adopted German expressionist techniques in his two-part film *Ivan the Terrible* (1942–6), thereby falling out of favor with the Bolshevik authorities. Eisenstein is known today for his theory of montage, which he derived from close study of Griffith's technique. Eisenstein stresses that it is the material of film itself, that is, how the film is cut, how the scenes are put together, how they fade in and out of each other, that distinguishes film as an art form and renders it important. The notions of textuality, self-referentiality and the ideas of Modernist painting are evident in this theory of film, which continues to be influential.

As did their colleagues in other fields upon the Nazi rise into power, many German film-makers too fled to the United States, and came to Hollywood. That the Hollywood film of the late thirties is the pinnacle of Hollywood creativity has diverse causes, but one of them was the arrival of the German expressionist film-makers. Fritz Lang found a following there, as did the young Austrian Billy Wilder. The Hollywood genre of the late thirties and early forties, the *film noir*, is so named for two reasons. Many of the scenes were shot at night to save on costs. But *film noir* is also a continuation of German expressionist film. Not only are the scenes sometimes very dark, but the topics are often very grim, with a heavy focus on the sado-masochistic. Many of the *films noirs* were directed by Lang and Wilder. Wilder's 1944 film *Double Indemnity* pursues the same theme of sado-masochistic sexuality as *The Blue Angel*. The German emigrants, applying their expressionist ideas, greatly raised the artistic level of the Hollywood film. It has never reached that level again.

Orson Welles' *Citizen Kane* (1941), generally regarded as the greatest American film ever made, is deeply indebted for its narrative method and its brooding ambience to the *film noir* and the German expressionist tradition in film-making. The resurgence of neo-Victorian sensibility during World War II ruptured the expressionist heritage in Hollywood and resulted in a monumental artistic decline in the Hollywood film of the 50's.

*   *   *

Classical and Expressionist Modernism

There is one fundamental polarity that cuts across the literature, music and visual and performing arts of the period of high Modernism which runs from 1905 to 1935. As fundamental to the philosophy of the period as it is to the arts, this polarity resides in what one might call classical and expressionist Modernism. One reason why historians do not find it easy to develop a clear perspective on Modernism has been their failure to discern the presence of two tendencies within the movement. The two sides of the polarity share important assumptions. They are both microcosmic, discontinuous, anti-historicist, and self-referential. They both reject sequential temporality and stress immediacy of perception.

Classical Modernism, which can also be called analytical or rationalist Modernism, is found in T.S. Eliot, Ezra Pound, the New Critics, in the American Southern Renaissance, the analytical philosophy of the period which will be described below, as well as in the science and most of the social science in the period.

This vein of Modernism holds emotions in check, represses them, and concentrates on the analysis of small phenomena brought under the scrutiny of the intellect. It acknowledges feeling but holds it in reserve. The emphasis is placed upon the critical and analytic mind. The term "classical" is T.S. Eliot's own for his method and precepts. Eliot saw this type of Modernism as recovering the rationalism of classical thought. Whether classical thought was really as rationalist as Eliot would have it, or what was the degree of selectiveness in his cultural appropriation is largely beside the point.

Classical Modernism envisaged a thick culture that was imparted through traditional institutions and which preserved social cohesion. You must never, warned Eliot, "neglect your shrines and churches"—not so much for their religion as for their ethical teaching and indoctrination of social solidarity. It is crucial to preserve "a certain uniformity of culture, expressed in education." There should be "a positive distinction . . . between the educated and the uneducated." Rationalist elitism was the hallmark of civilization and the preserver of social stability.

The term expressionist Modernism was also used at the time. The German painters of the Blue Rider school, like Kandinsky and Klee, thought of themselves as expressionists. Heinrich Mann too designated his novels as expressionist. Hence, like "classical," "expressionist" too is a contemporary term. The emphasis in expressionist Modernism is on short bursts of intensive energy and feeling. The mind is not so much a detached observer and analyst of experience; rather it is imbued in it. The individual integrates himself with the brief intense burst of energy. Truth and art—and perception of reality—lie in particles of energy that are permanently active in the world. The individual's salvation lies in integrating himself with this intermittently disseminated universal force. Blood and sex are the most visible forms of this universal energy.

The expressionist ethos can also be called "vitalism" after the concept of *élan vital*, vital force, propounded by the French cultural pundit Henri Bergson around the time of the First World War. In his day Bergson was regarded as an important philosopher. He was actually a cultural commentator who was trying to articulate what modern science meant to people of deep feeling. Very popular in his day, Bergson has become mostly unreadable. Yet some of the phrases he throws at the reader were eloquent in articulating expressionist concerns: "the thing we know most about in the world is ourself," "the creation of the self by the self", the "*élan vital*," all of which convey the vitalism, the energetic quality, and the sharply focused sentiment that marks the work of the German expressionists and is found also in the novels of D.H. Lawrence.

Lawrence is an interesting case in illustrating the problems that face historians when the duality in Modernism is not recognized. Many English department professors today deny that Lawrence was a Modernist on the basis of a comparison of his work with Eliot's. Lawrence was an expressionist, not a classical, Modernist. He focuses on a vital force in the blood, surges of deep, unrestrained emotion, and specially on sexual drives. He perceives short, intense bursts of sexual energy as reflecting or perhaps comprising the structural, systematic forces that drive personal behavior. And he exults in revealing this blood-force and sexual energy rather than conducting cerebral, clinical analyses of sexuality. Lawrence's is a world of powerful homoerotic masculinity and also decisive earth mother femininity that in the end androgynously blends together in the common, atavistic sexual drive of the human race. This is the theme of *Women in Love* (1920).

No wonder that even in the heyday of Modernism, Lawrence's reputation was mixed, that he had a hard time finding publishers, and that he had to wait until the 1960's to gain an unchallenged reputation as one of the great novelists. The classical Modernists thought him extreme, uncouth, unbalanced, not a little mad.

And certainly Lawrence's hard life and family pressures consumed him at the same time as they gave him the distinctive voice that he assumed. Lawrence's father was an alcoholic miner, his mother a lower middle class woman of genteel aspirations. His German wife—a distant cousin of the flying Red Baron Richthofen and with the same noble surname—would never let Lawrence forget she had abandoned a middle class professor husband and two children for an unstable bohemian life with him; also she wouldn't do the dishes. Lawrence's vision of primordial reintegration of the folk blood through expression of sexual energy can be seen as his way of trying to transcend these domestic agonies. But he was also a reflective, learned, and very decent man.

As we have already seen, Frank Leavis chose to give legitimacy to Lawrence's work as a Modernist, to move him from the margin to the cultural center. Leavis' criterion for including a novelist in the Great Tradition of the English novel was a writer's capability of communicating deep feeling, particularly a grave sensibility, a common moral seriousness, that Leavis thought always lurked just beneath the surface of working-class and middle class life. On this criterion, Lawrence was not only included in the Great Tradition; he marked its contemporary culmination.

Leavis spawned a large number of disciples who mostly became literature teachers in secondary schools. Sucking on their pipes, dressed in threadbare tweeds and baggy flannels, firmly reading from their paperback copies of the novels of the Great Tradition, never forgetting that Lawrence too had begun as a school teacher, the Leavisites were a small private army of expressionist advocates who had a major impact on English culture, not only through their role in education, but also through the BBC, which they began to infiltrate in the 30's.

Leavis and his disciples believed in and advocated a primordial life force, a pure and authentic tradition of deep-rooted national culture, which had not changed in its essentials over time. Literature of the Great Tradition prepared people and especially the young, to discover in their own hearts and minds this primordial life force and thereby to insulate themselves against the corrupting influence of a decadent, dehumanizing, technocratic environment.

The Surrealists and Dadaists of Paris in the 1920's also belong to the expressionist school of Modernism. The Dadaists claimed that the hegemonic culture and power system of the nineteenth century had been completely discredited. The Dadaists—like the hippies of the 60's—fomented happenings to demonstrate the absurdity of the old culture and shock observers into a recognition of the new. The Dadaists contended that the only starting-point for a new culture was the aesthetic vitalism of individual artists.

The similar Surrealist message was that the new technology had made all cultural forms obsolete. It was necessary to transcend the past with a new aesthetic vision that reflected the high tech present but which allowed for the singularly authentic expression of personal feelings and private visions. Of course there was an element of Nietzschean philosophy in Dadaism and Surrealism, but they would have probably said the same things without Nietzsche.

In the Irish Renaissance and particularly in the poetry and provocative essays of William Butler Yeats there was another outlet for expressionist vitalism. This was tied to a murky but deep conviction that there was something especially valuable in the mentality of traditional Irish peasant culture. Yeats' professed devotion to Irish folk culture appears somewhat ironic in view of the fact that he did not know the Celtic language beyond a few convenient words and until a patron gave him a country home in Eire, he lived most of the time as an expatriate in London.

Yeats is another figure that is not easily placed alongside Eliot, Pound and Rilke, because, in his poetry he is often more emotional than they, and because, especially in his essays, he stresses feeling and propounds what we have called vitalism. Yeats too expatiates on the folk blood, the primordial life force, that Lawrence and Leavis talk about, and in a modified way also Paul Klee. "Justify all those renowned generations,/ Justify all that have sunk in their blood . . . In every generation/ Must Irishmen's blood be shed." Yeats' writings sound this threnody again and again. Klee ruminated on the "passionate movement toward transfiguration," as did the composer Richard Strauss.

Finally there was the cultural pundit who was prominent in Vienna from 1910 into the twenties, Karl Kraus, a satirist and critic who was very influential among the most prominent German figures of the time. Kraus' fundamental message is simply that the most important thing is art. Everything else is inauthentic, superficial, bourgeois. The only permanent value and beauty lie in art. This theme and other expressionist attitudes, as we shall see, affected leading German philosophers of the period 1910–30.

Strongly influenced by Kraus was the novelist—and later political philosopher—Elias Canetti. His *Auto-da-Fe* (1935) is a prime example of the expressionist novel, dealing with a case of paranoid obsession. Later Canetti summed up the thought and method of expressionist fiction: "One day, the thought came to me that the world should not be depicted ... from one writer's standpoint, as it were; the world had *crumbled* and only if one had the courage to show it in its crumbled state could one possibly offer an authentic conception of it."

In both classical Modernism and expressionist Modernism there was a strong sense of individualism and a commitment to cultural solidarity. Both forms respected the capability of the individual mind to achieve truth telling. For the classicals, this was gained by a controlled rationality acting upon sensibility; for the expressionists, by some immediate charismatic vision. Adoration of the nuclear family, the stable force and dominant center in Victorian ethics, was abandoned both by the classical and expressionist Modernists.

The possibility that powerful individualism could lead to social disintegration and cultural and moral anarchy the classicals and the expressionists were both anxious to avoid. For Eliot and the classicals rationalized sensibility was to be placed in the service of traditional national institutions—the church, the university, and a social and cultural elite. The expressionists glimpsed an overpowering rebirth of national and group solidarity through a social experience characterized by the integrating impact of primordial vitality that somehow imploded spontaneously within a common consciousness.

Historians have generally seen this expressionist attitude as a seedbed for Fascism. But intrinsically it had no specific location on the political spectrum. If one can crudely specify the politics of the expressionists in the 1920's, many more were on the left than on the right. It was actually the rationalist classicists that were more inclined to the political right. Modernism eventually had political consequences; but it was a cultural revolution and an aesthetic and intellectual movement, not a political one.

*   *   *

Philosophy and Science

At the beginning of this century, philosophy underwent a fundamental transformation, both in the United States and in Europe, which resulted in the repudiation and almost total elimination of idealism, the dominant nineteenth-century philosophical school. Three new schools of philosophy emerged: in Germany, the phenomenological school whose leading exponent was Martin Heidegger; secondly, Ludwig Wittgenstein's Anglo-Austrian school which was originally called logical positivism and which is now, since the forties, referred to as the analytic school; and thirdly, the native American school of pragmatism whose most important names were William James and John Dewey.

The Heideggerian school is still dominant in departments of philosophy in Germany, and quite influential in France. Phenomenology has shown some influence on departments in the United States, but eighty percent of American philosophy professors, at least in the most prestigious departments, belong to the analytic school. In England, the analytic school is universal. There is no English professor of philosophy who is not a logical positivist. The leading figure of the analytic school, Ludwig Wittgenstein, was an Anglo-Austrian visionary and a Cambridge professor. The third school, pragmatism, is American. Of its two greatest figures, William James was a professor at Harvard and the brother of the novelist Henry James. The other, John Dewey, was both a professor at Columbia University's Teachers' College and a cultural guru in the 1930's with a large following.

Nineteenth-century idealist philosophy had two main principles. One was that mind created and constituted everything. Nothing, no facet of reality, existed in the world that did not stem from the mind. The more the empirical was refined, the greater the departure from the material and the experiential, the more the purely intellectual was approached, the closer one came to truth, morality, existence, joy, or to what was referred to as the absolute. This was the Hegelian doctrine.

The second principle of idealism was that mind was active. It was a vital force that actually imposed itself on the world. It shaped the world. In the 1890's a new form of idealism, the neo-Kantian school, emerged in German universities, which tried to modify idealism as the nineteenth century had conceived of it by allowing room for the empirical. Neo-Kantians accepted that ideas had shaping power; yet they revised this premise to mean that the intellect and typologies (ideal types) controlled and molded the empirical. But to a neo-Kantian this did not mean that the empirical was dispensible to philosophy.

Neo-Kantianism realized that one could not study the fields of sociology and anthropology, which were becoming established in the universities at the time, by means of pure idealism, since these social sciences had to work with data. Removing the empirical was tantamount to removing data, and what would then remain was pure ideology not social science. Neo-Kantians therefore generated room for data-based but idea-conditioned types. The greatest German sociologist Max Weber adhered to his neo-Kantian doctrine. The neo-Kantians retained the view, however, that the mind was a creative force. They preserved the conception of mind as capable of imposing itself on the world.

The new schools of philosophy after 1900 rebelled against this concept of mind. In the case of the analytic school, we find a total annihilation of every idealist precept. In the cases of phenomenology and pragmatism, the effort at elimination was not as blatant or comprehensive, but substantial nevertheless. They all rejected idealism and attempted to create new philosophies that generally cohered with Modernist culture. In consequence philosophy as taught in universities today is as far removed from Victorian ways of thinking as are literature and science courses. It would have dismayed the Victorians to discover that in the 1980's the only visible disciples of Hegel are to be found among Marxists.

Just as Modernist poetry found its forerunner in the 1880's in Stéphane Mallarmé, and the novel in Henry James in the same decade, so twentieth–century philosophy had a precursor in the American Charles Sanders Peirce in the eighties. Unfortunately for him, Peirce never quite found an outlet for his ideas which in many ways foreshadowed the new philosophy that was going to take shape after 1900. Many of Peirce's writings were unpublished in his life-time, and in fact, still remain unpublished. Some of Peirce's important papers that did find their way into print, found room only in *Popular Science Magazine* in a vulgarized form to suit the general audience. Nor did Peirce ever receive a university professorship. However, he had considerable influence on the American pragmatists William James and John Dewey. To some extent, he also anticipated the European philosophers of the early twentieth century, but the latter were not aware of the existence of this precursor. Peirce also foreshadowed the semiotic concerns of thinkers in the 1960's and 70's.

Martin Heidegger is currently regarded as one of the two most influential philosophers of the twentieth century, and even though this is much more the case in Europe than in the United States, here too Heidegger is finding an increasing following. He obtained a professorship in the early 1920's and continued as a prolific writer until shortly before his death in 1979. His complete works, including previously unpublished material, are currently in preparation, and are allegedly going to comprise fifty-seven volumes.

Always difficult to read and virtually untranslatable into English, personally as well Heidegger was not altogether a pleasant man. It would not be an overstatement to say that in the 1930's he was a prominent Nazi. He was the number one academic figure among the highest Nazi circles. Some of the speeches he gave during the thirties make for cruel reading today. Unsurpris-ingly, after the war he developed elaborate reinterpretations of what he had "actually" tried to say in those speeches. Regardless of what one might think of these reinterpretations, there is no question that Heidegger had been a vehement supporter of the Nazi regime.

Heidegger had a strong following in Germany starting in the 1920's, and had important influences on an entire generation of German thinkers, many of whom became émigrés and a considerable number of whom were Jewish. Among them were his student and sometime mistress Hannah Arendt, the famous political theorist, Gershom Scholem, who later became the Israeli authority on Jewish mysticism, and the guru of the new left of the late 1960's, Herbert Marcuse. All these diverse people had been students of Heidegger.

Heidegger is partly indebted for his ideas to his teacher Edmund Husserl, who claimed that the only source of knowledge is the intuitive action of individual consciousness. But putting Heidegger's debts aside, and concentrat-ing on his phenomenological system in itself, it can be claimed that Heidegger has three propositions. The first concerns the principle of authenticity, which is a principle that became widely used and strongly influenced French existentialism in the forties and fifties, and which has even entered into our own common language.

A person who has authenticity is one who is self-conscious of his wholeness and integrity as human being. Against the principle of authenticity are set alienation, artificiality and decadence. There is no doubt that Heidegger had very specific images in mind when he talked of authenticity. His concept of the authentic focuses on the rural world. He thought that there was nothing more authentic than a German peasant, that fresh air and individual labor, physical as well as mental, contributed to authenticity. He also thought of the life in art, of the appreciation and particularly the creation of art, when he thought of authenticity. On the other side, comprising the inauthentic and artificial, were large cities, industrialization, a tendency towards depressing the individual into large groups so as to destroy individuality, and a philistinism which lacked in appreciation for the arts. If this sounds remarkably like the American counter-culture of Woodstock of the late sixties, or of the Vermont woods in the 1980's, it is owing to a direct connection rather than to a fortuitous parallel. Heidegger's message of authenticity was preached by his disciples in this country, particularly by Herbert Marcuse, and was incorporated into the counter-culture movement of the 1960's.

Behind this principle of authenticity is the metaphysical doctrine—later seized upon by the French existentialists—that being is not fixed, but rather that it is temporal and has to be seen in relation to its corollary —death. Being is "becoming"; it is existential activity. It is participation, a commitment. Again there is a long heritage descending from Heidegger's doctrine, including the interest in death studies in colleges today, predicated on the principle that death is as much part of our existence as Being or life.

The second principle of Heideggerian thought is consciousness, that is, the idea that the only thing we really know is our own mind. This notion, Heidegger has adopted from his teacher Edmund Husserl: there is nothing outside our capacity to think. The only certainty that we humans are capable of obtaining is achieved through our mental processes. This proposition bears certain resemblances to idealism, but also produces a high degree of relativism. Because if the only thing one can know is what one thinks, then the world comes to us only as we think it; the world consists of our perception of it.

His third and most important principle distinguishes Heidegger's thought from nineteenth-century idealism. It is the principle of phenomenology *per se*. There are things outside the mind. Outside the mind, the thing lives and exists for itself. The mind does not completely absorb everything in the world which continues outside the mind. Furthermore, the mind cannot impose itself upon things exterior to itself, since it is not sufficiently domineering, powerful or creative to bring everything completely under its control. Instead, the fundamental act of the mind is to encounter, or to negotiate with, what lies exterior to itself. "That which shows itself should be seen from itself," claims Heidegger, meaning that we have to allow the authenticity of what exists outside the mind, whether it is the physical world or cultural and social processes, recognizing that we cannot dominate them.

What we can do is try to effect an interactive relationship with the world— an arbitrating, negotiating, encountering attitude. Phenomenology, as distinct from idealism, does not prescribe a fully active intellectuality. Its intellectuality is a more passive, less rigorous one, which encounters the world and, accepting it, attempts to live with it. Truth is a disclosure from the other. It is not something we control completely, as in idealism. The idealists had said in the words of Schopenhauer, "the world is my idea." The phenomenologists say "the world is my experience," a much less aggressive, non-hegemonic, accommodating attitude.

Especially the latter principle of phenomenology played important transformative roles in various areas of twentieth-century thought ranging from the social sciences to literary studies. It has also influenced our culture in more pervasive ways that extend as far as affecting our world view in the last fifteen years. Translating Heideggerian principles into Californian language, we might articulate its message as "Go with the flow" and "be laidback." Knowing that one cannot step outside one's consciousness and that mind cannot dominate the world, one is justified in surrendering oneself to a life of aerobic exercises, jogging, communing in the Vermont woods or California mountains, and above all, to the cultivation of the arts.

Heidegger is indeed an up-to-date philosopher, and as time goes on his intense flirtation with the Nazis is forgotten, or found to be relatively inconsequential, and his influence is constantly increasing. It is much greater today than it was, say, in 1945. Analytical philosophers may scoff at Heidegger's alleged murky neo-idealism, but in fact, phenomenology departed measurably from idealism. And we have to take seriously a philosophy that advocates authenticity, commitment, and mellowness.

Whatever Heidegger's motives in his accommodation with the Nazis, this behavior was fully in accordance with his philosophy. Phenomenology teaches accommodation, encountering the thing, whatever it might be. After 1945 Heidegger repudiated his French disciples, Sartre and the existentialists, not only because of their tendency to idealism but even more because in his view they advocated neo-Romantic confrontation and conflict against evil: that was not Heidegger's way. If only Lyndon Johnson had read Heidegger. If only Reagan would. Nixon and Kissinger acted as if they had.

The other influential philosopher of the twentieth century, and one of Modernism's personal gurus or culture-heroes, was Ludwig Wittgenstein. Beyond his influence as philosopher, Wittgenstein also commanded enormous admiration among those who knew him. He has become something of a secular saint, a kind of Socrates of the twentieth century as it were, besides being recognized as an important philosopher. He was Viennese. An enormously wealthy iron and steel baron, his father was the Carnegie of Austria. The family were highly assimilated Jews, but Jews they were, and two of his close relatives, one sister and one aunt, perished in the Nazi death camps. Wittgenstein probably would have too, had he been in Austria at the time of the Nazi take-over.

Like Einstein, Wittgenstein was educated as an engineer, and already as an engineer, he was sufficiently influenced by German physicists to begin to consider complicated mathematical and logical problems. In 1912 he went to Cambridge University's Trinity College to seek out Bertrand Russell. A genuine aristocrat whose grandfather had been a prime minister of England, Russell was even more a member of the social elite than Wittgenstein. Russell himself was at the time an extremely important mathematician and philosopher who, with the assistance of another Englishman, Alfred North Whitehead, was trying to construct a new philosophy along the lines of mathematical analysis. Whitehead later became a professor at Harvard.

Wittgenstein began writing his philosophical treatises. As Russell's version of the story goes, he turned up at Russell's office, or "rooms" as they say in

Cambridge, and told him that he had written something and that he wanted to know whether he was a genius. Russell told him that he would read it that night and that he should come back tomorrow. When Wittgenstein returned the next day, Russell replied to him, "Yes, you are a genius, Wittgenstein."

During the two years before the First World War, Wittgenstein retreated to a hut on the coast of Norway, and began to write his first and most influential philosophical treatise, *Tractatus Logico-Philosophicus*. (*Tractatus* is a Latin word that means "treatise.") He served in the Austrian army in the First World War. In 1918, his father died and left him several million dollars. Wittgenstein turned the entire sum over to a foundation that he established and which was committed to the support of artists and intellectuals. Among the first artists to receive a grant from the Wittgenstein foundation was the Modernist German poet Rainer Maria Rilke.

Wittgenstein's *Tractatus* was published in 1921 and had immediate impact. He himself decided that he had terminated not only his own philosophy but all philosophy. Since there was nothing left to be said after the publication of the *Tractatus*, he became a school teacher in the backwoods of Austria for six years. Finally, he heeded Russell's urging and accepted a position at Cambridge. Eventually, he succeeded Russell as professor of philosophy. By the mid-thirties, Wittgenstein held a monopoly over philosophy in Britain. No one who was not a Wittgenstein disciple could expect an appointment as professor of philosophy in the country. This is still the case.

After the Second World War, his influence made itself strongly felt in the United States, above all in the Ivy League schools. Even today, eighty percent of the philosophers in the top twenty-five universities in the United States are disciples of Wittgenstein. Outside Vienna, his influence on the continent has not been very great. Strangely enough, however, in France, interest in Wittgenstein has been increasing in the recent years. He has been the single most dominant name in philosophy in the English-speaking world. To a degree, this is unprecedented since the ascendency of John Locke and David Hume in the eighteenth century, with whom Wittgenstein shares certain similarities.

The occupation of professor did not make Wittgenstein very happy. He claimed that it was easy to impress students and to be a good teacher, but that he wanted to get people to think rather than win teaching prizes. He probably greeted the Second World War with a certain amount of relief, for he left his professorship during the war and worked first as a farm laborer, greatly damaging his health; later, following a physical breakdown, he worked as an orderly in a hospital. He died in 1951.

Wittgenstein's writings are oracular. They tend to consist of short paragraphs, often extremely opaque, and except for the *Tractatus* and a few short papers, he did not publish a book in his life time. His other four books were published posthumously, edited, in some cases, from fragments of drafts that he had written, in others, from students' notes. As with any other saintly guru, there is considerable dispute in the case of Wittgenstein as to what the master had actually said. Consequently, there has grown a vast body of commentary out of the controversy over the content of his thought. The contemporary

American philosopher Richard Rorty has remarked that Wittgenstein's impact on philosophy was very similar to that of Immanuel Kant in the early nineteenth century. His contemporaries knew that Kant had effected a philosophical revolution, but no one knew for certain what that revolution consisted in. Rorty finds this to be the case with Wittgenstein as well.

Nevertheless, what Wittgenstein has to say is fairly clear, especially in the *Tractatus*. He believes that the world as we see it is corrupt and rundown. We are living in a period of moral and intellectual decline, a period that is hazardous. This he wrote in 1921, and it turned out to be true. The problem, according to Wittgenstein, is reflected in, and to a large degree created by, language, for we do not speak clearly and honestly. Our language consists of endless strings of falsehoods, doubtful propositions, and obscurities. It is the purpose of philosophy to clarify and verify the language of ordinary life, that is, the ordinary language we use to communicate with each other, in order that we may speak truth to each other. "The limits of my language mean the limits of my world."

The project of philosophy is, then, to redeem language from corruption. It is to purify it of slogans, myths, falsehoods and perversions. Philosophy is to undertake the analysis of ordinary language. Every other subject matter with which philosophy has dealt until now, particularly metaphysics, abstract concepts, are unverifiable, meaningless, even dangerous. In a sense, Wittgenstein's message is the same as that of Voltaire who had said, in the eighteenth century, "remove the infamous." Wittgenstein's infamous is the metaphysical idealism of the nineteenth century, which becomes, in Wittgenstein's thought, a mere cover for power, cruelty, and confusion. This particular Wittgensteinean theme has been developed at length by the recent French theorist Michel Foucault.

It was no accident that Wittgenstein was the exact contemporary of Adolf Hitler, another Viennese, who was the great corrupter of the German language.

Since the propositions of ethics cannot be rationally verified, Wittgenstein claims that such propositions are philosophically not possible. Propositions cannot express, said Wittgenstein, anything pertaining to higher concepts. In his most famous and prophetic remark, he says, "Of all that matters in life, we must be silent." We cannot speak philosophically, rationally of momentous matters, including ethics and art. These fields are excluded from the domain of philosophy. Particularly to art Wittgenstein attributes the capacity to express the meaning of life, but art is exterior to philosophy.

Although Wittgenstein's analytic disciples generally regard Heidegger and the phenomenological school with contempt as bearers of continental idealism and mysticism as compared to hard-headed Anglo-American empiricism, there is a way in which Wittgenstein agrees with a key doctrine in Heidegger's philosophy. For Wittgenstein as for Heidegger, there is a great Other that exists outside of ourselves and which we cannot dominate, either metaphysically (Heidegger) or linguistically (Wittgenstein). "What expresses *itself* in language, *we* cannot express by means of language." This statement by

Wittgenstein is quite phenomenological; indeed it is reminiscent of Immanuel Kant.

Furthermore that the world exists is a super-rational fact: Wittgenstein maintains that we have to live with it as effectively as we can. "It is not how things are in the world that is mystical, but that it exists." Perhaps Wittgenstein has been perceived too much in the Vienna-Cambridge axis and not sufficiently within the context of historic German culture. The latter quotation recalls late medieval German mysticism.

The compatibility of extreme empiricism or skepticism with mysticism is a common theme in intellectual history, particularly in the later middle ages, and especially in England and Germany. When the writings of the great early fourteenth century Franciscan nominalists, Duns Scotus and William of Occam began to be studied closely for the first time in the 1930's and 40's, it was discovered that these Oxford Scholastics had in some respects anticipated Wittgenstein. This was no accident: these Franciscan friars were both mystics and empiricists. Was Wittgenstein conscious of this affinity? His biographers fail to deal with this issue.

Wittgenstein considered that philosophy deals not with the momentous, but with the marginalia of human communication, with the "limits of the world." But in our current corrupt situation, in a world in which vicious dictators and public monsters reign, purifying our language is critically important if we are to survive. With this in mind, Wittgenstein began to develop a new logic which deals with the analysis of ordinary language. In his later work, Wittgenstein argued that pragmatically the meaning of words is settled through usage which reflects a "form of life." But this settlement is difficult and problematic because we "stretch" langue beyond its limits. It is linguistic analysis which again can reduce this confusion and corruption and allow for authentic communication.

Wittgenstein did not complete this work of creating a new logic. He began it, and the project of completing it was continued by his most distinguished colleagues and disciples, one of whom was Rudolph Carnap who left Vienna to become a professor at the University of Chicago. Others were the English-men John Austin and A.J. Ayer and yet another the Viennese émigré to Britain, Karl Popper. In the younger generation of Wittgenstein's followers is the American Thomas Nagel, who teaches at New York University and continues to work on the project Wittgenstein left unfinished.

John Austin dominated the Wittgensteinian school of analytic philosophy at Oxford until his death in 1960. No statement—not even one expressed in mathematical language—is absolutely verifiable, Austin believed, because there is none that will not change its meaning in altered circumstances. Everything depends on context. In a discussion of good or evil it is our varied usage of these concepts that is to be scrutinized—not any inherent meaning of the words. Austin's philosophy bears some resemblance to American pragmatism.

Wittgenstein's school was originally called "logical positivism" in the twenties and thirties. Since the fifties, it has been known as "analytic philosophy," or simply as "philosophical analysis," or to use an even simpler term, "analysis." Wittgenstein's disciples have monopolized the term "analysis" for their own philosophical method.

Analytic philosophy is more temperament or a cast of mind than a precise set of doctrines—except that idealism is all wrong. The analytic philosopher examines a statement and asks: what are you really saying, if anything? What are the significations, if any of this sentence? Analytic philosophy excludes metaphysics, ignores history and concentrates closely upon what can and cannot be said in an arguably meaningful manner. This analytic approach resembles a lawyer's close examination of a case and one major impact of Wittgenstein, Austin and their group has been in jurisprudence and legal philosophy, particularly in the writings of H.L.A. Hart and Ronald Dworkin.

Of the two strands in Modernism, the classical and the expressionist, Wittgenstein belongs to the classical school, which is one reason for the welcome he received in England. Under Eliot and his friends and disciples, this particular strand of Modernism was achieving primacy in English culture, and Wittgenstein seemed to be a philosopher who cohered with the classical rationalism that the Eliot school propounded. A concern of Joyce, Pound and other Modernist writers was with an enclosed language world and Wittgenstein appeared to adhere remarkably well to this pursuit and indeed to justify it philosophically. Heidegger, on the other hand, is very much tied to the more intuitive, expressionist mode. In fact, he was inspired to a degree by German expressionist artists and writers, whom he, in turn, influenced as well.

The American school of pragmatism was famous in the twenties and thirties. In the American universities, it was at least as important as phenomenology and logical positivism. One of the two leading pragmatist philosophers, John Dewey, was extremely visible in the 1930's. He was, in a way, the court philosopher of The New Deal. Writing articles for newspapers, making speeches on the radio, delivering commencement addresses throughout the country, he was difficult to avoid. After the Second World War, pragmatism entered a deep decline, and was crushed, above all, by the tide of Wittgensteinean analysis. In the last decade, pragmatism has begun to make a comeback. Richard Rorty, who is one of the most important American philosophers today, has taken lead in trying to revalidate pragmatism.

William James, the brother of Henry James, came of a fiercely intellectual Boston family which was also not a little eccentric. The father was the disciple of a Scandinavian mystic who had formed a religious-philosophical clique in this country. James held the first chair of psychology at Harvard, and wrote the first important textbook in that field. In addition, he held a chair of philosophy and was also interested in religion. To the public at large, he was better known for a book he wrote by the title of *Varieties of Religious Experience*, which celebrates, so to speak, precisely the compelling variousness and intensity of this experience, than he was for his philosophical and psychological work.

William James has two main premises, the first of which is the presence of a strongly voluntarist element in thought. Thought does not come externally, but is worked out by the person in response to his environment in a way that is advantageous to him. We believe, in other words, what we want to believe, or what we think is to our advantage. What we think is what we feel we need to think. James postulates the existence of a will to believe, and given that the will is to think the advantageous, religion becomes a natural and even necessary component of human thought. He claims that issues of theology cannot be proved, for persons subscribe to religions for the comfort and integration they afford them. And that is sufficient in itself. The useful is the true.

The second premise, this time a psychological one, that James propounded was that consciousness is not separate from the physical. Consciousness can, at times, affect or mold the physical, and yet the process is reversible. The physical can affect consciousness. The physical and consciousness are distinct from each other. However, acting, doing something, we are capable of affecting our mental state. If we are depressed, for example, we can overcome this state by sheer activity. By some physical act of involvement, courage or commitment, we can affect the mind. The mind is molded by the physical action and by the material environment, just as the mind at times affects physical action. A behavioral pattern can be established which will affect consciousness. Out of this Jamesean principle arose the American behaviorist school of psychology.

John Dewey was a Midwesterner and a progressive liberal who first taught at the University of Chicago, and after establishing himself as a dominant thinker, became resident philosopher at the Teachers' College at Columbia University. In an era when Americans and particularly New Yorkers still had faith in their public schools, the College gained overwhelming prestige, influence and visibility in the twenties and thirties. It was a shaping force in American education for several decades.

Dewey's fundamental claim is that all thought is instrumental. A proposition is true if it can be used to attain a given end. Truth is not correspondence between ourselves and the external world, nor is it harmony or consistency. It is an instrument in the shape of a proposition that serves to attain an end. This, in a nutshell, is the philosophy of pragmatism. Of course, William James, and Charles Sanders Peirce before him, made the same claim. What is distinctive about Dewey, however, is his concentration on social instrumentalism as well as individual instrumentalism. There are, he claims, clusters of ideas in society which are true because they achieve social reform and progress, the general happiness sought by all, and the desired degree of common welfare. The criterion of truth as something effective in achieving a desired end renders arguments from history as well as formal logic obsolete.

Dewey's extreme epistemological relativism fitted in very well with the new meliorism and progressivism of The New Deal. It collaborated with Keynesian economics, and cohered with the new winds that were blowing in the American law schools in the thirties. Dewey stood in the long American tradition of social improvement. He was a public-spirited figure who would sign any liberal petition, and who played an early role in the civil rights movement. He was concerned to create schools that would serve as mini-workshops for democracy and he was immensely popular in his day. He profoundly influenced his generation.

Dewey found his disciples in the 1940's and 50's not among philosophers but among a prominent group of American social scientists led by the historian Richard Hofstadter and the political scientists Louis Hartz and Robert Dahl.

They identified American society as fundamentally different from Europe in that it was a pluralistic society made up of immigrants. In this perpetual condition of American exceptionalism, how could a consensus be achieved and maintained to bind together this pluralistic entity in a federal government? There were a variety of answers to this question; for instance, American history was claimed to have begun with the rejection of European feudalism and aristocracy. But the successful perpetuation of the exceptional pluralistic American consensus required that kind of democratic instrumental pragmatism that Dewey represented. His social instrumentalism was the kind of thinking that would maintain the American consensus and a democratic federalism within an intensely pluralistic society. For Hofstadter, Hartz, Dahl, and their many colleagues, Dewey's pragmatism was a central American social doctrine of crucial importance.

In spite of his close connection to the American political tradition of exceptionalism and pluralistic consensus, as a philosopher Dewey now makes for unpalatable reading. Wittgenstein is not readily accessible, even less so is Heidegger, but nevertheless, in these last two, there is a core that is immediately relevant to the reflective reader of today. To a degree, the same can be claimed of William James. Even though his language is pervaded by evening musicales in the Cambridge, Mass., of 1910, nevertheless James' ideas too strike one as relevant. But Dewey is out-of-date. Still, it is not possible to ignore a contemporary philosopher like Rorty who claims that Dewey will come back.

While this tremendous change was occurring in philosophy, an at least equally significant transformation was taking place in science. Particularly the field of physics witnessed the greatest change since the Newtonian revolution of the early eighteenth century—the triumph of a new paradigm to explain physical phenomena.

The twentieth century has seen two scientific revolutions, the first of which generated the new physics of the period starting around 1905 and culminated in the late thirties, or more precisely, in August 1945 in Hiroshima. This period of physics, and its culmination point, have yielded not only new knowledge in physics but have also made it necessary to reconsider the aims and the organization of scientific research, as well as generally transforming our view of the natural world.

The second scientific revolution of the twentieth century, which began in the mid-sixties, was the biological revolution which rendered critically important the field of microbiology. It is an astonishing story that the laboratory that played the most important role in the first scientific revolution also played initially the greatest role in the second one. That was the Cavendish Laboratory at Cambridge University. It was there that Rutherford and his team were able to penetrate the inside of the atom and to discover sub-atomic particles, a field which is today referred to as high-energy physics. It was again in the same place that microbiology registered its great breakthrough to the discovery of the DNA molecule by Watson and Crick in 1953.

The Cavendish Laboratory came into existence in the 1880's in a very peculiar English way. There was at the time no physics laboratory at

Cambridge, and it embarassed the university that an institution as young as Manchester University had what they lacked. Cambridge officials turned to Lord Cavendish, who was a trustee of the university and himself a considerable scientist, and told him of the problem over sherry one day. Lord Cavendish took out his checkbook and wrote a check for the amount necessary to establish the laboratory. The Lord's check was the equivalent of five million dollars today—an instance of typical English amateurism.

As is well known, the great personage of the new physics was Albert Einstein, although it would certainly be correct to place Ernest Rutherford's name next to his. Rutherford was the second director of the Cavendish Laboratory, when the seminal experimental work in atomic physics was accomplished by Rutherford and his students. It was Einstein, however, who became the mythic figure, and certainly he was the prime theoretical leader.

There is enormous controversy about Einstein among his biographers. It is possible to read two biographies of him and wonder whether one is reading about the same man. The views of the man presented by physicists and non-physicists—and among the latter the work of Ronald Clark stands out— vary greatly.

The reason for this is that at a certain point in his life, in 1933 when he was driven from Germany and was justifiably confused and frightened, Einstein recreated his persona. An American department store magnate created the Institute for Advanced Study in Princeton as a place of refuge for Einstein. Although he held the town and its upper middle class ambience secretly in contempt, Einstein in public was friendly and accommodating to his new environment. He became a different public person than in Berlin, transforming himself into an introverted guru, a Mahatma Gandhi, as it were, of science. Clad in tennis shoes and torn sweaters and puffing on his pipe, he became a man of peace and contentment, of gentility and joy. This is the way he wanted to be known to the world in his later years after he came to America, and this is too the way scientists now like to imagine him.

We know, however, that Einstein, from about 1910 to 1933, was a hellraiser, a subscriber to almost every radical cause imaginable, a leftist and probably too something of an anarchist. It is not easy to define what his politics were but they were certainly far to the left of center. A dedicated Zionist, a moral relativist, a pacifist, and an extremely vehement critic of everything in the upper reaches of German society, he terrified the German establishment, and particularly the staid German academic world.

Typical of the reversal Einstein effected in his image is his statement, dating from the thirties, that his theory of physical relativity had no relationship to moral relativism. It was, he claimed, an accident that the same word was used in both cases, causing an unfortunate confusion. Scientist after scientist has echoed this statement by Einstein. Yet in the 1920's, Einstein clearly understood that he was a leader in a comprehensive intellectual revolution. "Today," he wrote in 1928, "faith in unbroken causality is threatened" by the New Physics. Erosion of belief in causality removed the philosophical basis of normative ethics, making an extreme relativism the only possible moral theory. Although Einstein after coming to Princeton was almost universally revered as a saintly scientist, he never again achieved an intellectual breakthrough comparable in importance to the ideas of his earlier radical phase.

Einstein's early life has taken on a mythological quality that is familiar to most people today. The myth is substantially true. His family were middle-class German Jews. His father was an engineer who went into business and lost drastically. After this unsuccessful business attempt, the family moved to Italy where the father hoped to recuperate his fortunes. He abandoned Einstein when the latter was in high school. Unsurprisingly in these circumstances, Einstein finished high school with difficulty. He was not admitted to any university but only to an engineering school in Switzerland, where he received the only formal post-secondary education he was ever going to get. It is interesting that both Wittgenstein and Einstein received their formal education in engineering. These engineering schools were superior institutions, however.

Einstein then worked in the Swiss Patent Office, verifying, as an engineer would, proposals for patents. This job allowed him plenty of time to engage in intellectual and scientific work. There was one other person of some scientific background in the patent office with whom Einstein exchanged ideas. Unquestionably Einstein was an autodidact. At the time of the appearance of his first paper on the theory of relativity in 1905, he himself was ignorant of some other work in the field that had partly anticipated his own, particularly by the Dutch physicist Hendrik Lorentz.

Contrary, however, to the myth, Einstein was instantly recognized. Lorentz immediately acknowledged the importance of the work—which led to the slow, reluctant conversion of other German physicists—as did early on a leading physicist in Britain.

The problem with recognizing Einstein's theory was that it shattered the prevailing thought-world of physics. It made much of the theoretical work in contemporary physics obsolete. Physicists had to begin to think along radically novel lines. The pseudo-autobiographical novel *Night Thoughts of a Physicist*, written by the American physicist Russell McCormmach, describes how a German physicist of the old school around 1918 would have reacted to Einstein and recounts the terrifying professional disaster which Einstein's physics was likely to have meant for him. Einstein did nothing less than put scientists of the old school out of business.

The two important assumptions of Newtonian physics had been that mass and energy were distinct, in fact, that they constituted polarities and, in addition, that the dimensions of space and time were absolutely distinct and separable. Perceiving the significance of the research of James Clark Maxwell on electro-magnetism, Einstein eliminated both assumptions. He propounded the interaction of mass and energy, and showed that they were ultimately interrelated and that each could transform into the other at a certain point in the interactive process. He also argued that space and time were ultimately not separable, that they too were interactive. Beyond space and time lie other dimensions which absorb both of them. This meant that Newtonian assumptions were henceforth fit only for high school physics laboratories and that the science of physics at the theoretical level had to begin anew.

Based on his theories and on the formulae derived from them, Einstein in

1915 predicted how the curvature of space bending starlight would be demonstrated in a total solar eclipse that would occur in the year 1919. Data from the eclipse viewed from the Equator by a team of British scientists provided experimental verification for Einstein's theorizing. Einstein, who had held a research position in Berlin since 1913, became world famous overnight. Meanwhile Ernest (later Lord) Rutherford was effecting a similar upheaval in experimental physics.

Rutherford was a scholarship boy from New Zealand who hardly knew any advanced level science when he arrived at the Cavendish Laboratory in the 1890's. He began his serious experimental work when he was a professor of physics at McGill University in 1902. He continued his work at Manchester, which was then a university as important as Cambridge in intellectual and scientific vigor, especially in the fields of physics and mathematics. Shortly before the War, Rutherford became the director of the Cavendish Laboratory, a position he held until his death in 1937.

Rutherford, who eventually garnered every honor that a scientist can attain to, was the prototype of the high-powered, politically well-connected scientist of the twentieth century. He was an experimentalist who built big laboratories and gathered around him large teams of brilliant young people. He did not much bother about their educational background, but based his recruitment on the interviews he held with candidates, and then put them immediately to work on complex experiments. This sink-or-swim approach is still characteristic of important scientific experimental work and doctoral training laboratories.

Rutherford worked with teams that built much of their own equipment, which is still frequent practice, and often achieved great results using the crudest equipment. The latter method, however, is no longer so fashionable. During a series of Rutherford's experiments it was important to count the number of flashes of light per minute. Rutherford's team had no feasible means of doing this except hiring shop-girls to keep count. Once, so the anecdote has it, one of the girls missed count, which was realized after the results of the experiment had been made public. The papers had to be withdrawn.

The achievement of Rutherford and his group was nothing less than phenomenal. What they sought to discover, in Rutherford's words was "the constitution of the atom . . . the great problem that lies at the base of all physics and chemistry. And if we know the constitution of atoms we ought to be able to predict everything that is happening in the universe." Rutherford's teacher, the first head of the Cavendish Laboratory, J.J. Thomson, had already discovered one subatomic particle, the electron, although it was not until Rutherford's work that the meaning of this discovery was fully perceived. Rutherford and his team discovered other subatomic particles, protons, and neutrons. Rutherford speculated that atomic structure was a kind of solar system with particles moving around an extremely dense nucleus. Rutherford's student, the saintly Dane Niels Bohr, in 1913 drew the map of particle orbits that became the standardized conception of atomic structure.

Rutherford experimentally implemented the artifical release of atomic energy, the transformation of the mass of the nuclear atom into energy. In 1917, working alone in the war-reduced Cavendish Laboratory with only one research assistant, Rutherford split the nitrogen atom, the first instance of controlled nuclear fission. Busy with war work, he did not announce this breakthrough, equivalent in importance to Einstein's, until 1919— that incredible year of Modernist science—nor did he fully realize the implications of what he had achieved until the mid-twenties. Even then, Rutherford for several years insisted that his knowledge could not be used for military purposes. He said that if an atom bomb could actually be made, Cambridge would already have blown up. Finally, in the mid-thirties, shortly before his death, he was convinced by work done in Germany that it was indeed possible to make an atom bomb.

Rutherford is the prototype of the twentieth–century scientist in two further ways—first, in terms of the way in which he used data, namely according to the principle of quantified, aggregate data. The underlying conception of this principle is that the scientist never obtains an absolute, fully consistent set of data. The occurrence of anomalies—"outriders"—must always be acknowledged. This problem of inconsistency was to be circumvented by establishing a common aggregate pattern which reconciled most of the data, and which validated the verifiability of the experiment. The principle of aggregate quantification, which dispenses with the demand for total, complete consistency, has become a fundamental feature not only of natural science, but also of quantified social science in the twentieth century.

The other feature that renders Rutherford the prototype of the twentieth–century scientist was his war work. In 1916, he was asked by the Royal Navy to devise a system by which British ships could locate German submarines, which were sinking vast tonnage of British shipping in the Atlantic. Upon this request, Rutherford and his group developed sonar, very quickly, even before the war was over. Sonar is used today to locate objects both of a military and non-military nature far beneath the surface of the water—it works on the principle of echoing sound waves. However, it took Rutherford the rest of his life to convince the British Navy to use the system he had devised. Fortunately, the mechanism was finally put to use just in time for the Second World War, and it did make an enormous difference. Britain would not have survived the early years of the war without it.

Rutherford was paradigmatic of the great scientific patron of the twentieth century, in his readiness to gather an international group of scientists around him. Hans Geiger, the inventor of the radiation counter that bears his name, was a German physicist who was one of Rutherford's students. One of the physicists who began his work in Rutherford's laboratory, Robert Watson-Watt, was the inventor of radar without which Britain would not have won the air war in 1940 and without which commercial air travel would now be impossible. The prominent Soviet physicist Peter Kapitsa, who did the work on the Russian atom bomb, was also Rutherford's student. Rutherford loved to attend conferences. He read papers at conferences from Australia to Paris, and he also traveled in order to recruit workers for his lab and to meet with other leading researchers. In Rutherford's conception, Big Science was an international community.

Another team of experimental scientists, this time a husband and wife, were

Pierre and Marie Curie. Madame Curie was a Pole who came to Paris to get a doctorate in physics where she married another physicist, Pierre. The couple began their experimental work in the garage of their house under extremely difficult and hazardous conditions. They worked with radiation, discovered radium and conducted many of the important early studies of uranium radiation and x-rays. Of course, in the end, this work killed Madame Curie, a fate that is by no means atypical for the early twentieth–century physicist. They took risks with radiation that would now be considered suicidal. Many leading experimental physicists of this century have died of radiation, including several of those who worked on the atom bomb during the Second World War. Madame Curie was one of the first to suffer.

Partly because she was a woman, and in part because she was a Pole, Madame Curie received very little recognition and support in France until she won the Nobel Prize. But even so, her conditions for work improved but little. The recent British Television series about her life was accurate in showing her life-long struggles. It is hard to believe that people could do major scientific work, indeed win the Nobel Prize for that work, and still have to continue working in a shack. The physicists of the early twentieth century were heroic people and thought of themselves in those terms too.

In the first three decades of the twentieth century, physics was the queen of the sciences in the German universities. In addition to Einstein there were several German physicists of great importance for theoretical work. Max Planck followed through suggestions from Einstein himself, as well as from Niels Bohr, in undertaking speculations which led to the quantum theory of the mid-twenties. In the refinement of the quantum theory, important contributions were made by the aristocratic French scientist Prince Louis Victor de Broglie and the German mathemathical physicist Erwin Schrödinger.

Quantum mechanics, the basic theory of Modernist physics, conceives that all energy (not just light) moves not continuously but in short bursts or waves called quanta. Schrödinger—who was to be the Gentile German most vociferous in opposing Hitler and who went into early exile—stated the essentials of the quantum theory in its definitive form in 1925. Particles are only "a group of waves of relatively small dimension in every direction." The quantum theory was developed further by Paul Dirac in the late twenties. In spite of his name, Dirac was British—his father was a Swiss immigrant. Dirac proposed the theory demonstrating the spin motion of an electron in an electro–magnetic field, which constituted the inaugural basis of field theory.

Quantum field theory laid the foundation for theoretical physics of the following three decades. The idea of an interactive region in which quantitative relations can be determined at any given point was to be central not only to physics but to social science in the era of late Modernism. Field theory was as important as relativity to the Modernist vision of the world. Steven Weinberg, 1979 Nobel physics laureate, summed up the importance of the quantum field theory for his generation of quantum theoretical physicists: "Particles are bundles of energy and momentum ... The particle is nothing else but a representation of its symmetry group [field]."

Thus fully developed quantum field theory postulated two principles. The first was a principle of discontinuity, of brief, intense bursts of energy. The second was a principle of an interactive, definable field that could be quantitatively analyzed. Both discontinuity and field theory were conceptions central to Modernist culture as a whole. They are represented in literature and art, and they were to play as great a role in social science as in physics. Strangely enough, once the quantum theory was developed, Einstein had second thoughts about it and, to the end of his life, he never fully subscribed to it.

Even more celebrated than Schrödinger among German physicists was Werner Heisenberg, a tempestuous, vain, extremely ambitious person who was a full professor at the age of twenty-four. Heisenberg carried his extensive knowledge of the humanities into his scientific work: "Through the surface of atomic phenomena, I was looking at a strangely beautiful interior." He also carried into his science his intense nationalism. He was a willing collaborator with the Nazis, and although originally a theoretician rather than an experimental physicist, he was in the early 40's a member of the team of German physicists who worked on that atom bomb which, fortunately for mankind, was never constructed for reasons that are still under dispute. One side of the contention claims that the Germans "faked it," and only pretended to build an atom bomb for Hitler, that is, they sabotaged Hitler (obviously this is what Heisenberg and his collegues claimed after 1945). Or, a second explanation holds, the scientists working on the bomb simply had bad luck and took the wrong course in constructing it. A third view has it that the British and Americans bombed, to the point of total devastation, the place in Norway from which the Germans were obtaining critical material for their atomic experiments.

Heisenberg's major contribution to theoretical physics was in completing the relativist trend inaugurated by Einstein and in expounding a phenomenological interpretation of physics, compatible with Heidegger's philosophy. "Time and space," Heisenberg wrote in 1926, "are really only statistical concepts, something like, for instance, temperature, pressure and so on in a gas." No statement could more clearly articulate the Modernist character of the new physics. Just as literature had become sensibility and painting lines and materials, the physical world had become statistical categories.

Going on from this phenomenological assumption, Heisenberg developed his famous uncertainty or indeterminacy principle that won him the Nobel Prize in 1932. Heisenberg's argument is that the scientist cannot obtain an entirely objective view of the world, primarily because the researcher cannot remove himself absolutely from the scientific analysis or experiment. All scientific work is phenomenological, that is, it is to some degree conditioned by consciousness. The intrusion of the observer and his instruments prevents the measurement at the same time of both the position and momentum of an electron with complete accuracy. A minute but irreducible degree of uncertainty or indeterminacy intrudes.

The promulgation of Heisenberg's uncertainty principle in 1927 was hailed in the words of another leading German physicist, as "the dawn of a new era." In scientific practice, it did not have quite such a shattering impact. Experimental physicists generally ignored and still ignore the minute degree of indeterminacy in their work. Heisenberg's principle was, however, a theoretical contribution second only to Einstein's theory of relativity, of which it was an extension.

Indeterminacy and relativity were carried one step further in the thirties and forties by Bohr in his principle of complementarity. He stated that the subatomic particle can appear as a wave and as a particle in different contexts. Complementarity not only set the scene for the next generation of research in physics after 1945. It superseded Einstein's claim that God "does not play dice" with nature. Bohr was conscious of the extreme relativism of his theory if the same principle were applied in the social sciences. He speculated in the forties that societies are not hierarchically related, as the social Darwinists had believed, but were related in a complementary way. We shall see that this kind of social relativism came to prevail in anthropology where it is sometimes called the synchronic (comparative, complementary) approach as compared to the diachronic (historical) dimension of social categorization.

The uncertainty and complementarity principle thus spoke to the essentials of Modernist culture and bridged the scientific world with philosophical, sociological, literary, and artistic trends. The fixed, determinable macrocosmic Newtonian world had been displaced with the coming of relativity, uncertainty, and complementarity. A scientific revolution of unsurpassed magnitude had occurred, and this revolution extending itself beyond physics into biology is still playing itself out and deeply affecting our lives as well as our vision of the universe.

The media was for once quick to recognize the coming of a scientific revolution. "Revolution in Science: New Theory of the Universe. Newtonian Ideas Overthrown," the *London Times* proclaimed in 1919. "Einstein Theory Triumphs" echoed the *New York Times*. It is unfortunate that elementary and secondary education was so slow to respond, especially in the United States and Canada. In the forties, most American and Canadian public schools were still teaching Newtonian physics and setting bored and confused students to memorizing the laws of falling bodies.

The bovine inertia and parsimony of public school systems—new textbooks and informed physics teachers cost money—constituted a severe block for a generation in the dissemination of the new physics at the high school level, the only time most people ever took science courses. At least Hiroshima had the beneficial effect of disturbing the American secondary school universe, the most impenetrable element in the world.

*   *   *

Social and Behavioral Science

Social and behavioral science was the creation of Modernist culture. Except for some work in economics, there was nothing one would care to call or recognize as social science before the twentieth century. History was still entirely humanistic. Along with the novel approaches developed in other fields,

with new courses of research, theories, and the new attitudes of professional-
ism, the social and behavioral sciences habilitated themselves in the universities
for the first time during the Modernist era.

There were three economists of stature before the twentieth century whose
work remain significant. They were all British. Adam Smith was a Scottish
professor of ethics, whose book *The Wealth of Nations*, published in 1776,
created the theory of market economy, and of the self-regulating invisible hand
that is still central to the theory of market economy. This theory was fully
developed by David Ricardo, a London Jewish banker, in the 1820's. He
applied Adam Smith's precepts to labor, employment and wages, expanding
the former's simple market-oriented model to the whole of economic activity.
Ricardo elaborated on issues such as unemployment as well as developing an
elaborate theory of the workings of capital. Marx's knowledge of economics,
for example, came almost entirely from David Ricardo.

The third great pre-twentieth century economist was Alfred Marshall who
was a professor at Cambridge in the 1880's. Marshall's contribution was to
introduce quantitative analysis to economics, to make, in other words,
economic thought more analytic through quantitative projections.

John Maynard Keynes was a disciple of Marshall; he was a product of the
Cambridge school of economics. Keynes' family was one of the great
Cambridge academic families who achieved distinction in various fields, and
still continue to do so. Keynes was a member of the group of Cambridge
intellectuals of the closing years of the twentieth century that in the 1920's
came to be known as the Bloomsbury Group in London. He was a friend of
Virginia Woolf and her sister Vanessa Bell, as well as of Lytton Strachey and
the novelist E.M. Forster.

Like Strachey and Forster, Keynes was gay, or at least bisexual. He did
marry a prominent Russian ballerina and he was closely involved with the arts.
He became the treasurer of his college, King's College, at Cambridge, and
investing in the stock market for the College, greatly increased its income.
Keynes first achieved prominence in 1919 at the Versailles Peace Conference,
when the British and the French imposed on the defeated Germans what
Keynes called the Carthaginian Peace. He published a book on the economic
consequences of the peace in which he claimed that the heavy reparations that
were being imposed on Germany would cause chaos and vast problems in
Central Europe. Of course, he was absolutely right. Because of his public
protest, Keynes was forced to resign from the British Treasury.

For the next two decades, Keynes was an extremely influential professor at
Cambridge. He reentered public service in 1939 and spent most of the war in
Washington as economic liaison between the British and the Americans. After
the war, Keynes played the leading role in the establishment of a new
international fiscal order. He died at the age of 63 in 1946. Keynes'
contribution to economics was on par with Einstein's and Rutherford's to
physics. Keynes was one of the culture heroes of Modernism.

Keynes has three main ideas, two of which are commonly known, for his
principles have become part of our culture and, particularly in the period
between 1934 and 1974, were accepted as orthodoxy in the United States. As

President Richard Nixon said in 1971, "We are all Keynesians now." Americans were nearly all Keynesians from the thirties through the early seventies. Beginning in the late seventies, there has been a fundamental reversal in economic doctrine and public policy which is pointing once again in the direction of David Ricardo.

Keynes' first principle was that the market need not and should not be autonomous, that the state can intervene in order to make adjustments in the market. The argument of Smith, Ricardo and Marshall had been that state intervention would consistently result in disasters and bad choices, and that in case of deflation, inflation or unemployment, the market would have to be allowed, in spite of temporary mass miseration, to stabilize itself. They believed that eventually stability would reinstate itself, and that the state could and should not effect this result externally. Keynes interpreted this view as reflective of nineteenth-century historicism that did not meet modern standards, and claimed that the state could intervene in the economy through an act of will so as to reflate a depressed economy, actively reduce unemployment and restore business confidence and activity.

Keynes designated the variety of ways in which this could be done: adjusting the money supply by printing more money; reducing taxes; making credit more accessible by lowering interest rates, thereby encouraging business resumption and expansion; and above all by directly providing work, undertaking public works programs and so providing employment. The essential solution was to stimulate aggregate demand by encouraging investment and dealing directly with unemployment through public works.

The state, then, according to Keynes, can and should undertake the regulation of the economy to the extent this is necessary to maintain economic equilibrium, and to prevent depression and breakdown. Keynes also pointed out the other end of the spectrum of possibilities, and stated that when the economy overheated, in the case of labor shortage, runaway speculation, over-investment, and particularly in case of high inflation, the state ought to take restraining steps by, for example, increasing the price of credit. He never presented ways of dealing with inflation as clearly as he had set forth a program for dealing with deflation and depression. When he published his great treatise *The General Theory of Employment, Interest and Money* in 1936, the urgent problems were deflation and depression. When the Keynesians were in a position to deal with a booming economy in the sixties and seventies, a large-scale inflation occurred, and they did not have the means to contain it. Whether Keynes himself would have known how to deal with the inflationary crisis is an interesting question.

Keynes' ideas were taken up in American universities very quickly in the early thirties, with Harvard and Columbia universities in the lead. In the brains trust from the universities that F.D. Roosevelt brought to Washington in 1933 to help restore the economy and restabilize the market, were economists strongly committed to the Keynesian view of state intervention. The most prominent member of the Keynesian group at the time was the Harvard economist Seymour Harris, who became the chief Keynesian spokesman in the United States in the thirties and early forties. Another was Rexford G. Tugwell, political scientist from Columbia University and a formidable and capable person. There were also a couple of young economists who went to work in Washington in the late thirties: John Kenneth Galbraith and Paul Samuelson. The former became a Harvard economist, and in the sixties a public official and vehement advocate of the welfare state. The latter became enormously famous as a Harvard economist and public commentator in the 1950's and 60's. Samuelson's textbook of economics, published in the early fifties, became the standard textbook used at American universities and indoctrinated a whole generation of college students in Keynesian economics.

Keynes' second, and enormously influential, proposition was that we are entitled to the good life. We are morally *entitled* to economic security, to health care, and above all, to enjoy the most important thing in the world, the arts. We have a right, in other words, to hear a symphony, to see a ballet, and nowadays, to watch public television. These do not constitute a privilege but a right in modern society. Accordingly, the economy and the government must operate so as to provide these entitlements. During and after the War, this side of Keynesianism became increasingly more prominent. It became a dogma in Western Europe and informed the development of the welfare state in all European countries after the Second World War.

The first country to take up the Keynesian principle of entitlement on a grand scale was Sweden. The other Scandinavian countries followed suit, and have maintained the policy to this day, as did the new Federal German Republic, Britain and France. A prime disciple of Keynes in this context, aside from the large group of continental economists and politicians, was the English economist William Beveridge, who in 1942 published the Beveridge Plan which in turn became the blueprint for the British welfare state that was put into action between 1945 and 1951 under the socialist government.

In the United States, the Keynesian doctrine of entitlement became fully active in the 1960's under the Lyndon Johnson administration, and—although this fact may conflict with leftist mythology—it was continued vehemently under the Nixon and Ford administrations. It was only with the Carter administration that the idea of entitlement began to weaken, and continued to do so until its total reversal under Ronald Reagan. In the sixties and seventies, neo-Ricardian economists at the University of Chicago led by Milton Friedman, attacked the idea of entitlement, and argued that persons were entitled only to what the market afforded them. Efforts to reduce student aid, Medicare, and federal support for the arts in the early 80's is part of the neo-Ricardian, anti-Keynesian movement that achieved power in the Reagan administration.

The final proposition Keynes advocated was that the international economic system could only function effectively as an international fiscal order. The organized integration of the world's currency and fiscal standard was necessary so as to achieve stability. Keynes believed very strongly that the disaster which had led to Nazism was the consequence of the breakdown of fiscal order in the twenties, and that nothing could be more likely to lead to totalitarianism, either of the left or of the right, than fiscal disorder, since this was above all likely to impoverish and demoralize the middle class. At the Bretton Woods

Conference in New Hampshire in 1944, a world fiscal standard was achieved which related to the British pound and the American dollar. Eventually, by the mid-fifties, because of the impoverishment of England, the standard became simply a world-dollar currency, and every country's currency became fixed to the American dollar. In many cases, the relationship was fixed artificially high in order to protect weaker economies. This was the reason why American tourists could go to Europe in the fifties and buy local lire and marks on the black market at favorable rates of exchange.

Keynes had argued that this uniform fiscal standard would stabilize world economy, and again he turned out to be right. The rapid development of European prosperity and the unprecedented industrial growth in Japan, were made possible by the Breton Woods agreement. In 1972, the United States rashly abandoned this agreement, and allowed the dollar to float, with results that we have paid for very dearly. It has resulted in the fact that the Japanese could produce cars much more cheaply than comparable domestic cars, as well as in the fact that Americans could travel abroad very inexpensively while it was expensive to visit the United States from abroad. The overly strong floating American dollar has occasioned various kinds of dislocations of the world fiscal order since the United States abandoned the Keynesian agreement. The negative impact of this reversal on the Third World and Latin American countries has been particularly unfortunate. Once again Keynes has been shown to be an economic prophet.

It is agreed that the term sociology had been in existence before 1900. Looking at histories of sociological doctrine, one comes across nineteenth-century names like August Comte and Herbert Spencer, both of whom produced nothing more than garbled ideologies. The discipline of sociology truly finds its origins at the beginning of the twentieth century with the work of two great social thinkers, the German Max Weber and the French Émile Durkheim. They are the twin founders, the Romulus and Remus, of twentieth-century sociology. They were exact contemporaries and they died, respectively, in 1920 and 1917. Strangely enough, they never met, and it is doubtful whether they ever read each other's works. One reason why they may not have been familiar with one another's work was the deep political tension between Germany and France at the time.

Weber is a phenomenal figure whose influence began to be felt in the early years of the century, but has actually grown since the 1950's. He is only partly a Modernist. He is idealist to a considerable degree; a more precise designation of his thought would be neo-Kantian. Weber's background in nineteenth-century thought also explains the growth of his importance since the fifties, for this was the time when neo-Victorian ideas again began to receive attention. Weber is hard to read at times, and only about a quarter of his writings have been translated into English.

Weber came from a upper middle-class Prussian family of civil servants. He was trained as a historian, and did important work in the economic history of Rome. Then he proceeded to create a new discipline, and occupied the first chair of sociology in Germany. He was universally admired and respected. Shortly before the First World War, he had a nervous breakdown, after which he did not return to teaching, although he continued to write. It is a curious fact that the sister of D.H. Lawrence's aristocratic German wife was the mistress first of Max Weber and then of Weber's brother. Although the sisters occasionally corresponded, the novelist and sociologist had no contact with each other.

Weber makes two fundamental propositions, the first of which is contained in his theory of ideal types. The occurrence of social change is shaped by the interaction of ideal forces which are cultural and moral, and which interact in order to create a new ethos. He applied this idea to the rise of capitalism in his most famous book *The Protestant Ethic and the Spirit of Capitalism*. Here Weber explains the emergence of capitalism by the new ethic propounded by Protestantism. This ethic, Weber calls "the inner-worldly asceticism," that is, the asceticism of working in the world instead of in the monastery, as was allegedly done in the middle ages. Medieval asceticism was replaced by the new one that had been introduced by Protestantism into middle-class life.

This worldly asceticism, as it were, created a work ethic, and fostered capital accumulation. It advocated the postponement of personnal gratification, which translates into economic terms as savings. It was the Protestant ethic, advocating hard work and delayed satisfaction, that created capitalism. Without this work ethic, neither capital accumulation nor the capitalist mentality would have come about. Weber was self-consciously anti-Marxist. It is ideas that shape social forces, he believed, not vice versa, as Marx advocated.

Weber's second theory, which still enjoys influence among political scientists, pertains to government. He identifies three types of government: the traditional or tribal, which is found in early, communal societies; the charismatic government of religious, mystical, dynamic leaders who assume a religious vocation of leadership on the force of their personality, and are taken as gods; and modern bureaucratic government. Weber was the first to identify that the modern tendency in what we now call both the public and the private sector is in the direction of bureaucracy and management. This phenomenon was referred to in the thirties as the "managerial revolution." Modern government and administration, at all levels of public and business life, is marked by the managerial and bureaucratic domination. People working in offices—that is the shape of the future according to Weber, and his prediction has been proved correct. He foresaw the world populated by MBA's.

What he did not foresee, however, was that there could be a union of the tribal, charismatic and bureaucratic forms of government. This very explosive, terrible and catastrophic union, which occurred in Germany in the 1930's, Weber did not anticipate. Essentially, Weber was a neo-Kantian historicist who thought in terms of developmental stages over time. The possibility of a contraction of the past and the present into an explosive future was not discernible to him. Therein, he is very much a nineteenth–century mind who had visions of continuity. He explained how this continuity occurred through the interaction of ideal types. Because what happens in social change is the interaction of ideal types within consciousness, Weber was to a degree a phenomenologist. But he was concerned to plot the movement of value systems over time, making him a historicist.

Consequently, Weber did not get much of a hearing in the Modernist era, that is, in the 1920's and 30's, even though he was respected. It was only with the partial revival of historicism, after the Second World War, that Weber achieved his current prominence in sociology.

The seminal Modernist mind in sociology was the French professor Émile Durkheim, who was the immediate contemporary of Max Weber. Durkheim is the creator of sociology as we know it. Eighty per cent of the topics studied in sociology departments of universities today are in line with Durkheim's constitution of the discipline. Durkheim is a leading Modernist mind not only in terms of his thought, but also in terms of the way he behaved and conducted his professional life.

The characteristics of Durkheim's thought can be gathered around three essential principles. One is quantification. This principle, which, as we have seen, is also present in the work of Rutherford and the experimental physicists, prescribes the gathering of data for eventual quantification in an aggregate manner. It consists of establishing core data which will provide an observable pattern, and entails the rejection of anomalous outriders. In other words, it is not necessary according to this principle to have a hundred per cent correlation in data. It suffices to record data sufficiently correlated in an aggregate manner for a social pattern to emerge.

The principle of quantification was applied in particular to population and health statistics, as well as to the undertaking of public opinion polls, or, for what nowadays is called survey research. Graduate study in sociology today means above all training in conducting survey research for positions in political polling, market research, and advertising firms. Durkheim discerned this opportunity for applied social research.

The second idea Durkheim developed was that small marginal differences were significant. In evaluating the social data, attention is to be paid to the differences at the margins, which constitute the most compelling information to be obtained from a particular body of data. To cite an example from Durkheim's own work: that the annual suicide rate in Sweden is higher by two or three per cent than the one in France constitutes a significant factor. To a nineteenth-century mind, this difference would have had no significance whatsoever. Nineteenth-century sociologists would first have sought a very large body of data, and then looked for substantial difference in order to attribute any value to the data. Durkheim, however, saw the importance of small differences. Having established the validity of the small difference, Durkheim proceeded to try and determine why the difference occurred. Durkheim's identification of the importance of marginal differences and extrapolation of meaning from this number was made possible by the expansion of statistical science in his day.

Durkheim's third idea was the theory of social operation, which has come to be referred to as functionalism. Durkheim believed that a given society is an enclosed field in which the various aspects of this society, such as the political, the economic and the religious, interact with one another, that they are functions of one another. Therefore, one of the prime objects of sociological inquiry is to show the interaction of these enclosed social dimensions. How, in other words, religion is related to the political life in a given society, or what relationship exists between family structure and economic life, were questions the sociologist had to ask. To answer them was the main purpose of sociological thinking.

Furthermore, it was Durkheim's view that societies operate so as to sustain themselves. He believed that societies had strong self-preservative tendencies, and that when an anomaly or novelty appeared in one social domain, then all the other domains would operate upon the newcomer in order to socialize it. Socialization means the integration of the novelty into the customary operative mode of the society in order that that society may continue to function without engaging in disharmony or dislocation. An obvious example of the preservative or socializing quality from the the last twenty years in the United States would be that of the New Left of the late sixties. The tendency, strong and explicit, to socialize the left, not only transformed many leftists into professors, but also enabled an agitator like Jane Fonda to make a fortune from exercise videos, and her husband, Tom Hayden, one-time prominent radical leftist leader and a founder of the Students for a Democratic Society, to become a moderate and liberal California State Senator. This is a simple, obvious but telling example which Durkheim would have found to his taste. He would have pointed out how society had once again found ways to assimilate and socialize the most radical rebels.

A further aspect of Durkheim's theory was the notion of anomie. Durkheim believed that a society can be threatened with disintegration when the value system becomes discrepant with the institutional system. If, that is, the ways in which people behave and organize themselves in a given society develop into directions that are discordant with the value system, we are face to face with an anomic situation which can bring about a breakdown and a revolution. He also, however, finds this anomic rupture to be an extremely rare occurrence, although it can and does happen, owing to conservation and socialization in society.

These conservatizing or socializing societal forces are so powerful that the threat of anomie almost always remains momentary, and is normally overcome by resolution of the conflict. Values bend a little, as do institutions, behavior is adapted, ideas adjusted, and society continues to function as an integrated system. The anomaly or discordancy has been absorbed into the prevailing order, which is slightly modified to achieve the accommodation.

Durkheim's ideas are still central in sociological thinking. Until the late sixties, aside from the doctrines of Max Weber, sociology had no other systematic theory than that provided by Durkheim. Whether sociologists have actually gone much beyond Durkheim today is a moot point.

Durkheim's impact on sociology is ascribed not only to his way of thinking, but as well to his way of behaving. Durkheim was the grand patron, to adopt a French expression, of social science. His role in French social science was identical to that of Rutherford's in British physics. He was named to the Collège de France, which is the French equivalent of the Institute for Advanced Study, and used this position to amass extended patronage by which he could fund his students and the researchers sympathetic to his principles. He pioneered in making sociology an academic discipline, granting doctoral degrees, and finding research grants and employment for his students.

Durkheim also played an important role in the French educational system in the first quarter of this century, a role very similar to the one John Dewey played in the American educational world in the 1930's and 40's. In fact, Durkheim began his teaching career as a professor of education and, even after establishing himself as sociologist, he continued to teach prospective high school teachers. To these, he propounded a doctrine of secular rationalism, in order to divest education of Catholic teaching, to drive religion out of the schools, and to spread a message of patriotism based on sociology. The twentieth-century French lycée, or public high school, was in many ways his monument.

Durkheim was a liberal Parisian Jew (he was, like another paragon of social theory, the anthropologist Claude Levi-Strauss, the son of a rabbi) who was painfully conscious of the bitter conflicts over church-state relations in France during the early years of the century. He was aware that rightist Catholic intellectuals were not only combating efforts to secularize education but were also, in many instances, contributing to growing anti-Semitism in the French press. Durkheim brought all his intellectual and professional resources to the support of the liberal, anti-clerical majority in the Third Republic. For him, sociology represented the party of rationality that ought to prevail over religious traditions and clerical institutions. This attitude gave to his sociology a political relevance that attracted eager and capable young people from the liberal-left spectrum. It also predisposed the discipline of sociology to a left-wing orientation from which it has, with a few distinguished exceptions, never departed and on account of which the scientific credibility of the discipline has been questioned.

In the thirties and forties, Durkheim gained two important disciples in the United States, who shaped American sociology as it is practiced today. One of these was the American Talcott Parsons, who came from a fairly wealthy family and was educated in Europe, became professor of sociology at Harvard in the mid-thirties, and dominated theoretical sociology in this country for the next forty years. Parsons' classic, but largely unreadable book *The Structure of Social Action* (1937) is a lengthy presentation of Durkheim's functionalist theory. It remained unchallenged until the late 1960's.

The other disciple of Durkheim was a prolific scholar and academic entrepreneur who worked in the area of quantitative and survey research: Paul Lazarsfeld, an Austrian émigré who had come to the United States in the mid-thirties and become professor of sociology at Columbia. Lazarsfeld dominated applied research in sociology for the following three decades. He established the Bureau of Applied Social Research at Columbia, which was enormously influential and powerful through the sixties.

Lazarsfeld applied Durkheim's theories of quantitative survey research, organized vast numbers of graduate students and young researchers to undertake pioneering studies in political polling, and also entered into close collaboration with market research and advertising firms. Sociology was supported at Columbia, especially in the forties and fifties, by Lazarsfeld's contacts with polling and market research firms. Preferences shown for political party or one brand over another, the competition between Coca-Cola and Pepsi for example, were domains to which Lazarsfeld applied Durkheim's theory. He demonstrated that four per cent preferred one drink over another, and explained the marginal preference just as Durkheim had explained the rate of suicide in Sweden in relationship to suicide in France by using his method of quantitative analysis. Through Lazarsfeld, Durkheim's sociology had a strong impact on American business.

Contemporaneous with the rise of sociology along the lines of Modernist ideas was that of anthropology. Anthropology may be described as the Modernist behavioral science in its purest form. There had indeed been anthropologists in the nineteenth century. But as we have noted, their work, primarily social Darwinist or what would nowadays be called racist in orientation, is practically unreadable today. Today, nineteenth-century anthropology has only historical value; it is pre-scientific.

The beginning of a transition to Modernist anthropology occurred with the work of Sir James Frazer, a British ethnographer (student of early societies) who published in 1890 the first edition of his famous book *The Golden Bough*, which for many decades was esteemed as having primary importance in the field. Frazer pointed the way toward a departure from social Darwinism and nineteenth-century ideology in two respects. First, he was a functionalist, that is, he amassed a large body of data, about magic for instance, a topic he explored, without condemning it as superstitious or primitive, in order to discuss it in terms of how it operated in early societies. He treated magical practices as a form of social cohesion, and refrained from making moral judgments about them.

Frazer effected a transition to social relativism in his field, in that he was cautious about making distinctions between so-called advanced and primitive societies. He deliberately avoided using language which would evaluate societies in hierarchic terms.

Frazer lived until 1941. During his long lifetime, his *Golden Bough*, which originally consisted of two volumes, grew into a gigantic thirteen-volume compendium of anthropological data. However, Frazer could not break wholly away from evolutionary ideas. There remained in his work traces of historicism. Nor is he what might properly be called a twentieth-century anthropologist, for he remained, to the very end, an armchair-anthropologist. This is a typical feature of nineteenth-century social scientists, among whom Herbert Spencer could be cited. Frazer conducted his work in libraries, compiling data from reports written by missionaries and sea captains. He did not encounter the people he has described; he assimilated information about them from the libraries of Oxford University. This research method, needless to say, has become thoroughly obsolete and pre-scientific in anthropology.

The creator of scientific anthropology was the German Jew Franz Boas, who received his original training in Germany as a geographer. He became interested in ethnography, the science that studies early peoples. He came to the United States, partly because he was sensitive to the anti-Semitism which then prevailed in the German academic world, and began to work for the

Marshall Field Museum in Chicago, one of the three great museums of ethnography in America, the other two being the Smithsonian, which became a government operation in the late nineteenth century, and the Museum of Natural History in New York. The Field Museum was founded by the liberal Chicago department store magnate.

The Field Museum undertook to support research among pre-modern peoples, sending out scientists to live among the people to be studied and to gather information and acquire artifacts. Boas was dispatched to Vancouver Island, on the west coast of Canada, because the Field Museum, like most anthropological museums of his time, was interested in collecting totem poles. Although the first research team Boas worked on was mainly sent out to collect totem poles, he lived on Vancouver Island among the Indians, or "native Canadians," as they are called now, for several years and closely observed the Indian way of life.

Among his discoveries on this field trip was that the Canadian government was destroying the social nexus of the Indians who had devised their own monetary value, objects exchanged in a ceremony called "potlatch" by anthropologists, which the government arbitrarily declared to be useless. The native Indian currency was quickly devalued to point zero, with the result that families that had spent decades accumulating this distinctive wealth were pauperized overnight.

This led Boas to see that these societies presented very different qualities when considered from the inside, that they had their own systems, values, ways of functioning which to a Westerner appeared primitive and crude, but which were in many cases very elaborate and sophisticated "thick cultures." He saw, in other words, the necessity of comprehending these cultures in their own terms and in self-referential contexts. This constitutes precisely the main principle of twentieth-century anthropology. The twentieth-century anthropologist, of whom Boas is the prototype, lives with the people he studies, eats their food, attends their meetings, learns their language, and tries to experience their family and value systems and understand behavior patterns from within the culture.

Boas became the founder and chairman of the anthropology department at Columbia University, which under his aegis between 1910 and 1930, was the greatest anthropology department in the world. This is no longer the case since the university administration has allowed it to run down shamefully, but the scientific tradition that Boas started has been continued in other universities, particularly at Chicago and Berkeley.

Aside from the necessity of doing field work, which undertakes the "close reading" of societies while assuming that the alien culture that is studied is as thick and complicated as the anthropologist's own, Boas propounded the view of total cultural relativism. This doctrine enunciates the impossibility of establishing a hierarchy of societies, since every society, claims Boas, is valuable and must be evaluated in its own terms. This assumption about cultural relativity is accompanied by the dismantling of the evolutionary view. Boas holds that societies are not evolving toward a supreme telos; they simply exist. Each consists of its own self-enclosed system of functional operations.

Societies are not transforming themselves into each other. This is known as the synchronic (comparative), as opposed to the diachronic (historical), view of societies.

The diachronic was the nineteenth-century evolutionary view which holds that societies are moving in a predetermined direction and, needless to say, that direction is the state of England in 1890 or the United States in 1950. The other view, the synchronic, is non-historical, non-evolutionary, non-developmental, and relativistic; it studies cultures in themselves. These are the fundamental principles, established by Boas, upon which the discipline of social anthropology now operates.

Boas had many students. Perhaps the most interesting ones among them were two women, Ruth Benedict and Margaret Mead. Ruth Benedict came from a farming family in upstate New York. She went through a long struggle to obtain education. Eventually, she became Boas' prime disciple and a professor at Barnard College, and held the position until she died at a young age in 1945.

In the forties, it was possible to find copies of Ruth Benedict's *Patterns of Culture* not only in every bookstore, but practically in every drugstore in America. This book, of which hundreds of thousands of copies have been sold, is the all-time best-selling book of anthropology. It is a study of various early societies in the American southwest and the East Indies. It studies these cultures in terms of their own value systems from an entirely relativistic stance. Ruth Benedict was in addition a very fine writer. The book is a compelling piece of work that is still very much worth reading. It is, in fact, one of the great classics of Modernist literature.

Margaret Mead was Benedict's student—and, for a short while, her lover. Although Benedict never married, Margaret Mead had three husbands and a child who is also an anthropologist and a professor at Amherst. Although Columbia University often advertised her as a member of the faculty, in fact Margaret Mead never became more than an adjunct professor there. Through her long career she was a member of the staff of The Museum of Natural History.

Among her numerous books, the first and most famous is *Coming of Age in Samoa*, which she wrote on the basis of field research in Samoa in 1925. Although Mead's methods were not always controlled and systematic, *Coming of Age in Samoa* is still a fascinating book. Her aim was to show a complete alternative to repressive, puritanical, middle-class sexuality.

Margaret Mead's main interest was in comparative sexuality. She herself was a liberated woman who believed in open marriage. The purpose of *Samoa*, as well as many of her later books, was to remove what remained of Christian and puritan standards of sexual behavior and marriage. Mead had very considerable influence in this country in developing new sexual standards. Her visibility revived during the counterculture movement in the sixties, which she espoused and helped to legitimize.

Along with sociology and anthropology, Modernism manifests itself in the discipline of psychology as well. We shall see in the next chapter that early psychoanalysis and the work of Freud until 1920 fully cohere with Modernism, although later developments in psychoanalysis point in a different direction.

Psychoanalysis, however, was not the only approach to the psyche that was developed in the Modernist era. Behaviorism, which exhibits much of the radical, rationalist and microcosmic temperament that was so essential to Modernist thought, constitutes a second direction taken by psychology. It has been already pointed out that the philosopher William James was the founder of behaviorist psychology.

James' great European disciple was the Russian physiologist Ivan Pavlov who conducted the famous conditioning experiments with dogs. Pavlov exercised a dominant influence on Soviet psychology, which has rejected psychoanalysis, just as non-representational art has been rejected in that country, as a product of decadent bourgeois culture. Behaviorist psychology has been hailed as the psychology of the Soviet man and woman. The answer to the Soviet problem of breaking away from peasant forms of behavior was found in behaviorist psychology and in its tools of conditioning, which found wide application in Soviet society, including the Gulag.

James' important American disciple was John Watson, founder of the American school of behaviorist psychology. In departments of psychology today, at least sixty per cent of the work that is conducted is still along behavioral lines. This involves, above all, quantitative analysis, close scrutiny of minutiae, that is, very small segments of behavior, and the plotting of it quantitatively. To make this concrete: the quality of a behaviorist department of psychology can be recognized by the number of computers it owns.

There was a utopian strain in American behaviorial psychology that is implicit in the work of Watson and his disciples in the twenties and thirties. It became explicit in Watson's most prominent disciple B. F. Skinner, who was, for three decades, a leading professor at Harvard. Skinner's book, *Beyond Freedom and Dignity*, presents the social and ethical theory of behavioral psychology. There is a strong Modernist quality in his message.

Humanistic doctrines of freedom, Skinner claims, belong to the mystifications of nineteenth-century ethics. A good society is simply one in which people are appropriately conditioned to relate to their environment, and are adapted in their behavior patterns so as to be good citizens. Problems of crime are not solved by talking to and trying to persuade people; they are solved by conditioning environments from the time of a person's birth through their adolescence, as individuals are shaped to be the kind of people that are desired. Only this highly controlled environmental operation will preclude deviance and social pathology. Essentially, Skinner's message is identical to Pavlov's and that of Soviet behaviorists. This view has been much more strongly resisted in this country than in the Soviet Union.

In the field of legal education and legal theory there was also a great upheaval through the application of Modernist ideas in the first thirty years of this century. The first law school in the United States that is worthy of the name was Harvard Law School from about 1890 on. Before that, law schools were unintellectual places in which professors gave stereotyped lectures of either a rhetorical or a historical nature.

Two professors of law at Harvard University transformed the study of law between 1890 and 1920, and constituted law as an academic discipline. They also served as deans of the Harvard Law School. The first was the innovating educator Christopher Columbus Langdell, and the other and better-known one, was Roscoe Pound, who was regarded in his day as the greatest legal mind in America—an esteem he did not really deserve. Nevertheless, he, like Langdell, was a greater educator.

Instead of listening to lectures and memorizing text books, the students of Langdell and Pound did close readings of judicial decisions. Just as the Modernist conception of the effective method of understanding poetry was to read the poem word by word in order to reconstruct its imaginative structure, so the way to learn law was understood as reading the decisions of the Federal Court of Appeals, and reconstructing the (allegedly) rational minds and course of reasoning of the federal judges. This is known as the case method.

Instead of lecturing, the professor of law now discussed case studies in class, analyzing the matter from printed texts—much the same method that Eliot, Richards and Leavis used in literature. The close-reading method in law was similarly self-referential in its textuality. This Modernist method is still used in law schools.

Because of his application of the American philosophy of pragmatism and the Modernist doctrine of relativism to legal theory, Pound was also an influential theorist of law. Two prominent legal minds who advanced this doctrine further were Oliver Wendell Holmes, Jr., another product of Harvard Law School who became a Supreme Court judge, and Felix Frankfurter, who was a professor of law at Harvard before becoming a judge on the Supreme Court as well. The doctrine of legal pragmatism and relativism was most fully developed by Jerome Frank, a federal judge, and Karl Llewellyn, an academic legal scholar at Columbia University.

The pragmatist-relativist approach to law, which became very prominent in the thirties and forties, was called legal realism, although legal pragmatism would have been a more accurate designation for the approach. Legal realism stands in contrast to legal formalism. The latter entailed the derivation of law from abstract principles such as natural law, or inversely, the evolving discovery of abstract principles in laws. Where formalism sought to discern the perpetuation of abstracted historical patterns and philosophical and ethical principles, legal realism regarded the law as thoroughly flexible and instrumental. Law was viewed as synchronic, contemporary, relativist, and instrumental in the pragmatist's sense of the term.

According to legal realism, law is the servant of social reform and the means of exercising power. In order to understand the present state of the law, one does not begin by studying *Magna Carta*, or the intentions of the founders of the Constitution or the impact of natural law, but by investigating how legal decisions serve the interests of corporate or other groups that hold political power. Llewellyn's formulation of legal realism was particularly radical. He refused to give to law-making any special legitimacy or separation from other social acts. Whereas Pound, Holmes, Frankfurter, and Frank, in varying degrees sought to preserve some autonomy and distinctiveness for legal determinations, Llewellyn conceded that legal realism cannot sustain this traditional valorization of law.

American Legal realism, having eroded the legitimacy of prevailing legal doctrines associated with conservative economic and political groups, proceeds to envision new attitudes and principles that serve reforming and progressive interests and underprivileged groups.

This theory fitted in very well with the New Deal. When Franklin Roosevelt introduced the New Deal along with new regulations for business and social security, he encountered a conservative Supreme Court that felt that the changes proposed by Roosevelt conflicted with the Constitution. The legal realists replied to this by pointing out that the Constitution was not a fixed document, but that it always admitted of change in relation to social needs and the demands of those in power. From the realist point of view, to insist upon the conservative faith in abstract constitutionality, is to engage in fictive vestiging of Victorian formalism and historicism. The new approach did prevail, albeit with a lot of pressure from the White House. It the late 1930's Roscoe Pound warned that the legal realists, by divorcing law from ethics, legitimized the Nazi terror state as well as the New Deal.

*   *   *

History and Theology

There are two other areas to be discussed in which Modernism manifested itself before 1940, namely history and theology. These are not domains that immediately lend themselves to Modernist transformations because Modernism is intrinsically anti-historical, and Western theology is by its very nature related to the Judaic and Christian views of the world with their bias towards the traditional. It would be the measure of the power of Modernism if it were indeed seen to have penetrated even these fields. And it did. The results of the penetration yielded new frontiers in historical thinking and revivified theology.

In order for historians to remain intellectually current, they had to adapt themselves to Modernist ways of thinking. They encountered the formidable challenge of writing non-narrative history, a new mode of analytical history that reflected the method of close reading of a segment of past society and avoided the longitudinal projection of narrative histories that covered long-term developments, which was the fashionable mode of the nineteenth century.

A number of historians did rise to this challenge. The three most influential were the Dutchman Johann Huizinga, the Anglo-Polish Lewis Namier, and the American Frederick Jackson Turner. Huizinga was a graduate student at the University of Leiden when, in 1903, he organized the first exhibition of Van Gogh's paintings in the painter's native country. Huizinga, in fact, proceeded to write a history which resembled Van Gogh's paintings, at least the later Van Gogh of sunflowers. Huizinga is an impressionist historian who takes a certain moment in time, such as the fifteenth century in his famous book *The Waning of the Middle Ages*, and renders practically hundreds of detailed impressions of aspects of the culture, particularly stressing the arts and literature and what they communicate, as well as the behavioral patterns of the nobility. He attempts to construct an impressionistic model of fifteenth-century culture.

Lewis Namier came from the north-eastern (Polish) stretches of the Austro-Hungarian Empire. His family were wealthy Jewish landowners. He was educated in England, where he spent most of his adult life. He taught first at the University of Manchester, then at the University of London. In the thirties and forties, he was the dominant figure in British historiography.

Namier's approach can be described as radical positivism or realism. He focuses his attention on the eighteenth-century English consitution, and radically deconstructs it, eliminating the ideational content. Edmund Burke is dismissed as a mere propogandist as Namier assumes a severely functional apporach to eighteenth-century Parliament. He asks how exactly the parliament operated in the eighteenth century and what the realities were within which the party stystem functioned. He discards the ways in which people hoped the system functioned, or described it as functioning, and tries to uncover how it actually did function.

Namier too builds up a model from amassed data, the data being biographical for the most part. Namier set in motion the vast project of establishing the biography of every member of the eighteenth-century English Parliament. It took him and several associates twenty years to accomplish this, but they did construct a working model of the actual operations of the political system. Most relevant were patronage, corruption, and the actual reasons of "interest" for which people wind up in a particular political configuration as opposed to another. Namier dealt with the availability of jobs, wealth, influence, and gave no credence to ideology. Namier's is a highly functional, radical positivistic approach which aims primarily at political analysis without illusions or sentiments. Compared to the romanticization of the English past that had prevailed in the nineteenth and early twentieth centuries, Namier's work was revolutionary.

Not only because his middle name was Bernstein and because he was a fervent Zionist, but mainly because of his harsh Modernist delegitimizing of ethical constructs in the English political system, Namier aroused deep resentment at Oxford and Cambridge and was persistently denied a chair in the old universities. But he was Britain's leading historian from the mid-thirties to the early sixties.

The third of the great triumvirate of analytic Modernist historians was the American Frederick Jackson Turner, a Midwesterner who taught at the University of Wisconsin, and then at Harvard in the twenties and early thirties. Turner's approach was to find a reductionist or microcosmic factor in American history, some particle phenomenon, that is, that was not immediately visible but that lay underneath the surface of events, and had shaped the surface phenomena. Turner found this factor to be the frontier. It was the frontier, he claimed, that molded American culture and society, created its values and practices, at least down to the closing of the frontier in the 1890's.

Obviously, one way of dealing with the Modernist challenge to historical writing was to become more reductionist. The method was to find beneath the surface narrative a single factor that was driving the whole culture or society.

Turner presented one model of how this method could be put to work in his frontier thesis. Thereby, he also opened the way to the popularity of Marxist reductionism.

Although there are some common elements in modern developments in Catholic, Protestant and Jewish theology, each should be dealt with separately, with a view to their distinctive features. The greatest theologian of the twentieth century was the Swiss Calvinist Karl Barth who published his work in the twenties. Barth was closely affected by Modernist culture, and most immediately influenced by Heidegger and phenonemology. The catastrophe of the First World War is also among events to which he reacted very strongly.

Barthean theology owes a substantial debt to Saint Augustine. Barth is a neo-Augustinian, a school of which some aspects had been anticipated in the nineteenth century by the Danish theologian Søren Kierkegaard. In fact, Barth contributed significantly to the making of Kierkegaard's popularity in this century.

Barth's contention was that nineteenth-century liberal theology had been undermined by Modernist culture and proven bankrupt by the moral catastrophe of the First World War which showed that human society was not getting better, that man was not improving, and that the advancement of Christian morality was not as visible as Victorians had anticipated. These were the starting assumptions of Barth's radical neo-Augustinianism.

Man does not change, according to Barth, and human nature is not affected by history. Man is still old Adam, he is still sinful and as evil as he has always been. The fundamental fact of human nature is the micro-act of sin which constitutes man's rebellion against God, and the fundamental fact of human life, in turn, is the evil that exists in the human heart, and that we are rescued from it only by the love of God, or actually by God's love of us. We are so embedded in our corruption that we cannot escape from it save by divine grace.

Barth's theology was a revival of Augustinian and Lutheran ideas, and represented a rebellion against the nineteenth-century view that man was changing in history, and that modern liberalism was elevating man out of his sinfulness. Barth denies this optimism. Of course, the Holocaust, which was to come only twenty years after Barth wrote, even more than World War I, was going to prove how right he had been.

Barth had numerous disciples, including leading Lutheran opponents of Hitler such as Dietrich Bonhoeffer, who died at the hands of the Nazis. In the United States Barth had two main disciples: Reinhold Niebuhr, a professor at the Union Theological Seminary who was extremely visible and influential in his day, and Paul Tillich, a student of Barth's who immigrated to America and also taught at the Union Theological Seminary and later at Harvard. Barth's theology became dominant at the Union Theological Seminary, and spread, from there, to other Protestant American institutions. In their later writing and preaching both Niebuhr and Tillich modified Barth's severely Modernist theology with a revived historicism that was again, in the fifties, becoming fashionable.

About 1906, Albert Schweitzer had published a popular book entitled *The*

Quest for the Historical Jesus. Schweitzer was a German theologian who subsequently became the famous saint of Africa through his missionary work as a doctor in Congo. His book reviewed the vast body of nineteenth- literature in which historians and theologians tried to reconstruct the historical Jesus.

In the late twenties and the thirties, the German theologian and biblical scholar Rudolph Bultmann announced that the quest, which had been futile from the very beginning, should now end, since the historical Jesus could never be discovered. Bultmann's close reading of New testament literature, aided by his enormous learning in post-exilic Judaism, that is, the Judaism of the time of Jesus, demonstrated that the lives of Jesus that had come down to us in the Gospels were really Midrash—that is to say, they were Jewish commentary and legend. Bultmann showed that the Gospels consisted of a pastiche of stories about holy men that existed in the Jewish literature of the time. There may have been a historical Jesus, Bultmann argued, but endeavoring to reconstruct him from the available material was bootless.

Bultmann's claim substantiated Barth's theology. The Christian approach to Jesus must base itself on an entirely theological, non-historical stance. Faith in Jesus cannot be achieved through history, but solely by religious experience. Bultmann's work has had tremendous impact.

The most important names in Jewish Modernist thought belong to two disciples of Heidegger, Gershom Scholem and Martin Buber. Their thought was the product of an effort in the German-Jewish community from about 1910 to 1930 to apply modern scholarship to Judaism, and to undertake the close reading of the Jewish past and tradition, using the instruments of academic scholarship. There had not been much work done in this critical vein before then. Judaism was full of history, but it was largely a mythological history—the meretricious kind that is still propagated from the suburban synagogue pulpit on the Sabbath.

Both Scholem and Buber migrated to the newly founded university in Jerusalem shortly after its establishment in 1926. Gershom Scholem is the seminal twentieth-century scholar on the history of Judaism. It was his concern to undertake the phenomenological analysis of the Jewish past and to uncover the actual content of the Jewish consciousness, while asking what modern consciousness was capable of discovering in Jewish traditions.

Scholem established a very diverse Jewish heritage. Until his work, Judaism was founded on either a traditional orthodox heritage, or a more secular liberal past. Scholem demonstrated that Jewish religious tradition was extremely varied. He showed that there was imbedded within it a continuous strand of activist mysticism, as well as an equally strong apocalyptic, messianic movement. These aspects of the Jewish past had been largely buried because neither activist mysticism nor messianism fitted in with twentieth-century orthodox and liberal Judaism. Scholem showed that Judaism was an extremely complicated, rich, dynamic and volatile religion, or rather, that it had been so for many centuries until about 1850.

This message was not welcome in many quarters in the world Jewish community. It is precisely the narrowing and falsification of the Jewish past that Scholem's radical analysis sought to undermine.

His colleague Martin Buber was a philosopher and the visible embodiment of the mystical tradition. He reinterpreted Jewish mysticism in accordance with Heidegger's philosophy. Buber's famous vision of the relationship between the I and the Thou, that is between humanity and God, owed some of its inspiration to Kierkegaard, and much of it to Heidegger. The relationship between consciousness and the external world in Heidegger's thought is transformed in Buber into the I-Thou relationship.

At the beginning of this century, Catholicism was sunk in obscurantism and ignorance. These are harsh words, but nevertheless true. Nineteenth-century Catholicism, suffering a reaction against the French Revolution and the rise of secularism, tried to separate itself from modern thought. At the turn of the century, there was a movement in Catholicism called Modernism, which tried to bring Catholic theology into contact with modern thinking in the comprehensive sense of the latter term. But in 1907, the Catholic Modernist movement was suppressed by the Papacy as being dangerous to the faith.

It was therefore the task, during the 1920's and 30's, of Catholic thinkers who wished to modernize Catholic theology, to try and find a way around the disaster that had taken place in the early years of the century, a way around the papal condemnation. These thinkers were engaged in an activity which the overwhelming majority of the hierarchy, particularly of the Vatican, did not welcome. They were obliged to sneak, as it were, the modern world into Catholicism.

This movement found its two leaders in the Frenchmen Etienne Gilson and Jacques Maritain who were the constituters of what came to be called the Neo-Thomist movement. Thomist here refers to the thirteenth–century philosopher and theologian Thomas Aquinas. Gilson and Maritain were devout Catholics, needless to say, and prestigious scholars, but they also operated in the secular world. They taught not in Catholic, but in secular, French universities. They were both educated at the University of Paris and in the thirties held chairs there. Gilson taught as well at the University of Toronto, and Maritain came to Princeton University in 1940 as a professor of philosophy. He stayed there and never returned to France.

Gilson and Maritain believed that the Church had faced a comparable intellectual crisis only in the thirteenth century, when it had to find the means of circumventing the problems posed by the vanguard science and philosophy of the time, which were Aristotelian. Thomas Aquinas, a Dominican friar who was teaching at the University of Paris, tried to achieve a reconciliation between Aristotelian science and traditional theology. It was because Thomas presented them with a precedent that Gilson and Maritain selected Thomism as their governing doctrine. They sought to use Thomas as the Trojan Horse for bringing the Church into a more accommodating and mediating relationship with twentieth-century thought. Even with the base of their doctrine in Thomism, their task was not easy. They encountered stiff opposition, and if they had not been teaching in secular universities and had not both become very visible and celebrated in transatlantic academia, they would probably been supressed by the Church hierarchy. But Gilson and Maritain had acquired such fame and importance that the Papacy was obliged to allow them their way.

Even though Gilson and Maritain strike the contemporary reader as all too tame, and their thirteenth–century Thomison as rigid and tiresome, they must be read with an eye on the circumstances in which they were writing. They were using Thomas Aquinas as an instrument in order to overcome the prohibition against modern thought that prevailed in the Catholic Church, and continued to prevail until the Second Vatican Council of 1962.

A third Catholic thinker of the thirties was much more of a radical Modernist than Gilson and Maritain. This was the English Benedictine monk David Knowles. He subsequently became famous in the forties and fifties as the leading Catholic historian in the world, and held the senior chair of history at Cambridge University. But that was the later Knowles. The Knowles of the 1920's and early 30's was a young, intense Benedictine monk at Downside Abbey, the largest Catholic monastery in England. He was the editor of the *Downside Review*, which was the leading intellectual Catholic journal in England.

What Knowles advocated around 1930 was radical expressionism in Catholicism. Catholicism, he claimed, should aim towards a mystical, highly experimental recreation of medieval piety, not by emphasizing tradition and history, but through the teaching of existential commitment to a fully Christian life. He proposed, in other words, a mode of Christian activism. This view incurred the wrath of his order and of the Church. Knowles was exiled to a backwater monastery where he had a nervous breakdown.

Fortunately, Knowles' path converged with that of a Scandinavian woman doctor in England, who had converted to Catholicism and had become a mystic. For the next twenty-five years, they lived together in celibacy. She took care of him. During this period, Knowles wrote his marvelous histories of medieval monasticism and Catholic culture, and eventually he became extremely influential and important. He is one of those innovative Catholic thinkers who contributed to the intellectual revolution of the Second Vatican Council.

Even in Knowles' mature and celebrated work as a historian of medieval church and culture, the most inspired and original sections are those concentrating on charismatic religious personalities who expressed in concentrated form the dynamic of Catholic religiosity. These intense exponents of Catholic experience are elevated above the normal flow of Knowles' historical narrative.

*   *   *

The Expansion of Modernist Culture

We began this discussion of Modernism in the first four decades of the twentieth century by designating its fundamental characterics. Then we examined the manifestation of Modernism in many areas of culture. In conclusion, we shall now mention five areas of Modernist culture that are perceptible but have not been specifically discussed. Finally, we shall consider some general factors affecting Modernism.

Modernist culture was manifested by a novel, intense interest in sport, as well as the professionalization of sport. In the Modernist era, sport ceased to be a marginal, amateur activity and a gentleman's pastime. It became an object of full time pursuit that deserved intense concentration. Sport thereby also became a self-referential field in itself, acquiring a thick culture of its own. It came to constitute a world of its own, a feature it was henceforth to share, say, with Modernist painting, that is capable of absorbing everything around it and transforming it into its own terms. It developed its own microcosmic culture of intense density which was sufficiently powerful to absorb and attract that which approached its periphery.

This change occurred in the first quarter of the century. It is interesting to note that the particular sport in which this phenomenon first took place in the United States was baseball. In Europe, it was soccer. Both became sports that could be intensively pursued, that allowed people to make a living in them and masses to participate vicariously. Compared to American football or to European rugby, baseball and soccer are not sports in which serious injuries are common, and were therefore suitable for professional athletes. The development of these professional sports involves the establishing of patronage systems and exhibition stadia that closely parallel the role of art patrons and museums in the rise of Modernist painting.

A phenomenon and an emergence similar to those of sports can be detected in the case of the radio in the twenties and thirties. Radio broadcasting technologically became possible by 1920. Commercial radio stations were established already in the early twenties in the United States, and state-controlled broadcasting emerged at the same time in Europe, but it was not until the early thirties that anyone knew what to do with radio broadcasting. Until then, it was used mainly for providing information. In the early thirties, however, the radio came into being as a mass medium and developed a culture of its own. The principle of self-referentiality informs, in the case of radio, too, the formation of a microcosmic culture within the wider context of Modernism. Radio becomes a culture-point which develops a distinctive form of drama and especially of comedy.

Radio drama did not survive the 1940's. The situation-comedy that is still immensely popular originated in radio broadcasting in the 1930's and has not been significantly altered in its transition to television. Situation comedy is the distinctive genre of broadcasting. It is a thick point that draws everything to it. After about 1935, radio does not attempt to imitate the concert hall or the public platform, nor does it normally aspire to the lecture hall. It generates its own forms as did Modernist art. Jack Benny and Fibber McGee and Molly play the same role as Picasso and Klee in Modernist painting. They create a self-enclosed world that draws others into it. The situation comedy exhibits a perpetual world within its thirty minute frame—the same program that Cézanne identified for Modernist art.

Another cultural phenomenon of the Modernists has even now not yet been named. The term "folkish" is sometimes used to describe the ambience which manifests itself wherever movements for fresh air, clean bowels, long walks, mountain climbs and corn flakes (the latter being a vanguard phenomenon in its day, believed to re-make the individual) are found. The contiguous adoration of and devotion to youth must be added to this health list, perhaps as the most dynamic element on it. Through exercise and careful diet the middle-aged could preserve the physical exuberance and moral purity that were identified with youth.

Tied to this "folkishness" was theosophy, which blends together elements of eastern philosophy, mostly derived from yoga, Zen Buddhism, and Islam or perhaps from misinterpretations thereof, with bits and pieces of Heideggerian phenomenology, into movements that operate on the margin, propounding the kind of religious philosophy that can be described as secularized mysticism. Again, this movement appears early in the century in all European countries and in the United States, and by the 1920's develops the prototype of the wise man, the Guru, who is a conglomeration of the faith-healer, the visionary and the priest. The sophic guru cultural phenomenon, which almost disappears in the forties and fifties, comes back strong in the sixties.

The theosophical guru whose reputation is highest today is G.I. Gurdjieff. A Caucasian Russian, he became a theosophical leader first in Tashkent, then Moscow, Istanbul, and finally in Fountainbleu, France (1922) where he established his Institute for the Harmonious Development of Man. His method of "self observation" included sacred dance and components derived from the Moslem Sufi mystical sect. Since the 1960's recordings of Gurdjieff's music have been best sellers. What Gurdjieff and other theosophical leaders preached was a puritanical cultivation of the self through contemplation, diet and exercise, aiming for a disciplined inner harmony. This resulted in significant groups centering on strong leaders in the 1920's and has found a resounding echo in the 1980's.

Another cultural phenomenon of the Modernist era was feminism. Modernism was androgynous, and it represented a much greater acceptance of both feminism and homosexuality. The Modernist movement begins in the early twentieth century at the same time as the first great wave of twentieth–century feminism emerges. Feminism is conditioned by the social fact that the new bureaucracies and administrations of government and business that Weber had talked about needed large armies of office workers and so liberated women from the home. Bureaucracy possibly liberated women from the home in order to imprison them in the office, as some upscale feminists would now claim, but it did liberate them from the home nevertheless, giving them a certain amount of independence.

Prominent in early twentieth–century feminism was the suffragette movement that produced tremendous agitation in England and in the United States in the years before the First World War, in order to obtain for women the right to vote. The movement achieved its purpose shortly after the war as a reward for what women had done during the war in ammunition factories and hospitals and on farms. It is interesting that no sooner did women get the right to vote, than by a clear margin they voted for conservative parties in both countries. Why this should have been the case, no one has been able to explain.

Feminism was articulated in an ideology, as represented by Virginia Woolf in her book *A Room of One's Own*, a brief feminist treatise such as only Virgina Woolf could write, in which she advocated cultural and intellectual independence for women. Woolf spoke persuasively about the realization of women's artistic and intellectual possibilities and social benefits thereof. She herself was able to realize such possibilities because of a farseeing father and a very indulgent, or shall we say, egalitarian, husband.

Another aspect of the period's feminism was the recognition that women were sexual beings, that their sexual drive was as powerful as men's, and that women had an equal right in sexual relations. The psychoanalytic movement contributed substantially to this recognition. It was immediately translated into a revolution in women's clothes—the abandonment of corsets, the raising of the hemline, the advent of the brassiere.

By the late 1920's, the feminist movement had eroded. The trajectory of feminism is very similar to the trajectory of Modernism: it reaches its peak in the early twenties, as Modernism does, and it begins to run down in the late twenties as Modernism begins its decline. The job shortage in the Great Depression of the thirties fostered a return to the assumption that a woman's place is in the home. Feminism resurges in the prosperous, high employment sixties.

The most compelling book of the early feminist movement was Vera Brittain's *Testament of Youth* (1933), which is an autobiographical account by an English journalist from the lower middle class, of her struggle to gain an education, her hospital work during the war, her love life, her experiences at Oxford after the war and her hopes and disappointments. Vera Brittain's daughter is Shirley Williams, one of the three leaders of the British Social Democratic Party. Brittain's *Testament* is one of the major Modernist autobiographies. If it is less known now than Woolf's *Room*, that is because Woolf's book is polemically concentrated while Brittain's work is one of complex humanity.

Finally, there was the phenomenon of the rise of the university. Modernism arose in the same period as the one which witnessed the making of the modern university. By the 1930's, the university as we know it today had come into existence, and was teaching a significant portion of the college-age population, more in this country than in Europe. But the number of young people attending the university was on the increase in Europe as well. In addition, the university had already become the center of science and research. Not all these features were entirely novel to this period but only in the Modernist era did the university become the vital center of intellectual life in the Western world.

The departure signified the professionalization of learning, the emergence of a social recognition and institutional base for research and analysis. The most important didactic minds, especially in philosophy, science and in social science, were now university professors. This presents a very great difference from the situation in 1890. Between 1890 and 1930, the university had become the center of intellectual life and research.

Whereas in 1900, literary criticism was practiced almost entirely outside the university—by journalistic men of letters, poets, and novelists or combinations of these—by 1940 it had become a mostly (although not yet entirely) academic enterprise. The Modernist transformation of literary criticism into a central academic endeavor was accentuated after World War II, culminating in today's situation in which a respectable literary critic outside the university is as rare as one inside academe in 1900.

By 1930 the radical secular analysis, the microcosmic focus, the self-referentiality of learning that were central to Modernist thought had become characteristics of the scholarship done at the universities. The rise of the modern university involved the quality of constituting learning as a self-enclosed universe and as a value in itself, irrespective of whatever popular support and acceptance it might achieve. This elitist attitude was a fundamental feature of Modernist culture.

One of the most distinct features of Modernism is the extent to which expatriates were involved in its making, that is, the degree to which Modernism was a genuinely international movement. Expatriation played a prominent role in Modernist culture long before artistic and intellectual refugees from Fascism had to migrate to the United States in the 1930's.

More than nineteenth-century culture certainly, and significantly more than the culture that has been in the making since the Second World War, Modernism was carried forward by people who voluntarily left their own countries in order to make their mark as cultural leaders in a different environment. One might expect this internationalization process to be much more pronounced since the Second World War, especially given the facility of inexpensive air travel at this time, but to the contrary. Expatriation has played a much smaller role in cultural development since 1945. Indeed, more and more people now study abroad—international education has become a big business in itself—but cultural leadership tends to remain, in our day, nativist and national.

The jet plane compared to earlier steam transportation has actually worked against cultural expatriation by making short-term visits to foreign centers feasible. Travel abroad in the jet plane era is easily accessible to artists and intellectuals, but compared to the 1920's, they do not stay abroad and become cultural leaders in a foreign country. The exception to this pattern is the East European émigrés whose expatriation is largely involuntary.

Modernism was thus a movement in which expatriates played an important role, and in which there was a genuine internationalization of culture. Although it is well known that there was a large expatriate community in Paris in the 1920's, the case of England was equally remarkable as a phenomenon of cultural expatriation and internationalization. In 1935, the leading philosopher in England was an Austrian Jew, Ludwig Wittgenstein. The leading historian was a Polish Jew from the Austro-Hungarian Empire, Lewis Namier, while the foremost literary critic and poet was the American, T.S. Eliot. The most important British novelist of the time, one who at least wrote in English and spent part of his time in Britain, was the Irishman, James Joyce. The most distinguished British scientist was the New Zealander, Ernest Rutherford. The situation was unprecedented in English culture, and has certainly not repeated itself since the Second World War. Berlin's cultural life, in the 1920's, especially its painting, was also deeply affected by expatriates. The efflorescence of Modernist culture, in general, was characterized by a tendency towards expatriation and internationalization.

It was the cosmopolitan champions of Modernist culture who facilitated the relatively easy acceptance of refugees from Fascism in the United States in the thirties and early forties. The migration across boundaries and oceans of artists, intellectuals and academics had been made familiar and shown to be generally beneficial in the previous decade. The mostly involuntary expatriates from Fascist occupied countries in many instances struggled with underemployment and poverty in America and professors especially were disadvantaged until they mastered oral English. But the astonishing aspect of the cultured refugee migration in the thirties is the remarkably warm welcome and the rapid professional success the migrants enjoyed—and this during the Great Depression when academic and other intellectual jobs were hard to come by for the native-born.

It is true that many of the academic refugees were famous scholars and scientists who immediately magnified the quality of the university departments they joined. Princeton overnight became a world center for physics and mathematics, NYU gained celebrity in Art History, and the New School for Social Research greatly enhanced its reputation in social and behavioral sciences. Yale buttressed its standing in English literary criticism with giants in comparative and continental literature. Berkeley gained distinction in medieval studies and Chicago in analytic philosophy as a result of the European migration. Yet it is astonishing that when American Ph.D.'s had to teach in the boondocks or take clerical jobs in Washington or work in Macy's basement, American universities were filling academic chairs and establishing new ones for refugee scholars whose European level of thought and thick foreign accents made them largely incomprehensible to the fresh-faced but naive young Ronald Reagan and Lucille Ball types in the classroom. Nor did the émigrés sufficiently realize the instrinsic quality of indigenous American scholarship which they frequently crushed under their heavy German tread. "That man," the chairman of the history department at Columbia said of his distinguished émigré colleague in classical studies, "is a fool in six languages."

It was the previous modernist expatriation and internalization of culture that made the thirties intellectual emigration from Europe to American possible. It could not occur today on anywhere near the same scale.

A second general quality of Modernism was that it was carried out by urban groups, by groups of people, that is, living in the major cities of the Western world. It was in no sense a rural movement, nor a frontier movement, but entirely a metropolitan phenomenon whose leading centers were Paris, London, New York, Vienna, Berlin, as well as a number of subsidiary centers like Oslo and Dublin. Each of these centers harbored, not a few intellectuals, but large groups of people active in numerous facets of the visual and performing arts, who interacted with the philosophers and scientists. The arts and sciences impinged upon one another in these cities. Strong support groups in which artists and intellectuals assisted, encouraged, provoked and inspired each other marked these urban cultures.

The famous Parisian scene in the 1920's was led by three remarkable American women who acted as patrons of literature and art. These were, first, Sylvia Beach, who worked for a living by running a very important bookstore, "Shakespeare and Company." As is well known, she was the first publisher of James Joyce. Gertrude Stein, a graduate of Radcliffe, was a wealthy and somewhat eccentric American, a student of William James and herself a poet and a critic who sought a significant role as a patroness of culture. Although Stein never gained the public recognition she yearned for, her insights into the significance of Modernism were among the earlier and sharper descriptions of the movement.

Peggy Guggenheim, the American millionaire heiress and patroness of the arts, is the third of this phenomenal triumvirate. Peggy was a hell-raiser on two continents. She claimed that during her long and stormy life she had slept with a thousand men. Among them were a goodly number of prominent artists including Max Ernst, to whom Peggy was married for a short while. Forced to leave France during the Second World War, Peggy established a thriving commercial gallery in New York that became the model for the post-war art trade. Peggy's fabulous collection of Modernist painting—much of which, with visionary taste and on Ernst's recommendations, she bought for modest prices in the 20's, 30's and early 40's—is today in her former villa, now a museum in Venice, and in the Guggenheim Museum in New York, established by another member of her family. The Guggenheims originally made their money in Colorado copper mining.

In Paris too, were the Frenchmen Paul Valéry and Marcel Proust, as well as James Joyce and the American Ernest Hemingway, and the Canadian Morley Callaghan, who was perhaps the leading Canadian novelist of the early twentieth century. Further there were the Spanish artist Picasso, the Russian-Jewish painter Marc Chagall and the Italian sculptor Modigliani. Matisse and Braque headed the legion of native French artists. These figures knew each other, interacted with each other, and most important, influenced one another.

The same can be said of London at that time. In London there were two such Modernist groups. One was the cadre of poets and artists gathered around T.S. Eliot and Ezra Pound. Involved in this group were the Englishman Wyndham Lewis, a novelist and polemicist of Modernism, and the novelist Ford Madox Ford. The other one was the Bloomsbury group, led by Virginia Woolf and her sister Vanessa Bell. The group further consisted of Lytton Strachey, the novelist E.M. Forster, the economist John Maynard Keynes, the art critic Clive Bell and the artist Duncan Grant, as well as numerous others.

These urban movements were made possible by cheap housing, cheap food and steam transportation. The situation that prevailed as a result of these conditions no longer exists in the Western world. And it may be a long time before similar circumstances can again become possible. Yuppiedom is the enemy of cultural revolution, since it means high rents and expensive restaurants that force the artists to Hoboken, New Jersey and the further reaches of Queens. No renaissance will occur in these places.

A third characteristic of Modernism is that Jews played a major role in it. Modernism was not a Jewish plot, not a chapter in the Protocols of the Elders of Zion, but Jews did make major contributions in its conception and perpetuation. This fact is especially remarkable when it is remembered that the entire Jewish population of Europe west of Poland was less than 2 million people. Franz Kafka was not only Jewish but so conscious of his Jewishness as to become a learned Jewish scholar and sympathetic to Zionism. He was descended, on his mother's side, from a long line of distinguished Prague rabbis and mystic visionaries. Had Kafka lived into the thirties, he would, along with his friend and literary executor Max Brod, have migrated to Israel. Kafka's papers ended up in Israel, which is the reason why they have never been published in a definitive edition. They are in the hands of Brod's secretary who sells them off piecemeal to make a living.

Marcel Proust was Jewish on his mother's side. His mother came of the famous Weil family which produced a long line of distinguished businessmen, scholars and professional and literary people in France. Proust understood himself as Jewish, and when in the late 1890's the infamous Dreyfus case occurred, which maliciously charged a Jewish army captain with treason, Proust was one of the first to come to Dreyfus' aid and to organize a fund for his defense. One should not think of Proust entirely in terms of his later years, locked up in a cork-lined room, allegedly removed from the world. The myth of Proust as a recluse has been overdone. As a matter of fact, Proust was very much engaged in the arts and was intensely interested in politics.

The role of Jews in social and behavioral sciences is phenomenal. We need mention only Durkheim, the founder of modern sociology, Franz Boas, the founder of anthropology, and of course, Sigmund Freud himself, the founder of psychoanalysis, as well as most of his early disciples. The physicist Niels Bohr was also Jewish on the maternal side, and although he did not pay much attention to this heritage, the Nazis certainly did, and he had to leave Denmark quickly on a fishing boat and flee to England in 1943 after Denmark was overrun by the Nazis.

Einstein's physics was denounced as "Jewish physics" in Nazi Germany. Einstein too was extremely conscious of his Jewishness. A vehement Zionist, he was offered the first presidency of Israel in 1948 in recognition of his long support of Jewish Nationalism. He turned it down, giving his age as the reason. The first president of Israel was another Jewish scientist, Chaim Weizmann, who had a distinguished career as a professor of chemistry at the University of Manchester.

Although traditional Jewish religion had been hostile to the visual arts, there was a large group of important Jewish artists in Paris in the 1920's and 30, expatriated from eastern Europe, the most famous of whom were Marc Chagall and Chaim Soutine. About thirty of these Parisian Jewish artists died in the Nazi death-camps in the 1940's.

As we have noted the philosopher Ludwig Wittgenstein was a scion of an assimilated millionaire Viennese Jewish family. The leading European Modernist historian, and in some ways the most radical historical Modernist of the early thirties, Lewis Namier was, again, not only Jewish (his name had originally been Namierowski), a Polish Jew from the eastern frontier of the Austro-Hungarian Empire, but he was in the 1920's a vehement Zionist as well. It is interesting to note this recurrence of Zionism among Jewish Modernists. Namier very much wanted to become the first president of Israel, but lost the leadership of the Zionist movement in England to Chaim Weizmann in 1930. It was only after he was eliminated from the headship of the Jewish Zionist organization that Namier turned all his attention to the writing of history.

The fact that Jews played an important role in the shaping of Modernist culture has reasons intrinsic neither to the Jewish race, if we can indeed speak of such a thing, nor to traditional Jewish culture, but rather to the time and place in the history of Jewish culture in which Modernism appeared. Jewish Modernists were the first generation of liberated Jews. They belonged to the first generation of Ashkenazi (Western) Jews, stretching from Poland to Britain and to New York, who had a reasonable opportunity to attend universities, although discrimination still continued against them, and to advance in the learned and university professions.

People who belong to traditional but highly literate cultures, when initially given the opportunity to break out of them, and to participate fully in secular and academic culture, undergo, in that generation, intellectual explosion. The current situation of Asian-Americans in the United States is a comparable example. Asian-Americans are the rising intellectual group in this country today, just as Jews were in the generation of the twenties and thirties. It is said that if Columbia University had in the thirties accepted students entirely on the basis of their academic potential, seventy-five per cent of the entering freshman class in 1935 would have been Jewish. (The Jewish quota was fifteen per cent). Today, twenty-eight per cent of the entering class at Berkeley is Asian-American, a repetition of the pattern of Jewish achievement in Modernist culture.

Of course, the Jewish role as a vanguard group in Western culture is now over. Today, Jews are much more involved in real estate speculation, insider trading, conspicuous consumption and municipal corruption. The prominent role played by Jews in the formation of Modernist culture can be therefore explained as a sociological phenomenon typical of the first generation of a newly liberated and highly literate minority. A minority of this kind has to be one in which intellectual life is highly respected in the first place, even though its intellectual capacity has been previously devoted to sectarian religion.

The era of high Modernism, which stretches from 1900 to 1940 is also the era of the rise of anti-Semitism in the West. Never before, and not afterwards, since 1945, has an anti-Semitic explosion been seen, that affected the western world as strongly as the one that cuts through the decades between 1900 and the early 1940's. It came to an end only when General Eisenhower's armies reached Belsen and Dachau in the spring of 1945, and revealed the Holocaust to the world. It was only then that anti- Semitism collapsed. Even though there are some signs of a revival, particularly in Western Germany, Austria and to some extent among the left in Britain and the United States, nevertheless, it is still a comparatively muted form of anti-Semitism.

The important relationship between Modernism and anti-Semitism does not by any means cover the entire story of the phenomenon of anti-Semitism which is one of the fundamental facts of twentieth-century culture and has many roots. Yet it is impossible to ignore the fact that in diverse ways Modernism contributed to the rise of the anti-Semitic tide that overwhelmed the Jews.

The Jews were in a double bind. First, they played a very significant and visible role in Modernism. They occupied, albeit not exclusively, a vanguard position in it. In response, traditionalists, who felt that radical, secular Modernism was undermining, destructuring, as it were, traditional culture and Christianity, that its internationalist bent was threatening national cultures and traditions, attributed the ill they perceived to Jews and felt that the latter were serving Western culture poorly, and that they were effecting this through the vehicle of Modernism. Jews had launched an assault, according to this view, on traditional, Christian, historical, and national cultures, and Modernism, its secular internationalism, was their weapon. The traditionalists—especially Catholics—displaced their anti-Modernism into a fanatical hatred of Jews. Fervent nationalists often viewed Jewish intellectuals as cynical cosmopolites who were using Modernist ideas to delegitimize patriotism.

French anti-Semitism was particularly affected by an ideological reaction against Modernism. Right-wing French traditionalists were as strongly, and simultaneously, anti-Modernist as they were anti-Semitic. Yet the story is more complicated than that because in other places, particularly in England, it was the Modernists who themselves were anti-Semites. The Modernist movement in England, more specifically the circle of T.S. Eliot, Ezra Pound and Wyndham Lewis, was violently anti-Semitic. One could therefore be a leading Modernist intellectual and nurse anti-Semitism at the same time.

The main reason why T.S. Eliot's widow has not allowed general access to his papers by scholars is probably because when the archives are opened, it will be realized how extreme an anti-Semite T.S. Eliot had been. We do know for fact that he was an anti-Semite, particularly from a dreadful public lecture that he gave at the University of Virginia in 1931, which sounds like something that could have been written by Joseph Goebbels. Similar sentiments undoubtedly pervade his private papers. It is instructive and disturbing to read how delicately Eliot's biographers have dealt with his virulent anti-Semitism.

Ezra Pound, who may have been the greatest Modernist poet of the English language, one of the three at any rate, became a paranoid Fascist agitator, broadcasting from Rome during the war and denouncing Jews. Wyndham Lewis, a vanguard novelist, painter, and critic of major talent, produced several anti-Semitic pamphlets and articles in the thirties and lavished praise on Hitler. Lewis' reputation in Britain became so clouded that he had to seek refuge as a professor at a small Catholic college in Canada.

Anti-Semitism was present in German Expressionism as well. Contempt for the Jewish businessman, the Jewish bourgeois and capitalist is a paradigmatic theme in the art and literature of this school. It is not an overwhelming Expressionist theme, but it is present nevertheless. A search for the source of the caricature of Jews in the Nazi art of the thirties should not be too difficult.

It suffices to go back to the work of the prominent Expressionist artist Georg Grosz in the early twenties, to find the forefather of the bloated, decadent Jewish capitalist of Nazi cartoons.

The question why there should be an anti-Semitic strain in Modernism is a difficult one but answerable. The Jews were seen as the arch-representatives of the nineteenth-century culture against which Modernism was rebelling. The Jews were historically and religiously minded. Particularly so were the Jewish immigrants from Eastern Europe, who had been coming to Western Europe in larger numbers since 1900. The Jews, mostly Polish, who then came into the West, were traditionalist in their religious practices.

The Jews were an historical people. Their sense of identity was corporate and was expressed through historical consciousness—all of which were tendencies against which Modernism rebelled. Also, the Jews were the visible beneficiaries of nineteenth-century liberalism. Nineteenth-century liberal historicism had advocated the liberation of the Jews, had protected them, had given them civil rights, and had argued for the right of Jews to participate fully in European society. No British intellectual in the nineteenth century was more supportive of both political and civil rights of Jews than Thomas Macaulay—the leading Victorian historian. Therefore, the Jews were seen as the arch-representatives, but more important, as the arch-beneficiaries of that liberal historicist culture so disliked by Modernism.

The Jews were thus hit with a double bind. They were regarded as the arch-fiends of Modernism, who were eroding traditional European Christian and national culture, and, at once, they were perceived to be the arch-beneficiaries of everything that represented, to the radical Modernist mind, superseded nineteenth-century culture. The way in which Modernism developed contributed significantly to the rise of anti-Semitism between 1900 and 1940.

The final quality of Modernism, and one that has proved most permanent in the popular mind, is what might be called the Greenwich Village and Bloomsbury phenomenon, or the Parisian Left Bank and Munich university sector phenomenon. Modernism revived something which had been very strong in the period ranging between 1820 and 1860 in Romantic culture, namely, the bohemian—the middle-class artist who rebels against his own class, who retreats, not to the working class district, but to the attics and fringes of middle class living, and from there generates a vanguard artistic culture. In time, the rebellious culture so generated is incorporated or socialized into middle-class life and culture. This is the pattern and fate of bohemia.

Modernism reenacted this pattern, advocating a bohemian culture, art as the authentic form of human expression, one it deemed far more important than politics, far more noble and pure than economics. Modernism was expressed through a bohemian life. Many of the Modernists did live the bohemian life, and they certainly upheld the vanguard as the finest expression of European culture. This neo-bohemianism is central to the life of Modernism.

*   *   *

Modernism and World War I

The problematic relationship between World War I and Modernism has received much attention. World War I was essentially the consequence of arrogance on the part of the ruling groups in European society. Bloated with military power, the political elites had structured huge armies and developed novel forms of armament like artillery and the long-range machine gun. They were beginning to experiment with the use of airplanes and armored cars. In the period from about 1880 to about 1910, they had engaged in a vast international imperialist race to carve up Africa and spheres of influence in Asia.

In the years leading up to 1914, Western countries began to envision a military confrontation for rule and hegemony within Europe as well as for world power. That is, they could no longer export their military competition, since they had already divided up the world, and were also finding that overseas empires were ruinously expensive. They began to turn their military competition back into Europe. The political elite also suffered from a deep misconception as to what a future war to determine world-dominance, *Weltmacht*, would be like. They thought that the war would be much like the Franco-Prussian war of 1870, which had featured one battle and was over in six weeks. They also thought that with the tremendous military capability that they had built up, a "star wars" capability it seemed to them, the war would be brief and everyone would be home for Christmas.

What the Western powers did not understand was that the prototype for the first great war of the twentieth century was not the Franco-Prussian War, but the American Civil War of 1861–1865—a war, that is, fought with masses of infantry, a war of attrition which would cause tremendous loss of life (600,000 Americans were casualities in the Civil War, which is still the greatest war in American history in terms of loss of life), and a war that would eventually result in the impoverishment of the civilian population.

The exacerbation of the long-standing feud between Russia and Austria over who would dominate the Balkans was the immediate cause of the conflict in August 1914. But the German and British governments were most responsible for the war—the former for urging on their Austrian allies because the Berlin generals and politicians thought the moment was propitious for a German victory, the latter for not using its capability of interceding to prevent the outbreak.

The First World War was in fact one of unprecedented massacre in which ten million people died, nine million of them on the battlefield. One million consisted of civilians, mostly in eastern Europe. After the long-planned German thrust to Paris failed, there was deadlock on the Western Front by the Christmas of 1914, rather than triumph. Neither side was able to use its military power and advanced machinery to achieve the breakthrough it sought on the Western Front.

In the east the war fared differently. By 1917, the Russian army was shown to be a paper bear, there was a revolution in Russia and the new Bolshevik regime withdrew from the war. On the Western Front, military forces did not move more than a hundred miles in either direction during four incredibly horrible years, while vast numbers of young males were destroyed. Battles were fought in 1916 and 1917 in which each side suffered a quarter million casualties in two days. The British had developed the tank, whose deployment could have broken the deadlock, but conservative British generals, still dreaming of cavalry charges, resisted its use. By 1916, the war was impacting upon the civilian populations. The British were hungry, the Germans even more so. In 1917, massacre in the trenches and demoralization in Paris led to a huge mutiny in the French army, which was suppressed with great difficulty, and the French did little fighting in the next year.

The war came to an end for two reasons. First, by 1918 the Germans were suffering starvation and a left-wing revolution was threatening in Berlin. As a matter of fact, a communist revolution did occur, but it was aborted. The second reason the war ended was the United States' entry into the war in 1917. In 1918, one million fresh, untrained and inept American troops arrived in France, causing consternation among the Germans who did not realize how unprepared the American army was for the war. When the Allies began to penetrate the German lines, the German generals panicked and advised the government in Berlin to seek an armistice, which meant to surrender.

The war ended in a very peculiar way. It had never been fought on German soil. It took place entirely on Belgian and French (and in the East on Polish) soil, and the Germans surrendered before the battle reached Germany—in anticipation of what was going to happen now that the Yankees were over there.

There are two ways of interpreting the relationship between the coming of the War and Modernism. One would be to claim that the First World War, being the last gasp of the old order, had no relationship to Modernism. The old order, which was one of militarism, historicism, hierarchy, nationalism, and militant Christianity, separately played out in the War, its decadent manner, its tired ideology. On the other hand, it could be said that Modernism had played an unconscious role in the cause of First World War. The old culture in 1914 was threatened by cultural revolution, which was very much underway in the first decade of the twentieth century, involving philosophy, the social sciences, the arts and literature as much as the sciences themselves, developing in all fields new ways of perceiving the world that radically contradicted nineteenth-century modes of thinking.

The First World War could be seen as a desperate, although largely unconscious, effort of the old order to save itself. The path of self-preservation for the old culture ran through war. For the war reasserted nationalism, historical traditions, male chauvinism, social hierarchy, and the old ideological Christianity. The First World War was the way used by the old culture to stave off the advent of the new. The effort proved to be suicidal, to a degree, but it was, nevertheless, an unconscious strategy for warding off the threat of the total transformation of Western culture.

There is a point to the latter interpretation, a visible one too, that is discernible in the way the war broke out in August 1914 amidst the joyous welcome of the military and landed classes and among the leadership groups in politics. The war meant a moral revival for these populations, restoring them to an importance they were losing.

Among the effects of the war on Modernism, the one most frequently stressed is that the War strengthened the Modernist movement because it discredited the old order. The old order had caused the death of ten million people, destroyed the Tsarist and Hapsburg empires, had impoverished France, crushed Germany, and in acts of unprecedented horror wiped out an entire generation of young men between the ages of eighteen and thirty. The old order, in other words, proved itself incredibly foolish and inept in its last effort to assert itself. By discrediting itself, the old order gave renewed valorization to Modernism.

The literature of the post-war period stands as proof of this profound disillusion with the old order. The famous lines of William Butler Yeats, "Things fall apart, the center cannot hold/Mere anarchy is loosed upon the world," written in 1919, reveal the new pessimism and despair. Paul Valéry's comment, "The mind has been cruelly wounded, it doubts itself profoundly," points towards a sense of loss that concerns more than the biological, namely, the psychological. To the extent Modernism hated nationalism, militarism, historicism, and traditional Christianity, the First World War presented solid justification for its hatred. The War demonstrated that the Modernist hostile view of Victorian culture was well founded. Appropriately, Lytton Strachey's *Eminent Victorians* was published at the end of the War.

But Modernism lost as well as gained from the War. The First World War also begins the revival of Victorian culture. That it began the recovery of historicism, nationalism, and traditional Christian ethics, cannot be perceived very well during the years immediately following the end of the War, not clearly until the thirties. The vast military propaganda that had been possible in 1914 was again virulent in the thirties. The tremendous resurgence of Victorian historicism and national feeling that accompanied the War along with the assertion of male leadership and hierarchic order and the reaffirmation of traditional Christian ideals represented a powerful contradiction of Modernism. By the 1930's the impact of this neo–Victorianism was evident and operative.

While in the short term, approximately from 1918 to 1928, Modernism seemed to be given a new lease on life, a new vitality and validity, by the First World War, by the later years of the twenties, the neo-Victorian cultural qualities that the First World War had stimulated began to take hold and to threaten the new culture's vitality. Whereas some historians have seen the First World War as only a positive force for Modernism, its impact on Modernism was, in fact, mixed.

The War's immediate consequence was to accelerate disillusion with Victorian ideals. Its longer range outcome was to strengthen the reaction against Modernism.

There is one way in which the consequences of World War I and Modernism converge, and that is in a loss of conventional respect for human life.

Modernism eroded traditional humanism. It allowed for the expression of moral relativism, the recognition of sado-masochistic feelings as a genuine and inevitable component of the human personality, while the Victorians, who certainly knew about such emotions, hid both the knowledge and its expression. Modernism acknowledged as central to the human personality those violent impulses which Victorianism repressed.

In German Expressionism, French Surrealism and Dadaism, and even in some tendencies of the English Modernism, particularly as manifested in the writings of Ezra Pound and Wyndham Lewis, Modernism gave validity to cruelty, accepting cruelty not as something to be simply resisted, but as a human act that was to be understood as an inseparable part of life. We shall see that psychoanalysis also recognized the centrality of sado-masochism in the human psyche.

The War's legacy desensitized popular feeling and everywhere taught the same message graphically. That the unprecedented destruction of human life in the First World War, and its horrifying traces, wounded people, physically as well as mentally, could be seen in every European city in the twenties. Cities were full of people with severed limbs. Medicine not emerging from the dark ages until the 1940's, post-World War I medicine knew only one way of dealing with severely wounded limbs—to cut them off. The amputees as well as the psychologically traumatized ("shell-shocked") remained a prominent fixture of the inter-war period.

Europeans came to accept the brutal consequences of the war as a collective trauma: "In Flanders' fields the poppies blow/Between the crosses row on row." The vast cemeteries became an accepted fact, a part of the regular landscape. Signs of death and destruction were internalized into European culture and thereby normalized. Human life was devaluated, and cruelty assumed a new legitimacy as a result of the First World War.

This devaluation combined with the tendency in Modernism to erode traditional Christian humanism and normative ethics, to validate relativism, to recognize sado-masochism and cruelty. Modernism coalesced with the catastrophic consequences of the First World War to produce a new streak in European mentality—the streak of unrestrained destruction, legitimized massacre and socially acceptable holocaust. The roots of the Holocaust lie in several places, two of which are the First World War and Modernism.

3

Psychoanalysis

Psychoanalysis Today

It is commonly said these days that psychoanalysis is undergoing difficult and critical times. Recently a book appeared derived from a series of articles in *The New Yorker*, written by Janet Malcolm and entitled *Psychoanalysis: The Impossible Profession*. The title of the book expresses its theme directly.

Doubtlessly, psychoanalysis is currently facing a number of challenges. The conflict which has existed in this country since the 1930's between psychoanalysts with medical degrees, and lay analysts, many of whom have Ph.D.'s in clinical psychology, and some even degrees in clinical social work, has recently become exacerbated.

A primary question, which is by no means a new one, that psychoanalysis is currently entangled in is therefore whether psychoanalysis is a medical science or a cultural movement with a therapeutic branch. Does psychoanalysis have to be based on medical science? Sigmund Freud himself did not think that it had to be, even though in his case it was. He favored allowing lay analysis and training psychoanalysts who did not have a medical degree. His daughter Anna Freud, who was also one of his prime disciples, was not an M.D. Nor was his last student, Erik Erikson.

The second and perhaps more important issue that is facing psychoanalysis is that of the rise of what is called psychopharmacology, that is, the use of drugs to alleviate mental illness that had hitherto been treated by psychoanalysis. This concerns particularly the illness of mood-swing, or mood-polarization, called manic-depression. At least one third, and possibly one half of the patients that psychoanalysts normally treat are people whose moods undergo swings from mania to depression, remaining for the most part in depression and occasionally breaking into euphoric hyperactivity or mania. It became known in the fifties that Valium or a similar substance can help many people in a depressed or anxious state. But for those in a severe arc of moodswing another treatment had to be found.

About twenty years ago, largely by the trial-and-error method of experimentation, it was discovered that a certain lithium compound had the effect of flattening out the mood-swing, or at least of reducing the swing's curve, thus alleviating the depression to a significant degree for seventy per cent of manic-depressive patients. This lithium compound also almost eliminates the manic euphoria. Severe depression hurts work performance, impairs family relationships, and sometimes leads to suicide. The manic mood-swing can lead to reckless behavior such as overspending and gambling. Lithium greatly reduces these dangerous behavior patterns for most patients.

While the immediate effects of lithium are known, the reasons why or how it can produce these results remain unknown. The impact on the individual's health of the long-term use of lithium are also uncertain, but after two decades of use no toxic consequences are yet evident. The use of lithium against mood-swing may have another consequence. Many artists and other creative people are manic-depressive. Their creativity comes predominantly in the manic phase which lithium for the most part eliminates. Can society afford this threat to cultural creativity?

Valium is remarkably cheap. So are Lithium compounds. They do not cost much more than Tylenol and therefore pose as an attractive remedy in a variety of ways. Psychiatrists who are also psychoanalysts have in many instances abandoned treating manic-depressive mood-swings by means of the slow and difficult analytic process, which takes three to four years on the average, and do not hesitate to prescribe medication to these patients after very few sessions of therapy. In the majority of cases, there are visibly positive results within three or four weeks. This situation poses a growing threat to psychoanalytic therapy. Why go through a long and expensive psychoanalysis when drugs can do the job quickly and cheaply?

Paradoxically, the fathers of psychoanalysis, Freud and Jung, would probably have approved of the use of medication in the treatment of mental illness. Freud began his career as a neurologist, and he experimented with drugs in his earliest efforts to deal with neuroses. His most elaborate experiments concern the use of cocaine, which he abandoned because he could not control the effects. Even before the First World War, Jung foresaw that many mental illnesses including psychosis were the consequence of biochemical changes and hence might eventually be treated by pharmacology.

Nevertheless, the emergence of psychopharmacology is an important threat or, it could be claimed, raises interesting challenges to psychoanalysis. This is especially the case for lay analysts, that is, for those who are not M.D.'s and do not have the licence to prescribe drugs. Their professional credibility could be ultimately eroded by the spread of psychopharmacology.

A third challenge to psychoanalysis comes from philosophers of science, particularly from the disciples of Ludwig Wittgenstein, and specifically from Karl Popper, a Wittgensteinean who is professor of philosophy at the University of London, and Popper's disciples. Having devoted his early career to proving that Plato was a fascist and not a philosopher to be taken seriously, Popper devoted the latter part part of his career to proving that Freud from the standpoint of science was nothing less than a charlatan. For these unusual accomplishments Popper was given a knighthood.

Popper and his colleagues argue that whatever else psychoanalysis may be, it is not a science, primarily because it lacks that which is fundamental to science, which is in their view a principle of falsification. Psychoanalysis, they insist, is unable to posit a method by which a given proposition can be shown to be true or false. It is possible to regard psychoanalysis as a cultural theory, even as religion or poetry, they claim, but science it certainly is not.

This mode of anti-Freudianism has become popular in English academic circles. Although psychoanalysts have long held that they are engaged in verifiable science, that their field does not consist simply of articles of faith, recent criticisms both of their theory and practice have obliged them to assume a defensive position and to begin to face this criticism. The first line of response to Popper is that his definition of science is a very narrow one. A second would be that psychoanalysis has helped millions of people which constitutes verification. A third response points to recent research at Rockefeller University which claims significant experimental verification for Freud's theory of childhood development.

Despite the threats to the future of psychoanalysis, the field has had a remarkable history. It constitutes one of the great intellectual movements of the twentieth century. It has had a profound impact not only on individual self-image, but on our perception of the world as well. It has altered human sexual behavior in the Western world. It has recruited some of the leading minds of this century and influenced many other aspects of culture. Psychoanalysis, whatever its future, is a central cultural movement of this century.

Nothing separates us more dramatically from the Victorians than our attitude to and practice of sexuality, and psychoanalysis has played the greatest role in the sexual transformation of this century's culture. What an eminent French medievalist said of the impact of Christianity on the culture of the fourth-century Roman Empire may also be said of the impact of psychoanalysis on twentieth-century culture: it is as if a dreamer on waking had seen a different constellation of stars in the heavens.

Psychoanalysis offered to twentieth–century men and women a secular form of individual therapy to replace the therapeutic function that had been traditionally provided by religious organizations. Individuals suffer feelings of guilt, fear, depression, and mental agitation. To whom should they turn for help? Ecclesiastical systems traditionally affected people's lives more by their therapeutic responses than by their theologies, although theology conditioned the therapy a particular religious organization provided. The Catholic Church offered the comfort of good works—the sacraments, the moral priesthood, and the miraculous intervention of saints who were contemporaneously embodied in monks and nuns. The more conservative Protestant churches provided the therapeutic solace of belonging to the holy community and the Jewish solution to personal distress was similar. The more evangelical Protestant sects offered the services of charismatic faith healers.

Towards the end of the nineteenth century the therapeutic functions of religious groups carried less conviction. A process of secularization and withdrawal from church and synagogue membership meant that many people, particularly among the educated middle class, turned to novel secular agencies for comfort, guidance, and help with psychological distress. The decline of the therapeutic popularity of the churches is one of the more significant turning-points in the social history of the period. Many explanations have been given for this change: the impact of Darwinism and modern science; the result of the deracinating, materialist urban culture; the disturbing effect on confessional communities of long-distance immigration. One cause of the therapeutic change must be seen in the rise of public education at the secondary level in major Western countries in the late nineteenth century. In order to foster patriotism and avoid religious disputes among different groups, the new state-supported high schools taught a primarily secular culture, and this kind of instruction helped to shape the mentality of cohorts that looked beyond the churches and synagogues of their grandfathers and fathers to supportive agencies in the secular sector.

The religious organizations did not surrender a large segment of their therapeutic role without a struggle. In the twentieth century they took concerted measures to assert their traditional therapeutic dominance. The Catholic Church everywhere tightened up its administration and invested heavily in parochial schools to countervail the state-supported secular high schools. The Protestant churches sharpened their theoretical formulations in the direction of a social gospel or Karl Barth's neo-Augustinianism or a combination of the two doctrines. In Judaism there was a major expansion of the reform or liberal variety, designed to communicate easily with an educated, secularized clientele. Yet the churches and synagogues continued to experience a decline in their role dealing with the emotional and psychological problems of an increasingly educated and secularized public.

Behavioral psychology could offer environmental conditioning as a therapeutic function to this population, but this was a limited service. It was psychoanalysis that could deal on an individual basis with guilt, fear, depression, and mental disturbance. It was psychoanalysis that in the vision of Sigmund Freud aimed to replace traditional Christianity as the therapeutic agency of twentieth–century people, and to a major degree succeeded in doing this.

*   *   *

The Origins of Psychoanalysis

A remarkable early scene in the history of psychoanalysis took place at Clark University in Worcester, Mass. in the year 1909. Freud and Jung at that time received their first honorary degrees from Clark, then a newly founded university, in a ceremony that was the first moment of public recognition conferred upon them. It was Stanley Hall, the president of the University and a behavioral psychologist who was a disciple of William James, who invited Freud and Jung to Clark and celebrated them publicly. Included in the group of guests was the young British psychiatrist Ernest Jones, who later, in the 1950's, became Freud's official biographer. Following this public ceremony, one of the trustees of Clark University whisked Freud, Jung and Jones away to his fishing lodge on the Saint Lawrence, where they spent some days in unaccustomed upscale luxury.

This was the first public display of appreciation for the work of psychoanalysis, and it is significant that it should have occurred in the United States, where psychoanalysis has had warmer reception and greater intellectual impact than anywhere else in the world.

Among the cultural foundations of Freudianism, the Vienna of Freud's time plays a major role. This was a Vienna that was experiencing the political decline of the Hapsburg Empire simultaneously with important developments in the arts. Viennese culture was at the time highly sensitive to the complexities and depth of human emotions, and displayed this affectivity in the rich variety of arts, from music to painting, it was producing. The human possibility of being a monster as well as a saint is a perception that runs through the cultural productions of turn-of-the-century Vienna.

Secondly, Freud's Jewish background ought to be taken into account in explaining the origins of psychoanalysis. He came from a middle-class Jewish family, and belonged to that first generation of liberated Jewish intellectuals which has been described in the previous chapter. His realization of the discrepancy between appearance and reality, fundamental to psychoanalytic thought, can be traced to Freud's intimate experience of a formal religious culture that had lost its vitality, and was brewing, from its very core, motivations that were too deep-seated and novel to be immediately perceivable during occasional visits to the synagogue or the pleasantries exchanged around the Passover table. This is to say that amidst the religious-ceremonial formality that was continuing to be observed, and that was crumbling and becoming increasingly hollow, there were the individual Jews who were breaking away from formalism and moving toward an expression of their personal, individual feelings. The Jewish culture of Freud's time is a dualistic culture in which the formal structure cannot any longer contain and hold back individual experience. This cultural situation is paradigmatic of Freud's psychological theory.

Thirdly, the advancements of nineteenth-century Darwinism must be considered as background element in the shaping of Freudian thought. The claim that human life is governed by biological drives, the struggle for existence and natural selection, once again determined by biological processes, in which not reason but chance plays the determining role, is the fundamental precept of Darwinism. This conception implements the replacement of the notions of reason, teleology and divine purpose by the principle of chance and adaptation to a changing material environment. There is no doubt that Freud saw himself as the heir of Darwin. One of the more interesting books on Freud that have been published in recent years is entitled *Freud, Biologist of the Mind*. It argues that Freud was a biological reductionist who continued Darwin's work, albeit on a microcosmic scale rather than on the macrocosmic.

Not only Darwinian biology but the contemporary advances in physics influenced Freud. Just as the appreciation of the particle, of the microcosm and of descending beneath the surface become prominent in the domain of physics, that is, as physics develops around entities that are invisible not only to the human eye, but even under the microscope, Freud similarly develops an approach to the psyche that seeks the secret, hidden, and mysterious element in human behavior.

At the time that physicists developed the argument of the convertability of mass into energy, Freud was searching for the energy that drives the human psyche, which he discovered to be as dynamic as the energy conceived in physics. Freud repeats in psychology what Einstein and his colleagues were doing in the field of physics—and he did this consciously. He was cognizant of the intellectual revolution in physics. He wanted a similar revolution in psychology.

There is an element of Nietzscheanism in Freud. The Nietzschean search for the undiscovered country and the movement toward a realm that is not immediately experienced but which shall be eventually penetrated, inform Freud's concept of the unconscious.

A more simple, material factor that explains Freud's impact is the use of effective mechanical contraception. The rubber plantations in Malaysia did not busy themselves in the late nineteenth century as much with the production of tires as with making rubber for contraceptives. The discovery of the rubber condom, as the first viable and effective method of contraception, brought into the foreground the role of sexuality in human life. Previously there was not much to be done about sexual desire, except to repress it, unless one were willing to undergo unspeakable hazards. Before the invention of effective contraception, sexuality could not be separated from pregnancy and from its procreational function. Contraception opened up thinking about sexuality in ways that were divorced from its reproductive role. In a way, contraception rendered Freudianism, or at least the questions Freud asked, necessary.

Some recent biographers of Freud have tried to depict unflattering aspects of his personality. He altered a major theory to stave off professional and popular criticism, it is claimed. He recklessly experimented with drug-taking. He mistreated his family and conducted an ugly affair with his sister-in-law. He abused his disciples—so it is said. Despite the attacks and criticisms, Freud remains an imposing personality.

Freud was by nature a dualist. He engaged in polarities, and thought in terms of binary opposites like some other leading thinkers in the twentieth century. Jung was another one, as is Lévi-Strauss. Freud posits the conscious over against the unconscious as the primary duality of his system. Similarly, sexuality is opposed to moral conscience, love to desire, the normal to the abnormal and finally the illusion of Christianity to the truth of secular science.

It must be remembered that Freud was above all a therapist. He certainly did not start as one, but became a therapist nevertheless. Freud was a middle-class Jew who attended medical school even though he really wanted to be a research scientist, more specifically, a research biologist—in a field which was referred to as neurology at that time, and today would be called microbiology. However, Freud could not pursue the career he wished for because he was a Jew without money. While he could enter the medical profession, the prospects of obtaining a professorship at the University of Vienna were, in that anti-Semitic era, very remote. His family enjoyed modest circumstances, and he could not take the risk of choosing a profession that did not guarantee a living.

He got engaged when he was quite young. The engagement lasted five years, during which time his fiancée did not have sexual relations with him. (It is curious that Freud's uncle by marriage was the founder of modern American advertising, Edward Bernays.) The long engagement put additional fiscal—and psychological—pressures on the young Freud.

So Freud decided to become a psychiatrist because this was the branch of medicine which dealt with neuroses, and particularly with the hysteria of women, and he could practice as a therapist and earn a living. There was a tendency among middle-class women in those days to develop a variety of ticks, physical disorders, anxieties and delusions—collectively called hysteria— which guaranteed psychiatrists more than a modest income. After a brief period of post-doctoral work in Paris, conducted with two distinguished psychiatrists, Freud set up practice in a rather shabby neighborhood in Vienna. He did not leave this location until he had to flee the Nazis in 1938. On the ground floor of this modest building he set up his practice and began to treat neuroses, especially but not exclusively in women patients.

It is important to realize that Freud was a therapist and a clinician. He wanted, that is, to help his patients. All his early theories are based on his experience with patients and on ways of curing them. His theories grew out of his close observation of his patients.

Freud did not have grants to fund his work, nor was he sheltered by an institution such as a university. Even after he became famous, he did not rise at the University of Vienna to a position above that of an adjunct associate professor. At the university he was no more than a shadow that flitted in to give an occasional lecture. Even in the 1930's, with all his fame, Freud's colleagues in the medical school were not friendly towards him.

Freud was a heroic character. He was thoroughly inner-directed, courageous, and bold enough to make pronouncements that were bound to be ill-received and to make him unpopular. He continued in this manner to the end of his career. The occasions in which Freud tempered his statements were very few, if they existed at all. He changed his views, but never became a conformist. He said unusual and uncomfortable, disconcerting things from the beginning to the end of his career. Someone who could insist publicly again and again that children exhibited strong sexual feelings and that Christianity was a dangerous illusion, and say this in Catholic Vienna, had to be someone of extraordinary courage. That Freud rapidly gained fame and success does not detract from the hard road he chose to follow.

Freud saw himself as a Moses, about whom he later wrote a book. He understood himself as the founder of a new dispensation who was leading people toward a new Promised Land, a land of milk and honey where, at last, people could be free and happy. Beginning in his early days, when he was still a poor and obscure psychiatrist, Freud already saw himself as the founder of a school. Freud was the kind of person who, thoroughly rejected by the establishment, proceeds to create his own establishment. Such people are today usually regarded as highly neurotic and as badly in need of psychotherapy.

Within a year after he began his practice as a psychiatrist, Freud was envisaging himself as the creator of a new method, theory and school of psychology, even though he had no disciples and only three patients. He later said that he was an elder son, that elder sons, especially in Jewish families, were smothered in maternal love and developed high opinions of themselves. Fortified with maternal love, they became, among other things, extraordinarily brave. So went Freud's analysis of himself, on which he spent a great deal of time. His self-analysis usually proceeded on self-flattering grounds, but nevertheless he had a rather acute sense of who he was.

Freud was a domineering personality, both in his family and toward his disciples. A typical German *paterfamilias*, he had four children and was interested only in his youngest child, his daughter Anna, who, in turn, never married but who became a distinguished child psychiatrist and his literary executor. His other three surviving children, including his son, he ignored. His relationship with his wife, whom he thoroughly dominated, was quite conventional, almost formal. Although she seems to have been a highly intelligent and courageous woman, he never encouraged her to study, to develop her own mind or find a career. He was content that she raise their children and prepare the meals.

Freud may have had an affair with his wife's sister. He certainly had close feelings toward her, but whether the feelings were acted upon is a matter of dispute among his biographers.

From his disciples, Freud demanded absolute loyalty. He saw himself as Moses leading the Israelites, and those among his tribe who separated from him in order to worship foreign idols, he sent out into the desert to perish. Freud exhibited extremely acrimonious attitudes towards any of his disciples who disagreed with him. He did not hesitate to expel them from his group at the first sign of dissent. One either agreed with him or one left.

Freud got along very well with women disciples. He was eager to train women as analysts and several achieved distinction. The first was Lou Salomé, who had a long career as a courtesan, and had been the mistress of Nietzsche and many others. Becoming first Freud's patient, and then his disciple, eventually Frau Lou emerged as a psychotherapist.

Another of his female disciples was Marie Bonaparte, indeed of the aristocratic Bonaparte family. She became the founder of psychoanalysis in France and a renowned therapist. It was Marie Bonaparte's wealth and influence that saved Freud from the Nazis in 1938. A third woman disciple was Helen Deutsch who was prominent in American psychiatric circles in the forties and fifties.

Further among his female disciples was a leading child psychiatrist, Melanie Klein. A German who had studied with Freud, Klein set up practice in England where she was Anna Freud's chief competitor. A genuinely Freudian scenario of sibling rivalry and bitter psychosexual enmity ensued.

Most of Freud's male disciples, at least in his early years, were Jews. To the very end of Freud's life, psychoanalysis preserved its strong Jewish component, as it still continues to do in the United States. Freud spent a lot of time searching for gentile disciples. Embarrassed by his prominently Jewish following, he wanted a number of blond disciples around him. His unfortunate relationship with Carl Jung was a consequence of this desire—as we shall see. It is not surprising that Freud choose a British gentile, Ernest Jones, as his official biographer. On the whole, the choice was a fortunate one. Ironically, Jones' biography is known today principally not in its original three volume version but in a skillful one-volume abridgement made by a New York Jewish literary critic.

Freud's intellectual history falls into two periods: the first lasts from 1895 until about 1920; the second, from 1920 until his death in 1939. Even though he had contracted cancer of the palate by the late 20's, and underwent several serious operations none of which were successful, he continued to work and write with characteristic heroism until the end of his life. His last major book, *Civilization and its Discontents*, was published in 1930. Freud probably contracted mouth cancer because he chain-smoked cigars.

*   *   *

The Early Freud and Depth Psychology

In the first period of his career Freud produced what might be called the classic Freudian theory, or the theory of depth psychology. In this period, Freud is a reductionist, a microcosmicist, a behavioral scientist focusing on the particle of energy, a Darwinian, in brief a Modernist. The later Freud, on the other hand, was to a degree a cultural theorist who comes close to following Neo-Victorian precepts, and who modifies in significant ways the radical depth psychology of the early period.

There are seven doctrines of the depth psychology of the early Freud. The first is sexual reductionism, that is, the Freudian belief in the primacy of the libido, the sex drive, in motivating human behavior and more exactly, in making humans unhappy. It is the disfunctioning of the sex drive that produces neuroses. Both the individual and society would be far more content, Freud maintains, if the primacy of human sexuality, that we are sexual beings first of all, were recognized.

Freud was very much aware of what he referred to as the ambiguities of everyday life. The ambiguity is owing to the fact that things are not what they seem to be. The formal, immediately visible level of behavior conceals actual deep meaning. Freud posits a line above which resides the formal level of psychic phenomena. Below the line of formal behavior operates that primary sexual desire which drives and determines the readily visible level.

Freud was not the only thinker in his time to have made this claim. His contemporary, the English journalist Havelock Ellis, published book after book on the primacy of the sex drive and the value of sexual liberation. But even though others among his contemporaries assumed approximately the same premise, Freud alone was able to give a systematic theoretical description of this perception of psychic structure and sustain this theory with case studies drawn from his therapeutic practice.

The second aspect of Freud's theory is the assumption that there is no distinction between a normal and neurotic personality. Freud did not deal with psychosis (madness, such as schizophrenia), but with dysfunctions, the illusions of neurotics which prevent full participation in normal life, making it impossible to work and play effectively. Delusions of grandeur or of persecution, anxieties, hysteria, phobias, manic-depression, impotence, compulsive behavior are the anomalies that receive Freud's attention. Freud says that we are all normal and we are all abnormal. We are all equally affected by our sexuality, and by the devious ways of the libido. Freud claims that we never grow up, we can never escape from the libidinal impress upon us. We have no right to be arrogant, to make censurious judgments along sexual lines. We have no right to say that we compared to others have succeeded in repressing sexuality, because repressing sexuality would only make us neurotic and malfunctioning. Freud undresses people and makes them all into potential neurotics at the mercy of their sexuality.

The early Freud's third and most distinctive doctrine is that sexuality begins in earliest childhood. There is no clear distinction, psychoanalytically speaking, between adulthood and childhood. From at least the age of two, there is a strong sexuality in children which Freud finds himself able to identify. The only reason that the description of human sexuality begins with the age of two is that children cannot speak coherently before that age, thus making identification and proof problematic. Children are not innocent, if innocence means freedom from sexuality.

Freud maintained that between the ages two and four, children develop very strong sexual fixations toward the parent of the opposite sex. This, he termed the *Oedipal* feeling (after the Greek myth). According to this theory, the male child is attracted to the mother, as the female is to the father. One of the determinants of the process of growing up into a functioning human being is the capacity to socialize Oedipal feelings, that is, consciously to come to terms with them, to become aware of them and learn to live with them. The Oedipal feeling cannot be circumvented; it admits only of being compromised. When it is simply repressed, it becomes an insurmountable source of neurosis, and opens the way to a variety of disturbances centering on an inability to develop authentic relationships with the opposite sex. The repressed Oedipal feeling, which is always still present, profoundly intervenes in the adult's efforts to establish relationships with a member of the opposite sex other than the parent.

It was Freud's doctrine of childhood sexuality that was most controversial among his propositions, both in his time and since. Even though there were others claiming that sexuality constituted the main drive in human life, no one else had extended sexuality into the realm of childhood. The divestment of innocence from children, the view that children have strong sex drives, erotic fixations upon their parents—these are the Freudian claims that particularly disturbed and disconcerted his contemporaries.

Freud was fully aware of the controversial quality of his views on childhood sexuality. He could not but be aware when it brought down on him the contempt and wrath of the psychiatric faculty of the University of Vienna. But he developed his theory from data obtained from his patients and after discussing the issues with an early associate, Wilhelm Fliess, Freud felt compelled, as a true scientist would, to publish his controversial findings.

Childhood sexuality still remains the most controversial doctrine in Freudianism. As shall be discussed below, most post-Freudians have departed from this doctrine to a greater or lesser degree while preserving other aspects of Freudian thought. With the exception of the child psychologist Melanie Klein and of the radical psychoanalyst Wilhelm Reich, the leading post-Freudian psychoanalytic theorists have either modified or discarded his view on child-hood sexuality.

The fourth Freudian doctrine, a familiar one, is the doctrine of the unconscious. One does not have to look long at the paintings of Freud's Viennese contemporaries such as Gustav Klimt or Egon Schiele or attend for more than a few minutes to a Richard Strauss—Hugo von Hofmannsthal opera to know that in Freud's Vienna the unconscious realm was widely recognized. Indeed the idea of the unconscious had been a prime thesis of early nineteenth-century Romanticism. Freud did not discover the unconscious. He mapped it. He clinically defined its role in human behavior. And he associated the unconscious with sexuality.

Humans have conscious and unconscious lives that impinge drastically on each other, Freud claimed. The unconscious, massively driven by sexual feelings, is much stronger than the conscious. A sexual crisis is not at stake when one peruses a porno magazine like *Playboy*. The sexual trauma operates rather in the depths of the unconscious, when we are engaged in the repression of sexuality, when satisfaction is avoided and sexuality repressed. There are powerful repercussions in the unconscious that shape and possibly impair severely our conscious behavior.

The relationship between the unconscious and the conscious involves "the return of the repressed." Repressed sexuality constitutes the material of the unconscious, becoming unconscious memory, dominating the unconscious, and from there, it works back its way into consciousness in order to shape and determine conscious behavior. The unconscious, therefore, figures in conscious behavior, and impedes it, to the point of rendering the person visibly neurotic, unable to live, work and function as a human being. The repression of sexuality, for the earlier Freud, is not a theological or even a moral issue. It is a health problem, a segment of psychobiology. Neurosis that is always discernible in conscious behavior is the outcome of repression in the sphere of sexuality.

The repressed never fails to return into consciousness from unconsciousness, albeit always in altered form that needs be understood through analysis. While Freud's theories pertaining to childhood sexuality have met with resistance and although they have been modified or rejected even by his disciples, his theory of the unconscious has been accepted not only by specialists, but has even entered into general knowledge and become part of the cultural assumptions of the twentieth century. Just as in the old world, before the late nineteenth century, the man in the street believed, no matter how vaguely, in the existence of sin, so too in this century people believe in the return of the repressed.

The fifth principle of the early Freudian doctrine is the theory of dreams. Freud's first important book, the one that initially gained attention for him, is *The Interpretation of Dreams*. This is one of the more important books of the twentieth century. Freud expected it to become precisely that. The book was published in the latter part of the year 1899, but upon Freud's request, the publisher dated its publication as 1900. Freud knew that his book would have a profound effect on the coming century, and he was right.

In *The Interpretation of Dreams*, Freud argues that dreams reveal the imprint of sexual repression. Dreams constitute a screen upon which the consequences of repression, of fantasies as well as sexually motivated wishes, are projected. Therefore, he claims, dreams are crucial in the therapy of neuroses. One of the two prime ways by which the therapist can look into the unconscious is provided by the analysis of dreams. In fact, according to the tradition that runs back to Freud, analysands are still frequently instructed to keep a notebook of their dreams, in order not to forget them and to be able to report them to the analyst.

The sixth principle of the early Freud is the other entree into the unconscious that is psychoanalysis per se. This is the method of free association by which the patient talks freely under the questioning and guidance of the therapist, and eventually, so the expectation goes, reaches the point of catharsis when the unconscious makes itself conscious. The analysis is successful, in other words, when the repressions imbedded in the unconscious are clearly articulated.

The process of free association, along with the interpretation of dreams, are the two prime mechanisms by which psychoanalysis operates. Freud tried other means. Early in his career, he tried drugs, particularly cocaine. Like many medical researchers who, unable to find patients who will accept the risk of trying a new method and use themselves as subjects, Freud experimented with cocaine on himself. He decided to quit when he began to develop an addiction to it. The other method he tried was hypnosis, in which he had been trained while studying with Charcot in Paris in 1885. He also abandoned the hypnotic method because it met with resistance from some people and was therefore unreliable, and secondly, post-hypnotic suggestion posed problems as did other possible side-effects. He therefore replaced hypnosis with free association or psychoanalysis.

Psychoanalysis has two functions. One is to penetrate the unconscious, which requires highly trained, and gifted, therapists. The second function of psychoanalysis is to be the "talking cure." The psychoanalyst and the patient can bridge the unconscious to the conscious, and release the repressed, which has decisive therapeutic effect.

The final principle of early or classic Freudianism is the principle of transference. Transference signifies that in the relationship between the therapist and the patient there has to take place a close emotional bond, a symbiosis as it were, or else the analysis will not achieve its discovery and therapeutic goals. Therapist and patient must become bonded. The relationship can be a very stormy one; it can involve hatred as well as love, but it is necessary that there be the emotional involvement of transference for psychoanalysis to occur.

The psychotherapist himself or herself must undergo not only a very rigorous training, but complete psychoanalysis as well, which can last anywhere from five to twelve years, and which is absolutely necessary. This requirement, incidentally, is something that keeps some candidates from becoming analysts. Not only the duration, but also the requirement that the analysis be complete, represents an obstacle to them. While it is possible to become a surgeon without ever having to undergo an operation, it is not possible to become a psychotherapist without subjecting oneself to the process of transference with another psychoanalyst. In this training period, a very close bond is established between the psychoanalyst in training and the training psychoanalyst. The transference then is extended from the now-trained analyst to his patient, so establishing a chain of transference.

In some ways, the history of psychoanalysis is like the history of early Christianity: the immediate apostles of Jesus were followed by the bishops, the shepherds of the flock, who had been the disciples of the Apostles, and so on through and infinite chain of laying on of hands. The history of psychoanalysis recapitulates, in a way, this history of the early Church. Every psychoanalyst stands, at least in principle, in the pyramidic chain of analytic transference going back to Freud himself.

Freud's early life and career have undergone enormous amount of inquiry and are still being intensely debated. The official biography of Freud by Ernest Jones published in the 1950's under Anna Freud's scrutiny softpedalled some key issues. Not all of Freud's writings surviving from his early period have yet been made public. Freud's daughter Anna Freud, who died a couple of years ago in England where she had migrated with Freud in 1938, appointed herself the guardian of his writings. She and other aging disciples of the master suppressed some of the early material. Recently Freud's revealing correspondence with an early colleague and associate, Wilhelm Fliess, has finally been made public. But this does not exhaust the writings that still await publication. The material that still remains inaccessible is mainly in the Library of Congress.

Freud has recently received some rather bold criticism from a young psychoanalyst and historian of psychoanalysis, Jeffrey Masson, who raised such a storm that he was expelled from the psychoanalytic association. Nevertheless, what Masson has to say is worth listening to, even though he has articulated it in a highly polemical way. And there have been other critics of the early Freud.

First of all, it is pointed out that Freud's use of cocaine can be seen as proof that he was quite a reckless man in his early years. Perhaps it was so, but then, the use of drugs was much more common and not socially censured at the beginning of this century. In fact, in the nineteenth century, opiate-based cough syrups and other home remedies were widely in use. The use of drugs was rather thinly disguised in the nineteenth century, even in fashionable circles. Therefore, Freud's use of cocaine cannot be regarded from the perspective of today's controversy; it was not a highly controversial act in his day. As a matter of fact, the condemnation of hard drugs began only in the 1920's and was an offshoot of Prohibition.

The second argument about the early Freud is the particular point that Masson has made. Masson claims that Freud began by believing that having been abused while a child was a common experience among his patients and that many of their problems stemmed from these experiences of sexual abuse. Soon Freud abandoned the theory which his data indicated, Masson has said. This claim of Masson's caused nothing less than a storm among psychoanalysts.

According to Masson, Freud backtracked and changed his theory to claim that patients had fantasies of being subjected to child abuse, and that actual abuses had not occurred. Masson accuses Freud of lacking the courage to continue to report on the actual experience of his patients. Insisting on the reality of child abuse as the source of neurosis, Freud concluded (according to Masson), was not a socially acceptable proposition. Even today it would be immensely controversial.

If Freud indeed backed off from the child abuse theory because of the opposition it would encounter, then this was the only time in his life that Freud lacked the courage to report truthfully on his findings. However, we know from the recent controversies that have sprung up around child abuse, that this is an area that does not admit of easy probing. To accuse Freud of lacking courage is to accuse him of highly uncharacteristic behavior. Freud's revision of his earlier claim seems simply to have been the result of a change of diagnosis. It seems that he had decided, after talking further with patients, that the child abuse accounts were regressive fantasies rather than actual experiences.

A third critique of the early Freud is that he was a male chauvinist whose view of women was arrogant and excessively masculine, and that Freud could not, after all, break with nineteenth-century culture. Freud reported that many of his women patients had a sense of inferiority towards men. He reported on a phenomenon he termed "penis envy," that in analysis his female patients exhibited a wish that they had been males, and that this was part of their problem. These women, he held, were not able to come to terms with their own sexuality, and saw and judged themselves only in relationship to male sexuality. Part of this problem came from very strong Oedipal feelings on the part of women who had had intense attachment to their fathers, which in turn rendered them incapable of having full sexual relationship with men or coming to orgasm.

As a consequence of this, beginning with the psychiatrist Karen Horney in the 1940's, and developing with the feminist movement of the 1970's, Freud has been severely criticized as being anti-feminist. This position on Freud is again unfair. Freud was reporting what his patients told him, and these patients lived in a male-dominated world. They experienced a society in which even affluent women faced serious difficulties developing an image of themselves that did not take the male as its model. Freud was, to an extent, culture-bound, and he did not explicitly condemn this situation. But neither did he condone it; he simply reported on the psychoanalytic situation of his women patients.

If Freud were working today, he would report this sense of inferiority on the part of women much less commonly, since the feeling of inferiority towards males has been in the meantime often replaced by different problems which, however, are still frequently gender-specific. Freud was thus an observer and reporter of what the culture of his time produced in his female patients. It is difficult to see how he can be condemned for reporting the scientific truth that he found operating among his contemporaries.

Furthermore, no other twentieth-century thinker has contributed to the sexual liberation of women as much as Freud did. He had many women patients, but he also had many women disciples, whom he treated as equal to his male disciples. He accepted and encouraged them as psychotherapists. Among professional men of his day, he was far in advance of most in accepting women freely as colleagues.

Freud tried to help his women patients recover from mental illness, and from the terrible repressions of Victorian society. He helped them come to terms with their severe Oedipal problems, and tried to show them that their so-called hysteria was a result of sexual repression, and that physically and morally there was nothing wrong with them. Although Freud has paradoxically become a bogeyman for aggressive feminists in recent years, in fact the psychoanalytic movement marked a major meliorative turning point in the cultural status of women. That Freud is not a radical feminist of the 1970's does not need to be reiterated, but then, he lived and worked in the male-dominated society of early twentieth-century Vienna. A leading British feminist psychoanalyst, Juliet Mitchell, has in recent years come to Freud's defense against feminist censure.

The fourth accusation that is commonly directed against the early Freud is that he romanticized his autobiography by presenting himself as more of a hero than he really was. This is ultimately a matter of judgment and taste. In his own account of himself, the early Freud was an isolated thinker rejected by the academic and medical worlds of his day and subject to intense professional as well as popular criticism. This self-view is somewhat exaggerated. But anyone who works against the stream and must encounter as much antagonism on so many fronts as did Freud, is prone to such over-rationalization and dramatization.

It is true that as soon as Freud began to publish his work, he found disciples. He ceased to be alone. He found brilliant young people to support him not only in Vienna, but in Switzerland, Germany, Hungary, Britain, Italy, and after 1914, in the United States as well. He gained the attention and recognition of a very large segment of the more intelligent psychiatrists of the rising generation. Nevertheless it is also true that he became the butt of the press, that he was condemned from the pulpit, and, most important for Freud himself, he was rejected by the medical establishment, and particularly by the department of psychiatry of the University of Vienna.

Freud saw himself primarily as Viennese, and to be publicly condemned nearly every time he delivered a lecture or presented a paper at the University of Vienna, especially before the First World War, must have been deeply disappointing for him. The Viennese scene became disagreeable, if not ugly, for him as the leading professors of psychiatry pilloried him. The feeling of rejection he experienced in Vienna and in his own university remained with him for the rest of his life. He may have exaggerated his isolation, but it is understandable why he should have felt as heroic as he did.

Among the most significant products of his early career were Freud's clinical accounts of the actual processes of therapy he conducted with his patients. Two of the case histories he wrote in this period, *Dora* and the *Rat Man*, the names naturally being pseudonyms, are not only among the great works of psychiatric literature, but they also rank among prominent literary works of the twentieth century. Stephen Marcus, literary critic at Columbia University, has said that Freud's clinical accounts are among the great works of Modernist literature, fully comparable to Joyce's writings.

Inspite of, or perhaps because of, Freud's literary capability, there is a problem involving the English translation of Freud. The Standard Edition in English was prepared in the 1920's and early 30's by James Strachey (the brother of Lytton Strachey, the polemical Modernist biographer), with the assistance of his wife Alix. The Strachey translations do not entirely capture Freud's style, which becomes at times extremely facile and almost colloquial. Strachey's translation renders Freud's language and style more ceremonial, high and pseudo-scientific than they were in actuality. Freud is not easy to translate, partly because he frequently employs a simple and direct style. The Chicago psychiatrist Bruno Bettelheim recently published a book in which he claimed that Strachey's translation had engendered a rather stilted Freud that was at at variance with the German Freud. Yet Strachey's service to Freud, producing 24 volumes of fundamental psychoanalytic literature in the heyday of Modernism, was substantial.

*   *   *

The Later Freud and Cultural Theory

As he grew older (1920–1939), Freud became more of a guru, feeling compelled not only to develop means of psychotherapy and a theory to elucidate individual behavior, but to expand on these in order to comprise a theory of culture as well. The result of this Freudian enterprise, although always interesting, becomes at times rather unfortunate. His later theories are not infrequently vulnerable or at least problematic. Certainly, Freud is the case of a thinker becoming increasingly radical as he grows older—not radical in the sense of becoming more politically extreme, but in the sense of becoming bolder in theorizing and in speculation.

Freud was always conscious of and sensitive to competition, much of which came from his own disciples. In such cases, the disciple would be expelled from the Freudian circle, as in the example of Carl Gustav Jung. Jung and Freud were both interested in the cultural implications of psychoanalysis. Freud, always competitive, always insisting that the first and last words in psychoanalytic matters be his, could not resist developing a psychoanalytic theory of culture himself when he saw that other analysts, some of them his former students, were developing this new field.

The radical Modernism of Freud's early period became muted when he undertook the project of cultural theory, and he became idealistic in the philosophical sense of the term, as well as more historicist. A strain of neo-Victorianism began to develop in the thought of the later Freud, but certainly not as powerfully as it does in the work of most other psychoanalytic theorists of culture.

The trajectory of Freudian thought follows the trajectory of Modernism. In the early twenties, when Modernism reaches its climax, Freud the Modernist thinker too reaches his high point. Then, in the later twenties and the thirties, when neo-Victorianism makes headway and Modernism begins to lose ground, Freud moves with the times once again, modulating his radical Modernism in the context of a cultural theory.

Nevertheless, Freud's ideas from the later period are extremely interesting, delightfully bold, and have certainly roused much interest in the last twenty years. The resurgence of interest in Freud in the last two decades has been mediated primarily by the field of literary criticism, as well as by social and political theory. This resurgence has drawn more upon the later Freud than upon the early Freud.

The thoughts of the later Freud can be summarized in five principles. The first feature of later Freudianism is the viewing of life in terms of a dualistic conflict. On the one side, Freud posits "the pleasure principle," which is rooted in the libido or the sex drive. On the other side, there is what he calls "the reality principle," which is generated by the family and social institutions. Life, according to this conception, is a struggle between the pleasure principle and the reality principle, between the sex drive and the social institutions which surround us.

In his later writings, Freud develops new terms to describe this dualism, and articulates it as the struggle between *Eros* and *Thanatos*, two Greek words meaning "love" and "death." In Freud's view, the new terms were substantially expressing the same contention as the one expressed by the opposition between the reality and pleasure principles. The pleasure principle had become Eros, and the reality principle, Thanatos. The identification between the two sets of terms is not unproblematic, for it is not easy to see how the family and other social institutions can be equated with death. In any case, Freud understood himself as restating the same dualistic conflict the former pair of principles entailed.

Freud's dualistic conception introduces a biological dimension into the psyche which is contained in Eros and felt as pleasure. Thanatos, on the other hand, introduces a cultural and social principle which represents reality. The concepts of Eros and Thanatos opened up new possibilites for literary theorists to pursue in the last decade.

It is particularly in the context of this dualistic conflict, that Freud undertakes the critique of religion in the Judeo-Christian tradition. He says that the Judeo-Christian tradition is an illusion which impedes us from achieving appropriate compromise or transference, or concordance or symbiosis, between the pleasure principle and the reality principle. Theistic, puritanical religion is an illusion which impedes our efforts to attain a harmonious, healthy and functioning life, and repressively allows the sex drive to operate only within the limitations of the family and social institutions.

Therefore, religion makes life dysfunctional and induces neuroses. It does not allow for a personally effected compromise between reality and pleasure, or between biology and society, Eros and Thanatos, and it overweights the scale, producing unhappiness. As he grew older Freud became increasingly severe in his treatment of Christianity. Doubtlessly, the anti-Christian stance is not born suddenly with the later Freud. It is present in his earlier writings, too, but in the 1920's assumes a deliberateness and polemical edge that cannot be found in his earlier work. He devoted an entire book, entitled *The Future of an Illusion*, to the condemnation of Christianity and its abortive impact on human life.

The second principle of later Freudian thought is the famous three-fold division of the psyche into the *id*, the *ego* and the *superego*. The division caught on, so to speak, in the pop world, it entered the media, and became very well known in the 1930's. By this famous triad, Freud tries to map out the psyche.

The id consists of sexual desire. It operates in the unconscious, but is at work as well in the pre-conscious, which is the borderline between the unconscious and the conscious, and to a certain extent, it inhabits the conscious, too. Insofar as the id operates in the pre-conscious, in that dimly known border area, it becomes conscious. The id is Eros, the pleasure principle.

The superego consists of the moral principles, the constraining laws of the social world, which are internalized. It draws on parental authority as well as on the socialization we are subjected to in school, or by any other figure or institution construed as authority. The superego is therefore antithetical to the id. It is Thanatos and the reality principle.

The third component of the psychic triad is the ego, which refers to the conscious personality, as it consciously acts in and experiences the world. It resides between the sexual drive of the id and the constraints of the superego, striving to work out an effective compromise between the two and so to shape itself. Neurosis is precisely the result of an inability to work out such a compromise, and occurs whenever there is an over-powerful internalization of external authority. It is the development of a strong superego stifling the claims of the id that makes for neurosis.

The third principle posited by the later Freud is not as well-known as the concept of the triadic personality, and is propounded in the anthropological work *Totem and Taboo*. Freud's anthropology is bold enough to be called anthropological myth rather than anthropology proper. Freud certainly did not incline to extensive social research. He read only a few books on the subjects he wrote about, which were not always the most reliable ones, but sufficed at any rate to trigger his powerful imagination. So, too, with the anthropological myth, which was developed as part of his great competition with Carl Gustav Jung. Jung was extremely involved in anthropology, and actually took the trouble to gather a large body of anthropological materials.

At times, *Totem and Taboo* can embarrass the reader who admires Freud, but only upon first reading. Freud conjectures a transitional phase between the state of nature and civil society. He takes up the old problem, in other words, which had preoccupied seventeenth- and eighteenth-century political thinkers such as Thomas Hobbes, introduces some anthropology into it, and reinterprets it in terms of the Oedipal principle.

The beginning of organized society, Freud claims, was the result of the primordial killing of the Father by his sexually excited and Oedipally moti- vated sons. Instantaneously appalled by their deed, the sons organized themselves into civil society, the most distinct feature of which was the existence of the superego. In all taboos, according to all religious and moral precepts, the slaying of the father is prohibited. The horrible primordial, Oedipally motivated stain of patricide is thereby inhibited from recurring.

It is interesting to compare the Freudian myth with Hobbes' *Leviathan*. Hobbes claims that in the state of nature, all are at war against all, that man is fundamentally violent and brutish, and that the state of civil society and peace is attained only when power is handed over to the great Leviathan of the state. Only in the absolutist state is the human inclination to violence taken under control. Freud is rendering an updated, psychoanalytic version of Hobbes' theory, limiting to patricide the wider ranging violence that Hobbes had ascribed to pre-civil society. In both theories violence is circumvented and organized society achieved by positing taboos, figured by Leviathan or by the superego. In Freud's account, the establishment of the superego socializes the Oedipal feeling. Social organization came into being in order to control Oedipal feeling.

It is granted that the sexual life of civilized man is controlled and impaired, sometimes to such an extent that it causes neurosis. The function of psychotherapy is to provide a counter-veiling mechanism which enables one to deal with the limitations of sexuality that are necessary in civilized society. A terrible act in the distant past, a sado-masochistic one, that is endemic to human nature, has necessitated the development of a superego and attendent repressive social institutions. On the other hand, society must not go too far in the other direction. The same society that curbs the sexual drive must allow enough room for sexuality for the human race not to be become entirely neurotic. Psychotherapy helps find the balance between the two extremes.

The fourth principle of the later Freud, which is already implicit in Freud's anthropological myth, is that all existing social and cultural institutions, especially art and government, are the consequences of the sublimation of sexual desire. It is because of our need to control our sexual drive in civil society that we have mediating institutions. In this effort to control the forces of the psyche and to achieve a compromise between Eros and Thanatos, between pleasure and reality, between id and superego, we generate a cultural superstructure which expresses itself in various ways, of which art and government are perhaps the most significant.

The conception of social and cultural institutions as stemming from sublimation allowed Freud not only to write about Leonardo da Vinci and attempt other art criticism, but it also made his theory somewhat compatible with a particular brand of Marxism that flourished in the 1930's and is now undergoing a vigorous revival, a school of Marxist thought called "Critical Theory," which grew out of the Frankfurt School of Sociology of the early 30's.

The Neo-Marxists of the Frankfurt School and their disciples, who are very prominent today, believed in a cultural superstructure but one that comes out of economic conflict. They believed that institutions were generated out of the material conflicts in society. Freud, on the other hand, thinks that the superstructure develops out of sexual conflicts. Because of this particular Freudian conception, some Marxists thought that they could achieve a Freudian Marxism or a Marxist Freudianism. They could, that is, join together

Marxism and Freudianism and develop a theory of the cultural mediation of sexuality as well as of class conflict. This constitutes an important strand in radical thought, especially since the 1960's.

The final principle to be found in the late Freud is implied by anthropological myth, and is presented in his last book, *Civilization and its Discontents*. Long before the atom bomb, even before the Second World War (although by 1930 there were signs of imminent catastrophe) Freud, an anticipatory prophet of the nuclear age, was concerned that humanity was on the way to self-destruction. He argued for what might be called common sense or a middle way, saying that the repression of sexuality through social codes, the sense of guilt, and the bourgeois family are the price we have to pay for civilization.

Ultimately, Freud favors neither license nor repression, but opts for a middle path which will both enable civilization to preserve itself, and at once to acknowledge and relax its terrible grip on inherent human tendencies. The violent, destructive and sexual drives exist. This must be acknowledged. Sexuality cannot be repressed to the extent that we all become impaired. A balance must be struck between sexual repression on the one side, and sado-masochistic license on the other. Civilization resides precisely in this balance.

Civilization requires a cultural mediation. Culture incorporates the sense of guilt, but the sense of guilt, in turn, must not suffocate the sexual drive. There has to be a freedom in personal life, which cannot, however, grant the freedom to destroy other people. That the primordial feelings of man tend toward the sado-masochistic, towards destruction and patricide, does not justify fascism. It does not justify delirious violence, mass destruction or even unrestrained promiscuity. In the end, Freud opts for control and for the reality principle, but the reality principle he recommends does not totally annihilate or viscerate the sex drive.

Here too resides the importance of psychoanalysis. Psychoanalysis teaches the control of license, of patricide and primitivism, but at the same time, it helps create the space within which the individual can live without being emotionally viscerated. Freud knew very well that Western man stood on the brink of the volcano.

*   *   *

Jung

Freud's psychology, particularly the one of the earlier Freud, is referred to as depth psychology. Freud is here trying to deal with human behavior as it comes from the deep structures of biological drives. Subsequent development in psychoanalysis departs from Freud in two ways: first in developing what is called ego psychology, as a conception of psychology that is distinct from the Freudian depth psychology. It is sometimes also referred to as interpersonal psychology, and entails for the most part the study of adult psychology.

Ego psychology de-emphasizes childhood and the sex drive, or at least substantially reduces its importance. This approach tries to consider adults in terms of their personality or ego in relation to their social and cultural context. Ego psychology begins from Freudian principles, but it all but eliminates the theory of childhood sexuality and determinism, and greatly reduces the central importance of the depth of the sex drive. Instead, it concentrates on the functioning adult ego in relation to the social environment.

The other significant departure from Freud in modern psychology is effected by what might be termed radical Freudianism. This approach rejects Freud's plea for compromise between the pleasure principle and the reality principle. It rejects social control, and advocates the maximization of the pleasure principle and the unlimited achievement of sexual satisfaction. It condemns every social limitation that impedes the attainment of total gratification, and attempts to envision a world in which society is organized so as to allow for maximum pleasure. It looks upon Freud's compromise as a betrayal of his own premises, and interprets later Freudian theory as a conservative regression, and his compromise not as one aiming at self-preservation, but as one that yields to Thanatos.

These two branches in post-Freudian psychology do not, of course, exhaust all the nuances of later psychoanalysis, but are large enough to outline the main tendencies. Freud had to encounter both veins of departure in his own lifetime, and dealt with either side by means of denunciation. His great disappointment was with Carl Gustav Jung.

In 1909 when Freud received his first honorary degree from Clark University in Worcester, Massachusetts, so did Jung. It was Freud himself who had brought Jung with him in order to introduce him as the crown prince and his intellectual heir. On the way to the United states, Jung had a dream in which he killed Freud. Freud did not realize the significance of the dream, until a couple of years later Jung began to publish papers which sharply conflicted with Freud.

Carl Gustav Jung lived until 1961. He graduated from medical school and began to study psychiatry in his native Switzerland in the year 1900. He was a very brilliant, precocious person and rapidly moved to the front rank of Swiss psychiatrists who were already famous at the time for their clinical work. Jung worked for several years in a mental hospital. He read Freud's *Interpretation of Dreams* and was favorably impressed by it. Without entirely agreeing with him, he felt that Freud was a major figure who deserved respect.

Jung wrote to Freud, and so began the vigorous correspondence between the two psychoanalysts. Jung visited Vienna, and there were close contacts between them from 1908 until 1912. Freud was very conscious of the fact that most of his early disciples were Jews, and that the medical faculty at the University of Vienna were mocking Freud and his psychoanalysis for being a Judaic heresy. Freud was therefore eager to find gentile disciples, and certainly no one could be more gentile than Carl Gustav Jung who had descended from a long line of Calvinist ministers.

Jung was not only a gentile, but a devout Protestant as well, in addition to being a brilliant psychiatrist who was already greatly respected in Switzerland. So Freud rashly proclaimed Jung his disciple and intellectual heir—a designation, to be sure, which Jung never sought. Jung never said that he fully agreed with Freud, nor did he ever see himself as the heir of Freudianism. He continued to do his own work and eventually published papers that made it clear that he fundamentally disagreed with Freud in a number of very important areas. The only two areas upon which Jung agreed with Freud were the use of psychoanalysis and the importance of dream interpretation. When Jung began to publish his papers and the insurmountable differences between the two thinkers became evident, Freud denounced him as a traitor and expelled him from his circle.

Jung did not accept the theory of infant and child sexuality. He claimed that his clinical findings did not sustain the Freudian hypothesis. He rejected it, therefore, on clinical, scientific grounds.

Secondly, Jung rejected sexual reductionism. Even though he agreed that there was a strong sex drive at work through the libido, he nevertheless found that the libido was not a purely sexual force. It was, he said, a generalized psychic energy of which sexuality constitutes only a part. In Jung's own words: "Reality is not to be understood as a sexual function." No statement could articulate more clearly a fundamental diversion from the Freudian conception of psychic reality.

Thirdly, whereas Freud never dealt with psychotics and treated only neurotics, Jung, whose earliest work took place in mental hospitals, was very interested in schizophrenics. Indeed, one of his later patients was Joyce's schizophrenic daughter, whom Jung tried to help but could not, probably because her illness had already advanced too far. Jung propounded an innovative theory about schizophrenia. He found that in certain cases a genetic predisposition was at work. But in most instances, he claimed, schizophrenics had suffered a terrible trauma which had produced a biochemical reaction, "a toxin," in the brain.

Schizophrenia can totally remove a person from the world, making him unable to speak, to eat—these catatonic schizophrenics are often fed intravenously—and to enter into any form of interaction with the surrounding world. Or else, it makes the person hysteric, uncontrollably violent, so as to necessitate physical restraint of the patient. Jung traced this mental state to the production of a toxin in the brain, caused, in turn, by a trauma. While Freud acknowledged that Jung's conception of schizophrenia as the result of a biochemical alteration in the brain was possibly correct, he himself insisted that there had to be some kind of link between schizophrenia, or any other form of psychosis, for that matter, and sexuality. Jung, however, did not find that the originating trauma had necessarily to be a sexual one. Indeed, he found that extremely unhappy family life could in itself constitute a trauma strong enough to cause psychosis. Unlike Freud, Jung could conceive of a variety of situations which could prove so painfully traumatic for a person as to produce a biochemical reaction.

Jung claimed that he had some success in treating schizophrenics, and especially in the first half of his career he devoted himself extensively to their care. He proposed that paying close individual attention to the schizophrenics, placing them in novel beneficial environments, and assigning them simple work tasks obtained positive results in some instances. The illness is not entirely hopeless, in other words, but it requires careful, close work with the patient. Jung's method of working with schizophrenics was continued in the 1960's and 70's by the British psychiatrist R.D. Laing. Jung's approach to schizophrenia anticipates later research undertaken by others.

That there is a biochemical problem involved in schizophrenia, and that some melioration can occur through individualized treatment are only two of Jung's major contributions to psychology. Just about every precept in modern psychoanalysis and psychiatry that was not invented by Freud was suggested by Jung. His mind was almost as fertile as Freud's.

Jung also devoted attention in his early work to establishing personality types using non-sexual criteria. This attempt particularly annoyed Freud and his disciples, who claimed that Jung's nonsexual personality profiles were banal and useless, representing an absurd and unwelcome return to Victorianism.

It was Jung who invented the personality polarity of extrovert and introvert—a distinction that describes personality with respect to the individual's relationship to his environment, in terms, that is, of negative and positive responses to the world. On this basis, Jung worked out what he understood to be the entire spectrum of personality types.

This Jungian work is no longer considered very important, but from the 1930's through the 1950's, the extrovert/introvert dichotomy was very commonly pursued by therapists and psychologists. In the 1950's the Harvard sociologist David Reisman, in *The Lonely Crowd*, developed Jung's personality polarities into the concept of inner-directed and outer-directed people. The social psychologist William Whyte in *The Organization Man* applied the Reisman model to white collar workers in large organizations. The terms inner-directed and other-directed, which are direct adaptations of the corresponding Jungian concepts, entered everyday language in the fifties and sixties. A cottage industry developed in sociology and the media to cultivate this personality model. The concept found its way even into a novel and film entitled *The Man in the Grey Flannel Suit* which featured the other-directed person who was fit to work for large organizations and commute to the suburbs. The leftist wave of the sixties' countercultural movement dismissed this notion from the rather central place it had come to occupy.

By the 1920's, Jung had developed a very strong interest in mysticism and religion. He began to acquire data, mostly from libraries, and became an expert on oriental religions, concentrating mostly on Buddhism, Zen and yoga. If Freud had been the biologist of the mind, Jung, it could be claimed, was the anthropologist of the mind, who elaborated a complete anthropological theory of the psyche. This eventually developed into the Jungian model of the collective unconscious and the theory of archetypes—the doctrines for which he is best known and to which he devoted the last thirty years of his life. He published prolifically the results of his studies which were always based on anthropological data.

In 1928, when he first enunciated the theory of archetypes, Jung said that the structure of the unconscious was independent of individuals. This, of course, once again implies a strong conflict with Freud. There exists, Jung claimed, a universal psychic realm, the collective unconscious, in which the individual unconscious participates. The universal unconscious exists in and for itself, discrete from the individual. The universal collective unconscious is composed of mythological archetypes which play an active role in our psychic development.

The archetypes are known to us, partly through religion, and partly through literature and art. They are also embedded in our unconscious. They have a developmental as well as a therapeutic value, providing the channels through which we develop as human beings. To understand the world, to constitute a symbolic reality, which is tantamount to making sense of the world, we use these archetypes which we perceive in varying degrees of dimness and clarity. The archetypes can be described as the mythological guidelines which comprise the tracks of human behavior. The more we discover these tracks, the more secure we will feel about our development. The universal symbols point back toward infancy as well as forward to the yet to be realized possibilities of human life.

In the last two or three decades of his life, Jung increasingly propounded this view in terms of what might be described as a structural, neo-idealist historicism. He wrote that "the collective unconscious is an image of the world that takes aeons to form." There are certain features which have crytallized in the archetypes in the course of time, and these constitute "the powers" that rule the psyche. The development had begun already in the primitive world, and found its elaboration particularly in the great religions of mankind.

Archetypes are universal structures that allow us to develop personally, and to endow the world with meaning and order. Dreams are important because they reveal the workings of archetypes. In the symbolic implications of dreams, we can observe the connection between our individual unconscious and the universal. So, whereas for Freud, dreams constitute the screen which reveals the dysfunction of the individual sex drive, for Jung dreams represent the screen on which the associations between our individual psyche and the universal archetypes or collective unconscious are shown. Dreams are flashes on a screen which demonstrate the integration of the individual in the universal.

The theory of archetypes sounds mystical, and it is. It sounds neoreligious, which it also is. Further, it is historicist and idealistic. After about 1928, Jung turned away completely from Modernism and classic Freudianism, to a religiously-based idealistic and historicist stance. He anticipates Lévi-Strauss by noting in the archetypal symbols the presence of a strong duality at work. Like Lévi-Strauss' structures, Jung's archetypes come in pairs. Paradoxically, although Lévi-Strauss acknowledges a debt to Freud, his 1955 autobiography never mentions Jung. Nevertheless, the Jung of the 1930's resembles the Lévi-Strauss of the 1950's in some important ways.

In his later writings, Jung becomes increasingly religious as well as increasingly defensive about religious revelation. While the later Freud denounces religion as an illusion which wrecks mankind and destroys the balance of culture, Jung advocates revelation as "unveiling the depths of the human soul." No wonder, then, that Freud could feel as obsessive as he did on the subject of

Jung. Jung assumed the shape of Lucifer in Freud's mind, the fallen angel who committed the great betrayal.

Jung's influence in the English-speaking world was very small until about twenty years ago. This owes primarily to the fact that his work had not been translated. Jung is very difficult to translate because of the mystical and emotional qualities of his writing. Jung resembles Heidegger in terms of his career and impact outside of the German-speaking world. Like Heidegger, Jung is difficult to translate and it has taken a long time, in the case of both thinkers, for the writings to be rendered into English.

In the 1950's, a member of the Mellon family became a devoted follower of Jung, and established the multi-million dollar Bollingen Foundation whose principal function has been to translate and publish all of Jung's works, which comprise well over forty volumes, into English. The series has been published by Princeton University Press. So it is only in the last two decades that Jung's writings have become available in English. The Bollington translations of Jung are skillfully executed and beautifully printed. Jung had to wait a long time for his English face, but he was more fortunate than Freud in the final result.

There is a further similarity between Heidegger and Jung in that the latter's reputation was also scorched by his affiliation with the Nazis. In 1933, the Nazis established an anti-Freudian, Jew-free psychiatric association. Jung allowed himself to be designated the president of it. He did not occupy the post for more than a year, but did deliver a speech in the capacity of president in which he was critical of Freudian depth psychology, making remarks that could be construed as racist. The remarks are ambiguous, but allow for racist interpretation, especially since they were made in 1933. A year later, Jung resigned from the Nazi psyciatric association, and separated himself wholly from the Nazis long before Heidegger did. Of course, Jung was safely in Zurich, Switzerland, whereas Heidegger found himself in Marburg, Germany.

Jung's short-lived flirtation with the Nazis seriously damaged his reputation outside of Germany in the thirties and forties. It is only since the mid-sixties that this unfortunate association has been largely overlooked or forgotten. Furthermore, the rise of the counterculture in the 1960's, along with the accompanying interest in oriental religions and the fascination with archetypes, certainly contributed to stimulating interest in Jung. Jung's reputation is very much on the rise, and it can be anticipated that his influence will continue to grow.

The rise of structuralism in the sixties and seventies also reinforced Jung, because Jung had anticipated in various ways the attitudes, if not always the precise formulations, in Lévi-Strauss and French structuralist anthropology. Furthermore, as has already been mentioned, the results Jung obtained from his early work with schizophrenics, and his belief in the biochemical foundations of psychoses, have been confirmed by the recent trend in the direction of psychopharmacology.

It must be stressed that the later Jung represents very much a departure from Modernism. It assumes the prime form of neo-idealism and neohistoricism, and partakes of the resurgence of Christianity.

The most severe criticism that can be made against Jung is that he was too much a reversion to the Victorian system-builder in the Hegel mold. He wanted to develop a world philosophy that would explain just about everything. We have seen that the later Freud, as distinct from the arch-Modernist early Freud, had some inclinations in this direction also, with not always fortunate results, and partly in competition with his designated rival Jung. But Jung goes far beyond Freud in propounding a universal theory that incorporates all human experience. On the other hand, it is precisely this neo-Victorian macrocosmic kind of speculation that has contributed in a major way to Jung's enhanced reputation in recent years.

Jung's macrocosmic theory of archetypes was easily adaptable to artistic and literary criticism. He had a major impact on literary criticism, particularly in the work of the Canadian scholar Northrop Frye. In his *Anatomy of Criticism* (1957), which was regarded as a manifesto against Modernist New Criticism, Frye contended that the major function of literary criticism was the identification and elaboration of archetypes that are imbedded in literature, and particularly in poetry. Literature is comprised of an "order of words," of structural archetypes derived from "the context of its Classical and Christian principles." When the poet writes, he "imposes mythical form on his content." He makes "adaptations" of the archetypes comprising "Christian symbolism." Criticism therefore becomes archetypal criticism, the analysis of the way the language forms or structures are elaborated in poetry and fiction. Frye's Jungian approach to literature was well received in the fifties, just at the point when Modernist New Criticism appeared exhausted and its proponents to have lost their confidence and enthusiasm.

In 1965 the Yale critic Geoffrey Hartman praised Frye as in Copernican fashion, the "virile man standing in the sun . . . overlooking the planets." A short while later Hartman became a leading exponent of the application of French structuralism to literary theory. Obviously as New Criticism spent its force, the prominent critics had begun to look for a radically different approach, supplanting Modernism with macrocosmic speculation. Frye's Jungianism was immediately attractive. For a few years his Christian typology was regarded as the last word in criticism.

*   *   *

The Radical Freudians

Alfred Adler, the founder of the group of left-wing Freudians, was an early disciple of Freud. Adler was an Austrian psychiatrist who came to the United States in the 1930's. Although he died in 1937, he left a considerable heritage in America, which became particularly powerful in the 1960's. Adler completely desexualized Freud. He did not believe in childhood sexuality, nor did he find that sexual malfunctioning was the foundation of neurosis. Adler was a member of the strong Austrian Socialist Party, which was eliminated by the Nazis in 1938, and he wanted to achieve a just and neurosis-free society— something which Freud did not believe to be possible. Freud thought that a sane, balanced society was attainable, and that neurosis could be individually alleviated, but he believed that the attempt to achieve a neurosis-free society was in itself a dangerous illusion.

The problem, according to Adler, is not related to the libido or to the sex drive. It is posed by the aggressive tendencies in the ego, which stem from a sense of inferiority. Adler was closely concerned with the rise of Nazism, which was of course originally born in Austria—let us recall that Hitler was Viennese—and was as prevalent in the streets of Vienna as it was in the streets of Berlin. He was trying to find what it was that made people aggressive and violent, and to discover the source of what he called "the will to power." In other words, he investigated the dangerous type of neurosis that results in social harm, if not in destruction.

The road to just society ran for Adler through the identification and analysis of the causes of violence. In his view, violent acts constituted overcompensation for a sense of inferiority. Someone who grows up with a physical or psychic disability, if he is financially deprived, for example, or feels that he is ugly or is possibly handicapped in some way, or has a sense of some other kind of inferiority, will try to overcome the sense of deprivation by overcompensating in an aggressive manner. The way in which we can achieve this alleviation of the socially dangerous will to power, this aggressive bent for overcompensation, is to get individuals to recognize their problems without shame or guilt, and to enable them to live with their defects, to integrate their defects instead of going in the direction of overcompensation by harming others.

The biographies of Hitler and other Nazi leaders provide ample proof for the plausibility of Adler's theory. Many of the Nazi leaders suffered from a recognizable social or physical disability which—in Adler's theory—resulted in a paranoid eagerness to harm. In many cases Nazi leaders were extraordinarily brilliant and capable people, but became extremely perverse, hateful and socially dangerous out of an inability to deal with their sense of inferiority.

Adler's emphasis upon adults, his de-emphasis of sexuality, his stressing that the bases of neurosis lie in the dysfunctioning relationship between the ego, or the adult person, and the environment, opened the way to an important school of left-wing psychoanalysis. It also influenced a more moderate liberal American school of ego psychology, whose leading spokesman was Harry Stack Sullivan. This school continues to play an important role in American psychiatry to the present day. Sullivan and the liberal American school of ego psychology, as well as some of the left-wing Freudians, both find their start in the theories of Adler. Therefore, even though he is not very well known today, Adler's heritage in the development of psychoanalysis is an important one.

The approach of the remaining three leaders of the group of left-wing Freudians, Wilhelm Reich, Norman O. Brown and Herbert Marcuse, differs from the theory of Alfred Adler, and is indeed much more radical than Adler's. Reich, Brown and Marcuse believe in the total liberation of the pleasure principle and in the attainment of the full satisfaction of the erotic drive. Thanatos, or the reality principle, is indeed death, according to this group of analysts, and represents the suicidal wish for personal dehumanization and social destruction. In their view authentic humanity can be only achieved by the removal of the social barrier to erotic fulfillment.

This branch of left-wing Freudianism emphasizes the pleasure principle and speaks in the name of the complete triumph of the id. In their view, the later Freud compromised with his own theory, betraying his own early radical doctrines and departing from his biologically reductive theory, particularly in his last book, *Civilization and Its Discontents*, in which he proposed a compromise between sexuality and society. This, in the view of Reich, Brown and Marcuse, was the wrong way to go. We will never achieve either social justice or personal happiness, they claimed, by compromising between the reality principle and the pleasure principle.

Freud's mediative doctrine of culture, as a middle point between sexual freedom and sexual repression, can only lead to personal neurosis and to social oppression. This, in a nutshell, constitutes their fundamental message. It became a very popular message in the late 1960's, and permeated the culture of the New Left. It was proclaimed prominently among the message of the generation that filled the universities at the time, and generally by the rock and drug culture of the late sixties and early seventies.

Wilhelm Reich was an Austrian from Vienna, and a student and disciple of Freud, whom Freud regarded initially as an extremely brilliant theorist and one of his prime disciples. Then Reich became involved with Austrian socialism of a particularly militant brand, which was then, in the 1930's, engaged in street battles against the Austrian fascists. Freud increasingly believed that Reich was becoming too radical and dogmatic, and he finally decided that Reich was mentally ill. He said that Reich was clearly paranoid.

Reich came to the United States in 1938 and became a very successful psychotherapist. He was charismatic and built up a large following both of patients and of disciples. In the mid-forties, Reich moved to rural Maine and established an institute there, a successful one which gathered around him highly capable people. Among the latter was a brilliant young Harvard psychologist who later became Reich's biographer.

Reich upholds, quite vehemently, Freud's doctrine of childhood sexuality, but what he himself was most interested in was the sexual liberation of the adult. Reich increasingly encountered difficulties. He emphasized the special therapeutic value of orgasm, a view which does not constitute a departure from Freud. But he claimed that he could stimulate psychic energy and prepare for orgasm by placing people in an "orgone box." Reich seems to have appropriated some of the theosophic ideas of the 1920's and 30's. He believed in the existence of powerful energy forces in the universe. The subject placed in the orgone box could apply these energy forces to his unconscious in order to stimulate and liberate it. This was a kind of kinetic chiropractic. Reich's orgone box would have been much less controversial today than in the 50's. Reich's belief that the energy system which exists in the individual's psyche and body could be activated and stimulated to improve well-being would be readily welcomed in the 1980's.

Reich was warned by federal officials that selling this orgone box would be fraudulent. The first trouble he encountered was with the United States Postal

Service, and later with the FBI. When he persisted in his sales of the orgone box, he was indicted and convicted for fraud, and sentenced to five years in a federal penitentiary, where he died. His disciples, then and since, claim that Reich had been railroaded during the McCarthy era for his radical ideas, and that he had been the victim of a conspiracy plotted by the FBI. That there was a valid legal case against him is probable. That he was treated mercilessly is also true. Reich was a bit ahead of his time. In California of the seventies there would have been nothing extreme or reprehensible about his orgone box.

Like Adler, Reich in his younger and calmer days sought for a psychoanalytic explanation of Fascism. Reich's seminal book, published in 1934, *The Mass Psychology of Fascism*, is still one of the more interesting and original works on Nazi culture. He argued that the same attitudes and behavioral mechanisms that are at work in sexual repression constitute the phenomenon of Fascism. Fascism is the generalized death-wish, the Thanatos, of humanity. Reich claims that individual sexual repression translates into societal terms as the repression of sexual freedom. Therefore, whatever contributes to sexual liberation undercuts Fascism, and whatever in society favors sexual repression encourages and develops Fascism. Fascism signifies for Reich the crystallization of an aggravated and violent form of traditional repression in Western society.

Reich argues that sexually repressed persons are potential Fascists. They harbor strong Oedipal feelings, engage in behavior patterns that are repressive of their sexual feelings and their authentic humanity. The roots of Fascism, therefore, lie deep in the Victorian family and the repressive policies of Victorian church and society. Reich's is a plausible, albeit partial explanation of German Fascist culture.

Reich also presents the brilliant insight that Fascists in general, and the Nazis in particular, were aware of their connection to anti-sexuality. Their sado-masochistic institutions, their violent and destructive behavior, constitutes a persuasive and fatally attractive alternative to sexual freedom. He locates the root of Nazi violence in sado-masochistic displacement of sexuality. The members of the Nazi movement compensated for their sexual repression through sado-masochism and violence. This insight was later used by Lina Wertmuller in her remarkable film *Seven Beauties*—a film recognizably based upon Reich's theory.

The second of the sexual liberationists was Norman O. Brown, who has lived an interesting life, and certainly a much happier one than Wilhelm Reich. Brown is still alive and happily leading the existence of a guru in the Carmel Peninsula in California. "Nobby" Brown began his career as a classics professor at Wesleyan University and he continued in the same capacity at the University of Rochester. He was a distinguished classical scholar before, perhaps for personal reasons, he began to read Freud, and applied to Freud's text the same close reading he had to the classics. In 1954 he published his most famous book, *Life Against Death*, which was rejected by many commercial publishers and was finally brought out by the Wesleyan University Press. The book met at first with silence and was almost totally ignored, only to become immensely popular in the sixties among the New Left as a Bible of the counter-culture.

Brown published another seminal book in the late sixties, *Love's Body*. He became professor at the new campus of the University of California at Santa Cruz in the late sixties, which became the college of the flower children and of the counter-culture. The students on the Santa Cruz campus of the University of California still spend more time cultivating gardens than reading books in the library.

Brown became very prominent and has continued to write and publish. A saintly, impressive person in every way, he essentially follows the views of Wilhelm Reich, but borrows from Nietzsche as well. He is more interested in cultural liberation than in political upheaval. In his view, sexuality in its fullest cultivation wipes away both individual repression and social oppression. Through intense, unremitting and unending copulation, one can attain Nietzsche's "undiscovered country." Nietzsche had presented the concept of the undiscovered country as an image of transcending nineteenth-century culture. Brown specifies the method of realizing this cultural goal through unremitting copulation.

Through copulation, unrestrained promiscuity, we reach a new cultural plateau. Of course, this message was very much welcomed by the Woodstock generation. However, Brown's greatest contribution is as a cultural theorist, and his influence is mainly in literary and historical scholarship. It must be remembered that Brown never practiced as a psychotherapist, although his knowledge of Freud is deep and professional.

Brown argues that cultural structures can be read as psychoanalytic texts, that the culture of a society becomes a hypostatized, or mediated or raised, substance that can be read and studied as a text. So his aim is in a sense to combine the reductionist radicalism of the early Freud with the cultural theorizing of the later Freud, and introduce into this mixture the Nietzschean concept of the undiscovered country of a new transcendental culture, along with Modernist analytical scholarship. In his second book, *Love's Body*, Brown reads political and social theory as psychoanalytic text, that is, discourse on the "body politic" becomes, in Brown's reading, literally the sexual body politic. He tries to show the psychoanalytic and sexual underpinnings of this familiar concept of political theory.

Brown's work opened up a way for a large group of psychoanalytic cultural theorists and historians of the 1970's and 80's. Among the most prominent of these, are Peter Gay, holder of a distinguished chair at Yale University, Stephen Marcus, chairman of Columbia University's Department of English, and John Demos, who has a chair at Yale University. These highly visible scholars have followed the path opened by Brown in the late fifties and sixties, of in one way or another studying culture as a psychoanalytic text.

The third member of the group of left-wing Freudians, the one perhaps best known through the media because he became a pop figure for a while in the late sixties and early seventies, is Herbert Marcuse. There were times between 1968 and 1971, when Marcuse must have been seen on TV news once a week, haranguing college crowds from San Diego to Berlin in his thick and largely impenetrable German accent.

Herbert Marcuse started out as a member of the Marxist Frankfurt School of Critical Theory, but later came to the United States, where he struggled abysmally for many years, teaching in marginal institutions like The New School for Social Research, or working as an adjunct professor at Columbia University. He published at this time one of the best books published in English on Hegel, *Reason and Revolution*. In the late forties, when Brandeis University was founded, Marcuse was made professor of philosophy there.

In the 1950's and early 60's, Marcuse spoke softly about Marxism and presented himself for the most part as a radical Freudian. In the early sixties, he published what might be termed his best book, *Eros and Civilization*, a radical Freudian tract containing as well elements of a subdued Marxism. Marcuse freely owns his debt to Reich even though he does not entirely agree with him. In the late sixties and early seventies, perhaps overtaken by his new popularity among the flower children and the New Left, Marcuse began to shift more towards attempting a direct synthesis of Marxism and Freudianism. His later work, of which the most important is *One-Dimensional Man*, tries to achieve this synthesis.

The early Marcuse, that is, the Marcuse of the fifties and the sixties who produced *Eros and Civilization*, claims the need to achieve the fullest sexual liberation possible and the cultivation of the pleasure principle. He does note that Reich's interpretation of Fascism is important, but nevertheless he thinks that Reich's model is oversimplified because it ignores economic factors. Yet like Reich, Marcuse himself is a utopian with respect to what he expects a movement of sexual liberation to achieve. He believes that the intense cultivation of sexuality will unleash and magnify human energy, providing that extraordinary capability by which humanity will build the just society.

Through unlimited sexual practices, in other words, we will become not only full, but also super-human beings, which will enable us to ascend to a new social plane and achieve a just society. The sexual superman and superwoman will shake their chains to work like dew, and so create a new society that is both erotic and just. Unsurprisingly, Marcuse's message became immensely popular in the counter-culture of the sixties, and to a lesser extent his doctrine shaped the counter-culture's ideological expression. Thanks to the reception he found in this culture, Marcuse, after being totally ignored for nearly twenty years, became a guru almost overnight, and was lavished with invitations to address adoring multitudes from California to Germany. And once in a while, somebody in the audience understood what he was saying. Marcuse was not a very charismatic person and his heavy accent and opaque Hegelian terminology usually disappointed his audience.

The president of Brandeis was frightened by the discovery that he had a popular radical cultural hero on his faculty, and he refused to keep Marcuse on past retirement. But Marcuse found a ready welcome at the University of California at San Diego. Marcuse is a stimulating and learned thinker, and despite his appropriation by sixties movements, he is well worth reading even outside the context of that counter-culture.

*   *   *

The American School of Ego Psychology

Far more moderate than Reich and his disciples was the mainstream American school of Freudian therapy from the thirties on. The American school of ego psychology is also referred to as the school of developmental or interpersonal psychology. The school is an immensely influential one. The average New York psychotherapist today is likely to be the product of an ego-psychological training. The leading names of the school in its founding period were Abraham Cardner, Harry Stack Sullivan, Eric Fromm and Karen Horney, all of whom were well-known and important intellectual figures in the forties and fifties in the United States.

The American school emphasized the role of social conditioning in the formation of the psyche. It was the spokesman of the reasonable, moderate and liberal life. It de-emphasized sexual reductionism, and although it sought a happy sexual life for people, it did not nurse utopian expectations. The "undiscovered country," as well as magnified human energy through copulation and boxes and uncontaminated social justice, were, in the eyes of this school, remote fantasies. While sexuality was central to life, it had to be practiced in the context of social and familial framework.

The school of ego psychology presented a sensible, middle-of-the-road approach. It greatly admired John Dewey, and certainly could be seen, particularly as manifest in the work of Cardner and Sullivan, as an offshoot of the American philosophical school of pragmatism. Cardner was prominent in the late thirties and forties at which time he was a passionate advocate of the New Deal and a great admirer of John Dewey. He believed that personality is to a very large degree culturally conditioned, and that it is related to the needs of social institutions.

The superego, according to Cardner, is *not* the product of menacing repression caused by parental dictates, clerical traditions and social constraint. It is rather a category that society creates over time. The superego simply constitutes the sensible, moral substratum of a democratic society. In a progressive democratic society like the United States of Franklin Delano Roosevelt and Harry Truman, we need not take a negative view of the superego, and instead, recognize that the superego contains mostly liberal and progressive sense. We must, therefore, control our desires and direct our personality along the lines of these progressive ideals. The superego is culturally conditioned, which means that it changes with time, and at least in a democratic society, it can be looked upon as a positive force in life. This view represents a conservative departure from Freud, especially the younger Freud.

In sum, Cardner believes that the New Deal is a good superego. Of course, problems arise when one attempts to practice therapy according to this theory in a fascist or otherwise totalitarian country, but then Freudian psychotherapists do not usually last very long in those countries in any case.

The dominant personality in the American school and perhaps the single most influential figure after Freud himself in the history of American psychotherapy was Harry Stack Sullivan. Sullivan who died in 1949, was particularly influential in the thirties and forties. He began his work in Chicago, developed a large practice in Washington, and later became the most visible psychotherapist in New York. Not only was he the psychotherapist for the carriage trade, but he exercised enormous influence on the training of the new generation of New York psychotherapists, many of whom are still practicing. A reason for Sullivan's influence and power is that he became the hegemonic figure in the New York Psychoanalytic Institute, which accredits about seventy per cent of the psychotherapists in the metropolis.

Furthermore, Sullivan was the prime training analyst of the William Alanson White Foundation. The training analyst is the one who analyzes the candidate who wants to become an analyst and supervises the candidate's early clinical work. Every candidate has to undergo analysis for a number of years before he can become a psychoanalyst himself. Therefore, a significant number of an entire generation of analysts in New York were strongly under Sullivan's influence and, in many cases, were personally psychoanalyzed by him. Sullivan's enormous impact is still felt through his host of disciples.

Harry Stack Sullivan, it transpires, was a medical fraud. He always signed himself as Harry Stack Sullivan, M.D. yet his medical degree was inferior even to those quack off-shore medical schools with which Doonesbury amuses itself. In the early years of this century, down to the time of the First World War, there were many phoney medical schools in the United States that dispensed paper degrees. These were eventually closed down by the American Medical Association, but Sullivan managed to become an M.D. just before the last of these paper mills was eliminated.

Sullivan concentrates on the adult individual and on the need of the adult to "conform"—this is a word dear to Sullivan—to the social environment. Neurosis, in his view, is largely the result of a disconformity or of a conflict between the adult individual and the social environment. While this does not exhaust the problem for Sullivan, it does constitute the key problem. The function of the psychotherapist is to get the patient to adapt and conform to social norms. These social norms, in turn, prevail over personal feelings. Needless to say, this view presents a major departure from Freudian theory.

Society is right, according to Sullivan; individual rebellion is nearly always wrong. It was Sullivan who devised the psychoanalytic strategy which is still used by most psychotherapists in New York. He insisted that the first thing that the psychotherapist must do is to dismantle "the delusion of unique individuality" in the patient. No patient should believe that he is a special person with special problems. The therapist must persuade the patient that he is ordinary with common, universal problems. The initial period of therapy is devoted to convincing the patient of the ordinariness of his problems and the common quality of his identity. Suppose the patient were actually an Einstein or a Joyce? Would Sullivan advocate this approach? Presumably yes, unless the patient were already world-famous.

In the 1930's and 40's, Sullivan's theory had liberal connotations. That is, the people who were in conflict with the social order of the time were often reactionary misfits. The prevailing code was that of the liberal New Deal and of liberal secularism, and people who were in conflict with it were those of traditional or evangelical religious persuasion, and/or who believed in runaway capitalism, and who generally held retrograde cultural or political opinions. In the thirties and forties, Sullivan could therefore be viewed as advocating adaptation to a set of social norms that had progressive and secular content. However, by the 1950's, during the Eisenhower era, those social norms had been replaced by conservative ones which upheld the "togetherness" of the suburban family and the more competitive mode of capitalism. They were the norms of the man in the grey flannel suit, and Sullivan's teaching from being progressive became transformed into a conservative one. Now it was used to brand people who were leftists and socialists or otherwise critics of the establishment as neurotics. This reflexive conformism remains central in the New York psychiatric profession.

Sullivan made an enduring contribution to psychiatry through his work with schizophrenics. Like Jung, he believed that the therapist could work advantageously with psychotics, and he applied his doctrine of environmental conditioning to schizophrenics. He did not think that the "mad," the inhabitants of mental hospitals who were entirely dysfunctional, catatonic or violent, were hopeless. He thought that their problem was one of extreme disassociation from the environment, and he believed that placement in an appropriate environment would benefit many psychotic patients. The approach had been suggested by Jung. Sullivan worked at its application. This practice was continued by the British psychiatrist R.D. Laing in the 1960's.

Sullivan's greatest critic in the American school was Eric Fromm, who immigrated to the United States from Austria, where he had been a student and disciple of Freud. The ego psychology Fromm developed had a strong existential flavor. It bore distinct parallels to the existentialist philosophies of Jean-Paul Sartre and Albert Camus who were prominent in France in the forties and fifties.

Fromm began as a Marxist trying to combine the principles of the American ego-developmental school of psychology with Marxism. His Marxism became more muted with time, even though he always remained a leftist thinker. Ultimately, his approach can be identified as existential psychoanalysis.

Fromm claims that members of capitalist societies suffer from loneliness and alienation in an environment which is dehumanizing. This, of course, is a classic Marxist doctrine. Therefore, the problem of mental health stems from the loneliness of the individual in capitalist society. Unlike Cardner and Sullivan, Fromm does not whistle in the dark, claiming that all is right. He acknowledges that the majority is still suffering from adverse social and cultural conditions. On the other hand, he does not agree with Marcuse either, that capitalist society is totally dehumanizing and that freedom cannot be attained unless capitalist society be abolished as a totality.

Fromm believes that capitalism would yet continue for a while, and the main occupation of the psychotherapist is to teach people how to live in this society—thereby accepting the adaptationist assumption of the American School. And the way to live in it is to make rational choices. We have to learn to live with our loneliness, to prepare to live alone, to recognize that in our daily lives we are going to be in conflict with society. We have to be able to carve out a place for ourselves in a social and cultural environment that is inhospitable. The wrong thing to do is to "escape from freedom," to use the title of Fromm's most famous book which was very popular in the forties and the fifties. The escape from freedom is the work of false consciousness—here Fromm uses another Marxist idea—by which we convince ourselves that this society is good when it is not, and so try to conform to it. Sullivan was wrong. We have to recognize that society is not good, and that the individual is good.

The individual, by making rational choices, stays within himself, often living a life of psychological and physical loneliness, and yet preserves his dignity, knowing that the culture is dehumanizing, and struggles against this dehumanization. This view is the translation, as it were, into psychoanalytic terms of the teachings of Albert Camus. Camus, who was writing at the same time as Fromm, says that the world is absurd, the individual alone is good, and we must live with the absurd, knowing that the only good thing in the world is a good individual. Fromm is teaching essentially the same doctrine, expressed in psychoanalytic terms. Fromm's writings were very popular in the fifties and early sixties and they are still worth reading. There is a tough-minded dignity to his doctrine.

The final leading member of the American school was Karen Horney. Although Horney was influenced by Fromm, she was not as political as he was. She was further influenced by the anthropologists Ruth Benedict and Margaret Mead. Karen Horney was of Danish and German descent. She studied with Freud, came to the United states in the mid-thirties, practiced mainly in Chicago, and died in 1952. Late in her career, she was expelled from the American Psychoanalytic Association, probably because she wrote severe criticisms of Freud and because of her vehement, pioneering feminism.

As a psychoanalytic feminist, Horney was largely ignored in her day and had only a small following. She specialized in treating women patients. Her reputation was marginal until the feminist movement of the seventies rediscovered her. She is now very well known, and her writings have become best sellers in feminist circles.

Horney criticized Freud severely for what she regarded as his excessive male chauvinism. She believed that Freud had mistakenly applied his biological determinism to gender. She argued that gender differences were determined not biologically but culturally. It is moot point whether she was reading Freud rightly. Freud had discovered that his women patients were often conscious of the fact that they were not males, which perception he formulated in the theory of penis envy. It is not clear, however, whether he thought that this gender-sensitivity was a trait his patients had picked up from their cultural and familial environment or whether he thought it an inevitable, inherent feeling. In any case, he did not clearly say that it was culturally determined. Freud probably believed that it was both biologically and culturally determined, whereas Horney argued against any supposition of a real difference between men and women except as the culture makes them different.

One can imagine, Horney claimed, an androgynous culture which can be achieved by transforming the codes and institutions of society. This would remove not only repression from women, but also their consciousness of gender differences. At the same time, male consciousness of gender difference too would undergo transformation. This doctrine has become one of the leading doctrines of feminist thought, although not all feminists subscribe to it. It has a perpetual place in the mainstream of feminist theory.

*   *   *

Psychoanalytic Structuralism

Jean Piaget, Eric Erikson and Jacques Lacan are the three most prominent psychologists of more recent times. They may be described as comprising the school of psychoanalytic structuralism, and since structuralism has become very important in the sixties and seventies, this form of psychoanalysis has fitted in with the dominant cultural movement that will be discussed in a later chapter.

The three masters of psychoanalytic structuralism possibly had a forerunner in Otto Rank who died quite young in 1939 and has only in recent years begun to receive much attention. Erich Fromm denounced Rank in the thirties as a fascist and Freud, with whom Rank had once been very close, also repudiated him. The basic principle of Rank's "Will Therapy" is that we must learn to live with our illusions. Truth does not lie behind these illusions; truth lies in the structure of illusions itself. "This constantly effective process of self-deceiving, pretending and blundering . . . is the essence of reality." The task of the therapist is not to wean the subject away from his illusions but to get him to "learn to live with his split, his conflict, his ambivalence, which no therapy can take away." Freud saw this doctrine as another great betrayal of his message. It is only after the ideas of Piaget, Erikson, and Lacan have gained currency that in his rather crude and unreflective manner what Rank was trying to say has become more clear. We cannot break out of this structure. We have to learn to live with it and confront it.

Of all the leading Post-Freudian psychiatrists, Piaget appears to be least influenced by Freud. In fact, he has created his own system. One can plausibly claim that along with Freud and Jung, Piaget is one of the three most original minds of psychoanalytic thinking.

Piaget had a very long career which began around 1921 and spanned half a century. The greatest influence upon Piaget was the eighteenth century Swiss-French philosopher Jean-Jacques Rousseau, who argued in *Émile*, his book on child development, that a child will develop spontaneously and advantageously through innate structures of the mind. He advised to leave the child alone, not to intervene in the natural development of the innate mental structures. Rousseau further advocated that a pleasant environment be created for the child, within which he could pursue his own development. These psychological precepts were of course in accordance with Rousseau's idealist doctrine that society is fundamentally bad, and the individual good. "Man is born free and is everywhere in chains."

In Piaget's native Switzerland, in Rousseau's hometown of Geneva, there was an institute of child psychology devoted to studying and implementing Rousseau's theory. Piaget was trained principally there, and became, at the age of twenty-five, in 1921, its research director, and shortly after, he was made the head of the Rousseau Institute over which he presided for close to half a century.

In addition to the influence of Rousseau, Piaget acknowledges a debt to Bergson and Durkheim. How much anyone can owe to Bergson remains a matter of doubt. But Piaget's debt to Durkheim is a real one, as we shall see. There are also considerable resemblances between Piaget and some of the ideas of William James and John Dewey. There is a certain overlap in Piaget with the American philosophy of pragmatism.

Piaget's inital assertion concerns a stage theory in the mental growth of the child. He says that, from early age through adolescence, the child undergoes distinct developmental stages which Piaget finds himself on the basis of clinical evidence able to map out and describe year by year. He finds that each stage is marked by very distinct and visible changes which represent the gradual growth in the symbolic capability of the child—the capability, that is, of symbolizing the world and manipulating it mentally and internally. The process, Piaget says, is slow and strictly programmed: a child of four cannot do what a child of six is capable of achieving, and at six, a child cannot accomplish what he will easily manage at the age of eight, and so on. A child is only capable of achieving a certain level of symbolic rationality at a particular age. The child cannot and should not be asked to go beyond what Piaget terms "structures'" or the mental systems and capabilities suitable for his age.

The human psyche matures slowly. It cannot be rushed. Although a good environment is conducive to growth, nevertheless even the best environment cannot make a child of six do what he will not have the capacity for doing until he is eight. Piaget thus enunciates a principle that has become very widely accepted in children's education as well as in many other fields including athletics. Athletes can often be heard these days speaking of "staying within themselves," meaning that an athlete can achieve only what he can achieve. He can, that is to say, go only so far as his structural capacity allows. This is Piaget applied to athletics.

Even though the stages of childhood development cannot be significantly advanced, even under the most favorable conditions, they can be held back. The child can be inhibited by a negative, impoverished, fearful environment. Such environments can disturb the child's mental growth. Therefore, Piaget stands halfway between the idealism of Rousseau and the behaviorism of William James or Harry Stack Sullivan.

The second theory that Piaget develops, something we have already touched on, is that the most important part of mental development, which is fulfilled in late adolescence, is the attainment of a capacity to transform physical actions into mental operations. This capacity represents symbolic perception, that is, being able to perform a physical action as mental operation. It is the capability to see in the mind, to imagine oneself doing something without actually carrying out the action. And the development of this capacity is important not only with respect to performing mature mental operations, but also, most significantly, it enables one to understand oneself as a person, to grasp one's own identity. But if there has not been appropriate childhood development, if the child has grown up in a negative environment and therefore not lived fully through each developmental stage, he will undergo an identity crisis around the age of fifteen or sixteen. He will not be able to imagine and comprehend his identity and so develop an appropriate consciousness of himself—which is to say that he has not fully achieved the capacity for human symbolic operation.

This conception of Piaget approximates Durkheim's notion of *anomie*. A society is anomic, according to Durkheim, when the value system of that society, which signifies its symbolic understanding of itself, is out of phase with the institutional behavior. Similarly, if a child has not been allowed to develop appropriately, there is an imbalance between his external behavior and his symbolic consciousness. This, in turn, produces a poor sense of oneself, which leads to terrible frustration, crime and violence. Piaget would say that if one grows up in a pathological familial and educational environment, the result can be an underdeveloped sense of self. The only available means of self-expression that remains to such persons is socially dysfunctional behavior and ultimately violence, whose cost to society is likely to be formidable.

Piaget was not an armchair theorist. His clinical output was impressive. His theories are always based on clinical, experimental work with children as well as with adults. One eminent child psychiatrist who has been influenced by Piaget is the Chicago psychoanalyst Bruno Bettelheim. Bettelheim is an Austrian émigré and headed for forty years an institute at the University of Chicago for autistic, that is, schizophrenic, children. Bettelheim worked with autistic children along the lines of Piaget's findings. Bettelheim has had more success in his work with preadolescent schizophrenics than anyone else. Piaget's principles pervade Bettelheim's writings. He advocates above all that children have their own distinct culture, and reminds readers that children are not adults and that this simple but important fact should not be forgotten when environments and programs for children are designed.

The most interesting extension, however, of Piaget's theory, is to be found in the work of Erik Erikson, who became a national guru in the late sixties and early seventies, competing on public platforms with Norman O. Brown and Herbert Marcuse. He certainly is a very eminent psychoanalyst. Erikson is still alive, living and writing in California.

If Harry Stack Sullivan had a phoney degree, Erik Erikson, refreshingly honest, had no degree. He had no academic degrees except honorary ones. In spite of his Scandinavian name and Viking visage (which probably contributed to his guru image in the sixties) Erikson was a North German; he got his name from a Danish stepfather. Erikson was Freud's last student in Vienna, and came to the United States in 1938 at the age of twenty-one, and started work in a mental hospital near Boston. He was trained as a lay-therapist and began to publish papers as well as books which rapidly became influential. He ended up as professor of psychiatry at Harvard University. In the late sixties and seventies, he became world-famous.

Erikson essentially has three important ideas. The first of these consists of an application of Piaget's theory of the stages of childhood development to adults. Erikson combined Piaget with Harry Stack Sullivan and the American developmental school. Not only adolescents, but adults as well, Erikson found, go through distinct stages of development, and undergo identity crises approximately once every ten years. In the late 70's, the New York journalist Gail Sheehey wrote a book about this Eriksonian theory, *Passages*, which became a bestseller.

Erikson believes that the development of adulthood is affected both by an internal core as well as by the environment. Personality is significantly shaped by the period and society we live in, acting upon our innate personality. Identity, he says, "is located both in the core of the individual and in the core of communal culture." The innate capability and personality of the individual moves forward in a developmental way, and undergoes periodic crises and adjusts, effectively or ineffectively, to the cultural environment.

The second principle, already implicit in the first, that Erikson propounds is that neuroses have a strong cultural component. They are not fixed as in Freud's view, by the repression of the sex drive, but have a wider range according to period and culture. Erikson claims that different eras generate different neuroses. The form of neurosis dear to Freud's patients was hysteria, Erikson notes, and he agrees that this hysteria was indeed induced by sexual repression. But Erikson identified the emergence, in the 1960's, of a new kind of neurosis, which he called narcissism. Erikson's view of narcissism as a dominant modern form of neurosis was immediatly taken up and popularized by a number of writers. The American historian Christopher Lasch tried to develop Erikson's idea of narcissism into a theory of current social history.

Narcissism is the mental disease of late modern culture. It consists of "an inner uncertainty," Erikson writes, "and purposelessness concerning undefined avenues of life." In late modern culture, people have lost their bearings, their ideals, they have poor identity and lack purpose, which results in the problem that currently constitutes one of the biggest problems preoccupying psychoanalysts: well-educated, affluent people who have no moral purpose and low self-esteem. Narcissism has recently been identified as the common form of neurosis among yuppies, a view not so easy to agree with, since yuppies know very well where they are headed—toward a larger collection of CD's, IRA's and BMW's. There is not much uncertainty among them as to what their values are.

Erikson's third contribution to modern psychoanalysis was his development of psychobiography. Freud published provocative studies of Moses and Leonardo da Vinci but they were too abstract and formulaic to be regarded as biographies. His study of Woodrow Wilson, written in collaboration with the American ambassador to France, William Bullitt, is more of a circumstantial psychobiography, although highly polemical. It was withheld from publication for several decades because it was possibly libelous. In the 1920's, certain writers, most of whom were popular journalists, tried to apply Freudian analysis to circumstantial accounts of personalities of the past. Among them was the German journalist Emil Ludwig, who psychoanalyzed a number of historical people. Ludwig's psychobiographies sold very well, despite the strictures of professional historians against the practice of psychoanalyzing the past.

It was Erikson who legitimized psychobiography in the academic world. He claimed that it was possible, and intellectually profitable, to psychoanalyze historical personalities, granted that enough material could be found about the personality to be analyzed. He strongly advocated the writing of psychobiographies of great personalities, and he himself demonstrated how to pursue this genre with his book on *Young Man Luther*. He explained Luther's development in terms of an identity crisis the reformer had undergone in late adolescence. Erikson, to be sure, did not do original research to write Luther's psychobiography. He relied on standard biographical works, particularly on the work of the prominent German historian Heinrich Boehmer, whose study of the young Luther he subjected to psychoanalytic reinterpretation.

Erikson's other psychobiographical work was on Gandhi. In order to write this, however, he actually travelled to India in order to interview people who had known Gandhi. The latter book is not as successful as the one on Luther. It presents a Gandhi who is too good, too much a latter day Buddha, whereas the real Gandhi was a more complicated, problematic figure, perhaps more Machiavellian than angelic. Nevertheless, the book became very influential, and opened the way to a new psychoanalytic mode of writing.

Erikson outflanked the historical profession which had denied the legitimacy of psychobiography for half a century. With his formidable academic authority as well as popularity, Erikson forced the reluctant historical profession to accept the validity of psychobiography. By the early seventies this genre was at least grudgingly approved by the academic cadre of historians, with the proviso that such work had to be done not by intuition but by scholars whose mastery of psychoanalytic theory as well as historical method was professionally respectable. Such novel historian/psychoanalysts soon appeared in university history departments. Erikson had legitimized them.

Peter Lowenberg of the University of California in Los Angeles, and Rudolf Binion at Brandeis are the two best-known practitioners of psychobiography. Binion does voluminous original research for his psychobiographies. He is also an orthodox Freudian. *Frau Lou*, his psychobiography of Lou Salomé, the courtesan and mistress of Nietzsche become Freudian disciple become psychotherapist is methodologically superior to Erikson's work. Binion's psychoanalytic biography of Hitler, *Hitler and the Germans*, offers a convincing Oedipal account of why Hitler became a psychopathic antisemite.

The third of the structuralist psychoanalysts, who died in 1981, is Jacques Lacan. He was considered the most eminent French psychoanalyst of his day even though he was expelled in 1964 from the French Psychoanalytic Association. His expulsion appears to be mainly due to an allegation that he was abusing his therapeutic practice. Lacan decided that a psychotherapeutic session either brought about transference, an emotional action between the analyst and the analysand, or it did not; and, Lacan thought, if it did not give rise to transference, there was simply no point in holding a forty-five or fifty minute session. Therefore he would tell the patient when there was no transference to leave after five or ten minutes. On the other hand, if transference did occur early in the therapy session, Lacan sometimes dismissed the patient also in this instance, apparently feeling that no more could be accomplished at that session. These idiosyncratic choices on Lacan's part qualified as bad professional practice in the eyes of French therapists and led to his expulsion.

Lacan was a Freudian and he identified himself as Freudian. He wanted to improve on Freud, to build upon Freud's theory without ever essentialy leaving the orthodox line of the early Freud. By the 1930's, Lacan had already developed the rudiments of his own theory, and he published a small book at the time in which he propounded his views. The book went unnoticed at the time of its publication. It was not until the late sixties that Lacan gained wide attention and became the idol of the Left Bank. Not only did he gain a large practice but intellectuals flocked to study with him. He began to give seminars at the University of Paris. No theater could be found that was big enough to contain the audiences for his public lectures. He became so eminent a guru that students began to write autobiographical accounts of the privileged seminars they attended with him. Lacan was now frequently interviewed by the media. Every fragment of a word that dripped from the mouth of the master found its way into print.

Lacan was influenced by Ferdinand de Saussure, a Swiss-French Professor at the University of Geneva from 1891 to 1913. Saussure was a pioneer in the science of linguistics. Lacan made use of Saussure's theory and nomenclature to reinterpret the Freudian system as a psychoanalytic linguistics. Saussure's treatise on linguistics itself had oracular qualities. It was put together from Saussure's lectures and published posthumously, and it is an opaque, difficult work.

Lacan begins by abolishing the ego, claiming that the invention of the ego was a mistake Freud made. Contrary to the superego and the id, which were real, Lacan found that the ego was a fictive construct. What is experienced as the ego is nothing but the balance struck between the superego and the id. The focal point of psychoanalysis, Lacan claimed, must be the interaction of the id and the superego in the unconscious.

Lacan tries to carry on Freud's work of mapping the unconscious, and he thinks that by applying Saussure's linguistics, he can develop a closer map of the unconscious. He says that "the unconscious is structured as a language." The structure of language is the key to understanding the unconscious. Language shapes the unconscious, and an indispensable means of penetration into the unconscious is through the structure of language. The libido is submitted to linguistic order. There is no structure except through and in language. It is the order of words that constitutes the order of things.

Many Freudians found Lacan's pronouncements to be nonsensical, claiming that the Lacanian theory constitutes neo-idealist ravings under the influence of an arcane treatise on linguistics. But particularly in the sixties and seventies, Lacan was taken very seriously, first in France and then, to a degree, in the United States, although his following in this country has been much more among linguists and literary theorists than among psychoanalysts.

The world of words, the world of language, says Lacan consists of "the signifier." The signifier is the creative force that operates in the unconscious and generates and shapes everything else. By everything else is meant the signified. Words and the structure of language constitute the creative signifier operating in the unconscious that shape and order the signified perceptions that make their way into the unconscious. From this, Lacan derives the formula S/s, where S stands for the signifier, and s for the signified. The signifier S is the ordering principle at work in the unconscious by which the experiential material s is organized so as to generate meaning.

Lacan's view is certainly idealistic. It seeks to apply an idealistic theory to Freud, to combine Freudian Modernistic, sexualist reductionism with neoidealistic structuralism. But the merit of Lacanian theory does not reside as much in the elimination of the ego, nor in the formula of S/s—even though there is a genuine insight in the statement that linguistic structures play an important role in the workings of the unconscious—as it does in the Lacanian theory of the Other.

The theory of the Other can also be described as the theory of the divided self. This is really a Freudian concept, but Lacan develops it elaborately. Freud had introduced the notion of above the line and below the line. There is always a shadow personality that accompanies us, an Other that moves with the formal, social person. The Other lives in the unconscious. The idea of the shadow, of the Other, the secret sharer of our lives, the alternative person, is a Freudian theme that cuts across twentieth-century literature.

Lacan says that the Other is "man's radical extraneousness to himself." Man projects and becomes conscious of an Other that is always with him. "Man's desire finds its meaning in the desire of the Other." The Other, the unconscious or alternative self, is a more authentic person that is capable of expressing true desire. "The discourse of the unconscious is the discourse of the Other from which the subject receives his own forgotten message." The message is retrieved from the unconscious in the process of psychoanalysis.

Lacan claims that this Other is Oedipally generated. The Other is constituted in the struggle between the subject and the Oedipal object. The Other is the product of the primordeal estrangement, that is, the estrangement that derives from the subject's struggle against his Oedipal feelings. "The Other is the Name-of-the-Father." Lacan's re-articulation of Freudian theory accommodates Freudianism to literary theory. And that is why, aside from his direct interest in linguistics, Lacan has had such strong impact in the literary field.

Lacan was certainly influenced by French surrealism. Among other things, the jokes and puns that pervade his writings verify this. Lacan thinks that jokes and the use of paradox in language are the means of attaining the truth of the unconscious, since these discrepancies reflect the discourse of the unconscious. Freud in a famous essay had shown that "Freudian slips" and sometimes jokes gave out messages from the unconscious. Lacan extends this observation. The unconscious "always says an-other thing." Every act of speech says something that is an Other. Every discourse has a hidden meaning, the other meaning, from which the unconscious can be elucidated. Similarly, a surrealist like André Breton had said in 1920 that the way to truth lay in thinking in terms of opposites and paradoxes.

This aspect of Lacan is one of the foundation stones of what is called deconstruction. Deconstruction is the view in literary criticism and philosophy propounded by Jacques Derrida, who will be discussed in a later chapter. Deconstructionists hold that every statement deconstructs itself, that behind every statement is a hidden meaning which is very different from the statement's surface meaning. This view is fully compatible with, and in many respects inspired by, Lacan's theory of the Other.

The Other then is a concept that is valid not only with respect to the psyche, but can be applied to any statement or discourse. Every utterance contains an alternative meaning which contradicts the surface truth, regardless of the context in which it is spoken. Lacan is therefore not only a structuralist through his foregrounding of the structure of language as shaping the unconscious; he is also a father, so to speak, of deconstruction. His view that every discourse contradicts itself and harbors another meaning that is not immediately graspable is the foundation of deconstruction.

Thereby Lacan joins Piaget and Erikson not only in developing psychoanalytic theory but also in making a more general contribution to cultural theory.

*   *   *

Radical British Theorists

Two radical British theorists of psychoanalysis are R.D. Laing and Melanie Klein. Laing is from Scotland, a native British psychotherapist, and the head of the London psychoanalytic Tavestock Institute which is devoted to the treatment of schizophrenics. Laing spent twenty years of his career working with schizophrenics. From this work evolved Laing's theories of madness. He increasingly became a general theorist. For a while in the sixties and early seventies, he was very popular among the counter-culture and the New left.

His clinical work with schizophrenics convinced Laing of the destructive role of the family. Jung and Sullivan had already perceived this. But Laing extended their views into a provocative doctrine. In many ways, he found, the schizophrenics were rational personalities. They lived in such terrible familial environment that the only solution and exit out of the situation was either to become catatonic or violent. These people were not mad, said Laing. They resorted to the only approach to survival in horrifying situations. To "go mad" under such dire circumstances as his patients had been subjected to, Laing claims, is a perfectly rational response.

Laing organized his Institute like a commune, providing schizophrenics with a supportive, friendly environment in which they could communicate and work. He persisted in maintaining the semblance of a normal life in the clinic, and he frequently elicited positive therapeutic response from his patients. Laing acquired the reputation of being more successful in the treatment of schizophrenics than anyone else practicing in England in his time.

From this therapeutic base Laing began to propound generally radical doctrines. He asked the simple but interesting question as to who, after all, could be called mad and who sane. He went to the extent of suspecting that perhaps those we call mad were after all the truly sane, and those that are held to be sane, the mad. The "normal," repressed people, it could turn out, were the real mad. Rational society is really mad society, and the more extreme the form of that which we call madness, the more one approaches genuine sanity.

This conception of Laing's began to be used in the sixties as justification for heavy intake of drugs to induce artificial schizophrenia, in order to be able to reach toward a true sanity and to escape from the mad world. It is a matter of controversy whether Laing himself ever preached this pursuit or whether it was read into his work. He himself now claims never to have advocated drug-taking, and that this was a misinterpretation of his work. But the Laing who said this recently in a television interview appeared to be a somewhat calmed-down and sad figure, far removed from the counterculture guru of the sixties. Pirandello in the 1920s anticipated Laing's relativism.

There is an extreme relativism in Laing, characteristic of the sixties and early seventies. If he does not eliminate he certainly erodes the distinctions between sanity and insanity, and claims that we live in a world in which the insane may be the truly rational people. In the days of the counter-culture and the Vietnam War when Richard Nixon was in the White House, Laing had a compelling argument. Whatever his merits as a cultural theorist, it must be stressed that Laing was a formidable psychiatrist and a compassionate human being who helped many abandoned and desperate people.

Melanie Klein was a German, a disciple of Freud, and moved to England in the thirties after a very colorful career in Berlin. (She was famous for all-night non-stop dancing.) She became a very prominent and successful child psychologist in England and died in 1960. When Freud's daughter Anna arrived in England in 1938 to practice child psychology, the two women became great rivals.

If Harry Stack Sullivan can be called Doctor Feelgood, Melanie Klein can be called Doctor Feelbad. An interesting feature of her thought is that Klein is really a Neo-Augustinian. She believed in a secularized version of the old-fashioned Christian view of sin. If we were to go back and read the Puritan writers, we would find that they were convinced that children were full of sin, for which they had to be bound, whipped and checked in every possible way in order to be saved. The Puritan writers conceived of children as monsters. Strangely enough, Melanie Klein came to the same conclusion after decades of work with children.

Children were monsters, Klein found. They were full of aggressive and vicious fantasies, and of fantasies of fear and oppression. Klein does not find that it is so much infantile sexuality that is at work in the child's psyche as infantile monstrousness. Children had to be controlled and subjected to environmental conditioning in order to be brought to balance with the reality principle of social codes, lest they remain monsters. In her view, the violent and crime-prone adolescent is not so much somebody who has undergone improper structural development as a child, as is the view of Piaget, but rather is someone whose innate aggressive fantasy has not been acculturated and socialized. That Klein was a radical thinker is obvious, but her theory appears more supportive of a rightist than a leftist ideology.

The other important theory that Klein proposed was the principle of object relations. The growth of the child's personality centrally involves an attachment to an external object. This can be, for example, a mother's breast, a teddy bear, father's pipe and glasses, or—as in Orson Welles' *Citizen Kane*—a sled called Rosebud. The attachment to an object is an inevitable part of childhood psychology. But protracted or overly intense fixation on the object can produce severe neurosis, and prevent adequate socialization. One of the key things that the psychoanalyst has to discover is the pattern of object relationship in his patient's unconscious. Klein's theory, which is quite compatible with both Freud and Jung, has been well-received in the psychoanalytic profession and a whole Anglo-American school has developed around its exploration.

*   *   *

The Psychoanalytic Heritage

Psychoanalysis was the theory of the most sexualized culture since the Roman Empire. The Rome of the second and third centuries was given to highly free sexuality, as can be gathered from the accounts of contemporaries. There were no real limitations on the variety of sexual practices. This came to an end around 350 A.D., through what historical factors we do not know with certainty. But Christianity can be enumerated among them. Along with Christianity arose the repression of both heterosexuality and of homosexual practices.

The twentieth century had achieved, certainly by the 1960's, the freest sexual society since the Roman Empire, and psychoanalysis has helped bring that about by generating a justifying theory for sexual freedom. It both contributed to this freedom and was the consequence of the rising sexual tide. Yet the twentieth century may still turn out to be an intermediary sexual time in history. This may not be the end of the history of sexuality, but just a flashpoint in sexuality, as AIDS continues to wind its way, like the bubonic plague that befell the Roman Empire and the medieval world. There are already signs that AIDS is conducing a withdrawal from sexual freedom towards discretion and control.

We have previously witnessed a cyclic pattern in the history of sexuality. In the twelfth century, there was a partial departure, at least among the aristocracy, from repressive Christian attitudes which had prevailed approximately since 350 A.D. Then, in the late sixteenth century, there was a return to repression with the age of puritanism. The eighteenth century saw a liberation, and if we were to investigate the sexual lives of some of the fathers of this country like Benjamin Franklin and Thomas Jefferson we would find major disparities with the ethic of sexual control and family values. When Franklin was American ambassador in Paris no Frenchwoman was safe. Jefferson slept with his female slaves.

The nineteenth century marks a return to repression, but after 1900 only in order to yield to sexual liberation, aided by innovations in contraceptive methods and the theory of psychoanalysis. We may now once again be approaching a restrictive era in terms of sexual practices.

Putting aside whatever it may be that the future holds, and returning to the past, it is seen that of all the countries in the world, psychoanalysis had its greatest reception in the United States, with the single exception of Argentina, and particularly Buenos Aires. The two cities which harbor the largest number of psychoanalysts per capita are New York City and Buenos Aires. The case of the latter can be partly explained by the fact that there are many Germans and Jews living in that city.

The question is: Why the United States? How to account for the phenomenal impact of psychoanalysis in New York, Chicago and Los Angeles? One explanation is that between 1910 and 1940, when psychoanalysis developed in this country, the United States was very weak in its infrastructure, that is, in its social institutions. This was the period of the disintegration of the American family due to tremendous mobility, industrialization, and the decline of the churches as well as of public schools. The weakness of the societal infrastructure drove people back into themselves, and they needed a theory and a behavioral method which provided them with the means of functioning as individuals in a society with eroded and collapsing institutions. Psychotherapy, and in particular psychoanalysis in various Freudian derivatives, posed the solution or the alternative. If it had been possible to maintain the churches of the nineteenth century, psychotherapy would or could not have effected this penetration.

A second factor that has rendered the United States so receptive to psychotherapy is the peculiar history here of the medical profession. As has been mentioned with respect to the phoniness of Harry Stack Sullivan, the medical profession took hold in the United States suddenly, severely and arrogantly around 1910, just as psychoanalysis made its appearance. The state of the medical art between 1910 and 1940 was such that there was not much for medical doctors to do except surgery. It was not until the discovery of antibiotics in 1940 that the medical profession found means of treatment besides amputation and prescribing aspirin. Therefore, when psychoanalysis appeared on the scene, it presented doctors with a welcome alternative, with something to do as it were.

Psychoanalysis gave them an entire new branch of medicine to explore and to practice. The field had some basis in science, was socially valuable, had a market, and was financially rewarding. Therefore the American medical profession eagerly embraced and legitimized psychoanalysis. In the dark ages of twentieth-century medicine, before antibiotics, since doctors usually could not cure patients, they devoted themselves to primary care. They made housecalls. They offered psychotherapy.

Psychoanalysis also fitted in comfortably with current literary ideas, with the classicist literary Modernism of T.S. Eliot as well as with the continental expressionist branch of Modernism. It fitted in with the prominent literary theme of the *Doppelgaenger* (the double, the Other, the shadow), and with the microcosmic, word-centered, language-based approach to literary creativity and criticism. Psychoanalysis was a psychological theory that was immensely compatible with, and stimulative of, the literary trends of the first forty years of this century.

Psychoanalysis began as definitely a prime bastion of Modernism. If there is a single theorist of Modernism, it is the younger Sigmund Freud. Psychoanalysis began as Modernist, but increasingly, especially as witnessed in the writings of the later Freud and in the work of Jung, Piaget, Erikson, and Lacan, it takes more and more into structuralist or neo-idealist directions. It finds ways to reintroduce ideas such as that of macrocosmic forms operating within the individual as well as in culture, and to look upon the individual in the context of structural forms. While marking a radical departure from the doctrine established by the early Freud, this trend actually strengthened the cultural hold of psychoanalysis, as after the 1940's, there was a movement away from Modernism. A neo-idealist, neo-Victorian movement expressed itself in structuralist anthropology as well as in other fields.

Psychoanalysis, by departing from its early radical, microcosmic, biological reductionism, and by moving towards affirmation of various kinds of psycho-cultural systems and structures, remained compatible with the cultural history of the later twentieth century. Psychoanalysis demonstrated its historical resiliency and subtle adaptability to shifting intellectual trends. This later psychoanalysis, however, paid the price for adaptibility by losing its radical edge and its creative leadership in twentieth century culture. Somewhere in the 40's, 50's, and 60's psychoanalysis begins to be more concerned with keeping up with intellectual trends that originate elsewhere than with setting the trend in humanistic theory.

The therapeutic value of psychoanalysis must ultimately be stressed in judging its role in twentieth-century culture. Sexual and familial relationships lie at the root of a great deal of human misery in advanced industrial societies. At any given time in the United States there are five million people undergoing psychotherapy that is closely or loosely based on psychoanalytic theory, that follows from the Freudian heritage. The life of a sizable share of these people has been made happier and more stable and productive as a result of this psychotherapy. The psychoanalytic achievement as a therapeutic force in modern society is assuredly not less than the care offered by religious groups in earlier times, and one could surmise, it is probably more effective and more compassionate. Psychoanalysis has its problems and its vociferous enemies. But it has been a major positive dimension in twentieth-century culture. It has been a hallmark of the advance of civilization. It has reflected the application of reason and science to intimate human relationships. If life is in some ways more humane and beneficent in the later twentieth century as compared with society of a hundred years ago, psychoanalysis merits a substantial share of the credit.

4

Marxism and the Left

American Marxism Today

Twenty-five years ago, Marxism would not have been treated as a topic sufficiently important to occupy a special place among the historical themes of Western twentieth-century culture. It would have been considered marginal. Within these twenty-five years, however, Marxism has emerged as a major intellectual movement in the American university and in Western culture in general, and there is every sign that it will become increasingly more so in the decades to come.

The Marxist theorist Bertell Ollman in the Department of Politics at New York University has recently said that there are ten thousand Marxists currently teaching at American universities. Strangely enough, Ollman's antagonist Reid Irvine, who runs the right-wing Accuracy in the Academia, cites a similar figure. Whatever the accuracy of such figures, it is a fact that in the last ten years Marxism and cognate leftist doctrines have become central in leading universities in the United States.

There are three prominent history departments in the United States—the departments at Princeton, Rochester and New York Universities—where Marxists and scholars of similar persuasion are highly visible. There are also several sociology departments, particularly the department at the State University of New York at Binghamton, which are deeply committed to Marxism. The eminently prestigious Harvard Law School as well as the Harvard art history department have strong components of Marxists on their faculties. At Duke University, the holder of the senior chair in humanities is Marxist, and at Columbia University this important chair is held by an apologist for PLO terrorism.

One, and perhaps the most important, reason why Marxism has become so important in American academe is that the commitment to Marxism continues the trends of the sixties. Academic Marxism is the grand heritage of the disorderly sixties. This can be understood in very concrete terms. A generation of graduate students in the humanities and social sciences, who were in the universities in the sixties and early seventies during the height of the public agitation over the Vietnam War, developed strong left-wing commitments which continued through their academic careers. In the meantime, this generation of scholars have become senior faculty and department chairmen, occupying powerful positions. Many of them are distinguished scholars indeed, occupying prominent places among the scholars of their generation.

Furthermore, in the 1970's and 80's, the academic profession underwent severe impoverishment. In the seventies, academic salaries declined twenty percent in real dollars, which embittered many academics. This situation encouraged a left-wing orientation. If the power and money elite of this country does not want the university faculties to have a strongly leftist, anti-capitalist orientation, the way to achieve this is certainly not by reducing faculty salaries, particularly at a time when the income of other learned professions such as law and medicine is skyrocketing.

In 1966, between the salary for the new recipient of a Ph.D. in the humanities starting to teach at an Ivy League college and that of a new lawyer starting his career as an associate in a major New York law firm, there was only a thirty percent discrepancy. Currently the salary differential is three hundred percent. Under these conditions, resentment and radicalization is to be expected, which in turn encourages a left-wing orientation.

A third factor in the strengthening of Marxism is that in the 1970's, American universities suffered a failure of nerve, in the sense that they became increasingly dependent on ideas generated and developed in Europe, particularly those coming out of France and England. Between the two World Wars, American universities had developed strong intellectual autonomy and native intellectual traditions. The reliance on native production continued for a while in the fifties after the Second World War, but began to erode around the mid-sixties, when American scholars began to regard Paris and Oxbridge as the source of truth in many fields. At the time, the University of Paris was particularly dominated by Marxism in all its faculties, and for those who were already favorably disposed toward French ideas, importing and assimilating Marxism from France appeared salutary.

The same phenomenon can be observed in American academic relations with Oxford, Cambridge and the British universities. Indeed, Marxism was not dominant in British universities, but it had achieved a strong penetration there by the mid-sixties. Turning to Paris or Oxbridge for intellectual leadership and for imitation was therefore inevitably to result in the importation of Marxist ideas into American universities.

Finally, in the American academic world, there has always been a strong Emersonian strain. Most prominent American academics do not settle simply for teaching and engaging in research; they want nothing less than to change the world. From time to time, the Emersonian tradition becomes quite vibrant. It had been there in the thirties, returned in the sixties, and is still in the foreground. There is characteristically a restlessness in the American academic world. The self-image of the American academic is that of a would-be guru and social improver, and not merely that of someone who is conveying information and sponsoring research. The United States, not having been able to develop a powerful right-wing doctrine since John Calhoun in the 1840's, and William Graham Sumner in the 1880's, is bound to express utopian reformism in terms of a left-wing ideology.

*   *   *

Foundations of Socialism

Marxism and all brands of socialism were originally nineteenth-century creations. There was a variety of left-wing currents of thoughts in the nineteenth century. All of these socialist currents were conditioned by a rebellion against capitalism, market-economics and the dominion of the bourgeoisie, in other words, the upper middle class.

Especially after 1850 there was a persistent feeling in intellectual circles—a minority view but a determined one—that the achievements of capitalism were lacking in moral quality. Capitalism offended moral sensibilities, it was held, and bourgeois culture was philistine, that is, it assaulted aesthetic and artistic sensibility. Granted capitalism had altered the face of the world, which Marx himself was the first to recognize, but it had not necessarily changed the world for the better. Capitalism had perhaps been an inevitable stage in history, but it had to be transcended in the name of a better world. Capitalism and bourgeois rule were therefore not the end of history, but only constituted an intermediary stage which was deficient in moral and aesthetic qualities: this is a fundamental dogma of socialism.

Marxism was only one strand in nineteenth-century socialism. One group of socialists felt very strongly that capitalism had ravaged the environment, that the beautiful world of pre-industrial society had been ruthlessly pillaged by the railroad and the steel age. They objected that the atmosphere had been polluted, the world drenched in smoke and carbon deposits, and held that a socialist community would be able to transcend and remedy these conditions, saving and purifying the environment. This point of view was held by a talented group of artists and art critics in England, headed by John Ruskin and William Morris. The group was particularly influential in the period between 1870 and 1900, although Ruskin had advocated this point of view since the 1850's.

This group can be described as aesthetic socialists, who nursed the vision of a soulful community that would create a beautiful world. What they wanted was very much what environmental groups demand today. They wanted to control the ravages of capitalist materialism and to place an emphasis upon an aesthetic and healthy environment. The aesthetic socialists found that pre-capitalist societies, such as the medieval, were better than modern ones. While medieval people in fact did not respect the environment any more than modern people, they lacked the technology to ravage it as severely as the Industrial Revolution had made possible. Ruskin and Morris, however, convinced themselves that medieval men and women were more finely in tune with their environment than those of the nineteenth century.

In contrast with the beneficent medieval world, Francis Bacon's doctrine in the early seventeenth century that knowledge is power and Daniel Defoe's Robinson Crusoe as the prototype of the asocial individual entrepreneur—so socialist critics claimed—signified a new market ideology that meant disaster for beauty and refinement.

There was another group in the nineteenth century, which it is possible to describe as "welfare liberals," although they called themselves the New Liberals. They had a vision which became in effect the welfare state of the twentieth century. This group thought it had a mandate for its vision in the philosophy of Plato. Their political Bible was Plato's *Republic*, which presented them with the model for a strong communal organization and for the rule of the "philosopher kings." This elite would achieve a harmonious society whose citizens received their necessary rewards not on the basis of how well they competed economically, but in terms of what was best for society as a whole and according to what was beneficial for the individual in order to develop his intellectual and artistic qualities.

The New Liberals claimed that this social model could be achieved by the establishment of a strong central government which would severely regulate capitalist industry, expropriate some of it, engage in heavy taxation of capitalists and landlords, and redistribute income as well as provide for excellent educational and health services. A society would follow, it was claimed, in which every individual could develop his potential.

This view was enunciated most eloquently by Thomas Hill Green, who was a professor of philosophy at Balliol College, Oxford, in the 1880's, and Bernard Bosanquet, who was an innovative social and moral theorist working among the London poor in the 1890's. Bosanquet and Green gathered around them a group of influential disciples, particularly Graham Wallas. They exercised a strong influence upon the British Liberal Party, which, in the late nineteenth century transformed itself from being the party of capitalists, merchants and industrialists, to being the party of the lower middle class as well as, so they hoped, of the working class.

In 1906, this reconstituted Liberal Party won a landslide election in Britain. Three-quarters of their membership in Parliament were either school teachers or protestant ministers, which makes it quite clear who it was that believed in the uses of legislation for moral purposes and common benefits. The party introduced heavier taxation, particularly on land ownership, old-age pensions, and the first health insurance. Thus the reconstituted Liberal Party began to take the first steps in England toward the welfare state, representing a radical departure from the market ideals of nineteenth-century liberalism.

Behind the new welfare liberalism of the late nineteenth century was a pessimism about the capability of capitalism's growing further to the extent of eliminating poverty. The stubborn persistence of harsh poverty in British society was demonstrated by pioneering social work inquiries funded by Quaker philanthropists. The argument the New Liberals were making at the turn of the century was economic growth in itself would not eliminate poverty and positive state action was necessary.

It is under the heritage of the philosophy of Green and Bosanquet that the word liberal came to connote someone who believes in the welfare state—a meaning the word still holds—as opposed to designating one who believes in unlimited capitalist competition, which was the previous nineteenth-century meaning of the word. The opinionated British couple Beatrice and Sidney Webb were the prototype for the new breed of welfare liberals. That believed that in the welfare state the wasteful habits of the poor that offended their elitist sensibilities would be eroded while appropriate positions of power would be assured to enlightened social activists like themselves. Indeed more and better administrative jobs for the middle class has been the clearest outcome of the welfare state. In the United States the critical shift in liberalism began before the First World War in the presidency of Woodrow Wilson, when the welfare liberals were called "Progressives." It was fully achieved in the New Deal of the 30's.

Another group of socialists, a loud and radical one, called themselves anarchists in the nineteenth century. In the beginning of the twentieth century, particularly in France, they began to call themselves the syndicalists, which derives from the word "syndic," a French name for labor union. The movement can therefore be referred to as anarcho-syndicalism. The intellectual leader of nineteenth-century anarchism was the Russian émigré Peter Kropotkin. The movement found its twentieth century theorist in the French philosopher Georges Sorel. One of the leaders of this movement in the United States was Joe Hill, the one of the well-known folk-song by the same name. Joe Hill was a member of the I.W.W., the International Workers of the World, an anarcho-syndicalist union that was active primarily among the miners of Nevada. Joe Hill was shot by the State of Utah.

What the anarchists believed in was the destruction of the prevailing economic and political system by confrontation, and if necessary, by violent confrontation. They believed in general strike, in mobilizing all the workers so that in one ineffable moment, when all factories and industries had ceased functioning, capitalism and the state alike would grind to a halt, and the workers would take over. This was in fact attempted from time to time, but it never worked. It was certainly tried on a large scale in England in 1926 but only in order to fail. Closer to home, one such strike was attempted in Canada in 1919, and in the mining districts of the West in 1906 and 1916, which also failed. Nevertheless, the general strike was a revolutionary method dear to anarchists.

Anarchists believed in terrorism as well, and particularly in the assassination of political leaders. One such successful attempt was directed at President McKinley in the United States. The idea was to force the prevailing establishment to be repressive, to force it to take counter-terrorist tactics and so to discredit itself morally. This idea became very popular among the New Left in the 1960's, and is still occasionally propounded on the left.

Anarcho-syndicalists were essentially Rousseauists. Men and women are by nature good; it is the state and capitalism that corrupts them. Once the state and capitalism have been overthrown by the general strike, terrorism, and revolution, men and women will spontaneously form communes and cultivate their initial goodness. The New Left of the 60's spent a lot of time and energy trying to implement these anarchist principles, beginning with participatory democracy, a cardinal Rousseauist doctrine.

Anarcho-syndicalism found support in areas of Europe and the United States where the Industrial Revolution had been delayed, where it was coming in slowly at the turn of the century, and where, therefore, its ravages were particularly severe. Industrial revolutions treat their workers worst in their initial phases, and later improve the conditions of their existence. Therefore, places which remained marginal to the Industrial Revolution for a long while, like southern France, Spain, Sicily, the Rocky Mountain area, Arizona, and agricultural and mining regions therein, were areas where anarcho-syndicalism found support in the early 1900's.

Karl Marx loathed anarchists almost as much as he contended with capitalists. He found them "adventurous," hyper-romantic, irrational, and claimed that they would discredit the socialist movement. Marx vehemently disagreed with the anarchist view that the state was intrinsically evil.

Finally, the nineteenth century produced the doctrines of Karl Marx and his associate Friedrich Engels, and the Marxist movement in the First and Second International. Marxist theory has become so familiar that it can be summarized quite succinctly. Of primary importance to Marxist doctrine is the labor theory of value, which holds that it is the contribution of the actual manual worker or blue-collar worker that creates economic value. There is no value in management, in no aspect of economic activity in fact, other than in the actual product of the worker's labor. Nor does the capitalist have any social or moral rights to a return on his investment. Marx did not originate the labor theory of economic value. What is critical is the central importance he gave to it. Marx's labor theory of economic value is an extremely narrow and constricted one, and it is the foundation of everything else in his system.

Secondly, Marxism holds the view that capital is a substance, that is, it is a tremendous economic force which follows specific, idiosyncratic patterns of development and takes on an independence and life of its own. This notion will become central to the theory of the Frankfurt School of the 1920's and 30's. There is such a thing, an entity, as capital, which is capable of becoming a living force. Once it achieves a certain degree of accumulation of capital, capitalism enters a course of development which is irresistible. Eventually, of course, it runs out its course and breaks down, but on the upswing as capital reaches a certain level of vitality, it will inevitably continue to evolve.

There is here a close parallel between Marxism and Darwinism. Marx acknowledged his admiration for Darwin. Once a certain species has developed, said Darwin, by a process of natural selection and adaptation to the environment, the species will have been irreversibly constituted and prepared for a long course of endurance and further development, albeit one which, as in the case of the Marxian concept of capital, will not last forever. Marxism is founded on Victorian organicism.

Thirdly, Marxist doctrine speaks of alienation or dehumanization. This concept was particularly propounded, and quite eloquently too, by the younger Marx in the 1840's in the collection of essays now referred to as *The 1844 Manuscripts*. These writings were not published in Marx's lifetime and in fact, were not widely known until the 1930's. It is the unpublished 1844 manuscripts that present the doctrine of alienation most elaborately among Marx's works. Yet the doctrine appears in his other writings, particularly in

The German Ideology. It is also referred to in his major work *Capital*, but not fully developed there.

The doctrine of alienation describes the process of the dehumanization of the worker as he engages in industrial capitalist production. Laboring on the assembly line, the worker becomes an appendage to and an extension of the machine, which dehumanizes by subjecting him to the fragmented labor the modern industrial mode of production requires and by separating him from his authentic nature.

In the conditions of industrial capitalism the workers have become proletarians. They have been subjected to "naked, shameless, direct, brutal exploitation" by the bourgeoisie. "The work of the proletarians has lost all individual character and consequently all charm for the workman." The life of the worker in industrial capitalism is characterized by "accumulation of misery, agony of toil, slavery, ignorance, brutality, moral degradation." Nor can the intellectuals, artists, and learned professionals among the middle class themselves escape the dehumanizing effects of the capitalist Moloch. The bourgeoisie "has resolved personal worth into exchange value [and] . . . converted the physician, the lawyer, the priest, the poet, the man of science into its paid wage laborers . . . [Capitalism] has reduced the family relation to a mere money relation."

Marx and Engels were themselves products of the German middle class in the later years of the Romantic era. When they encountered the industrial revolution in England, where they migrated before and after the abortive revolutions of 1848, their sensibility was shocked by the material and social changes they encountered. Unquestionably some truly adverse consequences of industrialization were witnessed by them and found to be repulsive. Many men and women of sensibility in England, such as William Wordsworth, Charles Dickens and Thomas Carlyle, were also repelled by the social and environmental brutalities of the earlier phase of industrialization. The strange thing about Marx and Engels is that well before Marx's death in 1884 and Engels some years later, much more beneficent consequences of industrial capitalism were evident, and a significant proportion of the working class was relatively prosperous and contented. The professional middle class and to a substantial degree intellectuals and artists were much better off under the industrial and financial capitalism of the later nineteenth century than under the ancien régime. Yet Marx and Engels did not modify their judgment of capitalism, although they had ample opportunity to do so.

There is no more strange a phenomenon in twentieth-century culture than the many thousands of left-wing intellectuals assenting to an assessment of capitalism that was based on conditions in the 1840's and 50's that were rapidly superseded in advanced industrial countries. Obviously the Marxist doctrine of alienation has appeared convincing to so many in this century for other than objective economic and social conditions. An obvious explanation is that *any* social system that subjects human beings to control and regimentation in the interests of productivity is regarded as reprehensible to Marxists. At bottom there is a deep affinity between Marxism and aesthetic socialism.

This also explains why latter-day Marxists are so deeply concerned about the welfare of the masses in the Third World, a sentiment that was notably lacking in Marx and Engels. In the Third World with its involvement in the incipient phase of the industrial revolution, the Marxist vision of the unrelieved misery of the working class still is plausibly circumstantial. By the end of Marx's own lifetime his view of capitalism was incompatable with actual conditions in Britain, Germany and the United States.

The purpose of socialism in Marxist doctrine is precisely to rehumanize the industrial worker. It is under socialism, and particularly in the communist society which is the final stage of historical development, that the industrial worker will be restored to his full humanity.

Marx spent the last thirty years of his life trying to prove that the capitalist system would undergo a series of crises and disintegrate from within. In this final critical phase of capitalism a proletarian revolution would inaugurate "the Communist society" which in its "higher phase" would eliminate "the enslaving subordination of the individual to the division of labor . . . and with it the antagonisms between intellectual and manual labor." Then will come "the development of the individual in every sense . . . and all the springs of collective wealth will flow with abundance."

There is no essential difference between this view of the world and that of the radical Romantic poet Percy Shelley in the early 1820's. "Rise like lions after slumber/ In unvanquishable number/ Shake your chains to earth like dew/ Which in sleep had fallen on you." Marx—this learned, idealistic, pathetic son of a Rheinish lawyer, grinding away at statistical materials in the Reading Room of the British Museum year after year, beset with family and fiscal problems, living on handouts from his junior collaborator Engels, the rich son of a German textile magnate—it is all a poignant story. Marx's doctrines reflect his projection of his personal problems onto a society he held responsible and came to loathe.

Marxism also has a distinct doctrine of history which consists of the materialist version of the Hegelian theory of history, and which is based on the concept of class struggle. Marx, who studied with Hegel in Germany, can be described as a left-wing Hegelian.

The Marxian theory of history, or the doctrine of dialectical materialism, teaches that around 1500, feudalism, the social structure based on the rule of landlords over peasants, began to yield to the capitalist modes of production which did not, however, receive its fullest form before the Industrial Revolution of the eighteenth and early nineteenth centuries. This structure, in turn, Marx holds, will be replaced by that historical stage of development which will be dominated by proletarian rule. The late stage of capitalism is marked by periodic crisis and increasingly aggravated confrontation between the narrow stratum of capitalists on the one side and mass of increasingly impoverished workers on the other. So goes, according to Marx, the dialectical movement of history. It is a model of history that describes the entire development of human societies and is applicable to every society. Marxist historiography obviously constitutes a secularized version of the old Christian apocalyptic vision.

A key ingredient in the Marxian theory of history is the doctrine of false consciousness. This doctrine, which has been critically important for all of the more radical and activist socialists in this century, explains the inability of the proletarian to know and realize his own advantage. The worker's consciousness has been falsified and misguided by explicit propaganda as well as by subtler forms of ideological manipulation. This is why the Communist party, even without the majority support of the proletariat, is justified in undertaking the revolution against capitalism. The fact that the Communist movement may momentarily not receive strong support from the proletariat is explained by the fact that the working class is entrapped by false consciousness which prevents its members from perceiving the sordid operations of capitalism and the conditions of their victimization in full and clear light. This subtle paradox has enabled generations of Marxists to be democrats and oligarchs at the same time—or as communists said in the 1930's, to be adherents of "democratic centralism."

The doctrine of false consciousness finds an extended elaboration in the work of Lenin, who uses it to justify the revolutionary role of the Bolshevik Party in the revolution of 1917, although at the beginning of the revolution it was decidedly a minority party, even among Russian socialists. Those who remained outside the Bolshevik circle, Lenin believed, did so because of false consciousness. It never bothered Lenin to find himself and his cadre in a minority, even a very small minority. On the contrary, a minority role gave Lenin added confidence that he was right, the he was in tune with the forces of justice and history, while his opponents wallowed in evil and false consciousness.

Was this nineteenth-century socialist heritage at all compatible with Modernism or was the former a theory discrepant with main currents of the cultural revolution the early twentieth century witnessed? There are three ways in which the socialist legacy could be regarded as compatible with Modernism, the first of which is the aesthetic condemnation of the prevailing social system. The Modernists posited entitlement to participation in the arts as the highest social value, indeed, perhaps as the only social value. The only instance in which Modernists approach anything resembling a social theory is in the context of arguing for the universal right to cultivate the arts. This Modernist argument can be construed as compatible with the Marxist and socialist condemnation of capitalism on aesthetic grounds. Both Modernism and socialist thought find that the prevailing social system deprives persons of access to the arts as well as of full entitlement to artistic development. That Modernism and Marxism differ absolutely on the role of the state in control over the arts does not preclude a short-term alliance against alleged bourgeois philistinism.

Anarcho-syndicalism has some compatibility with the Expressionist tradition of Modernism. The latter believes in the possibility of capturing a glorious moment when humanity attains its highest degree of fulfillment. This Expressionist conception of the moment of truth, and of unlimited fulfillment of the deepest instincts of humanity, parallels the anarcho-syndicalist doctrine of the general strike and terrorism, the ineffable moment of social truth. Certainly Sorel's way of thinking was within the Expressionist tradition in Modernism.

Finally, the Marxist doctrine of alienation bears resemblance to Heidegger's doctrine of authenticity. Heidegger belonged to the right-wing and was vehemently anti-communist, but nevertheless the Heideggerian concept of authenticity and the Marxian concept of alienation both aim at the achievement and realization of the full humanity of the individual. Both assert that the purpose of life is to reach that moment of the deepest realization of one's authentic human quality, and Heidegger was indeed aware of this particular parallel between his philosophy and Marxism.

In spite of their fragmentary affinities, the socialist tradition, particularly in its Marxist form, was essentially incompatible and in conflict with Modernism. Marxism was moralistic, historicist, being entirely and inextricably based on a philosophy of history, and macrocosmic. Modernism strived to depart from Victorian moralism, whereas socialism is based precisely on Victorian moralism. Modernists wanted to remove history from the field of attention. They were ahistorical or antihistorical. According to the socialists, particularly to Marxists, every phenomenon is to be studied in the context of history, which is also very much a Victorian idea.

Where Modernism was microcosmic, socialism remained macrocosmic, once again complying with assumptions of Victorian culture. Socialism, in all its forms, believes in universal theories.

There are additional incompatibilities between Modernism and Marxism which become immediately evident whenever a Communist or Soviet regime gains power. Modernism was elitist and was concerned with a highly sophisticated intellectual and academic culture. Socialism has to believe that culture must serve the masses and that, for example, art and literature must be expressed in a style that the masses can comprehend. Hence, the Soviet emphasis on "Socialist Realism" and proscription of abstract art and experimental, non-narrative literature.

The most bitter conflict between Marxism and Modernism always comes over the question of whether art and literature are self-referential and whether artists and writers are independent of the state. Communist regimes always insist just the opposite: art, literature, and all forms of thought (even physics and biology) are to be developed in the context of the needs of the proletariat (in practice, according to state policy) and artists, writers, philosophers, and scientists are state functionaries as much as farmers and engineers.

The issue comes down to freedom: Modernism assumes the highest degree of automony for the arts, letters, and sciences. Marxism finds this anathema and treason to the revolution and the socialist state. In the later stages of the ancien régime, communist revolutionaries and Modernist artist appear momentarily to be allies. The former conspires against the dying order, the latter criticizes and satirizes it. Once the Marxists have come to power, however, Modernism suffers an early condemnation. This story has been repeated wherever communists have gained power in the twentieth century. The story is different where social democrats like the British Labor Party have held sway, only because in such political systems the socialists are subject to democratic processes and the rule of law and lack the mechanisms of state oppression, and because among the social democrats are mixed in welfare liberals who are only marginally Marxists.

One of the greatest problems for Marxist thinkers in the twentieth century—a problem which still continues to preoccupy Marxist intellectuals in the West—consists of the stresses and strains between Marxism, stemming from its Victorian legacy, and Modernism. Since Western Marxists see themselves as the progressives in every social and cultural dimension, they could not bring themselves, in many instances, to reject the artistic and intellectual avant-garde of Modernism. The problem remains how to bridge the gap between Marxism and Modernism. This posed a particularly important problem for American Modernists, which was investigated in *The Partisan Review* of the 1930's and still concerns *The Village Voice* of 1986. The *Voice* is still trying to keep one foot in Marxism, while it seeks to root the other in Modernism, just as *The Partisan Review* was trying to do in the 1930's. *The Partisan Review* solved the problem by abandoning Marxism in the 1950's.

In cultural history logic does not always prevail. The incompatible is sometimes made compatible and the union of very different modes of thinking in the end can prevail against very long odds. The task of bridging Marxism and Modernism represented almost insuperable difficulties, since they stood at such polar opposites from each other in the spectrum of cultural theory. Yet attempts made by left-wing intellectuals to affect a symbiosis of Marxism and Modernism were not without some interesting and partially fruitful results.

The understanding of twentieth century cultural history requires attention to this fundamental issue: socialism, especially in its Marxist form, represented a powerful manifestation of neo-Victorianism, contradicting Modernism in fundamental ways. The more Marxism gained credibility among intellectuals, the more this situation detracted from triumph of the Modernist cultural revolution.

Lenin and his Bolshevik colleagues saw this clearly in 1922 when they condemned Constructivism as reactionary bourgeois art, terminated a Modernist movement in Leningrad and Moscow that was of major consequence, and formulated the dogma that Modernist principles were anti-Bolshevik. The liberating efforts of luminaries among three generations of Soviet artists and intellectuals have essentially not been able to reverse this Bolshevik condemnation of Modernism, nor did Lenin err in his assessment of the ideological relationship of Modernism and Bolshevism. Stalin considered Modernists, whether in literature, painting, or music, to be enemies of the people. It is significant that whenever a new Soviet leader comes along, and Kremlinologists seek to discover his policy, they look for an easing of the proscriptions on Modernism as a prime indicator. Gorbachev is held to be taking a softer line on Leninism because he allows occasional exhibitions of abstract art. The history of Modernism in other Soviet regimes or in Red China has not been different than in Soviet Russia.

At most, a Communist state can tolerate some marginal Modernist activity in the arts but the Marxists-Leninists can never allow Modernist culture to take hold in the media and in education if they wish to retain their hold on the minds of the population. A strong, highly visible Modernist movement will always delegitimize Marxism as assuredly as twentieth-century culture departs from the nineteenth. It is only because Western Marxists have never exercised total power that they have the paradoxical luxury of denying this cardinal fact.

Because of the rooted conflict between Marxism and Modernism, the Communist triumph in Russia and the way in which the Soviet Union and its admirers became highly influential in Western socialism in the twenties, followed by the leftist advance during the Great Depression and the New Deal in the thirties, represented an adverse set of circumstances for the continued flourishing of high Modernist culture. The advance of Marxism and the left in Europe and the United States was a prime factor in the erosion of the Modernist consciousness in the thirties.

*   *   *

The Pre-War Era

Between 1900 and the First World War, there was a strong increase of support for socialism in Europe. By 1914, the Social Democratic Party, which was more or less Marxist, was the largest political party in Germany. This did not mean that it held political power, as Germany did not have a democratic system at the time. But the largest group in the German parliament were Social Democrats, most of whom were socialists and some even vehement Marxists, and if Germany had had a democratic political system then, the government would have been in the hands of the socialists.

Indeed, the socialists became so strong politically in the late nineteenth century, that the country's government under Chancellor Bismarck had to introduce the welfare state into Germany in the 1880's. Germany was the first European country to have the welfare state. Features of the welfare state were introduced into Germany as a way to pacify the German voter, to keep him from consistently voting for the Social Democrats. This political ploy could be glamorized as a hearkening back to the paternalism of the now superseded mercantilist state. But the method did not fulfil its aim, and the Germans continued to vote for the socialists.

In England, from 1906 to World War I, there was a strong group of welfare liberals in power. The same period saw the beginnings of the British Labor Party, which first formed a government in England in 1924, but which, by 1914, held a significant minority in the British House of Commons. The French socialists were already highly visible by 1914, under the leadership of Jean Jaurès, who was assassinated shortly before the First World War broke out. In the United States in 1912 and 1920, the socialists, under the leadership of Eugene Debs, received one million votes, which is the most that any socialist party has ever gained in an American presidential election.

The socialist political advance in the pre-war period was accompanied by significant development in Marxist theory. In Germany, the two leading Marxist intellectuals were Edward Bernstein and Rosa Luxemburg. Bernstein argued that socialism could come to power in Germany by the ballot. Revolution, he claimed, was not necessary. Eventually, as long as the German workers continued to vote for the Social Democrats, the Kaiser would have to give in and form a government of socialists. Bernstein may very well have been right. The war, however, intervened, followed by the Kaiser's abdication in 1918.

Rosa Luxemburg, on the other hand, believed that socialist victory by democratic means was not likely to happen, and that revolution was necessary. In 1918–19, she was one of the two leaders of a Communist revolution in Berlin which took place during the confusion that followed the collapse of Germany at the end of the First World War. Munich too was the site of a Communist revolution in the winter of 1918. The Munich revolution was momentarily successful and for three months a communist government held power in Bavaria. The Berlin revolution failed, and Rosa Luxemburg was murdered by a group of rightist naval officers. Luxemburg, a Polish Jew with a marginal anarchist penchant, is now revered by Marxist feminists.

In England, in 1902 the Labor Party theorist, J. A. Hobson, made a major contribution to Marxist theory. Marx himself had never vehemently condemned imperialism. He suggested that imperialism was tied in with capitalism, but Marx was very much a Western chauvinist who had a very low opinion of what is now referred to as the Third World. He thought that imperialism was good for the Third World, that it was a necessary stage which brought about the industrialization in these countries which they themselves could never have achieved. He did not see any intrinsic value in oriental culture, and thought that imperialism was an inevitable stage that these societies had to go through in order to be modernized.

Hobson produced a study of imperialism which condemned imperialism as the final stage of capitalism. According to Hobson, imperialism developed as capitalism deteriorated, as it exhausted its markets, and as it had to go in search for both new markets and for new sources of cheap raw materials. Imperialism is the way in which capitalism tries to stave off its terminal illness. Imperialism is the product of the crises of late capitalism which force the bourgeoisie to find new markets to deliver itself of the product of surplus manufacture. The colonial countries are also forced by the imperialists to surrender their raw material cheaply and assure the capitalists of continual profits.

Hobson's theory of imperialism was taken up by Lenin. Lenin was a leader of a far-left-wing revolutionary fringe in the Russian socialist movement, the Bolsheviks, who lived in exile in Zurich, Switzerland, until the 1917 revolution began. Lenin agreed with Rosa Luxemburg that revolution was the only way by which Communism could ever be brought about. He too was convinced that the overthrow of capitalism could not come about democratically, and that it necessitated revolution under the leadership of the vanguard cadre of the Communist Party at the appropriate time. Lenin remained in Zurich, read and wrote books, waiting for his moment. Lenin also took Hobson's theory of imperialism and inserted it into Communist theory where it has remained a dominant segment of Marxist-Leninist doctrine.

The period before the First World War also witnessed the beginnings of Marxist historical scholarship. Of all the academic or proto-academic scholarship, history is the easiest for Marxism, since Marxism is a historicist philosophy. The theoretical foundations of Marxism facilitate the writing of history, and the beginnings of a learned Marxist tradition of history occur in the ten years preceding the First World War, during which time four Marxist historians rose to eminence.

The first of these was Karl Kautsky, who was a colleague in the German Marxist movement of Bernstein and Luxemburg. His own views lie somewhere between the moderation of Bernstein and the radical authoritarianism of Rosa Luxemburg. Kautsky's contribution lay in his undertaking of a Marxist analysis of sixteenth- and seventeenth- century history in order to show in detail the emergence of capitalism out of medieval European society. Kautsky was not really in possession of the necessary scholarly equipment, but he did make the first efforts in this vein. It was Kautsky too, who first suggested that the English Civil War or Puritan Revolution of the 1640's was fundamentally a capitalist insurgence against feudalism, and he drew attention to democratic and proto-socialist ideas on the left wing of the Puritan Revolution.

Kautsky saw the revolution of the 1640's as the great turning point which marked the beginning of the modern era. This idea was taken up by the great historian Richard Henry Tawney, who became professor of economic history at the University of London around 1910. Tawney was the intellectual founder of the British Labor Party. It is his book *The Acquisitive Society* which became the theoretical Bible of the British Labor party until the 1930's. R.H. Tawney also was a prime founder of the adult education movement in England. He taught adult education classes for London workers in socialist theory, economics and in history. This was the first substantial adult education program in England.

Tawney also produced seminal historical works in the course of a long career. Tawney died in 1962. He became the dominant spokesman for Marxist historiography not only in England, but perhaps in the entire English- speaking world. Tawney envisaged the middle ages as having had strong communal structures. He believed that before 1500 the workers were taken care of by the Church, and that this relatively beneficent society was overthrown by the intrusion of capitalist agriculture into sixteenth- century England. The 1640's Puritan Revolution was conducted in the name of the rise of the capitalist gentry. The rural middle class, not being satisfied with what they had gained in the way of economic advancement in the sixteenth century, wanted to introduce the free market into England, and to eliminate the last vestiges of medieval regulation of the market by the crown. The purpose of the Puritan revolution was, in his view, to annihilate the remnants of medieval paternalism and institute unlimited capitalism.

Tawney advanced this argument in a series of eloquent books of which the most famous was *Religion and the Rise of Capitalism*, published in the early 1920's. Here Tawney disputed Max Weber on the meaning of the Reformation. Max Weber had said that the Protestant Reformation had made capitalism possible by introducing a work ethic and by valorizing capital accumulation. Tawney found that Weber had reversed the matter. He claimed that the causality ran in the opposite direction, namely, that capitalism advanced in the sixteenth-century and used Protestantism as its ideology.

Capitalism manipulates and assimilates Protestantism in order to endow itself with a moral ideology suitable to its interests. Protestantism is, then, the instrument of the sixteenth century capitalist revolution, rather than the Weberian shift in values that generated capitalism.

Tawney's *Religion and the Rise of Capitalism* is one of the all-time bestsellers of historical writing. Tawney was a master of English prose, and his book had enormous influence for a very long time. Through a host of Tawney's admirers and disciples, his grand Marxist interpretation of the Reformation endures as a legitimated model for the history of sixteenth and seventeenth centuries.

The third great historian on the radical left was Charles Beard, an American and a professor of political science at Columbia University until the United States entered the war in 1917. Beard vociferously opposed the entry into the war and was fired by the Columbia Board of Trustees. He never sought to regain his professorship. Having discovered that he could write bestselling history books, he retired to the Berkshires, where he became known as the sage of New Milford, Connecticut, and devoted himself to highly controversial historical writing well into the 1950's.

Beard's first and most famous book, which was published in 1913, was *An Economic Interpretation of the Constitution*, wherein he argued that the Constitution was created by a group of speculators, frontier developers and prominent merchants and their lawyers, who wanted a strong federal government in order to protect their interests as creditors and to allow them to gain entry into the western lands, western lands here meaning Western Pennsylvania, and the old "Northwest Territory"—Ohio, Indiana, Michigan and Illinois. There is of course some truth to Beard's argument, since George Washington was the leading investor in the Susquehanna Company, which controlled a third of New York State and what is now western Pennsylvania. The examples can be easily multiplied. Beard claimed provocatively that the Constitution was the document of a capitalist counter-revolution designed to protect the interests of the capitalist landlord and merchant class in the new nation, to deprive the proletariat and the small farmers of the benefits of the American Revolution, and to establish a market economy. His book had enormous impact and caused controversy both in and outside the academic world for several decades.

Finally, the last of the great quartet of pre-1914 Marxist historians was Albert Mathiez, who became professor of the history of the French Revolution at the University of Paris. He was the first Marxist historian to be appointed a professor in Paris. Around 1910, the University of Paris was the site of a bitter controversy about the interpretation of the French Revolution. The contention was primarily between the socialists and the conservatives, particularly those of the Catholic persuasion. The argument was finally settled by creating two chairs of history, one for the conservative interpretation of the Revolution, the other for the socialist—a tradition which still continues at the University of Paris.

Mathiez argued that the Jacobins, led by Robespierre, were left-wingers who wanted to establish a strong central government in order to limit unregulated capitalism and protect the interests of the common people. Even further to the left of Robespierre was Brabeuf, a doctinarian socialist. The democratic and prospective socialist revolutions were aborted by the Thermidorian Reaction, that is, by counter-revolution, but Robespierre and a few less celebrated personages even further to the left of him, were unquestionably on the road to socialism, said Mathiez. Thus the beginnings of the socialist tradition in France are found in the French Republic itself. The vision of Jean Jaures is firmly rooted in the traditions of Robespierre and Jacobinism. This view of the French Revolution is still regarded as gospel by all leftists in France, including François Mitterand.

*   *   *

Leninist and Western Marxism

Marx and Engels did not conceive of the communist revolution first occurring in Russia. They, and many others in Europe, thought that Germany would precede all other countries in the road to socialism, since the German Empire was the most advanced industrial society with the largest socialist party. What happened in Russia in 1917 was that there was first a liberal revolution which prevailed after terrible losses suffered by the Russian army in the First World War, combined with food shortages and rioting in Petrograd and Moscow, caused the Czar's government to collapse. The breakdown of the Russian economy and near starvation in the large cities enabled the liberal government, whose second chairman was the lawyer Alexander Kerensky, to come to power in February of 1917. The Czar abdicated in favor of another member of the royal family, who forthwith also abdicated, suddenly leaving Russia a Republic.

Kerensky was begged by the Western Allies to continue the Russian war against Germany, for the Allies were terrified that if the German army did not have to fight the Russians in the east any longer, then it would have enough power to achieve a breakthrough on the Western front. This in fact did not happen, but it was what motivated the Allies to urge Russia to remain in the war. Kerensky tried to continue the war and the result was increasing chaos and disorder. At this point, the German government provided a special train to carry Lenin from Zurich to the Finland Station in Petrograd (renamed Leningrad after the Revolution) because they felt that if Lenin appeared on the scene, he might be able to engender sufficient chaos so as to render the war effort of the Russians negligible. It is highly unlikely that it had ever occurred to the Germans that Lenin would gain complete power.

Even though Lenin's Bolshevik Party constituted a minority among the Russian Marxists, Lenin perceived that the organization of collectives (Soviets) of workers and soldiers in the major cities raised the possibility of a Communist takeover of power from the increasingly discredited liberal regime headed by Kerensky.

Lenin was assisted by Leon Trotsky, who rushed back to Russia from Brooklyn, where he had been doing nothing but waiting for the revolution.

Trotsky's real name was Bronstein. He was a Russian Jew. There was another East European Jew living in New York at the same time, who was named Rabinowitz, and who also adopted a pseudonym: Sholem Aleichem. He was the famous writer of the stories about the shtetl in Eastern Europe that half a century later were drawn upon for the musical comedy and film, *Fiddler on the Roof*. While Trotsky/Bronstein was writing turgid Bolshevik pamphlets that few wanted to read, Sholem Aleichem/Rabinowitz was gaining a vast reputation as a humorist in the Jewish press. When the two writers passed each other in Ratner's Dairy Restaurant on the lower East Side, they represented two main aspects of Jewish destiny in the twentieth century; the successful and prosperous immigrant to America from the shtetl and the Jewish Bolshevik leader who created a terror state that was to be worse for the millions of East European Jewry than the rotten anti-Semitic Czarist regime it replaced.

Great credit must be given to Lenin in that even though most of his own party did not believe that a successful *coup d'état* was possible, he insisted that there was sufficient support in the Russian armed forces, particularly in the navy, so that the Bolsheviks, the radical Communists, whom he led, could seize the Winter Palace where Kerensky's government was located. In the November of 1917 (October according to the old Russian calendar) with about two hundred sailors, the Bolsheviks seized the government which was housed in the Czar's Winter Palace. By this time, according to recent Marxist historians, the Bolshevik worker and military soviets or cadres had 250,000 members. Even if this figure is true, which is doubtful, this would represent only an insignificant minority of the Russian population.

Red October was not a mass revolution, but a *coup d'état*, conducted by a very small group of brave and determined revolutionaries, with the help of a handful of sailors and soldiers. The result was four years of civil war. The real decision in Russia was not made until 1921. In the meantime, the Bolsheviks were not only fighting the Whites, that is, the supporters of the Czar, the counter-revolutionaries. The Bolsheviks murdered the Czar and his family in the summer of 1918 in order to discourage the White Army. Between 1918 and 1921, Lenin's government also had to fight against Allied Armies that were sent into northern Russia as well as into Siberia to fight the Bolsheviks.

If the Bolshevik government has exhibited perpetual paranoia toward the West, it has to be remembered that it was partly because the English and the Americans tried to overthrow the Bolshevik government between 1918 and 1921. The Allied attempt failed because the Western governments would not commit to the enterprise armies that were large enough—a prototype for later failure against Communism in East Asia.

Trotsky, until then known mainly as a pamphlet writer, proved himself a military genius, and organized the Red army. Of course, he received help from former czarist officers who had gone over to the Bolshevik regime. Trotsky defeated the Whites in southern Russia and in the Ukraine, and fought the Allied Armies to a standstill. The latter had to withdraw ignominiously from the Russian front in 1921. Meanwhile, in order to get a free hand, the Bolsheviks had signed a peace treaty with the Germans in 1918 before the war ended on the Western Front. The peace treaty, which was signed in the spring of 1918, gave away enormous territory from the Czar's empire. Poland, Latvia, Lithuania and Estonia were given up by Lenin and Trotsky, to be regained in 1939 and 1945.

What happened in Russia was in one way a great triumph for Western Marxism, and in another way, it was an irrevocable disaster. The fact that the Russian Revolution had occurred meant that Marxism now had a power base in one of the leading countries in the world. Marxism was here to stay. Soviet Russia preserved high status in the international socialist community even though it had emerged impoverished from the war and the revolution. Russia did not regain the productive capacity that it had enjoyed in 1913 until the early 1960's.

On the other hand, the most left-wing and almost idiosyncratic form of Marxism had come to power. It believed in the use of violence to gain power and the mechanism of oligarchic dictatorship and the secret police to retain it. The Russian Revolution gave to the authoritarian view of Communism, as had been held by Rosa Luxemburg and Lenin, a tremendous and hitherto unprecedented prestige. This presented a constant challenge and complicated intellectual problem to Western Marxism. Western Marxists henceforth had to develop their doctrine in face of the prestige and influence held by the Soviet Union in the socialist world and the effort at manipulation of Western Communist parties engaged in by the Soviet Union well into the second half of the century.

Nevertheless, in the 1920's and 30's, there was a very important intellectual development in Western Marxism out of which arose some learned and subtle thinkers who were quite influential in their day, and who have become much more so since the 1950's. It is this non-Leninist group of Western Marxist thinkers of the 1920's and 30's who are worth the closest attention among socialists of the period. They made the most original contributions to twentieth-century Marxist theory. In spite of the enormous prestige which Soviet Communism now enjoyed in the West, this group of Western Marxist thinkers developed a cultural theory which contrasted sharply with Marxist-Leninism. If it was in the mainstream of the Marxist tradition, it was also closer to the younger, more idealist Marx of *The 1844 Manuscripts*, rather than the later, more materialist Marx of *Capital*.

The Hungarian Georg Lukács had a background in Hegelian philosophy and became a brilliant and original literary critic. For Lukács the advent of socialism implied primarily the triumph of a cultural liberation rather than a political one. He advocated the development of a society that would be devoted to the cultivation of the arts and literature, which he believed to be attainable only through socialism. Lukács also carried out pioneering Marxist interpretations of literary history, and particularly the history of the novel.

Lukács is most remembered for his theory of reification, which remains a central concept in Marxist theory. Reification means the controlled domination of the cultural, intellectual and artistic aspects of life by capitalism. Capitalism objectifies, or reifies, all human relationships including culture and art. It enslaves all aspects of cultural production, transforming all such products into its instrument. Capitalism is a strong substance, a great machinery, as it were, that runs through everything, from human relationships to artistic activity, subjecting all to its power and using them to perpetuate its own wealth. All art and literature that is so generated becomes, therefore, ideologically imprisoned in service of capitalism. This is the fundamental Lukácsian theory of reification. Just as industrial capitalism dehumanizes and alienates the individual, so capitalism dehumanizes, by reification or objectification, all culture. This culture is not free, since it is the instrument of capitalism.

Lukács was required in the twenties by the Hungarian Communist party, to which he belonged, to avow his loyalty to Leninism. He became a Stalinist after Stalinism came to dominate the Hungarian Communist Party in the 1930's. His own point of view, however, as ascertained in his early and creative work, is not in fact Stalinist, and his writings constitute the beginnings of a Western Marxism that departs from Leninist and Stalinist authoritarianism.

The second prominent Western Marxist thinker was Antonio Gramsci, who was the founder in 1921 of the Italian Communist Party. He spent most of his adult life in Fascist jails, and his main writings are entitled *The Prison Notebooks*. This material, which he wrote almost entirely in prison, was not published until after the Second World War and the end of the Fascist period in Italy. *The Prison Notebooks* produced immediate impact upon publication, and continued to exert influence until in the 1960's Gramsci became a revered theorist of the New Left. His reputation continues to grow. Marxist intellectual journals today constantly devote critical studies to Gramsci.

Gramsci can be said to be founder of the characteristic Western Marxist doctrine of base and superstructure. The foundation of every society consists in an economic base. It is out of this economic base that the cultural and institutional superstructure rises. The base is formed of the material aspects of existence, and the superstructure consists of the political and legal system, literature and the arts. Even though the superstructure arises from the base, it nevertheless assumes a life of its own. It is not entirely, immediately determined by the material base. To a significant degree, the superstructural aspects of a society assume a vitality, development and a history of their own.

The superstructure is part of what Gramsci calls the hegemony in society. That is to say, the ruling capitalists dominate not simply through economic control, but also through the hegemonic superstructure. Their hegemony or power is effected through institutions, law, art, and literature. This superstructure is therefore the means by which capitalist hegemony or rule consolidates itself. But, Gramsci continues, since the superstructure has a degree of autonomy, it can be used by the socialists to undercut capitalist rule. It is not necessary to wait for the moment of total transformation of the capitalist economic and social system. The superstructure itself can be used to confront and overthrow the capitalist hegemony. The arts and literature can occupy the vanguard of the revolution. The socialist revolution can be a cultural revolution.

Since capitalists rule through the hegemony of cultural superstructure, alterations in the superstructure can work back to erode the power of the capitalists and prepare for a socialist revolution. A cultural revolution can therefore anticipate and prepare the way for a social and economic revolution. This theory understandably became very popular in the 1960's in the United States as well as in France. It supported the view that if radical students could take over the university and if the counterculture could become dominant in society, capitalist hegemony would be eroded. Student radicals leading sit-ins and folk rock singers were in the vanguard of the Revolution—so Gramsci was interpreted.

Gramsci's theory has remained a very controversial and much debated reinterpretation of Marxism. The English Marxist Raymond Williams, for example, who is professor of literature at Cambridge University, finds that Gramsci's theory is attractive, but that it ignores the fact that the culture of capitalism is too thick, rich and complicated to admit of significant change. The counterculture can therefore only succeed in making very small inroads into the superstructural fabric of capitalist society. Gramsci, in Williams' view, underestimates the strength, and, in a sense, the creativity of the capitalist superstructure. The popularity of radical songs and the production of profound, rigorous Marxist literary theories do not necessarily signify substantial transformation of the capitalist superstructure.

On the other hand, there is the view of Juergen Habermas, the German philosopher and sociologist, who thought valid Gramsci's view that the strength of capitalism depended upon its moral visage and justification, and that capitalism would be delegitimized if it lost its moral presence and rationale. This, Habermas believed, could cause a severe breakdown in the entire bourgeois system. In other words, a cultural revolution focusing on the moral foundations of capitalism can in fact be effective. The debate in Marxist circles over Gramsci's theory still continues.

One characteristic of Gramsci's thought is clear: it is rooted in idealist philosophy. The leading school of Italian philosophy in the early twentieth century was the neo-Hegelian doctrine of Benedetto Croce. Gramsci's theory comes right out of this idealist background.

There is similarly an idealist vein in the work of the dominant German Marxist non-Leninist group of the inter-war period, the Frankfurt School of Critical Theory. The ideas of the Frankfurt School, whose organizer was Max Horkheimer and whose main intellectual luminairies were Walter Benjamin and Theodor W. Adorno, gained enormous prestige and attention in the transatlantic Marxist world in the sixties. Their work has now become habilitated in the academic world first in Germany, and since the early seventies in the United States under the leadership of Martin Jay and a group of disciples at the University of California.

In the eighties there has been an incessant stream of monographs and scholarly articles on the thought of the Frankfurt School. Benjamin has come to be recognized as one of the more important literary critics of the twentieth century even though his major work in the field was turned down by his university when in the twenties he offered it in support of his abortive effort to obtain a professorship. Adorno has come to be regarded in sociology departments and sometimes in philosophy departments as one of the leading theorists of the twentieth century and he has been placed alongside and perhaps even above Gramsci in the Marxist pantheon of great thinkers. As time goes on, as his collected works comprising some twenty-two volumes are published and translated into English, Adorno will gain recognition in academia generally as one of the half-dozen most influential thinkers of this century—or perhaps the twenty-first century.

As is the case with Heidegger and Jung, Adorno's writings require great effort and skill to translate into English, full as they are with Marxist and metaphysical jargon compounded with subtle paradoxes and asides that sometimes seem to be questioning the main argument. The best translated of Adorno's books and easiest introduction to his thought is *Prisms*, a collection of critical and expository essays. Of the torrent of recent monographs on Adorno, the most valuable and knowledgeable is by the Oxford scholar Gillian Rose.

In the late 1920's, a group of socialist thinkers in the industrial city of Frankfurt, which also had a large university, got together and founded the Institute for Social Research. At the time, the Institute was not part of the University of Frankfurt. It was founded as a counter- or free-school, designed to develop socialist ideas and a Marxist sociology outside the university. It raised funds from private sources, and was particularly funded by the sociologist who became its second director, Max Horkheimer. Not much had been done when Horkheimer took the Institute over in 1930. He became, in a way, its real founder as well as funder.

The three leaders of the Frankfurt School were Horkheimer, Walter Benjamin and Theodor W. Adorno. A younger member of the School was Herbert Marcuse, who has also been discussed above in his connection to Freudianism. Along with all left-wingers in Germany, at least with those who had not gone underground, Horkheimer, Benjamin and Adorno were dispersed by the Nazis in 1933, and their School eliminated. Horkheimer found his way to the United States, and with the help of Paul Lazarsfeld, the disciple of Durkheim who has been discussed previously, he reestablished the Institute for Social Research at Columbia University in 1938. Although Lazarsfeld was no Marxist, he was very protective of the Frankfurt School in exile and did much to help its members in their unfamiliar environment.

Adorno remained in Germany, changed his name and went into hiding. His father was a German-Jewish wine merchant, his mother was an Italian Catholic who was devoted to music, and from whom Adorno inherited his life-long interest in music. When the Nazis came to power, Adorno exchanged his father's German Jewish name for his mother's Italian name, which did not for long fool the Gestapo. Adorno had to leave the country. He too eventually made his way to Morningside Heights.

Walter Benjamin had a tragic end. Benjamin first decided he would go to Israel, which was then Palestine, and he asked his friend Gershom Scholem, the Jewish scholar of mysticism who had become a professor at the Hebrew University in Jerusalem, to obtain him a professorship at the same university. Scholem did that, but Benjamin turned down the offer, only in order to change his mind and to write Scholem once again, asking him to revive the offer. This time, Scholem did not reply. This account is from a recent book by Scholem himself.

Benjamin then fled to Paris, where he lived under impoverished circumstances, mainly on handouts from a Jewish refugee organization. The woman who ran the organization was herself a German émigrée named Hannah Arendt, the former student and mistress of Martin Heidegger and later a famous political theorist. Benjamin turning up once every two weeks to receive a handout from Hannah Arendt—there is material here for an interesting drama.

Finally, when the war broke out, Benjamin, unable to make up his mind about what course to take, remained in Paris. In 1940, however, when the German tanks rolled into Paris, he and a group of left-wing intellectuals obtained American visas and fled to the Spanish border, intending to go from Spain, which was neutral, to the United States. When they reached the Spanish border, they were stopped by the guards who refused them passage into Spain. They were told to come back the next day. Benjamin decided that the Spaniards would never admit him and that he would end up in Nazi hands. He returned to his hotel and killed himself. He was still in his late forties. It turned out that the problem on the Spanish border had been merely one of bureaucracy, and the next morning, his companions were admitted to Spain. Benjamin's fate constitutes a great loss to literary criticism as well as a personal tragedy.

Adorno was an extremely resilient person whose career in the United States was complicated and successful. Upon arrival, he went to work for Lazarsfeld on the new science of radio-polling. Adorno's job, which he enjoyed, involved telephoning people to ask which radio stations they preferred. Following this employment, he received a large grant from the American Jewish Congress to preside over an elaborate study of the authoritarian personality, which resulted in a famous work in social psychology that was published in the late forties. Although Adorno became known while in the United States as a social psychologist, this field was not his real interest. In fact, he believed that the foundations of Fascism were sociological rather than psychological. He did not really believe in an authoritarian personality type that—to make a living—he expounded so persuasively during his American exile.

In 1950, Horkheimer and Adorno returned in triumph to West Germany. Horkheimer became rector of Frankfurt University while Adorno held a senior chair of sociology and philosophy. Both were lionized by the students. They remained influential until the mid-sixties, until, that is, the rise of the radical New Left among the students in Berlin. Increasingly in his later years, Adorno devoted himself to music criticism, which had always been his great passion, and became increasingly moderate, almost apolitical. In his last years, Adorno came under severe criticism from the militant Marxist university students in Berlin. In the last year of his life, in 1969, his classes were disrupted by these radicals.

There are striking similarities within the Frankfurt School between the theories of Adorno and Benjamin. There are also similarities between the theories of the two Frankfurt thinkers and Lukács' and Gramsci's ideas, even though Benjamin and Adorno probably did not know about Gramsci's theory, since the latter's work was not published until the fifties.

Benjamin made significant contribution to literary criticism by stressing the importance of the change that had occurred in literature with the coming of the market, of mechanical reproduction and of mass culture. This change Benjamin located in the eighteenth century. At about the same time Queenie Leavis, the Cambridge critic, published a book making the same point, not from the Marxist point of view, but still arguing much the same theme. Leavis and Benjamin did not know each other's work.

Further, Benjamin developed a social and cultural theory. He said that out of literary and philosophical texts, there develops "an active figuration of constellated images." In other words, a cultural superstructure is generated out of a social context through the medium of words and concepts. The key word in the theory is "active." These constellated images take on a life of their own. While it is ultimately embedded in the social context, culture nevertheless has a high degree of autonomy, and operates its own world of symbols and dialectical images. Benjamin's theory is thus very similar to Gramsci's theory of the hegemonic superstructure.

Similarly, Adorno finds that in capitalist society a process of reification occurs in culture, which constitutes a kind of "fetishism." Capitalist cultural reification is "structural mystification." Capitalist society generates a system of symbols, literary and other artistic forms, a cultural superstructure, which has to be understood anthropologically. Just as in the study of primitive cultures, one realizes and takes into account that there are systems of magic, religion, kinship, an entire culture, which arises out of the economic base of that society, so too in studying capitalist society, the existence of a complicated fetishistic cultural mystification must be perceived.

In Adorno's theory, the generation of fetishism is a process of mediation. That is to say, this culture, the superstructural fetishism that inevitably emerges, is very thick. It is not simply an economic instrument to which one can readily refer as capitalist ideology. It becomes a form of mediation; it undertakes a life of its own, developing its own strengths and impact in the world. It is active and creative. Capitalism engenders a system of literature, the arts, and other symbolic forms which are structures of mediation.

As an example, jazz emerges out of American capitalist society, deeply conditioned by the exploitation of black people, but jazz constitutes neverthe- less an art form of its own, which has characteristics that cannot simply be attributed to the social and economic status of blacks. One cannot understand and fully describe what constitutes jazz as such by only describing the economic and social conditions of which it is a product. Jazz is a mediated culture that has to be understood on its own terms and not just as a social derivative.

The theory of structural mystification and cultural mediation represents a significant departure from the mature Marx of *Capital* although it has some affinities with the younger Marx of the *1844 Manuscripts*. This should occasion no surprise because the younger Marx was still somewhat of a philosophical idealist, still under the influence of his teacher Hegel. The mature

Marx stands Hegel on his head—that is, instead of ideas creating the world, the material world determines ideas. Adorno has now gone part way in turning Marx on his head because of the creative force and relative autonomy that he gives to culture.

Adorno's theory not only represents a partial resurgence of idealism in Marxism. His theory of cultural mediation bears a strong parallel to Freud's theory of mediation as propounded in *Civilization and its Discontents*. In Freud, culture is a consequence of the interaction of the pleasure and reality principles. In Adorno culture is the anthropological entity that arises out of economic practice. In both instances culture is a mediated structure.

It is not surprising then that Herbert Marcuse, a younger colleague of Adorno in the Frankfurt School, thought that a synthesis of Marxism and Freudianism was possible. Adorno's theory of structural mystification also to a degree anticipates Lévi-Strauss and the structuralism of the sixties and seventies. While there is no evidence from Lévi-Strauss' intellectual biography that he was influenced by Adorno, the affinity between their doctrines made possible efforts, still ongoing in the intellectual left, to achieve a synthesis of structuralism and critical theory.

Adorno's theory of cultural mediation is accompanied in his work by a doctrine of absolute relativism. Every "authentic" work of art and "true" philosophy Adorno tells us, has "always stood in relation to the actual life-process of society." The mind cannot escape from marketability and acts of exchange even when it consciously wants to. "Rather [the mind] grows to resemble ever more closely the status quo even where it subjectively refrains from making a commodity of itself." This statement can be construed as articulating in Marxist terminology Durkheim's principle of society's conservative capacity for functional socialization.

Adorno thus propounds a doctrine of false *un*conscious as well as consciousness and a doctrine of total, unavoidable reification. Even when the mind seeks to free itself from socialization and the dictates of market and commodity, it cannot do this, he claims. Here Adorno advances a theory of absolute cultural relativism that in the sixties was developed into the deconstructivist theory of Michel Foucault. The obvious question to be addressed to Adorno is whether he sees his own theory as exempt from unconscious relationship to the social network. And if not, what is its philosophical or scientific authority?

At times Adorno vigorously upholds an idealist humanism. "The reification of life results not from too much enlightenment but from too little." "Few things have contributed so greatly to dehumanization as has the universal belief that the products of the mind are justified only in so far as they exist for men." The latter statements make one think of Jung and Heidegger, or Jacques Maritain, but they are in fact Adorno's.

It is characteristic of the ambivalence of Adorno's thought that his proclivity to idealist humanism did not lead him towards utopianism, towards an affirmation of a social solution in which all contradictions are overcome and all problems resolved. He specifically rejected utopianism and advocated instead the principle of "negative dialectics." This concept, which got him into trouble with the New Left, utopian-minded students in the late sixties, essentially means that even in socialist thought there are no final answers. There is a negative dialectic or intrinsic weakness, within any theoretical propositions, including a Marxist one.

The historical dialectic never comes to a conclusion, not in Hegel's Prussian State nor even in Lenin's Communist state. There are always contradictions to be resolved, social issues to be addressed, novel factors to be integrated. Socialist perfection is an ongoing, endless process, according to Adorno. The actual problems of society are always greater than even the best-intentioned and most skillful socialist thinking to resolve them. We "must . . . reject the illusions . . . that the power of thought is sufficient to grasp the totality of the real." The dogmatism that characterizes Marxist intellectual journals today, particularly in the United States and Britain, reveals that Adorno's lesson of negative dialectics has not been learned by his followers. In Adorno's view, Marxism had an open-ended intellectual quality. Marxism was a never-ending story. This view would have got Adorno shot in the Soviet Union.

In his voluminous musical criticism Adorno frequently disarms us. As an eminent Marxist critic one would assume that he would unreservedly praise black jazz and condemn Arnold Schoenberg's modernism as bourgeois decadence. The reverse is true. He finds jazz lacking in developmental qualities—a view that would nowadays be regarded on the left as conservative or even racist (he is in fact wrong about jazz). On the other hand, Adorno thinks Schönberg is wonderful, one of the truly great composers. Adorno's inconsistency and idiosyncracy is refreshing and intriguing.

It is evident that Adorno wished to develop a sociology of culture along generally Marxist lines but he also wanted to preserve the independent character of critical judgment from ideological and political dictates. His temperament is very far from Leninism. Stalin would have sent him to the Gulag. Adorno remained a German philosopher in the idealist tradition. He was an immensely learned and creative sociologist whose ideas shifted from to time and he appears inconsistent in his theoretical exposition. That makes Adorno's writings all the more seminal as a bubbling spring of Marxist theory.

Consistency, in any case, has not been a characteristic of twentieth- century Marxist thought. Marxist theorists have in general sought to perpetuate the main doctrines developed by Marx and Engels. They have had to take account of the emergence of Soviet Russia and develop a perception, positive or negative, of the Soviet Russia that they can work into their theory. They have had a penchant to revive Victorian idealism from which Marx started and then repudiated and to reinsert it back into Marxist theory. And there has also been among many Marxist theorists a wish somehow to affiliate with the cultural avant-garde which has meant some kind of positive relationship to Modernism. Out of these diverse strands it has not been easy to fashion a consistent and comprehensive theory. Indeed it can be claimed that it is impossible to do so. But in cultural theory, the impossible sometimes bends to will and circumstance.

Because Adorno's thought is paradigmatic of the general intellectual agenda of Western Marxism from 1930 to the present day, and because of the intrinsic quality of this work, his influence and reputation is higher today in leftist circles than in his own lifetime. He has become the most seminal and admired of Marxist thinkers.

* * *

The Left in the Depression and World War II

The background of the socialist movement in the 1930's lies first of all in the Great Depression. The Depression began between 1929 and 1931, since it did not make itself felt everywhere at the same time, and it produced unprecedented economic disasters in the Western world, particularly deflation, decline in productivity, and massive unemployment. Not that the business cycle had not suffered crises before, for the West had lived through a serious depression in the 1870's and 80's, which nevertheless did not come anywhere near the decisiveness of the depression of the thirties. The level of unemployment in the United States had reached twenty-five percent by the time Franklin Roosevelt became president in 1932. It was indeed bold of Roosevelt to declare under those circumstances that the nation had "nothing to fear but fear itself." Even in 1940, the level of unemployment in America continued to remain over ten percent. There were industrial cities in northern England where unemployment approximated fifty percent—a record which England is once again approaching under Mrs. Thatcher. By 1931 the situation in Germany was as bad as in England and the United States.

Among the causes of the Great Depression was first of all the crisis in banking, which John Maynard Keynes had predicted as the probable result of the unwise Carthaginian peace settlement that had been imposed on Germany at the end of World War I, largely at the insistence of the French. The German democratic Weimar Republic, which had succeeded the empire in 1918, was saddled with enormous reparations. The German economy preserved its chaotic state until the mid-twenties. Under these adverse conditions, the Germans did not have the money to pay their reparations, and they borrowed from American banks, until, in 1928, they repudiated their debt to American banks, producing tremendous fiscal instability and a credit crisis first in the United States and then world-wide.

Therefore, the first cause of the depression was a banking collapse followed by a credit crisis. The implication of a credit crisis is that businesses cannot rely upon credit to sustain their loans and so preserve their current condition and remain in business, let alone, needless to say, have any prospect of expansion and growth. This will result in bankruptcy, not to mention the fear and panic any such adverse, wide-ranging phenomenon can produce.

Second among the causes of the depression was excessive speculation on an unregulated Wall Street, which brought about all manner of suspicions about the business world and the withdrawal of public support, to the extent of causing the collapse of October 1929.

Thirdly, in the 1920's, there had been an agricultural depression that cut across the Western world. The farming communities of the West had not been much affected by the First World War and they were tremendously productive in the 1920's with the result that there was an extensive overproduction along with the accompanying agricultural depression which made itself fully felt around 1926–27. The decline in rural consumption, in turn, eventually encouraged the depression in the industrial sector.

A fourth cause of the depression that historians have favored was the imposition of high tariffs on imports in the late twenties and early thirties, particularly by the United States. This rash protectionism disturbed international trade and encouraged a reversion to economic "autarchy" or self-subsistence. It is questionable, however, whether protectionism was a basic cause of the depression or more a response to the onset of bad times that exacerbated a deteriorating situation.

Finally, the depression was worsened in its impact and insured a long life by the unfortunate efforts of the governments in the Western world, in the critical period between 1929 and 1932, to deal with the depression. Their approach to the imminent collapse was sharply to reduce government spending; to do, in other words, the opposite of what Keynes advocated. They cut back in public works, laid off thousands of civil servants, and reduced the accessibility of government credit.

All the factors, mentioned above, which went into the making of the Great Depression, are in existence today. Pessimistic interpreters of the current economic scene, who claim that we are on the verge of another economic farflung disaster which will begin when Latin American countries repudiate their debts and so destroy New York banks, are drawing on the analogy between the current situation and the events of 1929–31. Of course, learning from history, we continue to extend loans to Latin American countries in order to save our banks from bankruptcy. We can only hope that the method will work.

The advance of the Great Depression—"Wall Street lays an egg," the entertainment newspaper *Variety* termed it at the time—generated a massive shift to the left in public opinion, particularly among educated people in the thirties. Within a few months, and certainly within three or four years, very significant numbers of university students and faculty throughout the Western world had shifted to democratic socialism, and in many cases, to support for the Soviet Communism. In 1932, Norman Thomas, running for president on the socialist ticket, gathered 900,000 votes, the second highest that a socialist presidential candidate has ever gained. Eugene Debs had received a slightly higher number of votes in 1912 and 1920.

The more important effect, however, of the advancement of the depression was on the opinion of the younger generation of people who were graduating from college without any prospect for jobs. A tremendous bitterness and massive withdrawal of faith in capitalism inevitably brought about the fundamental ideological shift to the left of an entire generation that was not significantly altered until the late 1940's.

The second factor that occurred in the 1930's was Stalinism. In 1927, after Lenin's death and a bitter feud in the Communist Party, Lenin's chief colleague

Trotsky was defeated and exiled, and Joseph Stalin became the Secretary of the Party and, in effect, the dictator of the Soviet Union. Stalin believed that Lenin and Trotsky had been far too soft on the Russian peasantry. He believed, and he was probably right, that if one were to achieve industrialization in the Soviet Union, the government had to break up the small farms of the kulaks, the wealthy peasants, that had come into being in the late nineteenth century, after the emancipation of the serfs. The way to achieve the modernization of the Russian economy was, according to Stalin, to destroy the conservative and entrenched peasantry.

Stalin had the lessons of history on his side. The Industrial Revolution had occurred in England only after the elimination of the old medieval peasantry between 1500 and 1800 along with their small holdings. Similarly, the rise of German industrial power in the late nineteenth century had occurred after the peasantry had been devastated in northern Germany. But what happened in the Soviet Union was deeply tragic in that Stalin moved too fast, and utilized the repressive engines of a police state, which had already been constructed by Lenin. Applying far more of an oppressive system than the one the czars had had at their command, Stalin engineered the slaughter of one to two million peasants, particularly in the Ukraine, in the early thirties. The exact number we do not know, and probably will never know, but it was a devastating massacre which did not even produce the intended effect. Russian agricultural productivity fell behind rather than increased under the forced collectivization scheme.

Stalin then became paranoid, believing that his colleagues in the Politburo, the executive body of the Party, were going to turn against him, and that they were going to remove him from power in collaboration with the army. This may very well have been the case; Stalin's fears may not have been groundless. He acted against his colleagues before they could undertake to act against him, although historians have not discovered any significant evidence that a coup against Stalin was in the making. The result was the infamous purge trials of the "old Bolsheviks" between 1934 and 1936. These were show trials in which the Bolshevik leaders confessed to elaborate treason, probably on the promise that they or their families would be freed, which, of course, usually did not occur. They were shot and their families either murdered or deported to Siberia. The huge secret police mechanism that Stalin had elaborated then got completely out of control and decimated not only the Bolshevik leaders but the rank and file of the Communist party.

These strange events presented a great problem for Western Communism. Were these trials genuine? Were the old Bolsheviks actually conspiring with Trotsky and the Nazis to surrender the Soviet Union, to overthrow the Soviet regime (as the purge trials contended)? It was difficult for Western Communists to decide these matters. Consequently, most of them in the thirties decided that the trials were genuine. Even Western journalists, observing these trials, including a reporter from *The New York Times*, decided, in most instances, that they were genuine. Even the American ambassador to Moscow decided the same. These purge trials produced a moral crisis for Western Communism and for Marxism in general, which reverberates to the present day.

In 1938, Stalin carried out a second wave of purges, and staged trials of the senior ranks of the army, including the commander-in-chief, with the result that the vast Soviet army, one that was larger and probably better equipped than the German army, became incapable of withstanding the initial phase of the German invasion in 1941. Contrary to common belief at the time, which accorded a specious invincibility to the German army, this is the main reason why the Germans succeeded in Russia for about twelve to fourteen months, and could penetrate to the gates of Moscow and Leningrad. Almost the whole senior echelon of the Soviet army had been purged by Stalin in 1938 because he feared they were going to overthrow him.

The second crisis after Stalinism, for Western Marxists, in the 1930's was the rise of Fascism. The crisis went along the following lines: Was Fascism a new phenomenon? Or was it simply a particularly vicious form of bourgeois capitalism in its final phase? Were the Fascists a threat to everybody, to bourgeois liberals and to Communists and democratic socialists alike? Should all these ranks therefore combine against Fascism, or was Fascism simply representative of the death throes of the decadent bourgeoisie? It took Communists, and even Western Marxists, the better part of a decade to come to a decision about the nature of Fascism.

One reason why Hitler was able to gain and consolidate power in 1931–33 was the belief of German Communists, whose number was a critical factor, that Hitler did not pose a great threat, but was merely an extreme extension of the bourgeoisie. This accorded with the advice given to German Communists by Moscow. Consequently, they would not cooperate with the social democrats, the moderate socialists and the liberals—"Social Fascists," they called them—against the Nazis. Because of this initial Communist view of Hitler, a united front against the Nazi advance to power was impossible.

Between 1936 and 1938 the international communist organization under Soviet leadership, the Comintern, pursued an alternative policy and created the international Popular Front against Fascism. This action was very well received by Western Marxists as well as by many liberals, and made Stalin popular. It cast a favorable image for him and helped cover up the significance of the purge trials which were reaching their height at the same time. Stalin presented himself as the patron and leader of the united crusade against Fascism.

In 1939 the Soviets changed their policy again, once again producing a crisis for Western Communists and Marxists, and signed the Hitler-Stalin pact of September 1939. The pact was based on the agreement of Hitler and Stalin to divide Poland and not to undertake war against each other. Stalin gave Hitler a free mandate to invade and conquer about sixty percent of Poland, retaining forty percent of the country for himself. Also, he promised to send war material, including oil and steel, to help the Nazis in their war against the decadent bourgeois Allies in France and England. He continued to send valuable war materiel to the Nazis until the very day, in June 1941, when Hitler invaded the Soviet Union.

The apologists for Stalin claim that he believed, rightly or wrongly, that he was about to be betrayed by the Allies. He believed that the British, under prime minister Neville Chamberlain, who had already made a pact with Hitler in 1938 at Munich, and the French were going to join up in a crusade against the Soviet Union. Stalin acted, so the apologetic argument runs, to forestall them and therefore signed his pact with Hitler. This is a controversial issue which diplomatic historians have not been able to untangle.

Whatever the reasons and justification for Stalin's act, it nevertheless presented one more crisis for the West. The Popular Front was of course repudiated by this time, and during the first year and a half of the Second World War, from September 1939 until Hitler invaded the Soviet Union in June of 1941, Western Communists opposed the Allied war effort. It was not easy to be a Communist in Britain, France or the United States in the late 1930's, trying to understand and deal with the unending series of crises and reversals of Soviet policy. "Their line has changed again" went the refrain of an anti-Communist leftist song of the thirties.

By the mid-thirties the long tradition of Marxist thought in Germany had been interrupted, not to resume again until the 1950's. While some German socialist thinkers, such as members of the Frankfurt School, continued their work in exile, all that remained of the large and diverse socialist movement within Nazi Germany was a small Communist underground. Until the Second World War began to go badly for Germany in 1943, this Communist underground was the only organized resistance movement to Hitler, irrespective of later self-serving myth-making. Similarly in German-occupied France from June 1940 until the Allied invasion of France became imminent early in 1944, the organized resistance to the Wehrmacht and Gestapo came mostly from the Communist underground, although there was also a smaller and less effective non-Communist underground lavishly supported and stimulated from London.

After the liberation of Paris in the summer of 1944, a glorious myth of extensive resistance to the Nazi occupiers was disseminated. While there were certain instances of exemplary heroism on the part of the non-Communist underground, many post-war French resistance heroes and heroines had actually done their service in the Left Bank cafés.

The Communist Party in the United States during the thirties flourished as never before or since. Its total membership remained insignificant, but it did manage to enroll temporarily in its membership a noticeable number of young intellectuals and media people, as well as gain momentarily representation in the executives of some labor unions. But the American Communist party was poorly led, faction-ridden, and periodically disturbed by changes in the Moscow line. The Popular Front motif of 1936–38 was highly beneficial to it, as it could thereby sponsor well-attended congresses of writers and intellectuals. The purge trials produced some unease among communist members and fellow-travellers. The Hitler-Stalin pact of 1939 was, however, the death-knell of Communism as a significant movement in the United States.

The most important development by far in the American left of the 1930's was the advancing tide of New Deal welfare liberalism. It absorbed the preponderance of progressive sentiment and assured that the Communist Party and other socialist groups would remain small and politically impotent factions, although not without some influence in academia, the media, and labor unions. Thus the patrician liberal FDR was indeed the savior of American capitalism; New Deal liberalism became the prime focus for the American left, not a variety of Marxism. The immediate access to power that the New Deal promised contributed to its attractiveness.

From the conservative public policy of the 1920's, the country went over to welfare liberalism in the 1930's. It is true that the New Deal was not as successful as Arthur Schlesinger and other historians of the New Deal claimed. Nevertheless, there was under its aegis considerable economic improvement, restoration of confidence and renewed vitality in business, and decline in unemployment between 1934 and 1938. However, the year 1938 brought another crash which continued until Americans began to build war materials for England in 1940. It was the coming of the Second World War, and not the New Deal, that ended the depression in America. The war, and the new needs and markets it provided, followed by the drafting of millions into the armed forces, totally ended unemployment and created unprecedented prosperity and power for American industry.

The defenders of the New Deal can plausibly claim that a conservative Supreme Court fought a bitter rear-guard action for a long time, and that some of the bolder and more imaginative ventures of the New Deal were rendered ineffective by the Court between 1933 and 1936. Whatever its intrinsic capability in controlling the Depression, the historical consensus remains that the New Deal changed American life. It brought about the federal regulation of commerce and industry, and governmental supervision of Wall Street and banking. The deployment of the Federal Reserve System to control credit supply was perhaps the single most important and effective New Deal enterprise. The establishment of the Social Security system and federally-funded public works were also consequential. The former brought the USA closer to Europe in providing for the elderly. The latter improved environmental conditions such as good roads and electric power dams and made a dent in the appalling unemployment rate.

What the New Deal program lacked was the establishment of a national health scheme, which America still needs, and a rigorous plan of Federal aid to education, which by and large did not commence until the 1960's. Nor did the New Deal do anything substantial by way of helping racial minorities, except to undertake some laudatory and ceremonial ventures such as an invitation for a black opera star to the White House, which caused nothing less than a sensation in 1937. Black people felt good about this novelty, but the first step in the liberation of blacks in this country came only during the War when there were some marginal efforts to integrate the armed forces. Yet, Roosevelt never showed the boldness and courage actually to effect the integration. It was not until Harry Truman held the presidential office that, in 1947, the United States army was integrated by presidential order. This event marks the real beginning of the civil rights movement in this country.

Whatever the actual accomplishments of the New Deal—still a moot issue— intellectuals, academics and media people lined up behind Roosevelt and the New Deal enthusiastically and in overwhelming numbers. Most American university professors in the 1920's probably voted Republican. The Ivy League faculties were then certainly overwhelmingly Republican and conservative. Even after the Depression began, many were still preaching social Darwinism and unregulated market economy in their classes. With Roosevelt's charismatic leadership and the New Deal's political success, there was a radical change. Even in the early 1950's, ninety per cent of the History Department at Princeton University were voting the straight Democratic ticket, just the opposite of what they were doing in the late 1920's.

The political transformation brought about in the New Deal era was profound and long-lasting. It moved the mass of American academics and intelligentsia to the left of center where it remains, although there were some significant neo-conservative defections among prominent scholars in the 1970's.

The paradigmatic New Deal intellectual was Lionel Trilling, the literary critic at Columbia University who became a leader of the New York intellectual world and gained enormous devotion and international prestige. He was the first Jew to become a professor of English at Columbia, and the last one until the 1950's. Another brilliant young Jewish literary scholar, Clifton Fadiman, applied for a job in the Columbia English Department shortly after Trilling, only to be told that the Jewish quota, which was one, was full. Fadiman had to find consolation in becoming rich and famous running a radio quiz program and the Book-of-the-Month Club.

What was there in Trilling that drew so much devotion and attention? He was able to associate the New Deal with the liberal traditions of the nineteenth century. Trilling was an authority on Matthew Arnold, the English humanist critic of the mid-nineteenth century, and by very skillful intellectual sleight-of-hand, he convinced his audience that the New Deal was in line with the best traditions of Victorian liberal humanism. It was not an infeasible argument; it is certainly not nonsense.

Trilling was thus an historicist. He placed the New Deal and the liberal-left in the grand tradition of Western Civilization. With his colleagues, he elaborated a core curriculum at Columbia College, which is still in use, called "Introduction to Contemporary Civilization in the West." In the sixties, the program was still using the canon that Trilling and his colleagues had prepared in the thirties. Every prominent name in Western Civilization from Plato through Thomas Aquinas, Machiavelli, Descartes, Kant—with the possible exception of Thomas Hobbes—belonged to Trilling's canon of the grand Western tradition which came to a crashing climax with FDR, John Maynard Keynes and the New Deal. Many other American colleges closely imitated the Columbia core curriculum. Two of Trilling's colleagues in the Columbia History department, Henry Steele Commager and Allan Nevins, rewrote American history to make the New Deal the triumphant culmination of national destiny. FDR was the heir of Jefferson, Jackson, and Lincoln.

The Trilling group developed a philosophy of history, and an educational theory and curriculum which came to occupy central place in academia and molded the mentality of two generations of American students. Trilling's historicizing of the liberal tradition and his placement of the New Deal within it effectively brought about the persuasion of public opinion. The media, led by the *New York Times* and the *Washington Post*, disseminated the Trilling model through its news and editorial columns (they still do.) By the late 30's the identification of FDR and the New Deal with the liberal tradition and humanist canons of Western Civilization encountered no effective dissent within either the media or academia. Under these cultural conditions, Roosevelt continued to win elections, and the Democrats, with the exception of the Eisenhower interlude (1952–60) which did not weaken the Democrats' dominance of college faculties, continued to hold power from 1932 until 1968.

Trilling's collection of critical essays *The Liberal Imagination* became a monument to his generation's efforts to combine New Deal politics with English humanism. His greatest accomplishment was actually as a novelist, not as a critic. In *The Middle of the Journey*, a work of the 50's, Trilling portrayed unflinchingly and honestly the Communist fellow- travelling of his New York friends in the 30's and 40's. This is one of the more important political novels of the century. But this more pessimistic side of Trilling was ignored.

Among the vanguard intellectuals in New York in the 1930's and 40's were a number who were instructors at the Washington Square College of New York University. Washington Square College goes back to the 1840's. Shortly before the First World War, Washington Square College was, for all practical purposes, closed down and became a night school run to make money. The trustees of NYU hated Jews and immigrants of all kinds. They established a new residential campus on University Heights in the Bronx, with very strict quotas against Jewish students. Washington Square College continued its existence as a mere milch-cow night school for immigrants.

However, in the 1920's, there were so many people, mostly Jews as well as some Italians and Irish, who wanted to attend NYU, that Washington Square College reopened as a day school. It was run on the cheap side, and most of the instructors were adjuncts, some of whom were extraordinarily brilliant people. These included William Phillips, Sidney Hook, and Delmore Schwartz, who belonged to *The Partisan Review* group, as well as the novelist Tom Wolfe. These formed New York's group of socialist intellectuals. They were mostly Trotskyites, that is, Communists who had decided already then against Stalin. Soon the group dispensed with Trotsky, too. Trotsky was by this time vegetating in his Mexican exile until he was assassinated in 1939 by a Stalin agent using an ice pick.

It was a remarkable group of free-floating intellectuals who produced the quarterly journal called *The Partisan Review*, which became the leading left-wing intellectual publication in the United States. It is still in existence and is now published at Boston University. Its two founding editors were Philip Rahv and William Phillips, both of whom originally had very foreign Jewish names which they changed. Phillips, now over eighty years old, still edits the journal. In 1939 *Partisan Review* had a paid circulation of five thousand, which even now would be considered a good circulation for a literary quarterly. Eash issue of *PR* must have been read by thirty or forty thousand intellectuals and academics.

Partisan Review exercised an enormous influence on the entire generation of the thirties and the forties. Those who worked for it comprised many of the leading literary minds of that generation: Dwight McDonald, the political theorist; Edmund Wilson, the literary critic who is regarded by many as one of the three or four greatest literary critics this country has ever produced; the nobel laureate novelist, Saul Bellow, and the poet, Delmore Schwartz; Harold Rosenberg, the modernist art critic; Irving Howe, who is still a university professor at City College and who gained fame in the sixties by writing about the Jewish immigrant culture, and who still writes about socialism; Mary McCarthy, the well-known novelist; Sidney Hook, chairman for thirty years of the philosophy department at Washington Square College; Daniel Bell, the Columbia and later Harvard sociologist; Irving Kristol, now a neo-conservative theorist. The *PR* list of names and achievements is long and highly distinguished.

The New York intelligentsia of the thirties and early forties, about eighty-five percent Jewish, began its formation for the most part in the Brooklyn ghetto and ended life in upscale apartments on Riverside Drive. The title of the autobiography of a younger member of this group, Norman Podhoretz, later editor of *Commentary—Making It*—speaks for this destiny. Quite a few members of this group have written their autobiographies in recent years, describing life in those days. They all portray themselves as poor, idealist geniuses whose lives bear a touch of sadness because their deep and somewhat simple socialist, and in some cases Communist, commitments could not always be maintained. The world changed and some of them became mere liberals in the 1950's and sixties, and even conservatives in the seventies.

The common theme in all of their writing is that they were intellectual and literary giants who saved American culture, that America would have been immensely impoverished without them. The *New Yorker* cartoon depicting the map of America according to New York intellectuals as consisting ninety per cent of Manhattan and ten percent of San Francisco cleverly approximates the perspective of these intellectuals on the United States. Hardly any of them went west of the Hudson except to go on lecture and book-signing tours.

The *Partisan Review* group and their affiliates—"the New York Intellectuals" as they are now called—have developed their own mythology. There are several graphic accounts, for example, of occurrences in the City College cafeteria in 1933–36, of heated conversations in Alcove I and Alcove II, where the young Jewish intellectuals, arrived by subway from Brooklyn, would sit and debate endlessly the Moscow purge trials or some new critical essay written by Edmund Wilson or some new pseudo-proletarian novel. They caricatured themselves in their memoirs. Their total achievement as theorists and writers is not anywhere as impressive as they themselves claim. Yet some of them gained a place in twentieth-century thought.

Sidney Hook is now a fellow of the Hoover Institute in Palo Alto, California, where he turns out brilliant right-wing pro-Reaganite treatises. In the 1930's, he was the leading authority on Marxist theory in this country. His book on the intellectual and particularly Hegelian origins of Marxism, *From Hegel to Marx*, is an astonishingly brilliant work, still the best on the subject. Hook is a very fine historian of ideas.

Edmund Wilson began as a critic of Modernism in the early thirties, when he wrote important essays on Modernist literature. He was very much taken by the left-wing trend of the thirties, and in 1939, published a book on the history of Marxism entitled *To the Finland Station*. The work became a bestseller and is still a fine, readable work. Even though it is now out- of-date and superseded by later scholarship, if one were asked to pick a book to be read on the history of Marxism as an intellectual movement down to the Russian Revolution, Wilson's would still be the consensus choice.

Wilson's greatest achievement, however, is *Patriotic Gore*, which was published in 1962. Unquestionably the most exciting work written on the culture of the American Civil war era, it is a study of the ideas prevailing in both South and North. Wilson is particularly brilliant and insightful on the South and when he describes the process wherein two cultures slowly separate and come into conflict. Wilson also wrote a pioneering study on the Dead Sea Scrolls, for which he taught himself Semitic languages. One can add to the list of his achievements that he wrote the first significant book on Canadian literature, and perhaps also the last interesting study of that remote topic. Wilson was an astonishing, brilliant and diverse man, an American original. One more reason to admire him was his refusal to pay income tax.

Harold Rosenberg was an important New York art critic from the late thirties to the sixties. He worked to achieve a symbiosis of Marxism and Modernism, starting from the principle that Modernism was a cultural vanguard while Marxism constituted the social and political vanguard, claiming, therefore, that they must be compatible, existing as two sides of the same coin. He did not find it easy to forge this argument, which necessitated twists such as claiming that T.S. Eliot was not a Modernist. To sustain his argument, Rosenberg had to purge Modernism of its rightist, conservative wing. To claim that T.S. Eliot is not a Modernist is tantamount to nothing less than arguing that the Pope is not a Catholic. There have indeed been people who have claimed both.

American socialists, while highly visible in the intellectual and literary world of the thirties, achieved only a small penetration of academia. This was a time when the university faculties were contracting. Because of the Depression, professors had been fired, and consequently, even though there was a generation of radical graduate students, few of them could get jobs in universities, since, regardless of the applicant's political stance, jobs were simply not available. Nevertheless, there were three important Marxist humanists in American academe by 1940. One of these was Sidney Hook, who used his chairmanship of the philosophy department at Washington Square to appoint his friends, such as William Barrett. A second was F.O. Matthiessen, who came from a prominent New England family, wrote a brilliant Marxist interpretation of the New England renaissance of the 1830's and 40's, rehabilitated the reputation of Melville as a novelist, and then committed suicide. He was a professor at Harvard University.

Finally, and perhaps most important, was Kenneth Burke, who became professor of English literature at Bennington College and later taught at many other institutions. He is still alive and still publishing, having produced a vast corpus of idiosyncratic Marxist or quasi-Marxist theory on literature. Because

Burke's most important work appeared in the 1950's, when there was a movement away from Marxism, he was not appreciated as much as he ought to have been. He has been rediscovered, however, by the recent Marxist cadre in the universities and generally febrile interest in literary theory. He is now receiving a great deal of attention, not only in Marxist publications but also in mainstream journals of literary criticism. Burke and Edmund Wilson will be recognized as the two leading left-wing literary critics that the United States produced before the sixties. There is an attractive nativist asperity about them. They worked things out for themselves. They did not take orders from Paris or London.

In the Britain of the thirties and early forties, there was a left-wing group that was comparable to the one that had gathered around *The Partisan Review* in the United States. Here too was a group that assumed a mythological aura, which they too later skillfully promoted. This was primarily a group of poets at Oxford and Cambridge Universities. The most distinguished among them was W.H. Auden, who came to the United States in 1939, and is still regarded as a major Modernist poet. Another was Stephen Spender, who is still alive and undertaking lecture tours in which he assiduously cultivates memories of the heroic thirties. The group also included Julian Bell as its member, the nephew of Virginia Woolf, who gained reverential martyrdom in the Spanish Civil War.

Among this generational cohort of British leftists were a group of students at Cambridge University who became Soviet moles. Writers, civil servants, and art historians were recruited by Soviet agents to enter the British intelligence services, where they spent twenty years causing havoc by selling state secrets to the Russians; and what was worse, betraying British and Allied agents. Homosexuality as well as ideology bound their group together; its leader was Kim Philby.

As regards the more academic and theoretically oriented representatives of British Marxism, two thirties' anthropologists stand out because they presented Marxist or quasi-Marxist interpretations of anthropology which gained credibility among the social scientists and the educated public at large. The first of these was the Polish émigré Bronislaw Malinowski, who began his field work during the First World War in the Trobriand isles, and in the 1920's became professor of anthropology at the University of London. Malinowski was a materialist who believed that all institutions in early society are outcomes of food-gathering activity and the satisfaction of other material wants. He was a good trainer of field workers, which enabled him to acquire many disciples. Malinowski trained many of the following generation of British anthropologists.

More theoretical as well as more dogmatically Marxist was V. Gordon Childe, who also became professor of anthropology at the University of London. He had originally been an Australian. Childe was an historian of early societies. In 1942 he published the first edition of his *What Happened in History?* that, along with Ruth Benedict's *Patterns of Culture*, remains the all-time best-selling anthropological book of the twentieth century. Childe raises the question of how civilization emerged in the Ancient Near East, and he describes it in terms of a class struggle, and more particularly, in terms of the emergence of a bourgeoisie in the cities of the ancient Near East, who gained control over the resources of their society and organized the technology of the society in their interest. Childe provides an early chapter to the Marxist historical theory of dialectical materialism by showing the beginnings of history in terms of class struggle.

Childe concludes his book by suggesting that the persistent class struggle continues into civilized societies of later eras. He comforted Marxists of his generation with the thoughts that the Marxist historical model was firmly grounded in archaeological and anthropological data from the Ancient Near East. Until the work of the Chicago anthropologist Robert Braidwood in the 60's, Childe's Marxist construct seemed credible.

Another Marxist working in Britain was Karl Polyani, a Hungarian who became a professor of economic history at the University of London, and later, in the 1950's, at Columbia until he and his wife found disfavor with the American immigration officers of the McCarthy era. Polyani published what is still the classic Marxist work on the Industrial Revolution, entitled *The Great Transformation*, which is a work of exceptional subtlety, and fully in line with the ideas of the Frankfurt School. Applying the Frankfurt School's ideas to history, Polyani attempts to show how the circumstances of the Industrial Revolution bring about the transformation from the old paternalistic view of economy and mercantilism to the development of market ideas in the service of industrial capitalism.

Finally, there was Harold Laski, famous in the 1930's and 40's. Everybody knew about Laski in Britain just as everybody knew of John Dewey in the United States. Every progressive petition would bear his name; at every mass meeting and leftist conference Laski would either appear in person or would send a telegram. He came of a wealthy Jewish Manchester family. He taught for a while at Harvard, and became professor of political science at the London School of Economics.

Laski provided opportunity, in the 1930's and 40's, for young people of Marxist views to get Ph.D.'s in political science and social theory. There were hardly any Marxists in that period who were political scientists, and Laski provided them the access route. He was also a prolific writer of books committed to pop-Marxist historiography, for example his account of economic individualism. Laski's books make painful reading today. His vulgar Marxist ideology and crude learning remind one that leftist academics were not necessarily more committed to high standards of scholarship in the 1930's than in the 1980's.

In retrospect two of the more original Marxist scholars in Britain in the late 1930's and 40's were art historians. In the German-speaking world in the late twenties, there were two centers of art history: the one in Berlin produced the Modernist school of iconology, which has been previously discussed, in the work of Abby Warburg and Erwin Panofsky. In Vienna, on the other hand, there was a group of left-wing art historians who tried to develop a social history of art, establishing the connection of the development of artistic schools and styles to social and economic history. Needless to say, this school was devastated by the rise of Fascism in Austria and by the union of Austria with Germany in 1938.

Two members of the Viennese school, however, managed to make their way to England: Arnold Hauser and Frederick Anthal. These two certainly did not get their due in England. Neither of them ever found a real academic post, and both ended up teaching adult education classes, never receiving a professorship. They met with difficulties in large part because England did not have a penchant for art history, not only of the Marxist bent, but for art history of any school. Outside the Warburg-Courtauld Institute in London, which was partly supported by Warburg's own money, there were no art history departments in England.

Anthal produced a very interesting Marxist interpretation of Florentine Renaissance art. Even though it was scathingly rejected by the iconological school, it is nevertheless a work worth looking at. Arnold Hauser, on the other hand, acquired fame with his four-volume *A Social History of Art*, which has become an all-time bestseller. Paradoxically, a very large number of people have received their introduction to the field of art history from Hauser's work. The book is a grab-bag of information some of which can become quite silly, establishing vulgar correspondences between the economic life of a society and its artistic products. Nevertheless, Hauser was a man of deep learning and is indeed capable of fertile insights. Doubtlessly, there is an economic and political side to art, and Hauser has a valid point.

Anthal and Hauser started a Marxist school of art history in Britain, which remained largely subterranean for several decades. But a product of this school, Timothy J. Clarke, a British scholar and disciple of Hauser and Anthal, is now senior professor and the leading influence in the art history department at Harvard University. In a way, Hauser and Anthal have triumphed in the end, and their Marxist ideas, carried from Vienna to the unwelcoming ground of England, have been eventually transplanted to Harvard, where they are now flourishing.

A new era of left-wing thought in France begins with Leon Blum's Popular Front in 1936, when a leftist coalition was established under Blum, the disciple of the socialist leader Jean Jaurès. Blum's doctrinal position within the left was rather vague. He was a mild socialist who can also be described as a welfare liberal. But a left-winger nevertheless, he headed the first leftist government of France, which lasted for only two years. Blum's government did not accomplish much, but it was a great rallying cry for socialists in France and provided a starting point for a French leftist intellectual tradition that persisted into the 1960's and beyond. François Mitterand is a disciple of Blum and his ultimate successor.

The two fields of intellectual accomplishment among the French left in the late thirties and forties were history and philosophy. Two historians, Lucien Febvre and Marc Bloch, were the founders of the seminal French school of social history called the *Annales*, named after the journal they had founded in the early thirties. Febvre and Bloch were first professors of history at the University of Strasbourg, which was at the time a vanguard institution. Until 1919, the University of Strasbourg had been a German university, and was reconstituted as a French university after the reconquest of Lorraine at the end the First World War, and endowed with a new, young faculty.

Febvre's interest was in the sixteenth and seventeenth centuries, while Bloch—who was killed by the Nazis in 1944 while he was in the resistance— was the most prominent French medievalist of his generation. Both Febvre and Bloch moved to the University of Paris in the 1930's, where they began to exert enormous influence on French historiography. Since the 1950's, the *Annales* school has gained strong influence in the United States as well.

Febvre was very much interested in geography and environmental history, in the effect of climate and topography, of material forces, that is, on social institutions such as religion. He applied the concepts and methods of early twentieth century French geography to the era of the Protestant Reformation, which he examined in terms of the influence of environmental and physical factors on religious values. Bloch attempted an understanding of feudalism in terms not only of its social structures, but also with reference to its cultural values. He examined feudal cultural values and ideology as generated by social structures.

Febvre and Bloch were committed to a program they termed "total history," which implies a combination of Durkheim's functionalist sociology with environmental determinism. Total history investigates how a social and cultural system is shaped by a variety of material factors and how a social "mentality" is conditioned by diverse forces, especially material ones. Neither Febvre nor Bloch were ideologically dogmatic, nor were they Marxists in the strict sense of the term. They can rather be described as left-wing functionalists, and as radical followers of Durkheim, who were interested in the ways in which a total social system operates in terms of the physical environment. They are concerned with values but of an impersonal, collective kind that comprise the mentality of social groups. What they really started was a school of historical sociology, which was to become widely popular in the fifties and sixties and to dominate the historical imagination of the late decades of the century throughout the Western world.

In the late forties, partly in response to Bloch's heroism, the *Annales* school became a well-endowed, state-supported Parisian institute and almost totally monopolized French historiography of the next generation. The deep learning and careful analyses that had distinguished the work of Febvre and Bloch were relaxed in the post-war era. The *Annales* school's commitment to total history and social mentalities became a convenient cover for a young, ambitious and energetic group of historians who were more ideologically committed to Marxism and to the political left than the two founding fathers.

The second area in which French leftists were productive was philosophy, in which the leading personalities were Maurice Merleau-Ponty, Jean-Paul Sartre, Simone de Beauvoir and Albert Camus. The philosophy they produced can be described as a left-wing phenomenology that drew on Hegel as well as on Heidegger, but transformed the ideas of the two German thinkers into a distinctly French philosophy. Out of the teaching of Merleau-Ponty, who was a professor of Hegelian philosophy at the University of Paris in the thirties and forties, and out of the elegant writings of Sartre, de Beauvoir and Camus, emerged the highly visible French school of left-wing existentialism of the forties and fifties.

French existentialism holds that the individual, committed to moral principles, stands over against an unfavorable social environment as well as against a cruel physical surrounding. The only thing that the individual knows that is good in the world, says Camus, is his own mind. Everything else for Camus, is absurd. The only way the individual can secure his existence, and achieve any degree of authenticity and integrity, is to continue struggling against the unfavorable environment, even though he knows that he cannot make much headway.

Camus uses the Greek myth of Sisyphus in order to describe life as tantamount to rolling a rock up a hill which will roll back downhill the moment it has reached the top. Nevertheless, despite the fact that one knows the fate of the rock that one is rolling uphill, one continues to work at it. There is no alternative to continuing to try. An individual's only means to maintaining his humanity consists of shouldering the struggle, knowing well that it is futile. "The absurd is born of this confrontation between the human need [for commitment] and the unreasonable silence of the world. This must not be forgotten. This must be clung to because the whole consequence of life can depend on it."

While Camus was fond of quoting Nietzsche and Kierkegaard, essentially his exentialism was an idealized version of Heidegger's phenomenological doctrine of authenticity. Camus—who died prematurely in an automobile accident in 1960—was a French colonial, a native of the French Algerian empire and the only philosopher of consequence to emerge out of vast array of European overseas imperialism. It is also possible to see in his writings the fatalism, the wistful romantic idealism that characterizes much of Moslem thought, particularly the Sufism that was popular in North Africa for centuries.

Yet existentialism was above all a response to the Second World War, the humiliating French defeat and surrender to Hitler in 1940, and the determination of De Gaulle and the Free French and the resistance at home to maintain the struggle against the Nazi occupation under circumstances that initially appeared hopeless. Camus was an active writer and theorist in the resistance and *The Myth of Sisyphus* was originally published by the underground press in 1942.

In the face of a dark situation that for a while seemed hopeless and promised no survival and no deliverance from the Nazis, the existentialists showed a way to continue to affirm one's humanity and moral integrity. We must, they said, resist the Nazis, not give in; any other mode of action would destroy our humanity. Existentialism became the philosophy of the resistance and then for the early years after the liberation in 1944, of the revived French republic.

That Camus and his two famous collegues, Sartre and de Beauvoir, in the existentialist movement were not academics, but made their living as professional writers and editors, that they were masters of French prose, that what they said was easily understood, increased their popularity. In spite of their leftist orientation (although Camus denounced Soviet Communism) the existentialists became popular figures even in the American media.

Jean-Paul Sartre and Simone de Beauvoir were middle-class philosophy students who took seminars in the late thirties with Merleau-Ponty in Hegelianism at the University of Paris, and visited the Left Bank cafés where they read Heidegger, and, according to de Beauvoir's memoirs, ignored the world around them. Even when the Nazis were attacking France, de Beauvoir writes, they did not pay much attention. Finally, partly as a result of Sartre's experiences as a prisoner of war in Germany in 1941, they became converted to a doctrine of left-wing existentialism and to the principles of the Resistance. The actual activities of Sartre and de Beauvoir in the Resistance did not entail anything of note, but they were part of the Resistance nevertheless, at least intellectually.

Sartre became a Communist. He tried to combine the existentialism of Merleau-Ponty and Albert Camus with Marxism—not an immediately intelligible project since existentialism is a highly individualistic philosophy, which would render it incompatible with Marxism. But Sartre's argument, stripped of jargon, runs as follows: granted, we find ourselves in a rotten world in which the only good is the individual. But Communism will create a new and better world, and the revolution will no longer have to be confined to individual members of the underground; no longer will they be in conflict with the absurd environment. The existentialist person will be reconciled both to the environment and to society. Society, the great other, will be changed, so making possible the process of the reunification of the individual with society.

Sartre contrasts existence with essence, and existentialism with essentialism. Essentialism is held to be the despicable bourgeois attitude—it believes in the fixed character of personality within the social and natural order. The rich are essentially rational and good, the poor shiftless and irrational—this is the contemptible bourgeois doctrine. Existentialism, according to Sartre, believes in the freedom of human existence, the freedom to grow and develop and become what the individual wants to become. Existentialism, according to Sartre, is the absolute freedom of existence, which precedes or overrules essence.

Yet in subscribing to Communism Sartre was committing himself to a neo-Victorian doctrine which rigidly defined the essence not only of individuals but of groups and classes. Marxism held to the mechanistic psychological theory that the essence of a bourgeois person was prescribed by his class which predetermines his behavior. This seems to be far from Sartre's existentialist freedom and radical individualism. Not only was bourgeois ideology essentialist; Marxism was as much or more so.

Sartre's was the dilemma of the leftist intellectual of the first half of the twentieth century who subscribed to a radical individualism and yet was politically committed to Marxism that was an enemy of such individualism. Sartre repeated the problem of the *Partisan Review* intellectuals of the thirties who wanted to combine modernism and Marxism. No wonder that Sartre was strongly admired in the same *PR* circles after the War. Camus was a clearer and more honest, if less philosophically capable thinker than Sartre. He sensed the incompatibility between existentialism and Marxism. Camus realized that existentialists could be vaguely on the left but not Communists and subscribers to Marxist doctrine. Truth to tell, existentialism was more compatible with anarchism than with Marxism—an insight that was indeed occasionally glimpsed in New Left circles in America and France in the late sixties.

Simone de Beauvoir agreed with Sartre's existentialist philosophy, as she did regarding everything else. Her own main interest, however, was in feminism. Her book *The Second Sex*, published in 1949, is the first great work in the feminist movement of the recent times. Her argument starts from the principle of existentialism that the individual can achieve authenticity and dignity against a rotten environment, and asserts the possibility, for women, of achieving the same. Women have as much right to this freedom, dignity, and authenticity as do men.

When Heidegger discovered, after the Second World War, what his now famous disciples in France were saying, he repudiated them, claiming that his French students had misunderstood phenomenology. Heidegger rejected the idea that the individual had to fight the environment, and claimed that instead, one had to negotiate with it. One has to encounter the world, Heidegger thought, but also to respect it, and so arrive at a solution and a compromise. He termed the French philosophers neo-romantics rather than phenomenologists. Whereas he was teaching accommodation and integration, he found that the French were Romantic revolutionaries.

The last of the prominent French left-wing intellectuals of the War era was André Malraux, who gained notoriety in the twenties for unsuccessfully trying to smuggle antiquities out of Cambodia, and who was famous in the 1930's as a left-wing novelist. He wrote revolutionary romantic novels—*Man's Fate, Man's Hope*—and then became known in the fifties and sixties as an art critic—*The Voices of Silence*. He also served as minister of culture in the Gaullist government of the 1960's. In that capacity, he did much useful work, refurbishing museums and becoming the greatest governmental patron of the arts since Louis XIV. In the interest of gaining a share of political power in which he could advance artistic creation and entitlement that had become his major concern, Malraux in his later years was willing to make a political pilgrimage from left to center. There had always been something of the buccaneer about him.

After the German victory in 1940, Malraux fled to the Riviera, where for three years he lived in his mistress's villa and consumed the entire wine cellar. In January of 1944, when it became evident that the Allies were going to invade France and the Germans were going to be driven out, Malraux dashed back to Paris and became an officer in the Resistance. He arrived just in time for the liberation and became a hero and a leading member of the Gaullist entourage.

Malraux's association with Gaullist centrism was a rarity in the political orientation of post-War French intellectuals. French academics by 1960, whether philosophers, anthropologists, sociologists, historians, or literary critics could not resist the leftist orbit of French intellectual life. If for no other reason than to maintain their credibility in the journals and cafés and among their students, they were compelled to do their work within the leftist context. In view of the Francophilia of American academia in the late sixties and seventies, this development had momentous consequences for American universities that sought a strong presence in the intellectual and disciplinary vanguard.

Simone de Beauvoir's novel of the mid-fifties, *The Mandarins*, subtly describes the elite leftist culture that emerged in post-war France and whose first wave was existential Marxism. The German conquest, the collaboration of many on the intellectual right with the Nazi occupiers or their participation in the now discredited Vichy regime devastated the intellectual right and disrupted the French conservative tradition. This right with its intense nationalism, fervent anti-Communism, and ties either culturally or religiously or both to the Catholic Church has not yet recovered from the events of the early forties.

In the three decades following the War, Parisian vanguard culture—its journals, publishing houses, its art and literature, and its vibrant academic wing—was completely dominated by the left, as never before in French history since the early 1790's. The left was not homogeneous and was deeply split over Soviet Communism, but there was a persistent leftist orientation in French intellectual life, a strong role for Marxism, and a reflexive hostility to American capitalism that only began to alleviate in the mid-seventies. For the French intellectual mandarins of the decades following the liberation in 1944, one began with a set of predisposed leftist assumptions and worked out one's cultural theory in that context.

There is a vast literature on the American, British and French intellectual left of the 1930's. An elaborate mythology about those heroic days has evolved, part of which is grounded in reality and part consisting of highly romanticized versions of real occurrences. The charismatic event for the American, British and French left in the thirties was the Spanish Civil War of 1936–39. It began as a *coup d'etat* undertaken by a group of right-wing military officers led by General Franco in alliance with a native Fascist movement, against the constitutionally elected socialist coalition government which was dominated by anarchists. The Civil War turned into the critical moment of truth for the international left. To the surprise of Franco and the militarists, the "loyalists" in the legitimate republican government resisted the *coup* and managed to fight on for two years against the overwhelming numbers of the Spanish armed forces which were battling to bring down their own government. As is the case in many Third World countries, for example in Argentina in recent times, the Spanish army was far to the right of the republican government. Spain was experiencing the agonizing impact of the early stages of industrialization. The country had become deeply divided between the traditional Catholic majority and the large minority of diverse leftists and secularists who were thoroughly hostile to the Church.

What actually happened during the Spanish Civil War still remains something of an enigma, despite the innumerable books that have been produced on the topic. There were atrocities committed on both sides. Aided by German and Italian planes, Franco and the Fascists bombed Spanish cities in loyalist hands and inflicted terror on the civilian population. On the other side, the loyalists and particularly the anarchists sacked monasteries and killed nuns.

The Civil War was an agonizing struggle for the soul of Spain, and it is perhaps only in recent years following the demise of the Franco regime that the Spaniards' moral and cultural wounds have begun to heal. In addition, the Basques in northern Spain, an ethnically separate group who have been resisting the unification with Spain for about seven hundred years, conducted their own civil war against every other party involved in the larger battle—and still do.

The chief external support for the loyalists, that is, for the legitimate socialist government, was provided by the Soviets. This meant that the Communists assumed an increasingly dominant role in the left-wing coalition. A significant number of British, French and Americans, all young leftists, formed volunteer brigades, such as the famous Abraham Lincoln brigade from New York, and went to Spain to fight on the loyalist side. In the view of the left, the Spanish Civil War was the rehearsal for a conflict between the left and the right, which eventually became the Second World War.

*   *   *

The God That Failed

Some of the non-Spanish intellectuals who joined the Loyalist cause in the Civil War became disillusioned by the heavy-handed Soviet involvement and the way in which the Soviets were attempting to expropriate the loyalist cause. Among these disillusioned participants from abroad was a celebrated left-wing journalist whom we know by his pen name of George Orwell. Orwell's second book, *Homage to Catalonia*, published in 1938, displays a visceral hatred of the Fascists, but it also shows a deep disillusionment with the Soviets and with communism. Orwell came from a British solidly middle-class family.

Orwell was one of the early and leading participants in an intellectual movement that began shortly before the Second World War, around 1938–39, and continued into the mid-sixties—a movement that might be called "The God That Failed," after a famous symposium-type book of the early fifties, setting forth individual pilgrimages to anti-Communism. Such writers had been active communists or fellow-travelers in the thirties before the massive disillusionment set in; some remained on the democratic left, while others moved further to the right. All believed the Soviet goal was to dismantle the democratic movement of Western Marxism, that the Soviet system was a ruthless tyranny, and that the Stalinist regime was a disaster for the Russian people and a threat to others.

The God-that-failed group was naturally greeted with enthusiasm by European and especially American centrists and conservatives. They often became heroes and heroines in the media. The CIA made covert efforts to use them and their leading journal, *Encounter*, was for many years secretly funded by the CIA. These indelicate facts do not discredit what they had to say.

Orwell set the course that many intellectuals, especially in Britain and the U.S.A., were to follow. He was a writer admired by many on the left, which made for the powerful impact of his critique and hatred of the Soviets. Toward the end of the Second World War, he published *Animal Farm*, an acidulous parable of life in a commune, where everybody is equal but some more so than others and the leaders are selfish and cynical. Orwell's novel reflects the growing belief at the time that the purges of the 1930's were fraudulent and manipulative and that Stalin was an oppressive dictator. It is a matter of dispute whether Orwell was any longer a socialist in his later years. His last and most famous book, *1984*, was a chilly and convincing vision of what the world would be like in a totalitarian regime. Orwell's vision of totalitarianism was constructed as much out of the Nazi as of the Soviet experience, but in the early fifties the book was construed as an anti-Communist polemic.

Orwell participated in the Cold War reaction of the fifties against the Soviet regime, which made him, during these years when he accomodated himself to the conservative forces in the media, the darling of rightist *Time* magazine. Orwell's later career and what he then really believed have engendered a Talmudic cottage industry of interpretation. When he wrote *1984* and even *Animal Farm*, it is a fact that he was anti-Soviet. To what extent he was by then also anti-socialist is an open question. Possibly Orwell himself did not know.

The other pioneer of the God-that-failed movement, an ex-communist who became a most severe and damaging critic of the Soviet regime, was Arthur Koestler. He has now somewhat faded from view, but from the forties through the early sixties, he was one of the most influential writers in the Western world. He exerted his influence particularly as a skillful political novelist. Originally a Hungarian-Jew with Zionist sympathies, Koestler in the early thirties was not only a Communist but a Soviet agent in Berlin. He belonged to the secret organization that later came to be called "The Red Orchestra," a Soviet spy-ring in Berlin. Koestler moved to Paris in the late thirties, and this was time of the crystallization of his deep disillusionment with the Soviet regime.

On the basis of his insider's knowledge of the Soviet system, acquired during the time he worked for the Soviet intelligence service, Koestler arrived at the decision that the great purge trials of the thirties had been thoroughly fraudulent and were instruments of monstrous tyranny. The result of this inference was his first novel, *Darkness at Noon*, which he originally wrote in Paris in 1939. But he lost the manuscript in 1940, while fleeing through Spain to Britain, and had to rewrite the book, this time in English, which was published in 1941. At the time, the novel presented a devastating exposé of the Soviets, a quality it still preserves, and it is still the most subtle explantion of what happened in the Soviet Union of the thirties.

Perhaps Koestler's novel is somewhat too subtle, since the book is the story of the elaborate brain-washing of former Bolshevik leaders, and of the processes whereby they become convinced of their guilt. The actual story of why they confessed, based on circumstantial historical accounts, is simpler than Koestler's reconstruction. They were beaten into submission and/or deceitfully promised that their families would be unharmed if they were to confess. Brain-washing played a relatively minor role. In any case, Koestler's novel will endure. It is one of the most influential anti-Soviet works of literature.

Koestler's later career was varied and successful. In addition to political novels, including a harshly critical view of life on an Israeli Kibbutz, he wrote books about the history of science, became closely involved in parapsychology and funded research in the field. When he committed suicide with his wife in 1980, Koestler left his substantial inheritance to support research in parapsychology.

Another outstanding figure of the God-that-failed movement was Hannah Arendt. The brilliant and ambitious daughter of a cultivated Berlin Jewish family, Arendt commenced her remarkable career as a student and mistress of Martin Heidegger. In fact, there still survives a series of letters between them, to which Miss Arendt's skillful, authorized biographer did not have access. Hannah Arendt in her early years was a strong Zionist and she worked for a Zionist organization in France in the thirties dispensing aid to other German Jewish refugees including the hapless Walter Benjamin. But she had married a gentile Communist, and so the couple immigrated to the United States.

In America, Arendt began to write for *The New Yorker*, as well as for other journals, and acquired an impressive reputation first as a political journalist and eventually, as a political theorist. She was offered a chair in political theory at the University of Chicago. She also taught for a while at Princeton University.

Hannah Arendt's major work in political theory is a study of totalitarianism, in which she argues that there is essentially no fundamental difference between Stalinism and Hitlerism. They are both movements of political autocracy and are terrorist states designed to perpetuate the power of a small oligarchy. Their instruments are terror and manipulation of public opinion.

Arendt's study of totalitarianism was very influential in the fifties, and sixties. Not only was it well received in moderate and conservative circles where Soviet Communism had always been a fearful anathema. Her thesis on totalitarianism provided learned and academically authoritative justification for the many intellectuals, especially in the United States, who were making the rightward journey to avowal that the Soviet system betrayed democracy and liberal humanity. The resurgent left of the late sixties and subsequently was less enthusiastic about Arendt's thesis. Today she is a controversial figure in left-wing circles and regarded by some leftist critics as a rightist thinker.

Arendt's other famous book, in which she reverted to her Zionist interest, is *Eichmann in Jerusalem*. The book elicited powerful reactions in the American Jewish community and in Israel when it appeared in the midsixties. It begins as an account of a trial, held in Jerusalem, of the Nazi mass murderer Eichmann, and continues as a discussion of the "banality of evil," the commonplace bureaucracy involved in the Holocaust, and of the occurrences in the Jewish communities in eastern Europe, particularly in Hungary, in 1943 and 1944. Her thesis is that the ordinary Jews were betrayed, in many cases, by the wealthier Jews, who were also the leaders of their communities. The thesis is not implausible. There is supporting evidence for it, particularly provided by events in Hungary, where Eichmann had been in charge of the deportation of Jews. Arendt, who was extraordinarily courageous and self-assured, effectively defended herself against the Jewish critics.

Another member of the group of ex-Communist intellectuals who did not spare the Soviets the criticism that was their due, was Karl Wittfogel, who was a German Marxist theoretician in the early thirties. Wittfogel came to the United States and pursued his career as professor of East Asian history at the University of Washington in Seattle. He published a big book in the late fifties, in which he argued that the Soviet system was merely a perpetuation of conventional oriental despotism. It was a manifestation of what he called a "hydraulic society," by which term he understands a society whose technological organization requires that a peasant society be ruthlessly controlled by a ruling oligarchy. This narrow political elite enslaves the people in order to be able to control the material and technological means and to keep itself in power. Such hydraulic tyrannies were endemic to the ancient Near East and East Asia, Wittfogel claimed.

Wittfogel's theory does not constitute a significant departure from Karl Marx's view of Eastern societies. Assuming that Marx would not have approved of the Soviet system, he might very well have said something similar to Wittfogel's perception of Stalinist Russia, for the thesis of oriental despotism was originally suggested by Marx himself. Wittfogel contributed to it the additional focus on the massive technological developments of which Marx could not have known much.

After the Second World War, and even more in the fifties, all sorts of circumstantial accounts appeared as to what had happened in Russia in the thirties, and about the continued existence of mass forced labor in the Gulags of Siberia. These revelations caused increasing doubt and confusion in Western socialist circles. Nevertheless, there were still many on the left who resisted accepting the evidence which came from Russian defectors and emigrés. As a matter of fact, in 1946, a Ukranian cipher clerk in the Soviet Embassy in Ottawa, Canada, defected with a host of documentary evidence about Soviet tyranny. But many Western leftists continued to claim that the documentation had been forged by the CIA.

In 1968, an English expert on the Soviet Union named Robert Conquest published *The Great Terror*, which elaborated in detail what had really passed in the Soviet Union in the thirties. The book included a mass of circumstantial and statistical information. In this case, too, there were American leftists who insisted that Conquest's research had been funded by the CIA, which was possibly true, but irrelevent. It was claimed that Conquest relied too heavily on accounts by Soviet emigrés and other opponents of the Stalinist regime. Presumably official Soviet documents were more reliable.

Finally, in the early seventies the last vestiges of Stalinist credibility appeared to be demolished by the publication of novels and other accounts by Soviet emigrés, the best-known being Alexander Solzhenitsyn, and especially by an authoritative, lengthy historical work by the Soviet Marxist scholar Roy Medvedev, whose *Let History Judge* was published in America in 1973. In 1958 the Soviet leader Khrushchev had denounced Stalin at the Communist Party Congress. Khrushchev's speech was kept secret, but a copy was obtained by the Israeli Intelligence and leaked to the CIA. In the Khrushchev "thaw," the short-lived relatively liberal period of the early sixties in Moscow, Medvedev gained access to Soviet archives and probably worked under Khrushchev's protection. Medvedev's book, which had probably been completed several years before it was published in the United States (it has not appeared in the Soviet Union), provided a detailed and devastating account of the dark period of Soviet history.

Substantially, *Let History Judge* confirms all the claims that had been made by Robert Conquest in 1968: the nefarious CIA was right after all in its assessment of the Stalinist regime. The Stalinist system competed with the Nazi regime for being the worst terrorist system of all time. Under Stalin possibly twenty million people lost their lives at the hands of the Soviet State, millions more were enslaved, millions upon millions of Russian families were made wretched, and the violence reached the point at which inevitably it became uncontrollable. Taking into account the research of Medvedev and others, as well as his own investigation, Conquest concluded in 1986 that in the Stalinist terror half of the Soviet Communist party perished and "about a tenth or twelfth of the remaining adult population." Only the Nazi Holocaust of the Jews and other peoples 1940–45 was a crime of comparable magnitude in human history. By the late thirties Stalin himself probably became unable to control and halt the terror system he had himself created. The mechanism of the police state that Stalin used was set in place by Lenin himself.

By 1980, shortly before his death, even Jean-Paul Sartre decided that the Stalinist system had been—shall we say—unfortunate. Sartre was probably the last prominent left-wing intellectual in the Western world to admit doubt about the morality and propriety of the Stalinist regime.

That it took so many years after the purge trials and after ample information on the details of the Stalinist terror system were available for Western leftists to turn overwhelmingly against the Soviet regime demonstrates the intensely religious character of the socialist faith. Stalinist terror having been finally acknowledged, a new question had to be addressed. Was the Soviet misfortune a grotesque aberration in the history of Marxism or reflective of an in-built structural defect in Marxism? This issue is still hotly debated in leftist circles.

Incredibly in the late eighties a group of neo-Stalinist English academic historians were again hard at work trying to discredit Conquest and Medvedev.

*   *   *

Resurgence of the Intellectual Left

In the sixties, and increasingly in the seventies and eighties, a new wave of intellectual Marxism appeared and has been systematically habilitated in the universities. Marxist theory was legitimized in the academic humanities and social sciences. The motivations that triggered this renewed Marxist intellectual movement have been discussed at the beginning of the present chapter, where the Marxist academic advent of the seventies and eighties was shown to have emerged in association with the New Left upheaval of the sixties.

Following the disillusionment of the fifties, Marxism resurged as a stronger and more credible theory. Disburdening itself of the Soviets and of the obligation to justify and come to terms with Stalinism, Western Marxism came of its own. Henceforth, Western Marxists did not have to devote their time and attention to defending the Soviet system, and were free to develop their own point of view.

Georges Lefebvre was a role model for this new brand of Western Marxist thinkers and scholars. He succeeded Albert Mathiez in the Marxist chair of the history of the French Revolution at the University of Paris. Already in the thirties, Lefebvre was working on a learned Marxist explanation of the origins of the French Revolution as grounded in class struggle. His argument was that the eighteenth-century aristocracy undertook a militant, reactionary attack upon the French monarchical state, and the confusion that resulted from the struggle between the reactionary aristocracy and the monarchy provided the opportune moment for a bourgeois revolution.

Lefebvre commanded a host of admirers and disciples, and by the 1950's, the dominant point of view in the historical faculty of the University of Paris was clearly along Marxist lines. Academic history moved consciously to unite with the leftist sentiment that prevailed in the cafés and literary journals. This was the cultural context in which the thought and career of Ferdinand Braudel developed. Braudel was the dominant figure in French historiography in the post-War era down to the eighties and the single most esteemed and influential historian in the Western World. As the disciple of Lucien Febvre and Marc Bloch, he assumed the directorship of their journal, the *Annales*, the prime outlet for radical historical writing, and what was more important, of the government-funded institute of social history that had been founded after the war.

This situation allowed Braudel to become the most powerful patron in French academic life since Durkheim. By the sixties, through the funding of student research and the placement of his disciples in professorships in the expanded French university system, the "Annalists" had become the over-whelmingly dominant group in French historiography. Catholic, liberal, and conservative historians were in danger of being blown away by the Braudelian surge; the media lavished attention on Braudel and his disciples and ignored other points of view; American universities fell over themselves to invite Braudel and his colleagues to come and give public lectures (even though, being French academicians, few of them could speak comprehensible English); and it was rare for a new French academic post in history to go to anyone except a Braudel nominee.

Braudel's first book, *The Mediterranean and the Mediterranean World in the Reign of Philip II* was based on the dissertation he had completed under Febvre's direction while teaching during the War and shortly thereafter in Algeria. It is not only the greatest single accomplishment of the Annales school, being a more finished work than Bloch's famous study of feudal society, but also stands out among the leading works of historical science in this century. Not since Maitland's history of English law in the 1890's had there appeared such an historical tour de force.

Braudel takes the entire Mediterranean world in the sixteenth century, both

Christian and Moslem, as a regional unit and tries to discuss every aspect of life, particularly material life in terms of climate, food, trade, industry. He shows how, in spite of the religious and political divisions, the Mediterranean remained an economic and social unit. Among Braudel's accomplishments in this book was his impressive capacity to do statistical or quantitative analysis, using very complicated and somewhat arcane materials from the sixteenth century. He showed that it was possible to use the quantitative methods to investigate the pre-modern period as well as the modern era. Braudel's model generated a vast tradition of quantitative history that dealt with the medieval and the early modern world. The social history of pre-modern societies was thoroughly transformed from dependency on anecdotal information to grounding in statistical structures.

Braudel's later work, the three-volume *Capitalism and Material Life*, adheres much more closely than the former work to Marxist dialectical lines. Braudel was obviously influenced by the Marxist atmosphere at the University of Paris in the sixties and the seventies. The work is a grand analysis of what might be called the cultural superstructure of capitalism between 1500 and 1800. What exactly the cultural value system was in the emerging capitalist world during these three centuries is the question Braudel seeks to answer in three volumes.

Capitalism and Material Life is conditioned by two principles. The first is the doctrine of "the long duration." The world changes very slowly, ephemeral political crises having been shunted to an allegedly minor, almost invisible role. Society continues to be governed by the same material forces and to exhibit the same class and group structures and behavior patterns over long periods. In writing about the period from 1400 to 1800, Braudel felt he was writing about the same enduring society. Marx would have enthusiastically agreed.

The second principle in Braudel's work was that capitalism existed as a structural entity; it was the force driving everything else. The historian's task was to show by a mass of anecdotal and statistical data the capitalist impact in operation. Braudel did not establish sociologically the existence of the capitalist structure; he assumed its existence and demonstrated its detailed impact. Braudel's work is the show and tell of capitalism.

As befits a French mandarin, Braudel's work is especially fascinating and amusing when he talks about diet. He tells the wonderful story—on the whole, true—of how the German invaders terrorized the inhabitants of the Mediterranean world in the early middle ages simply by their unusual proclivity for consuming barbecued steaks, in violent contrast to the largely grain and cereal based diet of Mediterranean (and of Asian) peoples.

The other leftist luminary in Parisian historical circles was Emmanuel Le Roy Ladurie, whose father had been a fascist collaborator. Ladurie became for a while a Communist and then a student and disciple of Braudel. A handsome and eloquent man, Ladurie became an internationally popular figure as lecturer and the darling of the French television and other media, as well as the holder of high academic preferment.

Ladurie's early work consists of orthodox quantitative Marxist social history. His study of the peasantry of Languedoc over 400 years is an example of strict class history that seeks evidence in statistics. More interesting is Ladurie's output since the early 1970's, which has been along the lines of an attempt at historical anthropology. The later Ladurie argues that there is no substantial difference in personal behavior between the medieval world and ours. The long duration appears to be infinite. The way a peasant living in an obscure village in the Pyrenees in 1380 behaved and the values he held, do not differ substantially from the behavior and values of a member of the modern world, particularly from those of a modern French peasant. Employment, sex, and piety dominate the mentality of the fourteenth-century peasant, as they would today. There is a constant in social history, according to Ladurie.

It could be argued that Ladurie's categories of mentality are at such a general, macrocosmic level as to make discrimination of fine but real differences over time imperceptible. Ladurie like the later Braudel follows the Marxist, anti-Modernist, neo-Victorian propensity to grossly large scale generalities. Viewed at that macrocosmic level, social mentalities are bound to be durable. It is like looking at the planet earth from a thousand miles away. Nothing seems to change over time; the continents and oceans remain.

In England, a group of voluble Marxist scholars emerged in the early 60's. The vibrance of intellectual and academic Marxism was bound to follow the election returns. From 1945 to 1951 the first Labor Party government with an effective parliamentary majority fully introduced the welfare state in Britain, and in spite of some marginal countervailing efforts by Margaret Thatcher's Conservatives since 1978, this anxious public commitment to welfare benefits for the population has not been reversed. The Beveridge plan of 1944 was realized and then some.

Whether it was wise for Britain, economically drained and physically exhausted by the War, to reduce sharply the pool of capital available for business investment and recovery of the private sector by the extremely high rates of taxation needed to finance the welfare state has been questioned more sharply in recent years than in the late forties. In the post-war period the concern was that the miserable conditions the working and lower middle class had experienced in the Depression should not be repeated and the priority was public spending and governmental regulation and outright control of industry to sustain this popular welfare. Even the empire had to give way to the needs of the welfare state. The Labor government, lacking the resources to maintain the British presence in India, abandoned it suddenly in 1947, leaving Hindus and Moslems to massacre each other. The dismantling of the rest of the empire followed steadily in the next two decades. Billions of pounds of Victorian investment were simply abandoned.

It was not widely recognized at the time that Britain's industry had been in an almost steady decline since the beginning of the century, that even before the War British investment capital had fled overseas, and that British human and technical resources for industrial productivity were at a low ebb, in spite of superhuman efforts in the early forties at arms production.

British higher education, both in terms of numbers of students and curricula, was all wrong for an advanced industrial society. Britain was so weak in business enterprise and applied engineering that two marvelous British inventions of the period 1938–40—radar and penicillin—could not be put into large scale production in the United Kingdom and were effectively developed in the United States. Nor could Britain capitalize on its early lead in nuclear weapons research and again had to give way to vastly superior American technology and resources.

In 1945 Britain still had the world's largest automobile industry, next to Detroit. Nowadays the only British cars built for export are upscale luxury items, and in Britain itself the largest-selling car is the Nissan. By 1985 Britain's industrial capacity was not only far behind Japan's; it was—a member of Thatcher's cabinet admitted—inferior to South Korea's. Socialism made the British people healthier and happier. It also made them technologically and fiscally a third world country.

British socialist theorists from T.H. Green to R.H. Tawney to Harold Laski had assumed that the social agenda was to redistribute the wealth of a fundamentally prosperous society. They had never considered that the wealth of Britain was itself fragile and temporary. They had not faced the issue that the commitment to the welfare state would be in itself a contributing factor in Britain's economic decline.

The Labor Party therefore never considered the possible consequences of heavy commitment to the welfare state in conditions of technological obsolescence, educational weakness, and investment shortage—a one-way ticket to economic decline of massive proportions. But the Conservatives who alternated in power with the Labor Government through out the sixties and seventies, before the advent of the neo-Ricardian Mrs. Thatcher in 1979, were not much better in perceiving fiscal and industrial realities. The almost unanimous admiration among university faculties for the welfare state and unlimited public spending provided a cultural and intellectual context and constant inspiration for hazardous public policy.

When Britain, following on the watershed Butler Education Act of 1944, quadrupled its post-secondary educational system in the three decades after the war, it still severely short-changed the engineering schools, created no American style business schools, and retained the late 19th century Oxbridge humanist curriculum as the dominant educational mode for college students. Nearly always the British civil servant of the post-War period was steeped in the humanities, wrote beautifully, understood little economics, and no science. The civil servant came out of his college years with a dogmatic faith in the utility of the welfare state, and with an acerbic contempt for capitalist enterprise and a horror of an untrammeled market economy.

The long shadow of Ruskin, Morris, T.H. Green and Tawney prevailed. Harold Laski was the chief theoretician of the Labor Party during its first creative period of power after 1945. Not only did he get the world he wanted, but the assumptions about public policy and human welfare that were central to his Marxist vision impinged themselves very deeply into British academic culture. Only since the mid-seventies has there been a modest alleviation of this socialist faith in British academic circles. The visceral anti-Americanism that surged during the War has also scarcely been moderated.

In the socialist era an array of publicly-acclaimed and well-rewarded academic British Marxists came to the fore, especially in the sixties and early seventies. Perhaps the most far-ranging and subtle mind among them was Raymond Williams, who is still a professor of literature at Cambridge. In the late fifties Williams founded the journal *The Universities and Left Review*, which is still in existence as the leading neo-Marxist intellectual publication in Britain. Williams' first major book, published in 1962, was the history of English literature since 1800 in relation to social and economic conditions. In it, Williams investigates the effects of the Industrial Revolution on the English novel, and how the novel, in turn, illuminates the Industrial Revolution. The influence here of Walter Benjamin and of the Frankfurt School is strong, but the indigenous influence of Queenie Leavis, the academically neglected wife of F.R. Leavis, too must be taken into account. Williams is an able writer, delightfully amusing and clever. Among his many books is also a consistently interesting history of twentieth-century drama.

Another pioneering English Marxist was Edward P. Thompson, who in recent years has become the leader of the unilateral nuclear disarmament movement in Britain. Edward Thompson comes from a wealthy family and has never had to teach. For a while he did hold a chair at the University of Warwick, which did not amuse him much, for he resigned quickly and continues to live from his private sources and the income of his books. He is in the great tradition of idiosyncratic leftist thinkers and personalities like Ruskin and William Morris, partaking of the same evangelical, puritanical English tradition.

Thompson's book, *The Making of the English Working Class*, published in the early sixties, was a vehement attack upon Namier, the conservative Modernist historian of the 1930's. Thompson claims that Namier's had been a narrow, conservative history that viewed the world from the perspective of the elite, and was interested more in the mechanisms by which they maintained their power than in the more significant phenomenon, around 1800, of the emergence of class consciousness and a democratic movement among the new industrial working class. Almost everything of substance in Thompson's book had been said many years before by an obscure scholar named S. Maccoby. Yet Thompson set forth the Marxist reinterpretation in a colorful and polemical fashion. He was hailed immediately on both sides of the Atlantic as the leftist and historicist liberator from Namier Modernism and conservatism. From Cambridge, England to Cambridge, Mass., droves of radical graduate students during the sixties clutched Thompson's book as a talisman.

There are four other important historical scholars who subscribed to Marxism, one of whom was Christopher Hill. Hill became very prominent as an Oxford professor and the Master of Balliol College, holding one of the half dozen most elite academic positions in England. He presented an orthodox Marxist interpretation of the English Civil War, which differs greatly, to say the least, from the royalist BBC version of this critical segment of British history, which has been prepared during Mrs. Thatcher's tenure. Hill continued the tradition established by Kautsky and R.H. Tawney early in the century, seeing the civil war as a bourgeois revolution and also the setting for the emergence of radical, proto-socialist ideology.

Eric Hobsbawm is professor of history at the University of London as well as at the New School for Social Research. He has presented skillful Marxist interpretations of various historical periods and phenomena, particularly of nineteenth-century England.

Lawrence Stone, another of the leading group of British Marxist historians, became a distinguished professor and director of an institute at Princeton University after a controversial career at Oxford. Stone too has presented an elaborate analysis of the English Civil War of the seventeenth century. The deferential culture which sustained the power of the aristocracy was eroded, and this aristocratic decline made way for the rising gentry. Stone's work on the English Civil War is very similar to Georges Lefebvre's interpretation of the origins of the French Revolution. Both analyses revolve around the perception of an ailing aristocracy which loses power and is overtaken by a bourgeois revolution. Stone was a direct disciple of Tawney, whose interpretation of the Civil War, he said in 1985, was "largely true." As director of a well-endowed institute at Princeton—funded by a very conservative oil magnate and alumnus—Stone had the patronage power to advance his leftist views of social history, as did Braudel in France. The influence of Adorno and the Frankfurt School on Stone is also obvious.

More interesting than the conventional Western Marxists like Stone and Hill is Perry Anderson, a self-educated free-wheeling dogmatic Leninist who acquired a special celebrity by marrying a prominent Rumanian film actress. Anderson's multi-volume history of European society from medieval feudalism to modern capitalism is curiously illuminative, not only because of its learning and clear presentation, but because of its commitment to an orthodox, pre-Frankfurt school Leninist view of the world. It is precisely on this difference between Western and Soviet Marxism that E.P. Thompson and Anderson engaged in a noisy and intellectually suggestive public dispute in the late seventies.

The efflorescence of Marxist historiography and literary criticism in the sixties and seventies in Britain represents a polar opposition to and rejection of the Modernists T.S. Eliot and L.B. Namier. Why did not only the provincial and new universities welcome and foster the advance of academic Marxism but also the Oxbridge citadel of the establishment? We have suggested one reason for this mainline cultural trend, the political triumphs of the Labor Party and the entrenchment of the welfare state. There is another, more long-range factor at work.

The triumph of British academic Marxism represents the revenge of landed Toryism upon modern industrial society. The rise of the industrial capitalists and the steam-engine entrepreneurial mentality in the nineteenth century had never sat well with the traditional gentry leaders of British society and their landed anti-technocratic patrician culture. They had no alternative, however, but to make way for the institutional power of the new entrepreneurial families, most of which originated in the midlands and the north rather than in the vested centers of inherited dominance in the south. What gentry culture did was to try to socialize the scions of the new industrial families through perpetuation of the old humanistic and gentlemanly curricula in the great preparatory schools and Oxbridge. But gentry culture was always on the lookout for additional ways to delegitimize and repudiate the capitalist entrepreneurial mind they intrinsically condemned and feared.

The rise of a generation of Tawney disciples after the War was therefore welcomed in conservative academic circles. Eliot and Namier were after all outsiders, the one an American Anglo-Catholic, the other an Austrian Polish Jew; and their Modernist critique could be construed as hazardous to cherished traditions of gentry culture. Marxist literary criticism and historiography was directed at capitalist entrepreneurship and the consequences of the Industrial Revolution. These departures had raised Britain to unprecedented world power and enriched the gentry as well as the manufacturers and merchants. But this was not enough for the gentry heirs in the twentieth century. They sought a restoration of a pre-Ricardian culture, one based on deference and sentiment rather than the pound sterling.

The myth-making and moralizing of the Marxist scholars was useful in this gaining of the cultural restitution of pre-capitalist Britain. That in so doing, the establishment risked shooting itself in the foot, divesting Britain of its entrepreneurial mentality and economic power, was not a matter of crucial concern. So Raymond Williams and Christopher Hill gained high preferment.

Marxist historiography emerged in the United States in the sixties and early seventies, and focused particularly on the American Civil War and on the old South, studying the pre-Civil War South and its slave system. The two names that stand out among those of American Marxist historians, are Eugene Genovese, who became chairman of the history department at the University of Rochester, and Eric Foner, who teaches at Columbia University.

Genovese is a colorful character. He began his career as historian at Rutgers University, and was an early opponent of the Vietnam War. His opposition was unwelcome to the extent of depriving him of his academic post at Rutgers and necessitating flight to Canada. He taught in Canada for some years, until he published work that earned him great distinction. Eventually, he became department chairman at the University of Rochester.

Genovese's work is Marxist in the tradition of the Frankfurt School. He has published elaborate studies of slave society in the early South, in which the superstructure of the plantation aristocracy assumes partial cultural independence and takes on a mediating vitality of its own.

Like Frank Leavis, Eugene Genovese is part of a husband and wife team, and again it is possibly the wife who is the real brains of the tandem. Elizabeth Fox-Genovese teaches Marxist feminist history at Emory University. She is the daughter of the respected Cornell scholar Edward Fox, is deeply learned, and brings a humanistic elegance to her writing. She is reputed to have the best wardrobe as well as one of the sharpest minds among radical feminist scholars.

Eric Foner is the nephew of Philip Foner, a leading American Communist historian and theorist of the 1930's and 40's who could be heard delivering speeches in New York City's Union Square every Sunday afternoon. Foner junior is a widely admired authority on the Civil War era. He was a student of the New Deal liberal historian Richard Hofstadter and his work subtly combines the intellectual strands represented by his uncle's circle and by Hofstadter.

With the rise of the New Left in the late sixties, Herbert Marcuse, the younger colleague in the Frankfurt School of Adorno and Benjamin, who was then a professor of philosophy at Brandeis University, reverted from radical Freudianism, which he had increasingly propounded since his arrival in the United States, to a Freudian Marxism, which had been his original position in the Frankfurt School. The result of this transformation was his most celebrated book, published in the late sixties, *One Dimensional Man*, which contains an argument for simultaneous revolution in the sexual and social realms. The notion is certainly present in Marcuse's early work too, but never as pronounced as it is in this later effort to synthesize Marxism and Freudianism.

In this book and later ones, Marcuse condemned the capitalist system with unsurpassed vigor. There is nothing that capitalism can undertake which will ensure the desired freedom. Even the freedom of speech and the relative tolerance of capitalist democracy are "repressive"—treacherously and insincerely manipulative. Capitalists can never do right, even when they offer civil liberties. These so-called freedoms are subtle repressive mechanisms by which the bourgeoisie seeks to pacify and so undermine opposition—a line of argument that continues to inform the columns of leftist publications such as *The Village Voice* or *The Nation*. Marcuse's doctrine of repressive tolerance remains a popular theory among many Marxist social scientists. Thereby Marxist academics can personally benefit from American capitalism and condemn it at the same time.

Marcuse was almost as critical of the Soviet system as he was of the capitalist. His position in his later work is actually closer to anarchism than to Marxism. He seeks to transcend the old industrial society, be it capitalist or Soviet, into a world of environmental bliss and libidinal freedom. It is not surprising that this message found warm welcome from the counter-cultural movement. Indeed Marcuse helped to articulate its doctrine. Among his disciples was the Yippie leader Abbie Hoffman (now much in demand on the college lecture circuit). There could not have been anyone who was further removed in personal style from a sixties flower child than was Herbert Marcuse—a buttoned-up, sober 1930's German professor. But his message certainly cohered with that of the counter- culture.

At the same time, in the social sciences an important group of left-wing and Marxist scholars had emerged. Especially in the anthropology and sociology departments at Columbia University, a movement, which gathered a number of remarkably brilliant scholars, became clearly discernible in the 1960's. One of the members of this group was the anthropologist Marvin Harris, for many years the chairman of the anthropology department at Columbia, who now lives in Florida. Harris continues to publish, becoming increasingly radical with age.

Harris is arguing for a strictly materialist interpretation in anthropological theory. He takes the Marxist approach of Malinowski and Childe, and drives it home even harder. Harris' *The Rise of Anthropological Theory*, which appeared in the late sixties, is the best history of anthropology, one can easily claim, that has ever been written. In his book, Harris runs through the entire history of anthropology, evaluating the workers in the field according to a Marxist scale, which does not, however, divest his work of credibility and insight. Margaret Mead is among those who suffer particularly from Harris' lucid and clever appraisal. He is the leading Marxist anthropological theorist in the United States.

Another distinguished Marxist spokesman among anthropologists is Eric Wolfe of the City University of New York. He is best known for his sympathetic and facile account of *Peasant Wars of the Twentieth Century*. The peasants, of course, are always seeking what justly belongs to them; the landlords are inevitably the embodiment of evil.

By the late fifties, metropolitan sociology departments in the United States had taken on the aura of bastions of moderation and conformity. They were heavily involved in political polling and market research, and following Talcott Parsons, they interpreted Durkheim's functionalist theory so as to cast grave doubts on the feasibility of radical movements. Ever eager to ride the crest of the trend, Daniel Bell proclaimed "the end of ideology." The strong exception to this conservative trend among sociologists was the dramatic figure of C. Wright Mills on the Columbia campus. Arriving on Morningside Heights in a leather jacket on his motorcycle (which soon killed him) from his home in Rockland County, Mills became the forerunner and role model for the large and influential group of Marxist sociologists that emerged later, in the closing years of the sixties. There is little to Mill's most celebrated book *The Power Elite* beyond the confrontational title. Mills discovered a power elite in society and he didn't like them. Nor was he satisfied with Parsons and Durkheim or Bell's eagerness to sound the retreat from sociological radicalism.

The other herald of a new day was Alvin Gouldner who taught first at Buffalo and then became Max Weber Professor of Sociology at Washington University in St. Louis. A group of radical graduate students migrated from Buffalo to St. Louis with Gouldner. Led by Paul Piccone, they established *Telos*, still the most interesting Marxist intellectual journal in the United States. (*Telos* is now published in Greenwich Village.)

Gouldner's polemical study of the sociological profession, *The Coming Crisis of Western Sociology*, was intended to be a leftist call to militancy and activism. Durkheim and Parsons—especially the latter—were condemned as political conservatives and functionalism in Gouldner's use became a dirty word, a synonym for conformity and surrender. How well Gouldner actually understood Durkheim and Parsons is questionable. The sociological profession was scathingly criticized in Gouldner's book for its involvements with governmental agencies and business corporations—its only sources of income outside of teaching. Gouldner overrated the opposition. There was no crisis of sociology. His view easily prevailed. In the late sixties, as a younger generation of social scientists came forward, there was a strongly sympathetic response to the student radicals and New Left of the era and a shift several degrees to the left on the part of the sociological profession in the United States. A similar trajectory occurred in France and West Germany. Marxism rapidly became— for the first time—the central theory in Western sociology.

Two young Columbia sociologists, Immanuel Wallerstein and Terence Hopkins, were the most vehement supporters of the student revolution in Columbia in 1968. They could not be fired for the support they lent the rebellious students, since both had tenure, but they did fall into disfavor. They went into exile: Wallerstein to Canada, to the same city, Montreal, to which Genovese had been obliged to withdraw, and Hopkins to the West Indies for a couple of years. They returned and in the early seventies found their way to the State University of New York at Binghamton, where they took over the sociology department and founded the Ferdinand Braudel Center, an institute of historical sociology along Marxist lines. Braudel came for the official opening of the Institute, which took place in 1976. In a huge tent pitched on the campus, Braudel cut the red ribbon himself.

The Braudel Center has become an important and influential agency in the field of Marxist sociology. No one asked the long-suffering taxpayers of New York State whether they wished to support a distinguished Marxist institute, especially respected by anti-American groups in the Third World.

What Wallerstein and Hopkins are pursuing is a universal historical science of sociology structured along the lines of what is called "dependency theory." This theory finds its origins in the theory of imperialism propounded by J.H. Hobson, the English socialist at the beginning of this century, and later by Lenin, and its elaboration in the work of Hopkins and Wallerstein. It was delineated by the Latin-American Marxist theorist Gunter Franck, who claims that the economy of Third World countries is thoroughly controlled and exploited by American capitalism. Wallerstein and Hopkins put this thesis on a historical projection, called world systems theory. They claimed that since the beginning of the sixteenth century, Western capitalism has organized the entire world economy so as to support itself and make non-Western economies dependent on Western capitalism. The phenomenon of Western imperialism's economic programs does not begin in the nineteenth century, with enterprises such as the United Fruit Company in Guatemala, say, but it originates in the sixteenth century.

An early case of this phenomenon is the famous enserfment of the peasantry in Eastern Europe around 1500. At the same time when most of the peasantry were enfranchised or liberated from serfdom in Western Europe, they were forced into serfdom in Poland and the Ukraine, for these regions were assigned in the capitalist world system the task of producing grain in order to support the Western economy. To ensure the availability of labor for the production of grain and in order to maintain production on the needed level, the Polish and Ukrainian peasantry had to be enserfed. This phenomenon, according to the dependency theorists, became the prototype of the global workings of Western capitalism.

The role of the Spaniards in Mexico and Peru, the Dutch in Indonesia, the Belgians in the Congo, and the British in India offered dramatic case studies to support Wallerstein's thesis.

Wallerstein's treatise on the capitalist world-system was crowned by the highest prize of the American Sociological Association. Among Latin American intellectuals he stands shoulder to shoulders with Marx, Lenin, Castro and Che

Guevara in the pantheon of heroes. Unfortunately, the dependency theory that Western capitalism, and especially the United States, made itself rich at the expense of the rest of the world, including Latin America and Africa, is vulnerable. Lawrence E. Harrison, in a persuasive critique of the dependency theory in 1986, pointed out that in the nineteenth century, the United States, Canada and Australia were exporters of primary materials and recipients of foreign investments—the same alleged victimized role as Third World countries occupied.

In spite of the Franck-Wallerstein-Hopkins vision of the bloated American capitalist octopus dominating the interlocked world economy, the American economy since the early twentieth century has been largely self-sufficient. As far as American trade is concerned, it is today largely with developed countries of Western Europe, Japan, and Canada rather than with Latin America. The U.S.A. trades with and invests more in Canada than in all of Central and South America. Harrison points out that "the total effective demand of the five Central American countries for U.S. products approximates that of Springfield, Mass."

Developments in the American and world economies during the past fifteen years have severely damaged Wallerstein's world-systems thesis. With the decline of the U.S. steel and automobile industries, the greater value of American exports has come to reside, as a hundred years ago, again in grain, lumber, and other primary materials. It is the peripheral and Third World countries, not the center of the capitalist world system, according to Wallerstein's vision, that should be providing the primary materials. If the Wallerstein thesis made sense, the current center of the capitalist world system would lie in Japan and West Germany, not the United States. But this would not suit the wish of Wallerstein and his Third World Marxist friends to blame the problems of Latin America and Africa on American capitalism. What Wallerstein wanted to do was to provide a historical thesis to disparage the United States (succeeding Britain in the nineteenth century as the center of capitalist world hegemony) and make the Third World feel and look good. In the sixties when he developed his thesis, with assistance from Franck and Hopkins, Wallerstein seemed momentarily to have some persuasive arguments. Unfortunately for him, economic history has moved into another era involving the decline of American heavy industry, and the probabilities in support of his thesis have diminished.

The Third World's problems are principally generated by their own weaknesses, especially in the political realm. The British economist, P.T. Bauer, has argued this point very effectively. In 1945 Argentina's gross national product was equal to Canada's; now it is much inferior. This has been due not to American interference but to the calamitous rule of crackpot dictators and greedy militarists.

A similar situation prevails in many other Latin American and African countries. Even the lavish U.S. (and, in some instances, Soviet) aid in these Third World countries has been grossly misused and has worked against making these economies self-subsisting. Bauer has pointed out that the greatest error the post-colonial states, especially in Africa, have made is to try to develop heavy industry long before their economies and cultures were ready for this departure. These countries lacked the educational infrastructure, technology, political stability, and capital necessary for industrial revolutions. At the same time, they neglected the fine agricultural legacies they inherited from the colonial era, leading to catastrophic poverty unknown in the 1950's. A 1986 conference at the U.N. reached the same conclusion.

For this disaster Wallerstein and other proponents of the Marxist dependency theory bear a large measure of blame. Following Wallerstein's view of economic history, it is easy to see how the liberated Third World governments would make these grievous errors. While Wallerstein was collecting scholarly honors and endowed chairs, his Third World disciples implemented his theory in a state policy of industrialization and embarked on a one-way trip to economic oblivion.

For earlier centuries, Wallerstein can point to some dramatic anecdotal instances to support his world-systems theory. Since statistical data are fragmentary, it is hard either to prove or disprove his longitudinal thesis. Yet the close survey of the European overseas empires reveals a mixed balance sheet. Sometimes the imperialist states made big profits from their colonial empires. Sometimes the governments lost money and only individuals profited. Sometimes nearly everybody lost in imperial ventures. If a generalization about the history of imperialism is needed, the facts appear to support the conservative view of Nathan Rosenberg and L.E. Birdsell, Jr. Western "economic growth seem[s] more a cause of imperialism . . . than its result." It is systematic cultural and economic factors intrinsic to the West, not its alleged domination of the Third World, that accounts for the rise of Western Europe and the United States. Wallerstein's elaborate and brilliant effort to foist a meta-historical guilt on the West is not convincing.

At the same time that Wallerstein and Hopkins developed their dependency theory, another approach—anarcho-syndicalist in spirit—was being propounded to elucidate the relations between Western capitalism and the Third World. This theory, formulated by Franz Fanon, became, at least momentarily in the sixties, very visible. Fanon was a West Indian physician who had been educated in France and came under the influence of Sartre and the existential Marxism of the fifties. He became the theorist of African liberation in the sixties. His theory has also had considerable influence on the black movement in the United States in the sixties and early seventies. There is no question that Fanon is also strongly influenced by Georges Sorel and French anarcho-syndicalism.

It is only the revolution against Western imperialism itself which will create a new man in Africa, Fanon argues. Whatever the problems of lack of education and other facets of underdevelopment, however insurmountable they may seem, the actual act of revolution will not fail to liberate the mentality of the African people, providing the basis for a new society. The question, therefore, as to whether the Africans are ready for freedom, is meaningless. Only the act of freedom itself will reconstruct African culture.

This romantic doctrine was influential in the Third World in the sixties and early seventies. It was embraced by the more radical wing of the Black

Liberation movement in the United States. The marginal destiny of African liberation and the doubtful history of many of the new African states has raised questions about its validity. Nigeria, Ghana and Zaire were in fact much more productive under white rule. The end of imperial rule in the countries lying between the Sahara and South Africa inaugurated an era of political ineptitude and corruption that adversely affected productivity and economic stability. Of course Third World advocates and Fanon disciples can respond that the political failures of the liberated African countries are the consequences of the devastating imperialist legacy. Colonial rule, it is said, destroyed the traditional political infrastructure in African societies and did not train a native elite to replace the European governors. When Black Africans can assume responsibility for their own shortcomings is unclear.

*　　*　　*

Recent Marxist Theory

The most important Marxist theorists of the sixties and seventies were Lucien Goldmann, Louis Althusser, both Parisian professors, and Juergen Habermas, professor of sociology and philosophy at the Free University of Berlin. Habermas is probably the most interesting and original Marxist theorist of the last twenty years.

Lucien Goldmann was a Marxist structuralist. His fundamental project consisted of the attempt to join the thought of Marx and Piaget. He argues that societies undergo specific stages characterized by cultural structures. Each social stage generates its cultural structures as well, such as, for example, Enlightenment culture and the culture of Romanticism. Cultural structures are then reflected in particular texts. The sequence is then, as follows: Social change produces cultural value systems or cultural superstructures, which are in turn reiterated, or represented, in specific textual formulations.

Goldmann's method is designed to write Marxist intellectual history, focusing on the culture and on the value systems as well as upon social and economic systems. It can be described as the academic outcome of the theories of Adorno, Benjamin and Gramsci with help from Piaget. It comprises a Marxist theory conducive to writing cultural history. Hayden White, of the University of California at Santa Cruz, who currently enjoys a high degree of visibility, is an important disciple of Goldmann in the United States.

Althusser is a Stalinist idealist—an unusual combination indeed. He was one of the few left-wing intellectuals in France who remained loyal to Stalinism, and justified it on the grounds that the world of ideology and the empirical world are not connected. One cannot, in other words, establish the two discrete systems of ideology and socio-economics as complementary and interrelated. They operate in disconnected realms, and therefore one is free to believe whatever one wants. The empirical data about the Gulag do not necessarily have to lead opinion to turn against Stalin or the Soviet Union. The world of ideology is not informed by the empirical world of data. Althusser is a twentieth-century Averroist or Occamist. He has resurrected the medieval double-faith theory.

Basing belief on the empirical can lead only to false consciousness, Althusser claims. Given this, belief is and must be radically divorced from data, and operates according to its own laws which leave the individual free to choose his ideological course. If one does want to believe in Stalinism, there is no empirical evidence that is capable of preventing one from doing so. This recalls William James' "will to believe."

Another way of arriving at this conclusion runs through the principle of over determination, which is a clever, historical theory of skepticism. Any given historical event is overdetermined. That is, there are so many factors, ranging from the social and economic through the political to the cultural that contribute to phenomena, that it is impossible to specify and exhaust the causes. There is, in other words, no such thing as a capability of determining the cause of a historical event. Therefore, one can decide for oneself what is at work in history, which decision then constitutes one's ideology. Just as economic determinism cannot be proved, it cannot be disproved either. The theory of history is something the individual works out for himself; necessarily so, since it does not admit of empirical and rational demonstration.

Althusser's theory can obtain the sympathy of historians who are familiar with the ambivalences of their discipline. His theory was immensely popular for a while with Parisian students who acknowledged at last the truth about Gulag, but did not want to stop being Communists. Althusser's theory can also be used by conservatives. Whatever the sleazebag qualities of the Nixon and Reagan administrations, there is no empirical need to give up rightist conservatism.

In 1980 Althusser murdered his wife and was found to be unfit to stand trial. These events adversely affected his reputation on the Left Bank.

Juergen Habermas is Adorno's principal disciple and the most celebrated German thinker of the last two decades. His work is not easy to read, but the effort is rewarding. Habermas has three theories, of which two are not particularly original, but the third one is extremely interesting and rather original.

The first theory strictly continues and revives the Frankfurt School. Following Adorno and Benjamin and their assertion that cultural superstructures assume independence from base-structures, Habermas claims that "social systems are life-worlds that are symbolically structured."

Secondly, there is the theory of displacement, which teaches that capitalist society is very tightly integrated and a crisis in one segment of society will bring about a displacement effect on another part. The breakdown of capitalism will not occur necessarily in the domain of technology or in the system of banking or in the economy, but it can occur anywhere. The principle of displacement will work, running through the entire system, regardless of the crisis' original domain. This supports Gramsci.

Habermas' third theory is the seminal one of legitimation crisis, in which he tries to deal with the cultural and moral issues in late capitalism, a specific problem of recent times. He proposes that late capitalism is threatened by a cultural crisis or a crisis of legitimation, owing to the fact that it has generated expectations and anxieties in important segments of the population, including the bourgeoisie itself, that the system cannot satisfy. Late capitalism is an ever-expanding balloon, as it were, that is bound to explode. The cultural values, the ethics, which have been generated by capitalism itself, demand so much from the capitalist system, they are so inflated, that inevitably they will render the system incapable of functioning.

There is an anomic split, according to Habermas, in late capitalism between values and social institutions. The anomie that Durkheim had identified as the possibility of a social crisis that heretofore remained hypothetical, Habermas finds to be in fact occurring. The recuperative, functionalizing, socializing capabilities of late capitalism are under unprecedented challenge. Why? What is happening at this stage of the development of capitalism is that grandiose expectations are being built up through the spread of education. The middle class are expecting a reward from their university education and professional training, to which the market society cannot respond. "The market is losing its credibility as a mechanism for the allocation of chances of life. . . . Market success is being replaced by professional success resulting from formal education." The rise of narcissism is a reflection of this novel situation, representing the critical decline of the bourgeois work ethic as well as increasing disappointment and frustration among the professional middle class. Capitalism cannot always satisfy the yuppies, with their "instrumental attitude to work." Their loyalty to the market system is fragile. Their loyalties to themselves, which capitalism has enormously fed and affirmed through its educational system, are incomparably stronger. The inevitable consequence of this is progressive demoralization among professionals. A momentous "erosion of bourgeois traditions" is occurring, accompanied by the emergence of "normative structures" that threaten the viability of capitalist culture.

At the same time, the scientific and technocratic culture of late capitalism has established a constant stream of information and legitimized criticism, which it, once again, cannot control. It has created a scientific, technocratic mechanism, which has become a modern Frankenstein monster that has assumed autonomy and is progressively becoming more critical of its parent system, feeding on the vast flow of information about the defects of society. The informational and scientific mechanisms that capitalism has created are undermining the system that spawned them. Habermas also sees modern art as the site on which a counter-culture is being generated, which provides one more important avenue of criticism and erosion of capitalist values. "Modern art is the cocoon in which the transformation of bourgeois art into counter-culture is bred."

Above all, there is emerging an unrestrained, universalistic morality in late capitalism. The civil rights movement for minorities, affirmative action, the women's liberation movement, (we might now add South African divestment)—in the last two decades capitalism has been unceasingly bombarded by universalitic ethical demands which, while it finds them intrinsically and serially justified, it now struggles anomically to satisfy. The values of capitalist society have exceeded "the dogma of mere tradition." Capitalism is constantly asked to fulfill absolute values which it cannot easily do, and when it does, this effort sends shock waves through the whole system. Capitalism is being eroded from within by its own ethical values.

Western society is deluding itself if it thinks it can integrate devastating egalitarianism without major outcomes. Until recently capitalism discriminated between the public sphere of activity, which is conditioned only marginally by ethical considerations, and family and private life, wherein absolute values play a much larger role. Now the barriers between the public and private spheres are being demolished. "Competitive capitalism has for the first time given binding force to strictly universal value systems." As a result late capitalism is in a condition of growing crisis. The traditional model of legitimation "is breaking down, while at the same time new and increased demands for legitimation are arising."

Habermas' theory of legitimation crisis is the most original and illuminating sociological doctrine since Durkheim. He is the only sociologist to deal realistically with the massive impact of the egalitarian changes of the past twenty years upon Western society. He has identified the upheavals that Western society is experiencing in the seventies and eighties as a result of civil rights extension, feminism, affirmative action, and cognate developments. He has broken the conspiracy of silence that social scientists have engaged in so as not to disturb the unimpeded advances of these radical departures that their leftist ideology advocates so vehemently. Habermas has in abundance the first quality of a great social scientist: honesty. Habermas' arguments can serve the conservative point of view as well as they can serve the left. There are Burkean overtones to the theory of legitimation crisis. If Reaganite conservatives were to read and understand Habermas, which is unthinkable, they would here find a social theory to support their efforts to slow down the civil right movements and women's liberation.

Lenin had said that the capitalist is so greedy that he will sell the rope that will hang him. Habermas suggests that the capitalist has become so driven by abstract moral principles that he will overextend and functionally impair the culture that has bred and sustained him. In the end, capitalism will find itself unable to justify its own continued existence and to maintain a stable institutional framework that will satisfy incessant demands and criticisms. The perpetual flow of information and the resultant criticism this occasions, as well as abstract moralizing, becomes even harder to respond to. Of course, a system such as the Soviets' would never have to encounter such a problem. That is why the Soviet government is so fanatical in restricting information. Legitimation is now a problem that is intrinsic to capitalism.

In recent years, there has been a fusion of Marxist literary and art criticism. We will here only mention the most outstanding Anglo-American workers in this field, without lingering on the details of their thought. The most prominent Englishman in this respect is Terry Eagleton, whose *Literary Theory* has become a bestseller and is a valuable source of information and very subtle Marxist polemics.

Students and the educated public at large in the eighties, as in the thirties, were anxious to acquire a basic knowledge of philosophy and cultural theory. In the 1930's a New Deal liberal who held marginal teaching jobs in New York colleges, Will Durant, satisfied the urge to gain this basic knowledge of Plato, Descartes, and Kant in his *The Story of Philosophy*, one of the all-time nonfiction bestsellers. In the eighties Terry Eagleton, a reputable Oxford scholar, achieved the same measure of success with his *Literary Theory*. This book could be seen stacked in huge piles at book stores on or near college campuses all over the country.

It is highly significant that Eagleton's orientation was aggressively Marxist, as Durant's had been blatantly New Deal liberal. The success of Eagleton's book represented the unquestioned habilitation of scholarly Marxism in the Anglo-American college world. For thousands of postadolescents, and also more mature students in the eighties, their introduction to the history of twentieth-century literary criticism was accompanied by a thick coating of Marxist interpretation. The traces of this pabulum in the readers' mentality would not soon or easily be eroded.

In the United States, the leading Marxist critics of the new generation are Frederic Jameson and Frank Lentricchia. Lentricchia is a capable historian of literary theory, while Jameson is a theorist. He applies the doctrines of Adorno and the Frankfurt School to the study of literary texts. Here is a passage that renders well the Marxist flavor of Jameson's style and thought: "Even hegemonic or ruling class culture and ideology are utopian, not in spite of their instrumental function to secure and perpetuate class privilege and power, but rather precisely because their function is also in and of itself the affirmation of collective solidarity." (Translation: Bourgeois culture ideally seeks class power sustained by group feeling.) Further: "The text liberates us from the empirical object, whether institution, event or individual work." The literary text, according to Jameson, becomes a cultural superstructure, taking on a life of its own, and is separated from the empirical world. This is Adorno–Benjamin with a flavoring of Althusser.

Several leading universities in the eighties vigorously competed for Jameson's services and he now occupies an endowed chair in the humanities at Duke. Why is Jameson so much in demand? He only presents cumbersome restatements of Adorno, Benjamin and the Frankfurt School. The Berkeley critic Frederick Crews has called Jameson "the Spruce Goose" of the academic world, after Howard Hughes' monstrous wooden plane that flew only once, and a few yards off the ground. What Jameson has to offer is what the trans-Atlantic academic world keenly wants in the late eighties. Quentin Skinner, the Oxford political philosopher, has, not facetiously, called this trend "the return of grand theory in the human sciences"—in other words, variants of Marxism applied to the humanities.

It is of great moment for the culture of the twentieth fin-de-siécle that writing authoritatively, as Jameson does, along the lines of the Frankfurt School is now the most valued commodity in the humanistic marketplace. Poor, poor Walter Benjamin, failing to get his seminal monograph accepted by his university, and later dying alone and by his own hand in 1940 in a bleak hotel on the Spanish border. Now he could have his pick of endowed chairs, visiting lectures and honorary degrees in American universities. Nothing could more dramatically signify the alteration in the academic legitimacy of Marxism than comparing the destinies of Benjamin and his intellectual heir Jameson.

The leading Marxist art critic, who has already been mentioned, is T.J. Clarke, a British scholar teaching at Harvard University. He is a disciple of the 1930's and 40's' Anglo-Austrian Marxist art historians Hauser and Anthel.

Also at Harvard University, there has emerged a Marxist school of legal interpretation, called Critical Legal Studies, which has its representatives at Stanford University as well. Harvard and Stanford house certainly two of the ten top law schools in the United States, and both have vibrant Marxist scholars on their faculties. The leading Marxist historian of law in America is Morton Horwitz, while the prominent Marxist theorists of law are Roberto Unger and Duncan Kennedy, all of whom teach at Harvard University. In fact, the law school of this university has been undergoing civil strife in the last few years, owing to the contentions between Marxist and non-Marxist faculty members. One of the leading anti-Marxists there left Harvard for the University of Chicago, which has the prominent conservative law school in this country.

Critical Legal Studies is well named. It joins legal realism of the thirties with the Frankfurt School's Critical Theory. Intellectually the result is conventional Marxist history and social theory. The importance of CLS is that it represents the penetration of Marxism into the intellectual bastions of the business corporations, the elite law schools. When the graduate of classes taught by CLS professors assume partnerships in corporate law firms during the next decade, its impact can be determined.

Finally, the formation of a Marxist-feminist group has occurred in recent years. Feminism will be discussed at greater length in a later chapter. There is in existence a very important group of Marxist feminist theorists, who use as their starting point a suggestion made by Friedrich Engels, the associate of Marx, to the effect that the subjection of women historically came about simultaneously with the introduction of private property.

Taking their cue from Engels, Marxist feminists claim that it is industrial capitalism that has played a particularly grievous part in the subjection of women. They hold that the removal of women from rural society, from the family farm, in which there had been a certain degree of equality between the husband and wife who worked side by side, and their transfer to the city have led to the reduction of equality, and the change of the role model for women, thus bringing about the deterioration of their position. The path to the liberation of women, so runs their conclusion, leads through a socialist society—not a Soviet one, which has evidently not released women from their former mode of existence, but through a genuinely socialistic society.

Among leading Marxist feminist theorists are Molly Nolan, who is in the history department of New York University, and Barbara Ehrenreich, who is prominent in New York feminist circles and frequently writes for *The New York Times*.

*   *   *

The Sixties and the New Left

The novelist Harold Brodkey, writing in *The New York Times Book Review* in 1986 disparaged the sixties by remarking, "Sixties culture changed everything and accomplished nothing." But the sixties did accomplish many things. First it produced the movements for civil rights and for black liberation. It advanced the Third World, as it did the feminist movement. All of these movements, even though their origins can be traced further back, do come out of the sixties. It was the sixties that placed them in the front of social action.

Secondly, the sixties produced a new popular culture—the rock culture—by taking an aspect of black culture and universalizing it. It commercialized rock, one could possibly claim, and corrupted it, but it did transform popular culture.

Thirdly, the sixties legitimated television. In the fifties, it was fashionable for intellectuals and many professionals to declare that one did not own a television set, and that even if one did, one hated it. The sixties altered this, making television an acceptable cultural element. Furthermore, the social impact of new forms of electronic communication was now a prominent concern of intellectuals and academics.

Fourthly, the sixties introduced Marxism into the universities, creating a large generation of young scholars who came from among the radical students. This phenomenon has been described at the beginning of the present chapter.

Fifthly, the sixties validated sects and subcultures within American life. Although many of the particular sects and subcultures of the sixties have died out, others have appeared to take their place. The new tolerance for non-orthodox and adversary groups that the sixties imparted appears to have become a permanent part of the American heritage, and a productive and worthy one, on the whole.

Finally, the sixties created the tradition of hating America as the bastion of capitalism and imperialism. It is true that there is a counter-tradition at work currently in the Reagan era. But the residual odium felt for "Amerika" was a prominent sixties' sentiment, according to which everything that came out of America had to become the object of protest, since this was also the country that produced every world evil, from acid rain and Vietnam to trashy movies. While there has been a reaction, an intensely cultivated one too, against this feeling, nevertheless the sixties' trend has left behind a powerful trail of pervasive, reflexive hatred against America, not least in the United States itself.

What factors contributed to laying the foundations of the sixties' phenomena described above? What forces triggered the upheaval that led to the May of 1968, when radical students took control of Columbia University, and when in Paris revolutionaries held not only the university but the streets as well, to cite a few among numerous other dramatic incidents?

The most prominent factor is the demographic one, for a population tidal wave had begun after the Second World War. By the late fifties, all demographers, that is, population experts, were agreeing that a population cohort of unprecedented size would reach maturity, or at least post-adolescence, in the mid-sixties, and that social institutions would not be able to cope with them.

Indeed, their predictions proved valid. That is precisely what happened in the sixties. One thing about which we can be absolutely certain as regards history, is that population cohort advances because, quite simply, people are born. The institutions of society, particularly the educational institutions, could not absorb in the sixties this vast generation of unprecedented size. No matter how many new state colleges were formed, regardless of how quickly faculties were expanded, educational institutions could not effectively absorb the tide of incoming students. Between 1960 and 1972 the number of college students increased from 3 to 7.5 million. But they were poorly socialized and deeply discontented.

After the upheaval at Columbia University of May 1968 was over, the university administration appointed a commission led by Archibald Cox, the old New Dealer and civil rights professor of law from Harvard, to investigate why the May 1968 events had taken place. His conclusion was that the greatest problem had been that the dormitories and the meals provided by the university had not been satisfactory. No wonder, was Cox' amazing conclusion, students were discontented. This is a realistic appraisal of the events, despite the humor it contains, and responsible for the severe deterioration of living conditions at the university was the demographic tidal wave. The proximity of Harlem, accessiblity of Greenwich Village radicals to the campus, and the Vietnam War also contributed to the Columbia upheaval.

The numbers of college students increased so rapidly in the Sixties that the normal socializing processes were rendered ineffective. The members of this vast generation taught each other, rather than being taught by adults. Youth culture became a thing in itself. The fifties, on the other hand, had produced a very conservative and conformist generation. Because there had been a very low birth rate during the Great Depression, the population that reached maturity around 1950 was abnormally small. This facilitated their easy control and socialization by adults. The sixties, however, saw the opposite of what had happened in the fifties.

Secondly, the period between 1958 and 1968 was also an era of unprecedented prosperity, featuring full employment. In periods when every college graduate, and even literate high school graduate, can easily secure employment, and livelihood itself does not pose problems, large segments of the population can devote themselves to the intellectual and artistic life and to radical political action. They are not frightened or anxious. They can become cultural and political radicals. This had been the case in the first decade of the twentieth century and again in the early 1920's; it occurred as well in the 1960's. To compound the favorable economic situation, there was a welfare liberal government in Washington, which generated even more jobs than the system of market economy could have done by itself. The Federal Government under the welfare state liberals in the Kennedy and Johnson administration vastly expanded during this period. It poured money into education as well as into social services. Particularly the Lyndon Johnson government generated jobs artificially.

Thirdly, one factor operating in the formation of the sixties is what might be called the heritage of moral absolutism. Beginning with the Second World War, "the last good war" as it has been called, the United States found itself drenched in ethics. Americans were saints, they were good people, who had first fought the evil Nazis, and secondly, in the fifties, had held back the malevolent Soviet communists. Then, beginning with the era of John F. Kennedy, they launched the crusade to improve society. The United States was provided with twenty years of unceasing ideological motivation towards rigorous ethical standards.

Eventually, this crusading mentality began to have its effect upon the behavior and outlook of people at large, particularly on those of the younger generation. They began to look for ways in which to be even more ethical. The civil rights movement was one such discovered channel. If America was striving to become the heavenly city, the problems that were plaguing the South could no longer be endured. So white students joined the blacks of the South in "Freedom Rides" to end segregation. The questioning of the war in Vietnam also took place in this context. A pure and moral society could not engage in the evils of imperialism, which this war was held to be.

The ethical shortcomings of the Vietnam conflict became especially evident after middle-class college students became eligible for the draft and after the Vietcong appeared to gain a big victory in the 1968 Tet Offensive (it was actually a Vietcong defeat but the leftist-inspired media claimed otherwise).

The establishment of this country allowed itself to slip into a situation where it preached ethics for two decades, and, unsurprisingly, it found itself soon face to face with a generation that cashed in the moral blank checks they had been issued. A new generation sought ever new areas for the application of ethical standards. Of course, the establishment was found wanting. This is precisely what Habermas points to in his argument about legitimation crises in late capitalism. The ruling groups of the United States, particularly when they got involved in the Vietnam War, could not defend their position in terms of abstract moral claims.

McGeorge Bundy had preached high standards of public ethics to students while Dean at Harvard. He preached ethics to the American people while National Security Adviser to President Johnson. Then he advocated involvement in Vietnam. He soon found himself drowning in the moral cauldron he had prepared so assiduously. Bundy and the rest of "the best and the brightest" liberal democrats lost their legitimacy. Unable to articulate a defense of their foreign and military policies as ethically determined, the Ivy League academics serving Lyndon Johnson, like Bundy and W.W. Rostow, went down with a resounding crash.

The fourth factor that shaped the sixties was the revolt against the fifties. The fifties had been the time of conformist suburbia, of middle class communality, and a time of boredom. How long could a culture be sustained, where people sat in Levittown and watched extremely primitive black and white television? It is hard to imagine how primitive television was a few decades ago. It was not enough to sustain suburban life at a time when restaurants, clubs, adequate movies and the like scarcely existed there.

Suburban life had little to offer the new, Post-modern generation. The shopping malls could not distract them for long. College students in the Fifties were called "the Silent Generation." They were putatively docile and conformist, supposed to be satisfied with studies and job searches and Doris Day movies. They could not be silent forever.

The rebellion against suburban conformity was first expressed by young men who wore pegged pants and greasy, duck-billed hair and who adulated the actor James Dean and the rock singer Elvis Presley. These nonconformists were denounced as "juvenile delinquents," a catch-all fifties phrase for young rebels.

The rebellion was further articulated by the "Beat" movement of the late fifties. Jack Kerouac, his *On the Road*, and his beat friends moving restlessly from San Francisco to New York—these reflected post-adolescent protest against the boredom of suburban life. It was bound to happen because the dullness of the fifties stood in sharp contrast to the exuberance of the American tradition of living. The twenties and the thirties provided a sharp comparison. Kerouac wrote most of *On the Road* on his mother's kitchen table in Lowell, Massachussetts, and the vision he presented of vanguard, North Beach San Francisco culture was really a revived image of the twenties' culture.

The Haight-Ashbury section of San Francisco, the eastern part of the Greenwich Village section of Manhattan, and the Near North Side of Chicago became the centers of the sixties folk rock counter-culture which played an indispensable role in the development of leftist influence and radical expression. The sources for this distinctive American subculture, which spread not only to most major American cities but the metropolises of Western Europe as well, were rock music and Black culture, the Beat movement, and the leftist folk-song brigades of the thirties. At summer camps, the Marxist-oriented Black Mountain College, Bennington College, and the New School, Union Square, New York and other places in the thirties the vehicle of the traditional Anglo-American folk song was transformed into consciously created ballads of political opinion. The Fascists and the Nazis did the same thing in the twenties and thirties—for example, the marching song of the Italians blackshirts was a snappy folk-type song significantly called "Youth."

It took a poet and musician of genius, Bob Dylan (formerly Robert Zimmerman, a Jewish boy improbably from the agricultural town of Hibbing, Minnesota), to merge these disparate elements into anthems for his generation. Carrying an acoustic guitar, Zimmerman appeared eagerly in folk-song taverns in Greenwich Village and was generously well-instructed by a veteran of the leftist folk song movement, Dave von Ronk. Dylan surpassed von Ronk and all his predecessors, even the thirties paragons of leftist folk songs, Woody Guthrie and Pete Seeger.

Dylan, in powerful musical lines that—initially to the dismay of the left—took on more and more of a rock beat, found the words to express the hearts and minds of a generation: "Come mothers and fathers throughout the land./Don't criticize what you can't understand./Your sons and daughters are beyond your command./The old world is rapidly changing/ . . . The order is rapidly fading./The first now will later be last./The times they are a'changing."

This is the best the Sixties' radical culture had to offer. Another Bob Dylan song became the anthem of the civil rights and anti-war movements: "How many roads must a man walk down/Before they call him a man?/How many seas must a white dove sail/Before it sleeps in the sand?/ . . . The answer my friend is blowing in the wind. . . ." Dylan and the radical folk rock singers were adulated by their generation and given maximum attention by the sympathetic media. They both reflected and stimulated rebellion and protest. "You don't need a weatherman to know which way the wind is blowing," sang Dylan again. He was sure it was blowing towards a revolution of some kind.

At the heart of the folk rock subculture was the idea of formation of communities by choice. Whether in Haight-Ashbury, Greenwich Village, or in northern Vermont groups of middle class students, artists, and political activists chose to live together affectively, pool their intellectual and fiscal resources, and devote themselves to a vanguard cause. In the worst case situations, these communes became infected by drug-taking and power struggles, and disintegrated after a few years or months. But in the best case scenario, these communities developed over many years, made enormous demands on their members, lived predominantly puritanical lives, and engaged in some form of socially valuable work.

A prime example of the latter was the Bread and Puppet Theater. It was founded by a scion of German Expressionist theater, Peter Schumann, in Greenwich Village in the late sixties and devoted itself to political theater involving giant puppets accompanied by music, dance, and circus effects. The Bread and Puppet Theater soon migrated to a commune in the depths of rural northern Vermont, became famous throughout the trans- Atlantic world, and was still going strong in the mid-80's. It made strenuous demands on its talented members that no commercial theater could claim. Each summer all its alumni and friends still gather for a two day puppet and circus festival in Vermont and celebrate an affective festival in the manner of the sixties. The Bread and Puppet Theater even has its own museum, in which retired giant puppets from past years are reverently preserved as totems of political theater.

Among the subcultures of the 60's were hippies who wanted to focus on communal and improved individual behavior, not political and economic slogans. This movement toward creating new subgroups did not want to clash with government so much as to be ignored by it. They were often in conflict with the political radicals that Bob Dylan represented, whom they saw as driven by psychological needs they would not face. The rock group The Grateful Dead were spokesmen for the hippie philosophy. And the Beatles sang: "If you're talking about destruction, brother you can count me out" and "with your pictures of Chairman Mao, ain't gonna make it with me anyhow."

The fifth factor in the shaping of the sixties was the reassertion of the old left. The fifties were an artificially reactionary period which featured the Cold War red scare, and the repressive McCarthy time, frequently referred to as an "era" even though it lasted no longer than four years. Left-wing intellectuals, particularly in academia and in the media, temporarily withdrew and kept a low profile. At most, they spoke about the purge trials and condemned Stalinism. But they did not abandon their socialist ideals and the old thirties' traditions. When the heat was off, which was largely true by 1958, and was completely the case the day liberal Democrat John F. Kennedy was sworn in as President in January 1961, these intellectuals began to reemerge. There is a strong continuity between the left of the thirties and early forties and the left of the sixties. The aging generation of leftists provided a strong support for the emerging radical generation.

The American New Left differed from the old left in only two ways. The New Left was the program of a new generation, more populous and affluent, bolder and more self-confident. Secondly, the New Left was much more sympathetic to anarcho-syndicalism than the old left.

How did the Students for a Democratic Society (SDS), the most important organization of New Left student radicals get started? It began as the youth division of an organization called The League for Industrial Democracy, an old Marxist organization of the 1930's. In its early years the SDS was supported by the League.

Elaborate sociological studies of the New Left student activists pointed to two clusters of data. A significant number of these young leftists were children of old left parents. An even larger number were Jewish. The discontents and ambitions of post-war suburbia extended the impact of inherited radical traditions from the thirties.

A sixth factor was a shift in Marxist theory due to the rise of Maoism. The sixties was the great age of Mao Tse Tung, not his age of greatest accomplishment, but the period when he was most visible. He was leading the Cultural Revolution at the time, and issuing a stream of theoretical pronouncements. The Chinese Communists came to power in 1949 in a society which was very far from an industrial revolution, even further removed, that is, than Russia had been in 1917. In the First World War, Russia was in the early stages of industrialization. China, however, was still, in 1949, a rural peasant society. Therefore, to justify the revolution in terms of Marxist theory, Mao developed the view that the revolution could be carried out by cadres other than the industrial proletariat. The revolution could be carried out by peasants as well as by students; there could even be a peasant-student front. Mao in the mid-sixties called upon the students to purify the revolution. The revolution would be initiated by the peasants, and purified and solidified by the students.

Maoist theory presented a revision of Marxist theory that also supported developments in America, where the left-wing penetration among industrial workers was extremely meager. In the sixties, American blue-collar workers were opposed to student radicalism. For the most part, the unions remained removed from the left. By and large, this was also true in France and West Germany at the time. It was therefore necessary for the New Left to hold that students could be the vanguard of the revolution, and this was essentially a Maoist position.

The seventh factor that went into the making of the sixties was the rise of subcultures, primarily of black and Spanish subcultures which were in many ways hostile to, or contradictory of, the white Protestant culture of America. In the sixties, the dominant culture was confronted by the emergence and legitimization of subcultures, which were very different from itself. Even if the subculture was Protestant in origin, then it was—among the blacks—evangelical Protestant. In the case of the Hispanic-American, the culture was Catholic, but this, in turn, was a Catholicism that had derived from Latin America rather than from Ireland or Italy. The history of this cultural conflict, a very important one, remains to be written.

The eighth, and final, factor is the electronic revolution that gave rise to the so-called "plugged-in generation." The cultural revolution produced by television and electronic media was identified by Marshall McLuhan in the mid-sixties. McLuhan had begun as a professor of English at the University of Toronto, where he had been an expert on Tennyson. However, he had a colleague in the economics department of the University of Toronto in the forties and the early fifties, an extraordinarily brilliant man named Harold Innes, of whom no American has ever heard, who taught McLuhan that the phenomena that transform culture are caused by changes in communication systems and methods, and in transportation. Changes in communication and transportation networks produce cultural revolutions. While Innes' great interest was the Canadian fishing and fur-trading industries, McLuhan applied this idea to the cases of television, stereo music, rock music and instantaneous forms of world communication.

The results of McLuhan's study can be distilled into two arguments. The first is the thesis of the "global village." We have been compacted into a world culture, he finds. Boundaries which hitherto isolated cultures have been broken down as a result of the development of television and film. Increasingly, the world is being assimilated into a homogeneous culture. There was much truth to McLuhan's argument when he first began to develop it, and it has assumed much greater truth since then, for in the meantime, satellites have been introduced, further transforming communication and hence culture. It must be remembered that McLuhan was writing at a time when, in order for CBS to bring to the television screen something that was happening in France, the company had to fly film across the Atlantic—a method that now seems almost medieval.

The other argument McLuhan presented was that television was a cool medium. The television viewer establishes an acutely personal, one-to-one relationship to the screen. The "hot" orator of the pre-television era used to address great crowds, which necessitated a specific form of loud address. That, McLuhan held, would not work any more. Hubert Humphrey's and Walter Mondale's formal and complicated rhetoric, for example, were wrong for television, which needs another rhetorical "cool" mode in order to be effective: a simple, sincere mode of address, such as is found in Reagan's style, by which he acts the old friend and fellow citizen talking to the viewer person to person. Once again, McLuhan's theory has been proved right. In a sense, he predicted what the politician of the future would be like.

McLuhan's theory is that television culture is on the one hand macrocosmic, instantaneously universalizing everything that happens, generating a world culture, but it is at the same time microscosmic and intimate, its focus being intensely individualistic and personal. With television, we have entered, McLuhan claimed, the greatest cultural revolution since the invention of printing. The medium is the message and the massage, McLuhan said. With electronic communication the rationalist, linear print culture, "the Gutenberg Galaxy" that emerged around 1500 A.D., is finally being transcended.

It was the young radicals who first perceived McLuhan as a cultural prophet. The people who were in charge in the sixties of political and educational life and of the media did not themselves clearly understand the nature of the transformation of the domains they commanded. They did not understand that a substantial transformation was taking place in the culture as a whole, even though they knew, of course, that they were dealing with a new communications technology. The transformation, however, was working not only in communications systems but also in interpersonal relations and in social mentality.

It was the younger generation, the students and the radicals, who more clearly sensed the meaning of what was happening. They were the first to understand why the seven o'clock news was important, to realize that it made a difference to watch it rather than wait for the following day's *New York Times*. More significant, it was the SDS who grasped the meaning of, and put to use, the seven o'clock news. The student left would plan and schedule its demonstrations and other events so that they could be filmed and be part of the seven o'clock news. The radicals understood the importance of doing this long before the politicians of this country did. Reagan certainly understands it very well, but the SDS were the pioneers. The slowness of the older generation to react to a cultural revolution that was in the making provided opportunity for the radicals, who knew how to utilize what the new system offered.

The dramatic scenes at Columbia, wherein New Left student radicals held a half dozen buildings for two weeks, brought the university to a halt, were dispersed only by violent police intervention, and achieved the resignation of the President and Provost—similar scenes were repeated on dozens of campuses, including Harvard. At Harvard the Dean of the faculty was sacrificed to leftist agitation. New Left demonstrators precipitated a confrontation with Chicago police during the Democratic Convention in August of 1968, discrediting the Democratic nominee, the welfare liberal Hubert Humphrey, and their constant verbal attacks on Humphrey brought about his defeat and election of Richard Nixon, the Republican candidate.

The principle upon which the New Left was operating was the same as the Communists in Germany between 1930 and 1933: the most important enemy was not the Right but the "social fascist" liberals. The election of Nixon would, they believed, bring about the ultimate confrontation between a conservative government and the radical movement, raising consciousness everywhere, and attaining the revolution.

This scenario appeared to be playing itself out in May 1970. American intervention in Cambodia led to a new wave of campus demonstrations. During one of these, at Kent State University in Ohio, a group of poorly led National Guard panicked and fired on student demonstrators, killing four of them. This was the climax of the New Left movement. Demonstrations and strikes erupted on hundreds of campuses. The middle class, the image of its scions slaughtered by the National Guard projected incessantly by the media, appeared momentarily to be on the verge of radicalization. Final exams were cancelled on hundreds of campuses.

The country, however, returned from the brink. The Nixon administration which, contrary to expectations, had done very little to retreat from the welfare state measures of the Johnson administration, finally pulled itself together and also turned down the Vietnamese War. In the end, 1968 did not inaugurate the age of revolution. 1968 was what the historian G.M. Trevelyan called 1848— "a turning-point in history that failed to turn". Ineptitude and corruption in the Nixon administration combined with media pressure and leftist agitation to bring down the President in the summer of 1974, but the succeeding Ford administration rapidly restored the dignity of the White House and the Federal Government. The resiliency of centrist and conservative forces in the country weathered this unprecedented crisis easily. By the time Gerald Ford acceded to the presidency, the revolutionary tide had receded beyond the horizon. Campuses had returned to peaceful routine. Most of the New Left leaders sought private careers, some highly lucrative ones in media, entertainment and academics.

The New Left revolution failed for three reasons. First, the so-called establishment learned to adjust to, appease and avoid radical confrontation. They negotiated; they made piecemeal concessions; they shamefully abandoned the Vietnamese people to their iron Stalinist fate. McGeorge Bundy fled Washington and became President of the Ford Foundation, which he used to fund radical causes and appease militants on the left.

It was the lawyer Edward Levi, as President of the University of Chicago, who demonstrated how the tide of campus sit-ins and occupation of buildings could be stemmed. The presidents of Columbia and Harvard summoned the police, thereby discrediting themselves and playing exactly the confrontational and delegitimizing role that anarchist theory prescribed. Levi did exactly nothing. He engaged in polite, desultory and token negotiations with the SDS occupiers of campus buildings. He made sure that university life continued as normally as possible around the occupied buildings. After a time, the bored and bewildered radicals quietly abandoned their citadels of confrontation. Levi showed hundreds of other college presidents how to deal with the student militants.

Secondly, the New Left revolution failed in the early 70's because the radicals could not maintain a united front. By 1970 they were split into a variety of factions. One of these, the Weathermen, engaged in terrorism and helped to discredit the movement in general among the middle classes.

At first the Weathermen were content to lead street demonstrations and "off the pigs" (fight with policemen). Then they made bombs in upscale apartments and townhouses or suburban "safe" houses, and used them against government installations and war industries, sometimes killing themselves in the process. Then, led by a scion of a prominent old left family, Kathy Boudin, a Bryn Mawr alumna, they went deeply into the underground, joined up with Black revolutionaries and just plain Black criminals and took to robbing banks and armored cars in order to furnace the revolution. The Weathermen justified all the critical remarks that Marx and Lenin had made about anarchist adventurists.

Thirdly, economic conditions began to worsen in the early seventies and under Republican government federal funding stopped expanding. The boom and boondoggle days when any college graduate could get a good job were over. The Big Chill set in. Anxiety about personal futures weakened the courage of the younger generation and eroded solidarity and activism. By the mid-70's the behavioral mode of the post-adolescent generation was again shifting from socialist activism to social Darwinist privatism.

Both the New Left and the yuppiedom that succeeded it were sociologically the outcome of the greatly expanded suburban middle class of the fifties and sixties. The children of this middle class, often programmed by their over-worked and frustrated parents, sought a share of national power. Their first avenue was radical politics in the shape of the New Left and the SDS and campus upheavals. When that possibility no longer looked feasible, the new middle class turned to private means of satisfying their ambition through advancement in the corporate world. The celebrated paradox is only a superficial one that contrasts the bearded, dishevelled radical or hippie of the sixties with the three-piece suited, finely coiffered executive of the eighties. There is a sociological—and in many instances personal —continuity here. The suburban middle class was struggling for a place in the sun, one way or another. Yet, while the New Left failed to sustain the mass support of the college population, its impact lived on in the academic and media worlds.

By the late eighties not only would *The New York Review of Books*, *The Village Voice*, *The Nation*, *The New Republic* and a host of other leftist publications issue a constant threnody of ideology. *The New York Times Book Review*, in the fifties and sixties a voice of centrism, even of moderation, would publish article after article advocating leftist doctrine. The network news would present a consistently left of center viewpoint, held back from full commitment to leftist ideology only by an uncomfortable need to maintain an uneasy and temporary amity with the Reagan administration. By the mid-1980's a new popular front against capitalist institutions and culture was solidifying in the academic and intellectual world. Strenuous efforts were being made to achieve a symbiosis of recent theoretical trends, that of structuralism and deconstruction, with Marxism and leftist doctrine. This trend will be discussed in a later chapter.

The student radicals and activists of the sixties have assumed diverse, interesting and in some cases leading roles in American life in the eighties. Tom Hayden, one of the key founders of the SDS, is a liberal Democratic state senator in California. He is married to the film actress and exercise impressario Jane Fonda, who was the Vietcong queen in the sixties, condemning Amerika vociferously from Hanoi. Fonda is now very quiet about subsequent events in Vietnam. Bernardine Dohrn, the leader for several years of the underground Weathermen, is a graduate of law school, works in an attorney's office, and regularly petitions the American Bar Association for admission to the Bar, claiming that she has the requisite good character. She is married to another militant of the sixties, whose father was a utilities magnate in Chicago.

Eldridge Cleaver, the Black activist, is a spokesman for the conservative Moral Majority. Staughton Lynd, once the highly visible Yale faculty radical, quietly practices labor law. Gary Hart became the familiar senator from Colorado and self-destructing presidential candidate from the "neo-liberal" wing of the Democratic party. Jerry Rubin, the one-time hippie militant, sells bonds on Wall Street and engages in other business enterprises.

David Stockman's dramatic career is paradigmatic of his generation. It has taken him from Marxism at Michigan State and anti-war activism at Harvard Divinity School to Republican congressman from Michigan, to Director of the Office of Management and Budget and self-proclaimed theoretican of the Reagan rightist revolution, to his current preferment on Wall Street.

Some biographies of sixties radicals ended in tragedy rather than prosperity. Sam Melville died in 1972 in the Attica prison riots, of which he was a leader. Two SDS leaders died in a townhouse on West 11th Street in 1971 when it blew up while it was being used as a bomb factory. Kathy Boudin, the daughter of an old left activist of the thirties, is serving a long prison sentence for murdering a policeman during an armored car holdup in Rockland County in 1981. This was the last of some twenty robberies of banks and armored cars by a gang of Weathermen and Black revolutionaries.

Some 60's radicals, on the other hand, had good lives. Carol Berkin, centrally involved in the Columbia rebellion, got her Ph.D. in American history at Columbia, and became a highly reputable scholar and an active feminist. She is now an administrator at one of the New York City colleges and is much in demand to lecture to chapters of the Daughters of the American Revolution. Jonathan Culler, an SDS member at Harvard in the sixties, is now a prominent deconstructionist critic and director of the Humanities Institute at Cornell.

These are classic American stories, products of the anxieties and ironies, paradoxes and tragedies of the sixties and since. These are the destinies of the American left in the late twentieth century. It is apparently a never-ending story.

A century after the death of Karl Marx, his intellectual progeny, in various shades of red and pink, are entrenched as never before in the academic, intellectual, and media circles of the Western world. As a quintessential Victorian form of thought, with emphasis on historicism, macrocosm, referentiality, and moral absolutism—all attitudes hateful and contemptible to High Modernism—the prosperity of Marxism and the triumph of leftist political culture signifies a continuing ebbing in the spirit of the Modernist cultural revolution.

Marxists, in their perpetually learned and informed manner, realizing that Modernism was the cutting edge of cultural inquiry and artistic form in this century, and wanting to identify with this intellectual vanguard and appropriate its prestige for their putative social and moral forces of progress, persist in attempting to claim that Marxism is no threat to Modernism, but on the contrary can be combined theoretically with Modernism in a popular front against alleged conservatism and reaction.

Perusal of *The New York Review of Books* and the *Village Voice* and other prominent leftist weeklies and study of the leading Marxist cultural journals such as *Telos* and *October*, reveals that the political left still dreams of a coordinated and comprehensive "adversary culture" to combat capitalism and the bourgeois ethos as currently personified by the hateful Ronald Reagan. The left passionately believes in the doctrine of Gramsci and the Frankfurt School that literature, the visual arts, and painting can be a hegemonic field of battle on which the left will triumph, no matter how decisively repudiated at the polls and the barricades.

The only problem for Marxists and the left in the articulation of this adversary culture is the precise ingredient of literature and the arts that should be expropriated in the interest of putative progress. The residual devotion to Modernism as the joint force with leftist ideology in a comprehensive adversary culture still prevails. There is, however, a minority opinion, expressed by Jameson among others, that raises the difficult question as to whether or not Modernism is not obsolete for political purposes. It is not too much identified with allegedly specious bourgeois individualism? A French Marxist critic, Serge Guilbaut, went so far as to suggest in the early eighties that American Modernist painting during the Cold War became an instrument of the CIA. Tom Bender, of N.Y.U's History Department, endorsed this thesis.

Where will the Marxists find the aesthetic balance of adversary culture? Assuredly Soviet realism will not do. Jameson has hailed Post-modernism as the ascending culture to be joined with Marxism in the adversary culture. This proposal, while given respectable consideration in the leftist weeklies and journals, has not won strong endorsement. Post-modernism is too novel, too fragmentary, too deficient in prestige, and perhaps too decadent to serve unequivocally as the literary and artistic ingredient of adversary culture the way Modernism was claimed to function ideologically.

Yet the Post-modernist era of the late seventies and eighties did make a novel contribution to leftist theory. This was the clever deployment in the political and juristic philosophies propounded by John Rawls of Harvard and Ronald Dworkin of Oxford and N.Y.U., of the forensic style of analytic philosophy. Rawls updated John Locke's social contract theory (1690). In the transition from the state of nature to civil society, the overwhelming majority of people are "screened" from knowing whether in the civil society they will be one of the few rich or the many and miserable poor. They play it safe by opting for egalitarian institutions and welfare policies to be written into the social contract. Dworkin's theory was suggested by Sir William Blackstone (1760). While rights are not founded in nature, they still determine laws because when wise "herculean" judges have to decide determinative hard cases they rely on principles derived from communal morality, which will have an egalitarian or at least generous cast to them. Rawls and Dworkin allowed an adhesion to leftist goals achieved by other than Marxist argumentation. In eclectic Post-modernist culture this was regarded as intellectual liberation and moral illumination.

5

Traditions on the Right

The American Right Today

A major threat to the visibility and durability of Western Marxism was the Stalinist terror that threatened the moral credibility of the left wing spectrum from the mid-thirties to the late fifties. Yet Western Marxism survived triumphantly the threat of ethical and emotional association with the discredited Stalinist legacy, achieved a popular revival in the sixties, and in the late seventies and eighties attained an unprecedented penetration of the more respectable academic circles.

The destiny of the right in the twentieth century Western world contrasts sharply with this beneficent course of Marxist development. The right suffered a devastating and near-mortal blow in the forties due to the militarist and genocidal conduct of the German Nazi dictatorship and similar terrorist behavior by other Fascist countries. The Holocaust of the Jews placed an irrevocable human stigma and divine damnation on the Fascist movements of the thirties and forties and dispatched into social and cultural oblivion a large part of the rightist program of the twenties and thirties.

The millions that died or suffered terribly at the hands of the Stalinist regime presented only momentarily an uncomfortable issue for Western Marxism— these devastations were after all, it was claimed and widely accepted, the product of an Eastern aberration for which Western Marxists were in no way responsible. On the other hand, the fifty million people, about half of them civilians, who died in the Second World War, were universally seen as the victims of Fascism, whose seedbed was held to be the rightist ideology of the early twentieth century. Hitler in reference to the right was seen by many people not as an aberration like Stalin on the left but as a polar extrapolation for whom rightist culture was responsible.

Hence a large part of the rightist program of the first four decades of the twentieth century was condemned to death with Hitler in the ashes of his bunker in devastated Berlin of April 1945. The expiation and penance that rightist culture had to undertake in the three following decades in consequence of association with and responsibilty for Fascist terror and holocaust obliterated several cardinal tenets of right-wing doctrine and fundamentally modified others. These were: racism and biological hierarchy among peoples, expiated by unprecedented social and political egalitarianism and negation of white and Western superiority; the end of Western colonialism and the independence of the Third World; a major diminution of anti-Semitism, the social and economic advancement of the Jews and the creation and rise of the State of Israel; the proliferation of social democracy, Keynesianism and the welfare state; and in the Catholic church, the decrease of papal power, the decentralization and democratization of authority and the belated doctrinal and cultural modernization of the church. By 1970 rightist culture as it had existed in the mid-thirties appeared to have all but vanished.

In the fifties and sixties the only alternative to the drift of leftist politics and ideology in the West appeared to be a kind of stodgy, inarticulate centrism represented by avuncular vestiges of the thirties: De Gasperi in Italy, De Gaulle in France, Adenauer in West Germany, and Eisenhower in the U.S.A. The vehemently anti-Communist movement in the United States identified retrospectively although not quite accurately as McCarthyism, was very short-lived. Although Republican Richard Nixon had first gained political visibility in the vanguard of anti-Communism, his presidency from 1969–74 perpetuated and even expanded upon the aggresive welfare liberal program of his immediate predecessor, the left-wing Democrat Lyndon Johnson.

Nixon's presidency involved Keynesian economics; no reduction of the welfare state; enhancement of affirmative action support for minorities and women; termination of the Vietnam War in an ignominious and chaotic manner, betraying the Vietnam people into Stalinist hands; and rapprochement with Red China. If welfare liberal Hubert Humphrey or New Leftist George McGovern, Nixon's Democratic Party opponents, had been elected in 1968 and 1972 respectively, and if they had followed the policies that Nixon actually implemented with the prime assistance of his Secretary of State, Henry Kissinger, the former Harvard professor, their presidencies would have been acceptable to most leftist circles.

Even Nixon's accommodation to leftist policies did not save him from destruction by the media, continuing into compulsive vendetta against the right—Tricky Dick had to be punished for his vehement anti-Communism of the early fifties, particularly his ruthless crusade against the traitor Alger Hiss. It is true that the Nixon White House exhibited marginally corrupt and illegal practices, but not more so than the Kennedy and Johnson administration, which were held safe harmless by the compliant, left- oriented media. Nixon arbitrarily and unconstitutionally made use of the IRS, FBI, and the CIA, but so did Kennedy and Johnson. Nor did Nixon, like Kennedy, bring upscale prostitution into the White House for his personal delectation, nor conduct an exploitive clandestine affair with a movie queen. What made Nixon vulnerable to his enemies was his arrogance and sense of impregnability and a self-destructive personality trait.

Nixon's error was to neglect the media luminaries from *The Washington Post* and *The New York Times* and the TV anchormen and not to court assiduously prominent Ivy League professors in the social sciences. These two groups had become the dominant opinion-makers in the United States during the sixties.

In the mid-seventies the political right in the Western world stirred from its three decades of somnolence. In the United States in 1980 and Israel in 1978, Britain in 1979, Western Germany in 1982, France and Canada in 1985, an array of conservative parties gained power. There were four reasons for this change. First, in the early seventies leftist regimes showed their incapacity to use Keynesian strategies to stem escalating inflation that threatened middle-class security, and the incessant bloating of the welfare state stagnated capital investment in economic expansion. Secondly, the conservative political revival was helped by the articulation of neo-rightist doctrine in academic and intellectual circles against the rising tide of the cultural left.

Thirdly, the mass of respectable, hard-working middle and working class people became concerned with the unrestrained egalitarianism that leftist governments endorsed and stimulated. They viscerally came to the the same conclusion as Habermas, that a legitimation crisis of Western capitalism was being precipitated. Finally, conservative political parties found effective popular leaders, especially in Ronald Reagan, Margaret Thatcher, Menachem Begin, and Kurt Waldheim.

There are four ideologies that comprise the intellectual American right today. Reaganism is the first of these four, and it has solid intellectual foundations which originated principally in the neo-Ricardian free market and monetarist economic theories of Milton Friedman at the University of Chicago. At Chicago Friedman spawned a group of true believers, such as George Gilder, and he gained many disciples in economics departments and business schools elsewhere. Friedman in turn was a follower of two central European émigré conservative theorists at Chicago in the forties, the political theorist Leo Strauss and the social theorist and anti-socialist polemicist Friedrich von Hayek.

In Friedman's view, the welfare state has become a burden on society. Even at the time when it had not yet become corrupt, the welfare state occasioned excessive government regulation of the economy and overspending. It withdrew capital from the private sector, and produced dysfunction in the economy.

Friedman offered the solution of adjustment in the monetary supply along with a cutback in the size of the government and reduction of taxation. In a relatively unregulated economy, conditioned only by changes in the money supply, economic expansion would be ensured. Unrestrained market forces could in a relatively short time bring more capital into the market and induce business recovery. Inflation would be reduced by the classic method of layoff of redundant workers, union-busting, and wage restraint. The ills of the American economy in the seventies, which resulted in high inflation and unemployment rates following from business stagnation, could then be remedied by these neo-Ricardian methods.

The most extreme statement of the Chicago school centered on Friedman came from his disciple George Gilder. He argued that capitalism is the true altruism, socialism a form of vicious selfishness serving only the needs and interests of a small oligarchy. "The heroes of capitalism are not arrogant producers of goods immaculately conceived in their own minds; capitalists imaginatively serve the minds and needs of others." A favorite theme of Gilder and the Chicago school is that the welfare state is the opposite of generous and humanitarian. It is in fact "a cheap charity that all too often spends the earnings of others in ways that degrade and demoralize the alleged beneficiaries." For example, the erosion of Black families was the consequence of federal aid to single parent families.

Why should the University of Chicago have become in the seventies and eighties the intellectual center of the American right? Not only its business school and economics department revived neo-Ricardianism, and indeed went beyond that conservative philosophy, but its law school also took a strongly rightist position. One of its former law professors, Antonin Scalia, was designated by Reagan for the Supreme Court. Scalia was famous not only for neo-Ricardianism but for hostility to affirmative action. In 1986 a prominent Harvard Law School professor fled to Chicago from the Critical Legal Studies Marxists who increasingly dominated the Harvard institution.

The rightist coloration of the University of Chicago was partly happenstance—the heritage of the dynamic two Central European émigré rightists Strauss and Hayek. It was partly the result of the physical location of the University in the mid-Western citadel of capitalism, and even more important, in its location on the South Side of Chicago, in the middle of a huge Black ghetto, a location that had the effect of stimulating the largely white academy. It forced the University inward, surrounding itself completely with walls and expensive real estate buffers (one of the faculty apartment houses had both a wall and a moat). Thereby the University was cut off from the city of Chicago and had to stress abstract theory.

But the most important reason for U.C.'s rightism is that the intellectual opening in the American academic world was on the right, the Ivy League and Berkeley having previously joined forces with the left. When Princeton was the stamping ground of Lawrence Stone and other academic Marxists and adherents of Frankfurt School of Critical Theory held sway at the University of California, the only place on the spectrum of political culture where the University of Chicago could distinguish itself in the seventies and eighties was on the right.

Founded by Rockefeller family in the early years of the century, the University of Chicago gained prominence between the wars in the social and behaviorial and physical sciences. In the forties and fifties it experienced an intellectual decline under the unfortunate leadership of President Robert Maynard Hutchins and his immediate successors, who stressed the undergraduate college and neo-Victorian core curriculum. Emerging from the doldrums in the late sixties under the shrewd lawyer and conqueror of the student left, Edward Levi, U.C. in the seventies, under a judicious president, Hannah Holborn Gray, became again a thriving center of research and scholarly inquiry. With a heavy infusion of new local money, it greatly improved its facilities and faculty, and Milton Friedman showed the university the intellectual road it could follow to regain the front-rank intellectual stature it had enjoyed in the halcyon pre-Hutchins era.

Gilder's rightist leaning was so extreme that he found highly laudatory things to say about Ayn Rand, an eccentric popular novelist of the forties who wrote best-selling stories about heroic, utterly selfish, rugged individualists. Gilder called one of Rand's works "the most important novel of ideas" since

Tolstoy. Ayn Rand (née Alice Rosenbaum) had heretofore been a laughing-stock in the academic world. Nothing demonstrates more dramatically the intellectual revolution that the Friedmanite school sought to achieve. Next: Reverend Falwell is the greatest theologian since Luther.

Friedman's program had considerable success under the aegis of the Reagan government. Inflation was greatly reduced and business recovery generated. Taxation was held in check and reduced for upper middle-class families, whose entrepreneurial ambition and investment capabilties were encouraged. The power of the labor unions, with help of the Reagan administration, was severely reduced. Unfortunately, high defense spending produced a sizable deficit but Reagan was no more inhibited by deficits than FDR had been.

A remarkable example of the effectiveness of Reaganism is to be found in the solution of the oil and gasoline problems. Twice in the seventies, first during the Nixon and later during the Carter administration, there were consumer gasoline shortages which reached critical dimensions. The Friedmanite econ-omists advised at the time that if the government would simply stop regulating oil and gasoline, the market would adjust itself and the shortage cease. They were proved right.

The other intellectual source of Reaganism was in the scientific theory of sociobiology, which was propounded principally by E.O. Wilson, a Harvard zoologist. If Friedmanist economic theory is neo-Ricardian, Wilson's social biology is neo-social Darwinist and entails belief in competition in every sphere of life, including the human. Wilson's research work was on insects and he applied the patterns he discovered in insect life, which were regulated by competitive principles, to human existence. The same reassertion of the competitive model among humanity can be found in Reaganism. Wilson did not rule out the occasional intrusion of altruism in sociobiology, but his world is essentially a modified version of the social Darwinist struggle for existence.

Wilson does not agree with Austrian population biologist Konrad Lorenz that constant aggression is prevalent in social groups. Wilson argues that the message of sociobiology is a reciprocal altruism, a social cooperation based on individual calculation and exchange of interest. He argues a paradoxical message of "true altruism" and "true selfishness" as distinct from the romantic leftist beliefs in a transcendent altruism over personal selfishness. "Human beings appear to be sufficiently selfish and calculating to be capable of infinitely greater harmony. . . . True selfishness, if obedient to the other constraints of mammalian biology is the key to a more nearly perfect social contract." In practical terms it is hard to see that this is in any way different from Friedman's and Gilder's neo-Ricardianism. It is a variant of the old social contract theory. In the nineteenth century there was a close colloboration between market economists and biological theorists like Darwin and Spencer. This seems to have happened again in the Age of Reagan.

While new leftists of the sixties and seventies had talked incessantly about participating in democracy and communal bonds, in fact they had aggressively sought power and preferment as much as any capitalist entrepreneur. Yet in the academic world and the leftist media it became the fashion to denigrate not only racism, imperialism, and capitalism but competitive strategies and judgmental structures of any kind. Leftist critics like Allen Chase and Stephen Jay Gould lumped IQ testing in the same category with nineteenth-century craniology (measuring brain cavities speciously to show white men had bigger brains) and early twentieth-century eugenics (theory of selective breeding to foster a vigorous white race). SAT tests were denounced as socially biased and discriminatory, against black, Hispanics, women—whomever.

Leading members of the federal Civil Rights Commission in the Carter administration, such as Eleanor Holmes Norton and Mary Berry, aimed to remove all competitive structure and standards as an obstacle to affirmative action and the perpetually egalitarian society. Quotas, euphemistically called goals, were enforced by federal agencies, since the new quotas were designed to assist the minorities and the underprivileged to get ahead.

Against leftist egalitarianism, Reaganism both reflected and fostered a resurgence of legitimate competitiveness, the last glimmer of social Darwinism. Harvard psychologist Arthur Jenson argued anew for the scientific validity of IQ tests as measuring an inheritable, biologically based intelligence and not just environmental impacts—nature as against nurture. The elite law schools fiercely held on to their LSAT tests as the most important criterion to admission, claiming a high correlation between the LSAT scores (combined with grade point averages) and law school performances. The yuppie generation, not marching to the barricades any more, but preferring to drive there in their BMWs, were comfortable with competitive standards in professional schools and the business world that assured them of high salaries, power, and interesting jobs. Because the egalitarian trumpeters of the left in their moment of power had in most instances not refrained from personal advantage, this minimalist new social Darwinism of the eighties exuded a freshly honest tone of cynical reality.

The second ideological strand on the American right, after Reaganism, was evangelical Christianity, whose most visible spokesmen, if not always its most skillful ones, were Reverend Jerry Falwell and Reverend Pat Robertson. In this country, not only in the South, but also in the Midwest and on the West Coast, albeit less so in the Northeast, there has been an upsurge of evangelical, Baptist, Seventh-day Adventist, Mormon and other more experiential forms of Christianity in the last thirty years. Access to television has greatly increased the reach and wealth of the evangelical churches. This important development, although it involves forty million people, has been underexamined. The attention it has received from the media is inadequate, and it has been largely ignored in the academic world. Nevertheless, evangelical Christianity constitutes a very important movement.

Evangelical Christianity has registered striking gains in some parts of this country, and this is a major right-wing phenomenon. Like evangelical and millenary Christians throughout history, the current group draws its support from the upwardly mobile lower middle class—or people not more than one generation removed from that class—who feel customarily disfranchised by the media elite and the limousine leftists in the Ivy League.

The evangelicals ("Born-Again Christians"), who might be described as neo-puritanical and neo-Victorian, support Reaganism. They are hostile to the

Soviet bloc, abortion, the teaching of contraception in schools, convenient divorce laws, sexual permissiveness and pornography, and Darwinian evolution. They have also become vehement supporters of Israel because this fits in with their apocalyptical model of history and because of Soviet hostility to Israel. In 1986 the evangelical clergymen themselves began to enter Republican primaries and thereby to seek direct access to political power. This could be the start of something big.

The third ideological stream in the American right today is constituted by a group of mainly New York neo-conservative intellectuals who have their leading outlet in the monthly journals *Commentary* and *The New Criterion*. This group has emerged as the New York intellectual crowd focused on *Partisan Review* in the forties has split asunder. *Commentary* and *The New Criterion* are the publications of the neo-conservative, rightist faction of the old *P.R.* crowd and their successors.

Commentary is funded by the American Jewish Committee, which is indicative of a partial right-wing shift in upper middle-class Jewish circles that has come about in the last fifteen or twenty years. *The New Criterion* is supported by a group of conservative foundations.

Both journals are edited by former Jewish liberals and Modernist critics— *Commentary* by Norman Podhoretz, who was a disciple of F.R. Leavis and of Lionel Trilling, the prominent Modernist critic of Columbia University in the thirties and forties. Podhoretz and his wife Midge Decter, who also writes frequently in *Commentary*, are committed to enlightenment traditions and preserving the manifestations of Modernist culture. They are also enthusiastic about Israel and Zionism. The consistency of their views is created by loyalty to Riverside Drive Jewish middle-class culture of the forties and fifties.

Theirs is the politics of liberal nostalgia. In their view, it is not they who have moved to the right. Their position has remained constant in their own eyes. It is the political fulcrum that since the mid-sixties has moved sharply to the left, they claim. They view themselves as loyal to the political and cultural ideals of forties liberalism. Meanwhile, the New Left serpent has intruded into the Edenic garden of forties liberalism with its extreme egalitarianism, erosion of American patriotism, advocacy of Third World production, support for allegedly Communist movements like the Sandinistas in Nicaragua, and hostility to Israel and Zionism and sympathy for the Palestinians and the terrorist P.L.O. Eternal vigilance must be exercised, according to *Commentary*, to challenge prospective anti-Semitic resurgence on the left and neo-Stalinist totalitarianism.

The editor of *The New Criterion*, Hilton Kramer, is a Modernist art critic of substantial reputation, who left his prominent and influential position at *The New York Times*, to establish a monthly journal of critical opinion in the spirit of T.S. Eliot's culturally Modernist and politically conservative *The Criterion* of the twenties and thirties. It is obviously not Eliot the genteel anti-Semite whom Kramer has in mind to emulate. It is Eliot the Modernist, the rationalist, the classicist, the visionary for a transatlantic community dedicated to a closely held and well-read elite culture stretching from Dante to Joyce who is recalled.

For Kramer, the West reached its cultural zenith in the late forties, with Eliot flourishing in London and the Museum of Modern Art in New York. Kramer sees Modernism as apolitical. The efforts of the left to politicize high culture and co-opt Modernism is a special heresy he contends against.

The New Criterion has rapidly exhibited itself as an important critical voice and anguished the left precisely because of its learning and sophistication, qualities that since the mid-sixties the American left has monopolistically claimed for itself as an exclusive privilege. *The New Criterion* challenges the leftist caricature of the right as a motley array of neanderthals and ignoramuses. This stereotype would not have been possible in the twenties and Kramer has vindicated his dedication to Eliot by severely eroding it. He has made the right a respectable intellectual force in America and thereby aroused the frightened fury of *The New Republic*, *The Nation*, the *Village Voice*, and the *Radical History Review*.

The New Criterion is also significant because its pages have served as an outlet for publication of critical essays of varying quality by young people whom Kramer has discovered, as Eliot and Leavis did in their own journals in the twenties and thirties. It is encouraging for American intellectual vitality in general, and not just for the right, to see this group emerge precisely because most of them are not academics yet are learned and perceptive. In 1986, *The London Times Literary Supplement* hailed *The New Criterion* as "probably more consistently worth reading than any other monthly magazine in English." Eliot would have been pleased.

Kramer and his collegues perform the service of acting as cultural whistle-blowers from a neo-Modernist and rationalist position. They perform the salutary service of pointing to the more vulnerable and hysterical cultural and artistic activities of the left that since the mid-sixties have been legitimized in the more prestigious leftist journals such as *The New York Review of Books*. Kramer sees the Modernist heritage as the best that twentieth-century culture has to offer and finds it threatened and betrayed by a leftist cultural movement that is not devoted to the arts *per se* but mainly wants to misuse the arts and manipulate the Modernist aura in the interest of pre-Modernist socialism.

The neo-conservative interpretation of the recent American past is generally that in the sixties and seventies, there was an excessive left-wing shift in the political views of Americans, which affected the universities, the media and the entire intellectual world, and which undermined traditions of rationality, liberal discourse, and civility. The rising tide of Marxism, neo-conservatives maintain, is accompanied by an excessive commitment to unrestrained egalitarianism expressed through affirmative action, which is in turn eroding and destabilizing professional and academic groups in the United States.

This neo-conservative view is not confined to the pages of *The New Criterion* and *Commentary*. It has gained powerful, if decidedly minority support in the academic world. The neo-conservative interpretation of the sixties was argued in the seventies by academician William O'Neill (Rutgers), Ronald Berman (California-San Diego), and Willam Bennett (Boston University). Berman became Director of the National Endowment for the Humanities under Nixon and Bennett held the same position (he is now Secretary of Education) under Reagan.

In 1985 Allan Matusow of Rice University published an extremely learned and convincing account of the sixties, *The Unraveling of America*. As the title implies, it takes a neo-conservative view, although expressed in a careful and mostly a non-polemical manner. What is doubly significant is that Matusow's volume appears in *The New American Nation*, a high-establishment, multi-volume history of the United States edited by two venerable New Deal liberal historians, Henry Steele Commager and Richard B. Morris.

From the point of view of cultural theory, what is most intriguing about Kramer-Podhoretz neo-conservatism is the unusual effort to combine Modernism with right-wing political theory. This is, however, by no means an unheard-of attempt. As shall be seen below, there were several points of coincidence between Modernism and Fascism in the twenties and thirties.

The neo-conservatives are in number a small group but because of their journals, and because of their representation in university circles, however limited, they manage to procure serious attention. The neo-conservatives and the evangelical Christians might not be thought to make very good allies, although one neo-conservative theorist, Irving Kristol, who teaches in the Business School of New York University, has made strenuous efforts to establish a feasible alliance between the evangelical group and the neo-conservatives. Hilton Kramer has lectured at evangelical colleges and has been well received there. The future relationship between the evangelicals and neoconservatives could be a crucial development in American politics.

There is certainly a connection between the neo-conservatives and the Reaganites. The former spill over into think-tanks in Washington, such as the Heritage Foundation, and from their ranks have come a considerable number of sub-cabinet personnel in the Reagan administration, such as assistant secretaries, have been drawn. The son-in-law of Norman Podhoretz, for example, is an assistant secretary in the State Department.

A fourth ideological strand on the American right in the late eighties is libertarianism, which has a substantial following but has not yet found a convincing intellectual statement unless it be in the novels of Ayn Rand. Libertarianism is a kind of underground movement on the right.

Libertarianism seems at first sight merely an extreme extension of the views of Milton Friedman and the Chicago school of market theorists. But there is a quite different ingredient in libertarianism. It is an anarchism of the right. It despairs of any moral or positive quality in the state and wishes to disassemble all political structure as far as possible. But how far is possible? This is unclear. There is a prominent strain of deep despair in libertarianism, a total rejection of the political road the Federal Government began to take, not just in the administration of FDR, but even in the time of Woodrow Wilson.

There appears to be a latent revolutionary consciousness in libertarianism, a Rousseauist yearning for a pristine return to nature and rejection of social constraints. It is a peculiar kind of quietist Fascism. Libertarianism makes little sense until one has to listen to Mario Cuomo speak for ten minutes.

Fundamentals of Rightist Culture

The right in the United States today, or at any time and place in the Western world in this century, whether France in 1910, Germany in 1930, or Britain in 1950, drew upon a common pool of ideas and traditions which comprises the spectrum of rightist theory. At any given time and place, what constitutes rightest thinking will make use of a majority of this spectrum of traditions or common pool of ideas, and frequently it will try to embrace all of them. The ideas and traditions are all not readily reconcilable with each other. It is the specific selection of traditions and ideas that will be made—frequently one or two from the total spectrum, such as anti-Semitism, being rejected—and the precise way in which the ideas and traditions are fitted together that will shape the direction and determine the polemical tone of a particular rightist doctrine.

Let us negate at the outset the claim that all this is a specious and futile undertaking, a false perception, that there is no such thing as a rightist culture in the way we have perceived it and now intend to explain it. It might be said that a point of view which places Hilton Kramer, Winston Churchill, and Herbert Hoover within a common spectrum of rightist thought and culture is heuristically useless. No more absurd than an interpretation that places Charles Beard, Walter Benjamin, and Joseph Stalin within a spectrum of leftist thought and culture, which was done in the previous chapter. As a matter of fact, neither of these perceptions and interpretations is wrong or absurd. They are both intellectually and heuristically viable.

These are two dominant political cultures or traditions in the twentieth-century West—the leftist and the rightist. Each culture is composed of a spectrum of ideas. The shape and direction of leftist and rightist thought is fashioned out of how these ideas and traditions are drawn upon and fitted together.

If a substantial majority of the ideas and traditions in the full spectrum of one of the political cultures is reflected in the writings of someone, that writer clearly belongs to the leftist or rightist political tradition. Kramer, Churchill, and Hoover do all belong to the right's tradition. It does not mean they agree on all issues. Similarly Beard and Benjamin were not personally responsible for Stalin and if they had lived in a Soviet country, they would have likely been liquidated by the Stalinists.

The fundamental fact remains that there is a leftist and a rightist political culture with distinctive sets of traditions and ideas in each case and Kramer, Churchill, and Hoover should be perceived—and can only be fully under-stood—in the context of the rightist tradition.

The spectrum of ideas on which right-wing theories have drawn in this century—which again is not to say that every rightist thinker has embraced all of them—consists of eight traditions. The first of these is inequality.

All right wing thought is discriminatory, hierarchically judgmental and exclusive, in some way. It believes in better and worse, upper and lower, whether it is considering a nation, an ethnic group, or a work of art. Marxist thought may point pejoratively to current inequalities but these are deemed only transient and will be obliterated in the egalitarian Communist society of the future when all class, national and ethnic barriers will vanish in a Communist system, and when all art will be equally devoted to the service of the proletariat. In practice this may be unattainable—"some are more equal than others"—and if attainable it will be in a totalitarian gulag nightmare, but that is what Marxism advocates and envisions—ultimate total equality, complete social and cultural homogeneity.

The rightist philosophy is fundamentally different. It believes in a necessary and salutory degree of inequality. The degree and form may vary momentously but the fundamental issue that separates left from right is the belief in equality versus inequality. The extreme and aggressive forms of inequality that some rightists adhere to—slavery, genocide, apartheid— will be condemned by other rightists in the strongest possible terms. Some rightists believe in inequality among groups. Others only in inequality of performance capability, and hence of gained social reward (status and income), among individuals. What binds all to the right is the conviction that some measure or criterion of differentiation and effective hierarchy is inevitable in nature and beneficial in human nurture.

This need not be the belief in the legitimacy of Western colonialism by the Aryan master race over so-called degenerate people. More often, especially since 1945, the rightist doctrine of inequality simply means some paintings are more beneficial than others; some works of literature more compelling and evocative—that a particular work is closer to true art than another. From Matthew Arnold in the 1860's to Hilton Kramer in the 1980's, conservative art and literary criticism has advocated a "touchstone" of superiority differing the quality of one work from another and therefore of the social value of the artist or writer who created it. The right of a individual to special rewards for superior performance is the controversial issue.

The rightist doctrine of inequality means minimally that some individuals are more or less intelligent or talented than the mean and this claimed fact implies that the superior intelligences or talents have a social and moral right to admission to elite college and professional schools in preference to the less capable. Adolescents of allegedly inferior intelligence should be satisfied with starting their post-secondary education at Bronx Community College rather than Princeton.

The rightist doctrine can also mean that when a specific nation or social group at a particular time shows itself more enterprising, whether in making war or making automobiles, it has the prescriptive right to enjoy the fruits of that superiority, whether through Israeli control of the West Bank and the Golan Heights or Toyota dealerships and plants in the United States.

The bitterest and most protracted debates in this country in the past two decades have been over the issue of affirmative action and this is because affirmative action strategies and policies speak directly to the issue of equality/inequality that separates the left from the right. It is to this question that the left's more subtle and learned intellects have addressed themselves, making very fine distinctions between "quotas" and "goals." There is no point considering the views of the ineffable Mary Berry, Assistant Secretary of

Education and leading member of the Civil Rights Commission majority in the Carter Administration, who went around the country in 1977 lavishing praise on Communist China's schools over ours because Red China's education stressed groupthink and was devoted during the Cultural Revolution to obliterating individual identity (as well as demolishing literacy and learning). Instead let us consider John Rawls and Ronald Dworkin, the most subtle contemporary exponents of equality and advocates of affirmative action.

Rawls at Harvard and Dworkin of NYU Law School have developed elaborate philosophical arguments justifying the more aggressive efforts to provide compensatory mechanisms for overcoming inequality. This means not just eradicating inequality of opportunity but obliterating measurable differences of intelligence and rational capability. Ethics demands, says Rawls, and the Constitution dictates, says Dworkin, that admission to elite schools and colleges and the giving of financial aid should nearly always favor the black applicant from Harlem rather than the Jewish applicant from Great Neck (assuming the Black candidate has a high school diploma and has met the minimal conceivable qualifications for admission). Rawls' and Dworkin's sophisticated and much applauded treatises come down to advocating the prescriptive right of levelling equality over existential inequality.

Another celebrated scholar of the left, Harvard biologist and historian of science Stephen Jay Gould takes out after Lewis Terman, the Stanford behavioral psychologist of the interwar period, and the father of school IQ tests and college admission SAT tests, with an avenging zeal usually reserved for the Eichmann mass-murderer type. All "hereditarian" views of intelligence lack scientific validity as well as ethical legitimacy, according to Gould's *The Mismeasure of Man*. In his view, biologically determinative differentiations among social groups, (as in nineteenth century craniology and social Darwinism and current sociobiology) are of without merit of any kind. It is also impossible, says Gould, to make such differentiation among individuals because personal intelligence is an immeasurable function. Against Terman and the Educational Testing Service, Gould opts for total "flexibility [as] the hallmark of evolution" and in assessing individual potential.

What this means in practice is that ethical and social considerations demand admission to Princeton with a full scholarship for the marginal applicant from Harlem in preference to the readily qualified middle class white applicant from Great Neck. You cannot compare their intelligence or rationally estimate their established potential, Gould believes. So political and ethical standards are the only criteria left. Gould would support the leftist view of affirmative action advocated by Rawls and Dworkin. It is indicative of the penetration of the left into the media and publishing world that Gould's political polemic won the National Book Critics' Circle award—the premier prize for nonfiction—in 1981.

It is the leftist doctrine of equality and its application in affirmative action that makes the right recoil in anger and frustration. The right has looked to the Supreme Court for succor but even the Reaganite government has thus far gained little help in that direction. Indeed the Supreme Court has affirmed the constitutionality of quotas as long as they compensate for previous racial discrimination. Thus the struggle between believers in the validity and legitimacy of a residual degree of inequality and the partisans of total equality—the first criterion separating the right from the left in this century—is infinitely perpetuated.

The dispute between the advocate of equality and inequality is directly related to the tension between Modernism and the preceding culture. Equality was a Romantic ideal—that Marx elaborated in gargantuan fashion—not a Modernist one. Modernism had a penchant for small-scale differentiation and fine discrimination. While rejecting facile nineteenth-century assumptions about macrocosmic social hierarchies, Modernism enthusiastically preserved distinctions at the microsocial and individual levels. It is precisely this particular kind of differentiation that affirmative action and its subtler advocates like Rawls, Dworkin, and Gould have recently sought to expunge. Thus the struggle between inequality and equality in the context of twentieth-century cultural history involves competition between the Modernist heritage and neo-Victorianism.

The second tradition that distinguished the right in the twentieth century is anti-Communism. Since 1917, be it Churchillian British conservatism or American McCarthyism, Reaganism, or Nazism, the right has consistently identified itself as anti-Communist. Next to inequality, anti-Communism is the most persistent and pervasive rightist belief.

The threat of the "red menace," that of the "evil empire," particularly of Communism in its Soviet form, of the persistent attack on the middle class by the left, and particularly by Marxists, has lent a solidarity to right-wing movements. If the right means anything in the twentieth century, it means anti-Communism and anti-Marxism. If the Russian Revolution had not taken place, if Russia were still ruled by Tsars and grand dukes, the history of the right in this century, as well as of the left, would have been very different.

The split between left and right in political culture in this century is along the seismic fault that separates on one side those who believe that the Bolshevik October Revolution, however unfortunate the Stalinist aberration and disappointing some of the other outcomes, signified a universal, irresistible summons to a better world. On the other side there are those who claim the October Revolution spawned a series of widespread tyrannies of the worst kind and treacherously exploited the moral traditions of the West in the interest of the Soviet thrust for world power.

The left thinks the October Revolution should in one way or another be emulated; the right believes it must be contained. Contained in the expectation that eventually the Soviet system will either disintegrate or transform itself into peaceful social democracy? Or contained while the capitalist, democratic West builds the military resource and finds the opportune moment to impose nuclear destruction on its irreconcilable enemy? Similarly, should Communist and Marxist fellow-travellers be excluded from positions of social responsibility and political influence in the civil service and education or should they have the full rights of citizenship, including free speech and employment anywhere, in the expectation that in the free trade of ideas the anti-Communists will prevail by the intrinsic merit of their case? Is there such a theory as an anti-Communist

Marxism, a liberal or Western Marxism or is there no real difference among the shades of red?

These are the issues that have divided the right, especially in the Cold War and so-called McCarthy era of the fifties, and increasingly again as the eighties draws to a close. But about the fundamental persistence of anti-Communism as a distinguishing tradition of the right there is no doubt. In any cocktail party in Cambridge, Mass., Berkeley, California, or Greenwich Village, New York, this is the issue, sometimes spoken, often unspoken, that divides the associated academics and other intellectuals and professionals. In the words of the 1930's leftist folk song, "Which side are you on?/ . . . There are no neutrals there."

The third tradition on which the right has drawn is theistic religion, central to Christianity and Judaism, that can be generally represented by the term *magisterium*. This is the doctrinal term espoused by the conservative majority of the Roman Catholic Church in recent years. In the Catholic context, the term has a twofold significance. It stands for its literal meaning of magistracy or authority and signifies those Catholics in Rome and elsewhere who uphold papal infallibility, the autocratic reserved power of the papal administration, and the plenary power of the hierarchy in faith and morals.

The term *magisterium* also refers to those Catholics who perpetuate the Augustinian tradition of stressing the majesty and goodness of God in comparison with the weakness and corruption of mankind. Without God, man is nothing good, and therefore the Christian ministry, the carrier of God's word in the world, is the focal point for the reformation and transformation of the world. To believe that a fiercely secular force, whether the Roman State in the time of St. Augustine or the Communist or Democratic parties nowadays can function as that focal point is blasphemy and anathema. Take away justice that comes into the world only from the Church, says Augustine, "and what is the state but a band of robbers?"

The Augustinian doctrine of God's majesty was espoused by the Protestant Reformation in the teachings of Luther and Calvin, again foregrounded in the early twentieth century by Karl Barth, and stressed in our time by the more conservative Protestant groups, especially the American evangelical churches. Along with the conservative majority in the Catholic Church that holds fast to papal authority, the Protestant evangelicals are the largest group on the right drawing upon the Christian tradition. Of course, these two groups, comprising together more than 100 million people in the United States alone, have no agreement or probably a future capacity for accommodation on the subject of papal authority. But conservative Catholics and Protestant evangelicals coincide on an Augustinian theology of *magisterium*—divine majesty and human weakness without God's gift of His love (grace). They do agree on the so-called "social issues" of abortion, contraception, and pornography and they have a common enemy in the Christian left.

In Catholicism this means determined opposition to those who interpret Vatican Council II of 1962–64 as sanction for the democratization and decentralization of the Catholic Church, the dismantling of papal authority, and a social activism in alliance with Marxists and other leftist activists—the "liberation theology."

The evangelicals on their part challenge a Protestant social gospel that believes in human freedom to change the world for the better through the secular means of the welfare state. The Protestant left over the past fifty years has come to acknowledge the anti-Augustinian principle that we live in the secular city—in the term of Harvard theologian Harvey Cox—and that the Protestant calling is an individual and internal matter, a source of personal inspiration, while in the public and communal sphere, it is the movement and ideology of the left that perpetuates Christian action. The good Christian today, this leftist gospel specifies, votes for Mario Cuomo, subscribes to *The Nation*, and studies with Immanuel Wallerstein or some other Marxist totem.

Where does the Reverend Jesse Jackson stand between the right and left Christian tradition as currently formulated? He walks a very fine line, aiming to conflate the theism of the Christian right with the policies of the Christian left.

Reverend Jackson's balancing act points to the political and social ambivalence that has always lain at the heart of the Augustinian tradition and still characterizes it. It is possible to begin with Augustinian theology and convince oneself to move in either a conservative or revolutionary political direction. The Catholic upholders of the *magisterium*, such as Cardinal O'Connor of New York, and the evangelical activists, like Rev. Jerry Falwell, have taken the rightist orientation. But they are not blind to the attraction of the other road in the political fork. If the papacy and the Catholic majority would embrace the teaching of Father Hans Küng and interpret the Vatican Council II in a radical way, if the bishops would espouse liberation theology, there would be a world-wide upheaval. Catholicism could threaten to take over the world. But this victory by a leftist Catholicism would be short-lived. The Catholic Church would in the midst of this turmoil fragment into pieces to a degree greater than it did in the sixteenth century.

Similarly, if the dynamism of the American evangelicals were committed to the left rather than to the right, the radical crusades momentarily threatening in the period from 1895–1910, in the form of southern and mid-western populism that in the days of William Jennings Bryan embraced the left-wing of the Democratic party, would revive. Early twentieth-century populists could never decide whether they belonged on the left or the right—their program embraced both welfare liberalism and a kind of visceral, grass-roots Fascism and anti-semitism. Nowadays evangelical Protestants, in response to the urbanization and partial industrialization and enrichment of the South, have chosen to stress the rightist implications of their theology of theistic majesty, but they are the heirs of populist dynamism.

In Judaism there is also a theological base for a rightist group and this potential has been effectively exploited by Menachem Begin, Itshak Shamir, Ariel Sharon, and the Likud party in Israel. The most important religious development in the Jewish world since 1945 has been the revival, in both the United States and Israel, of orthodoxy or traditional Judaism. In the first four decades of the century orthodox Judaism, devoted to the *Halacha* (traditional doctrine and ritual including twice-daily prayer, the Kashrut laws and sexual segregation), was relatively weak and politically of low visibility in both Israel (formerly Palestine) and the U.S.A. In Palestine/Israel the dominant Jewish group were the East European socialist and secularist kibbutzniks who founded the Labor Party and controlled the Israeli government for three decades after Israeli independence in 1948.

In the United States from the 1890's to 1924 (the closing of mass immigration) a vast and chaotic Jewish immigration from the East European shtetls pulverized traditional communal institutions, eviscerated the leadership of the Orthodox rabbinate and by absorbing Jews atomistically into secular life, compelled them defensively into leftist political groups. Since the fifties, there has been a renaissance of Orthodox Judaism, channelled largely through synagogues and parochial schools. Multi-party Israeli politics has given a disproportionately large share of power to the "religious parties." Similarly, in the United States, not only has there been a significant proportionate increase in number of Halacha-observant Jews (partly by persuasion and partly demography—i.e. larger size Orthodox families as well as due to the assimi-lation of secular Jews into the Gentile world). Orthodoxy has gained in visibility and influences as Conservative Judaism, the largest Jewish denomi-nation, has become stodgy and hesitant and Reform Judaism lost its vitality and became uncertain of its mission.

Orthodox Judaism is by no means homogenous. Halacha-observant Jews involve a broad array stretching from conventional liberals who pray a lot and eat only kosher food to Brooklyn hassidic mystics to ultra-orthodox sects in Jerusalem who await the Messiah, are technically therefore anti-Zionist, and who express themselves by stoning moving cars on the Sabbath and burning down bus shelters that show pictures of women in bikinis.

What the Orthodox renaissance has done—drawing upon the scholarship of Gershom Scholem and Martin Buber—is to reestablish contact with the explosive currents of the Jewish Reformation of the seventeenth and eighteenth centuries that was headed by messianism of Sabtai Zvi and the charismatic mysticism of the Bal Shem Tov, and which was plunged into obscurity by twentieth century Zionist, leftist, and secularist culture. In this respect, Orthodox Judaism runs parallel to the Catholic majority holding fast to the papal *magisterium* and to evangelical Protestantism.

Orthodox Judaism also resembles Catholicism in containing within it a coiled spring of homiletic dynamism that potentially can explode in any political direction. The key Jewish figure is Rabbi Irving Greenberg, a Ph.D. in American History from Harvard, for several years the venerated rabbi of the upscale Orthodox synagogue in the Riverdale section of the Bronx, N.Y., and now the organizer and leader of his own sectarian group obstensibly commit-ted to "religious educational research," but actually to a charismatic revolu-tion in Judaism. His wife Blu is the leader of Orthodox feminism. A magnificent preacher and a brilliant theologian, Greenberg frightens the conventional liberal, secular, Zionist leaders of the organized Jewish commu-nities such as the billionaire chairman of the N.Y.U Board of Trustees. In 1981 he vetoed Greenberg's well-merited appointment to the Chair of Jewish Studies at N.Y.U.

The volatility of the Judaeo-Christian tradition of prophecy makes political categorization of the future course hazardous. "He shall decide for many peoples" and "My kingdom is not of this world" can be read in a variety of ways—and has been through the centuries. But in this theistic religion there is a venerable, complex, and dynamic tradition for the right to draw upon and in turn to be conditioned by. As long as Marxism with its intense secularism dominates leftist thought, the continued affiliation of the right with the tradition of theistic religion is the more likely prospect.

The message of Augustine's *City of God*, written about 425 A.D., remains central to the Christian right: "The heavenly city . . . while in its state of pilgrimage, avails itself of the peace of earth, and so far as it can without injuring faith and godliness . . . makes this earthly peace bear upon the peace of heaven." Such is the plasticity and volatility of the miraculous Judaeo-Christian gospel that the Augustinian teaching can conceivably be incorporated into a Marxist Christianity, a liberation theology, but the more obvious and easiest accommodation is on the political right.

The fourth intellectual tradition that the right can draw upon is formalism. By formalism is meant a body of ideas and symbols or a cultural structure which conditions behavior along preconceived lines. Formalism allows a greater or lesser degree of individual choice. But it sets up a conditioning or confining program that strongly influences or predetermines the ultimate choice that the individual will make.

Formalism accords intrinsic legitimacy to this conditioning structure of individual and group behavior. This is formalism's most distinctive characteristic as compared with relativism, which may acknowledge the powerful influence of a conditioning structure, but divests this structure of intrinsic legitimacy. The formalist view of the world grants a positive, prescriptive quality to cultural structures controlling behavior. It not only perceives behavior as actually shaped by a body of ideas and symbols. It wants it to be conditioned in this manner, for the outcome will be deemed advantageous and as perpetuating beneficial and durable forces. Nor is this pragmatic justification sufficient; formalism believes in the intrinsic value of the system, program or law itself.

Formalism believes in extended cultural and intellectual systems and that the discipline of conforming to those systems makes the individual or group involved embrace civilization and affirm truth.

Several familiar manifestations of twentieth-century rightist thought and action are actually aspects of formalist tradition. Among these are rationalism and classicism; semiotics and iconology; and legalism.

Rationalism and classicism cultivate refined intellectuality and humanist learning expressed in elaborate formulations of precise language. Rationalism and classicism reject emotional affects and mass culture and demotic privilege. Truth and civilization are disclosed by and essentially integral with language patterns. Durable patterns of thought and expression that were for the most part established in ancient Greece and Rome, Renaissance Italy, and Baroque France form the core of rationalism and classicism.

Recondite imagery, complicated rhetoric, and allusion to venerable and esoteric motifs make rationalism and classicism an elite code. This formalist structuralism is normally accessible only through expensive education in highly selective schools, followed by long apprenticeship.

Rationalism and classicism disdain leftist ideology without having to engage in polemics against it. From the point of view of the rationalist and the classicist, the left is automatically excluded from genuine intellectual concerns because its language, fraught with vague neo-Victorianisms, is alien to the elite code and its mode of experience is generally vulgar and hysterical.

The left characteristically lays claims to moral traditions in Western civilization in order to capitalize on middle-class guilt. Rationalism and classicism, which indeed endorse a narrow and conventional ethic for the social and cultural elite, have moved the standards of legitimized intellectualizing and of authentic discourse to an alternative dimension, that of language and learning.

Obviously a substantial segment of the right will always find in rationalism and classicism immediate inspiration and comfort. They comprise a subset of formalism that is immediately accessible to the right, provided the latter are willing to be associated with elitism and intellectual privilege.

Similarly with semiotics and iconology. Semiotics is the study of signs built into language, literature, art and social gestures. Iconology is the study of themes and images in art history particularly as related to literary motifs. These scholarly pursuits extensively overlap, iconology being a vanguard discipline of the twenties and thirties, and semiotics playing the same role in the seventies and early eighties.

Semiotics and iconology have indeed attracted leftist scholars who are eager to show how literary symbols and artistic images have been employed as ideological signification by the bourgeoisie in its allegedly hegemonic culture. Yet the formalist quality of these disciplines is essentially remote from Marxist interpretation. They speak of a world of symbol, metaphor, allusion and illusion that constitutes continuing imaging of the pre-bourgeois aristocratic culture that Huizinga the Modernist historian c.1920 revealed as emerging in the late Middle Ages in Burgundian court culture. While a semiotics and iconology of bourgeois culture is feasible, such as in a study of advertising imagery or imperialist totems, the original and more substantial subject matter of these disciplines lies in the folio volumes and vast art works of the baroque and earlier aristocratic worlds. Here there was a very thick formal culture of elaborate signification—to take relatively plebian examples, the iconology of seventeenth-century wax and leaden seals is itself a demanding and complex subject, as is numismatics. This former culture can be summoned up and cultivated to fix the right in a venerable and durable structure infinitely distinct from the meretricious persiflage of leftist polemics.

The study of common law in the Anglo-American tradition is a third manifestation of formalism to go along with rationalism and classicism, semiotics and iconology as sources for a rightist culture. The common law is by its nature formalist since its only substantial quality is what has been called since the mid-fourteenth century the due process of the law found in writs, adversarial court procedure, judicial review, and lawyering. Legalism is the congealing of procedural and normative rationality—much more important than precedent—through the making of this miscellany into a social and cultural system.

The hallmark of the common law is not in legislative statutes, which are only an extraneous given—reflecting the frivolities of courtiers, the wiles of bureaucrats, and the scurvy ambitions of politicians—to be massaged and incorporated in the deployment of selectively accessible and coded language and in the signifying gestures of lawyering. Anglo-American legalism is as ritualized and rigidly formulary as the puberty rites of New Guinea natives.

Fully elaborated by the mid-fourteenth century in a culture that Cambridge historical anthropoligist Alan Macfarlane has called "English individualism" but which might more properly be termed common law formalism, the psychology of legalism has undergone little change between a justice of common pleas in the reign of Edward III and Lord Denning, the distinguished chief judge of civil appeal in the 1970's. In the United States, in reaction against New Deal legal realism and Marxist Critical Legal Studies, the University of Chicago Law School has become the center of legal formalism (joining up on the right there with the Friedman, neo-Ricardian group of economists—indeed they set up a joint program in law and economics).

We have seen that a product of this school, Antonin Scalia, has recently been appointed by President Reagan to the Supreme Court, the most important ideologically-motivated appointment to the court since the elevation of Frankfurter and Douglas, the legal realists. Another brilliant spokesman for legal formalism was former University of Pennsylvania Law School professor, Morris Arnold; he is now on the Federal district court in Arkansas. He is an excellent medieval scholar as well as a distinguished jurist (and also chairman of the Reagan reelection campaign in Arkansas). Arnold is able to bring a historical as well as theoretical understanding to his formulation of rightist legalism which stands prominently alongside other varieties of formalism as prospective foundations of rightist culture. Additional formalists appointed to the Federal circuit court are Richard Posner, from Chicago, and Robert Bork, from Yale.

The fifth intellectual tradition the right can draw upon is ethnic and national solidarity. Contemporary German sociologist Ernest Nolte terms this feeling "anti-transcendentalism," that is an anti-leveling reaction against leftist practices that transcendentally supersede and breakdown group, ethnic, and national loyalties. Whether in Germany in the twenties or the United States in the seventies there was a widespread feeling that the left, welfare liberalism, and the circumstances of life in late industrial society were leveling or transcending ethnic distinctions and community boundaries and undermining national traditions.

The consequences of this erosion were pervasive feelings of insecurity, the sense of being abandoned without a community to which a person can belong and take sustenance from. A process of atomization was taking place, driven by leftist ideology as well as by cultural changes derived from developments in technology and communications. It was feared that these ideological challenges and social changes, if undeflected, would destroy the vestiges of community life, regardless of whether by community is meant the Ukrainians of New York's East Village or the Jews of Brooklyn—or Gentile Berliners in 1930 or Catholic Parisians in 1936. That this leveling of community, which could destroy all roots as well as all ethnic and national communal identity, should be resisted is a pervasive and deeply felt conviction the right can draw on. In the 1920's the German rightists were exclaiming that the *"Gemeinschaft"* (community) had to be protected from the *"Gesellschaft"* (society) and *"Kultur"* from *"Civilization"*. These were code words for an ethos protective of ethnic and national feeling. A similar sense of ethnic solidarity inspired the railings against affirmative action by Podhoretz in *Commentary* magazine. Hilton Kramer envisages Modernism as an intellectual community threatened with dispersion by leftist activism in the cultural realm.

The phenomenal success of *Gone With the Wind*, both Margaret Mitchell's 1936 novel (still selling a quarter million copies a year) and the 1939 film made from it, must in large part be attributed to an "anti-transcendental," anti-leveling nostalgia for cultural solidarity that decadent late capitalism and leftist ideology and politics alike seek to devastate. *Gone With the Wind* not uncritically celebrated an aristocratic Southern culture that becomes a representative sign for all the ethnic subcultures that have flourished and declined on the soil of the United States, leaving behind a sense of regretful and irreplacable loss in younger generations deprived of this thick sustenance. For this loss, not even the learned tomes of leftist scholars like Genovese and Foner on slavery as an economic and social system can compensate even minimally.

Those who are not privileged to be among the handful of actual descendants of the ante-bellum gentry of Georgia or South Carolina, the dreamed flower of the doomed Confederacy, can project through the novel and film their own vicarious participation in *Gone With the Wind's* imaging of this superior if fragile culture, even if their own worlds they have lost were much less romantic and memorable—Irish peat-bog country, Sicilian illiterate villages, Jewish impoverished shtetls. The latter subcultures have also fallen victim to demotic and homogenous leveling that the left for its own purposes have foisted upon us (with the help of later twentieth-century communications and information technology) since the New Deal cultural earthquake of the late thirties, which was effected under the principal aegis of the metropolitan academic and intellectual crowd, the Lionel Trillings and their later epigones.

A sixth aspect of possible rightist tradition is the leadership principle, which does not appear in every right-wing movement, but when it does emerge, it does not fail to prove explosive. This principle derives from the belief that it is necessary to find a strong, charismatic leader on whom the lonely crowd of modern society can rely. A paternal figure that tends to his subjects, the leader will be the focal point of the communal feelings of society and he or she will demand and gain fervent loyalty. Not that there have not been strong leaders on the left, who could assume, as in the case of Stalin, the shape of a cult of leadership, but by and large it has been the right which has involved the *Fuehrer* principle, or the *Il duce* figure, or the Churchillian savior of a democratic nation.

Sometimes this principle has served as substitute for thought, in the absence of a coherent and elaborated rightist doctrine—just give absolute loyalty to the leader and forget about everybody else. The leadership principle can give emotional and unifying force to a broad array and perhaps not entirely reconcilable set of rightist traditions. It can demand a personal commitment that is so overpowering that it either slowly or immediately overrides and all but eliminates other doctrines on the right. The leadership principle is a stimulant but it can also be a dangerous intoxicant.

Intoxication with the personal charisma of the *Fuehrer* is what happened in Germany in the thirties and early forties and the absolutely horrendous consequences show the hazard of primary reliance on the leadership principle, unconstrained by other rightist traditions. The British story under Winston Churchill from 1940 to 1945 is a very different one. By the summer of 1940 the British people were so fearfully desperate and so immediately inspired by Churchill's rhetoric and visage that in their condition of isolation and military weakness, they would have probably been willing to surrender all power to him and abandon their democratic institutions. Yet Churchill did not seek to create a dictatorial position for himself. He continued to practice democracy which he once called the worst form of government until all others are considered. Churchill maintained legalistic formalism in war-torn Britain. He continued to respond traditionally to questions and criticism in the House of Commons, even in peacetime a time-consuming and wearisome task for a British prime minister. And he took great pains to frame his call for national salvation in the language of rationalism and classicism of which none was a greater master than he.

Churchill was very much a man of the right. All through the thirties and forties he remained a vociferous opponent of colonial independence and the dismemberment of the British Empire. He favored welfare measures, indeed he had been a pioneer in this area before World War I, but he was strongly opposed to socialist nationalization of industry. Churchill was the nephew of the Duke of Marlborough in whose Blenheim Palace he was born. He professed unbounded admiration for the first Duke of Marlborough of the early eighteenth century, whose biography he wrote. Yet that military hero had remained loyal and subservient to elected civilian governments. And this was also Winston Churchill's political ideal, although he was personally arrogant and possessed dynamic qualities of leadership comparable to Hitler's.

Adolf Hitler took a very different road and led himself and the German people to damnation. Hitler's version of the leadership principle was totalitarian in that he required his military officers to swear absolute personal loyalty to him that superseded their loyalty to the German State. This significantly postponed—as Hitler foresaw—the eventual effort of some senior officers to assassinate him, with terrible consequences for Germans as well as others, even when, by the summer of 1943, the war was irreparably lost. Hitler made the law courts just another personal element of tyranny and he polluted the German language, perhaps irretrievably, with his own coarse melodrama and hysteria. His leadership was such a personal one that the splendid German bureaucracy and brilliant general staff of the army could not effectively function, since all major and many minor decisions had to be carried back to him.

The leadership principle is a valuable tradition for the right and it is not easy to conceive of an effective rightist movement without its prominent display. But when deployed in virtual isolation, or even when it dwarfs other traditions we have discussed, the leadership principle becomes a dangerous one and one self-defeating for the best interests and higher purposes of the right. On modest scale, this effect has been exhibited in the presidency of Ronald Reagan. His personal leadership has been exercised so effectively and popularly that the long-range ideological and political structures for the right have not been as well developed during his time in the White House as they could and should have been. If Churchill finally came to put too much stock in his own charisma, his humiliating repudiation by the British electorate in 1945 and his replace-ment as prime minister by socialist Clement Attlee ("a modest man," said Churchill, "and he has much to be modest about") taught him a salutary lesson which he applied effectively when he returned to power in 1951. He worked to rebuild the Conservative Party for the long haul.

The seventh tradition of the right has been militarism. In the Western world of the twentieth century, beginning in Germany, France and England before the First World War and continuing into the age of Weinberger in the United States of the 1980's, the military has been on the right. This has by no means always been the case in Western civilization.

In the eighteenth century, the military in the Western world was often on the left. After all, George Washington, who led the American Revolution, was a military man. In France, the royal officer class went over in large numbers to join the French revolutionary state and give it almost incomparable military power, much to the astonishment and chagrin of monarchial regimes. Napo-leon Bonaparte, a Corsican aristocrat, and typical product of French military training under the auspices of the crown, was a member of this new officer class in the revolutionary state who were sufficiently radical to give their loyalty to what appeared to be the wave of the future. Thus in the Age of Enlightenment, the officer class did not necessarily support the right; it had a reputation in fact for abandoning the old regime in the interest of government reform and if necessary of revolution.

The military, in its pursuit of battlefield victory, could not afford to be sentimental about the disorders and incompetence of the old regime. The military was one professional group in eighteenth-century Western society, whether fighting on the American frontier or standing watch on the Rhine, that had to be committed to the radical standards of rationality and efficiency. Decadent monarchy and privileged and effete aristocracy often stood in the way of military reform and maximal capability in war. Hence the younger and more ambitious of the officer class could be persuaded to join the forces of the revolutionary state. This also happened in Russia in 1917–21 when Trotsky formed the Red Army, and with the help of former Tsarist officers, overcame the enemies of the Soviet regime.

Yet in the twentieth century, the tendency of the military in the trans-Atlantic world has always been on the right, to be associated with the privileged classes and rightist forces, to be hostile to the left and socialist movements. This was true of England and France in World War I; of the

German general staff—possibly the finest set of generals since Napoleon's marshals—in the Nazi era; of the French military during the Algerian revolution in the 1950's when some refused to accept the French withdrawal from empire and rebelled against even their mentor Charles De Gaulle; and of the graduates of West Point, Annapolis and the Air Force Academy in the Vietnam War and since.

Why are the military and military traditions associated with the right? There appear to be two reasons for this phenomenon. First, the right unequivocally accords legitimacy to war as a necessary expedient at critical moments and accords to participation in war a superior moral quality when pursued in a good cause. This tradition on the right has a long history—dating back to St. Augustine and the medieval church's preaching of a just war against its enemies. The right has not believed in pacificism. It has unambiguously embraced military force as a moral necessity.

The second reason why the military have been in the trans-Atlantic world almost unanananimously on the right is that the left has, since the early years of the century, not only denounced the military as myrmidons of reaction and enemies of justice and the workers. It has also flirted with pacificism and denial of the legitimacy of military solutions. This intrinsic leftist hostility to war certainly gave an edge to agitation against the Vietnam War. This pacificism is enshrined for us in Francis Coppola's 1974 film *Apocalypse Now* in which military iconology and semiotics are themselves depicted as evil. It is reflected in the ruthless vendetta in which the leftist media group pursued General Westmoreland and disgracefully denounced him as a liar and traitor in a notorious pseudo-documentary about the Vietnam War. It is reflected strongly in the way the trans-Atlantic left turned against Israel after its entirely-merited military victories over the Arab world in 1967.

The Soviets have taken great advantage of the reflexive anti-militarism of the left and have launched successive waves of disinformation "peace" campaigns against the Western military preparedness while maintaining the largest army in the world. This military force has futhermore been directed against efforts to liberalize the Soviet regimes, whether in Hungary in 1956, Czechoslavakia in 1968 or Poland in 1981. Much to the left's chagrin, only the right since 1945 has been consistently clear- headed about the implictions of Soviet military power. All the more reason why the military in the Western world is reflexively on the right.

The eighth and final ingredient in the rightist tradition has been anti-Semitism. Like the leadership principle, this factor too is not present in every rightist movement, but it is nevertheless common in right-wing thought. Anti-Semitism is not a universal but a frequent characteristic of the right.

While Soviet Communism has also drawn upon anti-Semitic traditions, and other leftist groups in the West have not entirely been free of antisemitism—for example, the British Labor Party and American populism—it is true that anti-Semitism has been mainly, while not exclusively, a rightist phenomenon in the twentieth century. The Holocaust and the recoil in horror in 1944–45 when the genocide of the Jews was fully revealed was therefore severely damaging to the right. Nowadays, when Catholicism no longer denounces the

Jews as Christ-killers, when evangelical Protestants bask in the glow of Israeli triumphs as signals of the Second Coming, when wealthy American Jews contribute millions to the coffers of the Republican as well as Democratic parties, and when Ronald Reagan is the most pro-Zionist President since the incomparable Harry Truman (who as much as any other single person created the State of Israel in 1948), the long and dreadfully consequential embrace of anti-Semitism by the right has begun to fade from history. Among intellectuals and writers in the trans-Atlantic world, anti-Semitism has become more a function of the left than the right.

Modern anti-Semitism in the Western world dates from the 1880's. Aside from residual and waning Christian Judophobia, there was very little of it in the nineteenth century before the last two decades. Indeed the Victorian record on the Jewish question was a noble one. Then the Jews in the Western world made greater strides towards political and economic emancipation, full status as citizens, and cultural assimilation than at any previous time in the second Christian millennium. There were, however, only tiny minorities of Jews in the Western countries and as in the case of Italy and France, these minute minorities had in many instances lived there since the time of the Caesars; they scarcely qualified as recent immigrants. Furthermore, the Jews were a learned, generally affluent, economically enterprising group with important contribution to make in professional, intellectual, and artistic life when they were given half a chance, and by the 1870's they were certainly given that.

Britain had a prime minister, in the 1870's, Benjamin Disraeli, who while converted as a child to the Church of England, went out of his way to remind everyone that he was not only a Jew ethnically but proud of it. In Disraeli's best-selling novels, written in the 1830's and 40's before his entry into political life, the blonde Christian hero and heroine are always saved by a swarthy, mysterious, immensely rich and learned Jewish sage. Disraeli never repudiated this view of the role of the Jews in European life. Indeed he acted upon it and applied it to himself. Not only did he take care that his dress and haircut would remind everyone that he was descended from Italian Sephardim who migrated to England in the eighteenth century (Disraeli's father was a distinguished literary critic and antiquary). When Disraeli as a prime minister needed funds to help Britain buy a controlling share in the Suez Canal, he borrowed the money from the most famous private Jewish bank in Europe, the Parisian Rothschilds. This act of chutzpah aroused little indignation about an international Jewish capitalist conspiracy as would such an action thirty years later—or today. Indeed Queen Victoria, the British aristocracy, and the usual majority of the British electorate alike found Disraeli completely charming and trustworthy.

The situation for Jews in the Western world changed radically in the period between the mid-80's and the First World War. Anti-Semitism became endemic in European life and raged uncontrolled until pictures of Auschwitz and Dachau appeared in newspapers and newsreels in the summer of 1944 (since 1967 anti-Semitism has been on the rise again). There are five reasons for the rise of anti-Semitism at the turn of the century: the demographic, the cultural, the economic, the political and the psychological.

For there to be anti-Semitism there had to be Jews, and in substantial numbers. Beginning in the 1880's millions of Jews poured westward out of the ghettos and shtetls of the Tsarist and Austro-Hungarian empires especially from Russia, Poland and the Ukraine and Austrian Galicia, impelled by discrimination, pogroms (in the case of Russia state-supported) and economic distress. It is well known and frequently sentimentally celebrated that three million Jews went to the United States before a racist-influenced new immigration law in 1924 closed the doors. But at least a million Jews also went into Western Europe, particularly Germany, Austria proper, France and Britain. While still remaining a small minority of the population, by the 1930's (there was another wave of Jewish westward immigration after World War I and the Bolshevik Revolution) there were 450,000 Jews in Germany, 300,000 in each of France and Britain, 190,000 in Austria, 40,000 in Italy and 75,000 in Greece. The figures today inspire reflection: 30,000 in Western Germany, 15,000 in Austria, 10,000 in Greece. Britain's Jewish population is about the same as in 1930, France's Jewish population has risen to half a million because of the Algerian Jewish expulsion in the 60's. In 1939 there were 140,000 Jews in Holland. Many families had been there since the seventeenth century. The Nazis killed 75% of the Dutch Jews. Of the 350,000 Jews in pre-War Czechoslovakia, only 25,000 survived the war. Let it not be said that Hitler did not have a long-term impact on Europe. In German-speaking countries at least, the Final Solution appears to have been final.

Of course, the Polish story is most thought-provoking: A Jewish population of 3.3 million is now about 25,000 (3 million were killed by Nazi and Polish anti-Semitism in 1941–44, with a further emigration of most of the remaining Jews in the fifties to escape renewed anti-Semitism). There are now far more Hungarian and Rumanian Jews in Israel than in their home countries. As far as can be statistically established, 5.8 million Jews perished under Nazi rule.

It was not just the number of Jewish immigrants between 1885 and 1920 that raised the Jewish question, but their character. There were very few, if any, Rothschilds or Disraelis or for that matter Felix Mendelssohn among them. While the great majority of immigrant Jews had some minimal literacy, they were impoverished, undereducated, superstitious, diseased, and criminal-ridden—just what any group of slum-dwellers would have been, whether from Poland or Sicily or Ireland.

American musical comedy and the general romanticization of their history which American Jews indulge in has cast a golden glow over life in the East European shtetl. But even the stories of Sholem Aleichem reflect the poverty and ignorance of Jewish life in the Russian Empire. Far worse is the bitter picture in the realistic novels of the writer who used the pseudonym Mendele the Bookseller. Here in a Zola-like vein are accounts of a sordid world of unrelieved misery and superstition. That immigrants from such a society would arouse loathing and fear in Western society is only to be expected. What is amazing is how quickly the Jews successfully adapted to their new environment. A prime reason is that the great emigration from Eastern Europe came at a low ebb in the organizational capacity of the Jewish communities, unable to withstand the intrusions of the industrial revolution. The further shock of emigration devastated rabbinical leadership and communal institutions and allowed Jewish immigrants to assimilate relatively rapidly to different cultures.

Unfortunately for the Jews, social and behavioral science at the turn of the century was still so steeped in Victorian prejudices and rigidities that these simple sociological facts were not understood. Given the racist and social Darwinist doctrine of the late nineteenth century, the unattractive and alien characteristics of the immigrant Jews were hypostasized into the belief that they were a degenerate, perpetually downscale race on the evolutionary scale. An American psychologist around 1920, after examining hundreds of Jewish immigrants at Ellis Island, pronounced them genetically deficient in intelligence.

When, however, the new Jewish settlers proved themselves industrious and commercially skillful and provided tough economic competition for the European middle and working classes, this racist contempt was inflamed by economic jealousy. The members of this scurvy race, while of course degenerate, were also, it transpired, unfair competitors for jobs and wealth. Of course, these prejudices were inconsistent—degenerate races should not be tough economic competition. But anti-Semitism was a set of irrational and inconsistent doctrines.

The position of the Jews deteriorated at the turn of the century when European politicians facing democratic electorates sought to capitalize on exploiting the hatred and fear of the Jews. It is regrettable that Winston Churchill in his early political career was one of these—as home secretary (minister of the interior), he personally led police in a tumultuous raid on the alleged headquarters of alleged Jewish anarchists and gangsters in London (they didn't find much).

It was in Germany, Austria and France, however, that political anti-Semitism became an elaborate art. Long before Hitler's regime, anti-Semitism was a central theme in Viennese politics. In Vienna, which critic Karl Kraus prophetically called "the proving ground of the world's destruction," Mayor Karl Lueger was elected on a mainly anti-Semitic platform in the 1890's. (In 1985, at a historical exhibition in Vienna there was a celebratory display on Lueger, without once mentioning that he was a prominent anti-Semite). In the years before World War I, young Adolf Hitler learned his anti-Semitic trade from the Viennese politicians—although Hitler was a little more sincere in his Jew-hatred.

The final factor conducive to anti-Semitism was psychological. Jews played the role that demons and witches had in the seventeenth century. They were the scapegoats for the troubles that racked the Western world in the first half of the twentieth century. Here is an example of demonization and reification on a grand scale. Jews were held responsible for all the troubles that plagued war-torn and depression-ridden Europe.

Jewish capitalists, it was claimed in the popular press, manipulated stock markets and caused banks to fail. Jewish Communists conspired against governments and betrayed their countries to the Bolsheviks. The Jewish proletariat took jobs away from Christian workers. Middle class Jews thronged the learned professions and destabilized them. Jewish intellectuals were Modernists who eroded traditional values. On the other hand, Jews maintained faith in a theistic religion that reason and science had long discredited intellectually. Jews were wanderers who had no country and therefore no patriotic soul. On the other hand, the Zionists were displacing the Arabs in Palestine from what was rightfully theirs. Jews were too ignorant and backward to be admitted to universities. On the other hand, if they had placed near the top in entrance exams, their admission had to be limited by narrow quotas lest they overrun academies and the learned professions. The Jews could do no good.

With this endemic and near universal feelings of hatred and resentment against Jews, it was not hard for Hitler to gain assent for removing "the Jewish bacillus infecting the life of people." "The annihilation of Jews," he said as early as 1922, "will be my first and foremost task." He kept his word.

When Hitler and his colleagues and followers began their persecution and then genocide, there was little intervention from anyone else, because Gentile society as a whole was implicated in the Holocaust. Sixty years of anti-Semitism had made the Holocaust possible. If universal hatred is vented on a defenseless minority, persistently and consistently and universally, only divine intervention will avoid a holocaust. Some group of thugs and gangsters will sooner or later carry out the murders that are in everyone's mind to do. God did not choose to intervene to save the European Jews. Capitalist and proletarian, rabbi and professor, elderly and children: they all perished in unimaginable numbers in the Hitlerian gas chambers.

It was the greatest crime in human history, for which twentieth-century culture as a whole was responsible. It is to the eternal discredit of the Western right that it succumbed so easily to anti-Semitism—in some cases passionately and sincerely, in others cynically, in most cases simply recklessly and reflexively.

What is most amazing is how hard-hearted Western people were in the early forties towards the pitiable Jewish victims of Nazism, even to children. The British under Churchill interned Jewish refugees as enemy aliens and potential spies and deported them to internment camps in the Quebec icefields. The American government persistently refused to admit Jewish refugees in significant numbers—not more than a handful were admitted during the early forties. One group was held in a prison camp in Oswego, New York. Although Canada was an empty country which desperately needed immigrants (Germans were intensively recruited after 1945), the title of a recent book—quoting a Canadian government official—aptly tells Canadian immigration policy toward Jewish refugees: "none is too many."

To placate the Arabs, Palestine under British rule remained sealed to Jewish refugees above a paltry annual number. Incredibly, three overloaded boatloads of desperate Jewish refugees from Nazi Europe in 1942–44 were turned back by the British navy from landing their desperate cargo on Palestinian shores. One such boat—the *Sturma*—sank off the coast of Turkey with 500 dead and two survivors. British and American military officials refused to use planes to destroy railroads bringing Jewish victims to the death camps. Until 1944, British and American government officials refused to authenticate fully reliable information on the Holocaust that was smuggled out of Germany through Switzerland.

Such was the intensity of popular anti-Semitism in the United States in the early forties that not only was F.D.R. afraid to help the Jewish victims of the Nazis, but the leaders of the Jewish community in the United States, Rabbi Stephen Wise of New York and Rabbi Abba Hillel Silver of Cleveland, were reluctant to protest American policy, especially immigration quotas, too loudly, lest anti-Semitism be stimulated. Wise and Silver and other establishment Jewish leaders made an occasional speech and delivered a few petitions to Washington. But they held no hunger strikes and conducted no sit-ins. It never entered their minds to chain themselves to the White House gate until President Roosevelt did something tangible to help their European brethren perishing daily in vast numbers in the death camps.

Wise and Silver were gentlemen who knew full well that in the Departments of State and Justice were droves of anti-Semitic graduates of Ivy League colleges. The only noise about saving Jews was conducted by a right wing Zionist agent (Hillel Cook, the nephew of a famous Israeli rabbi) who operated outside established American Jewish communal institutions. Cook stimulated the popular dramatist Ben Hecht to write a play about how the Jews were dying while the world looked on passively. Hecht's play was considered in more refined Jewish circles to be melodramatic and in bad taste.

The fact is not even Zionists liked Jews of ghetto and shtetl very much. The East European socialist Zionists who created Israel in the first half of the twentieth century were committed to the principle of creating a new Jew— secular, rational, close to the land, devoid of the same unpalatable characteristics that anti-Semites in Europe had condemned. The philosopher of Labor Zionism was A. D. Gordon who settled in Palestine in a large northern Kibbutz in Galilee on the shores of Lake Kinneret around 1903. Gordon, a self-pronounced disciple of Tolstoy, collected flora and fauna which has been reverentially preserved at Kibbutz Degania for inspection by today's puzzled American tourists (the Gordon natural history collection looks exactly like a bad American junior high school lab of the early twentieth century).

Working the land with their own hands in a socialist kibbutz, declared Gordon, would redeem Jews from centuries of putrid ghetto life and make them as healthy and powerful as in ancient times. Abandoning Yiddish, that accursed German medieval ghetto patois for Hebrew, the clean language, patriarchal and prophetic, would also have a redeeming effect. King David and Bar Kochba would live again. This indeed happened, but lounging in the Tel Aviv Hilton today and watching Israeli capitalists and politicians dash by to make their deals brings one light-years away from the world of A. D. Gordon. In the early eighties the big thrust in kibbutzism was to install closed-circuit cable TV and VCR's to play films nightly for the bored kibbutzniks. Collecting flora and fauna as A. D. Gordon had done wasn't enough for Jewish redemption.

The right wing Zionists of the interwar era went so far from ghetto and shtetl culture as to develop an affinity for Fascism. This group was led by the Polish intellectual Ze'ev Jabotinsky and became well known as the Revisionists. Menachem Begin came out of the Revisionist movement in Poland. He was a leader of the para-military Revisionist auxiliary, Betar, modelled consciously on the German stormtroopers and Mussolini's Fascist blackshirts. (Revisionists are now called the Herut party, the main component of the Likud coalition).

Jabotinsky and Begin welcomed the Nazis who, they thought, would drive the Jews out of Europe to Palestine. They also admired the militant and terrorist tactics of the Nazis. The future belonged, they concluded, to Fascist parties and terrorist groups and they formed their own. This was useful during the worst days of British rule in 1943–47. The Irgun Zvi Leumi (Begin) and Stern Gang (Itzhak Shamir) underground terrorist organizations grew out of the Revisionist movement and its Betar military organization. They specialized in taking reprisals against the calloused British colonialists who were still restricting Jewish immigration by hanging British army sergeants, assassinating diplomats, blowing up the British headquarters in the King David Hotel in Jerusalem, and massacring Arab peasants.

One thing is clear about this Zionist world: whether socialist or rightist, the Zionists didn't like European Jews as they had been, any more than Gentile anti-Semites did. Not genocide but redemption was their solution. Through collective agriculture or terrorist movements a new Jew would be created—as he and she were. The Zionists agreed with anti- Semites that the European Jews were indeed parasitical degenerates. But instead of exterminating them, the Zionists believed that the European Jew could be thoroughly tranformed. They were right—Auschwitz was unnecessary to get rid of the old Jews.

An apologist for Hitler would say that this outcome was indeed along the lines of one of Hitler's earlier proposals for solving the Jewish Problem. He wanted, like the Zionists, or at least rightist Zionists, to expel all Jews from Europe. Only the uncooperative stance of the British in not opening the immigration doors to Palestine forced the Nazis to use a more violent solution. The apologist would point out that Eichmann, the head Nazi exterminator in Hungary was still talking in 1944 about exchanging Jews for trucks and other war materiel the Germans needed.

How sincere Hitler and Eichmann were in those migratory rather than mortal proposals for solving the Jewish Problem we shall never know; not even Hitler and Eichmann themselves probably knew. It may have been just part of the endless stream of manic Nazi chatter. It is true, however, that Roosevelt and Churchill made no real effort to find out. They could not offend their electorates by proposing to transport Jews from occupied Europe to the United States or Palestine. To suggest that, the British felt, would have so inflamed anti-Semitic sentiment as to damage the war effort. Hard as it is now to believe this, there was a kernel of truth in this apology.

In addition to revulsion against the Holocaust, the reason for the decline of anti-Semitism on the right is that the old Jewish stereotype was eroded by mid-century. Degenerate Jews were either killed by the Nazis or transformed into muscular, bronzed, secular, victorious Israeli soldiers or into clean-visaged American Jewish business men and philanthropists. One way or another, the

old Jews were gone. This was one of the least controversial changes of the
twentieth century.

*   *   *

Rightist National Heritages

The national variations in rightist political culture in the West are greater
than the national differences on the left. Drawing upon the eight basic
ingredients of rightist thought, characteristic rightist doctrines and movements
have developed in the major countries of the West. While there is much in
common among the rightist doctrines across national lines, each country has
developed a distinctive blend of doctrines derived from the eight basic
traditions. Because a sense of national community is itself central to rightist
culture, the way in which each country has evolved its rightist traditions offer
a significant degree of distinctiveness.

A second characteristic of rightist thought is that like leftist thought it has
been subject to temporal variance, that is, it has flourished and waned at
different periods. Rightist thought reached a peak of influence around
1939–40, and greatly declined, with the collapse of Fascism, in 1944–45. In
the late seventies a partial revival in the strength of rightist thinking occurred,
although within a more limited set of ideas than in the thirties, and this rightist
renaissance continues in the late eighties. In the academic and media worlds,
rightist thought is not as powerful or influential as leftist ideology today, but
it has shown renewed vigor and creativity in recent years.

In discussing Modernism we pointed to the rightist intellectual group in
Britain—centered on T. S. Eliot, Ezra Pound, Wyndham Lewis, F. R. Leavis—
that constituted England's most astute rightist theorists of the interwar period.
Their outlook was characterized by four main attitudes. The first of these was
rationalism and classicism. The second was a desire to preserve not so much
Christian tradition as the sense of hierarchy and stability that they derived
from Christian culture. The third aspect of their rightist outlook was a
vehement anti-Semitism. Finally, they were fervent anti-Communists aiming at
the sustenance of group solidarity.

As high Modernists they were not historicists, but they wished to fashion in
education and elite culture a mythic content that contained ingredients
recruited from the past of which Augustinian theology and Dante's synthetic
Christian humanism predominated. They saw themselves as defending the
traditions of a timeless Western civilization against what they feared to be
witnessing, namely a deracinated, overly technocratic, atomizing culture. We
have noted the profound influence of this group on literature, criticism, the arts
and education.

Great efforts were made, especially in the United States, to sustain and
propagate the essential messages of this group while disguising its more
polemical rightist political teaching and particularly its blatant anti-Semitism,
which became sufficiently subliminal that the message of the Eliot group could
be enunciated even by American Jewish humanists who were fortunate enough

to penetrate discriminatory screening and obtain posts in humanities departments.

This kind of refined intellectual rightism, the heritage of Eliot and Leavis and the others, is still strong at Oxbridge. While the anti-Semitic component was muted after the revelation of the Holocaust, it slowly revived after the Israeli victory in 1967 and has now become again quite blatant, thinly disguised as anti-Zionism. The austere pages of *The Times Literary Supplement* and *The London Review of Books* are replete with this humanistic neo-anti-Semitism. Eliot, Pound and Lewis would have been delighted at the revival of this interwar era tradition.

A second rightist group in Britain consisted of Roman Catholics and their sympathizers. The most polemical members of this group were Gilbert Chesterton and Hilaire Belloc, who were two very prolific journalists and historians writing in the first forty years of the twentieth century. Both lived long and productive lives. Chesterton and Belloc had two things to say, namely that the Middle Ages were the best time that the world had ever known, since it was during that period when people were living under the happy guidance and rule of the Catholic Church; and that Jews were no good.

A more sophisticated member of the Catholic group was the novelist Evelyn Waugh, who was anti-Semitic as well, and very much committed to traditional Catholicism. But he was at the same time a novelist of extraordinary ingenuity. His most ambitious work, *Brideshead Revisited*, was published in 1945 and constitutes a lament for, and a panegyric upon, an old aristocratic Catholic family of the kind that had ruled England for centuries, but had become provincial, eccentric, and powerless after the Reformation as a result of its marginalization within English society and culture. Nevertheless, according to Waugh, these were the people who knew how to provide disinterested leadership, a decent ethic and a fine balance in English life. Had old England only survived—this is the longing of *Brideshead Revisited*, which is one of the major political novels in the English language.

The phenomenal popularity of the skillful TV version of *Brideshead Revisited* in the age of Thatcher and Reagan is not accidental. *Brideshead Revisited* is a passionate but rightist polemic from start to finish. Note who are the bad guys in Waugh's view of the world: businessmen, Jews, Americans, and academics. These are the traitors to the venerable and decent Roman Catholic hierarchical heritage.

Another important English Catholic thinker was the historian Christopher Dawson, a prolific writer who published several books about the medieval church. He never received much attention in England and held only an adjunct position at a small university. To the surprise of Englishmen, however, his books gained many admirers in the United States. In 1952, he was appointed to a chair at Harvard University. Nathan Pusey, who was then the president of Harvard and a right-wing Christian, created a chair for Dawson, enabling him to spend the latter part of his career teaching Protestants and Jews in Cambridge, Mass.

The central theme in Dawson's work is that the medieval world had achieved a synthesis between faith and reason under the beneficent rule of the

Roman Catholic Church, which the modern world has lost. Modern culture polarizes faith and reason, which makes for confusion and alienation, and for which the solution lies in a return to Catholic existence and Church rule. In a series of polemical, clever and often very learned books, Dawson propounded this thesis—essentially the same as Chesterton's and Belloc's but stated in a much more refined and learned manner.

Dawson had another argument, however, which held that the future of Catholicism lay in what is now referred to as the Third World, namely, in Africa and Asia. It would be Asia and Africa that would bring about the revival of Catholic leadership in the world. As the twentieth century draws to a close, Dawson's estimate of the best prospects for the Roman Church become ever more persuasive and sound.

A fringe member of this group, who, although not a Catholic, nevertheless thought in line with Catholicism, was Arnold Toynbee, the famous author of *A Study of History*. In the fifties, his six-volume work entered half of the literate homes in America in the one-volume abridged edition promoted by The Book-of-the-Month Club. Toynbee was honored at just about every major American university, and his portrait graced the cover of *Time* magazine. (Henry Luce, the publisher of *Time*, had a devout Catholic wife, Clare Booth Luce, the actress, dramatist and congresswoman.)

One of Toynbee's numerous theses fitted in with the views of the British Catholic group. This was also the idea which remained most permanent and ubiquitous in his thought. The outcome of a civilization, Toynbee claimed, was to produce a religion. Identifying exactly thirty-one civilizations in history, he delineated their progressional pattern of rise and fall, and argued that in the course of their inevitable decline, civilizations did not fail to produce religion. Out of the dying civilization emerges a universal religion which is the "chrysalis" of a new civilization. On the verge of its demise, the caterpillar transforms itself into a butterfly. In the course of its decline, the Roman Empire gave birth to Christianity. Toynbee, an authority on classical civilization began with this example and found, he claimed, many other examples to fit this distinctive pattern of historical change.

In *Civilization on Trial*, which he published in 1953, Toynbee argued that such was the intrinsic quality of Christianity, that this religion may be able to save Western civilization. Even though every civilization that the world has known hitherto has not been able to resist inevitable decline, Christianity, owing to its intrinsic superiority, will buttress and save Western civilization. This is a thesis in which Evelyn Waugh believed, and it is one in which Christopher Dawson, Education Secretary William Bennett, and, it can be supposed, Ronald Reagan, believes.

Toynbee incorporated a vigorous streak of anti-Semitism into his rightist opinion. As Director of the prestigious Royal Institute for International Affairs in the twenties and thirties, he advocated the pro-Arab and anti-Zionist policy that was adopted—with fateful consequences for millions of European Jews—by the British government. Toynbee's Arab-philia could be seen as character-istic of his generation of Englishmen (it has revived in the seventies and eighties.) Pro-Arabism was not merely strategic, however, in the interests of

British power and oil in the Middle East. It reflected a romantic attachment to the allegedly clean-limbed people of the desert, most romantically expressed in the idiosyncratic exploits of T.E. Lawrence in Saudi Arabia and the heading of the Transjordanian army by Glubb Pasha. But Toynbee genuinely held Jews in contempt as well. In his *Study of History*, he dismisses Judaism as a "fossilized" religion, a synonym for the condition of degeneracy that European anti-Semites of his generation universally attributed to Jews. Catholic and the rightist Christian thinkers of the interwar years summarily hated Jews both for religious and racial reasons. Toynbee belonged to this group.

Why was Catholic thought or proto-Catholic thought so vigorous on the British right during the interwar years? The answer would seem to lie in basic demographics. Between the mid-nineteenth century and the First World War the proportion of Catholics almost doubled within the British population due to Irish immigration, large families, and conversions. Catholic thought reflected this new prominence of Roman Church members in the British population. A second factor was that Catholics, like Jews, only entered into British academia, the learned professions, journalism, and publishing in significant numbers at the turn of the century. The inevitable effort to construct a social and political theory that was partial to traditional Catholicism followed. More reflective Catholics like David Knowles, who aimed at a more subtle doctrine and one more self-critical and sensitive to varying traditions within Catholicism, were ignored or suppressed.

Fascism was never a prominent doctrine in England, which had suffered too much in the First World War to become enthusiastic over militarism. The British were also not eager to embrace the leadership principle. Yet Fascism did make some inroads. We have noted the doctrine of expressive blood trumpeted by D.H. Lawrence and William Butler Yeats. A tiny Fascist movement per se emerged in the midst of the Great Depression of the thirties under the leadership of Sir Oswald Mosley, who led street demonstrations against Jewish shopkeepers and declared Hitler the savior of civilization. Mosley was related to the English aristocracy through marriage, and began his political career on the radical wing of the Labor Party, but soon found that the party was not sufficiently charismatic and that it lacked a leader. He declared himself to be the Fuehrer who would save England and ended up in prison. The English can be trusted not to have the boldness to produce serious Fascism.

In the forties Neville Chamberlain, conservative prime minister from 1937 to 1940, was pilloried by the left as a sympathizer with Fascism. In fact, Labor intellectuals even formed a book club, The Left Book Club, to darken Chamberlain's reputation. They published a new book every month in order to condemn Chamberlain as the one responsible for the crime of Munich, for the Second World War, the Depression, and for the terrible appeasement of Hitler.

Neville Chamberlain actually had inclinations towards welfare liberalism. He came from Birmingham, where his father had been a radical mayor. Even though his father later became a prominent imperialist, Chamberlain remained loyal to his radical heritage from Birmingham. He became Minister of Health in the twenties, and made important contributions to the government system of health insurance. He was a man of peace who believed that the First World

War had been the most futile and disastrous war of all time. He did not approve of Hitler even in the beginning, but he felt that Hitler would not last long, and that if he were appeased, by sacrificing, for example, a distant "little known" country like Czechoslovakia, he could be put under control. Chamberlain expected that Hitler would shortly demonstrate he was a toothless tiger or would be overthrown by the German generals, and so the cataclysm of the war be avoided. Chamberlain foresaw that a Second World War would produce unprecedented massacre, and he tried to avoid it. He failed, but he was right about the portending catastrophe. Fifty million people died during the war.

Chamberlain's policy was wrong. If England and France had gone to war in 1938 over Hitler's expansionist designs on Czechoslovakia, the German military, who at that time considered themselves unready to fight the Allies, might well have overthrown Hitler. At least Hitler, faced with internal opposition in the army and a determined Allied resistance, would have had to back down and thereby suffer a serious defeat. Chamberlain played the wrong card at Munich and capitulated to most of Hitler's demands, a move he almost immediately regretted when it became evident that not even a major concession could still Hitler's expansionism.

Yet Chamberlain was withal a decent man. He was not as much of a rightist as Churchill, being unenthusiastic about the Empire and willing to give India a substantial measure of self-government, a change that Churchill adamantly and for the moment successfully opposed.

The darkening of Chamberlain's reputation by denigrating him as a Fascist sympathizer, the repudiation of his successor Churchill by the British electorate in 1945, and the Labor government of 1945–51 and its introduction of a full-fledged welfare state with many socialist trimmings followed by the dismemberment of the Empire, were severe blows for the English right. Even more crippling were the heavy income and inheritance taxes that the socialists imposed, fiscally ruining many gentry families that had for centuries been the backbone of British conservatism. Aristocrats could always survive—they could make advertisements, join the diplomatic corps, or sell ice-cream to tourists visiting their ancestral homes for two shillings a head. But it was tougher for the gentry.

Notwithstanding these setbacks and the lamentable fact that Jews now had to be occasionally admitted to clubs and universities, a revived rightist doctrine was slowly constituted in the late forties and fifties. In spite of the triumph of the Labor Party in 1945 and several socialist governments in the sixties and early seventies, this British right-wing movement has remained steadfast and gained renewed political power in 1979 with Margaret Thatcher's election to office.

First among the intellectual generators of the reinstated British rightist tradition was the philosopher R.G. Collingwood, who taught at Oxford University for thirty years. He was unique for his time in that he was the only holder of a professorship in philosophy in England who was not a disciple of Wittgenstein. He was in fact an idealist, who held that history was a perception. History does not consist of mundane facts, he claimed, it does not exist objectively. It is what we imagine our past to be. And we have the right to create an image of the past that is non-Marxist. No view of history can legitimately claim exclusive objectivity, and neither can Marxism. If history is a mental image of the past, then an image can be created that suits mainstream conservatism.

Collingwood too was a neo-medievalist. He agreed with the Catholic group that the medieval world had achieved a fine integration and balance as well as a moral and religious structure which prevented alienation and lent people a means for self-understanding. He too advocated the return to this religion-centered order.

The second member of the conservative intellectual tradition in England was Herbert Butterfield, professor of modern history at Cambridge University in the forties and fifties. He is forgotten now. But in the fifties he was well-known, and popular enough to go on lecture tours in America. Butterfield is anti-"Whig". He argues that there are legitimate points of view other than the liberal. The historian can find a sanction and a legitimacy for the conservatives, the gentry, the Anglican Church (this, even though he was himself a Methodist), in other words, for people other than the secular liberals. History is not a field that lends itself only to elaboration from the secular liberal perspective.

Secondly, Butterfield was a neo-Augustinian. His famous book, *Christianity and History*, based on a BBC lecture series, argued against applying absolute moral standards to history. What happens in history is not a struggle between the saints and the sinners. It is a struggle among a lot of sinners. A conservative interpretation of history is one that recognizes that the City of God, as Augustine termed it, is inward, and that history consists of variants of the Earthly City—variants, that is, of partial people, of fallible people with partial ideas. It is a great mistake to write history as New Dealers like Arthur Schlesinger Jr. or Henry Steele Commager do, interpreting history as the development of one righteous party. No one party and its history can represent justice in the past since there is only a private morality which does not admit of such generalized, public representation. There is no public morality that can be accorded an historical triumph.

Among the more subtle and finely tuned statements of the rightist position in the bureaucratic, technological and Keynesian world of postwar Britain were the novels of C.P. Snow. Originally a physicist and a Cambridge don, Charles Snow (later Lord Snow) became a leading manpower expert in the civil service during the war, and afterwards one of the top corporate executives in Britain. His own experience thereby bridged the academic, bureaucratic, and corporate worlds. Snow's eleven-volume series of novels, entitled *Strangers and Brothers*, is concerned primarily with—to cite the titles of two of his novels—"the corridors of powers" and "the masters."

Writing in the nineteenth-century pre-modernist realist style, Snow reports through the eyes of his narrator, a prominent lawyer, how men and women in the circles of power react to the pressures of ambitions, crises, and moral concerns. Snow, perhaps under the influence of his wife, the accomplished novelist Pamela Hansford Johnson, is memorably effective at depicting the wives of powerful men, a special breed.

The message that Snow imparts is first that those in leadership positions and the learned professions are essentially decent and well-meaning people doing difficult and necessary jobs under great pressure. Some are able to function better than others; some deteriorate under the strain, a small minority become crooks of one sort or another. Later twentieth-century society demands proportionately more from these men and women in the corridors of power than it can possibly provide in compensation of whatever kind.

The second theme, an especially conservative one, is that the pragmatists, the compromising bureaucrats are not only necessary for an establishment (the term became popular in Britain around 1950) to function, but they are the most reliable types to entrust with power and wealth. The idealists, the romantics, the rebels are interesting personalities (here again Snow is adept at portraying them, especially academic radicals), but in the end they are untrustworthy. They either crack under the strain, or become dangerous and oppressive fanatics and ruin other people's lives.

The third message that Snow wishes to impart—and which he also propounded in expository fashion in a famous little book whose title entered the language, *The Two Cultures*—is that to benefit from the new science and advanced technology there has to be an interactive and mutually understanding dialogue between science and traditional humanism. It is the humanists who are more at fault for the chasm between the two cultures of the later twentieth century.

There are insightful subsidiary themes in Snow's novels: his ambiguous feelings about Cambridge, which appears as a mixture of the brilliant, the foolish, and the senile, and the composite picture is not flattering; a prominent and very wealthy London Jewish family which comes close to serving the same function of saving the Gentiles that Disraeli accorded to Jewish millionaire sages; and as a work of fiction his best effort, a study in the destruction of a marriage by the wife's schizophrenia, a highly convincing portrayal of extended psychological pain, yet hardly noticed by the critics.

Generally, Snow's rightist fiction on the world of power was well received by critics in the late forties and fifties but without enthusiasm after the sixties had laid its leftist, agitating glaze on the cultural world. He receives almost no critical attention nowadays, although the series continues to sell well.

An effort by the BBC in the early 80's to turn Snow's novels into a TV mini-series was an uncharacteristic disaster. The TV series by a large margin failed to capture the ambience and indeed obvious message of the novels. The TV characters came through as boring, tiresome, petty, and distinctly unpleasant people jabbering away at each other in overdecorated upper middle-class rooms. That is just the opposite of the point Snow was making. He believed that the masters who inhabit the corridors of power are critically important because their decisions shape our lives in the current world of a bureaucratic, technological, Keynesian state. Superficially they may seem dull, even appear as stuffed shirts at a distance, but they are distinct personalities. They have deep passions both about power and love (which Snow recognizes as interrelated—the Freudian heritage is delicately prevalent in his work), and on the whole they are doing very difficult jobs in a socially beneficial manner. Their feelings run deep and you cannot judge them by their public occasions. Whatever rewards they receive are relatively modest compared to the constant responsibilities and pressures that eat away at them. This conservative doctrine seemed to be beyond the comprehension of the TV producers and indeed it is a rightist rather than a leftist vision, and one more fashionable in the twenty years after the war (when Snow was writing) than since.

The heavyweight theorist on the Right in post-war Britain was Michael Oakeshott. Oakeshott became professor of political science at the London School of Economics in 1951, when he took over the chair of the pop-Marxist Harold Laski, the spokesman of the Labor Party. Much to everyone's surprise and to the annoyance of the leftist students, upon Laski's retirement, the university judiciously appointed a conservative in his place. Oakeshott held this important chair of political theory from 1951 until 1969.

Oakeshott found that there are two kinds of political systems: *societas* (society) and *universitas* (the corporation). He is opposed to the corporate state which tells people what to believe and how to behave. Oakeshott contends that the good society is one in which there is as great a degree of personal freedom as possible. The state cannot provide the important things in life. It cannot, for example, endow a person with moral goodness, make him see the truth. It has to allow people to work out the processes of their lives by private negotiations and exchange. The state should be as noninterventionist as possible, and should allow for the greatest opportunity for small group institutions like the family and local government. This Augustinian message had already been sounded by Herbert Butterfield, but Oakeshott elaborated it in a particularly persuasive manner, stressing secular rather than theological arguments.

There is a strong Burkian tone to Oakeshott—that is, in many ways he can be considered a disciple of the late eighteenth-century conservative thinker Edmund Burke. Oakeshott argues that law is of fundamental importance, not ethics. The state cannot impose a specific morality on people. What it can do is provide due process, a legal continuum, by which the rules of the game will be enforced. The rest is a personal matter, which must be worked through in a legal framework. Oakeshott draws upon the view of English law propounded by the great Modernist pioneer Frederick William Maitland in the 1890's, whose thought has been discussed in the first chapter. Maitland had described the rise of due process in English law as the result of thousands upon thousands of individual choices rather than of a mandate imposed by the state.

Oakeshott favored a deregulated economy. The practices of the Labor Party were anathema to him. The welfare state, Oakeshott concluded, took more than it gave: it destroyed people's lives, and eroded small group institutions. It deprived people of the opportunity of choice, and it overburdened the economy. Ever since the 1820's, leftist England had dreamed about the socialist state. The future finally arrived, Oakeshott contended, and it didn't work.

A group of British political intellectuals who emerged in the late sixties and seventies were very much influenced by Oakeshott. One member of this group was Margaret Thatcher, who along with many other officers in her government, is a disciple of Oakeshott, who, in turn, with some help from Butterfield and Collingwood, had reconstructed a distinctive rightist political theory.

The fact is, however, that another ingredient entered into Thatcherism beside Oakeshott's theory, namely, a very strong neo-Ricardian component. Indeed, while Thatcherism put into practice to the greatest degree Michael Oakeshott's political theory, the influence of Milton Friedman and of American Reaganism are also very much present in the policies followed by Thatcher's government. This includes a certain delight felt in humiliating people, particularly the unemployed of the old industrial towns of the North and people who are affiliated with the universities and with the more militant unions. This vengefulness directed at the poor, at university faculty and students, and at unions was a rightist revanche played against welfare liberals. In other words, Thatcherism is not only an outgrowth of Oakeshott's conservative theory; it also has neo-Ricardian and Friedmanite and Reaganite subtones.

A recent leader of the English rightist tradition, one who is currently highly visible and active, is Maurice Cowling, a history professor and philosopher at Cambridge University. Cowling has published two volumes advocating a return to what he calls the "confessional state," by which he means a state based upon religious principles. According to Cowling, the worst years in English history were 1828 and 1829. These were the two years during which the Anglican Church lost its monopoly, when civil rights were granted to Catholics and the more radical Protestants, and shortly after, to the Jews. Thereby, the Anglican Church lost the monopoly it had enjoyed within the political system since the 1670's.

In textbooks of English history, granting civil rights to Catholics, Protestant dissenters and Jews is conventionally regarded as one of the finest moments of English history, not, as Cowling assumes, its darkest. But for Cowling, this was the period when the opportunity to achieve the union of Church and State was lost. Cowling is trying to revive the ideas of the Oxford movement of the 1820's and 30's, particularly those of John Henry, later Cardinal Newman: a view of the state as joined together with the church in trying to attain a moral framework in society; a consistency of culture, morality and politics, merged in subjection to the Church of England. The influence of T. S. Eliot and F. R. Leavis is evident.

Understandably, Cowling does not yet enjoy a large following, but nevertheless he and his colleagues at Peterhouse College in Cambridge have effectively made known their point of view, which is very much an extreme rightist doctrine. This view lies far to the right of Thatcherism, and while Cowling professes that he has great admiration for Oakeshott, what he is arguing is a point of view that is closer to continental Fascism, particularly in the form it has assumed in Vichy France, Franco's Spain and Mussolini's Italy, than to anything that belongs in the English tradition. It is intriguing to see the far-right movement of the "confessional state," or religious corporatism, taking a foothold in English intellectual life at this time.

Nor is Cowling's thought free of anti-Semitism. He has a very ambivalent attitude toward Chesterton and Belloc, and to their anti-Semitic diatribes.

Thus at this time in England, at Cambridge University, in the highest reaches of the academic world, a genuine right-wing, quasi-Fascist intellectual movement is coming to the fore.

Along with Maurice Cowling, the most original rightist theorist in Britain of the 80's is Roger Scruton, philosophy professor at the University of London, who belongs to a group of conservative philosophers advising Prime Minister Thatcher on public policy. Scruton does not hesitate to address leftist theorists in polemical fashion. He rejects *The Communist Manifesto* as "schoolboy history". But his original contribution consists of arguing for the moral necessity of sexual restraint or "decency" in opposition to the sexual liberation of the 60's. Indeed it is standards of decency and restraint that make sexual activity desirable. One is the function of the other. "There could be neither arousal, nor desire, nor the pleasures that pertain to them, without the presence, in the very heart of these responses, of the moral scruples which limit them." And these standards of restraint, this ethic of decency is not bourgeois; they are classical, they are universal. They are propounded by the leading philosophers and the best writers in the history of Western culture. The so called bourgeois standards of sexuality and the family are the universal moral standards essential to civilization, Scruton claims.

Historians of Fascism frequently believe that the purest strain of Fascist theory emerged in France. In Germany, Italy and Spain, numerous idiosyncratic politics shaped Fascism, but it is in France in the 1930's and early 40's that a strong and genuine theoretical formulation of Fascism occurred. The French right and French Fascism grew out of, or at least found their generative occasion in the Dreyfus case which occurred at the beginning of the century. Dreyfus was a Jewish army captain who was railroaded by a group of anti-Semitic army officers, falsely convicted of treason, and sent to Devil's Island. Various liberals and Jews including Marcel Proust and Émile Zola came to his support, and eventually, after much commotion, another trial showed that he had been the victim of false evidence, and he was eventually pardoned. The real traitor, a rightist officer, fled to England and his accomplice committed suicide.

The Dreyfus controversy, which continued for a decade, produced an enormous public conflict, and the anti-Dreyfusards, those who felt that Dreyfus was guilty, and that even if he were shown to be innocent, he should have been guilty, incepted pervasive right-wing sentiments in France. The opponents of Dreyfus were those who were deeply concerned about the advancement of secularism, the de-confessionalization of French education, the progress of the left, the economic and social success of Jews, and the decline of Church influence and clerical traditions. Émile Durkheim was their bogeyman. They found their spokesman in Charles Maurras, who remained the leading right-wing intellectual in France in the twenties and the thirties.

Maurras and his colleagues formed a hyper-nationalist movement called *L'Action Française*, which was to constitute the base of the French Fascism of the thirties and forties. Maurras and his followers believed that French national honor was being betrayed by socialists, liberals, secularists, atheists and Jews. They found that France had achieved glory under a strong centralized government, as well as a powerful elite, a vigorous war policy and a homogeneous educational system which taught traditional Catholic values. The world was closing in on these native French traditions, corrupting France from within and weakening its military power. The "degenerate" Jews were taking over in political and academic life. France was losing its moral fiber, and its family structure, and its native traditions were being eroded.

Essentially what Maurras and his followers wanted was a medieval revival. They envisaged a society bound together by a code that upheld Christian values if not clericalism, a code that emphasized the corporate community of citizens working harmoniously for the common good. When they looked at the cathedral of Notre Dame they thought of the medieval guildsmen harmoniously working together, a hymn allegedly on their lips, to build this monument to Christian communal solidarity as much as it was a church dedicated to the Virgin Mary. Why could not this communal solidarity live again in France? Maurras and his followers were not anti-business, but they expected capitalists to devote themselves to the public interest and only marginally to entrepreneurial profit-taking. They wanted to recover the Victorian commitment to the nuclear family and they wanted an educational system and curriculum that provided training in values, tradition and citizenship rather then refinement of critical faculties. They disliked the party system in democracy which in their view inculcated corruption and petty deals. They wanted political parties to stand for comprehensive sets of ideals, not subtle combinations of interests.

They saw Jews as the enemies of all aspects of this program: the Jews were anti-Christian, cosmopolites, profit-takers, Communists, and political tricksters. Because of the fierce anti-Semitism of Maurras and his followers and because they increasingly became sympathetic to Hitler as an alternative to Leon Blum, it is easy in retrospect to dismiss their program as inherently wrong and them as evil. But leaving aside the anti-Semitism and the collaboration with the Nazis, it can be seen that Maurras was propounding a program that was central to rightist traditions in this century and was intellectually the most persuasive form of Fascism.

The *Action Française* group fought back vehemently against the left through newspapers and journals, all of which were unmistakably and consistently anti-Semitic. They also employed militant action, not only holding huge public meetings, but also forming paramilitary groups which undertook such activities as breaking up the meetings of leftists and attacking the offices of left-wing newspapers. In spite of the sympathy *L'Action Française* felt toward the Roman Catholic Church, and despite the reciprocated sympathy of French bishops in the twenties and the thirties, the Papacy condemned the organization in 1930 as excessively militant and violent. But then formal Papal condemnation did not mean much in the French context. It was, in fact, a cover for clerical support of Maurras and his followers on the local level.

While the leftist Popular Front of Léon Blum took shape in 1936–38, and while the Spanish Civil War was going on, French intellectuals and politicians became more and more polarized. There was a growing feeling among the right-wing that it would be better to collaborate with the Germans and to allow for a German victory over France than for the decadent, secular, leftist

Third Republic to win. In other words, many Frenchmen felt that the Third Republic was not worth saving, and that a German victory would at least prepare the way for a new kind of neo- Catholic French republic. This view prevailed in spite of the obvious fact that the Nazis were heathens and Hitler was no friend of the Church. With this sentiment, strong in intellectual circles, among the youth, in the media and in the French Catholic Church, it was not surprising that France's efforts to withstand the Germans in 1939 and 1940 presented a feeble record.

The French army was at the outbreak of war in 1939 larger than the German. It was better armed, and had more tanks and more airplanes. The French army was, however, abysmally led. The generals who were responsible for stopping the German attack in May of 1940 had been mostly trained in the Empire. They were mostly used to fighting defenseless people in Algeria and Vietnam, and in spite of the technological superiority of the French army, military technology was not put to full use. Some of the French officers were outright traitors, who agreed with *L'Action Française* in wishing for German victory.

Others, on the other hand, were simply defeatist and exaggerated the power of the Germans. The media in English-speaking countries also at the time characteristically exaggerated German strength and accorded an aura of invincibility to the Nazi *blitzkrieg* ("lightning war"). Among French officers, a defeatist attitude was especially prominent. As a matter of fact, if the French had been able to hold and had thrown back the German attack in the Spring of 1940, it is possible that the Germans would have had to sue for peace. Although the German army was very well-trained and superbly led, it was a relatively small army and Hitler had no reserves in June 1940.

Still other Frenchmen in 1940 were simply foolish. The head of the French army locked himself up in a chateau in a Parisian suburb, to which there was not even a telephone connection. Messages had to be taken there by motorcycle. Why? He was simply an obtuse person who had learned military tactics in the Empire in the twenties and stuck to them.

In any case, the Germans won an easy victory. The French in the interwar years had built at huge expense an impressive string of fortifications, the Maginot Line, to defend against a German attack through Belgium, as in World War I. The German Army simply moved at unprecedented speed around both ends of the Maginot Line, on the one side along the coastline, and on the other through the Ardennes Forest. The French generals convinced themselves that the German armored brigade could not move through the Ardennes. It is hard to see how the French came to this conclusion, because the French government had built an excellent paved road right through the forest. The German tanks rolled along as if on Sunday parade.

In spite of these disasters, the French army was not conclusively defeated. It surrendered before it lost Paris. While in August and September of 1914 the French had thrown back the Germans thirty miles from Paris, this time in May and June of 1940, when the Germans were not quite as close, the French republican government disintegrated and a new government, defeatist and to some extent pro-German in composition, surrendered on miserable terms. The desperate new British Prime Minister, Winston Churchill, flew to France and offered the French generals and politicians attractive terms for a political union with Britain if the French would only keep fighting. The French navy, second in Europe only to the British, was completely intact and there were still French armies in the colonies. But to no avail.

Had it not been for Hitler's Aryan cast of mind, the war on the Western Front would have ended then and there in a complete Nazi triumph and the extinction of Western civilization. The British expeditionary force in France, which numbered a quarter of a million, was cut off and surrounded in the French port of Dunkirk. But Hitler convinced himself that if he were generous, the fellow-Saxon British would negotiate peace with him. He allowed most of the British army, although without their arms, to escape across the channel. This was the famous miracle of Dunkirk. It was no more a miracle than the abysmal French defeat, the worst since the fourteenth century.

After the humiliating defeat and harsh peace, France was broken into two parts. The northern part was ruled directly by the occupying Germans out of Paris, whereas the new rightist government ruled the south from the old spa of Vichy, whose mineral water export we still consume. The government was presided over by Marshall Pétain and the prime minister was Pierre Laval. In Paris a group of very active collaborators readily appeared. They consisted of a large and vocal group of French Nazis basking under German protection and rule in 1941–44. The leading intellectual of the group was Drieu de la Rochelle, who was a disciple of Maurras, and a prominent critic and journalist. He advocated for the French a variant of German Nazism.

A leading novelist of the time was Louis-Fernand Céline. He immediately became the literary darling of the collaboration era. Céline specialized in foul-mouthed anti-Semitic diatribes. (Céline's novels are still read in French literature courses.) La Rochelle and Céline advocated a resurgence of French corporatist and clerical traditions under strong leadership, and above all they called for not only anti-Semite legislation but for the extermination of Jews. In fact, they elaborated extensively on a possible holocaust.

The head of the Vichy government, Marshall Pétain, had been a great hero of the First World War. He had been the man who had saved the French army in 1917 when the army had mutinied. Widely respected, Pétain claimed that France was being punished by God because it had surrendered its noble and venerable religious, aristocratic, familial and work traditions. The Vichy government would restore the genuinely French way of life. Léon Blum and his colleagues were tried for treason and sent to concentration camps.

Since Pétain was old and feeble, the government was mostly run by Pierre Laval, who not only collaborated with the Nazis but sometimes even exceeded their demands. When the Germans ordered him to round up Jews, for example, he rounded up not only the adults, but the children as well, even when he was not required to do so. Laval tried very hard to keep France staunchly on the German side. He was convinced that a permanent new European order had been created by Hitler and aimed to gain for France a prominent place in this order.

Vichy was opposed by the Free French, a group of French officials and soldiers who had fled overseas. These gathered around Charles De Gaulle in London. De Gaulle was only a colonel in 1940, but he had already achieved some celebrity by advocating a highly mobilized war strategy, a fast-moving war conducted mainly by tanks. It was mainly the German generals who had read his treatise. De Gaulle can be regarded as a centrist, a moderate conservative. He believed in strong government but was not clerical or anti-Semitic. He was intensely nationalist, was hostile to French Fascists, and believed in restoring an effective republican order under a strong presidency. Above all, he found it particularly important to create a France which was powerful on the international stage. De Gaulle's political vision was essentially Napoleonic.

After the Allied Liberation, in 1944, La Rochelle committed suicide, Laval was shot as a traitor, along with several hundred collaborators, Pétain was sent to prison for life, where he died, and Céline, after a brief hiatus in a Danish prison, managed to continue his illustrious literary career. De Gaulle became the first president of the Fourth Republic, which office he soon gave up because he felt that the restored government, specifically the executive, was too weak. He returned to power, however, in the late fifties and created a new Fifth Republic with a strong presidency and a constitution which France has preserved to this day.

By and large, the French rightist tradition—Catholic, corporatist, anti-Semitic—died in August 1944, when De Gaulle and the Allies liberated Paris. The remnants of the pre-war French rightist tradition are barely in existence today. The Gaullists have recently again regained power in France, but this is a group that is centrist and technocratic, and believe in a modernized France. While they advocate an aggressive, strong foreign policy, they are not rightists. The real French rightist tradition ended with the Second World War. The only rightist movement currently in existence belongs to the petit-bourgeoisie, and goes back to the old clerical ideology that cherishes the family and the Church and which is opposed to modernity, the Parisians, the intellectuals and the Jews. This group is, however, now a relatively small one that managed to obtain only ten per cent of the votes in the last French elections.

In the 1930's, during the Depression, there were two strong figures on the American right. The first of these was Father Coughlin, an eloquent, obstreperous priest in Detroit who gave political sermons on the radio every Sunday. His sermons were fervently anti-socialist, anti-New Deal and anti-Semitic. He was particularly popular in Boston as well as in some parts of Brooklyn. His point of view was very similar to that of the French Fascists. Coughlin was eventually silenced by the Catholic hierarchy, not because the latter disagreed with his opinions, but because he was gaining too much popular support.

The other right-wing figure was Huey Long, who emerged out of Louisiana populism and became the governor of that state. He was probably the only politician in the thirties who worried Franklin Roosevelt. Long appealed to the poor whites and, to some degree, also to the poor blacks of the south. There is a right-wing populist tradition in the United States that goes back to groups within the Democratic Party in the early years of the century, which had sought to forestall the modern world, find a way to redistribute wealth, and to provide for a right-wing welfare state, paradoxical as this may sound. Huey Long drew on this tradition which contains Fascist overtones. He was a brilliant orator and gained wide support. He was assassinated in a private quarrel in 1936.

The other allegedly right-wing figure in twentieth-century American history, one that has become extremely celebrated, was Senator Joseph McCarthy of Wisconsin. He has entered particularly into leftist demonology. Leftist mythology conveys the impression that McCarthy occupied the presidency of the United States for twenty years. The McCarthy "era" of the early fifties was a rather dark period, but it was not all that important, either in duration or in practice.

McCarthy was a cynical demagogue. When he was first elected to office in Wisconsin, it was actually as a left-winger and a populist. The year was 1950. He appraised the political tenor of the country. It was the period of the Cold War and the Communist takeover in China which aroused fear and loathing. There was an increasing concern in this country about loyalty among the government staff, particularly in the State department. Senator McCarthy detected an opportunity there. He claimed that he had a list of over three hundred traitors in the State Department. He never produced the list, of course, but he did make his political rounds generating extravagant accusations against people in the government as well as in the university and the media. He ruined the public careers of some worthy government officials, again concentrating mostly on the State Department, but contrary to subsequent leftist mythology, his influence in the universities was relatively trivial. Only about a dozen faculty in the whole country lost their jobs owing to McCarthyite accusations. Of course, McCarthy and his supporters fostered a repressively conservative atmosphere. Faculty leftists hunkered down and kept quiet until the storm passed. The most prominent refugee from McCarthyite accusation was the ancient historian Moses Finley who found refuge in Cambridge, England.

McCarthy's greatest influence was on Hollywood, where his followers succeeded in getting a group of actors, writers and directors in film and TV blacklisted because they had allegedly belonged to Communist and other left-wing organizations in the 1930's. Among those who were blacklisted was the prolific screenwriter Dalton Trumbo. Trumbo was certainly in the far left. In one of his films, United States capitalism is symbolized by a truckload of toilet paper. Another McCarthy victim was the director Joseph Losey, who continued his distinguished career in Britain. The president of the Screen Actors' Guild, Ronald Reagan, welcomed the McCarthyite intervention in Hollywood.

McCarthy came along at the same time as television, and he received high visibility from this new technological dimension in U.S. life as well as constant attention from the press. But his actual period of flourishing was brief, certainly not more than the period between 1950 to 1955. In the summer of 1955, McCarthy was publicly disgraced when he accused the army of harboring Communists. His claims were shown in televised hearings to be fraudulent. The army hired a very skillful Boston attorney from one of the top law firms in the country, who publicly demolished McCarthy. He was reprimanded by the Senate. Two years later McCarthy was dead of cancer.

There is no question that after the army hearings, the Republican party establishment turned against McCarthy. Even though President Dwight Eisenhower never clearly denounced him, he had been working behind the scenes to undermine McCarthy. McCarthy was a Republican Huey Long. In both cases, the wrong style had been adopted for the viability of the party system. Like Long, McCarthy was charismatic and uncontrollable. He would not heed the Party, which made him a dangerous man, and he had to be brought down. The only respect in which McCarthy was clearly right-wing was that he was an anti-Communist. He was an opportunist who used some rightist rhetoric.

The celebrated and now disbarred New York attorney Roy Cohn was one of McCarthy's three chief assistants. Another was Robert Kennedy, who later achieved considerable reputation on the left and became Attorney General and a candidate for the presidency, until he was assassinated by a P.L.O. lunatic. The third was another young man named Schine, who became a hotel executive in Florida and was never again heard from.

Senator McCarthy did do damage in American public life, but not so much by his coarse violation of civil rights and his actual ruination of the careers of a handful of government officials, academics, and media types. The long-range damage his jerky depredations accomplished was by his becoming the scapegoat demon of the left. Subsequently, in the late seventies and eighties, any effort to point to the hazardous penetration of Marxists into university departments and to the pop-left ambience prevalent in much of the media was immediately denounced as McCarthyism, which was *ipso facto* undiscussably evil. If the left did not create McCarthy they certainly perpetuated his reputation as a convenient demon, as a protective screen, a bogeyman they could denounce to distract attention from their own illiberal activities.

There is much controversy and discussion about General Dwight Eisenhower and what it was that he actually believed in, but even after reading the vast corpus on the issue, one cannot be very certain. It is likely that Eisenhower was a moderate conservative, a centrist. There are many similarities between Eisenhower and De Gaulle, except that De Gaulle produced a larger and more glamorous show, as well as more noise, than Eisenhower. The latter was an easy-going man, who as president seemed to spend an inordinate amount of time on the golf course. Subsequently, it has been claimed that he had a penetrating mind as well as phenomenal managerial skill, and that he always knew how to interpret events correctly as he played the fourteenth hole. His facility in government even surpassed his skill in his favorite sport, it is alleged.

As President from 1953 to 1961, Eisenhower was a centrist in domestic matters. He did not expand the welfare state or civil rights. On the other end, he did not shrink them either. He was very concerned about American presence abroad. Yet he was a man of peace and refused to let the British and French return to imperialism and gunboat diplomacy during the Suez Crisis in 1956. He had a right-wing activist Secretary of State, John Foster Dulles, and an equally activist and conspiratorial head of the CIA, Alan Dulles, another member of the the same peculiar, devout Protestant family. It now appears likely that Eisenhower was using these people as foils, as lightning rods to satisfy right-wing sentiments, while actually controlling them, keeping them on a very short leash.

The Reagan administration is the long-range successor to the Eisenhower administration, and is in many ways similar to its predecessor. It pursues an incomparably more negative policy than Eisenhower's toward the institutions of the welfare state, but then, there is much more of a welfare state today than there was in Eisenhower's time. The welfare state doubled, even tripled, during the Lyndon Johnson administration in the late sixties. Reagan has cut it back by ten or twenty percent—less than the fifty percent that had been the plan. The project of reducing the welfare state program by fifty percent may very well have been largely a matter of show, something the Reagan administration knew to be impossible to put into effect.

Both the Eisenhower and the Reagan administrations have been moderately rightist-center in domestic matters, strongly nationalistic in foreign matters. In between on the conservative spectrum was the Nixon-Ford administration, which did nothing against the welfare state. The welfare state continued pretty well along the lines established under Lyndon Johnson, and as a matter of fact, affirmative action was significantly expanded under Nixon and Ford. If affirmative action on behalf of women and blacks is a left-of-center advocation, then the Nixon-Ford administration had its opportunistic strain.

Their foreign policy was nationalist. Henry Kissinger, the opinionated former Harvard professor, taught and pursued an elaborate system of international power-politics, envisioning himself a combination of Machiavelli and Tallyrand. Nevertheless, the Nixon government did withdraw from Vietnam, although under public presssure. Nixon and Kissinger may have withdrawn because public agitation over the matter was reaching uncontrollable intensity, but the fact is that it was this administration that terminated the divisive war. The Nixon-Ford administration was ideologically on the right, but pragmatic in its policy. The Reagan administration is both ideologically and practically more on the right. It has done little, however, to establish a permanent intellectual bastion on the right. Reaganism has drawn more from academia than it has supported and shaped a rightist following in universities. This raises questions about the future viability of the American right.

There were four intellectuals in the Italian and Spanish world in the twenties and early thirties who contributed to a right-wing philosophy. The first of these was the Spaniard Ortega y Gasset, a philosopher whose most influential book was the 1928 *The Revolt of the Masses*. Ortega argues that civilization is a matter of and for the elite, and as Western civilization is absorbed by the masses—Ortega assumes that such absorption on the part of the masses takes place—and as democracy takes over, civilization, that elitist flower, will be vulgarized, resulting in the establishment of popular dictatorships. A similar argument was used at the same time by Michael Rostovtzeff, an émigré anti-Communist classical scholar of great distinction who taught at Wisconsin and Yale, to explain the decline of the Roman Empire. Ortega y Gasset did not advocate popular dictatorship. To the contrary, he favored the preservation of the traditional elite culture, which is the great bulwark against the rule of the masses.

Another conservative believer in elites was Ortega's somewhat older contemporary Vilfredo Pareto. He died in 1923, one year after the Fascist takeover in Italy. Pareto was an Italian aristocrat who spent the latter part of his long life teaching and writing in Switzerland. Originally a free market liberal and democrat, he came to believe in the falsity of liberal theory and sensed the grave danger to European civilization in the rise of Marxism. Although Pareto's style is far removed from Mussolini and the Fascists, his is a strongly right-wing doctrine that could be and was used to justify the Fascist takeover of Rome.

Pareto began as a civil engineer and the engineering principle of equilibrium is highly visible in his sociological theory. Essentially Pareto's theory represents the views of Edmund Burke, the English conservative of the eighteenth century reinterpreted and expressed through the medium of Durkheim's functionalist sociology.

Pareto has two main ideas. All societies, whatever their political form, are ruled by a small minority or elite and social processes operate so that over time one elite is replaced by another. Liberal democracy is merely a facade for one kind of elite that dominates by guile and artifice (Class I elite). Other ruling groups dominate by force and bureaucratic mechanisms (Class II elite). The former is more innovative an elite; it is also more materialistic. There is obviously a flash of plausibility in Pareto's elite theory. The second leading idea in Pareto's writing has recently won favor among rightist economic theorists in the United States. This is the view that whereas some human activities are rational or logical and some irrational, there is a tendency to logicalise irrational activity and make it seem logical. We must not fall into the dogma of the market economists, however, and over-rationalize human activity. We must recognize the value and influence of irrationalism—emotional belief systems, for example—in politics and economics. The social utility of a belief or theory is not coincident with its scientific, demonstrable truth.

How this austere aristocrat and Mussolini the street hustler would have got on is doubtful but unquestionably Pareto's rightist sociology could be used to justify Fascism, arguing the society is ruled in any case by an elite and democracy is a sham, and the highly emotional side of the Fascist program—its symbolism and political mysticism—accorded with social reality and human nature. It is thoroughly human to be a Fascist.

The Italian Benedetto Croce was an idealist philosopher arguing for historical Hegelianism against Marxism. With respect to politics itself Croce was centrist. Mussolini repeatedly tried to decorate him. Croce consistently did not attend the ceremonies scheduled on his behalf. But Croce did argue against Marxism.

Finally, among the right-wing intellectuals of the Mediterranean world, was Giovanni Gentile, who did attend Mussolini's ceremonies in order to receive his medals. Gentile argues for a coporatist Catholic state, which follows the lines of the precepts of French Fascists like Maurras and la Rochelle.

The Spanish General Francisco Franco was a right-wing Catholic militarist. There was indeed a Fascist movement in Spain called Falange, a radical, militant organization which was everything a rightist organization could be, including anti-Semitism in its program in a country which could not boast of a significant Jewish population. (The Jews were exiled from Spain in 1492.) The Falange supported Franco and his rightist military coup. Franco was a capable and clever man. His aim was to disarm the anarchists as well as the Communists, to centralize the government and the economy, to recover the Church's social influence in Spain and to regain the cultural life of the seventeenth century. Franco achieved everything he wanted. He was smart enough to keep Spain out of the War, in spite of Hitler's entreaties, so that the country could continue its political and cultural existence on more or less stable grounds.

Franco had two important problems. First, he could not figure out a means for industrializing Spain in a major way. Taking Spain culturally back to the age of the Bourbons did not provide a very efficient context for industrialization. Spaniards were praying and producing large families—none of which encouraged the penchant for economic progress. Secondly, like most military dictators, Franco could not devise the means to perpetuate his regime. Eventually, he gave in to the expedient of calling back the monarchy. After his death, the monarchy reinstituted the liberal constitution which Franco had sought to demolish.

In short, Spain went through tremendous turmoil between 1936 and the 1970's, and emerged from it approximately at the same point from which it had started. Now, it is facing the difficult tasks of modernizing industrially and absorbing twentieth-century culture, while trying to hold onto political unity.

The authoritative biography of Mussolini has been written by an Englishman, Dennis Mack Smith, which may say something about the dictator's reputation in his native country. Mack Smith, an Oxford professor, worked for thirty years on this book which finally appeared in 1985. According to Mack Smith, Mussolini was a fraud and a nihilist.

Mussolini actually began his political career as an effective socialist editor. He faced stiff opposition for leadership of the socialist party and above all Mussolini wanted to be *Il Duce*, the leader. He was also impressed with the following gained by the rightist activist poet Gabriele D'Annunzio. So in 1918 Mussolini switched over to a rightist, extreme nationalist position, dedicated to saving Italy from Communism and Marxism, ending the rule of inept liberal democratic governments, and above all giving glory in the world to the long-suffering and depressed Italian people. The Italians fought on the Allied side in the First World War. They endured heavy losses at the hands of the Austrians, and the rich compensation of reallocated Austrian territory they anticipated at the Versailles Peace Conference was only modestly granted. The Italian people were very disappointed that all those lives had been lost for so little and they were therefore susceptible to Mussolini's chauvinist rhetoric.

Mussolini gathered a group of discontented, demobilized veterans around him at a time when Italy was undergoing a deep depression. Under conditions of economic depression and national disappointment Mussolini found it easy to gather a few thousand toughs and criminals, to clad them in black shirts, announce they were Fascists, put on a Roman symbol, get on a train to Rome and make a *coup d'etat*. It is indicative of the nature of Italian Fascism that the Fascists arrived in Rome by train for their famous 1922 "March on Rome."

Mussolini was hospitable to the monarchy as well as to the church and to many industrialists. The Vatican, especially, welcomed him because he offered an alternative to the left. There was a disorganized but rather strong leftist movement in Italy, against which Mussolini offered comfort. He talked grandly about the corporatist state but did very little to improve the Italian economy. His philosopher companions like Gentile, who read and drew on French newspapers and journals to put together some ideas about what the aims of the new government would be, provided material for his eloquence. Aside from making long speeches from Roman balconies, Mussolini spent most of his time attending sporting events and indulging his insatiable appetite for women, food, and drink and talked confusedly about the military glory and the Communist danger. His career was one big fraud from beginning to end.

Mussolini's worst flaw was that he began to believe his own propaganda. He actually persuaded himself that Italy was a rising industrial power, that it had one of the greatest armies in Europe. Then, he witnessed, in anguish, the rise of Hitler. If Hitler had not come along, it is just as possible that Mussolini would have remained a bizarre interlude in Italian history, and would eventually have died of overeating and syphilis. The episode would have passed away as comic opera, had it not been for the advent of Hitler with the kind of substance that had eluded Mussolini.

In 1938 Mussolini established the Pact of Steel with Hitler. Although his generals warned Mussolini that they had a hard time fighting even the Ethiopians, let alone taking on the Allies, Mussolini did not heed them and blundered into war in 1940. The result was catastrophic. The Italian army could not even defeat the Greeks and the Yugoslavs. Mussolini was only kept in power by Hitler's support. Finally, in 1943, after the Allies had invaded Italy, even those closest to him forced his resignation. He was held in confinement in a winter resort, from which he was rescued by the German army which established him in a puppet regime in Northern Italy. Finally, in the spring of 1945, the Italian Communist partisans found Mussolini, shot him and his current mistress, and strung them up by their heels in Milan.

Mussolini was a megalomaniac poseur who left his country about as poor as he found it. During his regime, there was some industrial advance in the north, which would have occurred in any case, and Italian design—given impetus by Futurist art—moved to the front rank where it has stayed. Aside from a few bombastic buildings in Rome, there was no other legacy of his regime. Italian economic growth began in the fifties, with critical assistance from the United States.

Finally, there was Juan Perón, the right-wing dictator of Argentina in the forties and early fifties, who returned to power for a year and a half in the seventies. In 1945 the gross national product of Argentina was equal to that of Canada. Now it is about fifty percent of the GNP of Canada and is constantly falling. Perón is largely responsible for that.

Perón was an army colonel who belonged to a group of officers that carried out a military coup and then did not know what to do with the government they had seized. Perón was a populist, and appropriately found support in the labor unions and the peasantry. It was his idea to redistribute wealth. His government created innumerable artificial jobs. Merely a bulwark against the left, Perón was an extremely incompetent ruler. The only difference between him and Mussolini was that the Argentinian dictator had a very capable and determined wife—a former soap opera radio actress—who created a great image for herself among the people before she died of cancer. Eva Perón provided for much of the charismatic leadership during the early part of Perón's rule. Perón himself ruined the Argentinian economy, and demoralized the people, from which they have still not recovered.

*   *   *

Nazism and the Second World War

The literature on Nazism is vast and, as expected, a substantial part of the output is in German. In the mid-sixties the Germans began to publish furiously on this subject, which they still continue to do. Among the conclusions drawn from this research on Nazism is that there was such a thing as an intellectual component of Nazism. There were intellectuals, academics, scholars as well as serious writers, who generated views that were incorporated into Nazism. More than simply producing ideas for Nazism, many of these intellectuals also took active part in Nazi operations, either in an official capacity or privately.

Among the most important intellectual contributors to the rise of Nazism was Oswald Spengler, a flamboyant critic and writer who was famous in the 1920's as the author of *The Decline of the West*, a nine-hundred-page volume published shortly after the First World War. The book became a bestseller not only in Germany, but in the 1930's, in the English-speaking world as well. Spengler's name is not visible today, but between the two wars, it was prominent. All civilizations go through an organic cycle, Spengler tells us, and Western civilization has fallen into its winter of discontent; only charismatic leadership can save it.

Ernst Juenger was probably the most reflective and thoughtful among Nazi theorists, and the most comprehensive. He became the court intellectual. During the Nazi occupation of Paris, he was the designated intermediary between the occupying powers and the French right-wing intellectuals. Juenger is assumed to have played a key role in persuading the German commander of Paris in 1944 not to burn the city as the Allies were approaching. This was Juenger's main contribution to culture. He was a good European. Juenger's theory runs along the line of cultural order that appealed to T.S. Eliot.

Stefan George, the prominent German poet of the twenties, was the center of a right-wing intellectual circle. He is still regarded as a major lyric poet, albeit with a strong political bent in the direction of Fascism.

One of George's prime disciples was the flamboyant medievalist Ernst Kantorowicz, who enjoyed a wonderful career. His family were multimillionaire Prussian Jews, the Bronfmans of Germany, and dominated the whiskey business. Kantorowicz was close to Hermann Goering, the number two Nazi, although, being a Jew, he had to withdraw from professorial duties in 1934—the Nuremberg Laws of 1935 put an end to the scholarly careers of Jews. He continued to live in Berlin until 1938 and to draw a salary. Finally, he was persuaded by a prominent English academic who was visiting Berlin that his good fortune would not be long-lived and that he ought to leave Germany. He first went to Oxford, and, just as war broke out, to Berkeley.

Among Kantorowicz's many learned and imaginative volumes on medieval culture was a biography of Emperor Frederick II of Hohenstaufen; indeed this was his first book, and it created such a storm that it gained him a chair at a relatively young age. Young Kantorowicz's associations and opinions were extremely rightist; the book on Emperor Frederick has a swastika on the cover; the book ends with a hysterical call for a new great leader to save Germany.

In 1951 Kantorowicz was forced to resign his professorship at Berkeley during the famous "Loyalty Oath" controversy. In the fifties the California legislature required that all professors in the State University system swear an oath to show their innocence of Communism. Kantorowicz refused to swear the oath, finding that it violated academic freedom. He said that he had shot many Communists in Berlin in 1918 and 1919, which was true, and that he did not feel obliged to prove his loyalty. But he was nevertheless forced to resign. He then became professor at the Institute of Advanced Study at Princeton University as well as the recipient of numerous academic honors. Beyond doubt, Kantorowicz was a Nazi, as those who knew him personally could readily ascertain. Only the accident of his Jewish birth prevented Kantorowicz from ascending to the highest circles of the Nazi regime.

Percy Ernst Schramm, another important German medievalist, and probably the greatest medieval historian of the twentieth century, came from an old mercantile Hamburg family. He became an authority on medieval symbols of statecraft. He was certainly very closely involved with the Nazis, and was the official keeper of the war diaries of the German general staff. After the war, in 1952, he also published an edition of Hitler's table talk, a volume consisting of remarks Hitler made at dinner, presented with a rather laudatory introduction. One thing that must be admitted of Schramm is that he was unrepentant.

Another intellectual contributor to Nazism was Elizabeth Foerster, Nietzche's sister and his literary executor. She illicitly made Nietzsche the prophet of Nazism, interpreting his work so as to make him an advocate of a race of Aryan supermen who transcended moral standards and were free to push everyone else around. She even corrupted the text of Nietzsche's writings to make this Fascist message more unequivocal. The best scholarly opinion today is that while Nietzsche obviously had a repressive attitude towards women, and while he was sometimes careless in what he said, he was thinking of a transcendental group of intellectual, not physical or military over-men. Certainly Nietzsche was not a racist and he condemned his one-time colleague Richard Wagner for his anti-Semitic proclivity.

The philosopher Martin Heidegger, who without doubt was a Nazi collaborator for many years, has been discussed in a previous chapter, as has the psychoanalyst Carl Gustav Jung who had a short-lived flirtation with the Nazis.

What was there in Nazism that attracted these intellectuals? First among the factors historians enumerate is that of cultural despair. The cited intellectuals felt, in other words, that the traditions of Western civilization, the *Kultur*—a German word which may be rendered as "culture," but nevertheless remains untranslatable for its implications—were being destroyed by the rise of the masses, by technology, and by Communism and socialism, and the culture was on the ramparts, fighting for survival. Desperate times require desperate measures. They necessitated, so it seemed, the use of military force and the violent instruments of the state in order to repress the masses and bar the way of the Communist tide. The intellectuals who joined the Nazis shared this desperate vision of the future of Western culture.

Secondly, the intellectuals were antidemocratic. They believed that liberal democratic republics at best produced mediocrity, as in the case of England and the United States, and at worst, they produced chaos and disgrace, as in the case of the German Weimar Republic of the 1920's, which they saw as epitomizing the betrayal of national interest. Democratic politics were corrupt politics. It consisted of mean little men selling public interest for personal gain. Against such ills, the rule of an elite was needed, of learned, cultured people who were also physically superior, who were, in short, putative Nietzschean *overmen*, able to withstand the corruptions of democracy.

Thirdly, the Nazi intellectuals also shared the belief in the *Fuehrer Prinzip*, the leadership principle. In one way or another, each harbored visions of the great powerful leader who would be as charismatic and capable of controlling the masses as he would be able to activate the forces of the state in the interests of Western culture and national destiny. They shared a romantic faith in the advent of a leader in the great tradition of Charlemagne and Frederick Barbarossa, the medieval German emperor. In his person, in his heart, mind and body, this leader would be an expression of all that was best in Western culture and in the *Deutsches Volk*, the German people.

The fourth principle Nazi intellectuals commonly subscribed to was that of community and reintegration. They longed for an event that would reunite the German people, instead of being divisive, which was what democracy and socialism had been. Unification, reintegration, community were the desiderata, what the Germans called *Gemeinschaft*, that were pitted against the concept of atomizing society, or, *Gesellschaft*. The latter was conceived of as disorienting, disunited, selfish, whereas a *Gemeinschaft* would bring altruism, communality, unity, and join the people together in an endless chorus singing "Deutschland, ueber Alles."

The intellectuals thought they saw these qualities in the Nazi movement in the late twenties and early thirties. But they were not naive; they did not believe that the Nazi Party represented these ideas without qualification or without certain imperfections. Nevertheless, they did think that Nazism, the National Socialist Party, could develop a program disseminating and putting to work the ideas described above, and, in varying degrees, they committed themselves to the rising movement of national socialism.

These are the ideas that led intellectuals and scholars to support Nazism. What of the German people as a whole? Why did they in the elections of 1932 make Hitler the leader of the largest party in the German Parliament? The extensive research on this issue shows that while Nazism appeared to have special strengths among lower middle-class people and among Protestants rather than Catholics, support for Hitler was not class or group oriented. In roughly equal proportions Nazism gained adherents among all groups in German society. Support for Hitler in the early thirties appears to be more a psychological than a sociological phenomenon.

Hitler and the Nazi movement capitalized, to be sure, on the economic miseries of the Weimar Republic, but, far more important, they exploited the frustrated yearning for respect and dignity of all those who believed that in politics and society they were held in contemptuous disregard. The German soldier who returned from the front in World War I and had difficulty obtaining a job and keeping his head above water economically bore deep resentments. What impressed him above all was the ingratitude of the government. This experience accounts for the whining note that recurs constantly in these accounts of postwar personal struggles.

The German people, who were accustomed to regarding themselves as the salt of the earth who were supposed to dominate the twentieth century, found that the material and moral basis for their lives seemed to have vanished. Their indictment began to transcend purely political issues, and the suspicion grew that something was corrupt and rotten throughout German society, that a worm was not only eating away savings in the bank but also threatening to undermine family life, religious convictions, and moral standards. Many of the men who became activists in the Hitler movement were people who in normal times would have left politics and public life strictly alone, asking nothing more than to be allowed to rear their families and pursue their careers in tranquility.

The inability of the Weimar government to arouse confidence had many causes, which are lugubriously recited in all historical accounts of Nazism. There was the onerous burden of its "responsibility" for the Versailles Treaty, a myth that the republicans should have attacked at every opportunity—instead they allowed it to work its slow poison. There was also the inability to deal effectively with the Communist-led revolutions and strikes that plagued the government's early years. There were inflation and the painful question of reparations to the Allies.

But above all there was a critical psychological factor: the Weimar government was completely unable to establish any mystique. Republicanism in Germany had no roots, no traditions, to which it could appeal. There were no republican barricades in German history to which the government could hark back: no republican songs, no slogans like "Liberty, Equality, Fraternity." Indeed all the German traditions ran counter to republicanism; the German Republic's constitution was drafted at Weimar, but its capital was Prussian Berlin. The proliferation of postwar political parties and the resulting practice of political horse trading made the Weimar parliamentarians seem to be sordid political hustlers performing the continual sleight-of-hand tricks to stay in office, apparently striving for no higher goal than that of simply hanging on.

The frustrated idealism of the generation that had swallowed the exalted shibboleths of wartime propaganda could not endure this spectacle. The German bourgeois, who felt acutely his own insignificance, his own precarious hold on a livelihood, his own inadequacy at coping with defeat and the Depression, had no wish to see his own miserable struggles mirrored among the men who ruled Germany. The scorn that fell on the Weimar officials was an elaborate form of displaced self-hatred. The German people craved for strong and confident leadership.

In contrast to the tired, confused men of the Weimar government, the stress on youth in Germany of the 1920's became an ideology in itself, something of a fetish in fact, which Hitler was to incorporate as part of the Fascist image. German students, after the war as before it, sang paens of praise to the *Volk*, the great German people pure and simple in heart. Before the war the quest for the unspoiled *Volk* had produced activity of the sort that goes on anywhere when a people is in compulsive pursuit of its roots. Many folk songs had been resurrected for performance around campfires. Students had organized long hikes to explore the verdant beauties of pastoral Germany. Sports and gymnasiums were in fashion, and ancient pagan holidays like the feast of summer solstice had been self-consciously celebrated. These quasi-mystical celebrations of the *Volk* all looked toward the great "spiritual revolution" that the students and young people were supposed to be preparing. The myth of a great German, or Aryan, race was already blossoming.

Anti-Semitism was the perfect foil for the neo-romantic kind of political and social thought which characterized the youth groups. Before the war they had conducted soul-searching debates on whether or not Jews were themselves a *Volk* and whether or not they could ever be sufficiently assimilated to become part of the German *Volk*. The verdict had been various, though in the main negative. Around the turn of the century a fierce debate had taken place on whether or not Jews could participate in the time-honored university practice of dueling, the question revolving around whether or not Jews had any honor to defend. Jews were excluded from most fraternities, and in some universities the creation of Jewish fraternities was looked upon as a provocative act. Periodically petitions would circulate in the classrooms, asking that Jews be excluded from government jobs and the professions.

But it was during the Weimar period that "the Jewish question" came to assume a kind of absolute prominence. The regeneration of the *Volk* had once been the main motivation of the "youth movement"; a number of its leaders had looked upon the wrangle over Jews as merely an annoying distraction from the main task. They had wanted the self-consciousness of the German *Volk* to develop not merely negatively—that is, in opposition to Jews—but positively, through a rediscovery of roots, customs, and traditions.

During the Weimar period the old groups that had insisted on the importance of the folk dances, idyllic rambles in the countryside, and celebrations of festivals came to be regarded as naive and obsolete. They lost members to the more strident activist organizations. Anti-Semitism was no longer a subject for debate; it had become axiomatic, part of the dogma. The anti-Semitic obsession was exacerbated by general disrespect for the government, which was supposed to be riddled with Jews. Anti-Semitic riots became frequent in German universities in the 1920's.

The Nazis were infinitely rich and imaginative in symbolism, mythology, and pageantry. They had insignia, songs, slogans, salutes, and uniforms, the function of which was not so much to convince as to bewitch. The most famous symbol, the swastika, came from the Free Corps, a gang of terrorist army and navy officers who in 1918–19 assassinated Communists in Berlin, including Rosa Luxemburg. (Ernst Kantorowicz was a member of the Free Corps.) The red color of the Nazi flag came from socialism and the blood of soldiers. The salute came from Italian Fascism and, according to legend at least, from ancient Rome. The fervent "Heil" came from beer halls and ancient public gatherings. When Hitler spoke on public stages—at the annual Nuremburg rallies, for example—the production trappings assaulted the senses as if they were a part of a Hollywood extravaganza. The Nazi rallies were carefully choreographed and in the 1930's filmed by a woman director of genius, Leni Riefenstahl, nowadays much admired by feminists and film-makers. Thousands of torches held aloft by devout youngsters from the Hitler Youth groups lined the routes of march. Wagnerian music preceded the speeches.

Despite the essential paganism of Nazi philosophy, traditional religion was pressed into service, and Nazi speakers in small towns regularly found priests and Lutheran ministers sharing their platforms. The whole panoply of bourgeois fetishes was brought onto the political platform. The family, the sanctity of the home, and motherhood were invoked. (Hitler once promised an audience that under National Socialism every German girl would find a husband.) Politicians of other parties talked politics, but the Nazis talked about the whole man—his family, his fireside, his pocketbook, his vague aspirations to status and glory, his inchoate religious sentiments, his sense of decency.

Above all, Nazi speakers skillfully played on the deepest fears of German families: their fears of drowning in a Red bloodbath, of being unmanned, castrated by French imperialists, of losing golden-haired daughters to inferior races. (Julius Streicher, a fanatical early Hitler supporter, made his career as a journalist by "exposing" Jewish sexual crimes.) The Nazis tapped them all. While other parties spoke of interest and expediency the Nazis spoke of blood and race and thus summoned up what Joseph Conrad once called "fierce mouthings from pre-historic ages." The mysterious and formidable powers of ancient and other rituals, of "blood" and "soil," were constantly evoked by the Nazis.

This kind of appeal served the purpose of making National Socialism seem very much more than a mere political party. Hitler never liked the word "party." He led, he said, a "movement" that was in fact nothing less than the efflorescence of the ancient Aryan soul. He was no scurvy politician. He did not *represent* any group or individual, he claimed; rather he *embodied* the essence of German man. That was the secret of the Nazi leadership principle. It enabled Hitler to boast, years after he had come to power, that he was like a tree rooted in the people, deriving his existence and his sustenance from them. According to this formulation, Hitler was nothing less than Frederick Barbarossa, the German King Arthur, the once and future king who wakes now and then in the course of history and rouses his slumbering people, summoning them to their destiny and glory. During the Weimar years the Nazis appropriated all the best German myths.

Millions of Germans echoed Joseph Goebbels, Hitler's propaganda minister, who wrote in his diary, "Adolf Hitler, I love you because you are both great and simple." In the 1870's the historian Jacob Burckhardt, the friend of Nietzsche, had warned against the coming of the terrible simplifiers of the twentieth century. The warning was prophetic. Hitler was the most terrible simplifier of all. Hitler promised the German people that under National Socialism Germany would again enjoy wealth and power. The irreconcilable antagonisms between bankers and ditch diggers would be reconciled. When economists or generals produced blueprints of insurmountable obstacles, Hitler said to hell with them all. Versailles had produced maps of Germany's borders, but they had only to be torn up. Hitler recognized no borders. All obstacles could be effaced through struggle, through a determined effort of the will. The Nazi ascent to power was "the triumph of the will." Any obstacle could be surmounted by will. The German army could invade Russia in June of 1941 without a supply of winter clothing and be in Moscow before the snow fell. All it took was a supreme act of will.

This philosophy conformed exactly to Hitler's own experience. From the penniless derelict at the Vienna Home for Men he had risen to be Chancellor of Germany. Struggle, effort, and will power were at the center of Hitler's political creed. He impressed the exaltation of struggle on his followers and disciples. His was a philosophy of self-reliance applied collectively to the German people, or the Aryan race. It declared directly and brutally that there were no barriers, no anonymous and transcendent powers to limit and curb human potential. To still any final doubts, Hitler confided to his followers that they were part of a Nietzschean super race, that their triumph was preor-dained. German man was Prometheus unbound, and conquest was the test of virtue.

"That man for chancellor? I'll make him a postmaster and he can lick stamps with my head on them," old President Hindenburg is reputed to have said after his first meeting with Hitler in August 1932. But within two years Hitler and the Nazis had carried out a *Gleichschaltung* ("coordination"), a euphemism for state terrorism that eliminated all effective opposition. The only limits on the power of the Nazi dictatorship were internal to the regime itself—the constant struggles for power and privilege among party factions, the army, and the civil service.

At 8:00 P.M. on August 31, 1939, the German army faked a Polish attack on a German radio station. At dawn on September 1, German guns began to fire on Poland. The British Chamberlain government characteristically delayed sending an ultimatum to Berlin until the morning of September 3. The ultimatum expired that day at 11:00 A.M., and Britain at once declared war on Germany. France declared war on Germany at 5:00 in the afternoon.

The military struggle that began with Germany's Polish campaign was to reach a magnitude undreamed of by the diplomats of the interwar era or even generals of World War I. Tens of millions of men were to be engaged in campaigns in Europe, on the Asian mainland, on scores of Pacific islands, in North Africa, on the oceans, and in the air over much of the world. The amount of strategic materials produced and expended and the number of civilian and military casualties suffered would have seemed absolutely beyond the powers of the nations of the 1930's to survive.

Yet if the taking of human life can ever be justified, the Second World War was a just war—it prevented Europe, and perhaps the world, from falling under Nazi control. It must be remembered that in 1940 Hitler's triumph seemed highly likely. If Britain, like France, had betrayed its heritage and made peace with Hitler, the end of Western civilization might have been the result. It is to the eternal credit of the British that, rallied by a conservative from one of the first families of the British aristocracy, they chose to fight on, alone and against seemingly hopeless odds. As Churchill said, this was his country's "finest hour." What Churchill said of the R.A.F. fighter pilots in the Battle of Britain can be said of Great Britain's role in World War II: Never have so many owed so much to so few.

The main consequence of the Second World War was that it brought to a climax the trend that had begun in the First: Western Europe's power and influence in the world declined and global leadership passed to the Soviet Union and the United States. In 1945, Germany was in ashes, Japan thoroughly beaten, Britain exhausted and impoverished, France and Italy confused and demoralized. Victory lay with the United States and the Soviet Union. They were to be the superpowers of the postwar world.

The Second World War was called by Arthur Koestler, the ex-Communist novelist, a struggle "between a lie and a half-lie." More accurately, it has been called the last good war, the last war in which the West, and particularly the British and the Americans, had no doubt who was in the right. Italy entered the war in May of 1940 to participate in the spoils of Europe that were accruing to Hitler. Japan, which had come under the rule of an expansionist military clique in the 1930's, entered the war with the bombing of Pearl Harbor, "the day of infamy," on December 7, 1941.

Japan entered the war for two reasons. First, their German allies urged them to do so, so as to distract the Americans who had been giving extensive aid to Britain since 1939 and were thought by Hitler to be certain to come into the war sooner or later. Secondly, Japan's military expansion in China as well as Japan's intention to dominate the East Asian economy were opposed by the Roosevelt government. In retrospect, Roosevelt's judgment was laughable: by preventing Japan from taking control of China, he prepared the way for the Maoist Communists to do so in 1948. And Japan now dominates much more than the East Asian economy—good chunks of the U.S. economy as well. The Japanese did not seriously believe that they could defeat the Americans and the British. They aimed at getting spectacular early victories, which they did, and then holding on while Hitler won at least a negotiated peace in Europe. The Japanese were wrong about the German military capability, and they underrated the Americans. At the sea battle of Midway in May of 1942, the Americans—helped by phenomenal good luck—so badly crippled the Japanese fleet that the Japanese were immediately put on the defensive and slowly forced to yield their conquests in a half-forgotten war of incredible savagery.

The European War was the greatest military struggle in history. After the surrender of France in June of 1940 Hitler ruled a united Europe from Warsaw to the Channel Islands. While there were pockets of bitter resistance, especially in Holland and Denmark, the great majority of European people readily accomodated themselves to Hitler's New Order. Hitler offered a generous peace to the British, allowing their defeated army to escape from Dunkirk, France, and then promising Churchill Britain could retain its Empire (and even get pieces of French overseas territory) if Britain would make peace, and allow Hitler unimpeded to start his crusade against Bolshevik Russia. Although Churchill's advisors informed him explicitly that Britain's economic position would be ruined by a protracted war, Churchill told the Parliament and people he would never surrender and the British should never make peace with Hitler.

Frustrated in his plan to divide the world among the two Saxon races, Hitler turned his attention to Stalinist Russia and his armored divisions plunged into the Soviet heartland in June of 1941. Having purged and murdered his generals in 1938, Stalin was in no shape to fight the German army. Even puny Finland had been a formidable foe for the Red Army in a war during 1939–40. Stalin, much more appeasing of Hitler than Chamberlain had ever been, desperately sought to forestall war by shipping immense quantities of oil and metal to Germany. Even when war began, Stalin was indecisive for several weeks.

The Germans were within sight of Moscow and already fighting in the suburbs of Leningrad when the Russian winter descended unusually early in late October, 1941, and the advance came to a halt. The Germans had expected an early *Blitzkrieg* victory as in France; they were not prepared for a winter conflict.

Initially, many Soviet minorities, especially the Ukranian peasants who had suffered so terribly at Stalin's hands, welcomed the German army but Nazi rule turned out to be even more savage and bloody than Communist rule and the Soviet peoples rallied behind Stalin in the Great Patriotic War. Under the leadership of General Andrei Zhukov and other young generals who had learned their trade on the field of battle, the Russians fought back, although suffering incredible losses—so many, in fact, that the Soviet government has never revealed how many soldiers it lost in World War II: the figure is assuredly in excess of ten million. With tremendous national zeal and aid from the United States, the Soviet army slowly gained the upper hand. In the winter 1942–43, an army of 600,000 Germans was wiped out at Stalingrad on the Volga. In July of 1943, the Battle of Kurz, the largest tank battle in history (until the Battle of the Golan Heights in 1973), fought on the central plains near Minsk, was a draw but the Germans could not replace the devastating losses to their vaunted armored brigade. Germany was now a crippled giant and it was only a matter of time before the German resistance would collapse.

Western Allied victories in North Africa and Italy were of modest consequence compared to the Soviet triumph. Finally the Allies invaded Normandy, France on June 6, 1944, liberated Paris by August and pushed on to the Rhine. The Allied leaders and Stalin had agreed to accept only unconditional surrender, so Hitler and the Nazis fought on, hoping some miracle would save them. (As a matter of fact if the development of the ballistic missile—the V-2— and jet fighter by the Germans had come a year earlier and German physicists had made an atom bomb, the outcome might have been different.) German cities were leveled, ten million Germans were killed, eight million on the battlefield or in Soviet prison camps (the Germans on their side also let Soviet prisoners starve to death) and two million civilians before Hitler perished in his bunker under the Berlin Chancellory in April 1945.

The German defeat was by no means inevitable. Not only did Hitler come close to getting operative a ballistic missile (intra- if not inter- continental) with a possible atomic warhead. If he had not waited until 1943 to mobilize fully German industry and manpower, the war might have ended in his favor or at least in a forced negotiated peace. But Hitler had promised the German people in 1939 that the war would not be hard on them and until the middle of 1943—when he turned over industrial production to a brilliant engineer and manager, the architect Albert Speer—he pretended that the war was not interfering with German consumption of Volkswagens and Wienerschnitzel. This was his great error. Exterminating millions of Jewish skilled workers whom Speer badly needed in his slave labor factories was also severely damaging to the German war effort.

One thing Hitler had in abundance—a marvellous collection of superior generals, such as Erwin Rommel, who fought the Allies in North Africa to a standstill for two years with inferior armaments and personnel, and Heinz Guderian, perhaps the best tank commander in history, who rolled up the French defenses in May of 1940. The British lacked a first-rate general in the war (Bernard Montgomery was largely a P.R. stunt); the Americans had only one, Patton, who was unfortunately a psychotic paranoid, and the Russsians three or four. The Japanese had a naval commander of genius, Admiral Yamamoto, who planned and executed the Pearl Harbor attack, as well as some very good generals.

What the Allies had was the inexhaustible supply of Russian manpower and the incomparable dynamism of US industrial production. Even great generals could not overcome these long odds—Hitler, Mussolini, and the Japanese leaders all greatly underrated American military potential because they could not extrapolate from a depressed American industry to its full potential, and because in any case they believed Americans were too soft and peaceful a people to maximize their military capacity. By the end of 1942 it was evident the Fascist powers had made a fatal error.

*   *   *

Fascism and Modernism

As historians look back at the wild events and carnage in Germany, Italy, France, Spain, and possibly also Japan in the thirties and forties, a historiographical debate has raged for three decades as to what was the general pattern that occurred in that time and place—what exactly was Fascism?

The term Fascism is derived from *fasces*, the double-headed axe that was a symbol of state power in the Roman Empire and which Mussolini took as the symbol of his movement. A skeptical nominalist point of view on Fascism holds that the term is applicable only to Mussolini and his black-shirted followers. There are too many differences, it is said, with what was going on in other countries to use the term Fascism generically. Hitler and his followers for instance, called themselves National Socialists (abbreviated as Nazis); Fascism had no official standing as a term in Germany. A second view of Fascism holds that there never was a genuine ideology of that name anywhere. In various countries in the thirties and forties particular groups of militarists, gangsters, and terrorists sought power. These criminal gangs grasped pragmatically at any array of hysterical pronouncements to screen and justify their dreadful terror activities but there were no Fascist movements, only individual dictators and gangster followers.

A third view, to which we subscribe, holds that there was indeed a sociological phenomenon called Fascism and as such the phenomenon in appropriate circumstances endures. Granted that the word originated in Italy and that not all Fascist movements liked to use the term applied to themselves; granted that criminal activities were frequently involved and that ideology was often used cynically as a screen. Fascism was nevertheless a general phenomenon applicable to and an ideology determining political movements in various places and even in other times than the thirties and forties.

Fascism was a subset of rightist political culture, just as Stalinism was a political subset of the left. Fascism embraced all the eight rightist traditions we have spoken of, although its use of rationalism and classicism, and of formalism, was distinctive and highly manipulative. Fascism stressed inequality, militarism, the leadership principle, and anti-Semitism. When these traditions are joined with a particularly ruthless and violent kind of behavior, Fascism is in place, whether in Europe in the 1930's or Latin America in the 1980's. All systems of power provide an opportunity for corruption and looting of public resources; Fascism's proclivity in this regard is especially pronounced, but not unique. Nor is mass murder unique to Fascism; we have seen it also occur in Stalinism.

To say that Fascism is a subset of rightist culture and that it is founded upon rightist doctrines does not make others on the right responsible for Fascism any more than others on the left are responsible for Stalinism. Winston Churchill and Hilton Kramer are no more responsible for Auschwitz or recent rightist terrorism in Argentina than Walter Benjamin, Harold Laski, and Juergen Habermas for the Gulag.

Fascism emerged in the era of high Modernism in the 1920's. What was the relationship between the two movements? How did these two cultural phenomena positively or negatively affect each other?

There are clear points of contact between Fascism and Modernism. Firstly, both had deep respect for twentieth-century technology as well as for the novel technocratic, advanced industrial society. Fascism is a peculiar combination of efforts to restore nineteenth century mentalities, such as Romanticism and social Darwinism, within the framework of the modern technocratic state, which makes for an explosive fusion. Whereas the details of this view can be debated, Modernism and Fascism clearly share a fascination with technocracy. This appreciation manifests itself in two special ways in Fascism.

It was in the period of Italian Fascism that this country's important contribution to modern design was inaugurated. Probably the only legacy of Mussolini's Italy is the design industry in clothing and automobiles that developed in Milan under Fascist rule.

Similarly, the medium favored by the Nazis was film. The great propaganda films produced by Leni Riefenstahl—among which *The Triumph of the Will*, a documentation of a grand Nazi meeting, deserves special mention—were in the vanguard of their day and are paradigmatic not only for modern political art but as well in terms of motifs which are still at work in advertising today. The lighting techniques were especially subtle in Nazi films. The Nazis were not interested in books, except to burn them. Their interest rested with media developed by modern technology. The German film industry very much flourished under Nazi rule.

The second way in which Modernism and Fascism may be deemed compatible is their adherence to moral relativism. Although it did not entirely eliminate it, Modernism certainly eroded nineteenth-century normative ethics, whose standards, right or wrong, were deconstructed in Modernist thought. Much more radical than Modernism in this respect, Nazism did not have any faith whatsoever in normative ethics. Insofar as the Nazis subscribed to a moral system, it was that of power, violence and of a Master Race. Traditional moral standards, which prohibited violence, murder and genocide, went, needless to say, unrecognized by them. The moral relativism of Modernism does overlap, it must be admitted, with the moral nihilism of Fascism.

Thirdly, particularly in its psychoanalytic mode, Modernism recognizes the reality of sado-masochism in human nature. It admits that every individual has such tendencies, undeniably, and this constitutes one more trait that Nazism cultivates and shares with Modernism. Nor did Nazism only cultivate sado-masochistic tendencies, it exhibited them; it was proud of them. The Nazis built upon the sado-masochistic reality in human nature, which psychoanalysis had revealed, in order to legitimize the violence that was typical to them.

Fourthly, the Expressionist stream in Modernism valorized the beautiful moment, the climactic moment, one of whose streaks was violence. Also, it stressed blood, both as a visual figure which was a frequent motif in Expressionist art, and as a theme of reflection. The blood philosophy, the conception of blood as capable of spurting forth an ineffable moment of creativity, which existed in the Expressionist movement of the 1920's, and which was particularly strong in the writings of D.H. Lawrence and W.B. Yeats, recurs in Fascism.

Another common element Fascism and Modernism share is nonsense, or irrationalism. The rejection of traditional rational modes of thinking and representation, which is the basis of the Dadaist and Surrealist streams in Modernism, the fascination with chaos and the dominion of nonsense, are fundamental to Fascist culture. The rule of un-reason and of nonsense, therefore, is another priority Fascism and Modernism, at least in its Expressionist branch, have in common. Mussolini's career itself, from the time he marched on Rome in 1922, to the time he was hanged by partisans in 1945, exemplifies Dadaism to its fullest. His career contained nothing sincere or planned. It was spontaneous as well as phoney, one big rule of unreason from beginning to end.

Finally, Fascism and Modernism had a proclivity for the "thick point," that once again returns to the notion of the ineffable moment, in which the great personality and creativity congregate at the right time, and which makes for beauty, vitality, and joy. The result is one terrible moment of construction and destruction and violence. Here one can recognize that notion, equally dear to Modernism, of the thick, microcosmic, reductionist, and therefore, significant, moment. This Modernist conception is imitated in Fascism, albeit in caricature form, but it is the same notion nevertheless. The moment of the emergence of Hitler, of the Fuehrer who embodied, so to speak, one thousand years of German history, and who promised glory to Germans as he promised the destruction of the world, paradoxically foretelling liberation through violence, and the achievement of truth and beauty in the very act of destroying—for so Nazi ideology described it—finds a corresponding articulation in Modernism's concept of the microcosmic thick point.

However, it could be claimed with equal validity that on the other hand many features of Fascism are in conflict with those of Modernism. For Fascism was historical, and further, retold history in mythological terms. All Fascist movements, whether French, Italian or German, were historicist, and its kind of history was mythic rather than academic. Fascist thought was neo-Victorian. It believed in telling stories and in narrative art. It was opposed to nonrepresentational Modernist art, which it regarded as decadent.

In its approach to culture Fascism was populist, whereas Modernism was elitist. Even though Fascism believed in the rule of a political elite, the culture it propounded was that of ordinary, middle-class folk. The music, art and literature it favored were predominantly neo-Victorian. Therefore, while on the one hand Fascism gained from and capitalized on Modernism, and to a degree it became a terrible, deadly caricature of Modernism, on the other hand, in its historicism, neo-Victorianism, subscription to the narrative in art and to populism in cultural policy, it was antithetical to Modernism. It thereby helped to dam the advancing tide of Modernism in the 1930's.

Since Hitlerian Berlin was reduced to rubble in 1945, very little is now visible in Germany that is a legacy of Nazi culture. The best example, and one that shows the ambivalent relationship to Modernism, is Carl Orff's oratorio, *Carmina Burana*, first performed before an appreciative Nazi audience in 1937. Orff's music, if not atonal, is certainly in the expressionist, tone-poem mood, and there is a threnody of violence running through the work. The text, however, is a cycle of medieval student poems. Yet this historicism is artificial and in conflict with the music which could scarcely be less medieval. Its pulsating rhythms make us think of storm troopers and tanks, not medieval clerics and students. The words are essentially meaningless in this context, a mere mythic pretext; the burden of Orff's work lies in the remarkable music which sounds Modernist and like a military band at the same time.

Not only in Russia was the Second World War the Great Patriotic War. It was that too in Britain, the United States, and beginning in the summer of 1944, in France as well. For those not in the front lines or under Nazi rule, the War was in many respects a salutary event. The bitterness, poverty, and divisiveness of the thirties was replaced by national solidarity, good feelings about vicariously participating in a just war for freedom and human dignity, and in the case of the United States at least, full employment and unprecedented prosperity. The historicist, macrocosmic, and rigidly moralistic ambience of the War years ran directly counter to the Modernist mentality. Joined with central ingredients in Marxism and Fascism, revived neo-Victorian mentality during the War weakened and dispersed the Modernist movement.

Modernism persisted as a mentality and style of importance in the arts and humanities. It by no means disappeared—in architecture and painting for example, Modernism had a long way to go and analytic philosophy only reached its peak of influence in the postwar academic world. But Modernism as a broad-fronted cultural revolution was enervated in the thirties by Marxism and Fascism and was all but halted by the wartime ambience of historicism, patriotism, and nationalism.

*   *   *

The Emergence of Colossal Science

The Japanese continued to fight on after the end of the war against Germany in April, 1945. The Pacific conflict ended only after the U.S. Air Force dropped atomic bombs on Hiroshima and Nagasaki in August of 1945. Although almost universally applauded at the time, the atomic bombing of Japan has been a matter of great controversy since the mid-sixties. It was then revealed that some of the most distinguished physicists who had worked on the bomb, including Niels Bohr and Hans Bethe, later a Nobel laureate at Cornell, had after the German surrender urged that the atomic bomb project not be carried through to its terrible fruition, or at most, that a public demonstration of this unprecedented weapon be made and that the Japanese, after such a demonstration, be given the chance to surrender before it was used against them. (It was also disclosed that Nagasaki was the most Christian city in Japan and that it was only marginally a military target; Nagasaki was in fact only a fallback secondary target when the first choice was obscured by cloud cover).

The American government under its new president Harry Truman—who knew nothing of the atom bomb project until Roosevelt died in April 1945, a few days before Hitler—refused to listen to the dissident minority of physicists. When Bohr tried to appeal to Churchill, he was almost arrested. The official American view then and since was that the Pacific War had been an extremely costly one in American lives, that the Japanese had fought with incomparable ferocity, that the Japanese had been given ample opportunity to surrender but that the fanatical militarist clique in power since the early thirties was unmoved, and that not even the savage fire-bombing of Tokyo had brought about a Japanese collapse, that although the Japanese navy was virtually eliminated by 1945, Japan had many millions of experienced soldiers still under arms, and that the projected invasion of the imperial homeland would cost a million American lives. There was no alternative except the dropping of the bomb on Japan. A demonstration project on some uninhabited Pacific island would solve nothing: the Japanese fanatical militarists would not be impressed and no one knew whether the bomb would actually detonate. The bomb had to be dropped on a Japanese city for the dawning of a new era of military terror to be proved.

The contrary point of view laments the catastrophic impact on civilians in the two Japanese cities, and raises the question of whether a racist contempt for Asiatics was involved. It contends that the Japanese would have surrendered in at most a few weeks, possibly a few days, that the nuclear explosions were militarily unnecessary to end the Pacific War, that the real purpose of Hiroshima and Nagasaki was to impress and frighten the Russians, whose aggressive behavior in Central Europe in the Spring of 1945 had angered the Allies in what was the opening phase of what became the Cold War. Since nobody knows whether or not the Japanese would have surrendered without the atomic detonations—not even the Emperor knows, as he was before Hiroshima unsuccessfully trying to convince the militarists to agree to surrender—there is no way to resolve this interminable dispute.

Hiroshima not only inaugurated a new era in warfare that has threatened the future of the human race on this planet (the Russians had an atom bomb within a half dozen years under the leadership of Rutherford's disciple Peter Kapitsa and with the help of captured German physicists). Not only were the bombs used against the Japanese dwarfed by the hydrogen bomb developed by the U.S. by 1952 (and almost as quickly by the Soviets). The coming of age of nuclear war had the paradoxical effect of impeding the two superpowers from going to war against each other in the following decades at such moments of bitter conflict as the Cuban missile crisis of 1962 when errors in judgment on the part of both the Russian leader Nikita Khrushchev and U.S. President Kennedy brought the two countries into a position of direct confrontation, Khrushchev backing down and ruining his own political career.

Nuclear armaments meant that a U.S.-Soviet war would be the end of civilization as we know it, or worse; therefore the two countries could not bring themselves to press the nuclear button, and the Cold War never became a shooting war. Indeed the last two decades have seen an uneven but persistent easing of tensions and periods of actual détente or improvement in relations. Without the atom bomb, relying on so-called conventional weapons, it is likely that a Soviet-American armed conflict, such as in 1962, would have occurred. Here is an instance of the altruism of reciprocal selfishness.

The atom bomb also signaled the inauguration of a new age of colossal science. The labs in which British and German physicists had achieved nuclear fission in the twenties and thirties and made atomic warfare possible were incredibly puny affairs by later standards: they would not pass muster today at a good American college or even an affluent suburban high school. The monstrous Manhattan Project that made the atom bomb (beginning indeed in Manhattan at Columbia, migrating to a lab under an abandoned football stadium in Chicago; then to specially-created, secret international colonies of physicists and their families in Oak Ridge, Tennessee, and Los Alamos, New Mexico, with a subsidiary operation in Hanford, Washington) completely changed the way applied scientific research was done.

Now it was to involve vast establishments, usually but not exclusively on or contiguous to university campuses, and billions of dollars of annual government expenditure. It was to involve so-called peer review which meant in practice that a handful of established scientists decided how the government support for research should be distributed. And it involved close association between scientists on the one side and military and corporate worlds on the other.

Ten years after the war, the most powerful person on a university campus was certainly not the harrassed and overworked prexy, not even the football coach, but the Nobel laureate physicist. Colossal science was as important as a Rose Bowl football championship in establishing a university's national prestige. When the faculty of the University of California at Berkeley—which had been founded in a vegetable field at the turn of the century—was revealed around 1960 to have as many Nobel Laureates as the whole of Britain, its stature equivalent to Harvard, Princeton, and M.I.T. was confirmed.

The Manhattan Project taught scientists how to organize their collective endeavors. It is salutary to compare the making of the atom bomb with the one previous effort at colossal science in the United States, the making of the first cyclotron atom-smasher by Ernest Lawrence at Berkeley in 1937–38. He raised a million dollars (more than ten million in 1986 dollars) and recruited a large team. But Lawrence based his machine on a diagram of a model built by a German physicist. Unfortunately, Lawrence could not read German, and he did not realize that in the text accompanying the diagram, the German physicist admitted that his model was not operational. Neither did Lawrence's cyclotron work.

The Manhattan Project's success was due to the scientific and/or managerial genius of four tempestuous personalitites: Robert Oppenheimer, Leslie Grove, Enrico Fermi, and Edward Teller, although many others, including some British scientists transported to America (one was a Soviet spy, it later transpired) were involved. Oppenheimer was a brooding megalomaniac genius, an American trained in Germany and a professor at Berkeley, who had never up to this point fulfilled the high expectations held of him. He was the intellectual leader of the project, but he also exhibited superb leadership capacity and surprising managerial skill. Leslie Grove was an army engineer who was the managerial head of the project. Without his patience, tact, humor, and wisdom nothing much would have happened. He chose Oppenheimer to head the scientific research in spite of hysterical warnings from the FBI that Oppenheimer's extremely neurotic wife was an ex-communist and his brother was a communist. Fermi made the most important scientific discoveries establishing the immediate feasibility of the bomb. He left Italy, where he was the premiere physicist because Mussolini, after his ill-fated pact with Hitler in

1938, was pressured by the Nazis into anti-Semitic legislation, and Fermi's wife was Jewish. Teller was a mercurial Hungarian Jewish refugee and an applied researcher of unsurpassed capability. The relations between him and Oppenheimer were always tense. After the war Teller wanted to press on to make a hydrogen bomb, while Oppenheimer demurred. Teller denounced Oppenheimer, by that time director of Einstein's Institute for Advanced Study in Princeton, to the authorities and after a lengthy and highly controversial investigation, Oppenheimer lost his security clearance, which meant he no longer could work for his country.

After the expenditure of billions of dollars (Truman perhaps had no choice but to conclude the Manhattan Project at Hiroshima since this unprecedented secret expenditure eventually had to be justified to Congress) and the most intense labor by a small army of physicists and engineers, these four leaders of the project were successful. What Oppenheimer called the Day of Trinity occurred in the New Mexican desert in July of 1945 when an experimental bomb was detonated before a group of stunned scientists and military, followed three weeks later by the dropping of "Fat Man" on Japan.

Along with nuclear physicists, the pressure and opportunities of the wartime ambience also transformed medicine and biochemistry with the deployment of penicillin, the first effective antibiotic, to save the lives of hundreds of thousands of wounded men. Penicillin was discovered in a mold in the laboratory of a London biochemist Alexander Fleming as early as 1928. Fleming had an unusual approach to research; he believed in serendipity, that is, he never cleaned his lab, hoping that in the mess, something important would spontaneously be generated. After severe and rapid changes in temperature in London while Fleming was on summer vacation he returned to find this peculiar mold with unprecedented germkilling capacity. The problem was to synthesize penicillin, that is to make it artificially and in such quantities that it could be used in medical practice. This was accomplished by Ernest Chain and a team of researchers at Oxford in 1938. Chain offered his discovery to the British pharmaceutical industry; they were unwilling to take the risk of the huge investment involved in setting up new factories to manufacture penicillin. Realizing the potential for his new discovery among the wounded of the fast approaching war (in World War I, wounded soldiers died almost as miserably as in the Napoleonic Wars) Chain turned to America and found there the entrepreneurial attitude, risk capital, and the engineering skill required to make penicillin the miracle drug of World War II.

The coming of antibiotics revolutionized medical practice. Since the emergence of anesthesia and antiseptic surgery in the 1870's and psychoanalysis, there had been no major medical advance until the 1940's. In the thirties doctors still spent most of their time comforting dying patients they could not cure. Bedside manner, not science, characterized the medical profession. Antibiotics, headed by penicillin, changed all that. Medicine entered its modern, golden age. Doctors could actually fight disease and save patients. Medicine was henceforth built on extensive, often government supported, and like nuclear physics, very costly research.

In terms of applied science and technology, the success of the Manhattan

Project and the discovery of synthesized penicillin seemed to mean that Sir Francis Bacon's seventeenth-century vision of man's rational power over nature had been realized. It now appeared, in the postwar years, that with sufficient resources, scientists could put together teams of researchers that could do anything: build the hydrogen bomb, discover a vaccine for the dread disease of polio or an oral contraceptive that would alter sexual and family life for billions of people, carry out heart and organ transplants. It remains to be seen whether AIDS is similarly susceptible to massive scientific research.

These breakthroughs incomparably elevated the position of scientists not only on university campuses but on national horizons. In 1930, humanists still seemed to be in the same league as their colleagues in physics and biology departments. By 1970, scientists were operating in a separate dimension of intellect, power, and wealth. This was one of the major cultural consequences of the Second World War, one of the unforseen legacies of the Fascist era.

*   *   *

Expiation and the Revival of the Right

The left in the Western world took no responsibility for Stalinism and except for the United States during the Cold War in the 1950's, lost no ground therefrom. The right, on the contrary, was severely damaged by Fascism, the Holocaust and the Second World War that Fascism was reasonably held to have engendered. The two decades after the War were a period of expiation and penance for the right, and to some extent for Western Europe as a whole.

This expiation occurred in four directions: the ending of European militarism; the dissolution of the European empires; the creation and rise of the State of Israel; and the modernization and democratization of the Roman Catholic Church.

The great European wars had disturbed the human universe in the first half of the twentieth century. Amid the ashes of European and especially German cities in 1945, the determination arose: Never Again! At least not in our lifetime. The Europeans henceforth devoted themselves to the arts of peace, not the expertise of war. In the 1950's the West Europeans formed an economic community to facilitate trade and business recovery and as a stepping-stone to political union that is yet to occur. With generous assistance from the Americans, the Europeans rebuilt their cities and in the case of West Germany (Federal Republic), France and Italy, had by the 1960's reached an unprecedented level of industrial productivity and national prosperity. For really the first time, at least the northern half of Italy became a modern country economically. France resumed its aborted industrial revolution which had ground to a halt before World War I, and became by 1970 an advanced technological society. The greatest achievement was in West Germany, one of the two countries into which Hitler's Germany had been split apart between 1945 and 1948 because the Allies and the Russians could not agree on the political future of their fallen enemy (Berlin itself was divided into eastern and western zones.)

German cities were devastated in 1945 and ten million people, eighty per cent of them young men, had been lost. But the German road system (the most advanced in the world, due to Nazi building of autobahns) and rail network were largely intact. Within three years German agriculture had recovered. And most important of all, German technological skill, scientific knowledge, and entrepreneurial ambitions and work discipline had not been eroded under the Nazi regime. With American aid and investment, new cities rose on the ruins of the old, so that German cities by the seventies were the most modern, cleanest, best organized in the Western world. Although West Germany's population had a Catholic majority (even after a large migration of Protestants from East Germany), all the traditions of the Protestant work ethic in Weber's model were exhibited in the new Germany. Munich today glistens with a cleanliness that is undreamed of in the U.S. Not only affluent Americans but upper middle- class Japanese want to buy German cars. The hands that made the Blitzkrieg soon made German industry even more technologically and fiscally powerful and creative than it had been in 1914.

What the Germans, French and Italians now had in common was a distaste for militarism—let the U.S. army protect them against the Soviet armies massed on the borders between West and East Germany (German Democratic Republic). Of course, it will not stay like this forever. The Germans are still a people of ineffable pride and sense of superiority. They will not be satisfied with the division of their homeland forever. Nor will they be satisfied for all time being Volkswagen manufacturers, T.W.A. tour guides, and herdsmen of laundered cattle. Germany will rise again. But in expiation of the Nazi terror state, the rightist German traditions died away, and the leadership principle and militarism became something read about in illustrated history books about the Nazi era. (The Holocaust was sometimes described succinctly in such books, somtimes ignored.) German anti-Semitism was abated because the Jews were almost entirely gone.

How long the European empires would have lasted in Asia and Africa without World War II is unfathomable. They would not have lasted forever, but patches of empire would still be around today. As it happened, within two decades of World War II, most of the European colonies had gained independence, within three decades virtually all. It took three hundred years for the Roman Empire to fall; it took thirty years for the British Empire and the other European empires to fade away. But the Romans to the bitter end of the Gothic wars were proud of their empire and made it a literal synonym for civilization. The Europeans had deep doubts in the interwar years. By the mid-fifties, they could only speak of imperialism with shame and regret.

Japan showed that the European empires in East Asia were paper tigers. In the four months after December 7, 1941, Japan conquered 400 years of European empire in East Asia—one of the more formidable military accomplishments in history. Within a week after Pearl Harbor, Japanese carrier-based planes sent Britain's two best battleships to the bottom of the sea off the Malaysian peninsula. In February 1942, in what Churchill called the worst defeat in British history, the commander of Singapore surrendered 130,000 troops to a Japanese army that was less than half that size. It had landed 200 miles up the coast and advanced untouched on Singapore (whose big guns only pointed out to sea) on bicycles. The Americans had a large air fleet in Manila; the Japanese destroyed it by bombing while it was still on the ground and General Douglas MacArthur looked on in bewildered disgust.

The European empires never recovered from these incredible humiliations. Franklin Roosevelt, a fanatical anti-imperialist and consequently a man of the radical left on this issue, would not allow the Dutch to resume their rule in Indonesia, which they had governed quietly for 200 years. The French adamantly held on to Vietnam until they suffered a military disaster in 1954. Within a half-dozen years they had also abandoned Algeria, forcing hundreds of thousands of French families and Jews to flee before Arab rule.

The key decision that unhinged imperialism was Britain's abrupt withdrawal in 1947 from the Indian subcontinent leaving behind the new republics of India and Pakistan as well as unspeakable atrocities by contending religious and ethnic groups. Atlee's Labor government scuttled the Raj, and sent a member of the royal family, the rash Lord Mountbatten, to do its dirty work. Lord and Lady Mountbatten made a formidable team. As an Admiral in the War, he had established a record in the British navy for getting more ships shot out from underneath him than any other commanding officer. Then as senior officer with commandos, he became famous for designing unintended suicide missions. Lady Mountbatten, a famous millionaire debutante in her day, conducted an affair with the Indian leader Jawaharlal Nehru while her husband was negotiating with him; Lord Mountbatten appears to have not been offended by this.

There were several reasons why the British made the sudden, critical withdrawal from India, which doomed the vestige of the imperialist cause:

*British postwar poverty (Britain is the only European country worse off economically today than in 1939) meant lack of military and fiscal resources to combat determined independence movements led by Nehru and Gandhi (Hindu) and Jinnah (Moslem).

*British guilt about imperialism. In 1947 Churchill, no longer in power, was the only prominent political leader even on the right to insist that the jewel in the crown should be held on to at all costs. Since 1914 India's main value to Britain had been military manpower during the two World Wars. It was impossible to frame an argument to hold on to India for this reason (which was not publicized in any case).

*The disgrace and loss of Singapore and Hong Kong to the Japanese and the severe losses in the defense of Burma had made the British appear puny and used up in Asian eyes.

*The long-standing Labor Party commitment to give India its independence. Attlee felt this personally, since in 1937 he had spent several months in India as a member of one of an endless number of investigating commissions and decided that the British cause was hopeless.

The scuttling of the Raj set the stage for the abandonment of the British empire in Africa, beginning with the Gold Coast (Ghana) in 1957 and another ten colonies by the early seventies. The British believed around 1955 that they should hold fast in Africa for another twenty years. Thus they repressed the Mau Mau rebellion in Kenya with unaccustomed determination and skill. But it soon transpired that the whole African native leadership was already in rebellion against them and could not be trained to take over responsible leadership. The only thing to do was get out and hand over the keys to the governor's mansion, for better or worse, to the rebels against them. Insurgents in British jails on life sentences were a week or two later putting on snappy uniforms and becoming presidents of new banana republics. The British Colonial Office, always assiduous in paperwork, developed a special ceremony for running down the Union Jack for the last time.

Underlying the British withdrawal was a pervasive and thoroughly justified sense of guilt at not having done enough for the African people (the British did much more for India) and for allowing the numerous white settlers in South Africa, Kenya, and Southern Rhodesia to exploit and mistreat the natives. This guilt was inflamed by the egalitarian heritage of World War II.

The end of empire and the death of imperialism are encapsulated in fragmented memorials. One of these is South Africa itself, where the ruling Afrikaners (the Calvinist Dutch Boers), who were the heroes of the European left in the Boer War of 1899–1902, fight the last rearguard action for white hegemony of the continent. South Africa enjoys by far the most prosperous economy on the African continent. How long will this relatively viable economy survive the Afrikaner government that is doomed to be replaced by a leftist Black republic?

A second memorial to vanished empire is the Commonwealth (in 1945 called the British Commonwealth of Nations), the collective organization of all the states that once were under the British flag and on whom British, Canadian, and Australian schoolchildren were once proudly taught the sun never sets. The Commonwealth heads of state solemnly meet each year and do absolutely nothing. At most this meeting is an act of piety.

A third memorial to what existed before the imperialist collapse of the forties and fifties are the Rhodes Scholars at Oxford. In the early years of the century, billionaire South African politician Cecil Rhodes was so proud of the Empire that he left his vast fortune (he was a bachelor) in trust to train its future leaders at Oxford until the end of time. This is how the Rhodes Scholarships were founded. Rhodes seems to have forgotten about the American Revolution because he also provided for U.S. Rhodes Scholars. Rhodes' bones still lie under a monster rock on a hill in Zimbabwe (formerly Southern Rhodesia). But little else of his dream remains. Every year at Rhodes House in Oxford, a hundred or so of his Rhodes Scholars in residence and about to leave the old university (they now include women and even an occasional Black), rise while wearing evening clothes and toast "the Founder" who looks down on them from a bigger-than-life size portrait. Rhodes in this painting is appropriately wearing riding clothes and bears a remarkable resemblance to Hitler. Then the Rhodes Scholars go off, not to rule the Punjab or Zambesi but—in the case of the Americans—to attend Harvard Law School or take jobs on Wall Street, whose firms assiduously recruit this reputed elite each year.

Anti-Zionists in Britain and in the Arab world today are fond of saying that Hitler created the State of Israel. There is truth in this, as in many other sick jokes. Without the sympathy for the Jewish refugees in 1945–48 and revulsion against the implications of the Holocaust, Israel most likely would not have come into existence. The second creator of Israel was President Harry Truman who given his Southern Baptist background (unless it was just a bid for Jewish money and votes) doggedly supported Israel against the hysterical opposition of his own State Department. The third supporter was, strangely, the Soviets. It was widely anticipated that the Russians at the U.N. in 1947 would vote against the creation of Israel. But although the Soviets before this had been anti-Zionist and have been fiercely so every since, Russia endorsed the Zionist state.

Even more important for the survival of the new state was Czechoslovakia, and especially its military industry, which was legacy of Nazi rule in Prague. In 1947–48 Israel had to fight for existence against six invading Arab armies, one of which, the Jordanian, was well trained and equipped and led by British officers. The Israelis had to fight for survival while the United States and Western Europe had imposed an embargo on arms shipments to the Middle East. The Czechs provided the Israelis with armaments, especially the critical airplanes (basically Messerschmidts) bought with cash from U.S. Jews. Why did the Czechs do this? Perhaps the Russians, who wanted a long-term war in the Middle East and did not anticipate a relatively quick Israeli victory, told them to. Perhaps it was because the head of the Czech government, Rudolph Slansky, and some of his colleagues, were Jewish. In 1952, the Soviets purged and hanged Slansky and most of his colleagues.

In 1967, General Nasser of Egypt closed the Suez Canal and the Gulf of Aqaba to Israeli shipping—a blockade which was an act of war. The Israelis using military tactics of lightning attack employed by the Nazis and Japanese in World War II, won huge victories and greatly expanded their territories, some of which—East Jerusalem, the Gaza Strip, the West Bank and the Golan Heights—still remain in their hands in a Greater Israel. The Israeli victory in 1967 was generally applauded in the Western world—somehow it squared accounts with the Holocaust. But as Israel became an American client state in the 1970's and the Israelis maintained their control over large Arab populations, anti-Zionism, merging into anti-Semitism, returned to Western Europe. The ill-fated Israeli invasion of Lebanon in 1982 wiped away the Holocaust heritage in Western Europe, though not in the United States. Whether this is because Americans better remember the Holocaust or politicians of both parties remember how important Jewish money is in their campaigns, or Jewish votes in certain cities, is moot. Soviet hostility to Israel and evangelical Protestant belief that Israel fulfilled Biblical prophecy also help the Israeli cause in the U.S. By the mid-eighties, the American left was deeply divided on the Israeli question. The leftist weekly *The Nation* published in 1986 an anti-

Zionist and anti-Semitic diatribe that would have won a medal from Hitler. The American right is largely and sometimes fervently pro-Zionist.

Degania is the largest Israeli kibbutz. It is located in the Galilee on the shores of Lake Kinneret, some forty miles south of the Golan Heights and the current frontier with Syria. Degania was the home of Kibbutz philosopher A.D. Gordon. In 1948, it was twenty miles closer to the border. In the middle of the kibbutz, a few yards from the children's house, there stands today a peculiar monument, a rusting Syrian tank which in the War of Independence in 1948 broke into the kibbutz and was immobilized at that point, which became the limit of Arab advance against the newborn state. Its survival was a close thing.

That little Israel with an eventual Jewish population of three million, the same number as in New York City, emerged as the fourth military power in the world with an air force and tank brigade that even in 1973 turned back the Soviet-armed and trained armies after a surprise attack and have inflicted defeat after defeat on hundreds of millions of Arabs—that Israel should have become the Prussia of the Middle East, is partly explained by that salvage monument in Degania. Sheer desperation and the memory of the Holocaust forced the Israelis to be one of the great military powers on earth, demonstrating a military capability that only the Germans and Japanese in the early forties and perhaps the Russians in 1943–44 have matched.

Yet this necessary fact altered the character of Israel that its founders, headed by David Ben Gurion, and nearly all the Eastern European socialists of the generation of the Second Alyiah (immigrating around 1910) had envisaged. Israel was not to be a postage-stamp size little agricultural, socialist, secular, eighty-five per cent Jewish country. While still small (the size of Massachussetts), it controlled territory three times its original size and ruled over Arab populations almost as large as the Jewish population. Even in Israel proper (exclusive of the conquered territories in the West Bank and Gaza) thanks to Israeli medicine, and with full rights of citizenship exclusive of army service, the Arabs are one-quarter the population. Nor was Israel to be primarily agricultural: the kibbutzniks today comprise only three per cent of the population and only a minority of Israelis live on the land, however organized for agriculture. One-third of the Israeli Jewish population lives in Tel Aviv, which has certain affinities with Miami or Los Angeles and would be anathema to Gordon the Tolstoyan dreamer.

Nor is Israel secular: the religious parties are politically influential and are part of every government whether of the left or right. Orthodox and even ultraorthodox (messianic fanatics) from the large section of the population displaced from Arab countries or immigrants from Brooklyn have given a religious coloration to the country. The Israeli airlines and the bus lines do not run on the Sabbath. The government subsidizes Orthodox schools at an extravagant rate while charging heavy tuition for the secular high schools.

Nor is Israel socialist. Whoever is in power, it is a capitalist society with strong welfare components. Its economy and social system are therefore similar to most countries in Western Europe. The Israeli elite consists of unscrupulous, often corrupt politicians, ambitious Army officers and speculative entrepreneurs and scientists and scholars who spend a lot of time abroad.

The ambience of Tel Aviv is very close to that of the more affluent American cities of similar size. In addition, Israel is a garrison state. It requires three years military service of its sons and daughters and a month's annual reserve duty of every male (except the ultraorthodox) until the age of fifty-five. It has mild looking professors of archaeology and medieval history who are trained commandos and paratroopers of professional caliber.

Israel has shown that white colonies could have been made viable in the Afro-Asian world if enough settlers had immigrated, if they were fanatically determined and inspired by a great cause and not parasites, and if enough capital investment had been made. Imperialism failed, the case of Israel demonstrates (and South Africa shows the same to a lesser degree) because it was too half-hearted, the investment of human and material resources was simply not great enough. So it was easy to wipe out the results of one to two centuries of colonial history.

Israel will not go away, except by the second Holocaust that the P.L.O. advocates keep trying to implement. Walking the streets of Tel Aviv or Jerusalem, we are in a Middle Eastern Prussia or Sparta (in the course of being softened by American capitalism.) It will never disappear short of total physical destruction. If there is going to be a World War III, here is a likely cause.

It was the Jewish Question as much as any other factor that led to the upheaval in the Catholic Church in the early sixties, the biggest transformation for Rome since the sixteenth, possibly the twelfth, century. Pius XII, Pope during World War II, disgraced the papacy by failing to come to the help of the dying Jews (outside of Rome itself) and allowing the Holocaust to occur without significant public demur, let alone strong opposition from the Church. If there was ever a time when the Church had to confront the world in order to prove true to its confession, when the risk of martyrdom had to be broached, this was the moment. But Pius XII, a conservative diplomat who had been papal ambassador to Germany in the twenties and early thirties and was a Germanophile, remained steadfastly neutral. His silence gave no comfort at all to German Catholics wanting to oppose Hitler. His silence doomed the Jews.

In the fifties there was a huge controversy about the Pope's role in World War II. Both Jewish and German sources condemned him. Of course the Church vociferously defended Pius XII. A subtle argument was presented. It would have been all too easy to play the self-indulgent martyr and confront the Nazis; Pius saved millions of Catholic lives by his neutrality, it was claimed. This casuistry convinced no one. The *magisterium* had been disgraced and expiation for papal cowardice—or worse—collaboration—had to be made. It took the form of the Holy Spirit directing the electing cardinals to choose as an "interim pope" an elderly, obscure Venetian Archbishop of unknown views who became John XXIII, the greatest reforming pope since the thirteenth century.

John called the Vatican Council II of 1962–64 during whose later stages he died. It unequivocally condemned anti-Semitism; henceforth to denounce Jews as Christ-killers was wrong. It allowed, indeed demanded, that most of the liturgy be conducted in vernacular languages, rather than Latin which laymen rarely understood. At last billions of Catholics knew what they were saying in Church. It freed Catholic scholarship and theology from its narrow bonds of censorship and repression and liberated the friars and nuns and other Church intellectuals to follow reason and learning. It made the church much more of a consensual, democratic and decentralized institution—how much was left undecided. It entered into a greater spirit of cooperation with other faiths.

The spirit and theory of Vatican II was stated with unsurpassable clarity by Father Hans Küng, then a young German theologian who attended the Council as an adviser to the German archbishops: "Faith in . . . the Church . . . being maintained in truth . . . is related to the whole Church as believing community. It is not primarily related to certain ecclesiastical institutions or authorities, which for the most part did not exist at all or did not exist in this form from the beginning and will not exist or need not exist in this form forever." The core of the Church was community and not *magisterium.*

By the early seventies, a Benedictine monastery on the St. Lawrence was not only using a guitar and folk songs in its liturgy. It was using a Quaker-style speaking with tongues (spontaneous preaching by laymen) in its service. By this time most American nuns had abandoned their traditional habit (not ordained in fact by Christ—it was only modelled on widows' robes from seventeenth-century France). By this time Catholic schools of theology were carrying out a modernization of doctrine and synthesis with secular thought, as Thomas Aquinas had done in 1250, but which had been prohibited by the papacy for modern times in 1907. By this time the proportion of Catholics using artificial contraception was almost as large as among Protestants and Jews. By this time Jesuits in South America in some instances had turned Marxist, were cooperating with Communists and were preaching a liberation theology. The *magisterium* was losing its hold on the church.

In recent years, under the Polish Pope John Paul II, a reaction has set in; strenuous efforts to restore the *magisterium* have been partly successful. Father Hans Küng was evicted from his chair of Catholic theology at Marburg. Liberation theology has been condemned. Discipline over priests and friars and nuns has been restored. Contraception as well as abortion has been condemned unequivocally by Rome—although Catholics continue, with surreptitious assent from many priests, to practice both. John Paul II makes pilgrimages to the Catholic population all over the world, preaches personally to hundreds of thousands, tries to make the papacy a missionary force on the right. His style is a long way from Pius XII, the austere aristocrat who never left the Vatican. The colossal iceberg of the Church, however, having started to move toward reform and democratization, is hard to reverse. The leading churchmen in Germany and Holland and many in Latin American countries clearly remain on the left. The Archbishop of Chicago is a well-known liberal. In the United States, it is hard to discipline priests when there is a terrible shortage of clergy due to the monumental decline of new professions. It is hard to control what nuns and friars teach when the Catholic schools are entirely dependent on this highly-skilled, low-paid work force.

A Catholic scene of the eighties: the Bishop of Brooklyn, an elderly liberal, and apparently mortally ill. The nuns who run a college in Brooklyn gather to pray vehemently for his recovery, especially because should the bishop die, his replacement made by Rome might be a neo-conservative, Cardinal O'Connor type with whom the radical nuns will be in instant conflict. A miracle. The old bishop recovers.

How long can the Catholic Church endure such internal strains without a schism comparable in magnitude to the one that occurred in the Reformation era? God only knows. Whom will the Holy Spirit, acting through the Cardinals, choose as the next Pope? Having given up the Italian succession, possibly a Latin American Bishop will be the next pope and he will heal the divisions in the Church. Possibly the Church will split apart at the next papal election into its left and right polarities.

Having expiated its putative sins of association with Fascism and consequent responsibility for World War II, the right since the mid-seventies has begun to recreate a political culture. It is no longer willing to allow the left to occupy the dominant ground in the universe of discourse prevailing in the academic and media worlds. As of the mid-eighties, there was no question but that the left's position was still the hegemonic one; the playing field between the two camps of political culture was not level. It still favored the left by a significant interval. Serious weeklies, monthlies and quarterlies with a leftist tilt or blatant leftist orientation still greatly outnumbered the outlets of rightist opinion, and surpassed the latter too with very few exceptions, in terms of quality. From every TV network, upscale newspaper and a host of university chairs, leftist culture is disseminated on a very wide variety of topics. When threatened or confronted, the left never hesitates to use *ad hominem* arguments and concentrate firepower until the public credibility of their audacious opponent is shattered. Thus the problem for the right was a practical one—commanding its resources so as to gain as great a visibility as the left in academic and media worlds. In this application of resources to the cultural needs of the right, a handful of conservative foundations play the critical role. Unless the evangelical Christians exercise political power on the federal scene, the future of the American right is probably in the hands of these foundations.

The problem of the right was also intellectual—its theory was still anemic. From the eight traditions of the right came four formulations of rightist theory in the eighties. These were: Friedmanite-Reagan-Thatcher neo-Ricardian economics; E.O. Wilson's sociobiological neo-Darwinism; the more conservative forms of Christianity in the Catholic Church and evangelical Protestantism; and possibly the behavioral psychology of B.F. Skinner, although the latter while conventionally regarded as rightist by leftist spokesmen is mostly a method of social control and is devoutly believed in by the Soviets as well.

None of the theoretical expressions of rightist culture has gained overwhelming allegiance of intellectuals, although these theories have become much more popular since the mid-seventies in the trans-Atlantic world. It seems safe to conclude, however, that the right has still much more intellectual homework to do and the rightist theory of the early twenty-first century has not yet been clearly articulated. There are places to look for activity: among Maurice Cowling and his colleagues at Peterhouse, Cambridge; among *The New Criterion* group; at the University of Chicago's law and business schools;

among evangelical Protestants in the southeastern United States; in a Jesuit order over which the papacy reasserted its control in recent years. But all this is guesswork on past performance. The provenance as well as the specific contents of the message of the New Right remains obscure.

What is most intriguing about the rightist theoretical revival is that the more vigorous it becomes, with the exception of *The New Criterion* group, the less conscious it appears to be about the Modernist cultural revolution and the involvement of rightist thinkers and writers with the Modernist mentality. In recently reinvigorated rightism, there appears to be an absence of mind about twentieth-century intellectual history and particularly the Modernist heritage. The right nowadays seems inclined to let the left try to appropriate Modernism and thereby increase its legitimacy, although Marxism and Modernism were theoretically further apart than was Fascism from Modernism. The right nowadays appears at times to write off the Modernist era and hark back directly to Victorian modes and concepts.

This ingrained neo-Victorianism of the contemporary right does not *per se* distinguish it from the left, which exhibits also in Marxism a strong tendency towards neo-Victorianism. It does distinguish the right culturally from the vestiges of the liberal center which directly reflects the high Modernist tradition in two ways. In so far as the center is not just stodgy inertia, or unreflective ideological confusion—which it frequently is—it preserves the Modernist emphasis on individual rational judgment and Modernist advocacy of entitlement to self-fulfillment, particularly in the realms of the arts and the intellectual life. The more the right ignores the affiliation it once had with ingredients of Modernism, and subscribes to a mainline neo-Victorianism, the more does it become incompatible with the liberal center in a deep-rooted, philosophical way.

The diversion of the contemporary right from vestiges of the liberal center is not, however, a prime issue of the 1980's because creativity in the liberal center has mostly shrunk to pockets of juristic and constitutional intelligence in a handful of distinguished law schools. Here the heirs of Roscoe Pound refine their complicated common law heritage while preparing the brightest of the post-adolescent generation for high-paying jobs in arrogant law firms. Here alone, in these intellectualized law schools, the stream of juristic liberalism still runs pure and bracing. Yet these legatees of Coke and Blackstone, Marshall and Brandeis, resemble more and more the priesthood of an ancient religion whose meaning has been transformed by time and cultural change. Elsewhere in American culture the liberal center that was pulled leftwards by the New Deal explosion continues to submerge within the leftist ideological block, except for the significant margins that have broken away to join a revivified right.

6

Structuralism, Deconstruction, and Post-Modernism

The Coming of a New Age

In the 1970's a new age emerged without fanfare and almost imperceptibly. By the beginning of the eighties, the manifestations of a new era were in place. The coming of a new age was not announced by dramatic events like a war or depression, although the ending of the Vietnam War was a salutary and necessary preparation. After the dramatic events of the sixties, a new era whose characteristics were soft rather than hard news was bound not to be much celebrated by the media. But by the mid-eighties it was obvious to more intelligent journalistic commentators and to cultural critics that a new time was rapidly developing.

Three technological innovations comprised a material and scientific infrastructure for the new era: biotechnology, computer applications, and instantaneous world information distribution through communication satellites.

Biotechnology was the outgrowth of the discovery of the double-helix structure of the DNA molecule in 1953 at the Cavendish Laboratory in Cambridge, England (which Rutherford had once directed), by the joint efforts of the English biophysicist Francis Crick and the young American molecular biologist James Watson. For more than a decade DNA (deoxyribonucleic acid) had already been identified as the template of animate life. The issue was to identify its structure so that it could be controlled and manipulated by laboratory science. It was this possibility that Crick and Watson's discovery made possible, and for which they were awarded the Nobel Prize (although two other teams of scientists, one in London and one at CalTech, were on the verge of the same discovery.)

This was a scientific breakthrough in biology comparable to the work of Darwin and Mendel in the nineteenth century. It meant that the New Physics of Einstein, Rutherford, Bohr, and Heisenberg would now be applied in molecular biology and be committed to the analysis and shaping of life forms. By the mid-seventies advanced work in molecular biology had spawned vast new areas of biological engineering. A technology devoted to the artificial, lab-centered creation of life constituents emerged. By 1986 vaccines made of genetic mutants were introduced.

Biotechnology opened up unlimited horizons of accomplishment in science and engineering. It meant that mankind was beginning to control not just his physical environment—this reached a zenith when man first walked on the moon on July 20, 1969—but his own nature, the biochemistry of life itself. In some respects, molecular biology and DNA marked the ultimate fulfillment of the Modernist program that had begun with the century. The aim of finding the smallest particle had resulted in knowledge of the double-helix structure of DNA that is the chemical basis of animate matter.

The extended application of computers to research knowledge, industry, and government was the second material constituent of the infrastructure of a new age. The idea of a computer is not an invention of this century. Charles Babbage, a contemporary and friend of the author of *Alice in Wonderland*, had stipulated the main mathematical principle of automated computing (using the age-old binary theorem, i.e., a system whose only digits are 1 and 0 and all numbers are combinations of them) in the 1860's. In the 1930's Alan Turing, a young British mathematician had developed an elaborate project for a mathematical machine and something like it appears to have been built and put in use by British intelligence during World War II in the breaking of the German codes using the Enigma machine (a cipher machine that a Polish agent had sneaked out of Germany). The details remain secret.

In the period 1943–46, first at Iowa State University, then at the University of Pennsylvania, the first publicly known and commercially feasible computers were built. They used easily breakable vacuum tubes, needed intensive artificial cooling, and occupied enormous space. The computer power now provided by hardware about the size of a typewriter then required a machine larger than a basketball court. Further refinements were made in the postwar period by IBM, Sperry, and other corporations. The turning-point came, however, in the late sixties with the introduction of readily manufactured microchips to replace the large and cumbersome vacuum tubes. The microchip was developed simultaneously by engineers in Texas and Illinois.

By the early seventies businesses and universities with pretension to status and grandeur each had their computer center. A further major breakthrough in the late seventies, made possible by further miniaturization of the transistor and cheaper production—in which first the Japanese and then the South Koreans excelled—fostered the proliferation of desk-top and even portable "personal" mini-computers. This breakthrough revolutionized many age-old processes, including banking and book production, and carried further the revolution in the storage and retrieval and massaging of data that had begun in the sixties with the first feasible but still relatively large and awkward computers.

Both the biotech and the computer revolution used the same key words—code and program—to describe their basic functions. In both instances a structure of design and information drove processes that predetermined formulations: in the case of biotech and DNA, genetic histories; in the case of computers, knowledge for business and research, humanities or science, peace and war. Even the great achievements of the first three decades of the century in the application of science and technology were significantly transcended. A new interval in the evolution of the power of the human intellect had occurred.

Yet at the same time, since the biotech code and the computer program operated integrally for long stretches without human intervention, shaping life or crunching number sequences, a certain diminution of individual stature was also thought to have occurred. The biotech and computer breakthroughs both enhanced and diminished the power and value of the individual. They enhanced human mentality as a whole but made less necessary and valuable the mental capacity of any one individual. Such at least was the feeling.

It was the molecular biologists who especially articulated a theory of impersonal code overriding personal choices. Evolution, said Crick, has a creative "perfection of design" that operates outside the values of humanistic culture. "Scientific revelation," of which DNA is the highest dogma, takes the place of the nonsensical "modes of yesterday," he alleged. Life on earth started with a spaceship from a doomed civilization on another planet landing on earth; after that the genetic code functioned autonomously. Similarly Jacques Monod, another Nobel laureate in microbiology, spoke with contempt of those who continue to believe in "anthropocentric illusion." The discovery of life codes forces us to recognize at last that man "is alone in the universe's unfeeling immensity, out of which he emerged only by chance. His destiny is nowhere spelled out, nor is his duty." The Nazis would have applauded Monod's nihilist thesis.

Similarly, a group of computer scientists centering on Herbert Simon aimed to divest the human mentality of that distinctiveness that philosophers since Aristotle have accorded it. They believe that computers can function as artificial intelligence and think like humans as well as compute and remember in ways that exceed human capacity. Only a technological failure to get computers to equal human intelligence has impeded the full formulation of this mechanistic philosophy from the computer side to go along with microbiologists' proclamation of a scientific revelation in which the genetic code functions outside personal human intervention.

The placing of communication satellites in the heavens was an innovation of the mid-seventies. It realized McLuhan's prophetic vision of a global village. Now everyone around the globe in front of a TV set could see and hear the same event "live." This was a major advance in communications technology and it contributed not only to sports and entertainment, but also to the growth and proliferation of the multinational corporation, which through phone and TV linkups could now instantaneously straddle the earth. The citizenship of the world that eighteenth-century philosphers had dreamed about (when it took six weeks for a letter to cross the Atlantic), and the universalization of capitalist power against which Marx and Lenin had fulminated, were now indeed realized.

As in the case of computers, satellite communications seemed at the same time to increase human capability and efficiency and diminish human stature. The individual, any individual, now seemed small and feeble in comparison with the world communications network and the global corporations it made operative.

Satellite communications were the main practical outcome of the American space program that began in the early sixties when it was feared that the Soviets would conquer space before the U.S. The American space program combined German rocketry science carried over from World War II in the person of Wernher von Braun with American engineering and capital. The idea behind the moon landing project of 1969 was that somehow the attainment of this centuries-old dream would result in colonization of other planets. It turned out that the moon was several million square miles of useless rock and rubble and the other planets in the solar system were also lifeless and essentially uninhabitable except at prohibitive expense. The manned space program in the seventies then tried to make itself remunerative by serving as the means for launching communication satellites, and this program continued at a steady and largely successful pace until the disastrous explosion of the Challenger space vehicle in January 1986.

The second great change ushering in a new age in the late seventies was the rise of the Pacific Rim, involving not only Japan (whose success was most visible and celebrated), but other East Asian countries such as South Korea, Singapore and the Malay Republic. Western Europe continued its course of technological and economic progress it had started in the fifties, although dreams of political union, in spite of the creation of a largely powerless European parliament, evaporated. It was the United States that felt the crunch of competition from the Pacific Rim, and declined rapidly as an industrial power, losing large sections of its automobile, steel and electronics as well as textile manufacture capability to the Japanese and other Asian producers.

Fluctuations in oil supply and gas prices in the seventies seemed momentarily to play a key role in this development. But Japan had no oil while the U.S. produced the greater part of its own supply. The oil glut of the mid-eighties showed that oil and gas were not factors in this novel economic equation. The major factor was cultural: the decline of the work ethic in the U.S., the deterioration of its educational system, the loosening of family bonds and the weakening of socialization in disciplined behavior—these were the key factors.

Two other causes were involved in the rise of the Asian rim. The East Asian peoples were only one or two generations removed from feudalism, the historical moment of greatest industrial work capacity and social discipline for modern productivity. They were where Britain had been in 1780–1820 and Germany from 1870 to 1910. Beyond that, there was the factor of the Buddhist, Shinto and other highly austere religious traditions of East Asia, inculcating a fatalism, self-control, and group solidarity that Western Christianity, eroded by liberalism and leftism, could no longer duplicate—and perhaps never could because of its respect for personal conscience.

Had the American era in the twentieth century (1940–65) economy come and gone so quickly? Although the millions of Latin American emigrants pressing on U.S. borders had another view of the matter, it appeared to be so. Between 1981 and 1986 the U.S. lost one million manufacturing jobs. Since the mid-seventies in fact there had been no increase of real income for eighty per cent of the population.

The U.S. was still the land of freedom and individual opportunity. But its technological and industrial capacity had passed its peak by the late eighties. Only a thoroughly revamped educational system, restoration of the nuclear family, and regeneration of a public ethic of work, postponed gratification, and group solidarity could restore American economic hegemony.

No leadership was on the horizon in the mid-eighties to achieve these ends. Reagan knew some of the words but not the tune. He lacked the conceptual framework to understand the problem clearly, let alone articulate the solution. Public life in the U.S. was too corrupt, the media too venal, to expect anything better. By greatly increasing defense spending while gaining no increase in federal revenue, Reagan generated enormous deficits which created a special sort of fiscal problem, and imposed a further burden on a weakening economy.

The policy that began with the Carter administration, and was accentuated under Reagan, of stressing armament over industrial productivity, has sent the United States into the ranks of the debtor nations for the first time in a century. In 1982 the United States held nearly $150 billion of net foreign assests, exceeding any other country. But with the Reagan miltiary expenditures and accompanying tax cut, we have invited foreign nations, particularly the Japanese and the Germans, to fund our escalating debt. By the end of 1987 America's external debt will rise to $300 billion. By 1990, at the current rate of expenditure and taxation, the U.S. will owe the rest of the world $500 billion. This is not yet catastrophic since it represents only five per cent of Gross National Product. But we have entered a slippery slope of federal deficits and national indebtedness that will further enrich the Japanese and the Germans and will constitute a bitter legacy for our progeny.

Faced with U.S. economic decline in comparison with the Asian rim, and with a severe American trade deficit also with West Germany, neither the American left nor right had much to say of value. The left wept crocodile tears for Nicaragua and the South African blacks, and the right talked up bringing back the age of Teddy Roosevelt and Herbert Hoover. Neither proposal was very helpful when not only could the Japanese produce a better and cheaper auto in Tokyo but even in Ohio—using much-disparaged US workers (but not unionized ones)—Japanese managers could produce a better car for the same price than Detroit could.

A peculiar revelation of American loss of self-confidence occurred when General Motors and Toyota began to produce jointly Toyota Corollas in a new plant in California and agreed to have them marketed by GM as Chevrolet Novas. In 1986, these Novas were a drug on the market while American consumers were willing to pay several hundred dollars more for exactly the same car with a Toyota nameplate on it. In the early forties American industry was the master of the world. Four decades later American industry became a dirty word. This economic decline was based on cultural transformations that eroded work ethic and leadership capacity.

In the late eighties it appeared that the Americans had been infected by the British disease. Financial instruments became ever more subtle and complicated, what with a rash of unproductive takeovers of corporations by other corporations, and the devising of clever and expensive means to preclude this fiscal warfare, while industrial productivity stagnated, research and development of new products deteriorated, and family farmers were driven to ruin. The madcap dance of financiers surrounded by the gloom of industrial decline,

agricultural insolvency, unemployment and underemployment, and the deterioration of applied research: this distinguished the British economy and it now
threatened to become America's fate as well. Soon every American boy and girl
born alive would be fated to become an investment banker, a corporate lawyer,
or a hamburger chef or a motel maid.

Going along with the failure of American business leadership was the failure
of nerve of American academics. From about 1910 until the late 1930's, the
American university had developed its own distinctive forms and largely native
talent. It borrowed what it needed from Europe but it was proud of its own
emerging traditions and accomplishments. The advent of academic refugees
from Hitler in the 30's began to raise fissures in the self-confidence of U.S.
academics. In the postwar era these fissures widened into chasms as American
faculties were shaken, first by McCarthyite questioning of their loyalty in the
fifties, then by the onslaught of New Left students in the sixties, then by the
decline in real salaries and massive academic unemployment in the seventies.

The latter factor was probably the most important. The academic profession, except for law, medicine, and business schools, did not participate in the
American economic boom after about 1965 and its fiscal status deteriorated.
The professional devastation was worst in the humanities and soft social sciences
(excepting economics, which enjoyed affiliation with business schools) and it was
in these arrays of disciplines that efforts to create an indigenous American
academic culture were abandoned and there was a rush to adopt European
intellectual models, especially from France. This development shaped the rise of
structuralism, although some other dimensions of the new era also contributed to
the rise of structuralist theory.

Whether we call the new age post-industrial or post-Modern or eventually
find a new term is not important. It had a distinctive set of characteristics, in
addition to ones we have already delineated.

The visibility of psychoanalysis as a form of therapy is under attack and
being eroded by the rise of psychopharmacology. Perhaps more important,
psychoanalysis' leading position in cultural theory has softened. Psychoanalysis in the late eighties seems more prone to absorb cultural theory into its
canon than to go out front and shape it in an innovative manner. Psychoanalysis as vanguard theory has declined and it has become more reactive than
creative.

The welfare state has lost the internal impetus it had from the early years of
the century until the mid-seventies. While the welfare state is likely to be
around for a long time, probably forever, it has dissipated the capacity to
stimulate the imagination and elevate hopes. It has proved a costly burden on
federal, state, and municipal budgets, as conservatives had predicted. The faith
that somehow if only social security, state-generated employment, and health
insurance would be expanded all other problems would fall into place has
greatly weakened. We have social pathology such as drug traffic and one-
parent families that the welfare state seems to exacerbate, not alleviate. It is not
completely clear why the welfare state had fallen so far short of optimistic
expectations as the solution to social problems. But by the 1980's it was clearly
a failure.

On the other hand, if the left has no social panacea, the rightist claim that neo-Ricardian economics without compassion will solve all economic problems has likewise been proven vain. Neither ballooning nor shrinking the welfare state makes as great a difference as left and right polemicists believed in the early seventies. We appear to have reached a point at which debate about the welfare state is obsolete. We have to formulate a social doctrine and cultural theory along some other spectrum, such as group solidarity and personal discipline. Social progress seems unlikely without another cultural change.

There is a growing discordance, as there was not in the three decades after World War II, between the media and academic cultures. The latter have propounded theories that the media have difficulty comprehending or at least integrating into their work and are left either to ignore or satirize in vulgar fashion. As an example, in 1985 *The New York Times Sunday Magazine* set out to publish an article on deconstruction at Yale. The result was a miserable insult to common intelligence. The author failed to explain what deconstruction was, and clearly could not understand its social significance. He fell back on the bankrupt motifs of the dreamy professor and cloistered academic lifestyles.

The *Times* did not write about Einstein and relativity in 1919 in this futile, vulgar vein, nor would it today write about Wall Street brokers and investment practices in this cavalier manner. Another instructive example. In 1986 *The New Criterion*, the leading American rightist cultural journal, devoted a whole issue to a symposium on New York in the eighties. Not one of the eighteen contributors (they complained a lot about the real estate situation) was a professor from the two leading New York City universities, Columbia and N.Y.U. Would this have been possible in a similar symposium in 1936 or 1966? Absolutely not. "Things fall apart; the centre cannot hold."

There is an unprecedented amount of learning available today, abetted by storage, sample analysis, retrieval and dissemination by computers and communication satellites. There is lacking, however, fresh cultural and social theories to make sense and meaning out of all this information.

The way in which Modernism developed its revolutionary theories in challenge to Victorianism is no longer operational or feasible. There is no longer extant a systematic Victorian culture to push against and grow strong in conflict with. The wall which Modernism played off for four decades has dissolved into a nostalgic persiflage of artistic bricks and intellectual mortars. Furthermore, the resurgence of neo-Victorianism that began in the thirties and continues with vigor today has generated a nostalgic neo-Victorianism that makes the anti-Victorian Modernist program additionally obsolete.

The effort in the sixties to create a leftist culture adversary to capitalism and the putative bourgeois ethos—an effort which is still pursued in some quarters, especially university humanities departments—has produced a narrow band of thought that perpetuates partisan polemic rather than confronts the complex and novel circumstances of the new age.

Perhaps in desperation at the exhaustion of the Modernist program and the futility of New Left doctrine, the culture of the developing age exhibits a propensity to arbitrary and random appropriation and imitation of particular old themes and nostalgic traditions rather than comprehensive and original theorizing about contemporary culture. This quality of arbitrariness, random impetuosity, and pastiche characterizes post-Modernist culture as much as anything. Central to post-Modernism is the propensity to unresolved syncretism of diverse cultural strains, learned traditions, and diverse theories. Much is effortlessly imitated and distinctive cultures are blended together.

The new age has seen a reversal of the anti-urban ethos of the post-War era of the fifties and sixties. Then there was a flight to the suburbs and a pseudo-agricultural ethos that marginally harmed the continued progress of Modernist culture stemming from metropolitan life of the early decades of the century. Now there is a renewed appreciation for the civilities and sophistication of urbanism and particularly of urban centers. But the real estate situation has made New York and to a lesser extent London and Paris inaccessible to the avant-garde, the young artists and intellectuals who carry the aesthetic and cultural theory of the future.

We have seen a reversion to the metropolis as a fiscal and managerial center but we cannot find the means to regenerate it as a center of cultural revolution. We build bigger and more elaborate metropolitan museums, and at the same time drive the painters and sculptors who will replenish these elegant galleries to the urban fringes, provincial towns, and the boondocks. Here is a remarkable contrast between the infrastructure of the age of Modernism and the new era of post-Modernism. Then artists found support groups in the metropolis. Now lonely are the brave.

Perhaps a hundred or even fifty years from now, historians will see that the most important development in the new age was none of the above. Rather, it was the triumph of feminism and woman's liberation from domesticity. For the first time, middle-class women in large numbers are entering academia, the learned professions, and at least the middle ranks of business management. The historical profession itself, if current trends maintain themselves, by 2010 will be like nursing a century before, overwhelmingly a female profession. When fifty-one per cent of the entering class of N.Y.U. Law School, one of the top ten in the country, are women, what does this portend for the future not only of the legal profession but corporate management and the criminal justice system? We are possibly at the beginning of a matriarchical revolution that will reverse 5000 years of social history. Psychoanalytic and cultural theory has not begun to address this portending upheaval, whose psychological scars could run deep and ugly. The impact on men will be as great as the significance for women. Child-rearing and with it the delicate socialization of Oedipal feelings is changing.

The historian some decades from now may see the main difference between the era of Modernism and the age of post-Modernism to lie along a polarity of integration and fragmentation. Modernist culture of the first four decades of this century was characterized by a comprehensive cultural and aesthetic theory and by political and social fragmentation of a world reft by nationalism and fratricidal conflict within the human race and was still hampered by the relatively primitive steam and electro-mechanical means of transport and communication.

Post-Modernist culture comprises a world integrated by identification and manipulation of the universal genetic code, computer programs, communication satellites and the multi-national corporation, along with the relative obsolescence of national conflicts. It is, however, a world fragmented culturally and aesthetically, a world of subcultures and small group choices on aesthetic principles and idiosyncratic, nostalgic recapitulations of the past, but one in which a comprehensive, integrating cultural theory is lacking.

The Modernist era—to its great loss—allowed disfunctional political and economic decisions. The post-Modernist era—to what loss—allows random, privatist cultural decisions and the composition of arbitrary cultural pastiche.

Structuralism

The leading cultural theory that developed in the two decades after World War II was structuralism. It initially loomed large on the French intellectual horizon in 1955, with the publication of Claude Lévi-Strauss's intellectual autobiography and testament, *Tristes Tropiques*. This book ranks with Joyce's *Ulysses*, Proust's *Swann's Way*, and Freud's *The Interpretation of Dreams* as one of the enduring classics of the century.

By the early seventies structuralism was the leading cultural theory in France. It had come to dominate French anthropology and social sciences. It also deeply affected trans-Atlantic literary theory and criticism, eventually penetrating into the entire field of the humanities—"the human sciences," as the Parisians called them. In the late sixties, more specifically in 1969 with a special issue of *Yale French Studies*, structuralism migrated to the United States, beginning its penetration with the literary humanities, principally through the faculties of the English, French and Comparative Literature Departments of Yale University. From there, it spread out to several other universities including Johns Hopkins, Columbia, Cornell, and Chicago.

Since the mid-seventies, structuralism in its original form has been in decline in France, having been superseded by deconstruction as the main cultural theory. It has been challenged in the United States as well. Nevertheless, it does remain an important movement in the humanities in this country as well as in England and Germany. Therefore, even though it lost its initial thrust somewhere around 1975, structuralism is the single most important intellectual movement of the last thirty years. It could be claimed that had structuralism not come into being, there would have been no deconstruction either, since deconstruction developed as a movement responding to, growing out of and criticizing structuralism. Deconstruction can be seen as a subset and late variation of the intellectual movement called structuralism.

The reason for the emergence of structuralism can be located first of all in the exhaustion of existentialism, which had been the leading intellectual movement in France in the postwar period. We have seen that existentialism was a system of romantic phenomenology emphasizing the good individual against the absurd and hostile environment. It was a dramatic philosophy which had been valuable and meaningful in the early forties during the period of the Nazi rule. It had become the philosophy of resistance, as will be remembered from an earlier chapter. But existentialism was not a sophisticated philosophy, and it exhausted itself once the political conditions that rendered it important had disappeared—for how long can someone continue to shake his fist against the world before one begins to look juvenile and naive?

Lévi-Strauss realized the weakness of existentialism, he tells us, even when it was in its formative stage in the thirties. It was partly because of his antipathy to the then emerging existentialism that he abandoned his doctoral studies in philosophy at Paris, switched over to anthropology, and although a novice in this social science discipline, got a teaching job in Brazil. The position was obtained through his mentor Marcel Mauss, Durkheim's nephew and professional heir. When Lévi-Strauss returned from exile in New York in 1948 he found existentialism the rage of the cafés and the boulevards as well as the university. Nevertheless, he boldly declared not only his independence from Sartre and Camus, but his direct opposition to existentialism.

Structuralism moves the focus of reality and the center of attention from the individual to the system. It makes the structured system, rather than the individual, into the locus of the real and the meaningful. Structuralism signifies a transference of meaning and authenticity from the individual to the system, which makes structuralism a theory that rebels against the anthropomorphism of existentialism.

The second point of origin of the structuralist movement lay in the failure of the New Left and of the student upheaval in 1968. Existentialism was the mode of the 1968 rebellion, in that the uprising was primarily individualistic, conducted by a small group of highly self-conscious personalities who stood against the world at large. After a series of dramatic successes, the leftist heroes and heroines failed, and therefore, a reconsideration of the whole situation on the left became inevitable. The heroic individual or the heroic vanguard consisting of a handful of radicals who sought to dismantle the establishment had obviously suffered defeat, rendering necessary a revision of the entire system of belief. This caused a shift, rechanneling attention from the individual to the system.

Thus structuralism arose out of a reconsideration of what may be called the radical program, in view of the failure of the radical heroism of the late sixties. Instead of mounting the barricades, structuralism proposed to incorporate the barricades into a larger social system. Structuralism proposed to transcend the conflict between the individual and society by giving priority to universal structures in which both were subsumed.

Structuralism can lend itself to rightist interpretation, but in the hands of Lévi-Strauss and his French disciples it was intended to be a doctrine of the left. It was an effort to create a post-Marxist as well as post–existential leftist cultural theory, based on behavioral data and with impeccable intellectual credentials. The rise of structuralism is therefore a postscript to the tumult and defeat of 1968.

A third basis of structuralism lies in the economic and technological developments that were occurring in the late sixties and early seventies, one of which was the growing recognition of the central role of multinational corporations. Increasing attention was being paid for the first time to the elaborateness of economic institutions which extended over many countries. In a sense, such multinational corporations had been in existence for quite a while, at least since the late nineteenth century when they had been called cartels.

Unlike its parent institution, the cartel, which had received frequent moral condemnation, the multinational corporation received good press, to the extent that universities developed programs for the dispensation of special degrees, MBA's, for admission into the work force of these international companies. During the period in consideration, multinational corporations began to receive attention as complex computer-based economic and social systems, providing a springboard for general reflection on the elaborate, systemic quality of other institutional structures.

What now counted economically was not so much individual entrepreneurship or national distinctiveness but global corporate institutions with homogeneous behavior and universal fiscal instruments and data bases.

It was discovered that the modern world was increasingly tending toward rigorously defined system-building, and structuralism became the articulation of this insight in the domain of the humanities and the soft social sciences. The extension of computer applications and satellite communications in the seventies not only made the multinational corporation much more functional. It increased the attractiveness of a theory that gave prominence to codes and programs. This was structuralism.

A fourth general source of structuralism lay in formalism, which we identified as one of the foundations of rightist thinking. It usually finds its political place on the right, but Lévi-Strauss was not prepared to let the matter lie there. He sensed from his study of early people how much their lives were conditioned by behavioral codes, language structures, and symbols. He did not think that at bottom it was any different for people in more advanced societies, although the formalistic conditioning of behavior may be harder to trace in complex societies.

Lévi-Strauss and his disciples were not prepared to allow the right to appropriate formalism exclusively for their conservative programs. Lévi-Strauss, whose political sympathies lay in the left—he was a vehement anti-imperialist—wanted the left not to rely on simple-minded empiricism, vulnerable existentialism, and—in his eyes—discredited historicism. He wanted the best intellectual foundation for the leftist program and that meant formalism.

A Soviet theorist named Mikhail Bakhtin in the thirties had already perceived this point, but formalism stood perpetually condemned in the Soviet Union as bourgeois, counter-revolutionary reaction. Hence Bakhtin never exercised much influence in Russia (he has been rediscovered in the eighties by American critics.) Lévi-Strauss aimed to do what Bakhtin could not, namely create a highly visible leftist theory based on formalism. This was certainly an audacious and largely successful move.

Historically, structuralism goes back to Lévi-Strauss' work in the 1930's and

40's, and particularly to the early forties when he was a refugee teacher at the "University in Exile" in New York, which was a branch of the New School for Social Research. Claude Lévi-Strauss was the son of a Belgian rabbi, which lends him a certain affinity with Émile Durkheim, who was also a rabbinical son.

When Lévi-Strauss began his behavioral studies under Marcel Mauss, there was no major distinction at the time at the University of Paris between sociology and anthropology. After Mauss found a teaching position for Lévi-Strauss in Sao Paulo, Brazil, in 1934, Lévi-Strauss encountered the Third World. In 1938, shortly before the war broke out, he made an extensive trip up the Amazon, where he conducted field work. During this trip, he began to study the social codes, languages, and the diet of primitive peoples of the Amazon region. Anglo-American anthropologists find his field-work somewhat brief and also careless (he did not know the natives' languages and used interpreters.) Nevertheless, Lévi-Strauss' Amazon trip was a turning point in his intellectual development.

Soon after his return to France from Brazil, like many other Jewish professors Lévi-Strauss had to flee as the Nazi tanks rolled into Paris, making his way first to the French West Indies, and from there, to the United States. He taught at the New School as well as at Barnard College. This great anthropologist, Claude Lévi-Strauss, taught freshman anthropology in summer school at Barnard College in 1945. It would be interesting to get a look at a student's notes. In 1949 a position in Social Anthropology for Lévi-Strauss was created in Paris. He became Professor of Social Anthropology at the Collège de France in 1959.

At the New School, Lévi-Strauss encountered a remarkable polymath, Roman Jakobson, who was a product of the East European (mainly Russian and Czech) school of linguistic formalism. Jakobson's field is difficult to specify, given the wide range of work he produced, but his greatest interest was in the science of linguistics. He tried to develop a formalist theory of linguistics which would include the description of a code that underlay all language.

Jakobson's formalistic approach to linguistics drew on the one hand on Wittgenstein and the logical positivist school, which had been very strong in Prague. It was also indebted to early twentieth-century Russian literary theorists. There was a long East European ancestry in the tradition viewing all languages as generated by the one essential code. After the war, Jakobson became professor of linguistics, Russian and Comparative Literature at Harvard University. He died in 1982 at the age of eighty-five. He remained to the end a zealot and an advocate of formalist linguistic theory.

In his intellectual autobiography, Lévi-Strauss almost certainly underestimated the reality of his debt to Jakobson in the development of his structuralist theory. Instead he stressed the influence of the Swiss pioneer in linguistics of the second decade of the century, Ferdinand de Saussure, who also influenced Jacques Lacan. Yet at the time that Lévi-Strauss encountered Jakobson and his formalist system of linguistics in wartime New York, he could not have known very much of Saussure's similar linguistics theory, since Saussure never published a book in his lifetime. Saussure's treatise only appeared in the fifties, put together out of lecture notes by his students. Nor does Lévi-Strauss in *Tristes Tropiques* recognize a debt to Lacan, although they propounded some similar doctrines. Yet it is possible that Lévi-Strauss did not encounter Lacan's ideas until his own were formed. Lacan practiced as a private psychoanalyst and did not gain academic attention until the 1960's.

Why Lévi-Strauss does not mention Carl Gustav Jung among his forebearers is puzzling, since Jung's theory of archetypes contained some strong resemblances to Lévi-Strauss's structuralist anthropology. In his intellectual biography, Lévi-Strauss does express his debt to Marx, Freud, and Jean-Jacques Rousseau. While structuralist elements can be pointed out in the work of these three thinkers, beyond question, this appears to be mainly an act of formal piety on Lévi-Strauss's part, a typological bow to the masters that would please the Parisian Left Bank cafés and his students. Lévi-Strauss always exhibited superior skill in public relations. His theory is certainly closer to Piaget than to Rousseau.

Lévi-Strauss is a very prolific writer. He is currently in his late seventies and is still publishing. *Tristes Tropiques*, one of the great testaments of the twentieth century, is highly commendable as an introduction to his thought. Another of his books, *The Savage Mind*, is a more didactic introduction to his thinking, although unfortunately it is poorly translated. A four-volume collection of studies of which the first volume is entitled *The Raw and the Cooked* is very much worth reading as well.

Lévi-Strauss believes in an objective, universal social-mental code. That which constitutes a society and a culture is a universal code that runs through the culture and the institutional and behavioral forms of that society. The code is objective. That is, it is not ideational, only a mental image, but it exists independent of individuals and individual minds, and governs both human behavior and ways of thought. This universal cultural system objectively exists, structuring mental processes as well as social institutions. As humans we are involved in this code. It shapes our lives, our capacity to communicate, and how we function. But it is independent of us.

Secondly, Lévi-Strauss holds that this code exists in language and in myth. In order to discover the code and reduce it to its basic grid, one would have to look at the findings of the science of linguistics and at mythology. The former proposal suggests Jakobson's and Saussure's influence (Lacan said the same thing), whereas the latter points toward Jung. Furthermore, the code operates in the unconscious—not for nothing does Lévi-Strauss claim that he learned from Freud.

We have the hope, says Lévi-Strauss, "of overcoming the opposition between the collective nature of culture and its manifestation in the individual" because the collective unconscious is "no more than the expression, on the level of individual thought and behavior, of certain time and space modalities of the universal laws which make up the unconscious activity of the mind." (Jung would agree.) Thus Lévi-Strauss is not satisfied merely to eliminate the authenticity of existential heroism. He even eliminates meaningful individual thought, integrating it with universal laws that operate in the unconscious. Lévi-Strauss sounds the first great trumpet call for the project that runs through French thought since the late sixties, the project that is often called "the death of the subject," that is, the elimination of the value and significance of individual consciousness.

Lévi-Strauss' structuralism further claims that the savage, or primitive, mind and the *savant*, or learned mind of complex societies have the same deep structure. Just as Freud had said that there was no fundamental difference between the neurotic and the normal, so Lévi-Strauss argues that there is no fundamental difference between the savage mind and the *savant* mind in terms of the way in which they operate, and create mythological structures in order to explain reality. The same human mind, the same mental structures are at work in either case. Where the savage may create an elaborate mythology about the gods, the *savant* may produce a theory of physics, but at stake in both cases is the recourse to a structure of reality to explain ourselves, how we behave and how we exist.

The *savant* and the savage mind differ in this respect. The former is the mind of the engineer and is "adapted to perception and imagination." The primitive thinker is like a *bricoleur* or handyman. He is "adept at executing a great number of diversified tasks. . . . His instrumental universe is closed, and the rule of his game is always to make do with the means at hand." Thereby a special dignity and authenticity accrues to the primitive *bricoleur*. He remains close to his sources. He does not, like oversophisticated modern man, continually generate new concepts but constantly manipulates and refines pre-existing ones.

Lévi-Strauss the Parisian academic and left bank intellectual, the rabbinical scion, identifies the Amazon primitives with those weather-beaten, canny, diversely knowledgable *bricoleurs* he finds in the French countryside when he goes for his long summer vacation. These handymen possess a special intellectual power, they reflect an earlier thick French culture that cannot be matched in the halls of the Sorbonne or the upscale apartment houses on the right bank. There is something Rousseauesque in Lévi-Strauss' identification of the savage mind with the *bricoleur* temperament.

Lévi-Strauss is very sympathetic to primitive peoples. One of the main themes of *Tristes Tropiques*, aside from propounding his structuralist theory, is a dirge for primitive society and a regret about the transformations the Third World is undergoing. In primitive society, so Lévi-Strauss claims, people live on more intimate terms with fundamental structures. In primitive culture, there is no host of complicated and decadent interventions and corrupting obscurities to separate people from their basic structure of mind and society. Therefore, by implication, advanced society is repressive, confused, corrupt, decadent and inauthentic. Primitive society, on the other hand, is more humanly authentic for its proximity to basic structures. There is a parallel here with Heidegger's belief in the superior authenticity of the German farmer.

Lévi-Strauss sees in the primitive peoples of the Amazon basin a beauty, a simplicity and a closeness to nature that we have lost. They have been able to combine their institutions, their way of government, economy, mythology, religion, music, art and their food in a systemic whole. All facets of their life are closely integrated, while we, advanced peoples, have confused and disoriented all of the above. We are so bound down with the inhibitions, oversophistication, and the discordancies of advanced culture, that we have lost this authentic integration.

But Lévi-Strauss is a realist. He examines the present, rather than laments for the past. As he returns to the Amazon after a period of absence there, as he travels through India, he discerns how the dislocating, disorienting aspects of modern culture are affecting primitive people. He sees that we have done these cultures no service, that the greatest crime of imperialism is that of cultural disintegration.

In addition, Lévi-Strauss writes that as he searches for the universal code, he finds that it is always binary. The code exists and operates in terms of binary oppositions: space and time; the male and the female; the raw and the cooked. Complementary, reciprocal sets of oppositions, he proposes, cut through all areas of primitive life and thought. The kinship system of primitive peoples, which is the basis of their social organization, is based upon a binary system, which constitutes a form of the underlying code. He finds as well that the same code is at work in their diets. As we might expect of a French mandarin, he finds it easiest to extrapolate a universal code in diet along with language.

Finally, Lévi-Strauss emphasizes the synchronic plane rather than the diachronic, that is, the comparative, the universal, the mythic, the immediate rather than the historical and temporal. He has rather severe observations about history, one of which is that it is an impossibility, and even if it were possible to write history, it would be largely a waste of time. Gathering data, collecting information about the past does not guarantee that the information can be submitted to meaning. The heap of information is bound to remain precisely that—a heap of information, a bundle of nonsense.

Further, the accumulation of extensive information does not necessarily guarantee that one can obtain the needed information. It is just as likely that one ends up rather with misappropriated, misdirected information. History will not teach anything. Truth comes through a synchronic analysis of universal social codes in the present. The most fruitful activity is the analysis of what exists simultaneously in the present. To ask questions about the past and the origin of present phenomena is futile and, even if there were such a thing as history, in any case it could not be recovered. History is a waste and a foolishness. Lévi-Strauss' position is therefore strongly antihistorical and exclusively considers the synchronic.

Lévi-Strauss' powerful impact can be judged by the fact that, along with the historian Ferdinand Braudel, he was one of the two great intellectuals in the French-speaking world in the sixties and the seventies. Braudel indeed did much to accommodate himself to Lévi-Strauss. He agreed with Lévi-Strauss that the writing of fact-centered "eventual" history is an insignificant activity, and that what is needed is the delineation of broad historical structures. Lévi-Strauss was the darling of the French intellectual world in the sixties and the seventies, and has become almost as influential in the United States.

In the dissemination of his influence, in France as well as abroad and particularly in the United States, Lévi-Strauss was assisted by Roland Barthes, who was the central figure of the Parisian literary intelligentsia in the the sixties and seventies. Barthes began as a Modernist and an existentialist after the Second World War, but after Lévi-Strauss gained in importance, he became a structuralist. Barthes was a highly-skilled popularizer, or public communicator, of structuralist ideas. Barthes did eventually, near the end of his life, become a professor, but most of his career was spent as an intellectual journalist, like Albert Camus.

Editor of the prestigious journal entitled *Tel Quel*, the leading intellectual journal in France in the fifties and sixties, which it still is, Barthes cleverly propagated the structuralist gospel. Before he died prematurely in an accident in 1980 (crossing the street, he was run over by a truck), he became a deconstructionist. Barthes' career reiterates the development of French theory and intellectual fashion since the War. His views were disseminated in the United States by the prolific critic Susan Sontag.

In a 1966 essay that was extremely influential in the U.S. as well as in France, Barthes demonstrated how Lévi-Strauss' theories could be applied to literary criticism, indeed had to be applied if literary criticism was to remain intellectually respectable. Barthes advocated the creation of a science of narrative structure. "Either a narrative is merely a rambling collection of events . . . or else it shares with other narratives a common structure which is open to analysis." Structuralism's "constant aim," said Barthes, is "to master the infinity of utterances by describing the language [code] of which they are the products." "From the point of view of narrative, what we call time does not exist, or at least only exists functionally, as an element of a semiotic system." These propositions by Barthes set the direction of vanguard literary criticism in France and the United States, and to some extent also in West Germany and Britain, for the next two decades. Barthes' most remarkable tour de force was a little aphoristic work called *Barthes by Barthes*, published in 1975 (English translation in 1977). It combined autobiography, literary criticism, and expositions in postcard form of the messages of structuralism and deconstruction.

How can we account for Lévi-Strauss' popularity and influence, aside from his good fortune in having Roland Barthes as his press agent? First of all, the intellectual world of the time demanded emphasis upon system. It wanted some vehicle to approach the systemic level rather than the individual level, and this demand could be found in a wide range of disciplines. Secondly, there is a certain quality of honesty about Lévi-Strauss, who strikes one as a man without illusions. He seems to be a wise man, well-travelled and well-informed. He is one of the cultural gurus of this century.

He is, in brief, an eloquent writer who is able to draw on a wealth of experience, reading and observation. *Tristes Tropiques* has already become one of the great classics of French literature and has been read variously as an anthropological treatise, an autobiography and as *Bildungsroman*, or the story of one individual's development. One simple reason for his popularity, but a true one, given the typical French love for beautiful, elegant books, may be the simple fact that Lévi-Strauss can and often does write remarkable French prose.

At the time that Lévi-Strauss was beginning work, linguistics was making its appearance as the paradigm of human sciences. It became very popular at the University of Paris in the fifties and sixties, and Lévi-Strauss was showing why this difficult science was important, demonstrating that it was the basis of social science as well as of philosophy. His work fitted in with the rise of the central role of linguistics. It is interesting to note that in French films produced in the sixties and seventies, characters that are supposed to be university students frequently claim to be studying linguistics. In an American film this would strike one as nothing less than ridiculous.

Lévi-Strauss not only benefited from the connection of his theory with linguistics, but also with the emerging science of semiotics. We have seen that this variant of formalism is the study of signs within language, the visual arts, and other cultural expressions. As in the case of Barthes and literary criticism, Lévi-Strauss was fortunate in the appearance of another follower stimulated by his structuralist doctrine to develop a theory of semiotics. This was the Italian medievalist, literary critic, and best-selling novelist Umberto Eco. Following Lévi-Strauss' anthropology, Eco propounded the view that "every act of communication to or between human beings . . . presupposes a signification system as its necessary condition." Signs bounce off each other in an endless series of significations. "Signs are the provisional result of coding rules which establish *transitory* correlations of elements, each of these elements being entitled to enter—under coded circumstances—into another correlation and thus to form a new sign."

Since signs are cultural units interacting infinitely, and since semiotics embraces all forms of communication, not only language but also involving art history, film, and advertising, it is obvious that semiotics has much material to explore, and it is fun to pursue this enterprise as well. Hence its burgeoning popularity in the seventies and its academic respectability.

Semiotics was a wonderful subject for subliterate American college students. They didn't have to struggle with Milton or Keats. They could write essays on Coca-Cola ads. Since, according to Eco, signs are infinitely referential, it is possible plausibly to say anything about them. Appropriately enough, a student at Brown University in 1986 who was indicted for prostitution turned out to be a semiotics major.

Eco's theory of semiotics owes something to the philosophy of Charles Saunders Peirce, who propounded a theory of semiotics as early as the 1880's (hardly anybody noticed except William James and *Popular Science* magazine.) It owes a good deal to the developers of linguistics like Saussure and Jakobson. But above all it was inspired by Lévi-Strauss' structuralism. The emergence of semiotics as an academic discipline, and its popularity with students on both sides of the Atlantic, contributed further to Lévi-Strauss' fame and reputation.

Structuralism received another boost from the transformational grammar theory of the American Noam Chomsky, which achieved very high visibility in the sixties and early seventies. Chomsky as a theorist of lingistics was, as he acknowledged, saying essentially the same thing as Roman Jakobson. His celebrity owed not a little to his role as a spokesman against the Vietnam War and his superior skills as a controversialist and polemicist. There is a universal structure to language, says Chomsky, which we humans can discover because we are genetically endowed (a bow to microbiology) with a "language faculty." The transformations of language constructions are "invariably structure-dependent." Again: "Language is generated by a system of rules and principles [which] . . . are in large measure unconscious and beyond the reach of potential consciousness." This is pure Lévi-Strauss (and Lacan). Chomsky's fame contributed to Levi-Strauss's guru status in the Western world by the early seventies.

In the sixties the discovery of DNA and therein of the deep biological structure, along with the introduction of computers and their coded programs, posed seeming confirmations and proofs of the validity of Lévi-Strauss' approach. Even Lévi-Strauss' binary reductionism was confirmed by computer science. His structural anthropology fitted in with psychoanalysis as well, particularly the Jungian variant which was very much on the rise in the sixties.

Therefore, Lévi-Strauss' seemed to be a philosophy that cohered with developments in most other fields of learning, ranging from the hard sciences to the social. And structuralism opened up attractive new opportunities for literary and art criticism. It became a channel for a new cultural wave. It both stimulated and reflected this new wave. Like all hegemonic cultural movements, structuralism articulated widespread wants and feelings.

It could be claimed that Lévi-Strauss' theory was idealistic, since it subscribed to the notion of a universal code that runs through all areas of life. Lévi-Strauss himself would deny that his thought is idealist, replying that it is objective, not subjective, meaning that his is not a system that foresees the self-imposition of the mind upon the world, but rather that it is a system that is exterior even to the mind and locatable in everything, including the nonmental. The mind, according to Lévi-Strauss, does not create structure, it partakes of it.

This contention could lead into a long philosophical debate. Wittgenstein's student, the English logical positivist A.J. Ayer, claimed in his history of twentieth-century philosophy that structuralism is either idealism or it is rubbish. This is not to say that Ayer's judgment is right, but only to point out how a disciple of Wittgenstein, an exponent of high Modernist philosophy, responded to structuralism. Ayer's judgment indicated that structuralism could be perceived as tending towards idealism and therefore politically it could be construed as non-Marxist, not even politically radical, and susceptible to a conservative interpretation. If the world as it exists is an objective system, then the world must be accepted for what it is: this is the rightist implication of idealist philosophy in all times and places.

Lévi-Strauss did not see himself as a rightist idealist. Far from it. He thought of himself as left. He regarded his theory as a post-Marxist radicalism. And he was explicitly pro-Third World and critical of Western imperialism. In the fifties and sixties, colonialism was still an issue, and his views qualified Lévi-Strauss, in his own eyes, and in the eyes of the left, as staunchly leftist. But the Yale critics, who, stimulated by Barthes, hailed Lévi-Strauss as an intellectual savior around 1969 (at a time when American anthropologists were not very enthusiastic about him) overlooked his views on the Third World or deemed them politically inconsequential. Considering structuralism as a whole, they found it readily adaptable for exegesis without menacing political implications. It seemed indeed to mesh well with traditional New Deal academic liberalism.

Lévi-Strauss did not get a warm reception from American anthropologists before 1970 because his approach to anthropology did not conjoin with either of the dominant modes of ethnographic thinking on the American scene in the sixties. It was left for the humanists and literary critics initially to imbibe and propagate structuralism—after which, by the late seventies, the anthropologists fell into line and became more respectful of the Parisian master. The Marxists could not stomach Lévi-Strauss because whether or not he was a philosophical idealist, he was certainly not a materialist in the sense of Malinowski or Marvin Harris. The dominant group of ethnographic functionalists, intellectual descendants of Franz Boas, and admirers of Ruth Benedict and Margaret Mead, noticed the sharp distinction between Boas' and Lévi-Strauss' methodological argument, even though with respect to judgment on the Third World, they came in the end to approximately the same conclusion. As an anthropological thinker, Lévi-Strauss was anti-Modernist and anti-Boasian, even though their political views were close together.

Boas had to challenge social Darwinism, the universalist theory which claimed that the Third World was primitive, backward, or decadent, and that it was located lower on the hierarchical classification of cultures than the white West. The primitive people were culturally retarded and would never attain the level of civilization and high morality that the white man had achieved. The old cultures of East Asia were effete and exhausted. Therefore the white man deserved to rule the world.

Boas opposed this view, proposing that each culture be taken as a closed system in itself. Cultures cannot be compared, they cannot be classified in hierarchical terms. The primitive cannot be opposed to the advanced, or described as decadent over against what is arbitrarily selected as morally superior. Each cultural system must be taken in and for itself. Each has its own needs, values, and the features of each, their functions exist in order to respond to these needs and articulate those values. This view may have satisfied Marcel Mauss, Lévi-Strauss' early teacher, but it did not coincide at all with structuralism.

Lévi-Strauss reached the same egalitarian conclusion as Boas, but arrived there through different means. That is, he too vehemently opposed social Darwinism and imperialism, but not by means of the Modernist route. He did not claim that each culture is distinct, self-enclosed, self-referential and does not admit of comparison with others, but, quite to the contrary, he found that all cultures operated within the same system. Not only therefore is the Third World the same as the so-called civilized world, operating according to the same structural paradigm, but it is better than the latter, its cultural procedures being more immediately informed by the universal code.

Claude Lévi-Strauss thus arrived at a beautiful conclusion that comes close to Heidegger's ultimate message. In the end, he stressed the theme of authenticity that is found in phenomenology, except that Lévi-Strauss applied this superior quality to societies, to behavioral groups, whereas Heidegger was more inclined to speak of the authentic individual.

*   *   *

Deconstruction

Andy Warhol, the post-Modernist painter and cultural critic, remarked that soon everyone will be famous for fifteen minutes. Intellectual systems and their gurus wore out almost as fast in the seventies and eighties as celebrities in the gossip columns. And partly at least for the same reason: overexposure. After being delineated in the classroom in a major university, expounded in several books that appeared in rapid succession, explicated further in interviews with radical chic journals, taken on a road show of public lectures in American universities, and popularized in a spate of paperbacks, any new intellectual system began to look tired after a decade of such intensive exploitation.

Structuralism became so famous and got so much exposure that even though many academics and all but a handful of students still did not understand what it was, it began to face the challenge of a cognate but still distinctive alternative theory during the late seventies. This was deconstruction and its leading spokesmen were the Parisian masters Jacques Derrida and Michel Foucault, although Jacques Lacan had been saying and applying in therapy many of its key ideas for many years. Until his untimely death Roland Barthes was again a highly skillful popularizer of the new movement. He has had a host of successors, including Christopher Norris in Britain (the author of the best short treatment of deconstruction) and Jonathan Culler in the U.S.

It may be wondered why French culture produced so many influential mandarins in the postwar period and especially in the seventies and eighties. There appear to be three reasons, all quite mundane. First, France retained its superb elitist secondary school system, in which everyone received a rigorous training in traditional philosophy. Secondly, the top echelon of French professors, particularly but not exclusively those in the Collège de France, a sort of institute for advanced study, had little or no teaching to do and were free to speculate and write major books. Thirdly, French academics had an unequalled support system in the form of droves of admiring students, intellectual journals that propounded their more imaginative ideas, cafés where they were lionized, and a press and TV that took their ideas seriously.

While some of this exists in and around any major university, nowhere did it function with the intensity and rich stimulation as on the left bank of the Seine. Parisian professors asserted important ideas because a whole infrastructure existed to demand that they ought to expound important ideas, and when they did say something interesting, there was unbounded adulation and reward.

Deconstruction's formation took place in the context of the then dominant intellectual mode of structuralism. In fact, to realize that deconstruction emerges from within structuralism as defined by Lévi-Strauss is imperative for a thorough appraisal of the movement.

Deconstruction is therefore a radical variant of structuralism. It can be seen as a culturally and, to some extent, politically left-wing offshoot of structuralism. Or it can be understood too as a further development within structuralism, wherefore it is sometimes referred to as poststructuralism. The latter term is synonymous with deconstruction.

Deconstruction shares three fundamental doctrines with Lévi-Strauss' structuralism. The first of these is that authenticity, or reality, is given to the system rather than to the individual. By assuming that it is the system that has validity, deconstruction shares with structuralism a philosophical opposition to existentialism and traditional humanism, which hold that authenticity and meaning reside with the individual.

The second structuralist doctrine which deconstruction shares is the attribution to language systems the function of fundamental mental structures, thereby endowing the sciences of linguistics and semiotics with the property of constituting the interpretive code. "Mentality" consists of a systematic code of signification to which linguistics and semiotics hold the key. French deconstructionists share enthusiasm for the linguistics of Ferdinand de Saussure. It is not so easy to ascertain whether de Saussure's status arises from the intrinsic quality of his work or the fact that he was French.

The third doctrine that deconstruction and structuralism have in common is the assumption that the mental system or deep structure operates in the unconscious as well as in the conscious realm. Deconstruction accepts this psychoanalytic doctrine, fundamental to structuralism, of the continuity between the unconscious and the conscious.

How then does deconstruction differ from Lévi-Strauss' structuralism, rendering it a radical variant of the latter? Deconstruction begins with a concern that in Lévi-Strauss at any rate, structuralism is philosophically idealistic. From the doctrine that a common universal structure runs through all mind and all societies, which can be stated in terms of a general code, structuralism can be readily converted, deconstruction believes, into a conservative philosophy. Although personally he was on the left and passionately committed to the Third World, the political implications of Lévi-Strauss' system are nevertheless ambivalent, in the view of deconstruction. Structuralism *per se* can be interpreted as a theory which accepts the world as it is and looks for ideal deep structures within the world as it is.

Deconstruction, on the other hand, seeks to avoid precisely this potential in structuralism, which can be used to legitimize a conservative neo-idealism. It wants to save, as it were, structuralism from being put to work in a conservative way. Deconstruction wants to continue the radical leftist program of 1968, but it undertakes this by basing itself on structuralism rather than on existentialism.

In the 1960's it was a Marxist brand of existentialism, as expressed by Jean-Paul Sartre, which was the inspiring doctrine of the student left in France, and which was eventually repudiated, just as its American counterpart was discredited. The strong individualism and anarchism of the New Left lost vigor and value as a result of the failure of the revolution in 1968. Deconstruction, then, wants to fulfill the radical intent, but to do so by abandoning humanism and existentialism, and by building its radical philosophy on the new reigning doctrine of structuralism. For this purpose the revised structuralism of deconstruction is necessary. So runs, in brief, the intellectual history of the late sixties and early seventies.

Jacques Lacan was certainly the forerunner of deconstruction. For there are ideas in Lacan, which he was propounding as early as the thirties, and certainly publishing in the fifties, that can be understood as being in the deconstructionist mode. The two masters, however, who emerged in the sixties as the deconstructionist spokesmen, were first, Jacques Derrida, who is still very much alive, being about 56 years old, and holds a chair in Paris and also teaches frequently at Yale University, where he is a permanent visiting professor. The second master of deconstruction was Michel Foucault, who held a chair in the Collège de France in Paris until he died in 1984 at the age of sixty-two.

Roland Barthes, who began his intellectual career as an existentialist and a Modernist in the late forties, and continued as a structuralist in the fifties and sixties, was in his later years a popularizer of deconstruction. Barthes was thus the intellectual bellweather of his generation in France.

The prime missionaries of deconstruction in the U.S. have been a group of eminent critics at Yale, to which group a Chicago critic must be added. The Yale group consists of Paul de Man, who died in 1985, J. Hillis Miller, who has recently received attention from *The New York Times Sunday Magazine*, albeit not entirely to his credit; and Geoffrey Hartman. The fourth member of the Yale group is Harold Bloom, whose stance within or vis-á-vis deconstruction remains in dispute. Bloom thinks of himself as unique, understandably, and he is right to see himself in this singular light. An extraordinary man, his work can be construed even as Jungian.

Paul Ricoeur is another deconstructionist who, like Lacan, pursues a strongly psychoanalytic orientation. He teaches at Chicago and frequently at Paris as well.

An impressive group of disciples has emerged after these masters, including some in England. Among the prominent ones in this country are Jonathan Culler of Cornell University, as well as two scholars who are deeply engaged in trying to arrive at a synthesis of Marxism and deconstruction, Michael Ryan of the University of California and Frederic Jameson of Duke University.

There is not much doubt that the overwhelming elite of the younger generation of literary critics or scholars who have received their doctoral degrees in a field of literature in the Unites States in the 1980's are deconstructionists. It has in fact become difficult for a recent recipient of a Ph.D. in literature to find appointment at one of the top twenty American institutions without demonstrating considerable familiarity with deconstructionist theory.

Jacques Derrida's major book is entitled *Of Grammatology*. Even though Derrida may be accused of not being quite intelligible in this and other books, it is a fact that deconstruction is not easy to present in writing—paradoxically for a theory that so valorizes the written text. A good introduction to Derrida's thought can be found in the concise volume *Positions*, which consists of interviews with Derrida and presents his theory in a fully comprehensible manner.

Derrida's biography is unusual. He is an Algerian Jew. It is indeed difficult to be more of an outsider in French society than by belonging to this doubly alien background. In the late nineteenth century, a very substantial Jewish community had emerged in Algeria, which had become part of the French empire in the 1830's. The nucleus of this community went as far back as the middle-ages, but it grew with waves of immigration through the centuries. They were a thriving and highly literate, though not particularly wealthy, middle class community.

In the Vichy period during the early forties, Algerian Jews were stripped of their French citizenship by Marshall Pétain and the Vichy government, only in order to be restored to citizenship in 1944, under the aegis of General Eisenhower. Against the bitter opposition of the French government in Algeria, he insisted that the citizenship of Algerian Jews be reconfirmed. The Algerian Jews were squeezed out during the independence movement of the late fifties— something that is ignored in Pontecorvo's famous film on *The Battle Of Algiers*—and they had to flee. Twenty per cent of the 300,000 Jewish population left Algeria for Israel, while eighty per cent, including the poorer segments, went to France, with the result that France, who had until then one of the smaller Jewish populations in Europe, became the country with the largest Jewish community on the continent, west of Russia. The Algerian Jews are mainly congregated in Marseille and other Mediterranean cities, and they remain marginal and poor in French society. This is the background from which Derrida emerged, and if he occasionaly sounds like someone with a chip on his shoulder, then he comes by this condition honestly.

Derrida expresses his debt to Nietzsche, Freud and Heidegger. Although his greatest influence has been on literary criticism, he in fact holds a chair of philosophy. He spent the early years of his career lecturing on Heidegger and philosophy. Derrida never mentions Jacques Lacan as having exerted a real influence on him, for reasons that are not evident, but he does express debt to Mallarmé, the late nineteenth-century French proto-Modernist poet and critic. Derrida sees his deconstructionist stance as going back to the French culture of Mallarmé's time and to the Modernist movement in general. And it can indeed be claimed that deconstruction, as defined by Derrida, is a kind of neo-Modernism—let us here stress the words *a kind of*—for there are also incompatibilities between Derridean deconstruction and Modernism.

Modernist thought and deconstruction overlap in three ways, the first and most important of which is the notion of the self-referentiality of the text as an *epistémè*, which is one of the central concepts in deconstruction. *Epistémè* describes the self-enclosed structure of a system of knowledge. In other words, what Modernism referred to as the self-referentiality of the text, is subsumed in deconstruction under the rubric of the *epistémè*, according to which the text is a self-enclosed, structural world of knowledge.

Secondly, Derrida and the Modernists both display preference for *écriture*, the written text, as opposed to oral texts. This doctrine, which demonstrates one more similarity between deconstruction and Modernism, points as well at a major difference between Derrida and Lévi-Strauss. As a cultural anthropologist, Lévi-Strauss has a natural liking for oral evidence, whereas Derrida's emphasis, an unmistakably Modernist inclination, falls entirely on the written text. Modernist critics of the first two decades of the twentieth century fastened their theory on the written as deliberately opposed to the oral text.

The third compatibility between deconstruction and Modernism resides in the emphasis on close reading, or what the deconstructionists call *hermeneutics*, a term that has become a code word for deconstructionists. Originally used in Biblical criticism and familiarly by Talmudic scholars, the word hermeneutics, given that it figures so prominently in deconstruction, has interesting bearings on Derrida's thought and is telling in terms of the cultural and ethnic background he comes from. In its modern deconstructionist usage, hermeneutics means the close reading and interpretation of texts so as to yield the structure of knowledge and the signification contained therein. In a sense, this is precisely what T.S. Eliot, I.A. Richards, Cleanth Brooks, and R.P. Blackmur had in mind when they valorized the close reading of the text.

There is, therefore, a propensity in deconstruction to do as the Modernists: to assume the self-referentiality of the text, to emphasize the written text, and to engage in close reading. Except that now the process of reading and interpretation is described as the pursuit of the *epistémè* through a study of the *écriture* by the method of hermeneutics. This is essentially the same as the Modernist program.

This is a prime reason why Derrida has found such favorable reception at Yale University. In the forties and fifties, Yale had been the capital of Modernism in the United States. The Modernist movement in criticism in this country began at Harvard, but its center moved to Yale in the late thirties and forties, where critics like Cleanth Brooks and John Crowe Ransom were teaching. And Derrida, because his deconstruction carries some strong affinities to Modernism, was particularly welcomed at this institution.

At the same time, after four decades, Modernism appeared exhausted and redundant. The Yale critics in the mid-sixties looked around for something new. Geoffrey Hartman momentarily hailed the Jungian Northrop Frye as an intellectual savior. This prepared the way for reception of structuralism at the end of the sixties. But structuralism was diametrically opposed to Modernism and this forced the Yale critics towards an intellectual crisis they did not want to encounter. Derrida was a perfect solution for them. He emerged out of the structuralist tradition, maintained some of structuralism's cardinal principles, but he also reasserted Modernist traditions that Yale could not bring itself, after four decades, to surrender. Furthermore, Derrida was a philosophy professor at Paris and eminently respectable and he knew a lot about Heidegger and Nietzsche. He was made to order. He became Yale's main man.

The key concept in Derrida's thought is *différance*, not to be reduced to the word "difference," which is nevertheless contained in the Derridean concept. *Différance* is, and means, a combination of differences. He defines the concept as "the idea of conflictuality," which is the best translation in English of *différance*. It can also be described as intrinsic oppositions.

In each signifying text, in each text that holds meaning, there are by its nature oppositions or internal conflicts at work, by which the text deconstructs itself. This is the condition of *différance* or conflictuality. The process takes the surface signification, or the surface meaning, and breaks it down, disintegrates it, because of the oppositional and conflictual nature of language. The text, through a self-generating mechanism that is inscribed in the very being of language, breaks itself down into several simultaneous layers of meaning.

There is not one canonical signification to a text, as humanists have (allegedly) thought all along, but rather, there lies, beyond the surface meaning, one more meaning, and then additional layers of meaning. There are, in fact, infinite meanings in the text, moving from the immediate, conscious layer toward the unconscious, until finally one approaches the strata of meaning that border on the unconscious. Deconstruction is theoretically an objective, involuntary process because of the intrinsically fragmenting nature of the signifier.

This notion of the instability of signification is based on the oppositional, conflictual structures built into language. That this is the nature of language is not an assumption that admits of proof. Nor does one get the impression, upon having read Derrida's *Of Grammatology*, that he himself has succeeded in proving it. But building upon Saussure, from whom comes the notion of the arbitrariness of the sign, he claims an essential instability in language. The nature of language is such that it conceals meaning, but does not do so fully, leaving traces on the surface that yield to pursuit.

There is certainly an element of common sense in Derrida's theory of *différance*. We frequently observe in didactic theory of humanistic exposition fragmentary indices that do not fit the main thrust of the argument. Derrida is saying that this implies the return of the repressed opposition from the unconscious. Again this is not implausible.

Anomalies exist on the surface of the text. A text emits a message on the surface, but on the same surface it harbors as well, albeit sporadically, anomalies, or gaps, which, when taken into account, are found to conflict and put into question what is signified. Derrida stresses these gaps—between words, in meaning—which exist on the virtual margins of the text. As one focuses on these gaps, the text begins to deconstruct itself. The gaps spread, get bigger. The margins fall into the body of the text. It is not, however, the critic who is procuring that this happen, but the text itself, the signifier, systematically deconstructing itself before the reader's expectant eyes.

In the master's own words: "The play of *différance* . . . prevents any word, any concept, any major enunciation from coming to summarize, and to govern . . . the movement and textual spacing of differences." Because of the *différance* (conflictuality) at work in language, no single meaning can claim absolute authority over a given text, nor can the critic control, despite all effort, this movement of the text. Language is characterized by "the structural impossibility of limiting this [conceptual] network, of putting an edge on its weave," of "tracing a margin that would not be a new mark." There is, in other words, a structural impossibility of imposing a finity and a fixity, or a conclusion, to textual signification. When the humanist professor reads a text in order to find there a single, consecrated meaning, the text explodes in his face.

Derrida confronts Lévi-Strauss as a dangerous intellectual conservative, or at least, potentially so. Derrida advocates "a general strategy of deconstruction," writing that the latter is to avoid both "*neutralizing* the binary oppositions of metaphysics, [that is, idealism] and simply *residing* within the closed field of these oppositions, thereby confirming it [that is, conservatism]." The problem with Lévi-Strauss' structuralism as seen by Derrida is that it acknowledges the binary oppositions in mental and language codes, but it also tries to control and neutralize them, thereby attempting to keep them residual, rather than unbounding the text and the binary oppositions to the free play which is the aim of radical deconstruction. In Derrida's view, Lévi-Strauss wants to systematize and control binary conflicts while Derrida wants to liberate them into intellectual revolutions.

Derrida speaks of "the neccessity of an interminable analysis." We all have heard of the never ending story. Here is its counterpart, never ending criticism. He sounds the call for radical thinking: "The time for overturning is never a dead letter." That which is overturned are conventional meaning, traditional significations, surface readings. The perpetual overturning of meaning is in the nature of language, as is the interpenetration of layers of significations, reaching into the unconscious.

Derrida is aware of the radical social implications of his theory. His statement that "to deconstruct the opposition, first of all, is to overturn the hierarchy of a given moment" is tantamount to a call for an intellectual revolution which has broad cultural and social implications. Further he claims that "'thought' means nothing." "Thought" means, in this context, humanistic thought, that is, what the humanist tradition has hypothesized as thought, a canonical system or Western civilization itself. Derrida is putting into question consecrated, unquestioned entities such as "the humanities," "the classical tradition," "the medieval heritage" or "the liberal doctrine," all of which he regards as unstable and untenable concepts that mean, quite simply, nothing. The liberal humanists, in Derrida's view, are at best pathetically obsolete. At worst, they are the enemy who must be mercilessly overthrown.

The obvious implication of all this is that Derrida is an anti-humanist, since, first of all, he believes that there is no fixed meaning or canon or tradition. There is only an infinity of meaning. The humanists struggled over the centuries to create a canon, a received sacred tradition of valid texts that extended from Plato through Hegel. Derrida, by deconstructing the texts and by presumably pointing at significations in these texts which undercut both the continuity among and the meaning in them, demonstrates that the fixity of the humanist tradition is based on naught. All canons may be scrambled, all texts are subject to reevaluation, and their meanings are open to perpetual reconsideration. Derrida offers unlimited horizons for busy literary critics. No wonder they love him.

Derrida's position becomes clearer when he is compared with Lionel Trilling, who was the idol of literary criticism in the United States in the forties and fifties. Trilling and his colleagues at Columbia University, as will be remembered from a previous chapter, devoted much time to determining the essential texts of Western civilization which every student in Columbia College should have to read and reread, not only for what might be understood as their intrinsic worth, but as a tradition which culminates and finds its ulterior fulfillment in New Deal liberalism. Derrida's response to this project would be to point out that the number of canons are as numerous as the possible readings and combinations of texts, which is but to say that the number is practically infinite. What Trilling was doing was impossible and meretricious in its implications.

In the 1930's and 40's Trilling, the New York Jew, tried mightily to construct and valorize a canon of texts for Western civilization. In the sixties and seventies Derrida, the Algerian Jew, tried just as hard to deconstruct and devalue the same canon. This comparison illuminates the contrasting status of the Jewish intellectual in the Western world between 1940 and 1970. He moved from the defensive, from trying to show that he belonged within the humanist liberal Christian tradition, to flaunting his opposition, his expression of conflictuality, his disdain for that tradition. T.S. Eliot the anti-Semite would have had some interesting comments to make on this contrast.

Another reason why Derrida can be considered antihumanistic is his disbelief in the notion of the controlling mind. As the text deconstructs itself and generates its own multiplicity of meaning, the critic, or the reader, is a mere witness to the text's self-unraveling. There is of course some speciousness involved here, for when Derrida himself spends two hours deconstructing a brief philosophical or literary fragment (which he was prone to do from the lecture platform for a high fee), his mind is very much at work, not to say in control. Rather than the text working itself, it appears to be clever Derrida at work on the text. But he claims that he is himself acting as a *conduit*, transferring from the text into critical language the multiplicity of significations that comprise the text. He is rendering, in other words, what the text renders to him.

At this point, it becomes clear that Derrida's main departure from the Modernists of the twenties and the thirties is that the latter were committed humanists. Richards, Eliot and Cleanth Brooks believed first of all that there was very much a canonical tradition, and secondly that the canon in fact admitted of interpretation. Derrida, while also engaging in close reading, denies the real existence of both the canon and the canonical interpretation. In this sense, he is posthumanist and post-Modernist.

Derrida's published writings are concerned with philosophy, language studies, and literary and semiotic criticism. The radical political implications are present and are meant to be present, but in implicit rather than explicit form. Yet the leftist orientation is sufficient for Marxists to make a strenuous effort to bridge Marxism and Derrida's deconstruction. Frederic Jameson, Rosalind Krauss, and Michael Ryan, among others, are hard at work on his project, producing reams of dense literary and art criticism.

The enthusiasm of leftist theorists like Jameson, Krauss, and Ryan for Derrida derives from his appearing to be the long-sought fulfiller of the Frankfurt School. He was attacking the bourgeoisie at its hegemonic cultural center, its canonical texts embodying its faith in the Western consciousness. And Derrida was attaining the holy grail of the left with the blessing of a good part of the academic world. Whether it was the English department at Yale, the French department at N.Y.U., or the Humanities Institute at Cornell, Derrida was the recipient of lavish praise and public honor. Through Derrida, the left believed it was having its cultural epiphany at last.

A final reason for Derrida's popularity and influence is his familiarity with the language and concept formation of German phenomenology. Derrida first gained attention in Paris as a persuasive teacher of Heidegger's philosophy and his deconstructive theory can be viewed as having a certain compatibility with phenomenology. The text, in Derrida's interpretation, is an active Other with its own rules of conflictual *différance* separated from consciousness. The deconstructive process involves coming to terms, engaging interactively with this autonomous text. This view readily parallels the key ingredient in Heidegger's philosophy. Derrida's theory could be regarded as a skillful effort to blend French structuralism and German phenomenology. This intellectual bridging of the Rhine was unusual in the postwar era and contributed to Derrida's visibility and influence.

The other leading deconstructionist thinker, Michel Foucault, was a social theorist and cultural historian. His radical critique of culture and society was therefore entirely explicit, and he therefore gained extravagant adulation on the left in the seventies and eighties. On the whole, this leftist enthusiasm for Foucault is justified, although not quite in the unqualified form that it often takes, because there is a problem for the left in his doctrine.

It can be said that Marx and Nietzsche were Foucault's main inspiration with the influence of Durkheim, the *Annales* school, and Lacan also prevalent. With regard to Marx, Foucault frankly said that "it is impossible at the present time to write history without using a whole series of concepts directly or indirectly related to Marx's thought and situating itself within a horizon of thought which has been defined and described by Marx." Nietzsche was important because he was concerned with "power relation," which Foucault also wanted to explore. Indeed, he said that like Nietzsche, he was engaged in a study of the "genealogy of morals." Like Lacan, he thought that man is always accompanied by "an element of darkness . . . the unthought . . . the Other." Like Durkheim and Braudel and the *Annales* school, Foucault saw society as an integrated functioning whole. "Power comes from below; that is, there is no binary and all-encompassing opposition between rulers and ruled and the root of all power relations." Adorno's theory of cultural mediation is also reflected in Foucault's theory.

Obviously Foucault was a very learned scholar. The purpose of all this learning was to develop a theory of power. "The rules of right, the mechanisms of power, the effects of truth or if you like, the rules of power and the power of true discourses . . . formed the general terrain of my concern."

Michel Foucault had a distinguished but ordinary academic career as a historian of ideas. He became known initially, in the mid-fifties, for his first important book of intellectual history, entitled in English translation *Madness and Civilization*, a remarkable work on seventeenth-century French culture.

Those who read Foucault for the first time in the late fifties and early sixties, agreed that he was a clever and first-rate historian of ideas. It was realized only later that the book on madness was part of an entire new program.

In the sixties, Foucault represented himself as a structuralist, and in the seventies, as a deconstructionist. As shall be seen, there are some aspects of his thought that are strongly deconstructionist, while others remain as strongly structuralist. Of course, his deconstruction is a radical form of structuralism and generates no problematic contradiction between the two movements. Above all, it should be pointed out that ultimately Foucault did not like to describe himself in terms of any label but that of the human scientist.

Foucault died prematurely in 1985 of AIDS. He was gay and very conscious of being so. He contracted AIDS while in Los Angeles to give a lecture at U.C.L.A. and died within a year.

There are three basic concepts in Foucault's work. The first of these is the archeology of knowledge. Foucault tries to write non-historical, or discontinuous history. What are important are the *épistemés*, the deep structures of knowledge, that exist in society in particular eras. Although officially he was professor of the history of ideas, Foucault does not call himself a historian. He prefers the title of archeologist of knowledge. Like an archeologist, he sinks down shafts into the culture of a particular period and excavates its *épistémè* or the structure of knowledge at work in that society. In that sense, his work is deeply structural, for, in the last analysis, Foucault, like Braudel, is writing history that might be acceptable to Lévi-Strauss. Braudel presents the deep structures of society, and Foucault those of culture or systems of knowledge. His is the cultural or intellectual equivalent of Braudel's work in social history.

Foucault does not believe that the paths of change can be extrapolated. The study of the past comprises a series of discreet, discontinuous archaeological digs into culture and mentality.

The second Foucaultian theory that becomes increasingly pronounced in his work is ethical theory. Foucault is, entirely, thoroughly, a moral relativist. He writes that all the institutions of a society, as well as all its ethical principles and cultural forms, are instruments of power. It is the will to power which perpetually plays itself out in history, and no matter how brilliant and how admired, aesthetically or otherwise, cultural forms have as their fundamental function this instrumentality for power and serve, or seek, the interests of a ruling body. This theory obviously draws on a Nietzschean notion, as well as extrapolating a Marxian conception.

It was the Marxists who had held that the bourgeoisie used culture, residually, viscerally and fundamentally, in order to sustain their power. Foucault uses this idea, but unlike Marxists, who limit this cultural practice to the bourgeoisie, he includes all ruling groups—the aristocracy and monarchy, and democratic adversary groups—as much as the bourgeoisie, in the scheme. The hegemonic struggle for power is not terminated by the triumph of Communists, feminists, or Third World liberators. It is endemic, secular, and perpetual. Of course, this assumption begs the question whether Foucault's books are then designed to achieve *his* power. The answer is affirmative.

Foucault wrote a series of provocative books demonstrating power at work in manipulating culture. He is especially interested in showing that the progressive ideas in a culture are archetypical of this search for power. It is not merely the decadent or reactionary forces that partake of power structures, but the progressive ones, the innovators, the reputed great instruments of human progress that are in fact designed to enhance power.

Foucault considers first of all the insane asylum, which was the invention of the seventeenth century. Instead of letting the mad wander around the streets, as in New York today or in the middle ages, the seventeenth century incarcerated them in asylums. Whereas the middle ages had marginalized lepers, and appointed them for exclusion from society, the seventeenth century selected people it called "the mad" for incarceration. Who were these "mad"? They were mystics, nonconformists, misfits, and the unhappy, people in other words, who in one way or another were torn apart by social institutions such as the family and local government and were expressing their discontentment and resistance, and who thereby attracted attention either within the family or other small social groups. "'Dangerous' people had to be isolated . . . so that they could not act as a spearhead for popular resistance."

It may momentarily, and superficially, seem that the seventeenth-century introduction of insane asylums constituted an instance of human progress, since these, it could be construed, were shelters that protected the mad from abuse. But the same institution can be also regarded as segregatory, says Foucault, excluding from the world the nonconformist, who in the middle ages was placed in leper colonies.

In *Discipline and Punish* Foucault takes up the late eighteenth-early nineteenth century invention of the penitentiary, which marked the switch from the practice of either executing criminals or transporting them to Australia or other colonies. Now the criminal was locked up in the local penitentiary, where he was supposed to be restrained but also reeducated and so transformed into a good citizen. In this way, criminals were not only to pay their "debt to society," but they were to be disciplined into mental transformation as well.

Once again, Foucault claims the use of discipline and segregation to remove nonconformists from social life, since criminals too, like the mad, were people who were in conflict with the social order. Their criminality was very often inherited. They came, for the most part, from the vast ghettos of the late eighteenth and early nineteenth century city, whose dark panorama is so well drawn in the novels of Charles Dickens. The penitentiary, whose original rationale was that it would rediscipline and reform the criminal for reintegration into society, became one more means of segregating and removing threats to social order. This novel institution was much talked about, or talked up, as it were, and praised by the progressives of the day, and above all by Quaker reformers and liberal idealists, who were in fact instruments in the repression and segregation of dissenting and adversary people.

It must be realized that the issues Foucault has taken up were crucial for many developments in French culture in the post-World War II period. In the late forties and fifties, Frenchmen were fascinated by criminality, by what constituted the criminal, and whether the criminal was different from other, normal people. Foucault's book on punishment and the penitentiary draws upon this proclivity in the French culture of the post-war period which took a relativistic stance on criminality, which idea was perhaps made possible by experiencing the Gestapo at work in the streets of Paris, and its repression of the Resistance—an effective way of driving home the idea that the determination of what is criminal is a relative enterprise.

Another source of relativist attitude to criminality came from gays who still experienced social marginality. As a gay, Foucault imbibed their radically ambivalent view of criminality.

In his later years Foucault embarked on a multi-volume history of sexuality, and he died having completed three volumes, all of which are now available in English. This is a brilliant piece of work, very different from what we are accustomed to expect from that title. Another one of Foucault's demonstrations of the will to power, the *History of Sexuality* Vol. I, shows that the sexual liberation movement that began at the beginning of this century and went through successive phases, especially influential ones in the sixties and the seventies, has been once again the power play of those seeking hegemony in society. He asks us to remember that while the sexual liberation movement did indeed increase human happiness, the people who were leading it were also engaged in manipulation. For them it was another forum for achieving their desired place in the world. It was an instrument, a power mechanism, for advancing their situation within the power structure.

It is also Foucault the gay that is talking here, taking an acerbic and critical view of women's liberation as a form of instrumentation and assertion of power by one social group. Given Foucault's position on the sexual liberation movement, it becomes amusing to find publications such as *The Village Voice* hailing him as the champion of sexual liberation. He is, of course, that in some ways, but reading the *History of Sexuality*, one discovers that he does not exempt that movement from the same kind of moral and institutional ambivalence that he ascribes to all forms of progressive emancipation.

The deconstructive side of Foucault is much in evidence here. Just as for Derrida, all texts and concepts spontaneously fragment into their intrinsically conflictual segments, so for Foucault all moral affirmations disintegrate into thrusts for power and manipulative domination. There is no ethical system which rises above the corrosive force of total moral relativism.

The third important idea of Foucault is his proclamation of the end of man—the end of bourgeois and humanistic man. Man as he has been perceived in bourgeois liberal humanism is being dismantled, deconstructed, and cannot withstand the cold light of moral relativism that is cast upon him. The self-satisfied, self-congratulatory liberal humanism is disintegrating as it reveals itself as the instrument of class power and of the socially and educationally privileged. The individual subject with his conscience and reason that was the product of the cultural revolutions of the Reformation, the Enlightenment, and Romanticism is dying just as, according to Nietzsche, the idea of a transcendent, theistic God died in the nineteenth century.

Thus Derrida announces that humanist thought is nothing, and Foucault proclaims the end of bourgeois man. Both are the heralds of the decease of humanist bourgeois rationalism.

In the case of Derrida, the deconstruction movement has generated a theory of literary criticism, an extremely influential one. In the case of Foucault, on the other hand, it has led to a post-Marxist relativism. If Derrida spells literary or linguistic deconstruction, Foucault's is social and moral deconstruction. In both cases, there is found an instrument of radical theorizing against humanistic values and particularly against the liberal values of the 1940's and 50's. Therefore, both Derrida and Foucault have strongly appealed to the younger generation of Marxist scholars and theorists. Their deconstructive theories contain instruments for the further critique of bourgeois traditions and capitalist culture. They point at ways that step beyond Adorno and the Frankfurt School, and using deconstructionist theory, it is possible to propagate an additional erosion of contemporary culture.

There are three journals, lively ones and very much worthy of perusal—*Telos*, which began publication in St. Louis but is now being published in the East Village in New York; *October*, edited by Rosalind Krauss of the City University of New York; and *Social Text*, published by an international leftist collective, who are involved in the program of developing a new post-Marxist critique of capitalist culture using deconstruction.

Inspite of the enthusiasm of Western Marxists for deconstruction, it must be realized that neither Derrida nor Foucault would last very long in a country of the Soviet bloc. Their theory can be used with equal, if not greater, efficacy against Soviet culture. It would be interesting to see how Marxist scholars in Eastern Europe respond to deconstruction. They may not get the opportunity.

Derrida's deconstruction of Communist Party texts would immediately mark him as an extreme dissident. Foucault's enthusiasm for Marx would gain him Party plaudits in the short run, but it would be soon apparent that Foucault does not think history has stopped with the Dictatorship of the Proletariat. In Foucault's theory the Soviet state must also be seen as a mechanism for the gaining and retention of power by a particular group. Foucault would attempt to strip from the Communist apparatchiks their claim to moral superiority and would come into irreconcilable conflict with them.

Marx would see Derrida and Foucault as more within the anarchist tradition than as his own followers. That in part accounts for the immense popularity and prestige Derrida and Foucault gained in American universities in the late seventies and eighties. There had been a strong anarchist vein in the New Left. Now that the New Left was no longer marching to the barricades and offing the pigs, but had withdrawn into its academic citadel, studying and applying Derrida and Foucault offered a vicarious thrill of anarchist-type radicalism. What impact deconstruction will have on a generation of students who have had it preached to them in upscale colleges remains to be seen. Possibly no adverse impact whatsoever.

Indeed studying Derrida and Foucault may be construed as excellent preparation for intended lawyers and M.B.A.'s aiming at yuppiedom. The Parisian masters can reasonably be viewed as imparting an extreme relativism, indeed a virtual nihilism, that will allow the youthful law associates or investment banker to hold nothing sacred—either text or institution—in their ruthless pursuit of wealth and power. The historian of the future may see Derrida and Foucault as deconstructors of not only bourgeois rationality and morality but of any philosophy of altruism and public service. They are authentic nihilist voices of the new age.

*   *   *

The Decline of the American University

The culture of the postwar Western world was heavily focused on the expansion of universities and their enhanced role in intellectual life and national well-being. While this was particularly the case in the United States, where the campus came to play a major role even in the performing and visual arts, it was also true of Western society as a whole. By 1960 the importance of scientist and scholar to society was endorsed by governmental officials and corporate leaders alike and the need to provide the best possible college teaching and training facilities to the emerging generation was not questioned.

With the tidal demographic wave of the sixties, universities in the Western world experienced an unprecedented student demand and enjoyed a new level of prosperity and expansionary capacity. This high tide of social appreciation and fiscal affluence for universities turned out, however, to be relatively short-lived. Once again the American university was the bellwether institution and its destiny was shared, although again not as critically, by European universities.

One of the intriguing untold stories of the late sixites and early seventies was how the radical turmoil of the period particularly unsettled those white ethnic professors—particularly Jews, Italians and Slavs—who had finally broken their way into the departments and even some administrations of the old, established American universities. What they had wanted to conquer were the shining heights of the academic establishment. They had their sights on the pinnacle for half a century, and by the mid-sixties they had finally succeeded in scaling these heights. But open admissions and campus activism was threatening to change the nature of the American university overnight into a very different kind of democratizing, politically conditioned institution. It was not for this that they had struggled through City College in the forties, suffered privation and insults at Harvard, Columbia or Princeton in the fifties. They had not painfully internalized the tenuous, complex heritage of European aristocratic culture now to be publicly abused by black activists and S.D.S. ideologues, or to devote their exquisitely-tuned minds to teaching the rudiments of English composition to the semiliterate.

All the turmoil and disorder, which 1968 symbolized and in many instances directly caused, as well as the resurgence of conservatism on the campus and in society at large, led in the seventies to the downgrading of the experimental and more individualized curricula that had begun to appear fitfully in the sixties—and rarely as yet with any clear advance in learning. Instead in the late seventies there was a return toward the mandated distribution of course requirements and basic skills courses of the 1950's. Since the Eisenhower era was deemed to be a happy one in U.S. history, by the late seventies many colleges were making a bold, innovative step forward into the curriculum of the 1950's.

The reintroduction of distribution requirements at Harvard with much fanfare, under the leadership of Dean Henry Rosovsky, encouraged many other campuses, such as Stanford, N.Y.U. and Brooklyn to do the same. Rosovsky advertised his program as a "core curriculum." It was really a smorgasbord of allegedly tasty items from a stale menu culled out of Western civilization.

There were some very fine institutions—the colleges at Columbia, at the University of Chicago, St. John's College in Maryland—that had never departed from the intellectually demanding, highly structured great books core curricula in the humanities that they had established in the 1920's and 30's. A highly structured core curriculum adapted to the intellectual and social milieu of the eighties could be an interesting and beneficial experiment, especially if it involved the natural and social sciences as well as literature and philosophy. But the resurgence of mandatory distribution and basic skill requirements in a host of institutions in the 80's can scarcely be categorized as innovative and experimental. It was more a reflection of the cautious attitudes that affected the administrations and faculties at that time, and of the failure of the American university to stem the decline of the American high school.

The wide-felt need in the late seventies to establish in the first year of college basic skill courses in English composition and mathematical computation, and distribution requirements aiming to instruct freshmen and sophomores in the rudiments of history, literature, philosophy and natural and social scientific thinking, was a recognition that even high-prestige and very selective colleges found that students were emerging from high school in effect unprepared for university-level education. Instead of using its then rich available resources in the sixties to upgrade secondary education, the American higher education establishment now felt obligated in the more austere seventies to instruct the products of lamentably inadequate high schools in the kind of basic cognition that students in Europe gained at the secondary education level.

The American university had itself contributed to the decline in the quality of secondary education by developing schools of "professional education" and by getting state and municipal boards to require this kind of marginal training for certification to teach in public schools. It was the ineffective teaching in the high schools by the graduates of these schools of education which now required even highly selective colleges like Harvard and Stanford to compensate for the low quality of instruction and standardization in the high schools.

The 1960's, and extending into the early years of the 1970's, was an era of intellectual ferment and cognitive advancement in the American university. Through the latter part of the 70's and into the late 80's, there was a slowing down of intellectual advancement, a retreat from pedagogical experimentation, and a general conservatizing trend.

In the sciences, outside of biology and computer science, the American universities were no longer secure in their world-wide performance and in many disciplines their intellectual leadership was fast eroding. A 1980 study showed the severe decline in the quality of scientific research instrumentation on the major American campuses in the 1970's.

During the 1970's the most important discoveries in the physics of elementary particles were made at the laboratory of CERN (Conseil Européen pour Recherche Nucléaire) in Geneva—a European consortium center for advance work in physics. No laboratory in the United States could equal CERN's experimental facilities. While federal sponsorship of basic research increased in the mid-eighties, the extra margin of support was narrowly focused on five high speed computer centers and the Strategic Defense Initiative (S.D.I.).

In the humanities almost entirely and in the social sciences, outside of economics, the American university was looking for intellectual leadership to Western Europe, particularly to France, to some extent England and West Germany. Paris was again the intellectual capital of the West. As in the first three decades of this century, university professors were significantly better paid in West Germany and some of the other continental European countries than in the United States, with long-term consequences for the quality of research on campus.

The reduction of federal support for research, the aftershocks of the political upheavals of the late sixties, the return of a Great Depression in the academic world producing miserable job prospects for Ph.D.'s in the humanities and the soft social sciences that poured out of both the old and new graduate schools in the early seventies, were disincentives for the best minds to enter these professionally unrewarding fields in the early eighties. The loss of real income by faculty in the late seventies as salaries did not keep pace with inflation by a significant margin, the retrenchment of university budgets effected by state governments, and the fiscal difficulties of many private universities, even some of the more distinguished, all had a severely depressing effect on the intellectual vitality and cognitive ambience of the American campuses. The adverse labor market in the early eighties drove the college students so powerfully toward career-oriented undergraduate programs that professors in physics, philosophy, literature and history faced shrinking classes at both undergraduate and graduate levels.

In these adverse circumstances, arts and science faculty increasingly lost confidence in the value of what they were doing, or retreated into privatism and the pursuit of research that won the plaudits of a few colleagues in other institutions but could receive little recognition and no tangible reward in society at large.

Just as the tone and mode of American academic life changed rapidly in the early sixties as the upward swing of demographic revolution became visible, so the sharp decline in college-age population in the early eighties produced a widespread sense of futility and foreboding of defeat on the American campus. The talk was now all retrenchment, cost-cutting and the "management of decline."

One of the positive advances on the American campus in the seventies had indeed been improved planning and more effective management: would that the expansion of campuses and the creation of whole new universities in the sixties had been carried out with such care and skillful control as was now exhibited by a number of campus administrators.

The American academic world made some bad mistakes during the era of prosperity in the sixties and early seventies. Why was it so short-sighted, reckless and profligate? The 1950's had been a time of low risk-taking and relative rigidity on the campuses, both institutionally and intellectually. There was a constant fear that after the World War II veterans on the G.I. Bill were gone, the depressed condition of the thirties on the campus would return. This caution served as an unfavorable background for the expansionary and rapidly changing situation to be encountered in the 1960's, which required highly imaginative and novel strategies. Leadership was poor in the academic world, good planning and careful management virtually non-existent.

Unanticipated by the reckless expansionary campus policies of the sixties and seventies, the downside of the demographic revolution in the 1980's became a terrifying reality. The traditional college-age population declined nationally in the eighties by twenty to twenty-five per cent in at least three-quarters of the states. An optimistic view presented by some higher education analysts that the shrinkage of the national college age population would be balanced by an increased percentage of this group going to college— that is, the demographic base would shrink, but more of this cohort would attend college—did not occur. On the contrary, from 1973 to 1978 the proportion of the college age population going to college actually declined by a significant margin.

For those in the higher education establishment who could see nothing to do except manage decline and plan and implement retrenchment, history offered a certain sanction and authority. There have, after all, been only two short periods of creativity and affluence in the history of the American university. These eras—before the First World War and the sixties and the very early seventies—were, it could be claimed, moments of exception. Now with the late seventies and eighties, the American university was returning to the norm, to the shrinkage of the higher educational delivery system. It was said the U.S. could not now avoid the impoverishment of faculties, of a severe level of academic unemployment, of little or no pedagogical experimentation, and of research capacity lagging behind more prosperous countries such as the World War II vanquished foes, West Germany and Japan, to whom America did the favor of proscribing from heavy investment in defense so they could invest more of their internal resources than the U.S. could in scientific and techno-logical research.

It is not only in cars and electronic equipment that the U.S. was overtaken by other countries. In the humanities and human sciences, there was in the eighties a shrinking campus intellectual base that could not compete with the venerable, deep and ever-resilient aristocratic cultures of France and England. Incredible as it might have seemed in 1965, the U.S. in the mid-eighties was witness to the replaying of the Jamesian scenario in which the United States took the role of the intellectual colonial, the academic dependent of Europe.

David Reisman and Christopher Jencks, in their celebrated book *The Academic Revolution*, published in 1968, thought they had portrayed the shape of higher education in this country—dominated by the imperial research universities and their affluent elite faculty—for a long time to come. It actually described a very ephemeral moment in American higher education.

Not only this optimistic view of the American campus from the perspective of Harvard Square but just about everyone's perception of the American college and university in the late sixties and early seventies—N.Y.U. Chancellor Alan Cartter's was a lonely Cassandra voice on the future of the American college and university—was based on assumptions about an expanding American economy and affluent society that now appeared very doubtful. A situation prevailed at both the federal and state levels, in which higher education had to compete desperately and often disadvantageously for public support against other priorities within a stagnant or declining tax base.

By 1986 the downward spiral in the condition of the American university seemed to have levelled out. There appeared to be a renewed interest in humanities courses in the upscale colleges and a modest improvement in the academic job market for Ph.D.'s. But this meliorating situation was mostly illusory. For a dozen years, wave after wave of adverse circumstances had hit the campuses. By the mid-eighties, the prosperity and expansion of the sixties had been so much forgotten, and there had developed such desensitivity to growth and improvement, that even a hiatus in exploding disaster looked like a good thing.

The decline of the American univeristy in the seventies and eighties was by no means the consequence only of the external factors involving deterioration of fiscal resources, loss of public support, and the decline of the demographic curve. Weak leadership and defects in governance—internal structural problems—also affected the universities severely. While there are remarkable exceptions, the kind of people that now rose to the top level of university administration—presidents, provosts, and deans—were politicians, compromisers, apparatchiks, devoid of strong beliefs and lacking in visions of progress and reform.

The hegemony of these kinds of neutral people in university administration is partly a consequence of the upheavals of the sixties. Then it was discovered that university administrators with strongly held beliefs fared less well in dealing with student radicals than easier-going negotiator types who could bend to the wind and were spared the brittleness that often characterized the idealists among university leaders.

A second factor leading to the rise of the apparatchiks in university administration was the large increase in consensual instruments of university governance during the seventies. Faculty senates, student councils, or combined faculty-student assemblies gained much greater visibility and frequently held a significant measure of reserved decision-making power. With this politicization of the university, it became necessary, it was thought, for the president and other senior officials to be someone who was not distinguished by educational convictions or scholarly accomplishment but someone who was a skilled politician, able to manipulate assemblies. Thus the same qualifications for university leadership were inscribed as were valued in the political world at large.

Sometimes prominent politicians were simply appointed as university presidents. Terry Sanford, the former governor of North Carolina, became president of Duke. John Brademas, a welfare Democrat leader for twenty years, ascended to the presidency of New York University after as vehement a campaign as he ever waged in his Indiana congressional district. But more often, academia grew its politicians at home.

The kind of faculty who shone in university senates were professors who had lost interest in teaching and whose career in research and scholarship was on a downward trajectory. University politics became a viable and interesting substitute, with the immediate rewards of power and influence, and the longer-term possibility of gaining a top position in university administration.

Emerging out of this consensual governance structure, and with the aim of bringing cohesion and peace to the campus, the politician-type university administrator did succeed in healing the wounds and covering up the fissures inherited from the tumultuous sixties. This accomplishment was not without value. The price paid was, however, severe. It instilled in the eighties a mood of pliancy and caution in the university presidencies, an absence of strong and imaginative leadership either on the campus or in representing the university to society at large, and university administrations in the late eighties were devoid of specific programs to improve education and advance the life of the mind. There was not one new programatic idea in American education in the decade after 1975. Everything done on the campus was the cultivation of concepts and programs that had emerged in the previous half-century. Perhaps after the turmoil of the sixties a decade of stock-taking and reaffirmation was in order but by the late eighties the American campus was a quiescent and stultifying place. No wonder the brighter and more ambitious students chose programs and embarked on life careers on mostly material and selfish grounds. There was very little on the campus to fire imagination and inculcate high ideals.

There had been an exciting moment on the campus, from about 1962 to 1967, until the Stalinists and Trotskyites and anarchists took over the student movement and ruined everything, when an interactive engagement was in process between scholarly ideals and capacity on the one hand and education and pedagogy on the other. Professors talked meaningfully to students and tried to relate their learning and thought-world to the classroom and the seminar and to involve students in their concept formation. What characterized the campus of the late eighties was the polar opposite of this situation. Almost never now did a scientist of distinction teach a basic freshman-sophomore class in his discipline. That was left to the novice and the lame mediocrity. The leading social scientists devoted themselves to their separate research institutes, grant development, and consulting outside the campus. The humanists had become like medieval scholastics, talking to each other in the arcane rarified codes of analytic philosophy and deconstructionist criticism which only a few invited acolytes could fully comprehend and to which only partisans cared to listen closely.

The quiescence of the American campus in the late eighties and the dominance of its governance by neutral apparatchiks explains why the Marxists were able to have such a strong impact on the campuses. They were the only substantial group with strong convictions, ready to convert under-graduates, indoctrinate graduate students and use financial aid to bring the recalcitrant ones into line, and adept at taking advantage of every vacancy and recruitment in the humanities and social sciences to add to their numbers. University administrators in the interest of preserving campus peace and in the name of academic freedom were willing to allow this creeping politicization of the campus to occur, as long as it stopped short of the presidential suite or the provost's office.

There was therefore a tacit accommodation in the late eighties on the campus between the neutral apparatchik administrators and the deeply committed leftists. What suffered was the intellectual integrity and conceptual vitality of the American university. The momentary campus peace involved an appeasement of the left that raised very grave problems for the future.

Thus the decline of the American univeristy was not only a fiscal, demo-graphic and institutional problem. It reflected deep-rooted intellectual issues as well.

One of the salient features of twentieth-century culture since the age of Modernism has been the central place of the university in intellectual and scientific life. Therefore, the American academic decline threatened all other cultural dimensions that drew upon the power of the mind, not only the arts and education, but also in the corporate and governmental worlds. If the American university going into the 1990's did not recover its momentum and social recognition of its centrality in cultural and social life, and its intellectual and imaginative capability, the U.S. was in danger of following Britain on the sad one-way road from imperial grandeur to backwater status.

*   *   *

Feminism

Since the mid-sixties we have been living through the second wave of feminism in the twentieth century, the first of which occurred in the first two decades of the twentieth century and concentrated ultimately on the question of suffrage. The first phase was inspired by the absorption of women into the bureaucratic and business workplace and out of domestic work in an unprecendented degree. The invention of the Underwood typewriter in the 1880's had great impact on the employment opportunities for women. It was secretarial work, which still remains one major channel for the exploita-tion of the female worker, that withdrew women from domestic labor, within or without one's family, which, along with factory labor, had hitherto constituted the main occupation for women. Women now had the opportunity to work in offices.

Then, during the First World War, because of the labor shortage, women were employed in greater numbers in factories, frequently engaging in hard physical labor in ammunition production. They became, at this time as well, responsible for farm labor to an unprecedented degree. These social and economic situations, and their necessary results in terms of the use of women's labor, gave a validity or a compelling argument to the suffragette cause, resulting in the gaining of the vote by women at the end of the First World War in most Western countries.

The socialist movement favored the equality of women, and while middle-class liberals were split on the matter, they too eventually converted to the pro-women position. Then, with the Great Depression, there was a reversal in the advancement of women's liberation, which is a movement that always does poorly in times of high unemployment, since the economic crisis, whose solution inevitably lies in decreasing the competition on the job market, collaborates with those who prefer to see women at home.

There was a hiatus in the attempt to drive women back into the home during the Second World War, when women were once again needed in war work for four or five years. But then, in the late forties and the fifties, there emerged the motif of "togetherness", the reconstruction of the holy, middle-class family, comfortably settled in the suburban ranch house. Women were once again expected to stay at home, rear children, mix martinis and prepare extravagant meals for their spouses. During the early forties, it was feared that once the war ended, there would once again be massive unemployment. The prosperity that would become evident by the mid-fifties was not anticipated. Hence the recurrence of the outcry to segregate women into the home in the years immediately following the war.

Since the late fifties and particularly since the mid-sixties, the women's liberation movement has been pursued with unprecedented strength, taking the movement far beyond the demand for suffrage, which, it should be noted, women never used to a significant degree. Historians have always been rather taken by the fact that when women began to vote, in England and the United States, around 1920, they voted conservatively, following their husbands and fathers. They more rarely voted liberal or socialist, not that is, for those parties that sought their rights. Their direct participation in political life was negligible.

The factors that have produced, and continue to produce, the current wave of the women's liberation movement or feminism include the great economic expansion that began in the late fifties and was recognized by the mid-sixties, which produced again a demand, particularly for educated women in non-factory labor, including various kinds of professional as well as clerical positions. The first cause of the massive expansion of feminism was then the favorable labor market.

Secondly, the equally great educational expansion of the fifties and sixties, from which millions of women have benefited—fifty-one percent of students in the sixties when the state universities were expanding were women—is another factor and collaborates with the expansion of the labor market. By 1970, there were in fact millions of well-educated women active on the labor market. This could not but alter the situation in irreversible ways. Many of these women would decline returning to the former domestic mode of female life.

Thirdly, the egalitarian ideology of the sixties, which had produced the civil rights movement along with the movement for the liberation of the blacks and the New Left, presented an example for women. There is no doubt that the women's liberation movement was modeled on that of Black liberation, and in its early stages in the late sixties, it was not entirely welcomed by the Black leaders who thought that it would erode the thrust of their campaign. To some extent this did indeed happen.

The fourth factor fostering women's liberation was the Federal Affirmative Action program. It is well known that Federal Affirmative Action was never legislated. It was decreed by presidential order of President Johnson, and the Supreme Court is still debating whether Johnson and the succeeding presidents' Affirmative Action directives were in fact constitutional. The latest decision on the issue is that on the whole they were constitutional. It should be noted that the Affirmative Action program, begun under President Johnson, expanded first under the Nixon administration, and later under President Carter. Whatever we may think about Nixon and Carter, one a crook and the other a wimp, the fact remains that they very substantially expanded the Affirmative Action program, particularly in ways that were helpful to women. The fact that women began extensively to obtain academic posts outside of women's colleges was almost entirely due to federal Affirmative Action impositions.

The final impact was that of the private foundations, among which the role of the Ford Foundation under McGeorge Bundy was particularly important. Ford, and other foundations, poured vast amounts of money not only into the causes of civil rights, the Blacks, and of the Hispanics, but supported women's programs as well. All major universities, beginning with Northeastern University, developed women's reentry programs, which were designed to help women, especially college-educated and middle-aged ones, make the transition from home into professional careers. These programs, the first of which was started in 1964, were among those that received extensive help from private foundations. They also gained, needless to say, efficient sources of income for the universities.

The main question is of course what it is that has actually changed. What does "women's liberation" mean? In 1939 the average women's wage in the United States was sixty-three per cent of men's. In 1986, it was sixty-four per cent. Women's wages, in other words, as compared to men's, have gone up on average by one per cent in the forty-seven years. For some women, indeed, there was also a deterioration in their general situation during the sixties and seventies because one-parent families, which usually implies that the one parent is a woman, became much more common. The reason for this is the easing of the divorce laws. In a rather unimaginative and reckless moment, radical advocates began to deconstruct divorce laws, and in so doing, albeit unintentionally, they made it very difficult to reinforce alimony and child-support regulations upon most men, abandoning women to very difficult situations.

A study done in California in 1985 by a Stanford University sociologist argued that for middle-class women divorce means a deterioration in their income and their general economic well-being, whereas for their divorced spouse, it means an increase in income.

Nevertheless, the women's liberation movement has effected immense changes, the most positive among which have benefited professional women. A social revolution is occurring in this country, whose effects will probably not be fully perceived for another ten or twenty years. This is the case for professional women, academics, lawyers, physicians, accountants, economists, and for the few women engineers that there are. These women are advancing to the highest levels of the learned professions, which means that women will come to play an increasingly important role on the highest corporate levels. The leadership in the United States, the professional elite, has been undergoing the most radical change since the early nineteenth century.

Further, the decline of fertility in middle-class women, one cannot help but surmise, is a consequence of the liberation and professional advancement of women as well as the availiability of greatly improved forms of contraception. Women who engage in professional careers either do not marry, or they marry and do not bear children, and even if they do, the number of children they produce rarely exceeds the replacement level of two, remaining often at one. In fact, it is frequently the case that a professional married woman will bear one child when in her mid-thirties. The result of this is of course decline in aggregate fertility.

An unknown but possibly major consequence of the new status of women concerns the mindset of a generation of children brought up in hundreds of thousands, indeed millions of numbers, under various child care and surrogate facilities but without the daytime presence of their mothers, who by choice or necessity are employed outside of the home. Of course this was not unheard of in previous decades, but now its operation is on a much larger scale and among middle-class families as well as less privileged ones. Among American children under three, half have mothers that work. Eight million mothers of pre-school children are in the work force outside the home.

How will this affect socialization of Freud's Oedipal process? How will it impact, if at all, on Piaget's stages of childhood? Will such children become disassociated from Klein's object relations? Will personalities be changed by the absence of the nurturing mother? For the worse? For the better? Psychologists cannot tell us the answer to these questions, or rather their estimates now vary sharply. It is only when a generation has grown to maturity under the new familial regime of the working and absent mother that the outcomes will begin to become clear. It is to be hoped that these outcomes will not generate further social pathology. This could be a major dimension of the post-Modernist era.

The impact of women's liberation on men is very significant too. Nor is this the case only in terms of a decline of opportunity for men in the learned professions, owing to the competition presented by women. Even though these professions are expanding, men who rank below a certain point of intelligence and capability who previously would, for example, have been guaranteed a good position in a law firm, now have to go to work for legal aid or in the criminal justice system. They are, in brief, being pushed out of the better jobs by women. The increasing spread of male homosexuality deserves to be investigated in this context, as do the possible implications of the women's changing situation for other aspects of male personality.

Along with the social fact of the women's liberation movement, there has developed feminist theory which has in fact entered university curricula. Actually, it is more correct to speak of feminist theories, in the plural, since it is possible to group them under three doctrinal headings.

One of them is the egalitarian or liberal theory, which can also be described as the androgynous theory. This egalitarian approach holds that there is no difference between men and women, claiming that the biological differences are insignificant and the psychological ones nonexistent. Gender-specific cultural characteristics, further, are totally unitary and homogenous. Therefore, women are not different from men. Karen Horney, the psychoanalyst whose views were discussed in a previous chapter, was making these claims already in the forties, on pain of getting expelled from the New York Psychoanalytic Society. Currently, however, this school of feminism constitutes the more moderate branch. Among leading exponents are Carol Berkin of the City University of New York, and Mary Beth Norton of Cornell.

Berkin and Norton have widely disseminated their androgynous theory through school and college textbooks in U.S. history they have published from the feminist egalitarian point of view. Berkin's school text has been adopted by the whole state of Texas. Norton's college text has also been immensely successful. A generation of school children and college students is thereby imbibing the androgynous egalitarian theory of the sexes.

Secondly, there is the Marxist-feminist theory which, drawing on Engels, claims that the subjection of women was instituted at the same time as private property was. Therefore, women will not achieve full freedom until the demise of capitalism. Simple as this argument is, the Marxist branch of feminism has a strong hold in the universities. Alice Kessler-Harris, who teaches at Hofstra University, is one of the outstanding examples of this school. Another is Molly Nolan of N.Y.U.

The third category in feminism is the separatist theory, which is the entire opposite of the egalitarian theory. This holds that there are major differences between men and women, and further, that women are superior. This theory is still in the making, and many of its aspects still remain to be worked out. It was first propounded by women anthropologists in Britain the late 1960's. It was articulated in polemical form by the acerbic British feminist scholar Germaine Greer in *The Female Eunuch* (1971). "Women have very little idea how much men hate them. . . . Is it too much to ask that women be spared the daily struggle for superhuman beauty in order to offer it to the caresses of a subhumanly ugly mate?" The separatist theory has been developed further in the United States in a lengthy and learned 1986 book, which has received high visibility, by Gerda Lerner, who is the leading feminist historian in this country. She teaches at the University of Wisconsin.

Lerner's theory is based on an anthropological myth, which is by no means to accuse it of falseness, for Freud as well as Lévi-Strauss used myths as the starting point of their theories. Basing herself on anthropological data and historical evidence from early societies, Lerner maintains that societies in their original state were naturally matriarchal. Lerner proposes that the natural, original state of society be taken into account and that matriarchal power be restored.

In addition to the three, egalitarian, Marxist, and separatist theories, there is another position which, although its propounders claim it to be feminist, would not be acknowledged as such by the advocates of the three preceding theories. If nevertheless one were to give it a name, it would be the neoconservative feminist theory, which is mostly the work of the economist Sylvia Hewlett.

Hewlett asks that the single parent, the poor woman, and the woman in the black family or in the ghetto, in short, that the underprivileged woman, be emphasized. Institutional changes that are currently underway, she claims, are victimizing these women. While there are women who can look forward to top salaries as graduating professional students, there are also those who are direly underprivileged. What is needed in the United States are above all adequate child-care facilities—a major problem which Europeans have solved long ago, regardless of the fact that Americans are ideologically more advanced in feminism.

The traditionalist view enumerated by Hewlett and others claims that the feminist movement in the early eighties lost touch with the needs and feelings of the majority of women. It was women who defeated the Equal Rights Amendment (ERA) because they felt it would remove the protection of women's special status and further threaten the traditional family. The majority of women, it was claimed, needed not futher equality, but defense against cruel economic and social conditions. It is not certain whether this is a theory, but it is certainly a point of view. It harks back to the view of the thirties, when the emphasis was not on equality but on legislation to protect women and children.

It is possible that twenty years from today much of Heidegger, Wittgenstein, Derrida and Foucault will have passed away, but also that the impact of feminism will have exacted irreversible changes in culture and consciousness.

Post-Modernism

Post-Modernist culture is indeed post-Modernist. It comes after the great achievements of Modernism. It draws upon Modernism to some degree and also departs from it and partially reverts to Victorianism.

We are not in the midst of a great moment in the arts and literature. We are in a period after the fall, a period of fragmentation and reconsideration, perhaps of the beginning of a comprehensive new movement in literature and the arts but it is still too early to tell what the coalescing shape of this new movement will be. On the other hand, we may be in a time of frustration, doubling back, of essentially standing still.

There are three characteristics of post-Modernist culture in literature and the arts: partial perpetuation of Modernism; fabulism and fantasy; and arbitrary appropriation and imitation of the past.

There has been a strong neo-Modernist movement in drama. The dominant figure here is Samuel Beckett, the Irishman who spent his whole working life

Francis Bacon, *Painting*, 1946

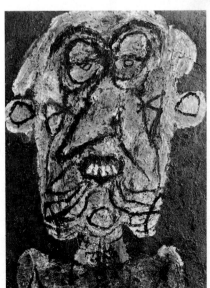

Jean Dubuffet, *Jules Supervielle,
Grand Portrait Bannière*, 1945

Henry Moore, *Reclining Figure*, 1939

Alexander Calder, *Black Widow*, 1959

Matta (Sebastian Antonio Matta Echaurren), *Le Vertige d'Eros*, 1944

Arshile Gorky, *Agony*, 1947

Willem de Kooning, *Woman, I*, 1950-52

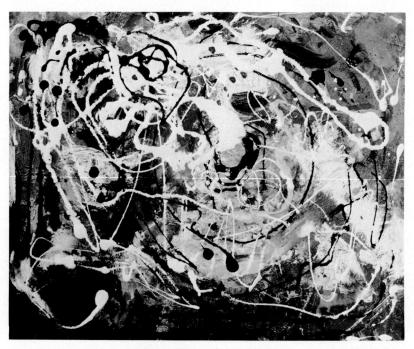

Hans Hofmann, *Spring*, 1944-45

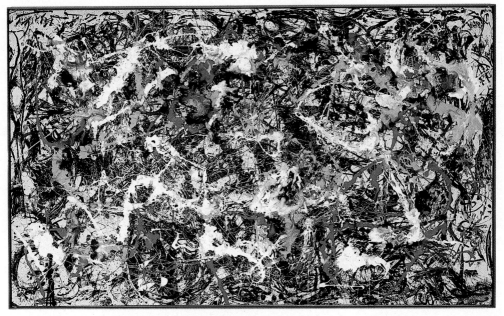

Jackson Pollock, *Convergence*, 1952

Barnett Newman, *Vir Heroicus Sublimis*, 1950-51

Robert Motherwell, *Elegy to the Spanish Republic, 54*, 1957-61

Ad Reinhardt, *Number 87*, 1957

Frank Stella, *Valpariso Flesh and Green*, 1963

Andy Warhol, *100 Cans*, 1962

Roy Lichtenstein, *WHAAM!*, 1963

Robert Rauschenberg, *Bed*, 1955

Jasper Johns, *Target with Four Faces*, 1955

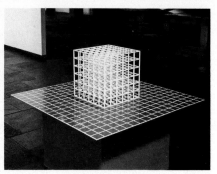

Sol Lewitt, *Untitled Cube (6)*, 1968

Claes Oldenburg, *Soft Toilet*, 1966   David Smith, *Cubi XIX*,
third view, 1964

George Segal, *Walk, Don't Walk*, 1976

Christo, *Surrounded Islands, Project for Biscayne Bay, Greater Miami, Florida*, 1983

Joseph Beuys, *Aus Berlin: Neues Vom Kojoten*, 1979

Richard Serra,
Vertical Parallelogram, 1983

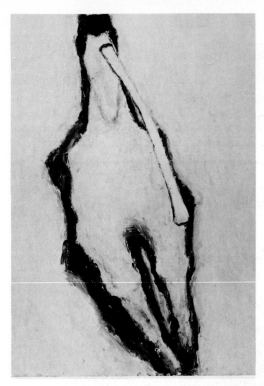

Susan Rothenberg,
For the Light, 1978-79

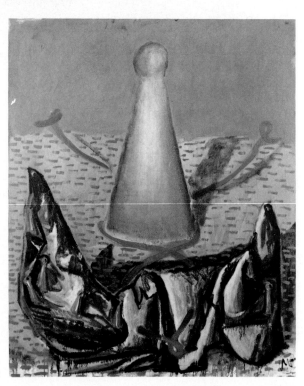

Marcus Lupertz, *Bewohner:*
Mittag (Das Collier des Siegers), 1983

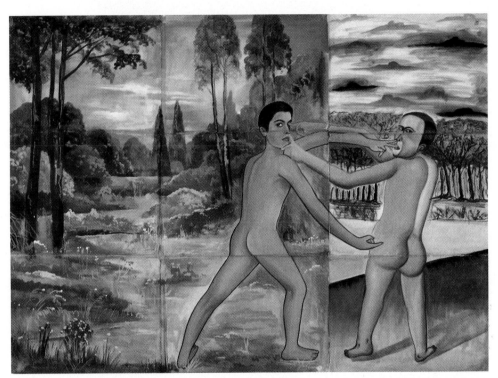

Francesco Clemente, *Two Painters*, 1980

Sandro Chia, *Poetic Declaration*, 1983

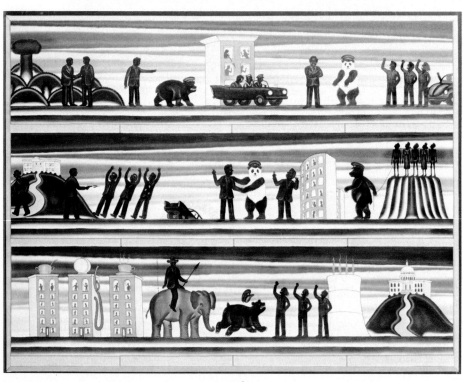

Roger Brown, *The Modern Story of Life: A Civics Diatribe*, 1983

Mies van der Rohe, The Seagram Building, New York, 1958

Robert Venturi, Vanna Venturi House, Chestnut Hill, Pennsylvania, 1962

Richard Meier & Partners Architects, Museum für Kunsthandwerk [Decorative Arts], Frankfurt, 1979-84

John Burgee Architects with Philip Johnson, AT&T Corporate Headquarters, New York, 1978

in Paris. He is a bridge between the thirties and the seventies. In the latter decade he was continuing to write and produce his highly self-referential, enclosed, depressing, intensively thick and relatively short plays. *Rockababy* is the quintessence of Modernist minimalism and despair: a one character play in which a very old woman sits in a rocking chair and unhappily but convincingly recollects her drab life.

Three dramatists of the new generation who worked in the Beckett tradition were the Englishman Harold Pinter and the Americans Sam Shepard and David Mamet. Pinter gained recognition in the late fifties with *The Caretaker*, a three character drama about poor, angry and miserable people speaking in a fragmentary manner. He became actively involved in film-writing and the result was first the drama and then the film of *Betrayal*, an astonishingly successful effort to combine upscale domestic drama with structuralist perception. The depersonalization of personalities is done very skillfully here; individual wills are involved but the objective system at the same time closes in and prevails.

Shepard is more in the expressionist tradition, touched up with 1980's deconstruction, which in *True West* takes place among lower middle-class characters over the kitchen sink. His is the theater of rage. David Mamet's *Glengary Glenn Ross* is a perfect neo-Modernist drama: a self-contained miserable little world in Chicago, lower middle-class shabby salesmen whose humanity does come through all too painfully.

The traditions of Modernism light up the film of the post-Modernist era. A gargantuan figure was the French director François Truffaut who as a critic first advocated a New Wave, postbourgeois French film and then showed everyone how to do it. *Jules and Jim* is an incomparable evocation of the second and third decades of the century in Paris. His later film *Day for Night* shows the strong influence of Roland Barthes and structuralism. In all of Truffaut's films, there is a sharp struggle between a Modernist and a neo-Romantic sensibility.

The American director Martin Scorsese is usually free of such tension. His is usually a straightforward, piercing neo-Modernist evocation of a lower middle-class world, not passive but strenuous, desperate and angry. This appears in three imposing films, *Mean Streets*, *Taxi Driver*, and *Raging Bull*. The latter was a conscious effort both in cinematography and story to evoke the late, high Modernist world of the early forties. Scorsese's one effort at neo-Romanticism, *New York, New York*, is held to be unsuccessful.

The Modernist music tradition was perpetuated in the highly improvisatory jazz compositions of John Coltrane and the abstract, almost Baroque sound produced by Wynton Marsalis.

The Modernist tradition in music is also perpetuated in the work of Steve Reich and Philip Glass, minimalists who use complex and repeated rhythms in orchestrated and complex frameworks. Glass is involved in a series of operatic productions on grandiose subjects while Reich works with large-scale orchestras. Their generally accessible, not difficult, although at times boring, music attempts to use the incantatory power of repetition to achieve a sparse, sonic structuralism.

In painting, Modernism came to late fruition in Britain and the United

States. Francis Bacon, who began his work in the late thirties, but is mostly known for his art of the fifties and sixties, must be regarded as one of the great later masters of Modernism. There is not only a strong sense of distortion but also of sado-masochism in his work.

The American school of abstract expressionism began in the late thirties with Jackson Pollock and reached its peak in the sixties and late seventies in the work of Pollock, Willem de Kooning (who is still active), Barnett Newman, Robert Rauschenberg and Mark Rothko. The direct influence of the German expressionism of Klee and Kandinsky, brought directly to America by Max Ernst and other refugee artists during the War, is readily apparent. Nevertheless, the work of the New York School, as they are called, should be seen as not derivative but as a distinctive late chapter in the history of Modernism and especially of post-impressionist and non-representational art.

The group was particularly effective in the use of color and in the case of Pollock and de Kooning, in "action painting," the dripping of paint on canvas or throwing it on. With the help of astute New York gallery owners, the group became immensely popular and wealthy. Modernist painting, particularly by the New York school, became integral to interior design for affluent people.

Two American sculptors in the sixties and seventies who represented the post-Modernist continuation and cultivation of the modernist tradition in art were Louise Nevelson and Claes Oldenburg. Nevelson, born in Russia, constructed a display wall (*Royal Tide IV*) of thirty-five wooden ordinary boxes arranged to form a collage and painted gold. In each box were customary pieces of finished wood objects. The result is to communicate a distinctive world of shape and signs through the arrangement of common objects. Oldenburg, born in Sweden, experimented in the late sixties with a series of sculptures in soft vinyl such as a wash basin and *The Great Swedish Soft Light Switch*. The purpose appears to be to force recognition through contrasting the soft shape of objects with the familiar hard shapes. Thus Oldenburg sought to realize Salvador Dali's proclaimed "era of the soft."

A leading neo-Modernist sculptor of the postwar era was David Smith whose stark, abstract, welded images perpetuated the work of Giacometti and other Modernists of the interwar period. An innovative sculptor of the seventies was George Segal whose life-size ghostly white plaster figures are a late and persuasive form of expressionism.

In poetry a leading late Modernist writer was an American resident in Britain, Sylvia Plath. Her early death by suicide removed a major talent. From her college studies, she learned the lesson of Modernist lyrical intensity and applied them well. Plath's near-contemporary, the Welsh poet Dylan Thomas, also played a significant role in perpetuating the pre-war Modernist tradition. A raging alcoholic and frenetic personality, Thomas also acted out on college campuses and in bars of two continents the popular conception of the existential poet raging against the world.

The leading neo-Modernist American novelist of the sixties was Vladimir Nabokov who follows in the tradition of the Mann brothers, particularly of Heinrich Mann. Nabokov's account of the life of a Cornell professor, *Pnin*, is a softened version of Mann's Professor Unrat. His account of the infatuation of a middle-aged man for a pubescent child, *Lolita*, is entirely in the sado-masochist, German expressionist tradition. The leading neo-Modernist novelist of the seventies was the Czech Milan Kundera. His stories of lives circumscribed by bureaucracy and technology are again a softened, more whimsical version of Kafkaesque themes.

In postwar France and continuing into the seventies there occurred an extremely self-conscious and doctrinaire flowering of the minimalist, non-narrative Modernist novel. Nathalie Sarraute, who began publishing in the thirties, served as a bridge from the era of Modernism to the new age of post-Modernism. The leading figure of this neo-Modernist movement in French fiction, called *le nouveau roman* (the new novel, although it was really not very new) was Alain Robbe-Grillet, a close collaborator in vanguard intellectual circles with Roland Barthes. His most influential work was *Les Gommes* (The Erasers), which was a minimalist work devoid of one discernible plot. It was a radicalized, more extreme version of Joyce and Virginia Woolf.

The second current in post-Modernist art and literature was fabulism and fantasy, a world of imaginative invention, whimsy and exotic referentiality that was far removed from the austerity of Modernism. Along with the outpouring of science fiction and Arthurian retellings, the leading exponents of this post-Modernist genre included two Latin American writers Gabriel García Márquez and Jorge Luis Borges. Fantasy and fabulism was a way of absorbing the pain of the terror and failures of their societies and the irresponsibility of the educated middle class from which they came. It was also a way of bridging the gap between the austere European, mainly French or English culture in which they were educated and the native Hispanic-Indian village life they knew about in their home countries, that is, a way of preserving their European cultural identities.

Somewhat similar is the fabulist inspiration of Isaac Bashevis Singer in his cycle of stories about his father's rabbinical court in a romanticized shtetl world of East Europe. Singer was capable of writing graphically Modernist, quite Freudian stories of the sex life of pressured immigrants in New York in the thirties. But when he came to write about Eastern Europe he felt compelled to screen the events with a romantic hassidic overlay to soften the pain of recollection. Two other prominent American novelists in the fabulist and fantastic tradition were John Gardner and Thomas Pynchon.

Thomas Mann's series of novels on Joseph and his brothers published in the thirties and forties had been a forecast of the fabulist stream in post-Modernism. A novelist of past years who now came to prominence was the prolific German writer, both novelist and poet, Herman Hesse. He was actually of the generation of high Modernism; he died in 1962 at the age of 85. His long series of novels dealt with stories of mythological and moral fabulism. One of these, *Steppenwolf*, originally published in 1927 and focusing on the theme of the struggle between man's animal instincts and bourgeois respectability, became a bestseller in the 1970's. Hesse's style is that of the neo-medieval moral and miracle story.

The fabulism and fantasy that is a central theme in the post-Modernist novel also conditions the historical writing of the period. The leading exponent of this interest is Natalie Zemon Davis, the highly visible Princeton historian, although Le Roy Ladurie and another French scholar Jacques Le Goff have also been active in this area.

Zemon Davis writes about carnivals, street theater, riots, adolescent and male-bonded high jinks in sixteenth-century France. Her work follows a principle proposed by the Soviet theorist Mikhail Bakhtin that such mini-explosions in society are an expression of adversary culture against authority in pre-Modern societies. Aside from this Marxist influence, Zemon Davis' work on activist fabulism in pre-Modern society reflects the doctrines of French structuralism and deconstruction. The marginal activities are part of the systemic structure of pre-industrial society and they also show the deconstructive operation of the social text. Following Zemon Davis, whose work has achieved such celebrity she has been elected president of the American Historical Association, there has been a rush of disciples to describe marginal activist fantasies in social history.

The influence of Lévi-Strauss' anthropology on Zemon Davis comes to her directly through the work of the American symbolic anthropologists Victor Turner and Clifford Geertz. They were concerned to identify the ritual symbols in early society that represent the dominant cultural forms expressing the thick culture that ethnography reveals. Transferring this to historical research, Zemon Davis is attempting the symbolic anthropology of thick culture of sixteenth-century peasant society. Applying Bakhtinian doctrines, she believes that this symbolic structure is readily perceived in fabulist and fantastic activity.

Another manifestation of post-Modernist fantasy and fabulism was science fiction films, making bold and ingenious use of computer graphics, that were Hollywood's prime achievement in the late seventies and early eighties. It is salutary to compare these science fiction films with the two previous genres in which Hollywood excelled. These were the *film noir* of the thirties and the musical comedy films of the forties and fifties. The latter musical comedy films, borrowing Broadway talent and techniques, went beyond anything Broadway could do in view of the elaborate sets, concentration of remarkable and expensive talents and innovative camera work. Metro-Goldwin-Mayer studios excelled and specialized in musical comedy and the genre reached its highpoint in Gene Kelly's *Singin' in the Rain* (1952). Changing public taste and the extreme expense of these films led to their decline in the sixties and the period of the sixties and early seventies were distinguished by the neo-Modernist New Wave French films. Now in the late seventies and early eighties Hollywood has made a comeback with the incomparable special effects of science fiction films such as *Star Wars* and *E.T.* The creative people were Steven Spielberg and George Lucas but the key to success was the skillful adaptation of computer graphics developed at the University of Illinois and other research centers. The science fiction film was a distinctive and novel subculture of post-Modernism. It is perhaps the most accomplished and skillful expression of post-Modernist fabulism and fantasy.

The third stream in post-Modernist culture—and one that became more prominent over the years—was the random appropriation of the past. This constituted a highly personal and idiosyncratic reaching back nostalgically for themes and motifs, especially but not exclusively to the Victorian past. There was a heavy neo-Victorian flavor to this historicizing at all times.

There is a random and arbitrary quality to the iconography and semiotics of these themes. The writers and artists of our day have a vast heritage behind them, not only as painterly and literary productions but a heritage that has produced, and finds support in, an equally extensive scholarly and theoretical output. The accessibility to all the materials of Western civilization is easy. Books, libraries and museums make everything available. In spite of this or perhaps because of this, post-Modern culture is fragmented and has a random and arbitrary quality to it. Its producers are aribitrarily picking up fragments of the past, which are found supremely appealing by post-Modern culture, and seek to revive them, but always in and as fragments. Every new year, in fact, reaches for different aspects of the past. This imitative quality of post-Modernist culture frequently gives it a pastiche character.

This historicizing and random appropriation of the past was very pronounced in architecture in the work of Philip Johnson and his associate John Burgee and also in the work of Robert Venturi. They were determined to break away from the internaitonal Bauhaus style (even though Johnson had begun his career as a junior associate of Mies van der Rohe) and they did this with the help of cornices, pediments and other pieces rescued from the past. The prime example is the neo-Edwardian top of the Johnson's and Burgee's AT&T building in New York. Another blatant piece of historicizing and random nostalgia-tripping by Johnson was his Bobst Library for New York University. Recalling Foucault, it is modelled on a Victorian penitentiary.

Neo-Victorian qualifications are well represented in music, poetry, and painting. In music a major talent, David Del Tredici, departed from discordant serialism and composed lyrical works with a strong neo-romantic flavor. Perhaps the most popular of these is his rendering of *Alice in Wonderland*, *Child Alice*, to which the Danish choreographer Eric Bruhn articulated an original ballet for the Canadian national company, combining Modernist and nostalgic ingredients. Del Tredici's work was enthusiastically received by critics and the concert public alike. He might well be the Stravinsky of his generation. In poetry Philip Larkin, the British laureate, tried to bring back the age of Tennyson and Kipling and was widely applauded.

In painting, the American Susan Rothenberg composed large representational canvases featuring horses, a random nostalgic icon. She described them as "charged images." The horses resemble those on the walls of neolithic caves. The Victorian ambience was consciously recreated by the immensely popular American painter Andrew Wyeth. His canvases could easily be products of the 1860's and there is in his work a distinct resemblance to British painters of that era. Wyeth is a neo-Victorian not only in his photographically representational style, but in his subjects, of which mysterious women of great beauty is the favorite.

The leading artist of post-Modernism was Frank Stella and he also stands as one of the cultural heroes of the closing years of the century. A brilliant history major at Princeton, he forsook a promising scholarly career to take up painting in the abstract expressionist mode. His geometric patterns were consciously done according to the Modernist theory of Cézanne, Klee and Picasso and Stella's skill, use of color and whimsical powers of invention made him immensely popular and wealthy. But Stella was not just a neo-Modernist. He incorporated the other two strands of post-Modernism as well. He saw himself as recovering the ideals and techniques of Baroque art, on which theme he wrote a lengthy paper at Princeton. He was especially interested in Caravaggio and gave a remarkable series of lectures on this Baroque artist at Harvard in 1984, combining criticism of unusual insight with deep learning.

In Stella's later work, there is a strong element of fantasy, constant experimentation with random objects and an effort to combine painting and sculpture (including welding), a neo-Victorian avocation. One wonders what Stella could have accomplished if he had not become a multi-millionaire so young, if collectors did not simply swoop down and stockpile whatever he produces, if there were a little bit of pressure and personal anxiety placed upon him. That he is one of the half dozen most accomplished and resourceful artists of the century is unquestionable.

In the sixties and early seventies, the Pop Art School of painting was in the forefront of post-Modernist painting. Andy Warhol, Jasper Johns, and Roy Lichtenstein constructed large canvases replicating soup can labels, panels from comic strips, U.S. flags or publicity stills of movie queens. Not only did museums and critics take these paintings seriously as vanguard art, but private collectors payed large sums for them (they were indeed effective against the blank white walls of the newly fashionable loft apartments.) Although the popularity of Pop Art waned in the late seventies, it has come to be recognized as a canonical constituent of post-Modernism.

There were three obvious principles that inspired Pop Art; indeed its theory was more convincing than its aesthetic results. First, since Modernism had legislated that it was the painterly constituents not the subject matter that counted, why not take as subject matter any random object from popular culture? Pop art could thus be regarded as the *reductio ad absurdem* of Modernism. Secondly, Pop Art accommodated to the new interest in semiotics and the Eco principle that all signs were infinitely referential. Anything was meaningful and ultimately related to everything else, so what difference did it make where one started? Mona Lisa was in the total semiotic scheme not much more sign-worthy than a soup can label. Thirdly, Pop Art reflected the post-Modernist tendency to arbitrariness, random appropriation, and pastiche.

One of the finest examples of Pop Art as a meaningful art form was Robert Rauschenberg's *Axle*. It was a vast silk screen collage of various semiotic totems of the 60's (e.g. J.F.K., space travel) put together in a way that suggested cultural patterns and communal feeling. It was Pop Art but it was persuasively symbolic and not decadent.

The quintessence of post-Modernist pastiche of art forms was performance art, whose most visible exponent was Laurie Anderson. Combining music, the visual arts, and dance, with theater and the use of elaborate lighting effects, performace art evoked the world of New York SoHo lofts and the special effects of science fiction films. At a time when each art form was cultivating its past and not breaking through to anything particularly new, blending traditionally distinct genres seemed an attractive program.

An art form that resembles performance art in its combination of several distinct genres is British rock opera. Its most creative people are Andrew Lloyd Webber and Trevor Nunn. It adapts the American musical comedy of the forties and fifties, rock music, and elaborate technical effects that are normally only seen on film. Leading examples of their works are *Evita* (on the life of Evita and Juan Perón), *Cats* (based loosely on a series of whimsical poems by T.S. Eliot), and *The Starlight Express*. The latter is performed at breakneck speed entirely on roller skates. This appears to be among post-Modernism's ultimate achievements in the performing arts.

A prime trend in the painting of the later eighties is the renewed internationalization of art and the blending of cultural motifs. A common figure is the German, Italian, or Israeli artist who has homes on two or three continents, always including a studio in Greenwich Village or Brooklyn Heights. New York remains the art capital of the world and the center of the art market but along with the decline of American academic leadership is the coming to the fore of European painters. The outstanding figure is Francesco Clemente, an Italian who live and works in his native country but also in India and New York. Clemente has gained high visibility in the New York art market. His expressionist-style canvasses are much in demand. He offers a kaleidoscopic blending of ideas, motifs, and cultural traces. "I like art that has no scale," he says, perhaps meaning art that is arbitrary in its iconography and is open to a variety of influences.

It is significant that the finely educated Clemente is drawn to the Baroque-type literature of the Roman Empire. *The Golden Ass* of Apuleius is one of his favorite books. And there is a similarity between this late Roman culture and Clemente's work: the eclectic, the pastiche, the exotic, the arbitrary, the decadent are terms that can describe this post-Modernist genre as it characterizes late Roman literature.

Of all the art forms, the one that most readily combined the three currents in post-Modernism—neo-Modernism, fabulism and random nostalgia—was rock music. In the sixties this was brilliantly accomplished in the work of the Beatles, Jefferson Starship and the Rolling Stones. They also achieved what the visionary Modernists of the early years of the century had foreseen: electronic music. It was rock music, however, not John Cage and other serialists, who created an electronic music joined to voice that attained a central cultural role.

The later development of rock music was somewhat disappointing. It came under the control of commercial entrepreneurs who controlled the recording studios and concert tours and pushed rock music to the lowest adolescent denominator. At the margins, however, creative work continued to be done by a handful of rock bands who were willing to sacrifice some of the loot that entrepreneurship offered. The outstanding groups were the Talking Heads, Crosby, Stills, Nash and Young, and Weather Report. Especially the Talking Heads remained loyal to the original post-Modernist program of the sixties and their work took on some of the abstract, Baroque quality that is reflected in the jazz of Wynton Marsalis and the painting of Frank Stella.

Post-Modernist culture has very little to say by way of political statement. The only thriving intellectual political theory of the late eighties is Marxism, but it is difficult to predict how far its vigor will extend and, very importantly, recent Marxism is a predominantly academic movement, and it is unable to produce any practical, political statements aside from its condemnation of imperialism. Excepting the rather vague feeling that Reagan's international politics is bad, and that the Third World inhabitants, as long as they are not terrorists who ruin vacation possibilities, are good, current forms of Marxism are theoretical.

One of the characteristics of post-Modernism is the use of Modernist analysis and concepts to sustain essentially leftist, pro-socialist arguments. We have seen in the last chapter that John Rawls and Ronald Dworkin used Wittgensteinean analysis and the mode of argument characteristic of analytic philosophy to sustain radical arguments on behalf of affirmative action. A similar use of Modernism against itself features the work of the Nobel laureate and Harvard economist Kenneth Arrow. On the surface Arrow appears to be working in the tradition of classical economics and to be using the traditions of Maynard Keynes. But Arrow's argument wends its way, by subtle dialectics, towards policies favored on the contemporary left. Arrow's close analysis of market operations leads him to affirmation of the intrinsic weakness of classical market economics. Its self-contradictions, inefficiency and irrationality necessitates ingredients of a welfare-state socialist system. "The logic and uncertainty of ideal competitive behavior. ... force us to recognize the incomplete description of reality supplied by the impersonal price system." Marx would cheer this conclusion.

Rawls and Dworkin use Modernist, Wittgensteinian philosophy to support radical left social policies. Arrow uses the language and concepts from the Modernist tradition but reasons towards welfare economics as the rational solution. Private individuals lack the information to make rational self-interested choices in an open market. Some kind of collective, statist intervention is therefore in the end frequently necessary. The texture of Arrow's work is far removed from historicist Marxism. The conclusions, however, frequently please the left.

Among the aspects of the culture in which we live is big science, which began with Rutherford and Einstein in the Modernist era, and now continues, drawing on vast resources and the close affiliations between science and the government and the corporate world. There are those that darkly predict that this spells the end of humanity, as well as those who claim that it will lead to unprecedented health and prosperity. It is hard to know which is the sounder prediction, but it is a fact that the resources are available to science to develop new technologies, military, health and otherwise, and to allow the scientists themselves to make decisions that are crucial for humanity. This process began before the First World War, but has reached a climax in our day.

A characteristic of the post-Modernist age is the Americanization of Europe and the beginnings of this process in Japan and the Pacific Rim. Middle-class

Europeans dress like Americans—including the extensive use of blue jeans as dress in the home and, away from business, in the street. All night long, radio stations in Britain and West Germany fill the airwaves with American popular music of the soft rock variety, making these stations' music indistinguishable from the American Forces Network broadcasting along side of them. Upper-class Europeans decorate their homes according to the standards of the upscale American magazine *Architectural Digest*. American TV programs, films and musical comedies are popular favorites. A similar cultural Americanization has set in among affluent Japanese, South Koreans, and Filipinos.

This process has occurred because of the admiration for the United States among ruling and wealthy groups in Western Europe and the Pacific Rim. The United States rescued them from Fascism and then has protected them against Communism for four decades. American culture has triumphed on several continents among the affluent groups the way the peoples of Spain and North Africa in the Roman Empire wore togas and taught their children Cicero and Virgil. To be an American in dress and manner is to be a citizen of a free world.

The United States is also the preferred place of investment for the rich of all countries that are free to export their capital. Japanese investment alone in U.S. real estate in 1986 totalled five billion dollars. The United States is the safest place for investing capital. The economy is held to be stable. Taxes are moderate. Socialism will never prevail to expropriate capital. So it is believed. To West Germans and Japanese, the deep fissures and critical problems of American society did not appear significant.

To be a European or denizen of the Pacific Rim in the post-Modernist era is to imitate American culture and exploit the American economy. This is at the center of their being. While on visits to the U.S. they lounge at the Plaza Hotel in New York and rush to Broadway shows. The homeless in the streets of Manhattan, the unemployed steel worker in Pittsburgh, the landless farmer in Minnesota mean nothing to them.

A fundamental characteristic of post-Modern culture is therefore the American homogenization of the lifestyle and taste of affluent people, whether in Greenwich, Conn., London, Hamburg, Tokyo, or Buenos Aires. Since they are the same people who are patrons of painting, opera, and the more expensive kinds of theater, their attitudes determine the greater part of the market for the visual and performing arts. Whereas it was a prominent feature of Modernism to establish a separate radical culture, this is largely lacking in the post-Modernist era. Adversary culture is mostly left by default to leftist polemicists. Post-Modernism tends to be the culture of the Americanized international bourgeoisie and the artist, writer, and performer who serves them, along with their usual entourage of domestic servants, chauffeurs, and bodyguards.

A prominent symbol of post-Modernist culture is the stretch limousine. But the capitalist scion riding therein behind the darkened window may well be wearing blue jeans and listening to rock music or watching *Dallas* on TV.

Another quality of contemporary culture is the decline of American public service, which may be the reverse side of political nihilism. One of the glories of the United States in the late thirties and forties was the high prestige and quality of public service. This was true to a degree also in Britain. Certainly, the United States would not have survived the Second World War if it were not for the high quality of the public service sector. To serve in the public domain, either as civilian or as military, was conceived of not as a way of dominating others, nor as a way of gaining money, but it was felt, in terms of citizenship, as dedication to the public need.

This country has never been blessed with more dedicated and wiser public servants than George C. Marshall, Secretary of Defense during World War II, and General Eisenhower, head of the allied armies and later President. Whether Eisenhower was a good president or not may be a matter of dispute, but that he was a skillful and wise military organizer and leader is a fact. These public servants did not acquire riches. They retired from service realtively poor men, with only their pensions. This was characteristic of numerous people in the forties. To serve in Washington was desirable at the time, and continued to be so until the early sixties. Now it is understood either as undesirable, or dangerous, or as the road to personal gain and corruption.

The decline of the public service of the republic is a fundamental fact of post-Modern culture. In the forties and fifties public service was regarded as a life for rich men like Averell Harriman and Nelson Rockefeller. In the post-Modernist era, it is viewed as a way to become rich.

We have witnessed the tremendous proliferation of communications, both in instantaneous satellite communication and in the use of computers. One feature of deconstruction theory that might justifiably cause worry is that given that more and more books are written on word processors, the question "What is the text?" assumes new implications. The text now seems to be not only deconstructing itself, but it is disappearing as well. It is only a floppy or hard disk. Yet the deconstructionists have not caught up with the word processor.

What is the most positive characteristic of the post-Modern culture in which we are living? It does give freedom to some remarkable people like Frank Stella, Martin Scorsese and David Del Tredici to cultivate a complex heritage to an unprecedented degree. This rich, intense historicizing, this versatile command of past heritages, makes post-Modernism similar to seventeenth-century Baroque culture.

On the other side, the culture of post-Modernism is reminiscent of the Baroque era of the seventeenth century in a more negative way. Both periods display astounding capability in detailed technique, the mastery of technology, whether this be the technology of science or art and language. Yet these capabilities are accompanied in both periods by the same redundancy and sterility of ideas. Seventeenth-century culture could not decide what it believed in, where it wanted to go, and above all, it could not decide on a political theory. It merely recirculated the ideologies of the past and devoted much time to trying to determine whether the medieval theory of representation or the Renaissance theory of absolutism was more suitable, and it did not go anywhere. The only outlet for this ideological frustration lay in civil wars and abortive rebellion.

Baroque culture was, in other words, socially and politically built on an *ancien régime* which is a culture of great literary, intellectual and technological capacity, but of political redundancy and ideological feebleness. Post-Modern culture exhibited this feature, and that is also why the iconology and themes of the art and literature of today are so much random recycling of the past, consisting of nostalgic appropriations and pastiches of segments of the past, without, however, any clear attendant theory of culture or philosophy of humanity. Only a new paradigm and a new vision will enable us to break out of the closure into which we seem to have drifted since the mid-seventies.

*   *   *

Conclusion

The first four decades of the twentieth century were characterized and shaped by a cultural revolution called Modernism that is represented in all major aspects of the humanities, the arts and the physical and behavioral sciences. Modernism was a self-conscious, broad-based rebellion against the main dimensions of Victorian mentality.

This age of high Modernism was the creative age of the twentieth century. Everything since then in the cultural and intellectual realms that is enduring and creative is largely the playing out and elaboration of the Modernist revolution. We are still spending the intellectual capital of Modernism.

The erosion of the Modernist revolution in the thirties and forties was the consequence of neo-Victorian modes of thinking arising from the two world wars, the Great Depression, and Marxism and Fascism. Although Marxism sought an affiliation with Modernism in a common adversary culture against the bourgeois ethos, it could on the whole not sustain this symbiosis because of the intrinsic oppositions between Marxism as a neo-Victorian mode of thought and Modernism. There was a closer affiliation between Fascism and Modernism but there were also ingredients in Fascism that strongly conflicted with Modernism and in any case Fascism was for the most part eliminated or at least discredited by the policies of Nazism and its demise.

Structuralism in significant ways constituted a reversion to nineteenth-century idealism. Deconstruction, a late development within structuralism, has a certain Modernist edge but the Modernist movement has not been reconstituted in a post-Modernist era, although certain manifestations of Modernism in literature and the arts are still appreciated and cultivated. Post-Modernism is characterized by omnivorous learning and an asserted freedom to appropriate whatever it wants in the past, leading to peculiar mixtures of Modernist and neo-Victorian elements.

Post-Modernism necessarily lacks Modernism's commitment to anti-Victorian rebellion. We are living now in a cultural age of diversity, eclecticism, and uncertainty of consciousness and goals, although skills and learning abound. We are in need of, and perhaps close to the point of the emergence of, a new paradigm, the construction of novel cultural theory. Although the left is currently flourishing academically and intellectually, it is from the right that novel creative movements are more likely to come.

Modernism was a release from the entropic quality of Victorian culture. It opened new vistas in the arts and architecture; it created social and behavioral science as we know it; it became modern science in physics and biology. It shaped a way of philosophical thinking that superseded nineteenth-century ideologies. It contributed to the coming of a revised economic doctrine and the welfare state. It enshrined the faith that all—rich or poor, young or old—are entitled to access to the arts, the refreshment and illumination of the soul. But it could not overcome the persistence of Victorian government and macrocosmic ways of thinking about war and peace and of acting upon this Victorian theory. It could not withstand the revival of historical nationalism, the impact of class consciousness, the dictates of group feelings, the flaunting of macrocosmic proportions. Out of the Romantic revolution, the two world wars, the Great Depression, the New Deal, the movements on the left and the right, neo-Victorianism reasserted itself and the Modernist cultural revolution was dissipated as a cohesive cultural force although it continued to have a strong impact in some specific areas.

This is what the history of the twentieth century reveals in summary form as we await expectantly the indices and traces of the next cultural revolution.

Our current Baroque condition is not as pathetic as Victorian fin-de-siècle entropy, since we can still profitably cultivate the culture of this century. But we are far from the blissful dawn that the intellectuals and artists of the first quarter of this century enjoyed and we now seek a new inspiration and renaissance. We hope that it will be as beneficent and enjoyable as Modernism was in its day.

One of the most intriguing questions with respect to the prospective cultural revolution is what its political mien will be. Modernism's essentially apolitical character made it vulnerable to the left and the right which tried to co-opt it for their own purposes. The integral strength of the next cultural revolution would be greater if it had a distinctive political stance.

On the other hand, each successive cultural revolution since 1500 has seen a progressive weakening of political content. The Reformation had a distinctive political quality from the beginning. It took the Enlightenment fifty years to develop its liberal ideology, but it was a momentous one when it emerged. Romanticism never achieved a single political view but polarized into the now familiar right and left. Modernism, except for a belief in social entitlement to the arts stayed apolitical. Is it too historicist a conception to conclude that the next cultural revolution will remain non-political as well?

A possible projection is that the next cultural revolution will expound a new politics, an ideology that will transcend the conflicts between the left and the right that have disadvantageously dominated the twentieth century.

In formulating a cultural policy for the closing years of the century that transcends the traditional boundaries of left and right, we have to consider what the U.S. can learn from other societies and alternative systems. It is not enough to try quick economic fixes by seeing what kinds of industrial organization and technique we can quickly copy from the Japanese or Germans. We also have to contemplate how deeply rooted are these alternatives in cultures and histories that are essentially at variance with our own. The current West German high-productive industrial system, including the maximal discipline of laboring populations and the extensive use of foreign "guest-workers," was developed for Hitler by Albert Speer in 1943. The Japanese are momentarily benefiting from the social discipline of early post-feudal society, which also helped England in its industrialization in the late eighteenth century and northern and western Germany in the mid-nineteenth century in its breakthrough to modern economy.

West German culture and education inculcates in its young people a uniform discipline and driving work ethic that the American ambience cannot sustain. The Japanese Shinto and Buddhist culture teaches a stern postponement of personal gratification and communal and cooperative work strategies that our culture and value system does not normally inculcate. Our industrial and fiscal shortfalls in comparison with West Germany and Japan are built upon cultural differences and educational deficiencies of more than marginal proportion. To begin with, the U.S. is paying a terrible price for allowing its school infrastructure to deteriorate severely and its secondary and college teachers to suffer massive demoralization. We also have to contemplate the insuperable fact that West German and Japanese societies are infinitely more ethnically homogeneous than our own and assess the pluses and minuses of our humane and permissive immigration policy.

We have to reconsider the whole issue of productive work in our society and the utility of novel apprenticeship and retraining programs within industry. We must reexamine the role of organized labor in our industrial organizations, how we can transcend the dysfunctional, adversarial system of management and labor, in turn an unfortunate and largely fortuitous British inheritance from the problematic adversary system of the common law and the agonizing trauma of the first Industrial Revolution. Institutionalized ongoing cooperation between management and labor, whether at the individual plant level or industry-wide, is the most immediate avenue for improving productivity and enhancing quality control.

In all advanced industrial societies in the 1980's—but next to Britain, in most aggravated form in the United States—there loom the agonizing problems arising from the atrophying of the value of human labor in a high-technology economy. Can our educational system and training programs within industry be revised so as to make the unemployed and chronically underemployed productive participants in our industrial and technological system? There is no greater problem faced by the elites—whether corporate, academic, or political—of our society. There is no problem more complex and frustrating, and which will only be resolved or at least substantially alleviated by the application of everything we know about human behavior and can envision relative to economic and social organization. In addressing this issue we need to abandon the demagogic slogans of both the left and right, and summon up the most dispassionate, rational and imaginative capabilities that exist in our culture, or we shall get nowhere in combating this ever-deepening social crisis.

Before we oscillate back to recapitalization of urban transportation systems, after several decades of fiscal incentives to dispersal of our urban populations, we have to reflect on what the newly interactive long-distance communication systems imply for the spatial organization of information and some other kinds of business.

We must consider that the greatest change in relations between men and women in recorded history that we are now experiencing raises psychological, sociological, and anthropological issues that are not going to be defined, let alone resolved, by political slogans and arbitrary legislation.

We have to reflect on whether being the most litigious society since fourteenth-century England is really to the common advantage of anyone besides the legal profession. Alternative forms of conflict resolution have to be considered and introduced. England, the home of common law, has a legal profession that in proportion to population is only one-third the size of the American one. There are special reasons for the relatively large size of the U.S. legal profession—a federal system multiplying courts and jurisdictions and the considerable size of the country. Nevertheless, there are aspects of American law that should give us pause. Resort to civil litigation is a much more common occurrence in the American as opposed to the English form of common law and resembles the English situation before the nineteenth century rather than today. The English now use a variety of offical conciliation boards and informal arbitrations as an alternative to litigation.

The American legal profession has been growing in recent years at a frenetic pace and is absorbing much of the best young brainpower in the country. A graduate in the top ten per cent of a first rate law school has a starting salary three to four times greater than a recent Ph.D. in the humanities from Harvard or Columbia, a disincentive for first-rate people to enter the academic profession. Since 1970 the number of new engineers in Japan equals the number of new lawyers in the United States. Is it a surprise that Japanese industry has outgained American industry?

We have to consider whether the sense of loneliness and alienation, the yearning for community that inspires the swelling ranks of evangelical religious communities, signals the need for voluntary, bonded communities focused on secular as well as religious idealism, a need that is not served any longer by the American family, its schools, and traditional forms of secular association. We have so severely turned our backs on the febrile experimentations of the 1960's that we don't perceive the large number of superbly talented and dedicated young people who would flock to join secular versions of monasteries and religious orders.

We have to recognize that there was something that was valuable in the cultural radicalism of the sixties and at the same time affirm that there was considerable merit in the intended policy of the Reagan Administration in reducing the congeries of federal social programs, in retrenching the size of the federal bureaucracy, and in decentralizing power away from Washington to state and local agencies.

There was merit in this policy of retrenchment and decentralization because, first, while millions of poor people found their lives more comfortable and dignified as a result of federal welfare programs, progress in making these people independent and capable of holding responsible jobs was marginal.

Penetration was particularly modest, or perhaps negligible, in dealing with the vast problem of the *lumpenproletariat*, the perpetual, hereditary underclass. Severely reducing federal subsidy for these poor, dependent, and sometimes homeless people is not in itself an advance: misery is always immoral. But it may force reconsideration of how to deal with this major, probably escalating social problem.

What was most wrong with the policies of federal welfare liberalism as it developed from the early sixties through 1980 (and certainly continued and even escalated through the Nixon and Ford administrations as well as in Democratic administrations) was not the actual funds spent on subsidizing the poor, even allowing for a degree of waste and corruption, but the massive increase in size and power of an authoritarian and dogmatic upper-level federal bureaucracy which molded as its constituency a large and often noisy (activist) set of interest groups, comprising university presidents as well as welfare mothers. There were definite signs of creeping Sovietism—the emergence of an ideologically directed, irresponsible group of high-level apparatchiks not always free even from temptation to succumb to personal corruption.

One example is the Office of Civil Rights which spent its time in the 1970's harassing university administrators to establish quota systems for hiring of minorities and women. This policy achieved only modest advances toward its ostensible goal. It had the additional effect of de-liberalizing the outlook of university administrators and faculty and driving thousands of upper middle-class Jews away from the Democratic to the Republican party.

The greatest failure of welfare liberalism was not its throwing billions of public dollars after social problems in a way that much more often constituted the dole rather than social reconstruction and modification of unproductive behavior patterns of impoverished groups. This was bad enough. What was worse was federal welfare liberalism's spawning, relatively unchecked by the Congress or the media, a power-crazed group of ideologically zany apparatchiks. Some of the top people in the NEH in the late 70's belonged to this group. The one positive thing the National Endowment for the Humanities could have done for the humanities in the late seventies and early eighties was (like the Mellon Foundation) to subsidize post-doctoral fellowships and new teaching jobs for recent Ph.D.'s. This it adamantly refused to do while getting involved in a host of doubtful projects. Among the silliest was bringing cadres of young academics thousands of miles to take summer seminars with senior academics at public expense. Apparently the NEH had never heard of that new form of communication: the book.

What was wrong with the decentralizing and retrenching policies of the Reagan Administration was not the essentials of its program, but its absence of feeling, sensitivity, imagination, subtlety and skill in implementing them. It has not effectively enlisted the good will of the American people.

At the heart of the radicalism of the sixties was a cultural movement away from centralizing structures and a tremendous yearning for the formation of communities by choice, e.g., agricultural and artistic communes, that had remarkable theoretical parallels with Reagan's devotion to voluntarism as against bureaucratic centralizing controls. The big problem was the one-dimensionality of Reaganist voluntarism. The Reaganites could only think of voluntarism in terms of millionaires handing out charity in the Scrooge manner, characteristic of the age of Charles Dickens or President McKinley. Where they completely missed the boat was in not capitalizing upon the personal yearning of young people to join local voluntary organizations committed to helping the poor and disenfranchised. The Reaganites wanted the rich to hand out crumbs to the poor (trickle down, or the horse feeding the sparrows). What they should have advocated and funded through corporate giving was a domestic kind of Peace Corps to work communally and interactively with the poor, the homeless, and the miserable. Instead of threatening the poor even further by proscribing abortions (for the poor, that is, the rich can always find a way), the federal government and the Moral Majority should now be stimulating and institutionalizing the idealism of the young to work in the South Bronx, Watts, Appalachia and the barrios.

The sad fact about the Reaganites was that even when their policy had much to recommend it in the abstract, they could not see where in American society lay the cultural forces that they could draw upon for alliance and activity that would make their policies appear idealistic and generate the formation of voluntary associations that could powerfully assist the implementation of their policies.

What all this means is that the idealism and moral fervor and proclivity to communities by choice (rather than by federal fiat) that was central to the cultural radicalism of the sixties must not be forgotten but rather should and can be re-activated in the era of post-Modernism.

There is another strand in Reaganism—its intense nationalism—that is a positive trend if it can be suitably articulated and which can have advantageous consequences for academic humanism. One of the disturbing and important phenomena in the history of the American university in the twentieth century has been the neglect of indigenous intellectual advances in favor of the later borrowing of ideas—with modest amendments, substantially the same ideas— from Europe. We have allowed academic colonialism and a suffocating Anglophilism and especially in recent years Francophilism to lobotomize memory of highly creative trends among American humanists and behavioral scientists which were replaced by wholesale importations of disciplinary innovations from Europe. Emerson forecast this issue long ago.

Here is an extremely important chapter in the recent intellectual history of the American university that raises a question parallel to current concerns about protecting American industry from Japanese competition (there is no technological advance whether in automobiles, electronics, or microchips that the Japanese haven't borrowed from American applied science and engineering). How can we similarly organize our universities so as to protect and cultivate our indigenous traditions and national culture?

We might start by trying to induce foundations and private benefactors to stop giving grants to American humanities institutes to bring over European thinkers for fat fees when a whole generation of our best humanities minds has been suffering terrible misery that is driving them out of the academic profession entirely or subjecting them, if they have the guts to hang on in the academic labor market, to dreadful working conditions with no opportunity for creative research.

A linear projection of current trends will make humanities departments in our leading universities by the mid-nineties derivative colonial outposts of the disciplinary research centers in Europe. No one can see this as anything but contrary to the best interests of American society and national power. The impoverishment of the humanities also facilitates the takeover of academic departments by Marxists and other leftists.

As long as conservative governments in Washington and London fail to appreciate the struggle for the soul of man, for an autonomous consciousness that is being fought out on college compuses today, as long as the Washington and London administrations at best neglect the academic world, and at worst occasionally beat upon and impoverish it, the only policy of survival for the non-left academic segment is through alliance and close cooperation with corporate capitalism, which it must seek to make more aware and intellectually oriented. As Marxism steadily penetrates into academia and seeks to spread its hegemony in university culture, the intellectual survival of the humanities and the human sciences depends on their capacity to integrate with a more enlightened and self-conscious corporate capitalism.

No one can say that this improved ambience, while not entirely absent from the current corporate scene, will be easy to realize. It will require the multiplication of novel tactical undertakings between the corporate executives and academics: joint corporate/academic non-profit institutes; exchange of visiting high-level personnel between corporations and university humanities departments; corporate involvement in sunset and start-up reviews of academic programs; recruitment of junior executives from humanities doctoral programs as well as from business and law and engineering schools.

The struggle for survival of the integrity of the non-left academic world is in some respects more difficult today than during the famous, highly visible conflicts of the sixties and the Vietnam years. Battle lines are more subtly drawn nowadays. The left has learned not to confront academia and denounce its intellectuality but to take over its cultural citadels from within. It has found in South African divestment a new issue to sow confusion and doubt in professional ranks, a new species of moonglow to blind the eyes of scholars and serve as a cloud of disinformation for well-intentioned but poorly informed and indecisive university trustees. Characteristically, it is not uncouth agitators and voluble polemicisits who lead the South African divestment contention, but distinguished leftist academicians. The intention, however, is the same as during the Vietnam agitation: to sow confusion and malaise on the campus, further delegitimize the right, and deconstruct the university as a conservative and cherishing institution.

Against the rising tide of the academic left, cultural conservatism has to elaborate its own program: a broad meliorative social role for business corporations, fostering of a national culture and indigenous intellectual traditions, a cooperative rather than adversarial relationship between management and organized labor, a symbiotic interaction between corporate executives and humanist intellectuals, the reconstruction of the nuclear family, and the stimulation of voluntary associations of mainly but not exclusively young people to engage in social service, including improvement of our public school systems, the rebuilding of urban infrastructures and industries, the securing of our farms, and the stemming of uncontrolled immigration.

Having tried welfare liberalism with disastrous consequences, having tried resurrecting market strategies with only partial results, the American people have to be given the opportunity to try another cultural strategy.

The options left to us in this country in the eighties and nineties are very few. In the United States the seventies were characterized by an erosion of popular confidence in federal welfare liberalism and a vast unease about the idealism and fitfulness of the federal bureaucracy. There occurred a movement of the public mind against the welfare state. Ronald Reagan sensed this shift but he unfortunately lacked the intellectual capacity to articulate and implement this monumental change in its fullest and most advantageous dimensions. The policies of his administration responded too crudely, simplistically, and cruelly to the popular yearning for a new policy. Instead of thinking through the dimensions of a new public policy that goes beyond the welfare state by utilizing maximally all the institutional and moral resources of American society, we have seen a policy based too narrowly upon a draconian market and social Darwinian philosophy. Now the welfare state and the federal bureaucracy are no longer the prime issues for the American people.

Since 1980, 200,000 steel workers in the United States have lost their jobs. Perhaps fifty thousand farm families by the end of the eighties will have lost the land which in many instances their families had worked for two or three generations. Allowing the market to run unchecked through society in this manner is both unjust and imprudent. At the same time, there is a national spirit that has been vigorously activated by the Reagan administration. But it has been used mostly for circuses, such as the tasteless Statue of Liberty display, and not for securing of bread and confidence for American families.

Friedmanism and sociobiology have had their day in court. The result has been some improvement over the corrupt and wasteful welfare state of the preceding years. But it is still a long way from a national policy of caring and solidarity.

The issue which the consequences of the Reagan years has posed is whether we shall be satisfied to allow international market forces to prevail unchecked or whether we shall develop policies protective of our national interests and large segments of our population. We have seen in the past fifteen years the export of industrial jobs to the Pacific Rim and the severe decline of our agricultural infrastructure.

A market theorist says that this change is further instance of economic rationalization and efficiency and will in the end rebound also to the benefit of the U.S. An alternative policy of national interest and social solidarity says that we cannot rely on the abstract imagining of a single world economy with no special consideration for the needs of particular groups in this country. It contributes neither to the well-being of steelworkers and farmers and other labor groups nor to our collective strength as a people to allow segments of our population to be overwhelmed by the draconian forces of the international market.

The issue which national leadership of the 1990's has to address is this one of public caring, social solidarity, and national interest. The emotional resources of the American people have to be stimulated and directed to these ends.

This is a policy of social texture and humanity rather than abstract reason and market ideology. It is a policy compatible with the era of post-Modernist culture.

While Reagan has expressed his support for the views of the religious right on the social issues of abortion and pornography, he has failed to perceive the significance of religious movements in the United States today. Twice in American history, in the 1740's and 1830's, great evangelical movements, bursts of great awakenings, have occurred. The atmosphere is increasingly charged for another awakening.

This is shown not only by the millions who belong to the evangelical "born again" churches and the tremendous response to charismatic preaching on television. It is shown by rock concerts, hand-holdings, collective gatherings of help for the underprivileged—these are all signs of a profound wish for communal evangelical experience. The badly led churches cannot organize themselves so as to turn these yearnings into an integrated, broadly participatory social program.

This is the greatest cultural challenge to public leadership in the U.S. in the later eighties: to channel the instincts for a religious awakening into a common endeavor for social improvement; to use it to save the family farms, provide employment for steelworkers, crush the drug traffic, return peace and safety to the cities, rebuild learning and discipline in the schools. Compared with this challenge, revising the tax system is of minor importance.

All these things, we were told by the market theorists and sociobiologists, would arise spontaneously from the market and calculations of altruistic self-interest. They did something, but they only made a dent in these problems. Their claims were oversold. Now if the American republic is to survive into the twenty-first century unimpaired, religious and communal instincts must be channeled in voluntary associations towards resolution of these problems through collective endeavor and communal integration. A much more complicated and comprehensive policy of national solidarity is needed to respond to the cultural and social upheavals that run torrentially through the recent and contemporary era.

This is not a policy of a revived and expanded welfare state which has proved to be a failure. It is not a policy of polemical Friedmanism and ideological sociobiology. It is a policy of conservative humanism, of voluntarism under corporate and academic leadership addressed to strengthening the social texture and the solution of critical problems.

The articulation and implementation of such a policy of social texture furthermore has world-wide significance, and not just because of the prominence of American power and wealth.

We have seen the Communist future and it doesn't work. The Soviet system

Conclusion

has already failed miserably in the economic sphere; now its total moral bankruptcy by the suppression of the Solidarity movement in Poland has been evidenced to the world. Especially for the lesser developed countries—what only yesterday was called the Third World—when they still have some flexibility to make synoptic choices, the meliorative transformation of the American system, given the anguished enfeeblement and discrediting of the Soviet system, may have major and enduring imitative consequences. Perhaps this salutary imitation of a revivified and reintegrated America will compensate for the unfortunate impact of dependency theory upon the Third World.

This century began with a cultural revolution that promised the liberation of the human spirit. And it did achieve as much in the arts and the realm of science and intellect as any of the great cultural movements of the past, perhaps more so. After all the destruction, death, and disappointment of this century, we have only a few more years in the nineteen hundreds to make good on the promise of Modernism.

There is no hope at this time of recreating the ambience of high Modernism. Many things have intervened, among them two world wars and the Great Depression as well as the Bolshevik revolution. Both the cultural and technological environments have changed since Modernism flourished. Even when deconstruction serves to reincarnate some of Modernism's critical principles, it only does so part way, and in the interests of a post-Marxist leftism. The right appears largely to have forgotten the points of affiliation between Fascism and Modernism, and for the most part committed itself to a straightforward neo-Victorianism.

We cannot recover the Modernist ambience. We can only hope to fulfill its promise of intellectual progress and cultural revolution. But this will have to be within a new paradigm, a new cultural theory, which may pick up ingredients from both Modernism and neo-Victorianism but which transcends them both in a new vision of humanity.

At the present, there is no indication where specifically this new theory will come from. The left constantly promises fresh insights but as long as it remains essentially loyal to Marxism it will not be able, at bottom, to transcend nineteenth-century modes of thinking, no matter how cleverly and vehemently claims to an adversary culture are advertised. The right has only in recent years awoken from the long somnolence it fell into while expiating the crimes of Fascism. The right has reflexively resorted to neo-Victorian modes of thought and policy proposals which neither resolve the many problems that we face nor quicken the imagination.

We are at the Baroque outer wall of a cultural *ancien régime*, arrogantly and expensively devouring the past and demonstrating our learning and technical skills, but we have not begun to find a new idea. Perhaps reflection on the complex history of twentieth-century culture will free us to begin dreaming of a different culture for the twenty-first century. It is now a hundred years since the first indications of what became the Modernist cultural revolution flashed on the trans-Atlantic horizon. Perhaps similar indices of the new culture of the twenty-first century are already with us, their significance not yet clearly perceived. This observer can perceive in post-Modernism only continuations of

Modernism, fabulism, and random nostalgia. But perhaps there is more here than meets the eye.

We have sent our last postcard from the volcano, in Wallace Stevens' phrase. We want to go home at last. As Herman Hesse wrote in his neo-medieval fable *Steppenwolf*, "we have to stumble through so much dirt and humbug before we reach home. And we have no one to guide us. Our only guide is homesickness."

In the closing years of the twentieth century, the intellectual homeland that we seek can no longer be Modernism. Perhaps this it to be greatly regretted. We have been, as it were, shut out of paradise by cultural residue of the political, economic, and military upheavals of the century and the bipolar condition of international relations.

From our vantage point, Virginia Woolf's pronouncement in 1910 that a post-impressionist art exhibition signalled a cultural revolution seems distant and naive. It is as removed from our feelings as Luther's posting of his Protestant theses on the church door of Wittenberg cathedral; as Rousseau's calling for a new social contract to liberate natural man from artificial government; as Goethe's and Byron's faith in the efficacy of the charismatic act.

We know all these things. We see them in our mind's eye: the art exhibition; the theological war; the French Revolution; the romantic gesture. But they are separated by our sensibility from stirring our imagination, from immediately converting our experience in any particular direction.

The Modernist art exhibition, along with the more distant symbolic aspects of cultural revolution, does not move us. Almost every month in New York City there are exhibitions of Modernist painting more elaborate than that which stirred Virginia Woolf. These exhibitions of Modernist art are massively witnessed, they are consumed like other consumer products, they are commented upon in learned and subtle ways in *The New York Times*, *The Village Voice*, and *The New Criterion*. It makes very little difference to consciousness and unconsciousness. It does not affect the limits of our imagination. The earth does not move. Modernist painting is something to which we immediately and reflexively respond because our vision of the world, its shapes and colors, has been instructed by Modernist art. Attending an exhibition of Modernist art is a semiotic confrontation of our perception of the world. But it is also routine, over-familiar, almost as redundant as the speeches and faces of welfare liberal politicians.

Modernism is paradise lost. We cannot return to it as a cultural entity, as theory for today. As deeply as we still drink from the bottomless well of Modernist culture, it is essentially a thing of the past. Its capability as a determining cultural revolution has played itself out at last. It has become an objectified historical entity like the Reformation, the Enlightenment, and Romanticism. Of course it is much more vibrant and meaningful to us than the three previous cultural revolutions, but it has already entered into past heritage. It is something we draw upon, not something we seek to create. Modernism is our past, not our future.

Although neo-Victorianism is a prime ingredient of current post-Modernist

culture, it neither can nor should be the cultural trend of the future.
Neo-Victorianism cannot prevail because it was too decisively discredited by
Modernism. The confusion characteristic of current post-Modernism, with its
neo-Victorian ingredients, reflect Modernism's persistent countervailing of
neo-Victorian culture. Nor should a full-fledged neo-Victorianism be the
culture of the coming decades, because this would bring back the historicism,
philosophic idealism, macrocosmic thinking, and perhaps the racism and
imperialism of the nineteenth century. After all the travails of this century, we
do not want to experience again all that to which we and our parents'
generation have wisely chosen to say goodbye.

We stand therefore at a Baroque interval between cultural waves, knowing
that Modernism has spent its force but not knowing the contrast of the next
wave. Deconstruction presently amuses because it scrapes away some of the
cant and unreflective arrogance that has been prominent in academic culture
since World War II. Fascism, or rather some similar peaceful rightist variant of
it, fascinates because it is the one cultural avenue of the twentieth century that
has not been pursued to the point of relative tedium. This does not imply that
it is the militaristic and racist aspect of Fascism that attracts, but its separable
rightist theory, its vision of a corporate community imbedded in tradition and
cultural forms.

The current Baroque interval gives momentary plausibility to the program of
the academic and intellectual left to declare the Death of the Subject, the end
of bourgeois man, and in the manner of Derrida and Foucault to post the death
notice of Western culture's individual consciousness.

Yet the elaborate funeral arrangements for Western culture appear prema-
ture. It may be granted that the culture of the future is likely to place a greater
emphasis on communal responsibility and group solidarity. We are socially in
need of this shift which structuralism stressed. But it does not seem likely that
self-consciousness and subjectivity which all the cultural revolutions from the
the Reformation to Modernism fostered in one way or another are going to
pass away. Derrida and Foucault themselves as sentient beings, whatever their
theoretical pronouncements, are very much within the Western tradition of
individual consciousness and personal affirmation. They may have been
prophetic of but they are not examplars of a new objective impersonal
dispensation.

The inexorable trend of Western civilization will continue to work its gently
ferocious manner as it has in the past. It will again generate a cultural
revolution. Eventually, if not next year or in the next decade, then in the next
century, we shall enter upon a new cultural homeland, yet another undiscovered country of the mind such as Nietzsche promised. In our present
post-Modernist situation we can anticipate this much of an outcome.

If there is one lesson that the twentieth century's history teaches, it is the
capacity of the human spirit over time to overcome seemingly impossible odds,
a capacity which makes predictions of the future hazardous. This fact is
represented by a tale of two cities—Tel Aviv, Israel, and Hamburg, West
Germany.

In 1939 Tel Aviv was a new city of 200,000 eager to welcome Jewish refugees from Europe but prevented from doing so by the British government's policy of appeasing the Arabs through blocking of Jewish immigration. Tel Aviv was then an impoverished, weak, marginal city. Now it is the marketplace of Israel with a population of over a million and eclipses its sister Arab city of Jaffa on which it steadily encroaches. It is a wealthy, self-confident Mediterranean metropolis that can welcome Jews or anyone it wants in a powerful, self-confident, and democratic state, the ultimate apotheosis of the medieval crusading kingdom centered on Jerusalem and Acre.

In 1945 Hamburg lay sixty per cent destroyed by Allied bombing raids. The core of the city was burned out, most of its historic buildings lay in ashes. Forty thousand of its population died in the war. The rest faced starvation and homelessness. Today, only four decades later, there is only one sign of the ashes of 1945—an old church that has intentionally been left in ruins as a memorial to the Nazi and wartime era. Hamburg is again the Venice of the North, its streets, buildings, parks and canals rebuilt well beyond the aesthetic level that existed before. It houses comfortably, often elegantly, 1.6 million people and is the largest city in West Germany. It is a city exhibiting the remarkable work ethic of social discipline, efficiency, and innovation that characterizes West Germany. It is a prosperous, gleaming, and democratic metropolis of the north, as Tel Aviv is of the south.

This tale of two cities demonstrates that happily the end of Western culture is not yet in sight.

Cultural Analysis Through Film

Film (and TV) is a highly effective medium for the expression of cultural history. In some respects the narrative and analytic qualities of film exceed the capability of expository prose in evoking complex and subtle aspects of twentieth century culture.

The following film and TV list includes works which are representative of cultural motifs at a particular moment as well as consciously contrived historical recreations of past cultural themes. While the list is far from exhaustive, viewing all these films would mean a substantial education in the main currents of twentieth century culture from 1900 to the present.

I. The Nineteenth Century Foundations of Twentieth Century Culture

Gunga Din

This 1937 Hollywood film, from a Rudyard Kipling poem, is not just a sentimental story about the nineteenth century British Raj. In itself it represents the ethos of imperialism and makes you wonder about American or at least Hollywood culture in the Age of Roosevelt. This film is so patronizingly racist it has to be seen to be believe. On the issues of imperialism and racism, the 1930's mentality is much closer, this film demonstrates, to the Victorians than to us.

Great Expectations

David Lean directed this 1947 film from Dickens' novel and if anything, improved upon it. The film subtly shows the meaning of getting ahead in Victorian society, and the tensions and anxieties it involved.

The Charge of the Light Brigade

Tony Richardson wanted his 1968 film to be a definitive critique of Victorian militarism and imperialism. He tried so hard the film was unsuccessful commercially and exhibits a hesitant, uncertain quality that was bound to confuse and annoy the mass audience (they much preferred the more simple-minded Hollywood version of the same incident, a companion piece to *Gunga Din*). What remains valuable in Richardson's film is the effort to get inside the minds of Victorian soldiers and show that behind their splendid uniforms, they were individuals—by no means were they all alike.

Burn!
The leftist Italian director Pontecorvo, with the help of Marlon Brando as a duplicitous British agent, unsympathetically scrutinizes imperialism in the nineteenth century West Indies. The first half of the film, on the transition from Spanish to British rule, is persuasive.

The Organizer
Marcello Mastroianni in a slow-moving but depressingly accurate account of a lonely and desperate labor union organizer during the earlier stages of industrialization in nineteenth-century Italy. The film indicates eloquently the roots of Italian anarchism.

Tess
Roman Polanski's faithful and convincing version of Hardy's controversial and bitter novel that reprimands Victorian culture and particularly its treatment of underprivileged women.

The Bostonians
James Ivory's respectful filming of Henry James' early novel; to be seen for Vanessa Redgrave's stunning portrayal of a frenetic, dominating, lesbian late 19th century feminist.

Buddenbrooks
A marvelous spare-no-expense German TV series closely derived from Thomas Mann's first great novel about the rise and decline of a wealthy north German mercantile family (his own). Dubbed skillfully in English. This is the best depiction of the 19th century bourgeoisie ever done on film or TV.

Hester Street
Jewish immigrant life on the lower East Side of Manhattan at the end of the nineteenth century, directed with compassion and care by Joan Micklin Silver.

The Godfather Part II
Francis Ford Coppola's reverent yet convincing account of the rise of a Sicilian immigrant on Mulberry Street in lower Manhattan in and through organized crime at the turn of the century.

The Go-Between
Joseph Losey's film from L.P. Hartley's novel subtly examines hierarchy and sensibility, passion and power in the Edwardian country house. A convincing evocation, at the same time nostalgic and critical, of a vanished world.

A Passage to India
E.M. Forster's novel described the British in India and their incapacity to communicate with the restless Indian middle class and comprehend ancient, deep Indian culture. The novel was published in 1924 but may have been written earlier and the world depicted is that of the Raj in 1914. David Lean's

film, which greatly accentuates the pomp and circumstance, elaborately shows the pre-war sahib ambience. Lean's film is not fully faithful to the novel because Forster depicts the Raj as tired and defensive, almost tattered and defeated, while Lean's nostalgic grandeur comes close to making the Raj attractive again. This is still one of the best films about imperialism and its decadence.

Heat and Dust
Similar in theme to *A Passage to India* if less grand in ambience, and more direct in exploring the intense sexuality involved in imperial power and racial tensions. Director James Ivory has a deep feeling for the complexities of the colonial world, perhaps more so than Lean.

A Room with a View
James Ivory's elegant and hilarious film of E.M. Forster's novel shows the Edwardians cracking under strain of sexual repression and contact with more liberated Italian culture. The novel is again somewhat different in tone: Forster glossed his comedy with a distant, critical view of the Edwardians that has almost disappeared from the nostalgic, delightful film.

II. Modernism

The Blue Angel
The classic 1930 film by Joseph von Sternberg with Marlene Dietrich and Emil Jannings, based on Heinrich Mann's expressionist novel about a school-teacher's self-destructive infatuation for a music hall girl. The film is a study in sado-masochism. This film, one of the seminal works of cinema, is both an exemplar of and memorial to German modernism at its zenith.

Ulysses
A bold but only modestly successful 1967 effort by Joseph Strick to illustrate parts of Joyce's novel. The film for the most part fails to capture Joyce's style but its Dublin scenes are helpful in memorializing the novel's environment. Molly Bloom's soliloquy is well done. Joyce would probably have admired this film more than the critics did.

Swann in Love
This recent film by Volker Schloendorff attempted to depict part of Proust's *Swann's Way*. It was savaged by the critics both of the literary and film variety. It fails to capture Proust's style and the film is quite dull. But it does faithfully illustrate the houses, clothes and faces of Proust's world and that is not insignificant.

Jules and Jim
Francois Truffaut's monumental effort to recreate the art nouveau world of early twentieth century France and in modernist vein to examine intensively human relationships in that world, does not always stay in historical focus.

Truffaut's innate neo-romanticism intervenes, but nevertheless this is one of the great films of cultural history, a piercing, incomparable evocation of a very important time and place. Pauline Kael has said that Truffaut's film is the best portrayal of the F. Scott Fitzgerald era; a valid assessment.

Raging Bull

Martin Scorsese's incredibly ambitious 1982 postmodernist effort to make a film in the Modernist style about professional boxing in the early 40's. This black and white film recovers the ambience of the era in a hundred subtle ways. The film is an entirely enclosed, self-referential, dirty, violent but somehow attractive little world. Since Scorsese's temperament leans to the Modernist mold, there are no disconcerting cultural cross-currents in the film. It might be said that Scorsese made the film that Hemingway tried in his novels to communicate, but never in as consistent and direct a manner as here (perhaps because Scorsese has more confidence in himself and feels less need than Hemingway to please the limousine liberals in media and academe.) The film was praised by most critics, who, however, often didn't understand what Scorsese was trying to do. The film was a disappointment commercially, not because the American audience does not want to see films about boxing. They love them—as witness the Rocky series, a license to print money—as long as the theme is presented in neo-romantic vein. The harsh Modernism of Scorsese's film disturbed and offended the popular audience and confused some of the critics. Until someone makes a good film of a Hemingway or Faulkner novel—the results have been close to zero thus far—Scorsese's boxing film will stand as the American cinematic effort at recreating the Modernist ethos, parallelling Truffaut's work in *Jules and Jim*.

The Day of the Locust

The plot of Nathaniel West's Modernist novel is preserved, but the film does not communicate the same harsh ambience and theme. The film is an exercise in nostalgia for the old Hollywood of pre-World War II.

Death in Venice

Visconti's earnest but only partly successful effort to illustrate Thomas Mann's Modernist novella, the film is instructive, if not inspiring. Dirk Bogarde as a character modeled on Gustav Mahler.

Women in Love

One of the great films, with two explosive sensibilities at work: Ken Russell on D.H. Lawrence. There has been much controversy as to whether Russell was faithful to Lawrence or went off on his own. This depends on what one thinks Lawrence was trying to do in the novel. Whatever the ultimate critical judgement, Russell does communicate Lawrence's masochistic fascination with intelligent and powerful women and strong but flawed men (i.e. his wife and himself) and his vitalist vision. Glenda Jackson plays the character based on Frieda Lawrence.

Long Day's Journey into Night

Jason Robards Jr. endlessly chews up the scenery as Eugene O'Neill's Irish-American, alcoholic, self-pitying actor father. For those who think O'Neill was a great Modernist writer, which includes the drama critics of the *New York Times* and some other people.

Double Indemnity

The highpoint of Hollywood film noir, this 1944 film directed by the Austrian emigre, Billy Wilder, presents a sadomasochistic theme similar in tone to *The Blue Angel*, and laced with violence derived from Wilder's mentor Fritz Lang and the German expressionist tradition as well as from the American detective novel of the 30's.

Madame Curie

Not the 1940's Hollywood weepie but the recent British TV series which accurately, depressingly depicts the poverty, misery and sacrificial courage in the life of Marie and Pierre Curie. The series captures the fanatical devotion and unlimited, foolish expectations of the new physicists of the early twentieth century.

The Horse's Mouth

Although painting is one of the glories of twentieth century culture, this British film of the fifties, based on the Joyce Cary novel, is the only good film ever made about a Modernist artist. Alec Guinness' painter is exclusively devoted to his avant-garde art and destructively treats everyone and everything else with contempt.

III. Psychoanalysis

Fanny and Alexander

Ingmar Bergman's passionate and powerful recreation of the family and sexual life of a middle class, turn of the century Swedish kin (his own). The oedipal and sexual rebellion against Christian patriarchialism and puritanism is better portrayed here than in any other film and it is precisely in this ambience that Freudianism emerged. Freud would have loved this film.

Freud

An enthusiastic but not altogether accurate Hollywood portrayal of Freud's early career, directed by John Huston. Nevertheless Montgomery Clift's depiction of an intense, groping Freud is a possible and certainly absorbing interpretation. A better film than critics have allowed.

Diary of a Country Priest

Based on a 1930's novel, this classic work by Robert Bresson depicts in shattering fashion the struggle between traditional Catholicism and modern sexuality. Again this is the cultural context in which Freud began his work. Not Cardinal O'Connor's version of the Catholic church but not incompatable with Vatican II.

Spellbound

This 1945 Hollywood view of psychiatry, directed by Alfred Hitchcock, is alternately interesting and silly, but it is a curious and valuable historical document, showing what psychiatry had come to mean in the popular American mind. Salvador Dali designed the dream sequence.

My Night at Maud's

Claire's Knee

Pauline at the Beach

Eric Rohmer's brilliant and delightful trilogy about all facets of sexuality in the life of the younger French generation of the late Sixties, Seventies, and early Eighties. The films fall under the category of comedy but they deal analytically with the ways in which sexuality affects the lives and thought of affluent, sophisticated middle class people. Rohmer was focusing on yuppiedom and narcissism before these terms had entered into common parlance. The vibrancy and originality of French culture as well as the technique of the New Wave of French film-making are reflected in these masterful films. The films furthermore are studies in the facets of the new West European culture of prosperity that followed from the tremendous post-war recovery. Rohmer doesn't miss a beat: his young people, when they attend university, take courses in linguistics, and we can assume they have been analyzed by Jacques Lacan.

Scenes from a Marriage

Bergman's view of modern marriage illustrates both the doctrines of Freud and his disciples and how these ideas, entering into middle class culture, have become as influential in human behavior as was Christianity in earlier centuries. If Freud could have seen this film early in his career, he might have had second thoughts about what he was trying to do.

IV. Marxism and the Left

Ten Days that Shook the World (October)

Eisenstein's offical propaganda version of the Russian Revolution, or how the Leninists wanted themselves to be memorialized. Everyone else will, or should be, depressed by this film.

Reds

The first half of Warren Beatty's film convincingly portrays leftist intellectuals in Greenwich Village c.1914, with a bravura cameo by Jack Nicholson as Eugene O'Neill. The film is about the pristine Communist John Reed (who wrote the original book *Ten Days that Shook the World*). The second half, after the revolution, is confused, but does convincingly portray the betrayal of noble ideals both in Moscow and New York. The uneven quality of this film offended the critics but it is withal a superior, undervalued historical work.

Dr Zhivago

David Lean's film from the celebrated autobiographical novel by Boris Pasternak depicts the Russian Revolution from the point of view of the liberal middle class. The harshness and sterility of Bolshevik rule and the relative well-being of life under the Tsarist regime is strongly portrayed. Not favorite viewing in the Kremlin.

1900

How the Italian Marxist Bertolucci visualizes the conflict of the rich and poor in his country since 1900. The first half is interesting and persuasive; the second half is dull Communist propaganda.

Dodsworth

This 1936 film by William Wyler, from the novel by Sincair Lewis, illustrates two aspects of the New Deal liberal mentality. First, successful business entrepreneurs, especially if they are self-made billionaire industrial magnates, are intrinsically creative and fascinating people. Secondly, there is no problem in American society that a good will on the part of someone in power cannot solve (anticipating the existential philosophy of the wartime and postwar era). This film also commemorates a now vanished era when entrepeneurs were admired for making something (in this instance, automobiles) rather than for financial manipulation or real estate speculation.

Mr Smith Goes to Washington

Frank Capra's 1939 film reveals how New Deal liberals wanted to see themselves. James Stewart is an idealistic senator struggling against conformity and corruption on the floor of the Senate. There are some thought-provoking touches. The heroic senator needs the advice and help of a sophisticated woman journalist. The senator triumphs through use of the filibuster, which later became a favorite technique of southern conservative senators battling against civil rights laws. The purity of the boondocks vs the cynical corruption of Washington theme that New Dealer Capra emphasizes was used three decades later very effectively in the campaigns of Carter and Reagan. What is disturbing in this monument to New Deal virtue is the sentimentality and self-righteousness.

Citizen Kane

Orson Welles' 1941 film is generally regarded as the greatest American film. It is a narrative account, using the techniques of German expressionist film as transmuted through Hollywood *film noir*, of the life of the right-wing newspaper magnate William Randolph Hearst. Welles' film shows the New Deal liberal mentality in its most effective and attractive form: as a critique of bloated and irresponsible capitalism, but still fascinated by capitalist power.

Yankee Doodle Dandy

James Cagney's charismatic performance as George M. Cohan, the flag-waving Irish-American songwriter and music hall performer. This 1942 film portrays in concentrated form the thick national patriotism and self-congratulatory ethic that the War, coming on the heels of the similarly oriented New Deal, generated. This thick public ethic and patriotism was to shape powerfully post-war American policy and ultimately to inspire the Vietnam disaster. This film unsurprisingly has received a lot of TV play in the Reagan era. What is not often noted is Cagney's careful, authentic depiction of Irish-American cultural traits, including the stiff-legged dancing style derived from the Irish jig.

From Here to Eternity
Fred Zinneman's 1953 film from the James Jones novel ostensibly depicts army life in Hawaii on the eve of World War II. The film is intellectually a hymn to New Deal liberal values and post-war existentialism.

Bound for Glory
This resounding 1977 commercial failure by Hal Ashby depicting the earlier life of Woody Guthrie, the folksinger, presents a wonderfully graphic account of the Great Depression and the heroic early days of union organization among agricultural workers in California, subjects that the American public now does not want to hear about. This film captures the spirit of the New Deal era and its leftist protagonists better than any other.

Daniel
Sidney Lumet's version of the Rosenberg case seen, as in the E.L. Doctorow novel on which it is based, from the point of view of the devastated children. This has got to be one of the most depressing films ever made, but its account is quite plausible.

Rebel Without a Cause
Nicholas Ray, an old leftist from the thirties, directed James Dean in this 1955 story about the rebellion of a "juvenile delinquent" against conformist society. The film was hortatory as well as expository. Dean became a symbol of teen age rebellion.

Easy Rider
Dennis Hopper's 1969 film about two hippie motorcyclists and drug dealers in the Southwest who are destroyed by corrupt and conformist society played a cultural role identical to *Rebel Without a Cause*. It not only depicted rebellion; it advocated it. *Easy Rider* is the essential anti-establishment film of the sixties. It was a box-office smash.

Odd Man Out
Carol Reed's 1949 film, with a subtle performance by a young James Mason as a fallen resistance hero on the run, deals with the Time of Troubles (1920–22) in Ireland, the period of independence of most of the island from British rule and the civil war among factions of the Irish liberation movement. It is instructive that in view of the time it was made, Reed's film is much more honest in showing conflicts and betrayals within the revolutionary movement

than later, more polemical and one-sided accounts of colonial liberation (compare *The Battle of Algiers* and *Gandhi*). It was still possible in 1949—as much more difficult a dozen years later—to show that the colonials were not all saints and heroes.

The Battle of Algiers
Pontecorvo's pseudo-documentary reconstructing the Algerian revolution against French rule in the 1950's, told entirely from the Arab revolutionaries' point of view. The French are cruel villains. The perspective is dogmatically that of the European left of the sixties, and is more accurate as reflecting the Maoist revolutionary ideology of the period than the subtleties (the Jews, many of whose families had lived in Algeria for millennia, were summarily driven out) of the Algerian war of liberation. Yet Pontecorvo's mise en scene is compelling: the black and white photography captures the North African sun-drenched, dessicated environment very well.

If . . .
The 1960's spawned a host of films about student revolution, all of them forgettable except this one by the British director Lindsay Anderson, which depicts a revolution in a British boys' school. The point of view is sympathetic to the students but the savage, nihilistic conclusion raises very disturbing—and appropriate—questions about 1960's radicalism.

The Confession
How the Communist dream became a nightmare of state terror. Costa-Gavras pulls no punches in depicting the show trials in Prague in the 1950's and how the party turned (as in Moscow in the 1930's) against many of its idealistic leaders and against human decency. The film is based on the autobiographical account by one of the victims—one of the few to survive the terror—and is fully accurate.

Apocalypse Now
Francis Ford Coppola's film about the Vietnam War, loosely based on Conrad's *Heart of Darkness*, is valuable not as an account of the War, but for the way in which the leftist discrediting of the war became firmly, probably eternally fixed in the popular mind as a very bad show in which the military acted discreditably and worse. Poor General Westmoreland; he never had a chance.

All the President's Men
The fall of Richard Nixon as perceived and engineered by the *Washington Post*. A liberal morality tale, possibly about sixty per cent true.

V. Traditions on the Right
Brideshead Revisited
This British TV series powerfully and eloquently expounded Evelyn Waugh's sympathetic portrayal of a patrician English Catholic family between

the Wars. Their lavish life style and conservative values comes through clearly, although Waugh's conviction that these are the kind of people who deserve to rule and prosper is somewhat muted and his anti-semitism is ignored. The type of aristocratic family that Waugh portrayed was easy prey for Fascism throughout Western Europe as a counterweight to communism and democracy.

The Garden of the Finzi-Continis

De Sica's masterpiece, based on an autobiographical Italian novel, delicately depicts the slow strangulation of a wealthy and aristocratic Jewish family in the fascist era—although Mussolini's fascism was initially and for many years not anti-semitic. The troubles of the Italian Jews really began in 1938 after Mussolini's alliance with Hitler. The family depicted in this film represents hundreds of cultivated, wealthy very old Jewish families throughout continental Europe who perished in the Nazi era, a unique, effete cultural and social group that can never be recreated. It is hard to imagine that the Finzi-Continis are only one generation removed from Arik Sharon.

The Sorrow and the Pity

Interviews with survivors of the Vichy era persuasively and not entirely unsympathetically explain what happened in France under Petain and the Nazi occupation. Marcel Ophuls' searching, intelligent indictment of rightist France and how the Jews became the victims.

Shoah

Claude Lanzmann's very lengthy series of interviews with survivors—victims, perpetrators, and not so innocent bystanders—of the Holocaust establishes the purpose and unspeakable horror of the greatest crime in the twentieth century. The film shows convincingly that East European ethnics—such as Poles—were almost as much involved as the Germans. This unpopular message has not gained sufficient public attention up to now, and its clear communication in this film has inevitably aroused resentment, especially in Poland. It is a wonder that this film, which took a decade to make, could have been made and that the participants were willing to speak so freely; this in itself is a disturbing message.

Mephisto

If you are going to see only one film on the Nazi era, this is the one to see. Through a study of a leading German actor and director of the period—from Klaus Mann's novel based on a true story—Istvan Szabo's film depicts the deceit, ambitions and fears that made possible the rise of Hitler and the willing surrender of educated Germans to the Nazis. A persuasive account of why relatively decent people became Nazis.

Seven Beauties

Lina Wertmuller's candid portrayal of the sexual sado-masochistic feelings that contributed to fascism and the Holocaust. The message appears to be the

Augustinian one that fascist terror is rooted in the universal evil in human nature.

The Bridge on the River Kwai
David Lean directs a thoroughly convincing portrayal by Alec Guinness of the authoritarian personality exhibited by a British officer in a Japanese prison camp. Fascism as a universal category.

Lawrence of Arabia
Another study by David Lean in the social psychology of fascism. What is remarkably suggested in Peter O'Toole's portrayal of the British leader of Arab nationalism is the hero's sado-masochism, homosexuality, and self-destructive qualities. A textbook example of Adler's psychoanalytic explanation of Fascism as rooted in a sense of inferiority.

The Third Man
Carol Reed's 1949 film, from a script by Graham Greene, depicts the malaise and corruption of postwar Europe, in this instance Vienna. The film also has the effect of contrasting a Nietzschean fascist (Orson Welles) against a good-hearted mid-American (Joseph Cotton). It also shows the Russians as heavies, reflecting the coming of the Cold War.

Oppenheimer
This lengthy British TV series was made in the early 80's and depicts Robert Oppenheimer and an international group of dedicated, brilliant, and ultimately agonized and divided group of physicists and engineers making the atom bomb in Los Alamos, New Mexico, 1943–45. The wives are not ignored, particularly Mrs. Oppenheimer, here truthfully portrayed as a brooding, difficult, ex-Communist. The look-alike American actor, Sam Waterston, plays Oppenheimer in a thoroughly convincing manner—except that he smiles too much—getting across the complex, Faustian character of this tormented, unique personality. The mise en scene is done very accurately: the claustrophobic quality of the environment in which the scientists worked comes through clearly. (There is also an American documentary film, *Day After Trinity*, about Oppenheimer and the making of the atom bomb that is powerful and instructive.) What is special about *Oppenheimer* are the nuanced explorations of the temperament and ideals of physicists in the age of colossal science, including their authoritarianism and arrogance. It is easy to envisage Oppenheimer, if he had occupied Werner Heisenberg's position, eagerly trying to make the atom bomb for Hitler and saying later he was sorry, as he accepts a chair at MIT. The British are fascinated with this theme of science in the service of government and destruction (compare the fifties film of exceptional value, *Breaking The Sound Barrier*, and the novels of C.P. Snow).

Enola Gay
Another film about the dropping of the bomb on Hiroshima is *Enola Gay*, a carefully crafted, historically accurate TV docudrama concerned with Col.

Paul Tibbets and the other men in the air force plane that delivered the bomb. The film evokes the simple idealism of the men who fought the last good war.

Z

Neo-fascism in Greece in the fifties. Costa-Gavras' film is left-wing propaganda but he does get an important point across: fascism is nothing special; it is rooted in militarism and bureaucracy. Cf. Arendt's banality of evil.

The Official Story

A subtle and complex account of the motivation and expectations involved in the rightist terror that produced the "disappeared" under the recent militarist regime in Argentina. This is a very good film because it is not leftist propaganda; it is not entirely unsympathetic to the businessmen who collaborated with the neo-Fascist regime and it grasps some of the subtle and complex motives that drive relatively decent people to the far right in times of stress.

Gandhi

An elaborate, very long epic of the Indian independence movement and its hero, and the end of the British Raj, told in wooden fashion by Richard Attenborough, and filmed in India at infinite expense. The film was a huge commercial success possibly because it carefully avoids subtlety and controversy. Except for a handful of British officers, who, after abusing the natives, slink off to drink gin and tonics and curse the darkness, everybody looks good. Gandhi is presented almost entirely in the conventional form of anti-colonialism's heroic saint. Yet the film is worth seeing because, with almost no help from the script, Ben Kingsley as Gandhi suggests some of the immense complexity of the Mahatma. As is customary in liberation epics, the early scenes under colonial rule are much more interesting—and historically accurate—than the later moments of triumph.

VI. Structuralism, Deconstruction and Post-Modernism

The Red Desert

Visconti's classic of nihilist boredom. What happened in economically recovered Europe when existential heroism was no longer believed in. Watching this film is like watching paint dry, but the rise of the structural system over the individual is evident.

A Clockwork Orange

The Anthony Burgess-Stanley Kubrick evocation of a near future of punk rock fascist terror. The Nietzschian deconstruction of middle class values turned into nightmare. Heavy metal.

Day for Night

Truffaut as Roland Barthes: signifier, signified, referents, and the whole semiotical structure subtly (and not paradoxically) inserted into film-making.

The Deerhunter

Michael Cimino's 1978 film about Vietnam disturbed the American left because of his post-Modernist, or at least post-sixties, ambivalences about the whole mess and his sympathy for the American servicemen involved, particularly those of white ethnic background. Cimino's vigorous appropriation of patriotic traditions and his faith in the integrity and decency of the silent majority were remarkably prophetic of the Age of Reagan.

Betrayal

Harold Pinter's structuralist love story; this is the best evocation on film of structuralist dehumanization of personality. Effectively directed by David Jones and brilliantly acted. An important and underrated film, that quintessentially represents post-Modernism as *The Blue Angel* reflected Modernist culture.

The Big Chill

This Hollywood film by Lawrence Kasdan doesn't stand up too well compared to Truffaut's and Pinter's versions of structuralism and postmodernism. Its theme of eighties cultural forms imposing themselves on nostalgia for the sixties doesn't quite come off, but it's fun.

The Return of Martin Guerre

This film is based on a historical work by the Princeton postmodernist historian Natalie Zemon Davis and she also acted as a consultant for the film. Based on court records, it describes unusual crises in a peasant family in 16th century France. The structuralism of Fernand Braudel and Claude Lévi-Strauss looms large in this film. The peasants are not only quite affluent but are highly articulate. Was that the way it was? Zemon Davis thinks so, audaciously citing a court record drawn up by a Protestant judge.

True West

Sam Shepherd deconstructs Western civilization over the kitchen sink. Why Nietzsche went mad. Foucault's revenge.

Stranger than Paradise

Jim Jarmish, a young graduate of N.Y.U. film school, pursues much of the same deconstructive, nihilist theme, but with delicacy and humor and in the end suggests that, contrary to Foucault, Man is not dead. There is also a nostalgic subtext of immigrant survival in the New World—a neo-Victorianism if there ever was one.

Chariots of Fire

This immensely popular 1981 film illustrates the way in which the postmodernist culture of the eighties arbitrarily appropriates in nostalgic vein segments of the past that Modernist culture considered an anathema. The heroes are two young Brits in 1924 who win races at the Olympics: a priggish, ambitious London Jew and an evangelical Bible-thumping Scot from a missionary family. On seeing this film, T.S. Eliot would have ruminated darkly on the decline of civilization; Joyce would have thought it hilarious. While the historicist sentimentality is laid on thick, what makes this a post-Modernist film is that the two heroes come through as yuppies more than as imperial idols. The early twenties ambience is constructed with infinite care by the director Hugh Hudson; yet the heroes are readily identified as eighties people. We know that following their athletic triumphs they will head respectively for Wall Street and CBS.

The Falcon and the Snowman

John Schlesinger's 1985 film about the actual case of two alienated California postadolescents who sold government secrets to the Russians was not a commercial success. It is a discomfiting portrayal of the nihilism and sullen hostility affecting many young people in the eighties. Habermas' legitimation crisis brought to life in an unusual way.

The Man Who Fell to Earth

This 1976 science fiction film by Nicolas Roeg had only modest commercial success but more than the famous *Star Wars* trilogy and without the blizzard of special effects and computer graphics, it was the finest achievement of science fiction movie-making of the seventies. It tells of a pilgrim from a dry, dying planet—played appropriately by the rock star David Bowie—who comes to earth in search of water. Of course this is an eschatalogical vision of the end of planet earth itself.

The Right Stuff

This detailed, historically careful account of the U.S. space program was a commercial disappointment. Its post-Modernist 1983 ambience mystified the mass audience who came to cheer a patriotic triumph that deconstructed before their eyes into non-triumphal, dismaying, acerbic levels of signification. The enormous cost of this film by Philip Kaufman indicates that it was intended for a mass audience, but the public at large is not prepared for the emotional downer of deconstruction.

Brazil

Monte Python's brilliant, original vision of retro-medievalism as post-Modernism. This current British film was much more favorably received by the Los Angeles film critics than by the New York ones, which suggests that in California they have seen the future and they know it doesn't work.

SELECT BIBLIOGRAPHY

I. The Nineteenth-Century Foundations of Twentieth-Century Culture

Walter Houghton, *The Victorian Frame of Mind*
Samuel Hynes, *The Edwardian Turn of Mind*
Gerhard Masur, *Prophets of Yesterday*
Helen Lynd, *England in the Eighteen-Eighties*
Charles Dellheim, *The Face of the Past*
Roger Shattuck, *The Banquet Years*
Henry Sussman, *The Hegelian Aftermath*
Carl Schorske, *Fin-de-Siecle Vienna*
Stephen Kern, *The Culture of Time and Space*
James Kloppenberg, *Uncertain Victory*
Robert Goldwater, *Symbolism*
Ronald Hayman, *Nietzsche*
Frederick Karl, *Joseph Conrad*
Leon Edel, *Henry James*
Margaret Drabble, *Arnold Bennett*
Ann Thwaite, *Edmund Gosse*
Michael Millgate, *Thomas Hardy*
Jackson Lears, *No Place of Grace*
Richard Shiff, *Cézanne and the End of Impressionism*
Barbara White, *Renoir*
Wayne Anderson, *Gaugin's Paradise Lost*
Peter Stansky, *Redesigning the World*
Robert Macleod, *Charles Rennie Mackintosh*
Hans Hofstaetter, *Art Nouveau*
Olof Lagercrantz, *Strindberg*
Martin Meyer, *Strindberg*
Michael Meyer, *Ibsen*
Jerrold Siegel, *Bohemian Paris*
Eugene Weber, *France: Fin de Siecle*
Michael Mitterauer and Reinhard Sieder, *The European Family*

II. Modernism

Robert Wohl, *The Generation of 1914*
Michael Levenson, *A Genealogy of Modernism*

Sanford Schwarz, *The Matrix of Modernism*
Paul Fussell, *The Great War and Modern Memory*
Ricardo Quinones, *Mapping Literary Modernism*
Paul Johnson, *Modern Times*
Richard Ellman, *James Joyce*
Quentin Bell, *Virginia Woolf*
Leon Edel, *Bloomsbury, A House of Lions*
Noel Stock, *Life of Ezra Pound*
Hugh Kenner, *The Pound Era*
Hugh Kenner, *A Colder Eye. Modern Irish Writers*
Ronald Bush, *T.S. Eliot*
Peter Ackroyd, *T.S. Eliot*
Michael MacLiammoir and Evan Boland, *W.B. Yeats*
Milton Bates, *Wallace Stevens*
Jeffrey Myers, *Hemingway*
Germaine Bree, *The World of Marcel Proust*
George Painter, *Marcel Proust* (2 vols)
Roger Shattuck, *Marcel Proust*
Paul Delancy, *D.H. Lawrence's Nightmare*
Anthony Burgess, *Flame Into Being: D.H. Lawrence*
Ernst Pawel, *The Nightmare of Reason. Kafka*
Nigel Hamilton, *The Brothers Mann*
Jacqueline Weld, *Peggy*
James Mellon, *Charmed Circle: Gertrude Stein and Company*
Wolfgang Leppman, *Rilke*
Hannah Hickman, *Robert Musil and the Culture of Vienna*
Howard Feinstein, *Becoming William James*
Richard Rorty, *Consequences of Pragmatism*
Allan Janik and Stephen Toulmin, *Wittgenstein's Vienna*
A.J. Ayer, *Philosophy in the Twentieth Century*
G.H. von Wright, *Wittgenstein*
A.J. Ayer, *Wittgenstein*
J.N. Findlay, *Wittgenstein*
Anthony Kenny, *Wittgenstein*
George Hamilton, *Painting and Sculpture in Europe 1880–1940*
Mathias Eberle, *World War I and the Weimar Artists*
Meyer Schapiro, *Modern Art*
Frederick Karl, *Modern and Modernism: The Sovereignty of the Artist*
Allan Greenberg, *Artists and Revolution*
Theda Shapiro, *Painters and Politics*
Reinhold Heller, *Munch*
Roland Penrose, *Picasso*
Pierre Schneider, *Matisse*
James Lord, *Giacometti*
Richard Verdi, *Klee and Nature*
G. di San Lazzaro (ed.), *Homage to Wassily Kandinsky*

Charles Harrison, *English Art and Modernism*
Anna Balakian, *André Breton*
Inez Hedges, *Languages of Revolt*
Francis Frascina and Charles Harrison (eds.), *Modern Art and Modernism*
Peter Selz, *German Expressionist Painting*
Paul Raabe, *The Era of German Expressionim*
Eberhard Roters, *Berlin, 1910–1933*
Peter Paret, *The Berlin Secession*
John Willett, *Art and Politics in the Weimar Period*
John Willett, *Expressionism*
Stephen Bronner and Douglas Kellner, *Passion and Rebellion: the
    Expressionist Heritage*
Meryle Secrest, *Kenneth Clark*
Richard Twombly, *Louis Sullivan*
Franz Schulze, *Mies van der Rohe*
Harry Levin, *Memories of the Moderns*
Robert Kiely (ed.), *Modernism Reconsidered*
Roger Shattuck, *The Innocent Eye*
Francis Mulhern, *The Moment of "Scrutiny"*
Martin Green, *The Von Richthofen Sisters*
Renato Pogglioli, *Theory of the Avant-Garde*
Raymond Williams, *Drama from Ibsen to Brecht*
Jeffrey Perl, *The Tradition of Return*
Jan Needle and Peter Thomson, *Brecht*
Martin Esslin, *Brecht*
Richard Schickel, *D.W. Griffith*
Gunther Schuller, *Early Jazz*
Leonard Meyer, *Music, the Arts, and Ideas*
Edward Shils, *The Calling of Sociology*
Steven Lukes, *Emile Durkheim*
Robert Jones, *Emile Durkheim*
Marvin Harris, *The Rise of Anthropological Theory*
Roy Harrod, *John Maynard Keynes*
Robert Skidelsky, *John Maynard Keynes*
Judith Modell, *Ruth Benedict*
Russell McCormmach, *Night Thoughts of a Classical Physicist*
Ronald Clark, *Einstein*
Lewis Feuer, *Einstein and the Generations of Science* 2nd ed.
Jeremy Bernstein, *Einstein*
Jamie Sayen, *Einstein in America*
Gerald Holton and Yehuda Elkana, eds., *Albert Einstein: Historical and
    Cultural Perspectives*
David Wilson, *Rutherford*
C.P. Snow, *The Physicists*
Arthur Marwick, *The Deluge*
Edward Purcell, *The Crisis of Democratic Theory*

III. Psychoanalysis

Ernest Jones, *The Life and Work of Sigmund Freud*
Steven Marcus, *Freud and the Culture of Psychoanalysis*
Paul Roazen, *Freud and His Followers*
Ronald Clark, *Freud*
J.N. Isbister, *Freud*
Ernst Freud et al, *Sigmund Freud*
Henri Ellenberger, *The Discovery of the Unconscious*
Reuben Fine, *A History of Psychoanalysis*
Clarence Karier, *Scientists of the Mind*
Max Schur, *Freud: Living and Dying*
William McGrath, *Freud's Discovery of Psychoanalysis*
Frank Sulloway, *Freud, Biologist of the Mind*
Peter Gay, *Freud, Jews and Other Germans*
Robert Steele, *Freud and Jung*
Murray Stein, ed, *Jungian Analysis*
Anthony Storr, *The Essential Jung*
Andrew Samuels, *Jung and the Post-Jungians*
James Lieberman, *Acts of the Will: Otto Rank*
Myron Sharaf, *Fury on Earth. Wilhelm Reich*
Philip Rieff, *Triumph of the Therapeutic*
Janet Malcolm, *Psychoanalysis: The Impossible Profession*
Adolf Gruenbaum, *The Foundations of Psychoanalysis*
Paul Ricoeur, *Freud and Philosophy*
Samuel Weber, *The Legend of Freud*
Jay Greenberg and Stephen Mitchell, *Object Relations in Psychoanalytic Theory*
Phyllis Grosskurth, *Melanie Klein*
Paul Roazen, *Helene Deutsch*
Sherry Turkle, *Psychoanalytic Politics*
Catherine Clement, *The Lives and Legend of Jacques Lacan*
Ellie Ragland-Sullivan, *Jacques Lacan and the Philosophy of Psychoanalysis*
Russell Jacoby, *Social Amnesia*
Joseph Smith and William Kerrigan, eds., *Taking Chances*

IV. Marxism and the Left

Jon Elster, *Making Sense of Marx*
Roy Medvedev, *Let History Judge*
Robert Conquest, *The Great Terror*
Adam Ulam, *Ideologies and Illusions*
John Erickson, *The Road to Berlin*
Eugene Lunn, *Marxism and Modernism*
Russell Jacoby, *Dialectic of Defeat*
David Held, *Introduction to Critical Theory*
Leszek Kolakowski, *Main Currents of Marxism* vol. III

Martin Jay, *The Dialectical Imagination*
Martin Jay, *Marxism and Totality*
Helmut Dubiel, *Theory and Poltics. The Development of Critical Theory*
George Friedman, *The Political Philosophy of the Frankfurt School*
Walter Adamson, *Marx and the Disillusionment of Marxism*
Gilian Rose, *The Melancholy Science. Adorno*
Richard Wolin, *Walter Benjamin*
Mary Gluck, *Georg Lukacs and His Generation*
Bernard Crick, *George Orwell*
Ross Terrill, *R.H. Tawney and His Times*
Elinor Langer, *Josephine Herbst*
William O'Neil, *A Better World*
Alexander Bloom, *Prodigal Sons*
Edward Abrahams, *The Lyrical Left*
Mark Krupnick, *Lionel Trilling and The Fate of Cultural Criticism*
Arthur Schlesinger, Jr., *The Age of Roosevelt* 3 vols.
Ted Morgan, *FDR*
Elizabeth Young-Bruehl, *Hannah Arendt*
Peter Nettl, *Rosa Luxemburg*
Joel Colton, *Leon Blum*
Herbert Lottman, *The Left Bank*
Anthony Heilbut, *Exiled in Paradise*
Richard Fox, *Reinhold Neibuhr*
Mark Poster, *Existential Marxism in Post-War France*
Stuart Hughes, *The Sea Change*
Alex Callinicos, *Marxism and Philosophy*
Susan Buck-Morss, *The Origin of Negative Dialectics*
Raymond Williams, *Marxism and Literature*
Dave Laing, *The Marxist Theory of Art*
David Castronovo, *Edmund Wilson*
Katerina Clark and Michael Holquist, *Mikhail Bakhtin*
Peter Hohendal, *The Institution of Criticism*
Kirkpatrick Sale, *SDS*
John Castellucci, *The Big Dance. Kathy Boudin*
Sohnya Sayers et al., eds., *The 60's without Apology*
Robert Skelton, *No Direction Home: Bob Dylan*
Peter Clecak, *Radical Paradoxes*
Brian Lapping, *The End of Empire*
Allan Matusow, *The Unraveling of America*
Douglas Kellner, *Herbert Marcuse and the Crisis of Marxism*
Thomas McCarthy, *The Critical Theory of Jurgen Habermas*
Steven Smith, *Reading Althusser*
Peter Burger, *Theory of the Avant-Garde*
P.T. Bauer, *Equality and the Third World*
Martin Pugia, *The Making of Modern British Politics*
Arthur Marwick, *British Society Since 1945*

V. Traditions on the Right

Ernest Nolte, *Three Faces of Fascism*
Karl Bracher, *The German Dictatorship*
George Mosse, *The Crisis of German Ideology*
Gordon Craig, *The Germans*
Pierre Aycoberry, *The Nazi Question*
V.R. Bergahn, *Modern Germany*
Klaus Hildebrand, *The Third Reich*
Lucy Dawidowicz, *The War against the Jews*
Robert Wistrich, *Hitler's Apocalypse*
Raul Hilberg, *The Destruction of the European Jews*, 2nd ed.
Martin Gilbert, *Auschwitz and the Allies*
David Wyman, *The Abandonment of the Jews*
Allan Bullock, *Hitler*
David Calleo, *The German Problem Reconsidered*
Rudolph Binion, *Hitler among the Germans*
Henry Turner, *German Business and the Rise of Hitler*
Joachim Fest, *The Face of the Third Reich*
George Stein, *The Waffen SS*
George Mosse, *Nazi Culture*
Jeffrey Herf, *Reactionary Modernism*
Alan Beyerchen, *Scientists under Hitler*
Woodruff Smith, *The Ideological Origins of Nazi Imperialism*
Peter Pulzer, *The Rise of Political Anti-Semitism*
Hannah Arendt, *Eichmann in Jerusalem*
Walter Struve, *Elites Against Democracy*
Albert Seaton, *The German Army*
Alan Clark, *Babarossa*
Hugh Thomas, *The Spanish Civil War*
Dennis Mack Smith, *Mussolini*
Eugen Weber, *Action Française*
John Toland, *The Rising Sun*
John Costello, *The Pacific War*
John Dower, *War Without Mercy*
Robert Paxton, *Vichy France*
Barnett Singer, *Modern France*
Frances Malino and Bernard Wasserstein, eds., *The Jews in Modern France*
Michael Marrus and Robert Paxton, *Vichy France and the Jews*
Herbert Lottman, *The Purge*
Laurence Shook, *Etienne Gilson*
Bernard Doering, *Jacques Maritain and the French Intellectuals*
Guenter Lewy, *The German Catholic Church and Nazi Germany*
Ernst Helmreich, *The German Churches under Hitler*
Derek Holmes, *The Papacy and the Modern World*
Saul Friedlander, *Pius XII and the Third Reich*
Anthony Rhodes, *The Vatican in the Age of the Dictators*

Maurice Cowling, *Religion and Public Doctrine in Modern England*, 2 vols.
Christina Scott, *A Historian and His World. Christopher Dawson*
Colin Holmes, *Anti-Semitism in British Society*
Robert Skidelsky, *Oswald Mosley*
Jonathan Guiness, *The House of Mitford*
John Harrison, *The Reactionaries: the Anti-Democratic Intelligentsia*
Cairns Craig, *Yeats, Eliot, Pound and the Politics of Poetry*
A.N. Wilson, *Hilaire Belloc*
Jeffrey Meyers, *The Enemy: Wyndham Lewis*
Christopher Sykes, *Evelyn Waugh*
John Fekete, *The Critical Twilight*
Alan Brinkley, *Voices of Protest*
Roger Waterhouse, *A Heiddeger Critique*
Lewis Coser, *Refugee Scholars in America*
Ronald Clark, *The Greatest Power on Earth*
Martin Jay, *Permanent Exiles*
Ellen Schecker, *No Ivory Tower: McCarthyism and the Universities*
Stephen Ambrose, *Eisenhower*, 2 vols.
Hans-George Gadamer, *Philosophical Apprenticeships*
Jan Morris, *Farewell the Trumpets*
Raymond Betts, *Uncertain Dimension*
Valerie Pakenham, *Out in the Noonday Sun*
Philip Ziegler, *Mountbatten*
Robert Pells, *The Liberal Mind in a Conservative Age*
Stephen Jay Gould, *The Mismeasure of Man*
Daniel Kevles, *In the Name of Eugenics*
Zeev Schiff and Ehud Yaari, *Israel's Lebanon War*
Ze'ev Chafets, *Heroes and Hustlers, Hard Hats and Crazy Men*

VI. Structuralism, Deconstruction, and Post-Modernism

Edith Kurzweil, *The Age of Structuralism*
John Sturrock (ed.), *Structuralism and Since*
Frank Lentricchia, *After the New Criticism*
William Cain, *The Crisis in Criticism*
Howard Felperin, *Beyond Deconstruction*
Vincent Descombes, *Modern French Philosophy*
Simon Clarke, *The Foundations of Structuralism*
Quentin Skinner (ed.), *The Return of Grand Theory in the Human Sciences*
Howard Gardner, *The Quest for Mind*
Miriam Glucksman, *Structuralist Analysis in Contemporary Social Thought*
Allan Megill, *Prophets of Extremity*
Christopher Norris, *Deconstruction. Theory and Practice*
Christopher Norris, *The Deconstructive Turn*
Terry Eagleton, *Literary Theory*
William Ray, *Literary Meaning*
Gerard Genette, *Figures of Literary Discourse*

Jonathan Culler, *Structuralist Poetics*
Jonathan Culler, *The Pursuit of Signs*
Jonathan Culler, *On Deconstruction*
Robert Scholes, *Structuralism in Literature*
Robert Scholes, *Semiotics and Interpretation*
Terence Hawkes, *Structuralism and Semiotics*
Vincent Leitch, *Deconstructive Criticism*
Jean-Pierre Mileur, *Literary Revisionism and the Burden of Modernity*
David Lodge, *Working with Structuralism*
Allen Thiker, *Words in Reflection*
John Fekete, *The Structural Allegory*
Denis Donoghue, *Ferocious Alphabets*
Dominick LaCapra, *A Preface to Sartre*
Henry Staten, *Wittgenstein and Derrida*
Michael Ryan, *Marxism and Deconstruction*
Donald Lowe, *History of Bourgeois Perception*
Ihab and Sally Hassan (eds.), *Innovation/Renovation*
Frank Lentricchia, *Criticism and Social change*
Christopher Butler, *Interpretation, Deconstruction, and Ideology*
W.J. Mitchell, ed., *The Politics of Interpretation*
Jose Harari (ed.), *Textual Strategies*
Gerald Graff, *Literature Against Itself*
Fredric Jameson, *The Political Unconscious*
Hester Eisenstein, *Contemporary Feminist Thought*
Nannerl Keohane, ed., *Feminist Theory*
Germaine Greer, *The Female Eunuch*
David Pace, *Claude Lévi-Strauss*
Edmund Leach, *Claude Lévi-Strauss*
Annette Lavers, *Roland Barthes*
Hubert Dreyfus and Paul Rabinow, *Michel Foucault*
Alan Sheridan, *Michel Foucault*
Charles Lemert and Garth Gillan, *Michel Foucault*
John Rachsman, *Michel Foucault*
Pamela Major-Poezl, *Michel Foucault's Archaeology of Western Culture*
Anika Lemaire, *Jacques Lacan*
John Lyons, *Noam Chomsky*
Jonathan Arac, et al. (eds.), *The Yale Critics*
Robert Davis and Ronald Schleiffer (eds.), *Rhetoric and Form:
    Deconstruction at Yale*
Paul Hernadi (ed.), *The Horizon of Literature*
Ralph Freedman, *Herman Hesse*
Dudley Andrew, *Concepts in Film Theory*
Peter Selz, *Art in Our Time*
Dore Ashton, *The New York School*
Dawn Ades and Andrew Forge, *Francis Bacon*
Serge Guilbaut, *How New York Stole the Idea of Modern Art*
Suzi Gablik, *Has Modernism Failed?*

Brian Wallis (ed.), *Art After Modernism*
Howard Becker, *Art Worlds*
Sam Hunter and John Jacobus, *American Art in the Twentieth Century*
Hilton Kramer, *The Revenge of the Philistines*
Rosalind Krauss, *The Originality of the Avant-Garde and Other Modernist Myths*
John Rockwell, *All American Music*
Charlie Gillett, *The Sound of the City* rev. ed.
Serge Denisoff, *Solid Gold*
Hal Foster (ed.), *The Anti-Aesthetic*
David Caroll, *The Subject in Question*
Jean-Francois Lyotard, *The Post Modern Condition*
Sherry Turkle, *The Second Self. Computers and the Human Spirit*
James Allen, *The Romance of Commerce and Culture*
Freeman Dyson, *Disturbing the Universe*
Horace Freeland Judson, *The Eighth Day of Creation*
Loren Graham, *Science and Values*
Ernst Mayr, *The Growth of Biological Thought*
Howard Kaye, *The Social Meaning of Modern Biology*
John Brockman, *Einstein, Gertrude Stein, Wittgenstein & Frankenstein*
Robert Crease and Charles Mann, *The Second Creation*
Edward Hartrich, *The Fourth and Richest Reich*
Richard Rosencrance, *Rise of the Trading State*
Allan Bloom, *The Closing of the American Mind*
Howard Gardner, *The Mind's New Science*

Index